THE APOSTLE OF PEACE

Volume Two

The Christian Commonwealth, September 20th, 1911.

NATIONAL BROTHERHOOD CONFERENCE.

The Christian Commonwealth

The Organ of the Progressive Movement in Religion and Social Ethics.

No. 1,562. Vol. XXXI. WEDNESDAY SEPT. 20, 1911. PRICE ONE PENNY.

"THOUGHTS ABOVE THE DIN."
AND OTHER POEMS.
By FRANK PEARCE.

PRICE, 1s. 3d., Post free.

Published at 2s., to be had of the Author, 119, Lake Road, Portsmouth.

"A Creed is not a stone to be hurled by the hand of a lie."

An attempt to suppress a new story by A. CURTIN SHERWOOD having been made, it is published to an unusual way, post free or one shilling from the address: A. SHERWOOD, Clifford, R.S.O., Herefordshire.

CLIFTON GUEST HOUSE.
Ideal for rest and change. Stimulating Thought Centre. Run on entirely original lines. Meat and Vegetarian Tables. Splendidly situated; cool and airy rooms. Fees 30s. weekly inclusive.
Prospectus from W. TUDOR POLE,
17, Royal York Crescent, BRISTOL.

CHRISTIANITY and SOCIALISM.
SOCIAL DEMOCRACY: Does it Mean Darkness or Light?
An Interpretation and summary of the work of HERMANN KUTTER, Pastor of the Neumünster, Zürich.
By RICHARD HEATH. 2s. 6d. net; by post, 2s. 10d.
"While admitting that Social Democracy presents itself a definitely atheistic and materialistic, Kutter sees behind it a Divine force compelling it to do the very work for which Christianity was called into existence."—RICHARD HEATH.

CHRISTIAN COMMONWEALTH CO.,
133, Salisbury Square, London, E.C.

By Rev. W. E. ORCHARD, D.D.
MODERN THEORIES OF SIN.
2s. 6d. net, post free 2s. 10d.
THE EVOLUTION OF OLD TESTAMENT RELIGION.
2s. 6d. net, post free 2s. 10d.
THE NEW SPIRIT IN RELIGION.
1d., by post 1½d.; 12 copies, 1s. 9d.
CHRISTIAN COMMONWEALTH CO.,
133, Salisbury Square, London, E.C.

WOLSEY HALL OXFORD

POSTAL TUITION
FOR MINISTERS & LAYMEN.
Beginners and Advanced Students in
THEOLOGY.
O.T. Hebrew Textual Criticism
N.T. Greek Comparative Religion
Bible Study Philosophy of Religion
Exegesis Christian Evidences
Dogmatics Philosophy
Homiletics Classics, &c., &c.
FOR INDEPENDENT STUDY
without any Examination in view, for
LONDON MATRICULATION,
Ministerial Exams. & all Degrees, viz.,
B.A., B.Sc., B.D. (Lond.), LL.B.

The Vanishing of the Veil.
Abdul Baha at St. John's, Westminster.
Archdeacon Wilberforce's Welcome.

Eighteen months ago Archdeacon Wilberforce, who had been watching the Bahai movement for some time with interest, sent a message to Abdul Baha. "We are all one," he said, "there, behind the veil." And Abdul Baha replied from his home in Akka, "Tell him the veil is very thin, and it will vanish quite."

All who were present in St. John's, Westminster, last Sunday evening, could not fail to realise that the veil was vanishing. Archdeacon Wilberforce's beautiful intercessory service was a means to that end. He asked that each one in the vast congregation should at

ABDUL BAHA (Abbas Effendi).

ness of the sick woman and the keen anxiety of the daughter hastening to her side. So the spirit of unity was spread abroad.

Then Dr. Wilberforce told of the teacher—"Master" he called him—who had come to London to emphasise unity, and who was present that evening at St. John's; to proclaim the meaning of it. "Whatever our views," the Archdeacon said, "we shall, I am sure, unite in welcoming a man who has been for forty years a prisoner for the cause of brotherhood and love."

Abdul Baha is not an orator or even a preacher, but, in view of all he stands

Baha. All eyes were fixed on the leader of the Bahai movement. In his customary Eastern robe and head-dress, a vibrating hand in hand with a leader of the West, it did indeed seem that the veil was vanishing.

Down the aisle they passed to the bishop's chair, which had been placed in front of the altar for Abdul Baha. Standing at the lectern, Archdeacon Wilberforce introduced the "wonderful" visitor. He told of his life in prison, of his sufferings and bravery, of his self-sacrifice, of his clear and shining faith. He voiced his own belief that religion is one, as God is love.

Then Abdul Baha rose. Speaking very clearly, with wonderful intonations in his voice and using his hands freely, it seemed to those who listened almost as if they grasped his meaning, though he spoke in Persian. When he had finished, Archdeacon Wilberforce read the translation of his address.

His theme was the Character of the Manifestations of God. He said that God the Infinite could not be comprehended of man; that whatever man understands of God is born of his imagination. For illustration he pointed to the mineral, which does not comprehend the vegetable, as the vegetable cannot understand the animal. So the animal cannot reach the intelligence of humanity. Neither, he said, is it possible for man, a created being, to understand the Almighty Creator. Nevertheless, the perfection and qualifications of God are seen in every created being and in the most perfect manner. In the manifestations of God, Abdul Baha likened those qualities to the rays of the sun focussed in a mirror. If we claim that the sun is seen in the mirror, we do not mean that the whole sun has descended from the holy heights of heaven and entered into the mirror, that is impossible. The eternal nature is seen in the manifestations, and its light and splendour are visible in extreme glory. Therefore men have always been taught and led by the prophets of God. The prophets of God are the mediators of God. All the prophets and messengers have come from one Holy Spirit and bear the message of God, suited to the age in which they appear.

It is the One Light in them, and they are one with each other. But the eternal does not become phenomenal, neither can the phenomenal become eternal. St. Paul, the great apostle, said, "We all, with open face, beholding as in a mirror the glory of God, are changed into the same image, from glory to glory."

Then, raising his hands, Abdul Baha prayed: "O God, the Forgiver! O Heavenly Educator! This assembly is adorned with the mention of thy holy name. Thy children turn their face towards thy kingdom. Hearts are made happy and souls are comforted. Merciful God! Cause us to repent of our shortcomings! Accept us in thy heavenly kingdom and give unto us an abode where there shall be no error. Give us peace. Give us knowledge, and open unto us the gates of thy heaven.

"Thou art the Giver of all! Thou art the Forgiver! Thou art the Merciful!"

The final note of a real chord of harmony was struck when Archdeacon Wilber-

THE APOSTLE OF PEACE

A Survey of References to
'Abdu'l-Bahá in the Western Press
1871–1921

Volume Two: 1912–1921

by

Amín Egea

GEORGE RONALD
OXFORD

George Ronald, Publisher
Oxford
www.grbooks.com

© Amín Egea 2018

All Rights Reserved

A catalogue record for this book is available from the British Library

ISBN 978-0-85398-616-4

Cover design: Steiner Graphics

CONTENTS

Frontispiece — ii
'Abdu'l-Bahá — vii
Preface — ix
Acknowledgments — xiii
Introduction — xv
A Note from the Publisher — xxi
Abbreviations — xxiii

PART I

26 Second Visit to England — 3
27 Edinburgh — 89
28 Second and Third Visits to Paris — 113
29 Central Europe — 131
30 Third Visit to Egypt — 155

PART II

31 Gender Equality and the Suffrage Movement — 169
32 Race Unity — 204
33 An International Language — 218
34 The Theosophical Society — 254
35 Spiritualism and Esotericism — 309
36 Opposition — 339

PART III

37 Return to Haifa — 367
38 The War Years — 402
39 The Passing of 'Abdu'l-Bahá — 439

APPENDIXES

1	Writings and Talks of 'Abdu'l-Bahá Published in General Periodicals	457
2	Photographs and Illustrations	467
3	Book Reviews	471
4	Invitations to 'Abdu'l-Bahá	478
5	*The Christian Commonwealth*	484
6	Arts and Artists	489

Bibliography — 493
Notes and References — 503
Index — 551

'ABDU'L-BAHÁ

'Abdu'l-Bahá (1844–1921) was the eldest surviving son of Bahá'u'lláh, the founder of the Bahá'í Faith. Named 'Abbás after his grandfather, 'Abdu'l-Bahá was known as 'Abbás Effendi outside the Bahá'í community. Bahá'u'lláh gave Him the titles the Most Great Branch, the Mystery of God and the Master. He chose the name 'Abdu'l-Bahá (Servant of Bahá) after the passing of Bahá'u'lláh.

Born in Tehran on 23 May 1844, 'Abdu'l-Bahá recognized His father's station even before it had been openly revealed. Later, He often served as His father's deputy when dealing with officials and the public. He shared Bahá'u'lláh's banishment and exile and was, like Bahá'u'lláh, eventually imprisoned in 'Akká, a remote outpost of the Ottoman Empire, in 1868.

Bahá'u'lláh described the station of 'Abdu'l-Bahá in the Tablet of the Branch (Súriy-i-Ghuṣn):

> There hath branched from the Sadratu'l-Muntahá this sacred and glorious Being, this Branch of Holiness; well is it with him that hath sought His shelter and abideth beneath His shadow. Verily the Limb of the Law of God hath sprung forth from this Root which God hath firmly implanted in the Ground of His Will, and Whose Branch hath been so uplifted as to encompass the whole of creation. Magnified be He, therefore, for this sublime, this blessed, this mighty, this exalted Handiwork! . . . Render thanks unto God, O people, for His appearance; for verily He is the most great Favor unto you, the most perfect bounty upon you; and through Him every mouldering bone is quickened. Whoso turneth towards Him hath turned towards God, and whoso turneth away from Him hath turned away from My beauty, hath repudiated My Proof, and transgressed against Me. He is the Trust of God amongst you, His charge

within you, His manifestation unto you and His appearance among His favored servants . . .

In the Book of the Covenant Bahá'u'lláh named 'Abdu'l-Bahá His successor and the authorized interpreter of His writings. He is the Center of the Covenant to whom all Bahá'ís were to turn after the passing of Bahá'u'lláh.

'. . . though essentially human and holding a station radically and fundamentally different from that occupied by Bahá'u'lláh and His Forerunner,' Shoghi Effendi, the Guardian of the Bahá'í Faith, explained, 'Abdu'l-Bahá was 'the perfect Exemplar of His Faith . . . endowed with super-human knowledge, and to be regarded as the stainless mirror reflecting His light'.[1]

Bahá'u'lláh passed away in 1892 and 'Abdu'l-Bahá became the head of the Bahá'í Faith. Largely confined to 'Akká by the Ottoman authorities, 'Abdu'l-Bahá began to receive a few western pilgrims from 1898.

In 1908 'Abdu'l-Bahá was set free after the Young Turks' revolution and in 1911 He began His historic journeys to Europe and North America to proclaim His father's message. The two volumes of *The Apostle of Peace* document those journeys through the eyes of journalists and commentators who encountered 'Abdu'l-Bahá.

PREFACE

This book was originally intended as a general survey of press references to the Bábí and Bahá'í religions during the period 1844 to 1921, known in Bahá'í history as the Heroic Age, and was to be based on research that began in 1996 and which, over the years, has resulted in more than five thousand documents that record many episodes of the early history of the religions of the Báb and Bahá'u'lláh.

While often inaccurate, inexact or even biased, these press articles stand as an important primary source for the study of the early history of the Bábí-Bahá'í Faith. They shed light on historical episodes, complement available sources and give an exact picture of how westerners received and perceived the new religion.

When in 2006 I started the process of writing this book, it soon became evident that one particular episode – the travels of 'Abdu'l-Bahá in the West (1911 to 1913) – had received so much attention in the press that it would have been impossible to give it a fair treatment if it were to share a volume with other periods in Bahá'í history. Thus, after consulting with the editors, it was decided to limit the scope of the book to press references about 'Abdu'l-Bahá published during His lifetime.

This book, therefore, attempts to present and contextualize over 2,200 press articles about 'Abdu'l-Bahá published between 1871 and 1921, most of them during the period of His travels. This has required two volumes, rather than the intended one.

The documents from the United Kingdom here included have been researched for the most part in the British Library (London). Research has also been conducted in the Bodleian Library (Oxford), the Library of the Religious Society of Friends (London), the Dr Williams and Congregationalist Library (London) and the library of the Theosophical Society of England (London).

Articles in English published in Egypt have also been researched at the British Library. Copies of articles from the Egyptian Arabic press were kindly supplied by the International Bahá'í Library (Haifa).

Many of the French articles were shared with me during my visit to the National Bahá'í Archives of France in Paris. Other documents were found at the National Library of France (Paris) or in its digital platform Gallica.

Some three hundred American newspaper clippings were acquired from the US National Bahá'í Archives. An equally large number of articles were found in different online databases and archives. Other documents were acquired from the Boston Public Library, the Bureau of State Library (Harrisburg, PA), the California State Library, the Carnegie Library of Pittsburgh, the Cleveland Public Library, the Minneapolis Historical Society Library, the New York Public Library, the Public Library of Cincinnati and Hamilton County, the Swarthmore College Peace Collection, the Toronto Public Library and the Wilmington (Delaware) Public Library, among others. Despite the large number of articles published in the American press that are presented in this volume, much more research is yet to be conducted in American journals and magazines, especially in the journals of various organizations and religious centers and in the many newspapers published by different ethnic and cultural communities in the United States.

For the most part, articles from Canadian newspapers were acquired from the Library and Archives of Canada or kindly shared by the National Bahá'í Archives of Canada.

Documents from Germany were generously sent to me by the National Spiritual Assembly of the Bahá'ís of Germany.

I had access to the bulk of newspaper articles published in Budapest when I visited the Hungarian National Bahá'í Archives. Other documents were acquired at the National Library of Hungary (Budapest).

Most articles in Esperanto journals presented in this book were found in the National Library of Austria (Vienna) and in two large private libraries in Spain: the Esperanto Biblioteko 'Ramon Molera Pedrals' (Moià, Barcelona) and the Esperanto-Muzeo de Subirats (Sant Pau d'Ordal, Barcelona).

The two volumes of this book are divided into sections. The first part of volume I includes those references made to 'Abdu'l-Bahá before His travels in the West. In the first chapter, the reader will find various articles written by authors who were not Bahá'ís who visited Him during His imprisonment in 'Akká. The second chapter presents accounts about 'Abdu'l-Bahá written by western Bahá'í pilgrims. From the early days of the Bahá'í Faith in America, most of the articles mentioning the Bahá'ís also mention 'Abdu'l-Bahá, therefore it was necessary to limit this chapter to only those references which provided information about Him. The third chapter presents accounts about 'Abdu'l-Bahá produced by non-Bahá'ís who visited Him in the Holy Land in the short period between His liberation and His first sojourn in Egypt.

The second part of this volume focuses on 'Abdu'l-Bahá's first two visits to Egypt, His early visits to Europe and His travels in North America. In addition to interviews, accounts of His public talks and texts written by 'Abdu'l-Bahá Himself, the reader will find a significant amount of contextual information which in many instances is not available from other sources. Some articles, for instance, will help to fix the exact time and place of some of His talks. Others give the names of people who visited Him, record the reactions of the audiences who listened to Him, or summarize the contents of talks of which no transcription has survived.

The chapters have been arranged chronologically and geographically. However, at the end of this section I have added one chapter of general articles about 'Abdu'l-Bahá in America.

The second volume opens with chapters concerning 'Abdu'l-Bahá's second tour of Europe and His third visit to Egypt. Its second section comprises chapters detailing His contact in Europe and North America with suffragist organizations, the civil rights movement, Esperantists, the Theosophical Society and with various figures and organizations linked with the spiritualist and esoteric movements. The second section closes with a chapter summarizing different instances of opposition to 'Abdu'l-Bahá.

The third part of volume 2 comprises articles about 'Abdu'l-Bahá published after His return to the Holy Land, including the many articles published about His passing.

As a general rule, the articles are reproduced in their entirety. However, to avoid an excessive redundancy and for the sake of brevity, I have not reproduced summaries of or introductions to the Bahá'í Faith found in the articles and have quoted only those texts that are devoted to 'Abdu'l-Bahá.

Where possible, the political or ideological tendency of each publication is indicated. Biographical notes of some of the authors who wrote about 'Abdu'l-Bahá or met Him have also been included. Where available, I have included the number of copies produced by each newspaper in the year a specific article was published or in the closest year for which statistics exist.

In my commentary, I have used the transliteration system standardized for Bahá'í literature for Persian and Arabic names and words. Similarly, I have chosen to capitalize the pronouns that refer to the central figures of the Bahá'í Faith, including 'Abdu'l-Bahá. The articles reproduced in this volume have not been edited and are reproduced as they appeared in the original periodicals .

Amín Egea
Sant Cugat del Vallés
March 2016

ACKNOWLEDGMENTS

I am indebted to many people for their valuable assistance and help during my research. First, I would like to mention my parents Emilio and Talieh, my sister Leili, and the rest of my family for their constant support and encouragement.

Since October 2011, and for a period of six months, I received the generous financial help of a friend, who does not wish his name to be mentioned, without which it would have been impossible for me to complete the research and dedicate the necessary time needed to finish the last stages of this book.

Dr Wendi Momen has patiently edited the manuscript and made many valuable suggestions for its improvement. Any mistakes are my sole responsibility.

Many friends have shared documents and information which has been used in this volume. I would like to thank Pedro Armindo, Frederic Autret, Jan Jaison, Chad Jones, Mona Khademi, Günter Maltz, Judit Manno, Eugenio Marcano, David Merrick, Tom Moritz, Ana María Molera, Zoltan Seress, Adam Thorne, Duane Troxel and Robert Weinberg. I am specially indebted to Parivash Ardei of the National Bahá'í Archives of France, to Joseph Keith of the Quaker library in London, and to Lewis Walker of the US National Bahá'í Archives. I also would like to mention Richard Arpi, Eric Biddy, Bob Brodbeck, Dr Wendy Chmielewski, Stephanie Hoover, Suzanne Johnston, Alice Kane, Rhonda Konig and Alice Morrow for their help in obtaining for me documents in different American libraries. I am also grateful to Heather Eason, Anneliese Garvie, Rodha Lane, Elham Simmons and Tina Vonhof for their translations.

A mi hijo Naim

INTRODUCTION

With the message 'What hath God wrought',[1] sent from Washington to Baltimore on 24 May 1844, Samuel Morse officially opened the first telegraphic line in the world. That historic occasion, which signaled a turning point in the history of human communications, was followed by the rapid development of a network of telegraphs across the world that in a few years transformed many areas of human endeavor, including that of journalism.

Only a few years earlier, in 1835, Charles Louis Havas (1783–1858) had founded the first international news agency. His Bureau in Paris, today known as Agence France-Press, compiled for its subscribers a bulletin with news published in European newspapers or received from correspondents, and would also send French news abroad. In its early stages the Bureau's news would be sent by pigeons or by messengers on horseback. But as telegraph lines were opened in Europe, Havas made extensive use of them, thus gaining immediacy and, with it, more subscribers to his news.

Soon after the establishment of the first telegraphic line to Berlin, one of Havas's employees, Bernhard Wolff (1811–79), opened in 1849 his own firm in Germany. The Wolffs Telegraphisches Bureau operated until the Second World War. In 1851, when a telegraphic line connecting England with the European continent was opened, Paul J. Reuter (1816–99), also one of Havas's workers, founded in London the agency bearing his name. Meanwhile, in America, five New York newspapers wanting to share the cost of covering the news of the war between the United States and Mexico established in 1846 the Associated Press, the first news agency on the American continent.

All these developments in the genesis of modern communications run in parallel with the birth of the Bábí-Bahá'í movement. Morse's first official telegram, for instance, was sent the day after the declaration of the Báb in Shiraz and the birth of 'Abdu'l-Bahá in Tehran.

From its inception the young religion was mentioned in the pages of hundreds of western newspapers. As early as 12 April 1845, *The Bombay Times* published a brief note about the sentencing to death of Mullá 'Alíy-i-Bastámí, which was later reproduced in a London weekly.[2] Just five months later *The Bombay Courier* reported the torture inflicted upon Quddús and other Bábís in Shiraz. Soon afterwards, this news was reproduced in several journals in England, France, Germany, the United States, Australia and New Zealand.[3] In 1848 at least one newspaper reported the trial of the Báb in Tabriz[4] and some months later news of the Shaykh Tabarsí upheaval was reported in various publications.[5] In 1850 news of the execution of the Báb was also published in no less than 320 newspapers in different countries. In that same year the press also reported the Zanján upheaval and the martyrdom of a group of Bábís in Tehran.[6]

When in 1852 Náṣiri'd-Dín Sháh suffered an attempt on his life, the Bábís and the persecutions they suffered were mentioned in hundreds of articles. Later, news of other episodes in the history of the Bahá'í religion such as the banishment of Bahá'u'lláh to 'Akká, the martyrdom of Badí', the execution of the King and the Prince of Martyrs, and the martyrdom of seven Bahá'ís in Yazd in 1891, amongst others, was also published in both Europe and North America. In the weeks following the death of Náṣiri'd-Dín Sháh in 1896, over six hundred news items mentioned the Bahá'ís.

As well as these references in popular newspapers, during this period many scholars and missionaries also wrote profusely about the new religion in specialized and scientific periodicals.

Thus, thanks to the press, and also to the work of authors such as Comte de Gobineau and Edward G. Browne, many westerners became acquainted with the existence of the new religion born in Persia. Familiarity with the terms 'Bab' and 'Babism' was such that, except for a few cases, the general public referred to the Bahá'ís as Bábís until well into the 20th century. Even the early Bahá'ís in the United States were called Bábís in the press for several years. That was more or less the situation when 'Abdu'l-Bahá visited the West. Through the publicity generated during His visit, one of the immediate results of His travels was the normalization of the term 'Bahá'í' and the clarification in the public mind of the differences – and at the same time continuity – between the religions of the Báb and Bahá'u'lláh.

By the time 'Abdu'l-Bahá visited the West, the press had reached a level of industrialization such as to allow some newspapers to produce more than one million copies per day. The first illustrated dailies were born only a few years before the arrival of 'Abdu'l-Bahá in England. Until then, the technique used to include pictures in a periodical was so slow that it was only viable for weekly publications.

The British daily press was divided between broadsheet newspapers and tabloids. The latter, with smaller dimensions, were born with the *Daily Mail* in 1896 and cost a halfpenny, while broadsheet journals cost one penny. Owing to their cheaper price, tabloids quickly became popular. Their contents focused on sensationalist information while broadsheets targeted a readership more interested in the editorial and political orientation of the newspaper. When in 1911 'Abdu'l-Bahá visited London, some 20 dailies were published simultaneously in the city.

In France, the press had developed along similar lines but was much more fragmented. In 1911, for instance, in the city of Paris alone, more than 70 daily journals were published simultaneously, not including financial and sports papers and newspapers in foreign languages.

In the United States the competition between the Hearst newspapers owned by William R. Hearst, son of the early American Bahá'í Phoebe Hearst, and Joseph Pulitzer at the end of the 1890s degenerated into the birth of yellow journalism, characterized by its sensationalism and the lack of informative rigor. The two-party system also resulted in the fragmentation of the media and, therefore, a smaller number of newspapers in big cities as compared to European capitals. Newspapers were simply categorized as Republican, Democrat or independent. In some cities, ethnic and national minorities and religious denominations also had their own daily or weekly publications.

'Abdu'l-Bahá gave much importance to the press. As will be shown, on several occasions He made interesting comments on the social role of journalism and gave recommendations to journalists about the ethical and moral values that they had to take into account in carrying out their profession. He also granted interviews in almost every city He visited, granted press conferences and even agreed to have pictures of Him taken, something that previously not even Bahá'ís visiting Him in the Holy Land were allowed to do. At the request of the editors of various periodicals 'Abdu'l-Bahá also wrote 'articles' for them. Some of these were published along with facsimiles of the originals. He also agreed that notes of some of His talks be sent to the press for publication and on many occasions He requested that several copies of a newspaper with Bahá'í content be bought and sent with their translations to the afflicted Bahá'ís in Persia.

In some European cities, 'Abdu'l-Bahá asked a few Bahá'ís, such as Isabel Fraser, to contact the media and inform them about the Bahá'í Faith. In the United States a 'Publicity Bureau' acting under the auspices of the Persian–American Educational Society was established in early 1912 to inform the media as well as different personalities, churches and organizations about the visit of 'Abdu'l-Bahá to America. A compilation of Bahá'í writings under the title *Universal Principles of the Bahai Movement* was sent to the major journals in the country as well as to many individuals.[7] It would be wrong, however, to conclude that the publicity given in the press to 'Abdu'l-Bahá was gained solely by the efforts made by the Bahá'ís. On the contrary, and as the reader will rapidly acknowledge, the media had a genuine interest in the Master, both as a religious figure and as a promulgator of progressive ideals.

In a Tablet written soon after the beginning of World War I, 'Abdu'l-Bahá mentioned as one of the outcomes of His travels the publicity gained for the Bahá'í Faith in the media:

> Undoubtedly you have read the contents of the American and European newspapers which are mirrors reflecting the public opinion of other nations. Verily, truth is that which is concurrently testified to by all wise men! The contents of these magazines and newspapers are the traces of the pen of the followers of Christ, the people of Moses, philosophers, professors and thinkers of the West. For example, amongst them might be mentioned the Palo Altan, published in the town wherein the Leland Stanford University is founded, the newspapers of Oxford, Christian Commonwealth, Century, Herald, Standard, Review of Reviews, the Arabic newspapers of New York, etc. etc. The philosophers, professors and literary men have expressed their opinions concerning this Cause in these periodicals. This was again through the mercy and providence of the Blessed Perfection whose Absolute Will had ordained the

promotion of the Cause of God in all parts of the world and who confirmed this servant of the Threshold in this service.⁸

It is impossible to estimate the number of people who read about 'Abdu'l-Bahá in the press. This volume includes the circulation figures of only some of the newspapers which mentioned Him between 1910 and 1913. Their total circulation number rises to over 221.72 million copies. At a time when the press was the only means of communication of news available to the masses, this figure is very significant.

The large number of articles about 'Abdu'l-Bahá that are presented in this volume is in itself evidence of His enormous fame and demonstrates that He was far better known by the public than previously thought. Further research will undoubtedly bring to light more evidence of this.

A NOTE FROM THE PUBLISHER

The first mention in the western press of the religion of the Báb and Bahá'u'lláh came as early as 1845 when on 19 April the *Illustrated London News* published a brief note regarding the death sentence passed on Mullá 'Alíy-i-Bastámí[1] and *The Times* of London on 1 November published an article about the arrest of the Báb.[2] Thereafter, the religion was mentioned more frequently in the print media. However, it was the travels of 'Abdu'l-Bahá in the West that attracted by far the most media interest, with literally thousands of articles appearing in the years 1911 to 1913.

However, at the time, the Bahá'í Faith was largely unknown in the West and most people knew nothing at all about it. Even those who were Bahá'ís had a very imperfect understanding of the religion and its teachings, and newspaper reporters had virtually no knowledge of it. Few understood the station of 'Abdu'l-Bahá as the Center of the Covenant, as the Perfect Exemplar of Bahá'u'lláh's teachings, as the Servant of the Glory of God. Therefore He was considered a prophet, a prince, the return of Christ. Thus the articles that were published were often inaccurate. Reporters sometimes framed their questions to 'Abdu'l-Bahá inappropriately and then cast His answers in ways that distorted His message. In addition, the interviews with 'Abdu'l-Bahá and His talks were translated from the Persian into English, which added another dimension of difficulty. The articles reproduced in this book reflect these challenges.

The spelling of names and terms relating to the Bahá'í Faith in the articles reproduced here reflects the uncertainty about the transliteration of these words in the early years of the religion. The spelling of words such as Bahá'í, Bahá'u'lláh and 'Abdu'l-Bahá did not become standardized until Shoghi Effendi provided a list of the transliteration of Bahá'í-related names, places and terms in 1923. The adoption of this system by the Baháʼís took many years and even today newspapers, journals and books written by those who are not Baháʼís adopt their own spellings of these words. Similarly, the articles appeared in publications from a number of countries and the spelling of common words varies, as, for example, with the American and British spellings of words such as center/centre and honor/honour. The publisher has not changed the spelling, punctuation or grammar of the articles reproduced or quoted in this book and therefore there are inconsistencies throughout the text.

The words, talks and letters of ʻAbduʼl-Bahá published in newspaper articles and in publications such as *Star of the West* are reproduced here as they appeared. They are not authorized translations of His words, which can be found in such books as *Selections from the Writings of ʻAbduʼl-Bahá*.

ABBREVIATIONS

American States

AL	Alabama	MT	Montana
AR	Arkansas	NC	North Carolina
AZ	Arizona	ND	North Dakota
CA	California	NE	Nebraska
CO	Colorado	NJ	New Jersey
CT	Connecticut	NM	New Mexico
DC	District of Columbia	NV	Nevada
DE	Delaware	NY	New York
FL	Florida	OH	Ohio
GA	Georgia	OK	Oklahoma
HI	Hawaii	OR	Oregon
IA	Iowa	PA	Pennsylvania
ID	Idaho	RI	Rhode Island
IL	Illinois	SC	South Carolina
IN	Indiana	SD	South Dakota
KS	Kansas	TN	Tennessee
KY	Kentucky	TX	Texas
LA	Louisiana	UT	Utah
MA	Massachusetts	VT	Vermont
MD	Maryland	WA	Washington
ME	Maine	WI	Wisconsin
MI	Michigan	WY	Wyoming
MN	Minnesota		

Months

Jan.	January	Sept.	September
Feb.	February	Oct.	October
Mar.	March	Nov.	November
Apr.	April	Dec.	December
Aug.	August		

PART I

26

SECOND VISIT TO ENGLAND

'Abdu'l-Bahá's Return to England Announced

After eight days of travel from New York, 'Abdu'l-Bahá arrived in Liverpool on board the SS *Celtic* at 7:50 p.m. on 13 December 1912.

His return to England was expected by many. Not only had He already received invitations before leaving New York to speak from various platforms, such as Liverpool's Pembroke Chapel and Oxford University,[1] but His new visit to England had also been anticipated in the British press. This was in part thanks to the efforts of Isabel Fraser, who sent articles about 'Abdu'l-Bahá to various journals and newspapers. The *Manchester Guardian*, for instance, pointed out that 'Timing his arrival with the assembly of the Balkan Peace Conference in London, Abd-ul-Baha, the "Prophet of Peace", is due to reach this country from America in a few days. This venerable Persian is the leader of the Bahais, a sect of Persian origin, which has gained some millions of adherents, in a few years.'[2] On 8 December the *London Budget* carried on its front page a lengthy article introducing the figure of 'Abdu'l-Bahá.[3] A similar article was published three days later in the *Evening Standard and St James Gazette* (London) stating that 'All who know him ['Abdu'l-Bahá] are impressed with his gentleness, patience and great wisdom.'[4] On 13 December the *Evening Express* (Liverpool) published a picture of 'Abdu'l-Bahá with the title 'Prophet of Peace' and reported in its caption that '['Abdu'l-Bahá] is due to arrive in this country in a few days'.[5] The same edition included an article which mentioned the fact that 'Abdu'l-Bahá 'has been invited by wireless to address the undergraduates at Oxford during his stay in England. He will also address the people of Liverpool.'[6] Other journals also published different versions of Fraser's articles.[7]

On 11 December, two days before the arrival of 'Abdu'l-Bahá in Europe, *The Christian Commonwealth* published a special Christmas

3

section which carried communications from religious leaders. 'Abdu'l-Bahá was among those asked to send a contribution and the following was printed as a message from Him:

> Convey my greetings to all your readers. I am extremely pleased and grateful for the attitude of The Christian Commonwealth, for its editor is indeed the servant of the world of humanity and the lover of universal peace. This noble editor is free from prejudice. Praise be to God that in America I established spiritual affinity between the hearts of various religions. It is my hope that through the favours of Baha'o'llah contention and strife may be abandoned entirely by the followers of various religions. All of them may be welded together. In the Synagogue of the Jews I established the validity of his holiness Jesus Christ, and demonstrated the prophethood of his holiness Mohammed. They all listened most attentively. In brief, I said that the Christians did believe in Moses. They believe that Moses was the prophet of God. They believe that the Torah is the Book of God, and they all believe in the Prophets of Israel. Why should you not believe in Christ, acknowledging that Christ was the Word of God? What harm will come to you thereby? The result of this confession will be the entire disappearance of the prejudice which has been existing between the Christians and the Jews for the last two thousand years. When this address, delivered in the synagogue, is read, the reader will be most pleased and most enlightened.[8]

Arrival in Liverpool

When 'Abdu'l-Bahá arrived in Liverpool, a group of Bahá'ís, including Isabel Fraser, Elizabeth Herrick and Hippolyte Dreyfus, boarded the *Celtic* to welcome Him.[9] Herrick, a Liverpool Bahá'í residing in London, had traveled to the city on the day before in order to arrange public meetings for 'Abdu'l-Bahá. With the party of Bahá'ís there were also four reporters wanting to interview the Master.

The following day, 14 December, the *Liverpool Daily Post and Mercury* briefly mentioned that 'The Persian mystic or new "Messiah", Abdul Baha, arrived in Liverpool last evening on the White Star liner Celtic. He will stay for some little time in this city and then proceed to London and Paris.'[10] A representative of the newspaper was among the reporters who boarded the *Celtic* to interview 'Abdu'l-Bahá and the following account was published on a different page of the same edition:

A PROPHET OF PEACE
Persian Mystic in Liverpool
INTERESTING INTERVIEW

Abdul Baha, variously described as the mystic Persian, Prophet of Peace, or the new Messiah, arrived in Liverpool last night from New York on the White Star liner Celtic. He is the leader, son of the founder of his sect, a new religion of humanity and peace, which is credited with 3,000,000 adherents, spread over all parts of the world. He has a strange, striking, and picturesque personality. Habited in the dress of the Persian learned or cultured class – a white fez on his head, a flowing chocolate under-garment, surmounted by a cloak of blueish tinge – all eyes on the stage were at once rivetted upon him as he peered over the ship's side into the rain and gloom of Liverpool. A closer view, which a 'Daily Post and Mercury' representative was privileged to have on board, revealed an old man, full of subdued fire, quietly resting in a luxurious alcove opposite the companion way. A mass of wrinkles upon his face, a gleam of Oriental enthusiasm in his eye, long grey hair streaming over his shoulders, there was something almost weird and bewitching about the 'Prophet of Peace' and the twentieth century 'Messiah', whose visit synchronised with the Balkan Peace Conference and the more pacific attitude generally of the European Great Powers towards each other. Round the prophet was gathered a circle of disciples, dressed more or less in the Persian fashion. The immediate retinue consisted of three persons: Ahmed Sohrab, who acts as translator of the speeches or sermons of the 'Messiah', Mirza Mahmoud, secretary, and Sayad Assadallah.

The 'prophet' speaking to our reporter reeled off the record of his travels. The burden of it was that he had 'presented' himself in all the large cities of the United States, delivered sermons, lectures, or speeches to men and women of all kinds of religion or no religion, he had addressed audiences at Church organisation meetings, treating men and everyone alike, Catholics, Protestants, nondescripts, or unbelievers, by all of whom he was well received. The keynote of his addresses was the distress of the world of humanity, and he summoned all men and all the religious bodies with which they were associated to cast away their prejudices, and unite on one common platform – that of peace and human love. He proclaimed, he went on, universal peace among all nations and religions. The differences which existed to-day, he proceeded, were caused by accretions, by dogmas, by imitations, incomprehensible blindness to the fundamental principle of real religion. There should be one language as a mode of communication to effect all this, which, when realised, the greed, the hurry and scurry of the world would disappear, and the highest form of spiritual and temporal well-being would be evolved.

Asked where his authority came from, he alleged that it was a direct inspiration from heaven.[11]

The *Evening Express* (Liverpool) also sent a reporter to interview 'Abdu'l-Bahá and published the following:

PEACE PROPHET
SAYS LIVERPOOL IS 'A LIVE CITY'

Abbas Effendi, or Abdul Baha (Servant of God), as he prefers to be called, will address the Theosophical Society to-night at eight o'clock at their headquarters in Colquitt Street, off Bold Street; and to-morrow evening he will address the evening service at Pembroke Chapel, at. 6.30.

Abdul Baha is the Great Peace Prophet, who suffered for 40 years in a Turkish prison that he might teach men how to attain the hitherto unattainable 'peace which passeth understanding'. He is stopping at the Adelphi Hotel, and when asked about the Liverpool people he said: –

'Liverpool is a live city. It has the Breath of Reality, and when in this spiritual springtime the Divine truth comes forth with renewed vigour, the people will be like fruitful trees, and the Holy Spirit will enable them to flourish in abundance. Then they will gain not only materially, but in what is of far more importance, spiritual progress. They realise that this is a brilliant century. Their eyes are open to the great necessity for union, if progress is to be made. Brotherly love will be born unto them. For, verily, you are all leaves of one tree, drops of one ocean. God is at peace with his children; why should they engage in strife among themselves!'[12]

Address at Pembroke Chapel

Among those who visited 'Abdu'l-Bahá on Saturday, 14 December, were Mrs Armour, president of the Liverpool Theosophical Lodge, where 'Abdu'l-Bahá was to speak in the afternoon of the same day (see chapter 34), and Rev. Donald B. Fraser, of the Pembroke Baptist Church, who invited the Master to speak on the following day at the regular service of his congregation.

The talk at Pembroke Chapel was programed for half past six on Sunday, 15 December. According to Sohrab, fifteen hundred people gathered to listen to the Master,[13] who spoke on the need for unity among religions. Sohrab further reports that 'after the address the Minister requested the Master to utter the benediction and the large audience arose with bowed heads, receiving the wondrous and effective words of the mainspring of prayer. The Minister was most pleased, the people came forward and shook hands.'[14] After His address 'Abdu'l-Bahá wrote a prayer for Rev. Fraser in the church book: 'O Thou Kind Almighty, confirm Thou this servant of Thine, Mr Fraser, in the service of Thy Kingdom. Make him illumined; make him heavenly; make him spiritual; make him divine! Thou art the Generous, the King.'[15]

Notes of the talk were taken by a certain Mr J. Stiles and from them a transcription was prepared by Elizabeth Herrick. This was published in the January issue of *Plain Truth*, the magazine of the Pembroke Chapel:

> A WORLD RELIGION AND UNIVERSAL PEACE
>
> At Pembroke Chapel, Sunday evening, December 15th, Abdul Baha, servant of God, arriving in Liverpool from America, where he had addressed large audiences of various denominations, gave an address in the Persian language to an attentive and deeply interested congregation. The Rev Donald B. Fraser, the recently chosen Pastor, in introducing the Prophet, remarked that Pembroke always opened its portals to every reformer. Hearing that Abdul Baha was to pass through Liverpool on his way to London, Paris and the East, he had approached this servant of Humanity.
>
> 'Abdul Baha,' said Mr. Fraser, 'is the son of Baha'u'llah, and, with his father, suffered 40 years' imprisonment and exile under Turkish rule for a very high form of religious ideal. Baha'u'llah and his predecessor, the Bab, who was martyred, believed it was possible

to bring into unity and fellowship the people of all religions, by the recognition of the fundamental truth that we are all the children of God, and that the bond between us all is Love. Our friend has undertaken at great cost to himself, and enormous labour, to make this truth known to every race and nation, and is going round the world to proclaim it. He has got something like three millions of people to believe what he says. There are three millions of Persians, some of them Mohammedans, a great many Americans and English, who really believe there is no bond nor free, but all are one in the Love of God. He has lately come from America, where he has been received with enthusiasm. Here in Pembroke we cannot be behind America! He speaks not only on Brotherhood, but on behalf of Peace throughout all nations, and if there is one thing more dear than another to the heart of the people who are in the habit of worshipping here, it is Peace. I just want for a moment to suggest to you that one of the great reasons why there is strife amongst the nations is because there is not perfect amity between individuals and classes. I am profoundly of the opinion that the strife between religious sects is very largely responsible for the more extended strife between nations. I believe that if we in this country could get peace established between the sections of the Church, it would go a long way indeed in bringing about a better understanding between nationalities. A quarrelsome house never makes friends. We do not like to have much to do with such a family. England is a quarrelsome family. The Catholics are quarrelling with the Protestants and the Protestants with the Catholics. Only some of us would unite on the basis of a creed, but it is possible for all of us to unite on the basis of a common Brotherhood. Our friend stands for coalescing, on the basis of love, of all creeds and sections in all parts of the Church Universal. That is the burden of his Message tonight. He brings with him a gentleman, Ahmad Sohrab, who is acting as interpreter, and you will get the best English of what our friend will speak in Persian.'

Abdul Baha said: 'To-night I am exceedingly pleased and happy to find myself in a revered assemblage, an assemblage, the members of which are well recognised throughout the world for civilisation and enlightenment; who are well known as factors in philanthropy and well-being. Therefore I supplicate on the threshold of God,

Divine confirmation for you, so that at all times you may become the manifestors of Divine mercy. May you serve faithfully the world of humanity. May you become the means of the welfare and prosperity of all mankind. The greatest prize this world can hold is the consummation of the Oneness of Humanity. All are the children of God, God is the Creator of all, the Provider and Protector of all. God is kind to all the children of men. The real Shepherd is God and we are all the sheep of His flock. He educates all of us and is compassionate towards men. Ponder, and you will see there is no restraint to the bounty of God. His grace encompasses all mankind. The sun of God shines upon all the children of men. The rain of God falls for all. The gentle breeze of God wafts over all His creatures. Humanity at large is sitting around the divine table of the Almighty. As long as we have a compassionate God, who overlooks our sins and rears us with great tenderness and affability, why should we be separate from each other? Why should we ever engage in strife? Why should we ever engage on the battlefield to kill each other? God is kind, is He not? Why should we be unkind? What is the reason? How are we benefited by being unkind? To-day, the chief means of dissension amongst the nations is religion; while in reality the foundation of the Religion of God is one. Differences lie in blind imitations which have crept into religion after its foundation. Religion is Reality, and reality is one. It does not permit of multiplicity. His holiness Abraham was the herald of reality. His holiness Moses was the spreader of reality. His Holiness Jesus was the Founder of reality. His holiness Mohammed was the spreader and promulgator of reality. His holiness Baha'u'llah was the establisher of reality. The reality of religion is one. Fundamentally there is no difference. The reality of religion consists in the love of God, in the faith of God, in the virtue of humanity, and in the means of communication between the hearts of men. The Reality of Religion is the Oneness of the whole of Humanity. All nations of the world are united and agreed on this fundamental principle. Every sect and every community has gathered around itself a certain set of doctrines and documents, and as these imitations and blind documents differ from each other, dissension and strife are visible amongst all mankind. If the world of Humanity forgets these differences and imitations, and investigates the reality of these religions, it will be found they are united and in accord. Behind every matter and every movement in existence there is Wisdom. For example, behind the body politic is Wisdom, behind sovereignty is Wisdom. Love and amity amongst the children of men is wisdom. Reciprocity and co-operation between men shows wisdom. Behind every universal movement is wisdom. What is the wisdom of religion may we ask? There is no doubt whatever that the wisdom of religion is love and amity amongst the people, that it establishes fellowship between the various organisations of man. God is love upon love with love. Therefore it is evident that the foundation of the Religion of God is love. The purpose of all religion is unity. It has not been given to create dissension. The Religion of God is for peace, not for war. It is the means of co-operation and mutual assistance, and must ever be the means of happiness to the children of humanity. Why should we ever make it a cause of separation and alienation? It is a remedy to bestow health, and recovery. Why should we ever make it a cause of pathology and sickness? Religion is the cause of the glorification of humanity; why should we ever make it the cause of degradation and debasement? Religion is the cause of the illumination of the world of humanity; why should we make it the cause of darkness and gloom? We are all the children of God. We are all the servants of God. The glances of His mercy encircle us all. He has bestowed religion that it may be the means of bringing together the various members of His family. Yet such illumination has become the cause of utter darkness. Such a means of amity and fellowship has become the cause of enmity and hatred! In the Orient, between the people of various religions, there was the utmost hatred and animosity. The greatest rancour existed between the various communities. They shed the blood of one another. They pillaged each others' property. They sacrificed each others' children. There was great commotion and constant warfare going on. Darkness had encircled this radiance. The horizon of reality was hidden by clouds of imitations and dogmas and no rays of the sun could penetrate through these clouds.

At such a time, his holiness Baha'u'llah appeared in Persia. He summoned the people of various religions to love and fellowship. At this time in Persia, the Jews, the Christians, the Mohammedans, the Zoroastrians, the Buddhists, all of contending religions, were ever fighting each other. Having heard the words of Baha'u'llah, they are now living together in the utmost love, and unity. They are in the utmost stage of co-operation and reciprocity. What harm can accrue if such amity becomes permanent throughout the civilised and uncivilised world? Strife and dissension should not remain. Warfare must disappear. It causes the destruction of humanity and must come entirely to an end. Baha'u'llah declared international peace. In Persia, many years ago he declared international peace amongst religions and nations and between the races of every clime. With the greatest power and penetration did he arise to spread principles of peace. For this he was thrown into prison and suffered great hardships. His properties were pillaged. His friends were martyred. More than 20,000 souls sacrificed their lives, so that the oneness of the world of humanity might be realised.

All his life Baha'u'llah endured great calamities and hardships. Often he was in chains. Sometimes he was living in exile. Again he was incarcerated in barracks. Notwithstanding these stumbling blocks, ever he strove, ever he worked, so that he became able to establish amity among the people of contending religions. Religion must become the cause of love. If it becomes the cause of enmity, what use is there for it? Religion must become the cause of prosperity. Alas! It is a thousand pities that it should have become the cause of hatred and rancour! Consider what has transpired in the Balkans lately. The blood of men has been spilled, women have been destroyed, children have been sacrificed, villages have been ransacked. How many fathers have become sonless? How many children have lost their parents? How many mothers are weeping to-day for their children lost on the battlefield? And these people call themselves the followers of religion! Well, religion must become the cause of love. It must create mercy, and be established in justice and equity. Religion must become illumination and enlightenment. Consider, ignorance has reached such a degree of folly, that it is the duty of humanity to ever investigate reality. No one must be satisfied with mere traditions. Traditions differ and cause misunderstandings to remain. These misunderstandings have created direful conditions.

Continuing my address to the Jews, I said: You are thinking that Christ destroyed the foundation of Moses; but let us be fair, let us be just, and investigate, reality. The cause of Moses, the religion of Moses for 1,500 years was circumscribed within the boundary of Jerusalem. The Bible was only found in that small locality. Other parts of the world never heard the name of Moses. Even the people of Persia never heard the name of Moses. They had never seen the Book of Moses. They had never seen the Book of Moses until His Holiness Jesus Christ appeared. He raised the name of Moses. His Holiness Christ promulgated the Old Testament throughout the Orient and the Occident. During the Mosaic Dispensation, the Bible was only translated into one language. But through the blessing of Christianity, the Bible was translated into many languages and spread throughout the world. Consider what love Christ had for Moses. His Holiness Christ promulgated the fundamental principles of Moses. The Ten Commandments He spread throughout the world. He made famous all the Israelitish Prophets. He made all the nations of the world believe in the priesthood of Moses. Were it not for the appearance of Christ, how could the people of America ever have heard the name of Moses? How could the Bible have become a household book? How could they have heard the names of the Israelitish prophets? All these services were rendered by Jesus Christ. Now let us find out, after these statements, whether Christ was the enemy of Moses, or his best friend. Be just. His Holiness Christ was the spreader of the Mosaic movement. He spread the Old Testament. Notwithstanding this, you are thinking that he was the enemy of Moses. Why not abandon these prejudices? The Christians believe that Moses was the Prophet of God, that the Bible is the Book of God, and that all the Israelitish prophets are the mouthpieces of God. What harm would there be if you came out and said: 'Christ is the Word of God', so that this dissension may cease? And so that fellowship may be established eternally between the Jews and the Christians? If you just say these words: 'Christ is the Word', this will show you have investigated reality, and dissension will be left behind. When we are not investigating reality there is dissension between religions. For example, in the Book of the Koran, his holiness Mohammed mentions the name of His Holiness the Christ. It is from the text of the Koran that Christ is called the Word of God, the Spirit of God. The text of the Koran says that Mary, the mother of Christ, was a virgin, and there is a long chapter in the Koran specially eulogising Mary, and it is very explicitly explained that Mary conceived by the power of the Holy Spirit. It is also written in the Koran that 'as soon as Christ was born He began to speak and that while He was a child in the cradle He could speak with all those who came to Him'. Such wonderful miracles are not recorded in the New Testament. It is the record of the Koran that Mary, the mother of Christ, was living in the Holy of Holies, that she had the fellowship of the Almighty, and that food descended from heaven for her. It is recorded in the Koran that the Holy Spirit addressing Mary said: 'Oh, Mary! Be faithful to God, for He has created thee pure and sanctified, and hath made thee superior over all the women of the world.' And again it is written in the Koran that 'Christ ascended into heaven, and that he will again return from heaven'. Again, that 'Christ is pure and unique'. So, most of the praises and commands of Christ are recorded in the Book which is considered sacred by 300 millions of Mohammedans. Just think of the present misunderstanding between these two religions! The presence of misunderstanding has caused the warfare of the last 1,300 years between Christians and Mohammedans! The warfare going on in the Balkans is through misunderstandings. Think of one crusade which lasted for 200 years! Yet religious warfare continues! There are more than 260 millions of Mohammedans throughout, the world. You cannot destroy this colossal number. Therefore, if there is love and fellowship amongst the Jews, the Christians and the Mohammedans, the Orient and the Occident will find the greatest composure and peace. The foundation of the religion of God is love. Even the idolaters are worshipping God in their own way. The foundation of the religion of God is compassion and mercy. It is not enmity and hatred. It is the illumination of the world of man, not darkness. Therefore, if we are truly religious in spirit, we must follow God, because there is no policy greater than His. We must treat all the members of humanity in the same manner that God deals with them. Is it possible for humanity to choose a better and wiser policy than God? There is no doubt that God is all-knowing and all-wise. His policy is kindness. Why should we be unkind? Do we know better than God? There is no doubt that He knows best. We see that God has created all, provides for all, and protects all. This ideal Shepherd takes care of all His flock. Why should we deal harshly with each other? Are we greater, wiser, than the Almighty – than the Omnipresent? Is our policy more consummate than His? It is evident that our policy is mere error. Therefore my advice is: We must all consider each other as the members of one family. Differences are the progeny of error. They only exist in the realm of imagination, imaginations have idle existence, but we have real existence, we have visible existence. No, our physiognomic differences are not the cause of hatred and animosity amongst the people. These have real existence. Why should imaginations which have only idle existence become the cause of alienation and differences? There is no doubt that they are compound ignorance, and the cause of destruction in the world of humanity. God is not pleased with the horrible events which have been transpiring in the Balkans. They are hated by Him. Every lover of humanity is displeased with them. There, people are killing each other like so many wolves. They tear each other to pieces. They shed each other's blood. They kill each other's innocent children. Just consider, the ferocious beasts do not treat their kith and kin like this. The wolf may tear to pieces one animal, which it does, for food – but wolves never tear each other in thousands. Are men not more ferocious than wolves? Are they not more unjust than birds of prey? What are the causes of all this strife? I say they are religious differences. The foundation of the world of God is Love. But nations say we want to increase our dominions.

I will only make one statement and close, and I want your careful attention. What is this land, this earth? Is it not this: That for five days we live on this earth; then it becomes our grave, our cemetery? Eternally shall we be beneath it. Now is it beneficial or kind to engage in war and strife for an eternal cemetery? Many generations have come, and have lived for a short time on this earth, and have gone under it. It is the universal graveyard of humanity. Is it praiseworthy that we engage in warfare, shedding blood, destroying houses, pillaging the wealth of nations and killing little children beneath the hoofs of horses? Is it worthy that we sacrifice eternal life and the everlasting soul of man, for the sake of a little dust? There is no doubt that God is displeased with this. There is no doubt that the perfect man will not approve. Justice and equity will not permit it. It is a pity man is to-day engaged in such warfare. Therefore, I hope that you who are members of a noble nation (praise be to God that you are a civilised nation) will strive with all your might, to raise the standard of the Oneness of Humanity and unfurl the flag of international peace over all regions of the earth. That peace amongst all nations, religions, and races, may be an accomplished fact. This is my request to you all. That you may be assisted and confirmed in this service. May you ever be manifestors of divine mercy. May you ever be protected beneath the shelter of God. And may you be submerged in the mercies of the Almighty.[16]

A few weeks afterwards, Rev Donald B. Fraser decided to dedicate the Sunday school classes of his parish to the study of the Bahá'í Faith and 'Abdu'l-Bahá through Elizabeth Herrick sent him a message suggesting some of the subjects that could be studied in the classes.[17]

In London a further report about 'Abdu'l-Bahá's activities in Liverpool was published in *The Christian Commonwealth*:

ARRIVAL IN ENGLAND

Abdul Baha arrived in Liverpool from New York on December 13 by the White Star liner 'Celtic.' Miss Elizabeth Herrick, formerly of Liverpool, now of London, had gone up to Liverpool a day ahead to arrange for the addresses; M. Hippolyte Dreyfus had come from Paris to meet the Master, and a group from Manchester, Liverpool, and Leeds – in all about a dozen – watched the great liner come slowly up the stream, literally out of the dark night. To the little group on the landing stage it seemed ages before the first, second, and third-class luggage was arranged in the Customs and the porters and reporters dashed aboard. Then we saw the Master's white-turbaned head and directly behind him, as they came slowly down the gang-plank, one of the Persians carried a tiny Japanese orange-tree from California. Laden with fruit, it looked like an offering from the tropics as it swayed in the gusts of the broad Mersey. Abdul Baha stopped two days in Liverpool, resting at the Adelphi Hotel. During that time he gave two addresses, one to the Theosophical Society on Saturday night, December 14, and one at Pembroke Chapel on Sunday evening, December 15. He left for London on the morning of the third day, Monday, December 16.[18]

'Abdu'l-Bahá left Liverpool by train on the morning of 16 December, reaching London at 1:40 p.m.[19] Two days later, 18 December, *The Christian Commonwealth* published a brief note stating that 'Abdul Baha Abbas landed at Liverpool on Friday evening and arrived in London on Monday. He will spend Christmas amongst us. This week he is attending several private and semi-private functions. More news about the Bahai leader will appear in our next issue.'[20]

Reception at the Westminster Palace Hotel

The London Bahá'ís arranged a public reception for 'Abdu'l-Bahá at the Westminster Palace Hotel on Friday, 20 December 1912. Over a thousand people attended the meeting. The audience included various personalities such as the Baron Weardale (1847–1923)[21] who had a private interview with 'Abdu'l-Bahá before the meeting started. The Master was introduced by Sir Thomas Barclay (1853–1941)[22] and after His address Charlotte Despard, the founder of the Women's Freedom League (see chapter 31), and Alice Buckton offered a few words about 'Abdu'l-Bahá and the Bahá'í Cause.

'Abdu'l-Bahá's talk focused on the subject of peace and made several references to the London Peace Conference. He closed the meeting by reciting a prayer for peace in the Balkans.[23] *The Christian Commonwealth* published two accounts of the meeting, the first of them appearing on 25 December:

> ### ABDUL BAHA'S RETURN
> #### RECEPTION AT THE WESTMINSTER PALACE HOTEL
>
> In a highly modern setting a picturesque meeting of East and West took place last Friday evening. Abdul Baha's return from his American tour gave his followers in this country their first opportunity of welcoming the Master, and a reception was held in the Westminster Palace Hotel, presided over by Sir Thomas Barclay. The numbers present were an indication of the interest now taken in the Bahai movement. Dark Eastern faces, impassive Japanese, and representatives of the Continental nations appeared in sharp contrast with the English people who formed the bulk of the assembly. But there was no diversity visible as these groups fused and intermingled.
>
> Into this animated assembly the Master came quietly, and a

sudden hush fell as the company realised his presence, followed by a rustle of dresses as they rose respectfully while he made his way to the raised daïs where the chairman awaited him. Sir Thomas Barclay said he was present in the capacity of a listener rather than a speaker, and as a Western European to learn the wisdom of the East. It was a great privilege to have the Master among them, and they rejoiced at the success which had attended his work in the cause of international peace and the unity of nations.

Abdul Baha spoke with great animation and vigour in some passages, and in others his voice fell into soft caressing cadences or rose with a sonorous solemnity as he intoned some great sentence. He spoke his native tongue, the sentences being interpreted as he proceeded. Mainly the address was an exposition of the teaching of Baha'o'llah. Love and affinity, he said, were the basis of religion; love is the cause of life, and hatred spells death. Hence the declaration that all the divine manifestations were meant to establish the law of love among men. In an interesting passage he spoke of an address delivered to nearly 6,000 Jews in California, in which he urged that 'his holiness Christ' had proclaimed the validity of the Mosaic law, and through him the name of Moses was spread abroad. Abdul Baha said he was very pleased that he was present in London while the conference was sitting to discuss the terms of peace in the Balkans.

He prayed that the deliberations might be fruitful of good, and that the English Government and people will do their utmost to further the cause of peace.

Brief addresses were delivered by Miss Monckton and Mrs Despard, the latter saying that she felt deeply privileged to have the opportunity of meeting and listening to the Eastern sage. We are living in strange times, and the unrest with which the world is seething has a profound significance for the future. At the conclusion of the speeches Abdul Baha gave his benediction on the gathering. The hope was expressed that this would be the first of many such assemblies while the Master is in this country.[24]

The second account, written by Isabel Fraser, was published a week later and contained a transcription of the talk delivered by 'Abdu'l-Bahá:

IN LONDON
RECEPTION AT WESTMINSTER PALACE HOTEL

A remarkable cosmopolitan gathering filled the large hall at the Westminster Palace Hotel, Friday evening, December 20, to listen to an address by Abdul Baha. His topic was one that is agitating many of the thinking minds of to-day – the vast subject of Peace. Sir Thomas Barclay, was in the chair, and among the audience were scientists, diplomats, and leaders of the great movements of the day, including a number of Orientals. So great was the overflow that many were compelled to sit on the floor, and a fringe standing at the outer edge extended beyond the door.

Sir Thomas Barclay, in introducing the Master, said he was present to listen as a Western European deeply interested in Persia, in Persian thought and in Persian literature and glad of an opportunity to do honour to a venerated Persian. Abdul Baha is known far beyond the immediate ranks of Bahaism, known not only for his own sake, but also, as the accredited messenger of the Bahai teaching. Persia has been a fatherland of religions, but Bahaism is a system of thought and conduct. 'If I have understood Bahaism,' said the chairman, after quoting some of the sayings of Baha'o'llah, 'it has a singularly good Christian ring; and I should interpret it to mean: Be a real Christian and you will be a good Bahaist. But I am merely presiding, not proselytising. I am proud to have been asked to preside at a meeting of those who have come together to do honour to one who deserves it so richly.'

Abdul Baha remained seated and spoke in Persian, Mirza Ahmad Sohrab translating. He spoke earnestly, with animated gestures, and one could almost divine the purport of his remarks from the play of his countenance. He spoke on the subject of unity and peace, and expounded some of the teachings Baha'o'llah gives for the attainment of these much-desired conditions.

ABDUL BAHA'S ADDRESS

Scientists tell us that the world of matter is made up of constellations of molecules which hold it in its various forms. Each molecule consists of a similar constellation of atoms, which, in turn, recent discovery shows, is made up, of tiny worlds of electrons. Thus we see that this law of affinity is the very basis of existence.

SECOND VISIT TO ENGLAND

As in the material so in the spiritual world, love is the attracting force that welds together the constituent elements into a composite unity and holds them firm against disintegration.

Love is the cause of life, and hatred or animosity spells death or disintegration. Just as affinity is the fundamental principle of composition, the greater affinity, love, is the light of unity, and the lack of love causes the darkness of separateness. Love is conducive to existence; difference is conducive to disintegration. Love is the cause of the illumination of the whole of humanity; discord and dissension are the cause of the destruction of the human race. All the divine messengers have come to this earth as specialists of the law of love. They came to teach a divine love to the children of men; to minister a divine healing between the nations; to cement in one the hearts of men, and to bring humanity into a state of unity and concord. In this pathway, each one of these divine manifestations of God's love has accepted innumerable calamities and hardships. For the sake of a realisation of love and concord amongst men, they have sacrificed their lives. How many persecutions have they suffered so that they might bring into a state of harmony those contending nations and religions and might create peace and conciliation, between these various peoples of the earth!

Let us consider his holiness Jesus Christ; how many trials he accepted along this pathway, how many difficulties and persecutions, even to giving up his life – he chose for himself the Cross – so that the light of love might shine in the hearts of men and the various contending nations come into a state of affinity and love: this was the purpose. When a holy and divine man shows us the way and sacrifices himself like Jesus Christ for the sake of love and affinity amongst the children of men, our duty is plain; it is evident that we, likewise, must follow in the footsteps of Jesus Christ. We, too, must be ready to sacrifice our lives that this love may live. We must accept every hardship that this love may come to the hearts of the people.

Consider carefully that for the last six thousand years there has been constant strife and warfare amongst the people. All the wars which have occurred in past history have been the basis of the destruction of the human race; love, on the other hand, has been the cause of cementing these people together.

Consider how Jesus Christ, through the power of his love, brought a state of harmony between the Egyptian nation, the Assyrian nation, and all the nations of ancient times. Such a unity and concord was realised amongst these various peoples that the pages of history are adorned with their accomplishments, although formerly they were in a state of constant strife and contention. Formerly their business was war; but, through the breath of the holy spirit, unity became a creative factor. The great and wise men of the world have ever striven hard, so that the hearts of humanity might be cemented together by the heavenly teachers, whose mission it is to bring into the world this divine state of love.

The foundation of all religion as taught by all the divine messengers has been love and affinity. A hundred thousand pities, alas, that the divine message has become the means of warfare and strife! In the Balkans blood has been freely and copiously shed, lives are being destroyed houses are pillaged, cities are razed to the ground – and all this through religious prejudice; while in reality the foundation of the religion of God is love. All the divine and holy manifestations invite the exercise of love. In reality we are living in the midst of the greatest proof of divine love. For at a time when in the Orient there existed the utmost state of strife and sedition, warfare raged between the nations, between the religions, and between the various sects; darkness encompassed the horizon of the Orient, and each religion asserted its claim over the other – at such a time, under such circumstances, his holiness Baha'o'llah shone from the horizon of the East. He declared that the reality of all religion is one, that all religions have the same foundation for their teaching. He taught men that the foundation of the religion of God is love. Alas, that they should have entirely forgotten this foundation! They have created blind dogmas, and as these blind dogmas develop, we observe constant bloodshed and strife.

If all the religions and sects were to quit themselves from all past limitations and search diligently for the foundation (as the foundation of the divine religion is one), there would follow unity and concord, these terrible events would not happen. Bloodshed would cease, and hatred between the hearts of men would be dispelled. Heavenly illumination would dawn, divine love would be created, the efforts of the divine teachers would be held and would yield results, hearts would be knit together, the basis of strife and quarrel would be forgotten, divine justice would be revealed and divine radiance diffused.

In order that the darkness of strife and sedition might be entirely banished from the human world, his holiness Baha'o'llah established and taught certain declarations or principles. The first principle which he proclaimed was the principle of the oneness of the human family. He said 'Humanity constitute the sheep of God's flock. The real shepherd is God.' The real shepherd is compassionate and kind towards all the members of his flock. Humanity is created by God; he provides for all, protects all; he is kind to all. Why should we treat each other harshly? He has made a plea for love, not for difference, or hatred, or animosity. None of us is created by Satan. All are edifices of God, therefore we must strive that these edifices be protected, and not seek to destroy them.

The second principle of Baha'o'llah concerned international peace, and to this end he wrote all the nations and sent special epistles to the rulers and kings of the earth. Likewise, he proclaimed peace amongst the religions – was not peace the foundation of religion? It is time that these limitations and dogmas be done away with that the foundation of religion of God may be the means of union and good fellowship.

Again, he proclaimed inter-racial peace, for humanity is the progeny of one Adam – all belong to one lineage. 'This sphere is one globe,' he said, 'and is not divided; the various continents on the face of the globe are, in reality, one native land, inhabited by one human family; therefore, there should not exist between the various countries this warfare and strife.

Another principle of Baha'o'llah was that religion must ever be the means of love. If religion is the cause of hatred and animosity, it is better to quit religion. Every affair, every matter which in the world of humanity is the cause of love, that matter is good; but if it is creative of difference amongst the children of men that matter is evil. If religion be a cause of hatred amongst the people, it is absolute evil. Irreligion is better than that so-called religion. The people have made religion the cause of warfare and strife, while the reality of religion is the cause of unity and love.

The fourth teaching of Baha'o'llah was relative to the conformity of science and reason with a true universal religion. If religion is contrary to science and reason, it is superstition. A theory which is not acceptable by the mind of man and which science rejects is devoid of reality. It is a vision of superstition.

The fifth teaching of Baha'o'llah is relative to prejudice, which must be abandoned. National prejudice must be forgotten, racial prejudice must be obliterated, and patriotic prejudice must likewise be lifted from amongst the people. Since the beginning of history all the wars which have occurred have been caused primarily through religious prejudice, or racial prejudice, or patriotic prejudice. As long as these prejudices are not broken the world of humanity will not attain to perfect peace and tranquillity.

Another teaching of Baha'o'llah is relative to the equality of men and women. In the human family of God there is no distinction. God is no respecter of gender. The religion of God is one. The human family share in common all the faculties; they share in common all the divine bounties. God has not accredited any difference between the male and female. The same education must be given to women as to men, so that they may acquire science and arts, and advance along the course of civilisation, in order that they may become proficient and attain to the level of men. In the Orient, woman has been very degraded in the past, men giving no importance to her, thinking themselves superior in creation, but through the teaching of Baha'o'llah, who declared that a great calling is destined for women, they promoted many facilities for the education and training of the girls. In a brief space of time, the girls and the women alike have advanced along the pathway of education. Now merely in the country of Persia alone, many schools are organised for the girls, and girls are engaged in the study of the sciences and arts.

The seventh teaching of Baha'o'llah concerns itself and is in accord with this system of universal education; it is that all the children should study and acquire a profession, that there should not remain a single individual without a profession whereby he can earn his livelihood. Baha'o'llah further declares that through the equipment of science and the misunderstandings which have prevailed between religion and science would become reconciled. The non-conformity of science and religion has been the greatest factor in keeping the religions apart.

The paramount declaration of Baha'o'llah is that peace must be realised between all the nations of the earth. International tribunals will be established and certain representatives from amongst all the Governments of the earth will be sent to that inter-parliamentary gathering.

The era of 'The Parliament of Man' will be ushered in. This international tribunal will be the court of appeals between the nations. Fifty years ago Baha'o'llah wrote to all the rulers of the world about this international tribunal of justice and arbitration.

These are some of the teachings in the religion of Baha'o'llah – all of which would take a great deal of time to expound. I will just add that it is my hope that during these days in which this Peace Conference is discussing negotiations for terms of peace you will strive to the utmost that peace measures and peaceful negotiations may be carried on among them. I am very pleased that I am living in London during these days. I supplicate that the conference may be crowned with success, so that peace may be established in the Balkans, this bloodshed may cease, and that this conference may become a working basis for the future international peace. May all the nations and all the countries of the world strive with us, that in the future there may be no war and no bloodshed.

As the English Government is a just Government, and as the British nation is a noble nation and they accomplish what they undertake, it is my hope that in this matter they will show their utmost wisdom and sagacity, so that the sun of peace may dawn on the horizon of the Balkans, eternal fellowship may be realised among them, and whenever in the future there is any difficult problem a conference may be called for its settlement, for through these various conferences all the troubles of humanity may be solved.

May there remain no more war and strife; and may tranquillity dawn on the world of humanity expressive of the world of light, so that this nether world may be transformed by love and concord and may become the foretaste of the other kingdom. Then all humanity will be sheltered under the shadow of the Almighty. This is my hope, the highest desire of my life day and night. I pray and I beg confirmation from God for this Government that this nation may be assisted to hold aloft the banner of international peace.

MISS ALICE BUCKTON

Following the Master's address, which was listened to in intense silence, Miss Alice Buckton, who for years has been closely associated with this great movement both here and in America, told how the wonderful words of Baha'o'llah, written from his prison at Acca, some of them smuggled out in bits of bread to the early followers, had been gathered and published and, during the last fifty years, spread throughout the world. Miss Buckton referred to the great significance of the Peace Conference, proceeding in London at the present time, and of the message which Queen Victoria sent to Baha'o'llah on receipt of his proclamation. 'If this is of God,' said the Queen, 'it will surely stand.' In a few words of explanation about the Bahai movement Miss Buckton made clear that it is not a new religion, but sought the reconciliation of all religions. It is a common meeting ground.

MRS DESPARD

The President of the Woman's Freedom League, who followed, said she was perfectly convinced that everyone who has heard him whom so many to-day are calling the Master – one of the great masters who have come to enlighten the world – felt deeply privileged to have had his presence here in our western isle. 'I had the joy of seeing him when he was last over in this country,' said Mrs. Despard. 'I have heard of the wonderful journeys that he has made. I know how he never falters. He believes that he is bringing a message to the world, and we believe it too. I sometimes think that when in the future the story of the present generation comes to be summed up we shall be shown it under two aspects: one aspect is that which is troubling us so much at the present moment. There is unrest everywhere; unrest in industry, unrest among the women of the country, intellectually and religiously, and some are frightened as they look out and wonder if these days mean the disintegration of which we have been hearing. But some of us think that this unrest at the present moment is actually a healthy symptom, that is on account of the unreality of things that people generally are troubled and anxious and longing for some settled thing. We have the mighty movements – the women's movement, the religious movement, the spiritual movement. At the basis of all the great religions that have moved the world there are the same great truths. This unrest at the moment, and of ancient times, though in different words and different forms, is still the same. God is one. There is nothing but God anywhere. He is the one eternal life; because we are in him therefore we are eternal; death is but the dropping of a garment. This is the principle of unity, and we are thankful beyond measure that it has been brought to us to-day.'

M. HIPPOLYTE DREYFUS

M. Hippolyte Dreyfus, of Paris, spoke of the wonderful interest that the movement has now awakened in London. 'Is it a religion, this movement?' he asked. 'Some say no, looking only to the philosophical aspect of the teachings, looking only to its code of ethics; but I say yes, and you certainly will say so too, after having heard what you have from this platform. It is a religion because it is founded upon the knowledge of God. The knowledge of God is the first thing we should try to acquire. It has, in former times, I think, been very difficult, for the esoteric part of religion was hidden from the people and the truth was only given by symbols. But in this day Baha'o'llah appeals to our reason.' M. Dreyfus concluded by thanking the chairman for presiding.

THE BENEDICTION

A deep hush fell on the people as Abdul Baha gave the blessing in Oriental fashion, with hands out-stretched and palms up-turned.

'O Thou Kind Almighty, we supplicate at the throne of grace for mercy for our sins; mercy for the great destruction of life, the blood that has been shed in the Balkans, the children that are being made orphans, the mothers losing their dear sons, the sons who have become fatherless, the cities that have been destroyed, the many hearts that have been filled with blood, the many tears that are shed and the many spirits that are in a state of agitation! O Lord, be merciful, extinguish this spirit of war, this peril, this gloomy darkness, from the face of the earth. Cement together these hearts. Let the Sun of thy Truth dawn upon all. O Lord! this world is dark. Guide us toward a brilliant light; the horizons are gloomy with the clouds of war; disperse these impenetrable clouds. Grant us a holiness and calm, dispose of these quarrels; illuminate the horizon of life, so that the sun of real loyalty may shine with his rays. May these dark hearts become illuminated, may these blind eyes become open, may these deaf ears become gifted with hearing. O Lord, cause thy divine justice to appear in this world. Summon these people to the banquet of international peace, so that they may live together in the utmost state of love. May all the religions and all nations embrace each other with this spirit of universal kindness, and may hatred be forgotten. O Lord! confirm this just government in the establishment of peace, so that it may hold aloft the banner of reconciliation in the Balkans. May the light of love shine and flame forth undefiled. O Lord! thou art almighty, thou art merciful, thou art clement, thou art kind!'[25]

Eager Heart

When 'Abdu'l-Bahá arrived in London, the famous play *Eager Heart*, written by the Bahá'í artist and educator Alice Buckton, was being staged at Westminster Church House. Another Bahá'í, Mary Blomfield, daughter of Lady Blomfield, played one of the characters. 'Abdu'l-Bahá was invited to attend the performance on Saturday, 21 December. He was seated in the first row of the theatre (there were over twelve hundred spectators) and it is reported that at some point during the play He was moved to tears.

After the performance, says Sohrab, the Master 'was invited behind the stage and congratulated the players and musicians for their delightful work'.[26] An account of the whole episode appeared in *Christian Commonwealth* on 1 January:

> ABDUL BAHA WITNESSES MYSTERY PLAY
> During Christmas week Abdul Baha was an interested spectator of 'Eager Heart', Miss Alice Buckton's mystery play, which was produced at Church House, Westminster. After the performance Abdul Baha went on the stage and gave an interesting talk to the little group who circled about him, emphasising how easy it is to overlook the promised One when he comes. After complimenting them on their presentation of the play, he went on to speak of its significance. "The people in the play thought they were waiting for Christ; they thought they were his intimate friends. Some there were who

used to cry day and night, saying, "O Lord, hasten the day when he will manifest himself on this earth." When he came they knew him not; they persecuted him and finally killed him, for they said, "This is not the true Messiah whose coming is to be under special conditions. How is it that he claims to be from heaven when we know he is from Nazareth, the son of Mary? He was to come with a sword; this man does not possess a stick. He was to sit on the throne of David; this man has not a mat to sit on. He must conquer the East and West; this man does not possess a shelter. He was to teach the laws of Moses; this man is abolishing them. In his day, justice was to encircle the world, the wolf and sheep drink from one fountain; the lion and deer graze in one pasture; the vulture and partridge live in one nest." The people could not see that these things were taking place. The reality of Christ was from heaven, though his physical body was from Mary. The sword was the tongue of Christ, which cut right from wrong. Many had swords, but that sword conquered the world. The kingdom of Christ was heavenly and not like the kingdom of Bonaparte; it was the reality of the ancient law Christ spread, not the words. He conquered East and West by the holy spirit, not by force. Sects which were in the utmost animosity drank from the one fountain – that is, the fountain of love. To-day I wept when I saw Christ in his mother's bosom, homeless and lonely in the world. But Christ's birthday was a glorious day; it was the day on which the sun of reality dawned; it was the day on which all beings were revolutionised; it was the beginning of a heavenly spring.'[27]

Interview with *The Christian Commonwealth*

On 22 December, Albert Dawson, editor of *The Christian Commonwealth*, visited the Master at Cadogan Gardens, dined with Him, and had a long interview with Him. In the course of the interview 'Abdu'l-Bahá thanked Dawson for his services to the Bahá'í Cause.[28] Just a few months before, *The Christian Commonwealth* had published 10,000 copies of a special issue dedicated to 'Abdu'l-Bahá and edited for its distribution in America. A new special edition dedicated to Him was also scheduled for 1 January 1913.[29] Dawson opened that issue with the following editorial:

TOWARDS SPIRITUAL UNITY

The adherents of the Bahai movement in England have taken advantage of ABDUL BAHA's second and probably final visit to hold a number of meetings for the exposition and advocacy of the principles of Baha'o'llah. With this issue of THE CHRISTIAN COMMONWEALTH we publish an additional four pages which we believe will be eagerly read not only by the followers of ABDUL BAHA throughout the world, but by many to whom the movement is at present only a name, and who desire to understand the significance of this new invasion of the West by the East. We welcome the opportunity which the Master's visit offers of helping to promote a mission fundamentally in accord with the principles we represent. The aim of the Bahai movement is identical with the spiritual purpose of Christianity, and in many respects closely parallels the history of the older faith. Its central doctrine of the unity of races and religions, and its dream of universal peace between all nations reinforce from the East the great spiritual movement of which we are conscious here in the West. The rise of a world-state, the vision of a moral order, the denial that strife and contention are sanctioned by the exigencies of human development have an immediate meaning for Western civilisation, which has exploited its material resources so enormously at the expense of its spiritual supremacy. In our secular struggles we have almost reached the point where collapse and disintegration must follow the neglect to restore the psychological balance, and to deepen the essential gravity and sanity which alone protect nations from decay. No clear-sighted observer can afford to ignore the symptoms of feverish excitement, of bluster, arrogance, and alarm, which meet him at every turn. Not only our own people, but the Continental nations and those overseas are being worked up to an unhealthy state of expectancy and apprehension which may at any moment precipitate the catastrophe that all wish to avoid. Mr. FREDERIC HARRISON's amazing outburst in the 'English Review' is typical of the heightening fever which may presage a mortal sickness unless spiritual healing comes quickly.

From what quarter will healing come for the human spirit if religion fails? The multiplication of armaments has increased the very danger they were meant to minimise. Treaties and alliances and international understandings have no value if the spirit which made them weakens in the crisis they were intended to avert. Religion, we say it deliberately, as the symbol of man's victory over the conspiracy of circumstances which threatens to overthrow his authority, is our final hope. It springs from the common sanity of mankind. It guarantees the continuity of the enduring human instincts for freedom, equality, and fraternity. The subtle poison which is infecting the life-blood of the race has religion as its only antidote. A rally of the moral forces of the world is now the most urgent need, if the world is to be saved from rattling back to barbarism. Happily, we believe, there is a real quickening of the religious consciousness of these times, and a clearer recognition of the fact that the world's peace may be conserved, given the will and desire, is beginning to gain ground. It is becoming more and more difficult to stampede the democracy, and evidence is not wanting that a collective will bent on the preservation of peace is emerging from the welter of rival interests, small patriotisms, and local greeds. It is the most dangerous of all superstitions which regards as inevitable an event which has not yet occurred. Nothing is inevitable until it has happened. And the real guarantees against war are to be found not in larger fleets or the treaties of diplomatists, but in the religious consciousness and the collective will.

For these reasons we feel it incumbent upon us to give full recognition to the work of the Eastern sage, and to the movement of which he is the head. ABDUL BAHA is not the founder of a new religion. The Bahais are not a new sect. They have created no new organisation, exact no formal pledges, and impose no dogmas or creeds. The Buddhist, the Mohammedan, and the Christian all find themselves at one with the spirit and aim of the Bahai movement. Its principles are common to all religions and alien to none. From the addresses of ABDUL BAHA which we publish this week it may be seen with what persistence he brings forward the ancient religious messengers, and bids his hearers perceive not merely the similarity but the identity of the truths they gave to their age. The Master simply reasserts the lost simplicities and purities of religion. With equal sincerity he discards the corruptions and distortions which have arisen to divide mankind into opposing sects. For him religion is undogmatic, unsectarian, and universal in its appeal. The famous gibe of GIBBON, the historian, that to the philosopher all religions are equally false, to the statesman all are equally useful, and to the people all are equally true, gains a new significance in the light of ABDUL BAHA's teaching.[30]

On 23 December a correspondent of *The Christian Commonwealth* interviewed the Master. The article that ensued was published in the above mentioned special edition of the magazine and included a very large picture of Him:

ABDUL BAHA IN ENGLAND
WARM WELCOME FROM HIS ENGLISH FOLLOWERS
ADDRESSES ON THE UNITY OF RELIGION AND UNIVERSAL PEACE

Abdul Baha is again in England on his way back from America to the Orient. London, the city where representatives of all races may be encountered, and the centre of a Government whose influence is heard at the far ends of the earth, has rarely sheltered a more significant and impressive personality than the leader of the Bahai movement. Three million followers call him Master, and the quality of their discipleship is compounded of reverence and love. Even the Western stranger coming into the Master's presence for the first time acknowledges an emotion akin to awe, and after a minute's speech with him, feels the stirring of a deeper spirit of devotion than the ordinary amenities of social intercourse are calculated to arouse. For Abdul Baha, whose mission of peace and universal brotherhood is like the coming of the four winds into the valley of dry bones, in Ezekiel's vision, is much more than a picturesque Eastern figure in the unromantic setting of Western civilisation. He is a prophet. A venerable figure, of rather less than medium stature, clothed in flowing Persian garments, his white beard lying upon his breast, silver-grey plaited hair falling over his shoulders, dark, brooding, pitiful eyes that yet light up when a smile of singular gentleness and sweetness passes across his face, and a low, mellow voice whose tones are charged with a strange solemnity – that is the Master as the stranger sees him. But to the Bahais he is the 'Servant of God', the symbol of the unity of religions and races which it is his mission to promote. Although nearly seventy years of age, he has undertaken this tour of the Western world to proclaim his message of universal peace, and to recall the nations from their armed madness to the forgotten simplicities of the spirit. For nine months he travelled in America, crossing the continent from coast to coast, from east to west, addressing large audiences in churches, synagogues, temples, halls, drawing-rooms, hotels, and in some of the universities. Wherever he spoke, it was at the invitation of the heads of the institution or movement which organised the meetings. He was a guest at the National Conference of Peace Societies held recently. The subject of his discourses everywhere was the same, an exposition of the teaching of Baha'o'llah, the source of the present-day Bahai faith . . .

Abdul Baha rose to receive me with a gentle courtesy and a murmured Persian sentence, which his interpreter, Mirza Ahmad Sohrab, explained meant that the Master was pleased to welcome a representative of THE CHRISTIAN COMMONWEALTH, which had done much to promote the progress of his mission. The stir and movement beyond the threshold of the room where Abdul Baha held his audience seemed to die away, and the familiar roar of London's traffic through which I had passed a little earlier receded into immense distances as we talked.

Sentence by sentence as they were translated to me, the Master told me of his itinerary through the American continent, of the messages he delivered before many different assemblies, and of the deepening desire everywhere manifested for the unifying of races and religions which will banish the nightmare of warfare and contention that now darkens the world. In America, he said, many societies are organised, whose purpose is the furtherance of universal peace. He has spoken before many of these organisations, 'and they have hearkened to my addresses with the greatest interest. And now I have returned to Europe. I observe that, praise be to God, in this capital a conference of peace is sitting. It is conducive to the utmost of joy to me that in this great centre of civilisation and culture such an important gathering is being held. Therefore I hope that the rays of universal peace may radiate from this great metropolis to all parts of the world and that the noble nation of England and its just Government, like the people of America, will strive their utmost in promoting the principles of international peace and brotherhood. I pray, that the war in the Balkans will be transformed into peace, and the rights of both sides may be protected.'

In answer to a question regarding the Master's impressions of

America, he said that material civilisation had advanced greatly, and he hoped that divine civilisation would be likewise established. The American universities were carrying on a most profitable and encouraging work, and he spoke of Dr Jordan, the head of the Stanford University, in California, whose guest he had been, as 'a very wise and erudite man, whose mind is full of thoughts of peace'.

A further question regarding the Master's plans elicited the information that he would visit Edinburgh, Oxford, Liverpool, and perhaps other provincial centres before he leaves for Paris. In Liverpool it is arranged that he will address a large gathering of workers. He returns to the Orient after this programme is completed, and told me that the possibility of a later visit to Europe is uncertain: 'It is not probable.' He has been very much encouraged by all that he has witnessed, and repeated his hope that the cause to which his life is dedicated would prosper in Europe. The Master rose again as I took my leave, and clasped my hand with a smile that was as much a benediction as his parting words. T.[31]

Parts of this text were the basis of articles that appeared in New Zealand.[32]

Visit to the Salvation Army

On Christmas Day, Wednesday, 25 December 1912, 'Abdu'l-Bahá received, as usual, many visitors, speaking to some of them about the real station of Christ. The Bahá'í Isabel Fraser recounted some of the events of that day in an article published in 1915 in the Californian magazine *Everywoman* (San Francisco). She is the 'American girl' mentioned in the article who gave 'Abdu'l-Bahá a sewing box as a present. According to Sohrab Ahmad, on the train from Liverpool to London the Master mentioned to Fraser that during His visit to America He also had to sew, cook and wash clothes and this prompted Fraser to make such a Christmas gift.[33]

CHRISTMAS DAY WITH ABDUL BAHA IN LONDON
SOME COMMENTS ON MODERN OBSERVANCE

Abdul Baha returned from America to the Holy Land via London, in 1912, and there spent Christmas day, amid the holly and chimes of old England – the home of Christmas as we know it – the

Christmas of cheer, gift-giving, and mutual well-wishing.

To have seen the world's greatest prisoner amid these surroundings was a never-to-be-forgotten picture, but one hard to reproduce in words. Many beautiful and touching incidents could be related of that Christmas had we the records of the hundreds that thronged to see him. Some he met in little groups in the dining room of his flat in Chelsea, and on request he would, at intervals, address a larger gathering in the drawing room, as people kept coming and going all day. Anon, some distressed soul wished for a conference alone, or a peace advocate sought his advice on an important issue.

Many came bearing gifts – the mighty and the lowly, the rich and the poor in this world's goods. A detailed account of the mere happenings of the day would mean nothing. The trivial details of life, even on a Christmas day, are seldom regarded in the light of a spiritual unfoldment, but it is through these seemingly small incidents that this master spirit brings out into the court of objectivity those principles which he teaches. Thus the very essence of his existence is vested with the penetration of the spirit – so much so that, save as his life manifests those principles for which he stands, he wishes to be forgotten as a personality.

To each who came to him on that Christmas day, he gave a spiritual present – compatible with the capacity of each; for Abdul Baha's method of teaching the people so they become moved with conviction, is through the heart.

Someone brought him an expensive gift. He accepted it graciously. Holding it lovingly for a moment, he told the wealthy giver of his own simple life. 'And now,' he said smilingly, 'you see I have accepted your beautiful present, and it has made me very happy. I thank you for it. And now I am going to give it back to you. Sell it, and give the money to the poor. The rich in England are too rich, and the poor are too poor.'

The man was at first astonished, but when, after further conversation, he arose and took his departure, one felt from his attitude toward the great master that a new impulse or seed had been planted.

Often Abdul Baha would laugh outright at some little gift that showed Yankee ingenuity, and many a compliment he wafted back to America, the land of his, then, recent sojourns.

One American girl was much amused at his rehearsal of

American experience. He concluded by saying, 'I learned much from my travels and hardships. Among other things, I learned to wash my handkerchiefs when occasion demanded, and to sew.'

On an impulse, she ran out to a nearby shop and bought the tiniest leather sewing box, and on her return, laughingly presented it, saying that it was impossible for her to imagine a prophet sewing on his buttons.

'I will accept the sewing case with gratitude, and will keep it,' he said, as he put it among his things, and then added, 'I am not a prophet. I am a man – like yourself.' He laughed, and we all laughed, for she was a well-known suffragette.

'He accepted it!' she exclaimed at the door, and so extremely overjoyed was she, that one felt that some deeper message or awakening beyond that which we had witnessed, had been accomplished through the simple transaction.

From laughter, Abdul Baha's face would become stern or expressive of a great weight of impersonal sorrow, the suffering induced by the realization of the hunger of humanity for spiritual rest.

THE REAL MEANING OF THE ADVENT OF CHRIST ON THIS EARTH

'Christ's birthday is a glorious day,' he said. It is necessary that these anniversary celebrations be observed, else man in his negligence would forget all about his Creator; but we should seek to penetrate the dark veils of custom and imitation of ancestors, perchance we may discover the reality of the meaning.

'The advent of Christ on this earth was a blessed day, for it was the day on which the sun of reality dawned; the day on which all beings were revivified. In the world's calendar, it was the beginning of a heavenly spring.

'Today they are celebrating this event, but they are dead to the reality of its meaning.

'His Holiness Christ did not appear on this earth in order that certain of the inhabitants should acknowledge his prophethood. He did not appear that we should acknowledge him as the Christ, and form a separate sect, and adore him. He did not appear for the purpose of founding a nation, though in the heavenly realm, Christ was a king. The unlimited reality of Christ cannot be bounded by man-made forms and rituals.

'Nay, this great sun of reality dawned from the eastern horizon in order to illumine the human world, and render man celestial in nature; to free men from the bonds of dependence, and usher them into the kingdom of God.

'Today the mention of Christ is on a thousand tongues, but when he was on earth, he was not thought much of, notwithstanding they were awaiting his coming with great impatience. They thought that they would be his intimate friends. Some there were who used to cry day and night, saying, 'O God, hasten the day when the promised one will manifest himself on this earth.' When he came, they knew him not; they persecuted him and finally killed him, for they said, 'This is not the true Messiah whose coming is to be under special conditions. How is it that he claims to be from Nazareth, the son of Mary? He was to come with a sword; this man does not possess even a staff. He was to sit on the throne of David; this man does not possess a mat to sit on. He must conquer the East and the West; this man does not possess a shelter. He was to teach the law of Moses; this man is abolishing it. In his day, justice was to encircle the world, the wolf and the sheep drink from one fountain; the lion and the deer to graze in one pasture; the vulture and partridge live in one nest.

'The people could not see that these things were taking place. The reality of Christ was from heaven, though his physical body was from Mary. The sword was the tongue of Christ, which cut right from wrong. Many had swords, but his sword conquered the world.

'The kingdom of Christ was heavenly and not like the kingdom of Bonaparte; it was the reality of the ancient law Christ spread, not the words. He conquered East and West by the Holy Spirit, not by force. Sects which were in the utmost animosity drank from the one fountain – that is, the fountain of love.'[34]

In the afternoon of the same day, 'Abdu'l-Bahá visited the headquarters of the Salvation Army in London and addressed the many people who had gathered there for Christmas dinner. An account of this episode written by Isabel Fraser was published in *The Christian Commonwealth* and was later included in the above mentioned article in *Everywoman*:

ABDUL BAHA AT A SALVATION ARMY SHELTER

On Christmas night Abdul Baha visited the poor of the Salvation Army Shelter, Westminster, where each year a Christmas dinner is provided for those who have no homes and no friends, and, but for the shelter, would have no lodgings. There were about 1,000 present on this occasion. It was a most impressive scene – the dinner for the homeless and the Master from the East delivering Christ's message to the poor. As a true test of attention many of the hungry men forgot to eat and listened intently. In conformity with the wonderful tact Abdul Baha displays on all occasions, his message to the homeless was simple, direct and short.

I feel to-night, he said, great joy and happiness to be in this place, because hitherto my meetings and visits have been mostly with the poor, and I think of myself as one of them. My lot has ever been with those who have not the goods of this world. The world consists of brothers. The poor have ever been the cause of the freedom of the world of humanity; have ever been the cause of the upbuilding of the country; and have ever laboured for the world's production. The morals of the poor have ever been above those of the rich; the poor are ever nearer to the threshold of God; the humanitarianism of the poor has ever been more acceptable to God. Consider his holiness Christ. He appeared in the world as one of the poor. He was born of a lowly family; all the apostles of Christ were of humble origin and his followers were of the very poorest of the community. This is what Christ states in the gospels, 'It is easier for a camel to go through the eye of a needle than for a rich man to enter into the kingdom of God.' This testimony of Christ to the exalted state of the poor ones is sufficient. It is easy for the poor, very easy for them, to enter into the kingdom of the Almighty. The poor have capacity. They are favoured at the threshold of God. If wealth was a necessity, Christ would have wished it for himself. He lived a simple life, and one of the titles of Baha'o'llah was the 'the poor one.' In Persian his title was 'darvish', and that means one who has not a slave. All the prophets of God were poor. His holiness Moses was a mere shepherd. This will show you that in the estimation of God poverty is greater than the accumulation of wealth – that the poor are more acceptable than the lazy rich. A rich man who spends his wealth for the poor is praiseworthy. Consider that the poor are not born in a state of solvency; they are not tyrannous. All the tyranny and injustice in this world comes from accumulation. The poor have ever been humble and lowly. Their hearts are tender. The rich are not so. Sorrow not, grieve not! Be not unhappy because you are not wealthy! You are the brothers of Jesus Christ. Christ was poor. Baha'o'llah was poor. For forty years he was imprisoned in poverty. The great ones of the world have come from a lowly station. Be ever happy; be not sad. Trust in God, and if in this world you undergo dire vicissitudes, I hope that in the kingdom of God you will have the utmost happiness.'

In generous conformity with Baha'o'llah's teachings that 'our words should not exceed our deeds', the Master left twenty sovereigns and many handfuls of silver with Colonel Spencer of the Salvation Army so that the poor might enjoy a similar dinner on New Year's night. Colonel Spencer told the men that they were to have this New Year's dinner in Abdu'l-Baha's honour. The Master was just leaving the hall when this announcement was made. With one accord the men jumped up and, waving their knives and forks, gave a rousing farewell cheer. Before leaving, the Master was shown all over the shelter, and at the outer door he said to the officer in charge: 'May God prosper you! May you all be under the protection of the Almighty!'[35]

Months afterwards *The Suffolk and Essex Press* (Sudbury) quoted one sentence of 'Abdu'l-Bahá's talk at the Salvation Army in its section 'Words of Wisdom': 'The great ones of the world have come from a lowly station.'[36]

Interview with *The Standard*

On 27 December, the Unionist newspaper *The Standard* (London) published a sympathetic general article about the Bahá'í Faith apropos of the arrival of the Master in England.[37] Two days later, on the morning of Sunday, 29 December, 'Abdu'l-Bahá received a representative of the newspaper who interviewed the Master for an hour and a half.[38] The next day this leading political newspaper carried the following article:

THE GOSPEL OF BAHAISM
ITS TEN COMMANDMENTS

Abdul Baha, the Persian prophet of the new teaching, who has spent 40 years of his 68 of life in the Turkish fortress of Akka in Northern Palestine, is in London, and yesterday expounded his gospel of peace in the King's Weigh House Church, W. The announcement previously made of the date of his sailing from New York was incorrect, as he was already on his way here at the time . . .

He has just returned from a triumphal tour of the United States, and is now at Lady Blomfield's flat in Cadogan Gardens, where his services are attended by a large number of well-known people who regard the new doctrine as the faith which is to illuminate and redeem the world.

Abdul Baha is a picturesque figure – a typical Wise Man from the East. In features he bears a strong resemblance to the late General Booth, but his face is brown – the same shade of brown as the long Jaeger gown he wears. His beard is white, and so is his turban, and there is about him much of the peace on earth and goodwill to men which he preaches. Through an interpreter he yesterday gave a representative an outline of the teachings of Bahaism, and during the interview two secretaries made a careful note of his statements, which were as follows:

'In the Orient for some centuries the real foundations of religion have been forgotten. Darkness and ignorance have prevailed. All the religions and all the nations of the Orient were submerged in a sea of blind dogma and religious imitations. Therefore, they constantly fought against each other. They were thirsty for the blood of each other. They shunned each other's company. Not a trace was left of the illuminations of the Sun of religions. Even the various races living in the Orient exercised hostility. In brief, it was at the time constant strife, warfare and battle. At such a time his Holiness Baha-Ullah (father of Abdul Baha) appeared, like unto a sun. He proclaimed the principle of the oneness of the world of humanity, saying, 'Humanity constitutes the sheep of God. He is the real Shepherd. He is kind to all.' He (Baha-Ullah) proclaimed that all religions have one foundation. A world of misunderstanding has crept in owing to accidental dogma. His Holiness instituted certain new teachings: –

'1. The unity of the human race. God is the Creator of all, the Provider for all, and kind to all. If He was not kind we cannot have creation. Therefore we must all associate with a spirit of fellowship and love. All religions and nations must love each other from the hearts and souls.

'2. The declaration of a universal peace amongst all religions, races, nations, and fatherlands. With regard to these lofty principles, he wrote many epistles to the reigning kings and queens of the world, including one to Queen Victoria (to which her late Majesty did not reply).

'3. Religion must be the cause of amity and love. If religion is to be the means of hatred and rancour, it is better to be an irreligious man – an atheist.

'4. Religion must ever conform with science and reason. If religion does not do so, it is a heap of superstitions, because when we study the bases of Christianity, the Mosaic law, Confucianism, Mahometanism, and Brahmanism, we find that they all conform, in their origins, to science and reason.

'5. Religious prejudice, racial bias, national prejudice, patriotic prejudice, political prejudice are the destroyers of the foundation of the human race. As long as these prejudices exist humanity will not attain to universal peace. The human kind are one family.

'6. Men and women are equal. We must give the highest education to women, and cause them to enter the university of learning, so that they may acquire science and art and craft equal to the level of men. Equality obtained by force is not to be commended. In Nature the fact that there is no difference between the sexes is manifest.

'7. Universal spread of education. All children everywhere are to be educated; none are to remain ignorant. If the parents are unable to supply education, the Government must give it and make it compulsory.

'8. The establishment of a readjustment in the economic conditions of society; justice and fairness for all, but the classes not to be disturbed.

'9. The organisation of an international court of arbitration. The laws of this court to be binding on all humanity.

'10. The inauguration of an auxiliary universal language that must become part of the curriculum of all primary schools of the world. This will dispel long misunderstandings. No one will be obliged to study a large number of languages. Two will be enough.

'There are many other teachings, but these are the principal tenets of Bahaism.'[39]

This article was later the basis of an article that appeared in *The West Australian* (Perth) on 12 and 21 February 1913.[40]

Address at the King's Weigh House

On 29 December, 'Abdu'l-Bahá gave another address, this time at the King's Weigh House Congregational Church. Its minister, Rev Edward Lewis, and his wife had visited the Master on Christmas day and in a private meeting with Him arranged the details of His visit to the church.

Many people attended the service to hear the Master, which was briefly reported in the London *Times*.[41] *The Christian Commonwealth* published the following account:

> ### ABDUL BAHA AT THE KING'S WEIGH HOUSE
> #### MR LEWIS ON THE MOVEMENT
>
> The announcement that Abdul Baha would be present at the evening service in the King's Weigh House drew last Sunday a large congregation. The Eastern teacher was not present during the earlier stages of the service, but at 7:45 Rev E. W. Lewis went into the pulpit and prepared the way for the coming of Abdul Baha by giving a general sketch of the rise of the Bahai movement. Mr Lewis explained that it was not a new sect, and that it had not committed itself to any form of organisation; it was essentially a spiritual movement, very much on the lines of what Jesus wanted his movement to be.
>
> On the entrance of Abdul Baha the whole congregation rose to their feet and stood while Mr Lewis in a brief sentence conveyed their greetings to the Master. Abdul Baha then advanced to the front of the chancel, with his interpreter behind him, and spoke animatedly and impressively, the interpreter translating as the address proceeded. The Master appeared to be quite at home, pacing backwards and forwards in the intervals between the

sentences. 'I praise God,' he began, 'that a number of reverent souls are gathered in this congregation to serve the Almighty. Their hearts are cemented together. Their faces are joyous with the glad tidings of the Kingdom of God.' Abdul Baha went on to speak of love as the greatest power in the world to bring about unity, peace, and the federation of man. A brief sentence or two from Mr Lewis brought the service to a close.[42]

A similar account was also published in the *Christian World* (London).[43]

Address at Manchester College, Oxford

During His second visit to England 'Abdu'l-Bahá visited Oxford at the invitation of Prof. Thomas K. Cheyne (1841–1915), with whom He had been in contact since as early as His first visit to England in 1911.[44]

'Abdu'l-Bahá arrived in Oxford at 11:30 in the morning of 31 December. His first visit was to the home of Prof. Cheyne, who at the time was severely sick but nevertheless embarked on the project of writing his celebrated *The Reconciliation of Races and Religions* (1914). After having lunch with the Cheyne family, the Master proceeded to Manchester College at three in the afternoon where He delivered an address to a large group of professors and students of the university.[45] Dr Estlin Carpenter (1844–1927),[46] the principal of Manchester College, introduced the Master to the audience.

At least three accounts of the talk were published after the meeting. *The Oxford Chronicle*, a weekly newspaper, published on 3 January 1913 a complete report of the talk.[47] A shorter but very similar account was also published on 4 January in the *Oxford Times*.[48] On 22 January *The Christian Commonwealth* published the following account based on the above mentioned two articles:

> ABDUL BAHA AT OXFORD
> Abdul Baha addressed a large and deeply interested audience at Manchester College, Oxford, on December 31. The Persian leader spoke in his native tongue, Mirza Ahmad Sohrab interpreting. Principal Estlin Carpenter presided and introduced the speaker by saying that they owed the honour and pleasure of meeting Abdul Baha to their revered friend Dr Cheyne, who was deeply interested

in the Bahai teaching. The movement sprung up during the middle of the last century in Persia, with the advent of a young Mohammedan who took to himself the title of the Bab (meaning door or gate, through which men could arrive at the knowledge of truth of God), and who commenced teaching in Persia in the year 1844. The purity of his character, the nobility of his words, aroused great enthusiasm. He was, however, subjected to great hostility by the authorities, who secured his arrest and imprisonment, and he was finally executed in 1850. But the movement went on, and the writings of the Bab, which had been copious, were widely read. The movement has been brought into India, Europe, and the United States. It does not seek to create a new sect, but to inspire all sects with a deep fundamental love. The late Dr Jowett once said to him that he had been so deeply impressed with the teachings and character of the Bab that he thought Babism, as the present movement was then known, might become the greatest religious movement since the birth of Christ.[49]

The same issue included the text of the talk together with a photograph of the original Persian text from which it was translated. According to Sohrab, on 18 January 'Abdu'l-Bahá gave to Isabel Fraser the Persian and English texts of the talk for their publication in *The Christian Commonwealth*.[50] Thus the text of the talk published in *The Christian Commonwealth* – if Sohrab's statement is true – was based on Persian notes approved by the Master and translated by Sohrab.

ABDUL BAHA'S ADDRESS

Abdul Baha, following in the main the Arabic which begins on the preceding page, said: – This is indeed a blessed gathering, in the centre of science and learning. In the world of existence to-day the greatest achievements of man have been made possible through the scientific uncovering of realities. Through the knowledge of science, the mystery of past ages and the possibilities of the future are unfolded before our eyes. The world of existence is like unto the human body; science is like unto the Spirit which animates that body. Science distinguishes man from the animal. Were it not for science man and the animal would be on the same level. Science leads us to the understanding of the power invisible, and enables us to comprehend the mysteries of God. Knowledge is the greatest foundation of human prosperity and happiness. If we do not exert ourselves to investigate we can never arrive at any comprehensive conclusion. All the sciences and crafts were once the hidden mysteries of nature but out of the plane of invisibility man has brought them into the realm of visibility. Let us look at the material universe. The sun, so colossal, is the captive of nature, and all the stellar bodies in the boundless heavens move submissively under this heavenly domination. They cannot use their force against the strength of these laws or deviate from their mandate even by the width of a needle. On this globe all things alike are held captive – the mountain and the little ant. Nothing escapes. The ocean with its rebellious force cannot free its neck from the chains which encompass the spheres.

Man alone is free from these laws. He is endowed with a power which enables him to break the confines of the material prison, wrest the sword from the hand of nature, and use it against her head. He calls to the elements, 'I will make you my servants.' By the strength of his will power and intellect he can contradict the laws that govern the material world, annihilating its terrors and using its powers for his own convenience and comfort.

According to these laws, considering the exigencies of his birth, man should remain on the face of the earth, but he flies in the air and travels over and under the seas. These acts are apparently in opposition to the laws of Nature. The power of electricity, which has strength enough to cut mountains to pieces, man captures and imprisons in a little lamp. The voice which according to Nature spreads only to an echo, he imprisons in a little instrument which carries the voice for many miles. Also through the power of electricity east and west are brought into communication within the twinkling of an eye. He catches the passing light and shade, and fixes it in a photograph. Man is enabled to break though the confines of matter and wrest from Nature her treasures, for Nature cannot keep her own secrets. Man has intelligence; he has perceptive, inventive, contemplative, sensitive faculties; why should he turn and adore Nature? Why, having freed himself through the cultivation of these faculties should he again confine himself in her domain? In his primeval state he was ignorant and the collective centre of all the vices and sins. But man, on being educated, freed himself from these defects and adorned his being with the perfections of civilization. Nature is a traitor, and when man again places himself under the laws which govern her domain, this is eternal loss, this is sorrow, this is death. Man must not forget to look toward the divine gifts. What a blessed power there is in man! What a wonderful effulgence is the morality of man! There is warfare in the world of nature. The wind tries to uproot the trees. Thunder and lightning destroy and the earth quakes. How pitiful it is that in humanity there is something akin to the material warfare, not only in the warfare that is the working of the principle of the survival of the fittest, but in the warfare that is carried on in the minds of men. The foundation of all the religions of God is one. Pure religion invites men to love each other. The Balkan War is the result of the fundamental basis of religion having been set aside. All the horrors of that war have been brought about by religious prejudice, while all the religious teachings of God beckoned to love and unity. Through dogmas and superstitions, religion, which should have become the cause of love, prosperity and happiness, has become the cause of hatred, destruction, and strife. Praise be to God, the intellect of man is broadening; his perceptions are becoming cleaner, and the enlightened universities are carrying on a great work of peace and reconciliation. This is the century for the establishment of universal peace between all countries. This is the day-spring of the future. It is my hope that all of you with tongues, pens, and hands will help to spread the keeping of peace amongst the children of men so that they will be enabled to uproot the trees of difference and consequent warfare. Then all nations and religions will accord. This is my hope for you. May the bounties of God descend upon you.

The Chairman proposed a hearty vote of thanks to the speaker who, he said, was going to reside in future in Alexandria, under the protection of the Khedive and Great Britain.[51]

A few weeks after the visit of 'Abdu'l-Bahá to Oxford, Cheyne wrote an interesting article expounding some of his thoughts about the Master and the Bahá'í Faith:

THE UNION OF RELIGIONS

Is it possible that there should be a union of religions? An increasing number of persons would answer in the affirmative, because ideally the union of religions exists already. Religion is not of earthly, but of heavenly origin; it is not a branch of magic, not a department of State policy, but a revelation. Now revelation is worldwide; there is probably no people in which the light of sympathetic study does not disclose signs of contact between the human and the divine. More especially is revelation a characteristic of the great religions – those which have had the advantage of a rich and varied development. Jews would have no right to place their prophetic revealer (MOSES, or those unknown personages for whom MOSES may stand) above the prophetic revealer or revealers of the Zoroastrians nor are Mohammedans justified in promoting their prophet MOHAMMED to a place above JESUS, the revealer worshipped by the Christians.

This appears a favourable time for asking English Christians to reconsider their attitude towards Eastern religions, because of the visit of the leader of the Bahai movement, ABDUL BABA ('Servant of the All-Glorious'), who is conspicuous for his avoidance of the errors into which so many leaders have fallen. Of greater or lesser rank he says nothing; each prophet must be studied with reference to his period and surroundings. That his own father stands for him in the foreground becomes natural and right as soon as we recognise that BAHA'O'LLAH has a special mission to this age, and acknowledge the transcendent beauty and grandeur of his character. There have been many who have set a noble moral example, but there are elements in BAHA'O'LLAH's inner life and consciousness for which the biographer would find it difficult to produce a parallel.

Space forbids us to dilate upon the singular phenomena of the lives of this father and this son. It is only necessary to add that writers in the newspapers have done what in them lay to make known ABDUL BAHA's deep love for all his fellow-men. His love of GOD is a secret between him and EL-ABHA ('the Most Glorious One'). Nor must we enter into details respecting ABDUL BAHA's teaching. He is doubtless not original; he claims only to be an interpreter of his father's written revelations. These are in a high degree adapted to the wants of the present age. But the central truths are those of Judaism and Christianity – the love of GOD and the love of man.

ABDUL BABA is not a Mohammedan, and it is a mistake to describe Bahaism as a Mohammedan sect. But there is no reason why a really broad-minded Mohammedan should not be a Bahai, or, for that matter, why a broad-minded Christian or Jew or Zoroastrian should not enter the community. Just as the moulders of the doctrine gather pearls of truth in all seas, so neophytes of the community may adhere with affection to the church, synagogue, or sect to which they owe their spiritual birth. The Bahai community is really not so much a church as a fighting religious order, whose members are, to adopt the beautiful phrase of HEINRICH HEINE, *Ritter des Theologengeist*.

Bahais are not subject to the decrees of any Council or Pope; both BAHA'O'LLAH and ABDUL BAHA have had to make pronouncements on difficult points which involve disputable matters of historical criticism and Biblical exegesis. Those of us who have spent life and energy in the battle for freedom of inquiry are not likely to change even for the sake of a new spiritual power. There is no ground for supposing that in this new Catholic Church any real difficulty from the presence of free inquirers will arise. There will, however, always be differences between North and South, East and West.

T. K. CHEYNE[52]

A Tablet by 'Abdu'l-Bahá

In its edition of 1 January 1913 *The Christian Commonwealth* published a translation of a Tablet by 'Abdu'l-Bahá addressed to the Bahá'ís of the world; it was accompanied by a facsimile of the original Tablet in Persian:

ABDUL BAHA'S MESSAGE TO BAHAIS ALL OVER THE WORLD
TRANSLATION OF THE TABLET

GOD, the Maker of the worlds, hath created the realm of humanity to be the Paradise of Eden (or the Garden of Paradise) of the edifice of Peace.

Reconciliation, Love, and Faithfulness is founded on a solid and firm basis; nay, rather, He hath willed it to become the mirror, reflecting the Delectable Paradise. Then, and not until then, will all the divine bounties become manifold; happiness and well being infinite; the virtues of the world of humanity revealed and resplendent; and the rays of the Sun of Reality visible from every direction.

Consider that his holiness Adam and others were living in Paradise. But as soon as strife became known between him and Satan, everyone was driven away from Eden, so that the children of humanity might learn a lesson and realize that quarrels and strife, even though with Satan, are conducive to deprivation.

Therefore, in this radiant century, according to the heavenly teachings, altercation and dispute are not allowable, even though assailed by Satan himself.

Astonishing is it, that notwithstanding the inculcation of this lesson, yet man has remained ignorant. From one end of the world to the other, the realm of humanity is engaged in hostilities and war. There is enmity between the religions.

There is hatred between the classes. There is war between the fatherlands. There is contention between the diplomats. How delightful it would now be could these black clouds be dispersed from the horizon of the world, letting the light of Reality shine; the dust of slaughter and the crime of shedding blood be swept away; the breeze of providence from the Dawning Place of Peace and Salvation be wafted; thus the world would become a new world, and the face of the earth receive new life from the rays of the divinely effulgent light of God.

Our hope is in the favours of the glorious Lord, trusting that His providence and protection will encircle us. May the bitterness of struggle, warfare, and the cruelty of the blood shedding sword be changed into the sweetness of friendship, reconciliation, righteousness, and justice! May the tastes become sweetened, the nostrils perfumed, with the essence of the rose.

May this New Year be made the occasion of the New Peace! May this conference be assisted and aided to inaugurate an era of peace with justice, and to establish the basis of a fair treaty and agreement, so that their work may be blessed for ever and ever.[53]

Talk for the Cosmos Club

On 19 December 1912, a few days after His arrival in London, 'Abdu'l-Bahá received a member of the Cosmos Club (London), who invited Him to speak to this society. The meeting took place on the evening of Wednesday, 1 January 1913.

'Abdu'l-Bahá was introduced by the president of the Cosmos Club to an audience of more than three hundred people. After some introductory words about the Bahá'í Faith by Lady Blomfield, 'Abdu'l-Bahá spoke on the human soul and spirit. At the close of the meeting He was invited by some participants to a vegetarian dinner. Among those who were present at this dinner were Sir Richard Stapley, who is mentioned in chapter 6, volume 1, and Felix Moscheles, who is mentioned in chapter 33 below.[54]

Notes of the translation of 'Abdu'l-Bahá's talk were taken by 'three lady disciples'. One of them was probably Lady Blomfield, who was present at the meeting, and the other two were perhaps Ethel Rosenberg and Mary Thornburgh-Cropper, who on that day had visited the Master. Their notes appeared in the March issue of the *International Psychic Gazette*.

ABDUL BAHA'S ADDRESS TO COSMOS CLUB
AS REPORTED BY THREE LADY DISCIPLES

Tonight I wish to speak before this loving assembly on the subject of the Spirit. All phenomena are endowed with spirit, but the spirit is manifested in varying degrees of life according to the capacity and ability of the manifester.

It has been demonstrated that mineral life is endowed with spirit, or soul. A step higher than the mineral is the vegetable kingdom, and when we observe carefully we see that the vegetable is also endowed with this virtue of life, or spirit. It is evident that the spirit in the vegetable kingdom is of a higher order than that of the mineral.

A degree higher still, and we enter into the animal kingdom. The animal likewise possesses this spirit. A sphere yet higher, and more comprehensive, is that spirit possessed by man. This life and this spirit has been bestowed upon man. These four categories of spirit are in the realm of matter. They belong to the materialities of life.

There is yet a higher spirit which belongs to the world of idealisation – that is the real spirit. In this connection, his Holiness, the Christ, says, 'Let the dead bury their dead', while in reality those who desired to bury their dead were endowed with spirit – that is, they were living. Although they were endowed with the spirit of the vegetable, the animal, and human kingdoms, you will see clearly how Christ classed them as dead people, because they had not the spiritual life.

Unknown and insignificant, humble fishermen became known throughout the heaven of the Almighty, and their glory was like unto a brilliant star, ever shining on the horizon of life. Therefore we must ever strive so that this spirit may become resuscitated through the breath of the Holy Spirit; so that He may draw these illumined ones to the kingdom of God; so that the rays of the sun of reality may shine upon us, and that invisible reality of man which is immortal may ascend to the supreme concourse.

Illumination is of two kinds. There are two kinds of bodies which bestow light: one kind enjoys light from itself and independently, like the sun. It does not receive these rays from any other source. There is another light-giving body, like unto the moon. The moon is not itself a light-giving body, it is a recipient of the light from the sun. Likewise, the realities of humanity are not independent light-giving bodies. They must receive these rays from the sun of reality, because from this centre of illumination and its rays all phenomena are educated and cultured.

This sun is one sun, although it may have many dawning places. For example, the dawning place of the sun during the summer differs from its dawning place during the season of winter. Sometimes the sun dawns from the equinoxial point, again from another horizon, and at another time it may shine from a southern horizon. Although the dawning places may differ, yet the sun is ever the same sun. Those beholding the sun will receive the rays of the sun, no matter from which horizon it may dawn. But those who are limited to a certain definite horizon, while the sun is shining from that point, turn their faces in that direction, but later on when the sun directs its course to another horizon, they stay just where they are and do not turn their gaze to the new rising and dawning place; they worship the dawning place and not the sun. For example, there was a time when the sun of reality shone from the Mosaic place of dawning. Then, when the sun of reality shone from the Mosaic horizon, the Jews worshipped that horizon. Then that light of reality was transformed into the sun of reality which appeared from the Messianic dawning place. If the Jews had been adorers of the light, they would have turned their gaze to the horizon upon which the light was dawning, and from which Christ appeared; but because they were worshippers of the horizon, and were gazing towards the Mosaic point, they were consequently deprived from beholding the rays of the sun of reality.

Man must never be limited; he must be the adorer of reality. He must be the seeker of the light of reality, no matter from what dawning place it may arise. No matter from what point or from what lamp the light is shining, we must be lovers of the light. We must be athirst for water, no matter from what fountain it may be flowing. We must be seekers of fruit, no matter from what tree it is plucked. Let no one be subject to his own limitations, for if he be limited he will be deprived of that bounty which God has willed that man may enjoy, from the benefit which He has showered upon this world, and from the effulgence of the sun of reality. In short, that spirit of God shines upon all the creation. It is my hope that all of you may become illumined through the light of reality; that each one of you may become quickened by the spirit of God; that you may all turn your attention towards the kingdom of God; that you all may become manifestations of the bounties and favours of God.

Again, Christ says: 'Those who are born of the spirit are spirit, and those who are born of the flesh are flesh.' Man enjoys two kinds of realities – a reality which is visible or seen, and a reality which is invisible or unseen; a reality which is limited, another reality which is unlimited. His limited reality belongs to the world of matter, and through these limitations he belongs to the animal kingdom, but his illimitable reality belongs to the world of God. His visible reality is circumscribed, and is captive in the claws of the natural world. All the catastrophes in the material realm are contingent upon this visible and limited reality. If the body of man is exposed, he catches a severe cold. He may become submerged and drowned in the sea through an accident, and the animals attack likewise the outward body of man.

But as regards the invisible reality of man, that reality is infinite. It is the discoverer of the reality of beings; it is endowed with supernatural power; it can withstand all creation, it can withstand attacks from the Occident or the Orient. All phenomena are humbled before it. A mountain becomes as nothing before that invisible reality. A lion is caged through that invisible reality.

This radiant reality which is in man is like unto a clear mirror through which the secrets of the Kingdom are reflected. The rays of the sun of reality mirror forth through it the breath of the Holy Spirit which bestows life. This invisible reality is of the world of light. It is of the world of eternity. This is why spirit is changeless and immutable.

In the beginning of every dispensation, at the dawn of every new manifestation of God, this spirit is breathed through the body of men, and by it people become renewed. Their qualities and attributes are changed. It transforms man from the lower degrees of life to the higher realm or state of existence. Whereas a man was imperfect, he becomes wise, whereas he was imperfect, he becomes perfect, though but a dead body he enjoys a new life.

Consider how, during the time of Christ, this spirit of reality was breathed through the body of the Apostles, who, though ignorant, became wise, and who, though living in darkness, became illuminated.[55]

Addresses to the Society of Friends and the New Congregational Church

As seen in a previous chapter, during His first sojourn in Egypt, 'Abdu'l-Bahá corresponded with British Quakers and His letters to them were published in various newspapers. This correspondence generated some tension between those members of the Society of Friends who had a favorable view of the Bahá'í Faith and those who perceived it as essentially anti-Christian. These fractures were reproduced when 'Abdu'l-Bahá was invited to address the Sunday service of the Westminster Quaker community on 12 January 1913 at the Friends' Meeting House, 52 St Martin's Lane. According to Sohrab, several hundred people attended the meeting, and the topic of 'Abdu'l-Bahá's talk was meditation.[56] *The Friend* (London), organ of the Society of Friends, published a short report of the visit:

ABDUL BAHA AND WESTMINSTER MEETING

While Friends at Westminster were quietly worshipping the other Sunday, they were surprised to see enter two Persians, one a patriarchal old man, and the other much younger, accompanied by an English woman Friend. The two Persians evidently understood the Friends' manner of worship, and before very long the Bab (otherwise known as Abdul Baha or Abbas Effendi, who, indeed he proved to be) addressed the meeting. He spoke in Persian, and his companion translated, and appeared to be doing it very well. The burden of what the Bab said was not, of course, Christianity, but was what one would expect to hear from the leader of a mystical offshoot from orthodox Mohammedanism. He made lengthy references to eastern mythology, and some Friends were exercised at what they heard in a meeting for worship, while others were glad to see and hear such a distinguished visitor, even if they could not understand or agree with all he said.[57]

This report prompted a letter to the editor from one of readers of the magazine who was present at the meeting and wanted to clarify some points:

Dear Friend – Some of us who were at Westminster meeting when it was visited by Abdul Baha, received a different impression from that of your correspondent (page 61). Most of the elders and overseers had been informed that this visit was intended that morning and some Friends were waiting to welcome him before meeting began. It was not until a quarter to twelve that he arrived, accompanied as described. A friend was speaking at the moment when he came in and he was shown to his seat. Another friend in the body of the meeting also spoke, and then Abdul Baha rose and addressed us in Persian Arabic. Those of us who were following closely would have felt more interested had the interpretation been more literal. As an Armenian Christian, who speaks Arabic, remarked afterwards: 'the interpreter added many things.' After describing the rise in Persia of a sect which he said resembled the 'Society of Friends' (sic), and referring to 'His Holiness', the father of Abdul, who founded 'Bahaism', he gave us a rather flowery dissertation on the value of meditation, with a few Quaker phrases about the 'Inner

Light,' &c, thrown in. The Baha had no time to enter into the spirit of our meeting for worship . . .
Yours sincerely,
A Westminster Elder[58]

A note in the same issue directed the readers to an article against the Bahá'í Faith which had been published recently: 'Friends interested in the personality and aims of Abdul Baha (Abbas Effendi) will find a serious criticism by one familiar with the subject (W.A. Rice of Persia) in the January issue of *The East and The West*. The writer argues that "as Christians, we find ourselves in disagreement with the fundamental views of Bahaism as to nature, man, the soul, and God, which are mainly a mixture of sufism and pantheism". (S.P.G. 15 Tufton St., Westminster, S.W.).'[59] The same newspaper, however, published on 11 April 1913 a positive review of Myron Phelps's book *Abbas Effendi, His Life and Teachings*.[60]

The Christian Commonwealth briefly stated regarding this visit that 'Last Sunday morning Abdul Baha was present at the meeting of the Society of Friends at Westminster. A small body of Friends, he said, had settled in Persia 100 years ago, and persisted there to this day.'[61]

In the afternoon of 12 January, 'Abdu'l-Bahá also spoke at the New Congregational Church which was filled to capacity by an audience eager to listen to Him and which twice stood as a sign of respect. The Master was introduced by Rev J. J. Poole, who in his remarks stated, 'I prefer to call him my Master and myself his servant'. *The Christian Commonwealth* reported the meeting:

> On Sunday night Abdul Baha paid a visit to the New Congregational Church, Woolwich, where Rev J. J. Poole, the pastor, introduced him to a large gathering, which was keenly interested in the service which followed. Mr Poole said that Abdul Baha was no ordinary person, but a religious teacher whose message was laying hold of the people in the West and in the East, and he hoped and believed that what the Master taught would be realised. At the conclusion of the service many people expressed their wish to know more about the movement and of the personality of its venerable leader.[62]

Visit to Bristol

On Wednesday, 15 January, 'Abdu'l-Bahá left London to visit Clifton, in Bristol. The same day *The Christian Commonwealth* announced: 'Abdul Baha visits the Clifton Guest House, Bristol, January 15–16. On January 15 at 8 p.m. he gives an address.'[63]

The party that traveled with the Master to Bristol included a special guest, Dúst Muḥammad Khán, a son of a former Persian prime minister and a son-in-law of Náṣiri'd-Dín Sháh, who had recently made several visits to the Master. On one of them, on 14 January, he listened the Master speak on the subject of reincarnation and the immortality of the soul. That night, says Sohrab, 'he went to his room and sat all night thinking it over. He did not even take off his coat. He thought and thought till eight o'clock when he left the Hotel to come to the Master'[64] and it was at that moment that he was invited to join Him on His visit to Clifton.

The train reached Bristol at ten in the evening. Wellesley Tudor Pole took the Master and His companions to the Clifton Guest House – the same place where 'Abdu'l-Bahá had stayed during His first visit to the city in 1911 – occupying a room on the third floor. On the night of His arrival, 'Abdu'l-Bahá gave a public address introducing some of the Bahá'í principles and granted two interviews to local reporters. The Western Edition of the *Daily Chronicle* (Bristol) published the following report:

TURKS' PRISONER FOR 40 YEARS
A FAMOUS PERSIAN CHIEF IN BRISTOL
STRIKING MESSAGE IN AN INTERVIEW

After travelling half-way around the world, Abdul Baha Abbas has paid a return visit to Bristol, before turning his steps once more towards his homeland in the East. He is the head of the Bahai movement which, it is estimated, has upwards of three million followers.

'One of the most remarkable and far-reaching of modern times,' said the Rev R. J. Campbell of the movement when Abdul Baha was recently welcomed to the City Temple.

A picturesque figure in Oriental dress, Abdul Baha attracted a good deal of attention as he stepped from the train at Temple

Meads, welcomed to Bristol by Mr Tudor Pole, whose visitor he was at the Clifton Guest House . . .

He employed one English phrase in conversation with a 'Daily Chronicle' representative at Bristol, and that was 'Thank you'.

TANGLE AND CONFLICT

In his native tongue Abdul Baha gave a message to 'Daily Chronicle' readers and it was interpreted by Mirza Ahmad Sohrab thus: –

'His holiness Christ stepped into this world about 2,000 years ago. The birth of Christ into this world is considered a blessed inaugural day for humanity. Before this the world was dark. Like unto a brilliant luminary He shone forth and flooded the regions with his light: He spread divine teachings; He enunciated certain heavenly principles whereby humanity should be led so that the human kind may become enlightened, warfare and battle be swept away, the foundations of estrangement be razed to the ground and the human race elevated. All this teachings spelt love between the children of men.

'But these peoples have forgotten those cardinal laws. They have abandoned the pathway in which he walked; and the fire of hatred and enmity is raging all around to-day. That is why you witness every day a new international tangle and conflicting interests clashing with each other. Anarchy, darkness, has encompassed the world. The East and the West have become estranged.'

Then Abdul Baha spoke of the coming at such a time of Baha-u-llah, with his message of universal peace and the federation of men, creating love between the nations.

'Here,' continued the interpreted message of Abdul Baha, 'our mission is to cry out Peace, peace, amongst all the nations, spreading and promulgating this all-encircling peace amongst all the peoples.

'As the inhabitants of Clifton' – where the interview took place – 'are honourable and noble people, it is our hope that they may become the advocates of international peace, and devotees of the oneness of the world of humanity. May their eyes be opened and may they behold the lights of the Master's great guidance. May they walk in the straight path all their lives. May they become the recipients of the light of the sun of reality. May they spread the lambent lights of righteousness, straightforwardness, trustfulness, and fidelity.'

AGE OF HUMAN FRATRICIDE

After this, Abdul Baha addressed an invitation meeting at the Guest House, at which Mr Tudor Pole presided.

It was a notable gathering of East and West – the central stately figure in flowing robes, with Oriental headdress setting off the long hair and flowing beard and striking countenance; around a group of coadjutors; whilst amongst the audience of Westerners was here and there a scarlet fez which denoted the presence of Eastern students.

It was a courtly greeting from Abdul Baha as on entering he raised the palms of the hands to the forehead. He commenced his speech – interpreted sentence by sentence – while seated on a couch, but warming to his subject he was soon on his feet, occasionally striding to and fro, sometimes expressing his thoughts with bent head in studious mood, and then directing his eyes to his listeners as, with upraised hand, he emphasised weighty points.

It was not long before his plea for world-wide peace came, with a reminder of empires having become 'like unto arsenals and nations as an armed camp' ready for the ignition of a spark to threaten universal conflagration.

He contrasted vaunted civilisation with the unrest and strife and the activity in manufacturing armaments which were to be noted, and asked, 'Is not this an age of human fratricide rather than the best of the cycles?'

He put it that the fundamental principles of all Heavenly teachings are the unity and love, lamenting that humanity is yet asleep, and he laid stress on the need of the movement for international conciliation and the institution of new principles for the establishment of the brotherhood of man.

As exposition of the teachings of Baha-u-llah included a recognition of the equality of man and woman – a point which was quaintly elaborated, going close to, but without expressly mentioning the suffrage question; and besides international peace councils and universal education, the teachings advocated a universal language as an auxiliary to one mother tongue.[65]

The same day the *Western Daily Press* (Bristol) reported that the 'Clifton Guest House was crowded on Wednesday evening on the occasion of

the visit of Abdul Baha Abbas, chief of the Bahai movement, who, with his disciples revisited Clifton after a tour of the world. Our correspondent mentions that "Abdul Baha, in short, sweet, rhythmic sentences, gave expression to the Gospel of International Peace and Concord, based on eternal realities". Mr Tudor Pole presided.'[66]

On 22 January the weekly *Clifton Chronicle and Directory* published an article reproducing the talk delivered by the Master and including a message for the citizens of Clifton:

ABDUL BAHA
PERSIAN REFORMER'S MESSAGE TO CLIFTON
THE BAHAI MOVEMENT

On Wednesday evening a large number accepted invitations to meet Abdul Baha at the Clifton Guest House, Royal York Crescent, and all followed with deep interest his address on the Bahai movement.

Who is Abdul Baha? What is the Bahai movement? These are questions which readers will probably at once ask themselves. In a sentence, then, the Bahai movement may be described as having for its object the establishment of unity and the 'most great peace'; throughout the world, when man shall no longer make war and when he shall have learned the fact that there is only one religion, that which is based on ultimate reality, and which is recognizable as spiritual truth. Its founders claim to have depended absolutely and entirely upon spiritual inspiration and illumination . . .

THE MASTER

Abdul Baha, called by his followers 'The Master', is an aged man of venerable appearance, with flowing grey beard, massive brow, and large kindly eyes, and he presents a striking figure clad in his loose Persian robes. His address at the Clifton Guest House, where Mr W. Tudor Pole occupied the chair, was delivered in Persian, and translated into excellent English by his interpreter, Mirza Ahmad Sohrab.

Abdul Baha commenced by observing that every age requires a central impetus or movement, and asked: What is the spirit of this age? What is its focal point? It is the establishment of universal peace, the establishment of the knowledge that humanity is one family. Think on the existing conditions.

Nations have become like unto armed camps waiting to be ignited by the combustion of war. God has created man for love's sake. He has endowed man with creation so that He may illumine the world with the flame of brotherhood and express the utmost state of unity and accord. This would express God's good pleasure; this would be the prosperity of the world of humanity. A thousand times alas, that this glorious century has been besmeared with war and strife, hatred and rancour. Bloodthirsty wolves are tearing the sheep of God so that destruction is more widespread than in all the ages of the past. We hear on every side praises of the wonders of this cycle; its achievements; its refinements; its genius calling the past the age of mediaeval horror. What mediaeval age held the horror of a Krupp gun, a Mauser rifle, or a grape cannon charge that kills a whole camp at a volley?. In the sea we have the submarine and dreadnought. If you compare the past with this age in impartial judgement, you will call this the age of human fratricide.

FUNDAMENTALS OF RELIGION

All the religions of God are revealed for the sake of good fellowship. The fundamental foundations of all are fellowship, unity and love. The Heavenly books were revealed and divine love bestowed to bring about peace. What has man made of religion? He has made it the cause of bloodshed and strife; enmity and hatred. Religion was destined to be a remedy for the sickness of humanity; an illumination for the darkness of uncertainty. Have we, then, forgotten the divine teachings, cast aside the Heavenly books, created imaginary thoughts and illusions and made them the basis of rancour and strife? The Bible commands the practice of peace and justice; God desires love. In the Gospel we find the golden statement that man should be expressive of love even unto his enemy; he should be expressive of love to his ill-wishers; he should be expressive of love to all his fellow men. He must have an eye to pardon; he must have an eye to benevolence. All the divine books invite men to these teachings. All the divine prophets suffered that men might realize these teachings. Alas, that all the travail of these holy souls and sanctified prophets should be wasted. The world of humanity is in a stupor of sleep and it cannot grasp the realities. The horizons of the minds are still beclouded and the hearts are occupied with phantasmal longings. We seem never to think of the reason of creation; never to strive to proclaim those principles which enlighten humanity. In the sea of materialism are we sinking and of the kingdom of God know we nothing!

Nearly 60 years ago, when the horizon of the Orient was in a state of the utmost gloom, warfare existed and there was enmity between the various creeds; darkness and doubt hovered over humanity and foul clouds of ignorance hid the sky. At such a time, his Highness Baha-u-llah rose from the horizon of Persia like unto a shining sun. He boldly proclaimed peace, writing to the kings of the earth and calling upon them to assist in the hoisting of this banner. In order to bring peace out of chaos, Baha-u-llah established certain precepts or principles. The first principle concerned itself with the unity of truth. Baha-u-llah urged the independent investigation of truth. If each investigate for himself he will find that reality is one. It does not admit of multiplicity; it is not divisible. All will find the same foundation and all will be at peace. The second principle of Baha-u-llah proclaims the oneness of the human race. He compares humanity to the sheep of God. God is the real shepherd. When this shepherd is compassionate and kind, why should the members of the flock quarrel among themselves? The third principle of the revealed religion of Baha-u-llah is in regard to international peace. There must be peace between the fatherlands, peace between the religions. In this period of its evolution, the world of humanity is in danger. Every war is against the good pleasure of the Lord of mankind. Man is the edifice of God. War destroys the divine edifice. Peace is the stay of life; war the cause of death. If an active, actual peace is brought about, the human world will attain to the utmost serenity and composure. The wolves will be transformed into lambs, devils into angels, and terrors into divine splendours in less than the twinkling of an eye. The fifth principle declares that religion must be in conformity to science and reason. If a religion does not agree with the postulates of science nor accord with the regulations of reason it is a bundle of superstitions; a phantasm of the brain. Science and religion are realities, and if that religion to which we adhere be a reality it must needs conform to the foundational reality of all things. The sixth principle of Baha-u-llah is that religious, racial, political, and patriotic prejudices are the destroyers of human society. As long as these threatening clouds are in the sky of humanity, the sun of reality cannot dawn.

EQUALITY OF THE SEXES

The seventh principle of Baha'u'llah is in regard to the equality of men and women. The male and female of the human kingdom are equal before God. God is no respecter of gender. Whosoever practices more faith, whosoever practices more humanitarianism, is nearer to God; but between the male and female there is no innate difference, because they share in common all the faculties. The world of humanity has two wings, one the male; the other the female. When both wings are reinforced with the same impulse the bird will be enabled to soar in its flight heavenward to the summit of progress. God has created the man and the woman equal, why should she be deprived of exercising the fullest opportunities afforded by life? The eighth teaching suggests a plan whereby all the individual members may enjoy the utmost comfort and welfare. The degrees of society must be preserved. The farmer will continue to till the soil; the artist pursue his art and the banker to finance the nation. But in this Bahai plan there is no class hatred. Each is to be protected and each individual member of the body politic is to live in the greatest comfort and happiness. Work is to be provided for all and there will be no needy ones to be seen in the streets. The ninth principle declares that there must needs be the establishment of a parliament of men, a court of last appeal for international questions. The members of this arbitral court of justice will be representatives of all the nations. The tenth admonition is in regard to education. All the children must be educated so that there will not remain one single individual without an education. In cases of inability on the part of the parents through sickness, death, etc., the State must educate the child. In addition to this widespread education, each child must be taught a profession or trade so that every member of the body politic will be enabled to earn his own living and at the same time serve the community. Work done in the spirit of service is worship. From this universal system of education misunderstandings will be expelled from amongst the children of men. The eleventh principle is the establishment of a universal language, so that we shall not have to acquire so many languages in the future.

In the schools children will study two – the mother tongue and the international auxiliary language. The use of an international auxiliary language will be one means of dispelling the differences between nations.

MESSAGE TO CLIFTON

To a representative of the 'Clifton Chronicle' Abdul Baha, through his interpreter, gave the following message to Clifton: – I am most delighted and pleased with the situation of Clifton and its surrounding valleys and hills.

Therefore, before returning to the Orient I have again come here to spend one night. In reality the people of Clifton are very intelligent. They have the capability of understanding every problem. Their consciousness yearns for the search of reality. They understand selfless objects and they are willing to work for philanthropy. It is my hope that they will be assisted to serve the whole of humanity. May they become the means of creating good fellowship between the children of men. May they entirely relinquish those blind dogmas which have created strife in the world of humanity. May they become instrumental in putting into practice the Heavenly teaching. May each one of them become a Heavenly lamp to enlighten humanity, so that this gloomy darkness of strife and contention between peoples may be entirely dispelled, and nation and nation show friendlier fellowship towards each other, and the day of universal justice and the day of the unification of all the races and all religions may become apparent. This is my message to Clifton people.

Abdul Baha, who recently returned from America, was accompanied by his Highness the Moayer el Mamelck Doust Mohamed Khan, the late Prime Minister of Persia, one of the wealthiest noblemen in that country and son-in-law of the late Shah, who was the guest of Mr W. Tudor Pole at the Clifton Guest House.

Abdul Baha told Mr Tudor Pole that of all the places he had visited in Europe and America he had found the climate most temperate and delightful at Denver in America and Clifton in this hemisphere, and he gave Clifton by far the preference.[67]

The weekly *Clifton Society* also published a short notice about the presence of the Master in the area: 'His Excellency Abdul Baha Abbas, the great Persian religious and social reformer visited Clifton last evening. He is on his way back to the East from America, where he has spoken all over the States to audiences sometimes amounting to over four or five thousand. An informal reception, at which Abdul Baha spoke was held at the Clifton Guest House, Royal York Crescent.'[68]

The *Western Daily Press*[69] and the *Clifton Society* published in the next few days further notes reproducing information that had already appeared in *The Clifton Chronicle and Directory*.[70] Both newspapers identified Wellesley Tudor Pole as their informant. Other local periodicals, like the *Clifton Free Press* and the *Horfield and Bishopston Record*, also published short notes reporting 'Abdu'l-Bahá's visit.[71] Outside the Bristol area, *The Christian Commonwealth* offered on 29 January a further account of the talk based on what had already been published in Bristol and Clifton.[72]

Visit to the Woking Mosque

The Oriental Institute invited 'Abdu'l-Bahá to visit the Woking mosque on Friday, 17 January. This Institute was created in 1883 by Sir Dr Gottlieb Wilhelm Leitner, a Hungarian of Jewish background who had converted to Islam and was responsible for the building of the Woking mosque which was opened in 1889 but soon fell into disuse.

Some leading British newspapers had announced the visit of the Master to Woking. *The Manchester Guardian*, for instance, mentioned on the same day that 'Abdul Baha, the Persian religious reformer and leader of the Bahai movement, will address a gathering arranged by the "Asiatic Quarterly Review" in the Mosque attached to the Oriental Institute at Woking to-day.'[73] A similar announcement published in the *Daily Mail* stated that the public meeting was to start at 3:15 p.m.[74]

The Master traveled from London to Woking in the car of the philanthropist Sir Richard Stapley (1843–1920) and his wife. Many personalities had gathered at the mosque to receive Him. Besides members of the Oriental Institute and the Muslim Mission such as Khwaja Kamal-ud-Din, other visitors included Princess Cheref Ouroussoff; Dúst Muḥammad Khán, who traveled to Woking with 'Abdu'l-Bahá and the Stapleys; Lady Barclay, wife of Lord Barclay; Sir Arundel and his wife; Henry Leitner (1869–1945), son of the founder of the Oriental Institute; George R. S. Mead (1863–1933), editor of the *Vahan* and *Quest* magazines; Lord Lamington; Dr John Pollen (1848–1923), president of the East India Association; and Miss Alice Buckton, who had a residence in the Woking area and who, according Sohrab, was instrumental in arranging the meeting.

A lunch in honour of the Master was served and afterwards all those present were invited to take part in prayers at the mosque. 'Abdu'l-Bahá took off His boots and joined the Muslims in their prayers. Afterwards, outside the mosque, the Master gave an address about the unity of religions to those assembled. Before returning to London 'Abdu'l-Bahá visited the home of Henry Leitner.[75]

The Asiatic Quarterly Review, the organ of the Oriental Institute, and newspapers published in Surrey sent reporters to the meeting and afterwards published several accounts of it.

The weekly newspapers *Woking News and Mail* and the *Surrey Times* (Guildford) published detailed accounts of the events of that day:

'AND NEVER THE TWAIN –'?
HOW EAST AND WEST MAY MEET ORIENTAL PREACHER AT WOKING

Friday last was a day of much interest for those interested in the Mosque at Woking. A large and unique gathering of Asiatics, including Christians, Mohammedans and Jews, assembled to meet Abdul Baha (His Excellency Abbas Effendi), the leader of the Bahai doctrine, which seeks to unite East and West, who is visiting England on his way home to Persia after touring America. The gathering was held under the auspices of 'The Asiatic Quarterly Review', which is published at the Oriental Institute, Woking, and a great number of distinguished personages were present.

This beautiful Mosque, which adjoins the Oriental Institute, was founded by the late Dr Leitner and the Begum of Bhopal about 30 years ago. Hitherto it has been used only on special occasions, the last time being on the occasion of the memorial service to the late Shah of Persia, some six or seven years back. There is only one other building like it in England. The other building is in a busy quarter of Liverpool.

General approval was expressed on Friday when it was announced that the Mosque would in future be open for Mohammedans to worship there whenever they liked.

Abdul Baha, who travelled from London in a motorcar, was

greeted at the Memorial House, adjoining the Mosque, on his arrival, by Mr. H. Leitner (son of the founder). Here he partook of a meal which was prepared in an Oriental style, prepared by native servants. There were about 40 present, principally Persians.

Afterwards his Excellency Abbas Effendi made a few remarks. Indicating a banner on the wall, bearing a representation of an Eastern and a Western woman with a globe dividing them and the word 'Concordia', he said it was a great thing to establish the unity of the globe. (This banner, which, by the way, was worked by poor women in London, has just been returned from the Peace Congress held in Rome).

Later Abdul Baba was also greeted at the Mosque by Rt. Hon. Lord Lamington, Rt Hon Ameer Ali, P.C., and Dr J. Pollen (representing the East India Association) and the large gathering, which included many local people, was photographed in front of the building by Mr A. Wildman. A prayer having been offered by his Excellency, a number of the Asiatic visitors worshipped in the building, and then Abdul Baha, who was attired in native robes, addressed the audience in Persian on 'The unity of all the religions of the earth', his remarks being repeated in English by his interpreter (Mr Sohrab).

DISTINGUISHED VISITORS

Among the visitors were the Turkish Princess Ouroussoff, Prince and Princess Sherriff, His Highness Mehmet, (ex-Prime Minister of Persia). Lady Blomfield, Lady Barclay, Sir Arundel, J.P. and Lady Arundel, Sir Richard and Lady Stepley, Dr. Abdul Mazid, Khaja Kamaluddbi, Maimutullah Shah, Shah Mohamed Yehya, Zafrulla Khan, S. Bashir Uddin (Middle Temple), Zafar Ali Khan, Sheik Atta Ullah, Abdul Ghani, Mohamed Nawas Khan, Habid Ullah Khan, Mohamed Hasan, Mr G. R. S. Mead (Theosophical Quest Society), Miss Alice Buckton and a number of representatives from the Asiatic Society, the India Office, the Mohammedan Brotherhood and Oriental students from Oxford and Cambridge.

In the course of his address, Abdul Baha said that whilst in America he was invited to speak at many churches, societies and clubs, and even in the Jewish Synagogue. In every one of these gatherings he summoned the people to the unity of the human race, and invited all to become the advocates of universal peace. He mentioned the fundamental principle of all the religions of God, stating that the foundation of all was one. That one foundation was absolute reality, and was not subjected to multiplicity. Therefore, they concluded that all the religions of God were the means of human cultivation and education. The religions led men to the virtues of humanity and encouraged the people to uphold universal peace. The foundation of the religions of God was love; it was the basis of reciprocity, cooperation and affection, and was conducive to the establishment of communication between the children of men. That which was the cause of difference was the folly of blind dogmas and imitation, for as these blind imitations varied, they had become the means of difference.

Each one of the religions of God was divided into two parts, the first part being the foundation which belonged to the world of morality. This first part was immutable. Its foundation was faith, belief in God, love, justice, equality and benevolence. So this part of religion was not subjected to any transformation. It was the basis of the Holy Writ, and these were the principles which all the prophets had promulgated.

THE DAWN OF PEACE

The second part belonged to the world of transactions and business, and these laws changed according to the exigencies of the times. Therefore, it was incumbent upon them to relinquish all those counterfeits and investigate the fundamental teachings of the religions of God. Clergymen or priests might entertain the idea that Mohammed was against Christ, but this was erroneous. All these prophets entertained love for each other, praised each other and were friends. Why should not they, the followers of these religions, be friends? These were at peace, and why should they of the present be at war? Why should they falsify instead of acknowledge each other? Praise be to God that the century of light had dawned, that, the intellects had advanced and the horizon of the minds extended.

Now was the time when universal love must be established amongst all the people. All the religions must show affection and good fellowship towards each other. For 6,000 years the children of humanity had been engaged in war and strife, but now the period of love had come and the day of peace had dawned. God had created all men to show the attributes of humanity. Why should they lower their station and be characterised with animal instincts? Why should they be unkind? There had been strife and warfare between the nations; Oriental people shedding each other's blood, and the utmost enmity between them.

At such a time a prophet arrived who established affection between the nations and encouraged love between the religions. He proclaimed the law of the oneness of the world of humanity and enunciated universal peace between the nations and communities. He gathered in his flock various communities who to-day bore the utmost love and unity toward one another, and considered the whole world as one commonwealth.

Another principle of the Bahai religion was that religion must become the cause of love, the means of illumination and the cause of the oneness of the world of humanity. If religion ever were the cause of hatred and rancour, if it were the means of bloodshed and strife, it was better to leave that so-called religion, for God created religion to be the means of love and not hatred. Again, religion must conform with science and reason and if any of the religious theories were not in accord with science and reason, it was superstition.

A GREAT DOCTRINE

This prophet established a strong affiliation between the tribes of the East and to-day, according to the estimation of the Bahai, the Gospels, Old and New Testament, the Koran and all the other Holy books, formed the Bible of the world. In these Holy books it was clearly seen that they invited the people to affection and love. Therefore, why should they shun each other? Why should they practise hatred and rancour? All those prophets of God had sacrificed everything, gone through a thousand ordeals and had been ready to give up their lives for the sake of cementing the hearts of men together. Why should they let go the wonderful results of these prophets' teachings? Why should they let the law of God remain fruitless? Praise be to God that they were the servants of one God and the sheep of one Shepherd whose bounties were all enriching. Let war and strife be banished from the face of the earth. These were the cause of the humiliation of the human race, and were the blameworthy attributes of the lower grades of humanity, and the imperfections of the people. Peace and love were better than enmity, and affiliation was better than hatred. They should not be so inadvertent; they should not make themselves bloodthirsty animals, or be unjust. In the past when there were not the communications between the various sections of the human race, ignorance and misunderstanding were predominant, but these things were banished to-day. Misunderstandings were being wiped away, and the reality of the religions of God unfolded.

Dr Pollen expressed thanks to those present, and bid them welcome in the name of the West and the East. Abdul Baha, he said, was presenting a great doctrine, and would hasten the day when all men would work in a noble brotherhood. The speaker, on behalf of Mr Leitner, announced that the Mosque would in future be open for Mohammedans, to worship in at any time.

Afterwards a number of the local visitors put on sandals and inspected the interior of the Mosque, as well as the magnificent Koran, in three volumes, which was presented by the late Queen Victoria.

In the visitors book Abdul Baha, referring to the Asiatic Quarterly Review, wrote in Persian: 'O God, illumine this review and ignite this society like unto a lamp so that it may spread the light in all directions . . .'[76]

The Surrey Herald and Middlesex News (Chertsey) published a further account, which included a picture of the Master in front of the Woking mosque surrounded by all the people who had gathered to listen to Him. The article also mentioned the names of some of the attendants and summarized the words of the Master. 'The spectacle will live long in the memory of those who saw it,' stated the reporter. 'The Prophet, a venerable figure, wearing a long brown robe and a white turban, which emphasized the keen alert eyes, stood on the steps of the Mosque surrounded by Asiatics and Europeans and delivered his message of love, peace, goodwill and fellowship to all nations.'[77]

The Woking Observer and the *Surrey Advertiser and County Times* published accounts containing information very similar to that published in other journals.[78]

In London, *The Christian Commonwealth* published a further account based on what was published in Surrey's newspapers.[79] The same edition included notes of the prayer recited by the Master after His address:

ABDUL BAHA'S PRAYER AT THE DOOR OF THE MOHAMMEDAN MOSQUE

O God! I supplicate thee. In thee I put my trust. Guide us toward the straight path. Direct us toward the strong fortress. Dilate our hearts with the light of thy knowledge. Reinforce us with thy power, so that we may arise in thy service. Inflame us with the eye of thy compassion. O God! I beg of thee by the manifestation of thyself and of thy great messenger to submerge us in the sea of thy mercy. Verily the darkness of error hath encompassed the world. I invoke thee by thy merciful light to guide us toward the path of salvation so that we may behold the manifest signs! Verily thou art the Clement! Verily thou art the Omnipotent! Verily thou art the Compassionate and the Merciful![80]

The Daily Telegraph furnished its readers with information about the event in a brief note in which it was stated that no less that one hundred people attended the meeting.[81]

In April 1913 the *Asiatic Quarterly Review* published an account of the visit of 'Abdu'l-Bahá to Woking which included one of the pictures of the meeting taken by A. Wildman but did not add any new information to what had already been published in local newspapers. In explaining the reasons for the invitation extended to 'Abdu'l-Bahá to visit the mosque the article stated that 'It occurred to some friends interested in those matters of East and West with which this *Review* is concerned, that the presence in London recently of the Head of the Bahai movement (H. E. Abbas Effendi) afforded a fitting opportunity for bringing the mosque once more into prominence. Abdul Baha was accordingly invited to give there, under the auspices of the *Asiatic Quarterly Review*, a discourse on "World Unity".' Dr Pollen 'was hastening that "diviner day", when all men would work together in noble brotherhood'.[82]

Outside England the magazine *Al-Badr* (Qadian, India), organ of the Ahmadiyya movement, published a letter by Khwaja Kamal-ud-Din in which he described his encounter with 'Abdu'l-Bahá at the Woking mosque. The article contained a large section that is not directly connected with the visit and thus is not reproduced here:

> On Tuesday of last week we went to the funeral of a young Muslim and discovered there that this Friday the Head of the Babi religion, Abdul Baha, will come to Woking with his followers and the opening of the mosque will also take place. To my knowledge, the Babi religion is not a sect of Islam but a separate religion. I was deeply saddened at this combination of the Head of the Babi religion and the opening of an Islamic mosque. At the funeral some Muslim friends were present. Anyhow, at the invitation of the Secretary of the Anjuman Islam the young Muslims of London were invited to Woking at 12 midday. The invitation card stated that the *Jumu'a* prayer would be held and led by Khwaja Kamal-ud-Din . . .
>
> I have forgotten to write that as I was standing delivering the *khutba* Abdul Baha arrived with a few friends in a motor car and stood at the gate of the mosque, some fifty yards from me. He saw us, stood there for a few minutes and then went towards the guest house. He is after all the son of a Muslim, and used to be a Muslim and knows what the *Jumu'a* prayer is. After finishing the prayer, when we went to the guest house, we found Abdul Baha seated at a table with his food. Our eating arrangements were in the same room. When they finished and emerged from the room, Abdul Baha extended his hand towards me and greeted me. After a formal exchange of words, I said to him: You came here in connection with the opening of the mosque and today was Friday. Why didn't you join the prayer? Being familiar with worldly expediency, he replied: The prayer time came when we were still at home, so we performed this duty there. I said: Yes, but now the time for *asr* is approaching. He would have to join in it. He had no choice but to answer in the affirmative.
>
> Anyhow, we entered the dining room, and as I emerged after the meal Abdul Baha approached me and began to walk with me, taking me to the mosque while talking to me. Finding the mosque empty he immediately entered it, called out the *takbir* and pointed to me to lead the prayer. If he had said his prayer at that time no one else would have known what happened in the mosque. I said to him that there were many Muslims who had yet to pray and he

should wait till the congregation was ready. He was about to say something when I went outside and called everyone to come inside. Immediately I had the *adhan* called loudly for the *asr* prayers. People started to gather. Meanwhile Abdul Baha had started praying and performed the prayer in the manner of Sunni Muslims. While the *adhan* was being called out he finished his prayer. However, when the *adhan* came to an end he said loudly *La ilaha illallah Muhammad-ur Rasulullah* like Muslims. Then we stood for prayers, which I led. Abdul Baha joined us in the congregation and two Europeans who were with him, probably Bahais, also joined. Others just watched. His Persian companions, including Hakim Mahmud, also joined the prayer.

After the prayer Abdul Baha stood outside at the threshold of the mosque and some forty people were present in the courtyard to listen to him, including ourselves and some other Muslim students who had not been able to come in time for the *Jumu'a* prayer. The gist of Abdul Baha's speech was that the basis of religion is harmony and love, and it was the mission of every prophet to spread harmony and love in mankind. This was also the real mission of Moses, Jesus and the Holy Prophet Muhammad. In past times there was much discord and ignorance. Now Bahaullah had brought light and his mission was to teach love, harmony and brotherhood. The reason for man's existence is to show humanity and love, so we must adhere to love and brotherhood.

There was a Persian interpreter with him who translated each sentence into English. No doubt the speech was well constructed but it was certainly not impromptu.

Anyhow, after *asr*, having listened to this speech, we went to the railway station and reached home safely.[83]

Talk for the Higher Thought Centre

On Sunday, 19 January, the day before He left London, 'Abdu'l-Bahá addressed a public meeting arranged by the Higher Thought Centre. This was the second time this organization invited 'Abdu'l-Bahá to speak and the event was publicized in the Socialist *Daily Herald*.[84]

The Higher Thought Centre used to organize two Sunday meetings simultaneously. One of them was held at their headquarters in

10 Cheniston Gardens, Kensington, where 'Abdu'l-Bahá had been invited to speak in 1911, while those Sunday meetings open to the general public were held at the Doré Gallery, 35 New Bond Street, a building today used by Sotheby's.

The *Quarterly Record of Higher Thought Work* offered an account of the meeting at the Doré Gallery:

> ABDUL BAHA'S VISIT TO THE DORÉ GALLERY
>
> It was a deep satisfaction to the members of the Higher Thought Centre that their invitation to Abdul Baha to address them at the Doré Gallery was accepted. On his former visit he had come to the Centre itself and had been received in the rooms where the Bahais of London had met weekly for the past few years. It seemed fitting that the great Advocate of Unity should also be welcomed in the beautiful Gallery where the more public work of the Centre is carried on. Accordingly, on Sunday afternoon, January 19th, on the eve of his leaving England, a meeting was organised, and after the singing of one of the Truth Songs by the large concourse assembled, Mr Charles Spencer gave a short pregnant address of welcome and of deep appreciation for the occasion. This was followed by an account of the Bahai Movement from its inception in 1847, by Lady Blomfield. The address which followed was given by Abdul Baha in Persian, translated, sentence by sentence by an able and sympathetic interpreter. It was a veritable trumpet call to the higher and nobler part of man – to rise and manifest the inherent brotherhood lying fundamentally beneath external differences of race, nation and creed. 'Children of One Father' was the recurring note, and all went forth with the spiritual uplift of a great message delivered by a great messenger.[85]

The Christian Commonwealth also published its own account of the meeting. In outlining some of the contents of 'Abdu'l-Bahá's address, the article stated that 'Abdul Baha entered the hall, and, through the medium of an able interpreter, addressed the meeting in stirring terms. He spoke of the Fatherhood of God, and the consequent unity and brotherhood of all human beings. Lines of separation – religious and secular – arose out of the lower or animal nature, and not out of the higher or spiritual nature of man. Hence in the coming new dispensation, upon which we are now entering, war and discord would tend more and more to disappear until finally peace, unity, and the higher spiritual powers of mankind would rule.'[86]

Message to the Editor of the *Asiatic Quarterly Review*

On Monday, 20 January, three days after 'Abdu'l-Bahá's visit to the Woking mosque, the editor of the *Asiatic Quarterly Review* visited the Master in London and had a private interview with Him. In the course of their conversation 'Abdu'l-Bahá was asked to contribute an article for the magazine. 'Abdu'l-Bahá agreed and weeks later, while in Paris, dictated a message which was translated by Ahmad Sohrab and published on April 1913 together with a facsimile of the original Persian notes and a section with notes of a talk of 'Abdu'l-Bahá on education.[87]

ON THE IMPORTANCE OF DIVINE CIVILIZATION
BY ABDUL BAHA – HIS EXCELLENCY ABBAS EFFENDI

When listening to Abbas Effendi's address at the Mosque at Woking (of which a brief report is given elsewhere in the present number), it occurred to us that readers of the 'Asiatic Quarterly Review' would be interested to have from so distinguished and widely revered a visitor some account of the impressions made upon him by our Western life and institutions during his recent tour through America and Europe, which tour may be briefly characterized as a pilgrimage among the many shrines which are being erected of late to the Spirit of International Concord. We therefore asked him would he be good enough to write an article for our pages. The result is here given, and affords a typical instance –with its Eastern warmth of metaphor and simple directness of phrase – of that 'Contact and Comprehension' which is becoming possible between the mind of the East and the mind of the West, on which Mr Anderson wrote in our January issue, which also is one of the chief aims of the 'Asiatic Quarterly Review'. – ED.

TO THE EDITOR OF THE 'ASIATIC QUARTERLY REVIEW'
YOUR letter was received. It indicated the spiritual susceptibilities which emanate from your spirit and consciousness, and it imparted the utmost happiness.

During this journey it has become manifest and evident to me that the Western world has made extraordinary progress in material civilization, but Divine civilization is well-nigh forgotten.

This is the result of the submission of all human thought to the world of nature.

All that one observes in the Western Hemisphere are the appearances of the material world and not of the Divine world.

As there are many defects in the world of nature the lights of Divine civilization are hidden, and nature has become the ruler over all things.

In the world of nature the greatest dominant note is the struggle for existence – the result of which is the survival of the fittest. The law of the survival of the fittest is the origin of all difficulties. It is the cause of war and strife, hatred and animosity, between human beings.

In the world of nature there is tyranny, egoism, aggression, overbearance, usurpation of the rights of others and other blameworthy attributes which are the defects of the animal world. Therefore so long as the requirements of the natural world play a paramount part among the children of men, success and prosperity are impossible. For the success and prosperity of the human world depend upon the qualities and virtues with which the reality of humanity is adorned; while the exigencies of the natural world work against the realization of this object.

Nature is warlike, nature is blood-thirsty, nature is tyrannical, nature is unaware of His Highness the Almighty. That is why these cruel qualities are natural to the animal world.

Therefore His Highness the Lord of mankind, having great love and mercy, has caused the appearance of the prophets and the revelations of the holy books, so that through Divine education the world of humanity may be released from the corruption of nature and the darkness of ignorance; be confirmed with ideal virtues, the susceptibilities of consciousness and the spiritual attributes, and become the dawning-place of merciful emotions. This is Divine civilization. To-day in the world of humanity material civilization is like unto a lamp of the utmost transparency, but this lamp – a thousand times alas! – is deprived of light. This light is Divine civilization, which is instituted by the Holy Divine Manifestations.

This century is the century of light. This century is the century of the appearance of reality. This century is the century of universal progress.

A hundred thousand times alas! that ignorant prejudices, unnatural differences and antagonistic and inimical principles are yet displayed by the nations of the world toward one another, thus causing the retardation of general progress. This retrogression comes from the fact that the principles of Divine civilization are completely abandoned, and the teachings of the prophets of God are forgotten.

For instance, it is the clear text of the Old Testament, that all humanity are the creatures of God. They are under the protection of the Almighty. 'The devil' had nothing to do with their creation. It is the text of the New Testament that the sun of God shines upon the just and the unjust alike. It is likewise written in the Koran, 'Thou shalt not see any difference in the creations of thy Lord.' These expressions, which convey the same idea, are the foundation of the Holy Divine Manifestations of God.

A thousand times alas! that misunderstanding has completely uprooted this basis.

Firstly, religion must become the means of love and amity; secondly, it must proclaim the oneness of the world of humanity.

But the leaders among the people have caused it to become the means of hatred and enmity. For the last 6,000 years there has been bloodshed and rapacity amongst the children of men. These blameworthy attributes are the manifestations of the animal nature. Outwardly it has been called religious prejudice, racial prejudice and patriotic prejudice. Men have taken an axe and cut through the root of the tree of humanity. A hundred thousand times alas!

In short, I have travelled throughout many countries in the Western World, especially America. In many big churches and large meetings I proclaimed the oneness of the world of humanity in accord with the teachings of His Holiness Baha' Allah. I promoted the principle of universal peace, and with resonant voice I summoned all to enter into the Kingdom of God.

I said: Praise be to God that the Sun of Reality has shone forth with the utmost brilliancy from the Eastern horizon. The regions of the world are flooded with its glorious light. There are many rays to this Sun:

The first ray is heavenly teachings.

The second ray is the oneness of the world of humanity.

The third ray is the establishment of universal peace.

The fourth ray is the investigation of reality.

The fifth ray is the promotion of universal fellowship.

The sixth ray is the inculcation of Divine love through the power of religion.

The seventh ray is the conformity of religion with science and reason.

The eighth ray is the abandonment of religious, racial, patriotic and political prejudices.

The ninth ray is the universal spread of education.

The tenth ray is the organization of the arbitral court of justice, or the Parliament of Man, before the members of which all the international and inter-governmental problems, are arbitrated.

The eleventh ray is the equality of the sexes – the giving of the same educational facilities to women as to men, so that they may become adorned with all the virtues of humanity.

The twelfth ray is the solution of the economic problems of the world, so that each individual member of humanity may enjoy the utmost comfort and well-being.

The thirteenth ray is the spread of an auxiliary world-language.

Just as the rays of the phenomenal Sun are infinite, likewise the rays of the Sun of Reality are infinite. The above summary only contains a few of its rays.

The spreading of these rays will deliver the world of humanity from the darkness of ignorance, strangeness, and narrowness, and will guide it to the centre of all these rays. Then the foundation of warfare and strife, animosity and hatred, will be destroyed from amongst the people, and the misunderstandings existing between the religions will be dispelled. The foundation of the religions of God is one, and that is the *oneness* of the world of humanity.

Praise be to God! while travelling in America I found attentive ears. I associated and became intimate with many people. I observed that their object is the spread of fellowship amongst all people, and their highest hope is the extraordinary advancement of the human world. Similarly in London I met many blessed and enlightened souls who are striving with heart and soul to create love and amity between the various nations and races. It is my hope that from day unto day these lofty ideals may find greater spread, and these philanthropic intentions may more and more appear, so that all the nations of the world may become the manifestors of merciful attributes, and there may remain no strife and ill-feeling amongst religions and communities. This is the everlasting glory! This is eternal prosperity! This is the paradise of the world of humanity!

ON MATERIAL AND SPIRITUAL EDUCATION

Education in the world of humanity is divided into two parts:
1. Material education.
2. Spiritual education.

Material education confers upon man the means of physical comfort; the complicated physical needs of humanity are assured and material advancement is made possible in worldly affairs. For example, the European nations, through the blessings of material education, have made marvellous progress.

The founders of the school of material education are the past and contemporary philosophers and thinkers. Scientists and inventors, through the application of their mental faculties, bring forth upon the arena of existence wonderful enterprises and undertakings; thus man enjoys the benefit of the labours of these leaders of thought.

However, the teachings of these material educators do not have effect in the world of morality, and if they display any effect it is very small, for material education simply develops the physical side of humanity. It is incapable of illumining the dark regions of the great world of morality. Eternal beatitude is not made possible through the spread of material education.

Consider, after all, how the sphere of material education is limited. Even if man satisfies his greatest desires for material comfort he is but like unto a bird! Imagine the happy state of a bird which flies in the immensity of space, hops from one branch to another, and builds its nest upon the loftiest branch, whence it can view the whole panorama of nature spread before its eyes – a scene of ravishing beauty and enchantment. Its tiny nest is more beautiful than a King's most sumptuous palace. Its wealth consists of all the seeds in the fields, of the cooling springs flowing from the breast of the mountains, and of the green meadows. This is the highest point of physical bliss and enjoyment, which is made possible in a more perfect manner for the birds of the fields than for men. These things are prepared for them without any hard labour or suffering. They know not sorrow, neither any danger or fear, such as men experience in their lives. In the utmost ease and happiness they live.

Such, then, is the happiness of the animal world. But the happiness of the human world comes from the virtues of the world of humanity, which enjoyment the animals know not of. That comes from the extension of the range of vision, the excellencies of the world of humanity: the love of God, the knowledge of God, equality between the people, justice and equity and ideal communication between hearts.

These are the principles upon which the structure of human happiness is built. Spiritual education consists of the inculcation of these ideals of Divine morality, promotes these high thoughts. This spiritual education is made possible through the power of the Holy Spirit. As long as the breath of the Holy Spirit does not display any influence, spiritual education is not obtained; whereas if a soul is inspired by the Holy Spirit, he will be enabled to educate a nation.

Consider the records of bygone philosophers: the utmost that they could do was to educate themselves. The circle of their influence was very limited; all that they could do was to instruct a few pupils. Of such a type was the influence of Plato and Aristotle. These philosophers were only able to train a limited number of people. But those souls who are assisted by the breath of the Holy Spirit can educate a nation. The prophets of God were neither philosophers nor celebrated for their genius. Outwardly they belonged to the common people, but as they were encircled with the all-comprehending power of the Holy Spirit, they were thus enabled to impart a general education to all men. For instance, His Holiness the Christ and His Holiness Muhammad were not among the thinkers of the age, neither were they counted great geniuses; but through the power of the Holy Spirit they were able to confer universal instruction upon many nations.

They illumined the world of morality. They laid the foundation of a spiritual sovereignty which is everlasting. Similarly with those souls who have entered the Tabernacle of the Cause of God.

Although not important in appearance, yet everyone is confirmed in stimulating the cause of general moral instruction. Therefore it has become evident that real spiritual universal education cannot be realized save through the breath of the Holy Spirit. Man must not look at his own capabilities, but think of the power of the Holy Spirit.

In this age His Holiness Baha' Ullah has breathed the Holy Spirit into the dead body of the world, consequently every weak soul is strengthened by these fresh Divine out-breathings – every poor man will become rich, every darkened soul will become illumined, every ignorant one will become wise, because the confirmations of the Holy Spirit are descending like unto torrents. A new era of Divine consciousness is upon us. The world of humanity is going through a process of transformation. A new race is being developed. The thoughts of human brotherhood are permeating all regions. New ideals are stirring the depths of hearts, and a new spirit of universal consciousness is being profoundly felt by all men.[88]

Interview with the *Daily Herald*

The *Daily Herald* was a national labor movement journal founded in April 1912, which claimed to have a circulation of over 50,000 copies daily. Besides supporting the work of trade unions and the protests of workers, the journal also extended its unconditional support for the suffrage movement, specially for the most militant wing. Among those who contributed articles to this journal were the Nobel prize winners Norman Angell and the writer G. K. Chesterton.

On 21 January this newspaper published what purported to be an interview between 'Abdu'l-Bahá and the author, W. F. Rean, a former Anarchist and one of the founders of the journal. "I stood the other morning", stated Rean in introducing the article "in the presence of one of the most remarkable men that even Persia has given to the world of humanity". The text consisted of two parts. The first, not included here, was just a copy of comments by 'Abdu'l-Bahá already published by other journals. The second reproduced a very brief conversation between the writer and the Master:

'Tell me', said 'The Master', 'about the origin of your paper and your League.'

'It was born of oppression; it was born of the toilers; it was the result of a strike of London printers. The men knew the English Press was the Press of the rich; that they had no voice to support their cause. They demanded a Press for the poor. The *Daily Herald* is the poor man's and the poor woman's paper. It speaks as no other paper in the history of England has spoken before – for Justice, for Humanity, and Peace; it defends the oppressed nationality: it defends your people, Abdul Baha, as it defends all peoples against the powers of darkness and of death.'

The wonderful soul of Abdul Baha awoke; the rugged face, serene but saddened by the world around him, brightened:

'Tell the readers of the *Daily Herald*; tell the people who form your League that the Poor can never expect of the rich a Press to voice their rights; tell all that Justice, Humanity, and Peace among all peoples be the watchword.'

For there is neither East nor West,
Border, nor Breed, nor Birth.
When two strong men stand face to face
Though they come from the ends of the
Earth.[89]

Farewell and Departure

'Abdu'l-Bahá left London for Paris on 21 January. A few days before, on Saturday, 11 January, a farewell reception in honor of 'Abdu'l-Bahá was held at Caxton Hall, London, a place frequently used by the local Bahá'ís for their public meetings and also used as a meeting centre for various women's organizations and other social and progressive movements. An account of the meeting was published in *The Christian Commonwealth*:

ABDUL BAHA'S FAREWELL
JOYOUS GATHERING AT THE CAXTON HALL

The friends and followers of Abdul Baha came together in large numbers last Saturday afternoon to take farewell of their leader, who leaves England next Monday for Paris. It was an animated assembly and there was none of the 'sadness of farewell', so closely knit are the Bahais. After Abdul Baha had delivered his address an hour of social intercourse gave his followers opportunity to approach him, and for each he had a message and a hand clasp. Some of his messages will probably be cherished by their recipients for a long time. While I was speaking to the Bahai leader a lady drew near with a little girl and both were introduced as mother and adopted daughter. Abdul Baha's eyes kindled as he said that the lady had undertaken a good work and that God would assist her in carrying it out. To another group I heard him say that this was the age of eloquence and that the message of Baha'o'llah must be uttered by all who had been taught its meaning. The master passed from group to group attended by the interpreter, Mirza Ahmad Sohrab, speaking freely and copiously to all.

Mr Eric Hammond, author of the 'Splendour of God', acted as chairman of the meeting, and among the speakers were Mrs Cobden Sanderson, Bishop Bacon, Captain St John, Miss Buckton, Mrs Sidley, Prof. Margoliouth, of Oxford, and Maharajah Rana of Jalawar.[90]

A week later the same journal offered an account of 'Abdu'l-Bahá's departure from London:

ABDUL BAHA'S MOVEMENTS

Abdul Baha Abbas left Victoria, with his retinue, last Tuesday morning, en route for Paris. He is returning to the Orient after a visit which has lasted some four years. During the Young Turk rising he was released from the prison at Acca, in 1908, and has since travelled widely in Europe and America. We understand that his plans are to spend a few weeks in Paris, where a great deal of work awaits him, and then to pass over into Germany. There also keen anticipation has been aroused, and a considerable programme will be carried out. Thence the Master proceeds East to his home at Haifa, at the foot of Mount Carmel, in Syria. Many of the descendants of the early martyrs of the Bab movement have settled at Haifa, and naturally to the children of those who followed Baha'o'llah Abdul Baha is the central figure to whom they would turn in every crisis of their lives. It has been stated that he will later go to Alexandria, but we are informed that nothing is yet settled beyond his journey to Haifa, where he is expected to remain for some time.[91]

The Near East also reported that 'On Saturday week he addressed a crowded meeting of his English sympathisers at the Westminster Palace Hotel, and left for Egypt on Tuesday morning. Abdul Baha will break the journey in Paris, where he has a large number of fervent admirers, and hopes to arrive at Port Said or Alexandria about the end of February.'[92]

A correspondent of the French weekly newspaper *Gil Blas* (Paris) visited 'Abdu'l-Bahá at Cadogan Gardens soon before His departure for France. He wrote an account of the meeting which was published in Paris just a few days after 'Abdu'l-Bahá's arrival in the French capital:

> A little groom in white gloves shows to the visitors the residence of Abdul Baha, the prophet's refuge. A courtyard, the elevator to the third floor . . . and one suddenly finds himself in the middle of a heterogeneous meeting. The faithful and the curious are gathered, sitting on 'chintz' chairs or leaning on the piano covered by photographs, flowers, and piles of books. Men interested in the Orient, ladies in golf costumes, young girls with fresh faces adorned with huge glasses, all seem to wait. They have their ecstatic eyes directed to heaven from where they will get some beneficial light. For the English, the deep concern for the daily realities exalts the dream for the contrast. As they hasten around the Asiatic prophet who, surrounded by his disciples, has come to give them a guide to spiritual life and practice . . .
>
> The prophet speaks. In his Persian language, slow and melodious, he gives his precepts and speaks of Universal Truth. A young woman [Laura Barney] is with him gathering his thoughts and giving them to the visitors. And these are the phrases that still fascinate us. 'Happiness should always live in us. Welcome others not only with the affability of your manners, but more importantly, with the affability of the heart.'
>
> 'I desire', said also Abdul Baha, 'to unify the spiritual life of the peoples. The advanced civilization of the West I want to substitute for another: that which gives a truly human religion.'
>
> This descendant of Zarathustra, this prophet who seems to have been created with the divine gift of persuasion, has gathered in London many people who listened to him and wins every day new disciples. He will be in Paris tomorrow. What kind of welcome will

the city of heedlessness and scepticism give to the prophet? Will he vivify everyone with the warm of his persuasion? Or will he rise antagonism and disrespect towards his fervour? . . .[93]

Message to the Bahá'ís of London

Several weeks after the departure of 'Abdu'l-Bahá from England, a group of London Bahá'ís visited Him in Paris. The Master conveyed through them an oral message for the Bahá'ís in London and notes of it were published in *The Christian Commonwealth*:

ABDUL BAHA TO HIS FRIENDS
WORDS OF GREETINGS AND ENCOURAGEMENT

Certain London Bahais, who have been visiting Paris, have been questioned closely by Abdul Baha Abbas as to the welfare of his friends in this country.

'Are they happy? Are they spreading the call of the Kingdom? Are they full of zeal? Do they comfort the unhappy? Do they raise the fallen? Do they serve the cause of universal peace and goodwill among the nations? Are they the stars of the heaven of Baha? Are they illuminating the dark path of the travellers? Are they the bright torch of Reality?'

'Convey to them,' he said, 'when thou art returning to London, my longing and greeting, for I love these friends of God. They are faithful followers of the Light, firm in the covenant. They are calling the people to the kingdom of God on earth.

'They must not rest, but strive to illumine the children of men. This is not the day of silence. Each one of you must become a crier of the kingdom, a herald of the glad tidings of the supreme concourse, for each one has heard the call. This is the great privilege, as yet you do not realize how great. But in the future you will know.

'The apostles of Christ were vilified and scorned in their day, because they were followers of the humble Nazarene, but now the light they spread had flooded the world with knowledge and wisdom, and each one shines like a star on the horizon of the eternal glory. So you live in a new dispensation, and to you the call has come to be the friends of the light. No one can estimate to-day the greatness of the calling, but if you are faithful the future will reveal it.

'I will never forget the London friends and will always pray for them.'⁹⁴

Addenda: The Ethical Movement

After the publication of the first volume of the present book further documents were found in the British Library regarding the first visit of 'Abdu'l-Bahá to England in 1911. One of them deserves particular attention and is therefore included here.

In 1877 the intellectual of German birth Felix Adler (1851–1933) founded in New York the Society of Ethical Culture and started the so-called ethical movement, a kind of secular religion centering its efforts on the promotion of ethics and values from a rational standpoint. A few years afterwards, Stanton G. Coit (1857–1944) introduced the movement into Britain, attracting some interest among Fabian Socialists, Free-Thinkers and Christian Non-conformists. Soon several ethical societies were founded in London and elsewhere and an Ethical Union was created to assemble and coordinate all these groups. The organization launched its own periodical, the monthly magazine *The Ethical World* (London).⁹⁵

Many members of the Ethical Movement had some direct or indirect relationship with 'Abdu'l-Bahá. Felix Adler, for instance, was the father of the Universal Races Congress held in 1911 in London to which 'Abdu'l-Bahá was invited (see chapter 32). Adler was also the vice-president of the Free Religious Association when this organization invited 'Abdu'l-Bahá to speak at its annual meeting in Boston (see vol. I, chapter 16, pp. 327–35). Gustav Spiller met 'Abdu'l-Bahá in London in 1911 (see vol. I, chapter 6, pp. 98–9) and published His message to the Universal Races Congress in the proceedings of that event. Harrold Johnson was the secretary of the Moral Instruction League, an organization closely linked with the Ethical Union, and as such he was one of the organizers, with Gustav Spiller and others, of the Second Universal Congress on Moral Education to which 'Abdu'l-Bahá was also invited (see vol. I, chapter 8, pp. 184–8). Johnson not only met 'Abdu'l-Bahá on different occasions and wrote about the Bahá'í Faith (see vol. I, chapter 6, pp. 92, 144, 153; chapter 8, pp. 184–5) but he also delivered a lecture on the Bahá'í religion on 3 December 1911 at Toynbee Hall, London, a usual meeting place for the Ethical Union.⁹⁶

The educationalist Michael Sadler (see vol. 1, chapter 6, pp. 134–7) was also connected with the Ethical Movement.

Among those members of the Ethical Movement who met 'Abdu'l-Bahá in 1911 was Richard Dimsdale Stocker (1877–1935), a writer with interests in the fields of psychology, graphology and physiognomy. After visiting Him on several occasions, Stocker wrote a two-column article for *The Ethical World* summarizing his impressions of the Master. In assessing the importance of 'Abdu'l-Bahá, Stocker stressed the fact that while the Ethical Movement was one based on academic and philosophical study, 'Abdu'l-Bahá was the embodiment, the experience, of those ethical principles pursued by the Ethical Movement:

ABDUL BAHA: AN IMPRESSION

We cannot, perhaps, too often recall to mind the thought that ethics, in the deepest and profoundest sense, is no mere academic question, to appreciate which we are required to sequester ourselves in the seclusion of the study. Those who mistake it for a barren philosophy, or confuse it with so many abstract rules of behaviour, cannot fail to lose sight of its outstanding significance and appeal, which, after all, goes to emphasise the belief that ethical principles, in so far as they have genuine interest and reality, must be embodied in persons, without whom they can possess no actual and concrete existence.

This fact, it appears, has always won acceptance among the religious-minded, who have invariably maintained that the ultimate worth and vitality of their faith have reposed upon the life, legendary or otherwise, of its assumed inspirer. To reject such a source for religion would certainly involve its speedy collapse and extinction; for, whether we seek in the mists of antiquity or in the calm, clear light of the present, precisely the same principle is disclosed.

This thought came vividly before me when, a few days ago, I was privileged to meet Abdul Baha. 'The Master', as he is reverently designated by his disciples, was spending a few weeks in England, where he has been enlightening innumerable inquirers upon the principles which are professed and advocated by the Bahais. These inquirers have included dignitaries of the Church, eminent Nonconformist divines, and others, all of whom appear to have been considerably impressed by the personality of the man.

And, indeed, their admiration is scarcely surprising, for, in spite of the inevitable diversity of opinion which may have existed in their minds, the principles for which the 'Servant of God', as Abdul Baha styles himself, comes forward are of so lofty and comprehensive a nature as to compel the assent of all who have the eternal welfare of the race at heart. There is, we cannot too often remember, a higher agreement than that of intellectual opinion. To be at one in regard to one's reasoned convictions with another may be gratifying, and, in a measure, essential for practical purposes. But, under such circumstances, there is always the danger that the stronger mind may dominate the weaker, and that the less critical may make such agreement the pretext for avoiding intellectual effort; whereas, with emotional or ethical union, precisely the reverse is true. While holding in common certain ideals, aims, purposes, and aspirations, men are conscious that, though they are bound by the ties of the spirit of goodness and fellowship, they are yet at liberty to view truth under whatever aspect their individual conscience and experience may decree.

'The Bahais have no priesthood, and, beyond proclaiming, in addition to the fellowship of man, the fatherhood of God, they advance no specific doctrines. Nor is their theism, I may observe, more than a mystical intuition, which many humanists themselves imply by their theory of the 'social soul'. The metaphysic of Bahaism, we have to remember, comes to us from the East, and it therefore bears traces of a long tradition. What it is accomplishing, however, in the way of breaking up sectarian bigotry and prejudice serves to show that its appeal is primarily to the enlightened understanding. In Persia alone, it is said, no less than one-third of the people are Bahais; and elsewhere – in India, in America, and in Europe – the movement has attracted many thousands, who find in it something that the orthodox creeds have failed to supply.

The movement was inaugurated in Persia in 1844, by a young man who came to be known as the Bab, or 'gate'. He it was whose mission was to prepare the people to discover the truth of their own faith. Not unnaturally, such an innovation was denounced and anathematised by the Mohammedan authorities; and his exertions on behalf of the cause were rewarded by subsequent death. Numbers were martyred for giving their adherence to his teachings. But the cause, nevertheless, grew and multiplied.

Later arose Baha Ullah, whose ministry did much to advance Bahaism. He, however, spent years in exile, and lived a life of seclusion. Baha Ullah died in 1892, and was afterwards succeeded by his son, Abdul Baha.

This remarkable man, who is no less revered than his illustrious predecessors, was born in 1844, in Teheran. For years he also was an exile from his native land, and has been a prisoner of the Turkish Government. For upwards of forty years he has suffered persecution, rejection, and imprisonment, having been confined in the fortress town of Akka, at the foot of Mount Carmel, his release taking place only three years ago.

Small wonder that he should be treated with the honour that is due to him! Never have I beheld one more full of grace and truth, or in whom the majesty of simple devotion exhibited itself more impressively. Neither have I confronted a man who seemed more at peace with himself or with mankind.

What is the secret of his power? His message – what of that? He makes no claims to supernatural gifts; he denies all exclusive disclosures of divine wisdom. All the faiths and their teachings, he tells us, are of relative worth. Their virtue is derived not from their absolute value, but from the devotion and beauty of the lives of their followers. The time has come when men must feel that they stand not for themselves, but for the whole human race. We must rid ourselves of egotism, surmount our selfishness, and eradicate the root of all error – 'the sense of separateness'.

Abdul Baha, 'the servant of God', is a true mystic. He believes not in theories, but in men. He knows because he has proved for himself. Love is the secret of life. 'Love for man is love for God. To serve men is to serve God,' he says. After a long life – nigh upon seventy years – you see him serene, calm, and trustful as a child; and he has the wisdom of a child. He has accepted the assurance of Jesus, and in him the kingdom has visibly appeared. 'You can', he said in my presence, 'be in heaven now. No matter what life may be, you may be angels here.' And he should know – he who has endured so much.

Heaven and hell, he teaches, are not places. They are conditions of the mind and heart. 'Good thoughts, good resolves, and good deeds bring men nearer to God; and that is heaven.'

It is the ethical note distinguishing Bahaism that must commend it to ourselves. It is thoroughly democratic. The light within must be our guide. By its aid we must reach our ultimate decision. It is on the moral side alone that the teaching of Bahaism is explicit. All are to work. Temperance and self-control are obligatory. Murder, theft, and adultery are condemned; backbiting and slander are prohibited; cleanliness is insisted upon; love and courtesy to all are enjoined; even the animals are to be treated with kindness.

But above it all rises the stately figure of Abdul Baha. Hero-worship has its dangers, yet the life – the life of man – is the supreme thing. And as Abdul Baha advanced to me, took my hand, and murmured the words 'My son, my son', I realised it as I had never done before.

R. Dimsdale Stocker[97]

In 1913 Stocker published *The Times Spirit*, a work in which he surveyed some of the 'contemporary spiritual tendencies' and dedicated about half of chapter 3 to a discussion of the Bahá'í religion. In the course of his commentary Stocker again mentioned 'Abdu'l-Bahá and his impressions of Him, a text that is worth including here:

Abdul Baha only recently (1911) paid a visit to this country: and on several occasions it was my privilege to meet and hold converse with him – or rather it would be truer to say that he conversed with me; for, when we met, I did but listen to him. He speaks in his native tongue, Persian, and through an interpreter. But his expression is so benignant and gracious, and withal so full of sympathy and kindness, that one catches the spirit of the man long before the words have passed his lips . . .

Few people perhaps whom we meet fail altogether to impress us – at least in some particulars: for good, for ill – powerfully, intensely, or otherwise, as the case may be. Some of us are more susceptible than others; but we are influenced accordingly nevertheless. But what a force lies in the personality of Abdul Baha! Rarely, if ever, have I beheld one so imbued with truth and grace as this man. Seldom or never have I been more profoundly affected than when, in taking leave of me at our last interview, he embraced and kissed me in oriental fashion, and charged me that my life should be fruitful – an influence for good – a means of aiding and uplifting others.

Never perhaps before had I so well realized as then the infinity of the human soul, or the incomprehensible potency of its appeal. The personality of Abdul Baha was, and remains, a mighty mystery to me. All men are wonderful. But this man seems to include so much. And when we reflect upon his significance, he becomes more wonderful still.[98]

27

EDINBURGH

6–10 January 1913

As early as 16 December, the day of His arrival in London, 'Abdu'l-Bahá received an invitation from the Scottish Bahá'í Jane Elizabeth Whyte (1857–1944), wife of the noted scholar and church leader Dr Alexander Whyte, to visit Edinburgh. Mrs Whyte had met 'Abdu'l-Bahá on a pilgrimage to the Holy Land in 1906 and visited Him again in London in 1911. Her continuous efforts in propagating the Bahá'í teachings in Edinburgh and her acquaintance with various prominent people and organizations of the city allowed her to arrange public meetings and private interviews for the Master. On 1 January 'Abdu'l-Bahá was presented with a complete plan for His visit to Edinburgh which included addresses at meetings convened by the Edinburgh Esperanto Society (see chapter 33), the Theosophical Society (see chapter 34) and the Outlook Tower Committee.

On 6 January, at ten o'clock, 'Abdu'l-Bahá left London from Euston train station, arriving in Edinburgh some eight hours later. During His sojourn in the city He stayed at the house of Mrs Whyte at 7 Charlotte Square.

Isabel Fraser traveled to Edinburgh a few days in advance to maintain contacts with the local press and furnish them with information about 'Abdu'l-Bahá and the Bahá'í Faith.[1] Local newspapers responded very favorably and several articles about 'Abdu'l-Bahá and the Bahá'í Faith were published in the Scottish press. Interestingly, when He returned to London, 'Abdu'l-Bahá was invited to a dinner in His honor at the Persian Legation and the ambassador presented Him with a collection of clippings from Edinburgh newspapers with articles about Him which were provided to the embassy by a clippings bureau.[2]

Visit to Edinburgh Announced

The visit of 'Abdu'l-Bahá to Edinburgh was announced as early as 1 January in an article appearing in *The Christian Commonwealth* (London) that offered details of the Master's schedule in the Scottish capital:

> ABDUL BAHA IN EDINBURGH
>
> Great interest is being manifested in Edinburgh over the forthcoming visit of Abdul Baha to that city. He arrives in Edinburgh next Monday evening, Jan. 6. On Tuesday afternoon a meeting with students from the East attending the University of Edinburgh will be held, and in the evening a great public meeting, arranged by the Edinburgh Esperanto Society, will take place in the Freemasons' Hall, one of the finest halls in the city. On Wednesday Abdul Baha will be present at a meeting in the Rainy Hall, New College, arranged by the Outlook Tower Committee, with Professor Geddes as chairman, and that evening it is hoped he will be present at a recital of Handel's 'Messiah' in St Giles' Cathedral. This recital is unique in its way, as the audience is strictly limited to poor people selected by invitation ticket. The oratorio is to be rendered by the Edinburgh Royal Choral Union, assisted by the Scottish Orchestra, and the soloists are some of the finest oratorio singers of the day. On Thursday Abdul Baha is to take part in a public meeting arranged by the Edinburgh Theosophical Society in its rooms, 28, Great King Street.[3]

On 8 January the same newspaper reported that 'His Excellency Abdul Baha Abbas and party left London on Monday to fulfill the series of engagements in Scotland mentioned in our last issue. While in Edinburgh Abdul Baha will be the guest of Principal Alexander Whyte, the greatly respected head of the United Free Church'. A Scottish correspondent wonders 'when London's Bishop will follow Dr Whyte's excellent lead and entertain the Bahai leader at Fulham Palace'.[4]

On 3 January the *Evening Dispatch* published an article announcing the arrival of 'Abdu'l-Bahá which was accompanied by a large portrait of Him. It also included an introduction to the Bahá'í Faith and offered some details about His planned activities in the city.[5] Similar but briefer articles were published on the same day in the *Evening News*,[6] which also carried a portrait, in the *Glasgow Herald*[7] and in the *Evening Telegraph* of Dundee.[8]

On 7 January the *Evening Dispatch* published under the title 'A New World Teacher'[9] an article by Alice Buckton introducing the Bahá'í Faith. The same newspaper published further information about the Bahá'í Faith in its report of 'Abdu'l-Bahá's address to the Esperanto Society that appeared on 8 January.[10]

Address at the Rainy Hall

After His address at the meeting of the Esperanto Society, which will be discussed in another chapter, 'Abdu'l-Bahá's second talk in Edinburgh was delivered on Wednesday, 8 January 1913, at the Rainy Hall, New College, in the Faculty of Divinity of the Presbyterian United Free Church of Scotland. The meeting was organized by the Outlook Tower Committee and it was chaired by its president, Patrick Geddes.

Patrick Geddes (1854–1932) was a noted biologist, urban planner and philanthropist. In 1892 he acquired Edinburgh's Outlook Tower and transformed it into a museum and cultural centre. 'Abdu'l-Bahá visited the museum on the morning of Tuesday, 7 January, and was shown around the building by Geddes himself and by John Scott Haldane (1860–1936), the inventor of the gas-mask and a prominent physiologist. Geddes, who was knighted in 1932, was also among the speakers who welcomed 'Abdu'l-Bahá at the meeting arranged by the Esperanto Society.

The meeting at Rainy Hall was announced in the press in the preceding days. It was scheduled for 4:40 p.m.; the admission for the members of the Outlook Tower Society was free and the price for the rest of the public was one shilling.[11]

In His talk 'Abdu'l-Bahá gave a general presentation on the Bahá'í Faith and expounded some of its principles. Other speakers were Dr Alexander H. Freeland Barbour, professor of medicine at Edinburgh University and brother of Mrs Whyte, and two Christian priests, Rev. Alexander B. Robb and Rev. R. B. Drummond.

The Scotsman published on 9 January a detailed account of the meeting in which significant portions of 'Abdu'l-Bahá's address were paraphrased:

ABDUL BAHA IN EDINBURGH
A NEW UNIVERSAL RELIGION

The Persian Reformer, Abdul Baha, appeared for the second time before an Edinburgh audience yesterday afternoon, and delivered an address in the Rainy Hall to a large audience mostly ladies. The meeting had been arranged by the Outlook Tower Committee to give Abdul Baha an opportunity of expounding to the people of Edinburgh the principles of Baha Ullah, whose object was to 'show the way to divine union of man with God and its manifestation in the brotherhood of mankind'.

Professor Patrick Geddes, who presided, said that on Monday night Abdul Baha spoke of a universal language, on which he set much value as a means of international communication in commerce, in science, and in sympathy; that day he would speak of the ideas and ideals of the movement with which he was identified. That Bahai movement, which had struggled for half a century through persecution and difficulty, recalled the martyrdoms of old. It was now widely known in the Persian world and from it made its appeal to the surrounding Mohammedan countries, to the Jews, and to the Christians. Arising as it did in the cell of the mystic, it was at the same time strongly fitted to interest the modern Western world.

AT BAHA ULLAH'S COMING

Abdul Baha, who was in the costume of the Orient, spoke in Persian, and had his remarks interpreted into English by Mirza Ahmad Sohrab. I have, he said, pleasure in presenting myself to this gathering, so that I may explain to you certain of the principles of Baha Ullah. Nearly sixty years ago, at a time when the Orient was engaged in warfare, when there was enmity between the different religions, his Holiness Baha Ullah appeared. Darkness brooded over the horizon of the Orient; foul clouds of ignorance hid the sky; religious prejudice and race prejudice prevailed. The peoples of the Orient were as though submerged in a sea of blind dogma and tradition. The votaries of the different religions hated each other; they never associated with each other in the same building. Had they done so they would have considered themselves contaminated. His Holiness Baha Ullah, under such conditions appeared, and boldly proclaimed the doctrine of the oneness of the whole of humanity.

THE UNITY OF THE RACE

He stated that humanity were the sheep of God; that God was the real and kind shepherd. When this great shepherd was compassionate and kind, why should the sheep fall out with each other? Addressing the whole of humanity Baha Ullah says: – 'Ye are the fruits of one tree and the leaves of one branch. All the nations, peoples, and tongues are the branches leaves, blossoms, and fruits of this great tree of humanity.' God created all; God provides for all; God protects all; and as he is kind and good, why should you be unkind?

INTERNATIONAL PEACE

The second principle of the religion of Baha Ullah has regard to international peace. Concerning this weighty matter, Baha Ullah had written to many rulers and kings. In these epistles he had brought forward certain unanswerable principles that the whole of humanity could not enjoy security and composure without the establishment of universal peace. Every war, he says, is against the good pleasure of the Lord of mankind. God has created men so that they may enjoy fellowship with each other. Man is the edifice of God. War destroys the divine edifice, and cannot, therefore, be pleasing to God. Peace is the stay of life; war the cause death. The third principle of Baha Ullah is this: religion must ever be the cause of love and amity. If religion breeds rancor and strife it is only a so-called religion, and it is better to do without it. God made religion a means of fellowship. When His Holiness Moses appeared, instantly good fellowship prevailed amongst the Israelites, and with the dawn of the Christian era there was wonderful concord between Egyptians, Chaldeans, Assyrians, Europeans, and other nations of the world. When His Holiness Mohammed appeared in Arabia with his presence and his mission there arose light out of the ashes of discord, and between tribes of Arabs who had warred like wild beasts against each other for 2000 years there was peace. These three examples show that religion in its nascent stages has been the cause of union. In the Old Testament it is recorded that God created man in his own image. His Holiness Jesus says that God sends His sun to shine on the just and unjust, and in the Koran it is written that between the creation and God thou shall not see any difference.

Therefore, if religion brings about warfare between nations you are better without that sort of religion.

SCIENCE AND RELIGION

The fourth teaching of Baha Ullah relates to the conformity of religion with science and reason. If religion is not conformable to science and reason it is superstition. God has given us an absolute mind, so that we may distinguish between error and that which is just, differentiate between right and wrong. If religion does not correspond with science and reason, it is a phantasm of the brain; for science and religion are realities, and if that religion to which we adhere is a reality, it must conform to other realities.

RELIGION AND RACIAL PREJUDICE

The fifth teaching of Baha Ullah is this – that religious, racial, political and patriotic prejudices are the destroyers of the foundation of the edifice of man. As long as these prejudices last, the world of humanity will not attain to peace and composure. If we consult history, we shall find that every war was due to one or other of these prejudices. These prejudices are phantasmagoria, breeding hostility and dissension; if we investigate the object of the religion of God we shall be united. As regards racial prejudice, is not all humanity the progeny of Adam – members of one family, though the family has grown quite large? How ridiculous it is to sow division between members of one family! As regards patriotic prejudice, how small is this terrestrial sphere as compared with the great astral regions; how evanescent is the life of man! What is this native land, this fatherland that we glory over so much? We live but a few years on the surface of the earth; afterwards it becomes our eternal cemetery, as it has been the cemetery of all the men and women that have lived since Adam. In these circumstances, is patriotic prejudice worth all the divisions it has caused?

THE EQUALITY OF MEN AND WOMEN

The sixth teaching of Baha Ullah is as regards the equality of men and women. Male and female belong to the same stock of humanity. They share in common the same faculties. God created men and women alike; why should we cause a difference between these two partners? The world of humanity has two wings – one wing the male, the other the female. If the male wing is strong and the female wing is weak, the higher flight is impossible. But if both wings are strong, there will be a flight heavenwards to the higher dominions of human perfection. Then if the same curriculum of education is given to women as has been given to men in the past; if they are allowed to acquire all the virtues which they can possibly acquire they will become peers of men. As up to this time the means of education have not been given in an equal degree to women as to men, women lag behind to a certain degree. Praise be to God however, that this glorious century has given the means of education and culture to women, and if men cooperate with them, there is no doubt that they will advance extraordinarily and attain to the level of men. Then the world of humanity will attain to a higher pitch of perfection.

ECONOMICS AND EDUCATION

The seventh teaching of Baha Ullah is what we call solidarity, or, in your terminology economics, and it suggests a plan whereby all the individual members of the social body may enjoy the utmost comfort and welfare. There is a special programme concerning this Socialism, but I will only give of it bare details. He says the degrees of society must be preserved. These degrees in the body politic must not be disintegrated. An army has need of a general, a colonel, a captain, and of private soldiers. In the body politic as in the army, these degrees are essential; at the same time each individual member of the various classes must enjoy the utmost comfort and happiness. The eighth teaching of Baha Ullah concerns universal education. That means the education of all the children of all the communities. If the parents are capable of giving a thorough education to their children well and good; if not, the state must take care of them. Every child must also learn a profession so that he may not be left helpless. The ninth teaching of Baha Ullah is that work done well is as acceptable to God as prayer in the Churches; the tenth principle relates to the necessity for having an international auxiliary language. Each person, need only study two languages in their classes – their own native tongue and the auxiliary language. The eleventh of the Baha Ullah's teaching is that there must be a standardization of education or the system of the training of children in all countries, so that the children as they grow up may lose their prejudices in reference to foreigners. Were this done misunderstandings would be swept away from amongst the peoples. There are many other principles, but I have spoken of a few of them to you, and from these you will understand the spirit of the Bahai revelation.

THE MARTYRS OF BAHAISM

His holiness Baha Ullah instituted this teaching in Persia. Those who adopted his views became entirely free from their former shackles and limitations. Nowadays meetings and assemblies are organised in Persia, in which you will find Mahommedans and Christians, Jews and Zoroastrians, and Buddhists gathered together in the same room in the utmost fellowship and amity, so that if an outsider were to enter he should find such a spirit of love prevailing and so complete an elimination of the ego or self that he would be unable to distinguish between one religion and another. But in the days of Baha Ullah, the Mahommedan clergy stirred up enmity against the leaders of the new movement. They represented to the ex-Shah of Persia, Nazir, that this community was a political party striving to dethrone him. So the Shah rose in his wrath and tried to destroy the Bahaists, caused all the possessions of Baha Ullah to be pillaged and threw him into prison. Then he exiled him from Persia. But the Baha Ullah met these persecutions with the greatest resolution and firmness, and in his exile continued to promulgate these principles to humanity. From Bagdad the Baha was exiled to Roumelia, thence to Akka, near Mount Carmel, where he died in 1892.

Nearly all the days of the life of Baha Ullah were spent in prison or exile, and many of his friends and followers were martyred and pillaged. More than 20,000 people sealed their faith with their blood. Notwithstanding all this, Baha Ullah never wavered or had a faint heart. Nay, rather the cause spread more rapidly like wildfire from day to day, so that all the Orient was covered with the rays of this revelation. From his prison in Akka Baha Ullah ascended to the throne of God. Those who were his followers were left in prison until the flag of revolution was raised in Constantinople, and they were free. Before that the Shah had fallen before the Democratic movement in Persia, and they were free to return to their own land.

THANKS TO THE BAHA

Dr. Barbour expressed the thanks of the audience to Abdul Baha for his eloquent exposition of one of the great movements of their time. It was a plant which had spread rapidly in the Persia of to-day. Yet one recognised in it a great similarity to plants that were growing nearer home. What struck him when their friend was speaking was that he was giving expression to some wishes of their own heart. They approved of the ideal he laid before them of education and of the necessity of each one learning a trade, and his beautiful simile of the two wings on which society was to rise into a purer and clearer atmosphere put into beautiful words what was in the minds of many of them. What impressed them most was that courage which had enabled him during long years of imprisonment, and even in the face of death, to hold fast to his convictions.

AN EASTERN MISSIONARY

The Rev. A. B. Robb, Falkirk, said they had been in the habit of sending missionaries from the West to the East to preach the Gospel; that day they had a missionary from the East to preach the old Gospel, and to preach it in a new and original way. After all, it was not the words which had impressed them so much as the life. He had a right to speak, for he had spent forty years of his life in prison for the sake of the truth which was revealed to him. Dr. Kelman, he thought, said last night that Abdul Baha was not here to proselytise. He (Mr. Robb) was not so sure of that. He felt they were not preaching quite the Gospel they had heard that day, though they were all longing to preach it, and perhaps Abdul Baha's address would give some of them assistance to do so.

The Rev. R. B. Drummond, late of Castle Terrace Chapel, also said a few words, and the Chairman having conveyed the thanks of the meeting to Abdul Baha, the interesting meeting terminated.[12]

A briefer but similar account was also published in the *Glasgow Herald*[13] and in the *Dundee Courier* (Angus).[14] In reporting the words of Alexander Barbour, the article indicated that he 'cordially thanked Abdul

Baha for drawing aside the veil from one of the great movements of our time. One recognised, he said, great similarity to movements at home.'

On 9 January, the *Evening News* (Edinburgh) published an editorial on the Bahá'í Faith apropos the meeting in the Outlook Tower. Its author clearly entertained a suspicion towards the Bahá'í Faith. Considering it as an offshoot of Islam, he lamented that some members of the clergy were 'taking a prominent part in these meetings, eulogising the Bahai teaching, and indicating that much is to be learned from it'.

> A MORE complete exposition of the Bahai faith was given in Edinburgh yesterday afternoon. As the reformer's son outlined it in the Rainy Hall, it suggests a form of Mohammedanism, in several important respects purified and liberalised. Its humanity is broad, it gives to women a status of respect hitherto unknown in the East, it clears out a number of gross superstitions by the declaration that religion must be consonant with reason. In the Mohammedan world, the Bahai movement may represent a process akin to our Reformation. But we find Christian clergymen taking a prominent part in these meetings, eulogising the Bahai teaching, and indicating that much is to be learned from it. For example, the Rev. A. B. Robb, Falkirk, at the close of the address yesterday, said they had had a missionary from the East preaching the old Gospel. It had been said Abdul Baha was not here to proselytise. He (Mr Robb) was not so sure of that. He felt they were not preaching quite the Gospel they had heard that day, though they were all longing to preach it. From these remarks, it would appear how easily even educated men may be impressed by a personality. If all Mr. Robb's reverend brethren were as susceptible, we might have mosques and mullahs springing up over Scotland to replace kirks and ministers. Since edifying generalities produce so great an effect, let us look at one or two expressions used by Abdul Baha yesterday, and ask: How do these accord with Christian doctrine? First then, what has Bahaism to say about a future life? That is a cardinal belief of Christianity. How does it fit in with the following passage from Abdul Baha's address yesterday? 'We live but a few years on the surface of the earth; afterwards it becomes our eternal cemetery, as it has been the cemetery of all the men and women that have lived since Adam.' Is Bahaism able to present a future to the individual soul? That highly

important point is not made at all clear by yesterday's discourse. A second question is even more critical. What place does Bahaism assign to Christ? Most, if not all, of us, were brought up to believe that one supreme and essential revelation was given to mankind. Taking the references in Abdul Baha's address yesterday, it will be observed that a common title expressive of respect is applied to Moses, to Mohammed, to Christ, and to Baha Ullah, father of the Persian preacher. Each is spoken of as 'Holiness'. Bahaism, then, would appear to claim rank alongside of Christianity. Christianity is relegated to a place as but one revelation among many. Is this a propaganda hastily to be welcomed by Christian ministers? What becomes of the unique authority of the Christian Gospel?[15]

As will be shown in another chapter, the presence of 'Abdu'l-Bahá in Edinburgh generated some opposition among Christian circles and some local newspapers were used to voice this opposition.

Geddes continued his contact with the Bahá'í Faith throughout his life. In 1920 he traveled to Haifa in his capacity as town planner for various cities in Palestine. There, he again met 'Abdu'l-Bahá and was somehow involved in the launching of the project of the stairs uniting the main avenue of the German Colony with the Shrine of the Báb.[16] He also attended the Bahá'í Convention held in Bombay, India, in late December 1920. In one of its sessions Geddes explained his experiences with 'Abdu'l-Bahá in Haifa.[17]

Interview for the *Scots Pictorial*

'Abdu'l-Bahá granted an interview to the *Scots Pictorial* (Glasgow),[18] an illustrated weekly specializing in social and general information that circulated across Scotland. The interview was published on 18 January and its author was Ion S. Munro (1887–1970),[19] editor of the *Scots Pictorial*. The text was accompanied by a picture of the Master and included some historical information about the Bahá'í Faith.

Judging from the tone employed by Munro it is certain that 'Abdu'l-Bahá, whom he described as 'an embodiment of the prophets of old', left a great impression on him:

THE APOSTLE OF PEACE

ABDUL BAHA
THE TEACHINGS OF BAHAISM. UNITY OF ALL RELIGIONS. UNIVERSAL PEACE

INTERVIEW WITH ABBAS EFFENDI – 'THE SERVANT OF GOD'. BY ION

To be ushered into the presence of Abdul Baha, Abbas Effendi, 'the Servant of God', is to have the curtains of time lifted back and to hold converse with a prophet of Israel. The artistic dignity of his quietly coloured Eastern gown, the white folds of his turban, and the patriarchal beard which hangs upon his bosom all contribute towards giving the immediate impression of an Eastern scholar and divine. But it is the finely moulded contour of his face, the gentle movements of his hands, and the deep expression in his eyes which make it manifest that here, indeed, is an embodiment of the prophets of old. In comparing Abdul Baha to the Biblical prophets, there is a distinction to be made. The early prophets descended upon mankind as the scourgers of iniquity and as swords of the Lord. This messenger comes as a great reconciler of all faiths, as the forerunner of universal peace. In his eyes there is suffering and love. He is a man who has looked aghast and with pity upon the turmoil of life, and has heartfelt thoughts to utter.

When I entered the dimly-lit room, Abdul Baha was seated deep in a great arm-chair. At his feet reclined a companion in quiet conversation with him. Nearby there sat one of his secretaries, a slenderly-built young Persian, with a delicately-shaped nose and a short square-cut black beard. He looked like a figure from an Assyrian statue. A gentle and courteously-mannered Persian, Mirza Ahmad Sohrab, acted as interpreter.

In a low and gentle voice Abdul Baha spoke to his interpreter, who translated his message into English, sentence by sentence.

'I come as the preacher of the religion of Bahai, which recognises the fundamental unity of *all* religions. Jews and Christians. Mohammedans and Buddhists, worship the same great God of mankind. The mission of Bahaism is to unite all religions in one, and to propagate universal peace. When I speak of religions I mean, of course, the *foundations* of religions, and not the dogmas or blind imitations which have gradually stolen in here and there. These are ever destructive and hinder the progress of nations.

'The foundations of the religions of God are one. They are not multiple, for they are realities. (Reality does not accept multiplicity, though every one of the divine religions can be divided into two distinct departments, one concerned with the world of *morality*, and that is essential, the other with *conduct*, which is subject to transformation and change with the times and customs.) The foundation of these divine religions is ever the cause of progress, and the mission of these divers prophets has been no other than the education and advancement of the world. If a prophet is a true prophet it will be found that he has educated the people, lifting them from the abyss of ignorance. Whatever religion it is that the true prophets have preached, they have all been sent by the same God. Christ and Mohammet, Moses and Buddha, all teach the fatherhood of God. The followers of Bahaism have a religion which selects from the great religions of the world that which is common to them all.

'Men of every land and thought believe and know that God is kind. Now, so long as we have a kind God, why should we be unkind? He is our Creator, our Provider, and Help. Why, therefore, should we say, 'This is a Christian, this a Jew, that a Mussulman, or Mohammedan, or Buddhist? It is really none of our business. God has created us all and it is our care to be kind to everybody. That is our duty. As to our speculative beliefs, that is a matter between each individual and the universal God.

'Religionists have considered each other as contaminating, and have shunned and reviled each other, exercising the severest enmity. Then dawned His Holiness Baha'u'llah, the founder of the Bahais. He has laid institutes and teachings which unite all the nations, cause fellowship among the various religions, and which dispel political, religious, and racial prejudice, and usher under the tabernacle of its Oneness of humanity all the peoples of reality, just as if they were one household.

'That is why his Holiness Baha'o'llah addresses humanity, saying, 'Ye are all the leaves of one tree and the drops of one sea.' That is to say, the world of humanity, representing all the religions, representing all the races, may be likened to a tree. Every nation of the nations is like a branch thereof, and every soul among them is like unto a leaf. But all of them belong to one tree, and that tree is the blessed tree, and that tree is the tree of life, and that tree is the tree of sacrifice.

'Therefore it is not allowable that among human individuals there should linger any strife. All must live in the utmost kindness, in the utmost love, the utmost of fellowship, and must pass their days pleasantly, for this will win the bounties of God and the bestowals shall surround them, and the Kingdom of God will become personified in the human kingdom. And this is our wish in its entirety.'

When he had finished speaking the prophet smiled gently. With a feeling of deep reverence I clasped his hand as he wished me goodnight. When I had left the presence of Abbas Effendi I asked Mirza Ahmad Sohrab for the history of the Bahai movement . . .'[20]

Reports after 'Abdu'l-Bahá's departure from Edinburgh

'Abdu'l-Bahá left Edinburgh on the morning of 10 January arriving in London around 7 p.m. of the same day. After his departure articles about His visit to Edinburgh continued to be published inside and outside Scotland. The news of His address to the Esperanto Society, for instance, was to be published around virtually the whole globe (see chapter 33). In Edinburgh, the press continued publishing letters by a particular Christian group warning public opinion of the dangers posed by the Bahá'í Faith (see chapter 36). Also some reports about the Master's activities in the Scottish capital continued to be published inside and outside Edinburgh. *The Weekly Scotsman*, for instance, published on 11 January a general article introducing 'Abdu'l-Bahá and the Bahá'í Faith that also carried a summary of some of His activities in Edinburgh.[21]

In London *The Christian World* (London), a magazine to which Alexander Whyte contributed regularly, carried on 9 January a brief report by a correspondent on 'Abdu'l-Bahá's movements in Edinburgh which besides giving other details mentioned that 'the meetings were nominally held in the interests of International amity, but a considerable amount of curiosity and interest were also entertained with regard to the personality of the world-renowned Persian'.[22]

The Christian Commonwealth (London) published in its issue of 15 January three articles dedicated to the visit of 'Abdu'l-Bahá to Edinburgh. One of them was an editorial that discussed the reactions produced by 'Abdu'l-Bahá among the Christian circles in the Scottish capital and also replied to the statements published in the editorial of the *Evening News* which had appeared on 9 January:

ABDUL BAHA AND PERSONAL IMMORTALITY

The accounts we are able to publish this week of Abdul Baha's visit to Edinburgh prove that the Persian leader aroused intense interest in his mission and teaching. Religious leaders north of the Tweed appear to understand the significance of the Bahai movement better than their brethren on the south side. The International Free Church Council has missed a great opportunity in not giving a reception to the distinguished visitor from the East, or in some way taking friendly note of his presence amongst us. During his stay in Edinburgh, Abdul Baha was the guest of Dr. Alexander Whyte, and at the meeting in the Freemasons' Hall Dr. Kelman presided; a subsequent meeting in the Rainy Hall was presided over by Professor Patrick Geddes, who contributes to this issue an entirely favourable impression of the visit. The 'Edinburgh Evening News' devotes a leaderette to a discussion of certain points in Abdul Baha's address, with particular reference to a statement made by Rev. A. B. Robb, Falkirk, who said that they were listening to a missionary from the East preaching the old gospel. Mr. Robb added that he felt they were not preaching quite the gospel they had heard from Abdul Baha, although they were all longing to preach it. The 'Evening News' asks whether the Bahai faith included a doctrine of personal immortality. There is not the slightest doubt that it does, even if it happened not to be clearly stated in the address at Edinburgh. The same journal appears to find difficulty in the fact that Christianity, in the Bahai teaching, is regarded as but one revelation among many, and asks what becomes of the unique authority of the Christian gospel. It is clear that the meaning of the Bahai movement is not appreciated by the 'Evening News'. It is not a new religion, but an effort to unify all religions.[23]

The same issue contained a complete and detailed report of 'Abdu'l-Bahá's movements in Edinburgh and also offered a glimpse of the different reactions that His visit generated in public opinion:

ABDUL BAHA IN EDINBURGH
COMMANDS BAHAIS TO LEARN ESPERANTO
(From Our Own Correspondent)

The visit of Abdul Baha to Edinburgh has been the event of the week in the Scottish capital. Everybody is talking about him and his utterances, not all of them with favour. The evening newspapers have printed his portrait and special articles dealing with the Bahai movement, and have given extensive reports of his addresses. The 'Scotsman' reports in particular have been very full. Some of the papers have published leading articles, from which it seems difficult to conclude whether they think that Bahaism is a new religion or is as old as the hills. It is not surprising that in a citadel of orthodoxy like Edinburgh there should have been many who have regarded Abdul Baha as 'the propagandist of a false religion', and have been scandalised at the idea of his consorting with eminent Christian divines and making his chief public declaration of the Bahai teachings in the Rainy Hall of the New College, one of 'the 'holy of holies' of Scottish Presbyterianism. We rejoice, however, that the tolerant spirit, of which Abdul Baha is so fervent a preacher, has been so finely manifested in Scotland, and we honour for their exhibition of this supreme virtue Abdul Baha's distinguished host, Principal Whyte, his amiable wife, Mrs. Whyte, his able colleague, Dr. John Kelman, whose speech on the Tuesday evening meeting was a brave and refreshing utterance, and those Christian ministers and layman who took pains in the meetings.

Like ancient Athens, the 'modern Athens' contains many people who 'spend their time in nothing else but either to tell or to hear some new thing', and a man with a message can always depend on a crowded audience. Abdul Baha's first public appearance was on Tuesday evening, when in the Freemasons' Hall, one of the largest and most beautiful halls in the city, he confined his remarks entirely to the benefits of an international auxiliary language. The meeting was arranged by the Edinburgh Esperanto Society, and among those who accompanied Rev. Dr. Kelman, the chairman, to the platform were Professor Patrick Geddes, the eminent scientist, and Dr. Sarolea, editor of 'Everyman' and initiator of the local Esperanto Society ten years ago. The Esperantists were greatly pleased at Abdul Baha's unhesitating approval of their language, and at his important declaration, 'Let us thank the Lord that this Esperanto language has been created. Therefore we have, commanded all the Bahais in the Orient to study this language very carefully, and ere long it will spread all over the East.' That Abdul Baha intends this command to be carried into effect is evidenced by the fact that he has ordered a supply of Esperanto books to be sent to Haifa, to be studied by his students there, and four hundred copies of the programme of the meeting, a beautiful production, are being sent to Persia for distribution among the Bahais there. The programme has a portrait of Abdul Baha, the photo block for which was lent by THE CHRISTIAN COMMONWEALTH, and contains the Esperanto poem, 'Prego sub la verda standardo', by Dr. Zamenhof, Dr. George Matheson's 'Gather us in', and quotations from the Bible, Baha'o'llah, and Burns.

On Wednesday afternoon Abdul Baha, in a meeting arranged by the Outlook Tower Committee, and presided over by Prof. Patrick Geddes, expounded in detail the principles of Baha'o'Uah, which are familiar to readers of THE CHRISTIAN COMMONWEALTH. Dr. Barbour, in moving a vote of thanks, referred to Bahaism as one of the great movements of our time, a plant which had spread rapidly in the Persia of to-day; but one recognised in it a great similarity to plants that were growing nearer home. Rev. A. B. Robb, Falkirk, said that they had been in the habit of sending missionaries from the West to the East to preach the Gospel; that day they had a missionary from the East to preach the old gospel, and to preach it in a new and original way. He felt that they were not preaching quite the Gospel they had heard that day, though they were all longing to preach it, and perhaps Abdul Baha's address would give some of them assistance to do so. On Thursday Abdul Baha addressed the Theosophical Society, when he spoke of the rational evidences of immortality to a sympathetic audience, and concluded with an impressive benediction. In addition to these public gatherings he spoke to a remarkable gathering of Oriental students on Tuesday afternoon in Principal Whyte's house, and on Thursday afternoon he addressed another meeting in the same place, where he told the story of Kurratul-Ayn, the beautiful and eloquent Persian woman who was strangled at Teheran in 1849 for her devotion to the cause of freedom and truth. On Wednesday evening he attended a recital of Handel's Messiah' in St. Giles' Cathedral. During the meetings 300 copies of the Abdul Baha special number of THE CHRISTIAN COMMONWEALTH were sold, and members of the C.C Fellowship found a congenial sphere for active service.

[We propose to give in our next issue a report of Dr. Kelman's speech, referred to above.][24]

Patrick Geddes also contributed to *The Christian Commonwealth* with his own account of the visit of 'Abdu'l-Bahá to Edinburgh focusing on the two public talks at which he was present.

ABDUL BAHA'S VISIT TO EDINBURGH
BY PROF. PATRICK GEDDES

It is impossible to estimate what definite results may remain or arise from Abdul Baha's three public appearances and private meetings; but his friends may fairly congratulate themselves on his reception in every case, which must certainly have exceeded even the most sanguine anticipations of their organisers, and this alike as regards numbers and receptivity of audiences. Never has Esperanto had so excellent a recommendation to the public who crowded the magnificent new Freemasons' Hall, as this ardent appeal for it on the international and specific, and the moral and spiritual grounds, which, although realised by Esperantists themselves, have seldom, if ever, to the same extent been put by an effective preacher. Some disappointment, however, was felt that at this meeting the advocacy of internationalism through a common language should have left no time for a statement of the Bahai system as a whole. This, however, was presented next day in a systematic discourse, and with numbered headings, in the lecture in the Rainy Hall, under the auspices of the committee of Outlook Tower, which he had visited with intelligent appreciation and sympathy rising at times to enthusiastic approval. This exposition was at once a sermon and a lecture, according as one viewed it from its beginning or recalled it from its close. Its beginning was an ardent expression of the spiritual unity of humanity, an appreciation of the historic religions, and an insistence upon the need and practicability of their increasing unison, and of their needed public action from inward goodwill towards international peace. Its later passages gave a no less cordial appreciation of science and industry, a demand for technical education and universal efficiency, and insistence upon the full equality of woman. Here, in fact, was made plain what is surely one of the greatest merits and recommendations of the Bahai system, its wide catholicity. For though all over the world old controversies are dying out, old hatreds abating, and though the need of reconciling us with the past and leading us onward into a renascent idealism, permeating modern life and directing its progress, is being widely felt, it is doubtful if any of our Western preachers, men of science or of affairs, has yet learned to give so simple, direct and categorical a statement of all this, at once from the spiritual and the material side, as in this long meditated, simply stated, teaching of Abdul Baha.[25]

This report was reproduced on 16 January in the Socialist newspaper *Daily Herald* (London).[26] The same day, the *British Weekly* (London), a magazine that used to publish many of the sermons of Alexander Whyte, 'Abdu'l-Bahá's host in Edinburgh, published a report of the visit,[27] which was published in Canada in the *Manitoba Free Press* on 10 February,[28] and was also the basis of a critical editorial published in the *Herald of Gospel Liberty* (Dayton, Ohio).[29] In the United States the Presbyterian *The Continent* (Chicago) also mentioned briefly 'Abdu'l-Bahá in connection with Edinburgh and emphasized that the Christian ministers that received Him 'understood that Abdul is not trying to proselytize Christians, and they accepted him as a worker for the kingdom of God.'[30]

Tablet to Andrew Carnegie

On His last day in Scotland, 'Abdu'l-Bahá wrote a Tablet for the Scottish-born American businessman Andrew Carnegie (1835–1919), the famous steel trader and industrialist who possessed one of the largest fortunes in the United States. He was also an important philanthropist and social activist who created and sponsored many charitable, social and scientific institutions – among them the Carnegie Endowment for International Peace (1910) – and built a large number of cultural and educational institutions across the United States.

According to Maḥmúd, 'Abdu'l-Bahá and Carnegie met but it is not clear from his comment where and when that encounter took place.[31] They both certainly met at the Lake Mohonk Conference and probably again on 13 May when, as has already been shown in a previous chapter, 'Abdu'l-Bahá addressed a meeting organized for Him by the New York Peace Society, an organization of which Andrew Carnegie was president. From the notes taken by Howard Colby Ives of a conversation between 'Abdu'l-Bahá and William H. Short (1868–1935), secretary of the Peace Society, it is inferred that illness prevented Carnegie from visiting 'Abdu'l-Bahá at the Ansonia on 15 April and that he expressed himself 'glad to receive Abdul-Baha at his home'.[32]

In 1889 Carnegie published in the *North American Review* his essay 'Wealth'[33] which was later published as the first part of his collection of essays *The Gospel of Wealth* and became popular under that name. In it, Carnegie made a series of proposals for social and economic development and for the redistribution of wealth.

'Abdu'l-Bahá read this essay and mentioned it in His letter to Carnegie which also dealt with the question of socioeconomic development. While composed in Edinburgh it was apparently sent from London to Hayozoun H. Topakyan, the Persian Consul in New York, who in turn delivered it to Carnegie.[34] A copy of the translation was also sent by Ahmad Sohrab to Harriet Magee, a Canadian Bahá'í residing in New York, with the express instruction that 'no copy of it should be given to anyone'.[35]

With the consent of Andrew Carnegie himself the *New York Times* published on 9 February the text of the letter He had received from 'Abdu'l-Bahá as well as the letter to Topakyan. The two letters were accompanied by a photograph of 'Abdu'l-Bahá with the Persian Consul.

ABDUL BAHA'S TRIBUTE TO MR. CARNEGIE
FAMOUS PERSIAN PROPHET PRAISES THE 'GOSPEL OF WEALTH' AND TELLS WHEN THE RICH MAY GIVE TO THE POOR

ANDREW CARNEGIE has received a letter conveying to him the fervent blessing of one as devoted as himself to the cause of international peace, a letter from Abdul Baha Abbas, the Persian philosopher and interpreter of the Bahai revelation, whose robed figure during his seven months' tour of this country was one of America's most picturesque sights in 1912. From London Abdul Baha writes of his incessant prayer that the ironmaster may shine as a luminous star from the horizon of eternity, and expresses this conviction from his sociology: 'It is not well that the poor should coerce the rich to contribute to them.'

Here is the letter:

97, Cadogan Gardens, S.W.
January 10, 1913

To the Hon. Andrew Carnegie,
New York City.

He is God!

O thou revered personage! Your article entitled the 'Gospel of Wealth' was read. Of a truth it contains sound opinion and ideas which, if followed, would lead to happier conditions in the world of Humanity. The doctrine of 'Human Solidarity' is well developed in the Teaching of Baha Ullah. 'Human Solidarity' is greater than 'Equality'. 'Equality' is obtained, more or less, through force (or legislation), but 'Human Solidarity' is realized through the exercise of free will. The Virtue of man made manifest through voluntary philanthropy, based upon the idea of 'Human Solidarity' is as follows:–

Rich men give to the poor; that is, they may assist the poor, but by their own desire. It is not well that the poor should coerce the rich to contribute to them! For such coercion would be followed by disintegration, and the organization of the affairs of society would be disturbed. But the idea of 'Human Solidarity', based upon mutual help and understanding, would lead to the peace and comfort of the world of Humanity, would be the cause of the illumination of the world of Humanity, and the means of prosperity and glory of the world.

As an evidence of this fact during my journey throughout the cities of America, my visits to various universities and associations, and my presence in educational circles, I witnessed the philanthropic traces of your honor scattered abroad. Therefore, I will pray for you that incessantly you may be encircled with Heavenly blessings and graces, and your philanthropic deeds may cover the East and West, so that you may become like unto a brilliant lamp in the kingdom of God, attain unto Everlasting Life and Glory, and shine as a luminous star from the horizon of Eternity. I beg of you to accept the consideration of my highest respect.

                        (Signed) ABDUL BAHA ABBAS

Mr. Carnegie granted permission for the reproduction here of this letter, which was written from London and translated by Mirza Ahmad Sohrab. It was conveyed to Mr. Carnegie through H.H. Topakyan, Consul General of Persia in New York, who opened wide his doors to the gray-bearded prophet when he was in this country and who served as his guide, counselor and friend on many occasions during that memorable tour.

Here is the letter which accompanied the letter to Mr. Carnegie:

7 Charlotte Square,
Edinburgh

Hon. Mr. H. H. Topakyan,
Consul General of Persia:

He is God!

O thou my revered friend! Your letter was received.

The Kind susceptibilities of conscious[ness] imported the utmost of rejoicing. Truly, I say, during my stay in America the signs of love became manifest from you from every side. Therefore, I am extremely pleased with you.

I will pray for you and Madame so that the Doors of the Kingdom of God be always open before your faces and the Infinite Divine bestowals may descend upon you uninterruptedly so that according to the statement of Christ, you may be of those who are chosen and not of those who are called.

May God encompass your family with His Heavenly Benediction! Upon thee be Baha El Abha.(Signed) Abdul Baha Abbas.[36]

Parts of the letter were later reproduced in other newspapers.[37] As will be shown, 'Abdu'l-Bahá wrote at least one more letter to Carnegie (see chapter 38).

***

'Abdu'l-Bahá requested Isabel Fraser, Marion Jack and Alice Buckton to travel to Edinburgh and continue His work with the many admirers and contacts He had established during His visit. Accounts of some of these activities were reported in *The Scotsman* and in *The Christian Commonwealth*. On 23 April the latter newspaper gave the following details about their program:

> In response to the deep interest that is being taken in the Bahai movement in Edinburgh, Miss Alice Buckton, who is widely known as a lecturer and leader of various thought movements of the day, and who for the last few years has made a special study of the Bahai movement, will deliver four addresses at the Outlook Tower, Edinburgh, on the following subjects:– 'The Waking of Woman in the East and the West', Sat., April 26; 'The History of the Bahai Movement' (with lantern slides), Mon., 28th; 'The Opening of the Gates of the Most Great Peace, 29th; 'The Relation of the Bahai Teachings to the Religious Life and Thought', 30th. In connection with these lectures, Miss Marian Jack and Mrs. Isabel Fraser, who have been privileged to be much with Abdul Baha in Palestine, London, and Paris, will be at home to inquirers every afternoon, 5–7 p.m., at the Royal Hotel, Princes Street, Edinburgh.[38]

In the first of these meetings there was also an exhibition of paintings by Marion Jack of places associated with the Bahá'í Faith in the Holy Land.[39] The chairman of the meeting was Dr. Otto Shlapp of Edinburgh University and another speaker was Patrick Geddes.

At the meeting of Monday, 28 April 1913, Alice Buckton and the engineer George G. Andre gave an address on the Bahá'í Faith which was chaired by Andrew Young (1858–1943), headmaster of the North Canongate School and later M.P. for Glasgow. His school had been visited by 'Abdu'l-Bahá on 8 January and in the course of his address Young recalled that 'the head of this great movement when he was in Scotland had the splendid courtesy to come down to the North Canongate School, and bless the bairns and their noon-day meal. Abdul Baha had won the hearts of the children by his great generosity and kindness.'[40] According to the same report, on the following day the children of the North Canongate School were shown some slides of the Holy Land and 'When at the end they saw the picture of Abdul Baha, they cried out with delight, and sent their love to him.'[41] The meeting held on 29 April was chaired by Rev. W. H. Bridge of the St.

John's Episcopal Church.[42] The fourth and last lecture was presided over by D. G. Pole and explored the relation of the Bahá'í faith to 'Theosophy, Modern Science and Social Work'.[43]

Theosophy in Scotland published in June 1913 a brief report about the public addresses of Alice Buckton and George Andre.[44] Accounts of some of the talks by the latter were also published on June 4, June 18 and July 16 in *The Christian Commonwealth* and they reported that Andre spoke 'as a convinced adherent of the founders of Bahaism'.[45]

28

SECOND AND THIRD VISITS TO PARIS

'Abdu'l-Bahá arrived in Paris on Tuesday 21 January at 7 p.m. He made a prolonged sojourn in France which He interrupted for one month in order to visit Stuttgart, Vienna and Budapest.

This second visit to France aroused less attention in general journals but, as will be seen in chapters 33, 34 and 35, His contacts with French Theosophists, Esperantists and Spiritualists were covered in great detail by the respective organs and publications of each organization.

As discussed in chapter 26, two days after the arrival of 'Abdu'l-Bahá in Paris, His visit was announced in *Gil Blas* (Paris).[1] On 10 February the European edition of the *New York Herald* (Paris) also reported that 'Abdu'l-Bahá 'has begun a series of morning conferences at 30 rue Saint-Didier, which are free to the public' and gave some biographical notes about Him.[2]

Visit to a Bahá'í-Inspired Social Project

Victor and Fanny Ponsonaille were two French Bahá'ís who had established an educational center to assist children in one of Paris's slums. 'Abdu'l-Bahá visited the center for the first time on 15 October 1911. An interesting article by Alice R. Beede published in *Star of the West* recounted the visit and reproduced some of the words of 'Abdu'l-Bahá, who told the couple that because of their work among the poor, 'Your names will go down through all the ages.'[3]

On His second sojourn in Paris 'Abdu'l-Bahá visited the center again. *The Christian Commonwealth* published an article by Isabel Fraser about the visit:

ABDUL BAHA IN PARIS
A BAHAI SLUM SETTLEMENT

It was just outside the fortifications of Paris that a little group of Bahais gathered to meet Abdul Baha, on the afternoon of Sunday, February 2, at 22, Rue Ledru-Rollin, près Saint Germain (Seine). Here a real Bahai settlement work is carried on by efforts made through self-denial, patience, and disinterested love of the children of the poor. Mons. Ponsonaille and his good wife are poor people who found that by giving up their noonday meal they had the wherewithal to give to those who were poorer than themselves. They looked about for the best way to serve, and, feeling that the present generation were practically hopeless of results, they decided to direct their efforts to the coming race. Each Sunday they gather together the children of the poor and the outcast to hear the sweet lore of love and brotherhood through the tablets of Abdul Baha and the hidden words of Baha'-o'-llah.

Mons. Ponsonaille, who is employed as a collector for one of the large department stores in Paris, took up his residence in this quarter and pioneered the work in a discarded car in a back lot.

The band of children grew and the clergy of various sects suggested a consolidation. Mons. Ponsonaille saw a war of creeds imminent and declined their offers. Growing jealous, the opposing forces consolidated and took the car from him.

The Bahais of Paris offered to build a place for his work, but M. Ponsonaille said that if they would buy the boards and nails he would build a board cabin himself.

The place is difficult of access. After leaving the train at the Gambetta Station there is a tram and then unpaved by-streets and narrow lanes, off which open barrack-like tenements. It is a noisy, rebellious, ragged, squalid quarter just outside the remnants of the old wall of Paris. To add to the desolation of that never-to-be forgotten trip the wind was howling and a drenching rain was falling. By dint of constant inquiry we finally found M. Ponsonaille's self-constructed cabin hard by the discarded car. The cabin, about 20 by 30 feet, was full of singing children. Mme. Ponsonaille, who has a radiant face, and who has evidently taught the children how to sing, was beating time and singing, as they have no instrument. On a raised platform at the further end was a huge Christmas tree which had been left, at the request of the children, for Abdul Baha to see. On this glad occasion there was gift-giving. One of the Bahais had sent a warm garment to each of the children and a consignment of oranges and cakes came in a taxi with four other Bahais.

The children, after reciting some words from a tablet of Baha'o'llah, were singing 'Jesus de Nazareth est ici' (Jesus of Nazareth is here) as Abdul Baha entered and swung down the aisle bestowing on them his radiant smile. He spoke but a few words, preferring to spend the time with them individually. To the mothers who had brought their offspring for him to bless he gave his oft-repeated admonition to educate, educate, educate the children to the very best of their ability. 'Always strive', he said, 'to give them a better chance than you have had. I am glad to be here with you to-day. You are all my children, and I love you very much. I will pray that these children may grow up in the light of education and spiritual guidance, and that they may reward you and show true appreciation by enkindling others. M. and Mme. Ponsonaille are your spiritual teachers. You must love these good friends very much. They are giving you spiritual food so that you may be strengthened in the life everlasting.' To the Ponsonaines he said, 'You are doing a noble work here. May you be strengthened from day to day. May the blessings of El Abha descend upon you. You will be rewarded, and future ages will see the results of your work.' M. Ponsonaille modestly remarked that God's favour was the only reward he sought. The Master blessed the place, and as he, with M. Ponsonaille, again stood out in the rain, prior to his departure, he pressed into this good man's hand the material blessing of several hundred francs.[4]

This article was later translated into Dutch and published in the Theosophist weekly magazine *Eenheid*.[5]

Meeting of Inayat Khan and Albert L. Caillet

On Thursday, 6 February 1913, 'Abdu'l-Bahá received Albert L. Caillet (1869–1928)[6] at His residence in 30 Rue St Didier. Caillet was the president and one of the founders of the Société Unitive, a society created in 1912 and linked with the New Thought movement.[7] He was also editor of the monthly organ of the society. In his meeting with 'Abdu'l-Bahá, Caillet presented Him with a signed copy of his recently published book, *Traitement Mental et Culture Spirituel* (1912), in which, among other things, he discussed the possibility of healing illness through the mind. Caillet also informed 'Abdu'l-Bahá that he had planned to publish in his magazine an article on the Bahá'í Faith and requested an interview with Him.

Soon after the arrival of Caillet, another guest arrived to see the Master. He was the renowned Indian musician and Sufi leader Inayat Khan (1882–1927)[8] who in those days was visiting France for the first time to give a series of lectures and performances. It was probably Caillet, to whom Inayat refers in his memoirs as his disciple and who arranged his lectures in Paris, who suggested that Inayat Khan visit 'Abdu'l-Bahá.

During their meeting Inayat Khan performed for 'Abdu'l-Bahá, who praised his work and talked to him about the history of music.[9] According to Khan's published memoirs, the Master inquired from him whether or not, as a mystic, he had attained the goal of his search. From Inayat Khan's answer, it seems that he evaded the question:

> I had the pleasure of meeting Abdul Baha when he was in Paris, who showed great interest in my music and with whom I had an interesting talk about our experiences in the Western world. During the conversation we had, he exclaimed, 'There should be no secret, you must speak; either you know or you do not know.' I answered, 'The whole nature of things and beings has a secret; each thing and each being has a secret which reveals its nature and character and the life itself has its secret and it is the uncovering of its secret which is the purpose of life. Speaking out loud does not prove a person to be the knower of the secret. Neither is every occasion a suitable occasion, nor is every person a person fitted for the truth to be spoken to.' 'You are also preaching the brotherhood of nations?' I said, 'I am not preaching brotherhood, but sowing the seed of Tawhid, the unity of God, that from the plant of Sufism may spring up fruits and flowers of brotherhood.'[10]

The February issue of the *Bulletin de la Société Unitive* carried a long article by Caillet in two parts. The first, not reproduced here, contained a long exposition of the origins and tenets of the Bahá'í Faith.

In the second part Caillet reproduced the notes of his interview with 'Abdu'l-Bahá and of His comments to Inayat Khan:

BAHAISM
RELIGION OF UNITY, LOVE AND UNIVERSAL PEACE

We had the occasion of greeting in the name of the UNITIVE SOCIETY the venerable prophet Abdu'l-Baha during his current stay among us in Paris, and we had the good fortune to attend on the same evening, Thursday February 6th, a musical recital of Sufi poetry accompanied by the *vina* (guitar) and the *tabla* (drum) – offered by our friend and brother, the professor Inayat Khan, to the great leader of the Bahais.

Bahaism is *par excellence*, as we said, the religion of unity, love, devotion and brotherhood.

It makes a warm appeal to men of all races and all religions to gather themselves under the banner of unity and to bring forth today the Kingdom of God on earth, that is to say, a true and real brotherhood of all mankind.

The venerable prophet, having learned that we constituted ourselves precisely in the name of such UNITY, symbolized by our UNITIVE SOCIETY, was willing to give us some lofty thoughts about our beautiful doctrine.

Unity among men, he said, speaking through his devoted interpreter, Mirza Ahmad Sohrab, is manifested in four ways.

First there is the *Unity of the Family*, which cannot fail to be somewhat imperfect and subject to certain conditions and differing views.

Then there is the *Unity of the Nation*, represented by each nationality, which, unfortunately is also not always free of problems, such as civil war, for example.

There is still the *Unity of Race*, or parts of the world: that of Asia, Europe or America, for example, which generally provides only a weak equilibrium, with frequent convulsions and crises.

And finally, there is true unity, the *Spiritual and Conscious Unity*, which is based on the consciousness of the common origin of all Men, and that makes of Humanity even more of a bouquet than this one here – and the venerable prophet indicated the beautiful flowers that adorned the room – rather, *one single flower*, immense and indivisible.

This is really the only fixed and durable UNITY, he continued, the one for which those of us who have a consciousness of our being must work ceaselessly and in perfect agreement.

This is the unity that Bahaism is establishing on the earth, and it is for this unity that your UNITIVE SOCIETY must also collaborate.

We deeply and warmly thanked the Master on behalf of all and assured him of our sincere and ardent collaboration in the common work of Unity, without distinctions or limitations of any kind.

Our distinguished honorary member Professor Inayat Khan, who was guided by the same feelings and beliefs as ours, and who was sympathetic to the revered prophet and with an even greater closeness, if possible, born of shared Eastern origins, kindly let us attend, afterwards, the interview and musical recital that followed.

Abdul-Baha first expressed some interesting thoughts on the materialist philosophy that makes a God of Nature and he recounted a conversation he had had with one of them on the ship that brought him back from America.

Only animals, he says, are deprived of the concept of the Creator and there is no cause for boasting about it when one is human and one suffers from this affliction.

If one but relies on the testimony of the senses one will be certain to remain in error: a mundane mirror does not show us, for example, an image as it looks to the eye, identical to reality. And don't some meteorological phenomena in the polar regions occasionally make one sun look like four?

So consider: to reason on the evidence provided by the senses is to reason as animals do, and so, using the forceful terms of the prophet, to reason 'like a cow who also has these five senses, and these five senses only'.

Then in a language rich with beautiful imagery, BAHA'U'LLAH shows us our planet as a single atom in the grand immensity of the universe, and the very smallness of the scale implies its singleness, since the atom, itself, is one and indivisible.

With this beautiful image the philosophical interview was over, and Professor Inayat Khan, accompanied on the *plen* (Indian drum), and Mr Ramakrishna, with the *vina* (guitar), sang a repertoire of Persian poetry of great symbolism and spiritual elevation, borrowed from the works of the great Sufis.

It had been more than sixty years, the Prophet told us, since he had heard the songs of his homeland sung with the quality with which the professor sang them, and at that time he was only five or six years old.

Then the evening ended with a discussion of Persian and Eastern music, which covered more or less the following:

Music is a great art to reach the emotional depths of the soul – and that is because it comes directly from the soul itself.

The voice that we hear, for example, can be material, but it comes from the 'sound of the abstract', *Anhad nada*, it comes directly from the soul to the body and to the thoughts of the one who expresses it through the intermediary of his material body.

As the Qur'an puts it: 'All things are of God and unto Him must all return.'

The music of the Greeks was very ancient, and the philosophers, who used to teach in public places, liked to present the science of music and to explain philosophy through it: music is the food of the soul, and as the soul is invisible, so must its food be invisible.

Long before the days of Islam, music was highly developed in Persia and considered one of the most essential arts and sciences.

In Bukhara, music, in all its varieties, was the main topic of education. It was there that Avicenna, the famous disciple of Farabi, learned music.

During the splendour of Eastern civilization, music made its way to Spain through Arabia, and it was taught in the Arab University of Cordova.

This explains the introduction of Eastern 'color' in western music: which is found even today, to some extent, in Spanish music.

To this the Professor Inayat Khan replied that music had always been the chosen method for the Sufis to elevate their souls to the highest spiritual state . . .'[11]

The same issue also told readers, 'We also learn that the Venerable Persian Prophet ABDUL BAHA . . . the Founder of the great religion of peace, BAHAISM, is currently in Paris, and he receives guests every morning from 10:00 to 12:00, at 30 Saint-Didier, sixteenth district.'[12] Caillet announced the launching of a new magazine with the title *Revue Universelle*, which was to serve as an organ for any progressive movement working in any way for the betterment of the world, including the Bahá'í Faith.[13]

The day after meeting with Caillet and Inayat Khan, 'Abdu'l-Bahá and His visitors heard the neighbor living in the flat above playing the piano and some music in the street. This circumstance prompted 'Abdu'l-Bahá to speak about music as a metaphor of the different religious and intellectual ideals in the world. Ahmad Sohrab prepared a translation of the Persian notes of this talk and Isabel Fraser submitted it to the *International Psychic Gazette* (London), which published it in September 1913:

ABDUL BAHA ON MUSIC
BY MRS. ISABEL FRASER

ONE morning during Abdul Baha's recent sojourn in Paris, he entered the room asking after the health of the little group that had gathered to meet him. As he seated himself in his usual chair by the window, a band of noisy street singers held forth just below. A girl in the flat above was practising on the piano. The result was like some pandemonium. Abdul Baha sat perfectly quiet till the noise ceased, and still looking out of the window, gave the following talk on music:–

Last night a Hindu professor of music came here to see me. He brought with him a musical instrument called the Vina and played for us certain Oriental strains, accompanying himself while singing. Overhead our neighbour was playing the piano, but as soon as the professor started to play, the piano became silent till the Hindu finished. This teaches us a lesson: whenever we hear better music we must stop to listen; then we can forget all inferior music. For instance, when a lover of music hearkens once to the entrancing notes of a great master, his love for music will no longer be satisfied by the playing of a pupil. If he listened with equal pleasure to the pupil, it would show a lack of artistic appreciation, a non-capacity for any spiritual upliftment.

Let us suppose that the most accomplished artist of Paris is playing for us in this room, inspiring the heart by immortal songs and charming us with sweet celestial harmonies. Is it possible that any one of us could leave this room afterwards and, going through the streets, stop to enjoy the crude notes of a hurdy-gurdy? Should we do so, it would indicate that we could not appreciate the melodies of the great master.

To-day there are many melodies to be heard, in the world. From every studio diverse strains are floated to our ears, but many of these melodies have become antiquated and covered with the rust of time. For thousands of years the same notes have been heard. They have lost their original charm and purity, for the singers have grown old and decrepit and lost their voices. The song of life has become so changed with time that it is no longer recognised. In short, from every direction melodies are sounded and we must needs have discriminating ears to discern the most beautiful and artistic.

Let us seek the song with the sweetest strain which will be taken up by the angels and carried to the supreme concourse. Let us hearken to the melody which will stir the world of humanity so that the people may dance with joy. Let us listen to a music which will confer life on man. Then we can obtain universal results; then we shall receive a new spirit; then we shall become illumined. But if we attend to all the different kinds of music we shall have nothing but discord, for they are being played by inferior artists. If we follow all the distracting sounds we will be lost in a wilderness of deprivation.

Therefore let us investigate a song which is superior and above all these other songs; one which will develop the spirit and produce harmony and exhilaration, unfolding the inner potentialities of life. It has been proved before that whenever the Divine Song is raised on earth, the world of humanity is quickened with a new impulse, and the realm of existence receives a new lease of life; the sphere of thought is rejuvenated; sciences progress; the world of morality is resuscitated, and humankind is reborn into a new era of civilisation and refinement. Again and again this has been experienced and its results and benefits are the records of past history.

We must not run after untried songs, the effects of which are uncertain, or we may fail in our pursuit of harmony. Perchance the effect of a given song may not be praiseworthy; perhaps it may not have the sweet quality which is the characteristic of a true melody. Therefore, let us search and find out the one glorious song which has run throughout all ages with thousands of entrancing accompaniments, the effects of which have changed millions of human beings. Often have we sown the seed, and as a result have gathered many harvests. Now, is it wise for us to overlook this goodly seed, and experiment with another variety? Instead of a harvest, we may reap only thorns and thistles. There is a course of treatment which has been tried a thousand times, and has always healed the sick ones. Is it wise for us to relinquish it and go for consultations to charlatans? It is evident that the world of humanity cannot be rejuvenated through weak instrumentality. Except through the power of God, mankind cannot be imbued as a whole with divine virtues. Except through the rays of the sun, the entire surface of the earth cannot be warmed. There may be a lamp or a torch or electric light, or there may be even the countless stars and planets, but notwithstanding these luminous orbs, this globe in its entirety cannot be illumined. It is through the rays of the sun that the various kingdoms of existence on this globe are imbued with life; therefore, let us follow the sun so that we may become illumined.

When the sun appeared from the eastern horizon, the mantle of winter had fallen over the meadows and pastures, the soil was black. As soon as the sun rose from its dawning place, flooding the regions with glorious light, the gentle breezes wafted and the clouds of mercy descended. Winter passed, spring appeared. The meadows and prairies became verdant; all the trees were adorned with blossoms, and multi-coloured roses and hyacinths perfumed the air. The trees attained to fruition, and our nostrils inhaled the fragrance. The surface of the earth became transformed, and this world became the mirror of the Kingdom.

The lower spheres expressed the virtues of the higher work. These have ever been the results whenever the Sun of Reality dawned. Now is it fitting that we turn our backs to the sun and hold fast to a dim, flickering candle? Is it right that we should forget the boundless sea and follow after a little brook? Is it wise that we should close our eyes to the luscious fruits of this tree, to run wild in the jungle collecting wild fruits? Is it not shortsightedness to fling away the quick-healing remedy and take into our system a poisonous drug? Is it not ignorance to renounce the skilled physician and go to charlatans? Praise be to God, the sun of reality has shone forth, illuminating all the continents with its effulgent rays, warming the cold bodies and causing vegetation to appear in the earth. The flowers of the Kingdom are springing up in the East and the West, in the North and the South. Now consider how negligent are the people who do not turn towards this sun, but try to illumine themselves with dim lamps. They have forgotten the waves of the most great sea, and they try to assuage their thirst at dried-up streams. They do not listen to the soul-stirring music of the Supreme Concourse, but run wild with joy over the jarring notes of a street organ.

Strive day and night. Perchance these sleeping ones may be awakened, these blind ones may see and the dead arise to listen to the soft mellow music which is streaming down from the Kingdom of El Abha.[14]

Inayat Khan again visited 'Abdu'l-Bahá on 29 May and asked Him questions regarding Nirvana and other subjects.[15]

Visit to the Theological Seminary

On Sunday, 16 February, 'Abdu'l-Bahá was invited to speak at the Theological Seminary of Pastor Henri Monnier (1881–1941) of the French Reformed Church.[16] The staff and students of the theology faculty attended the meeting at which 'Abdu'l-Bahá and Monnier initiated a dialogue on the unity of religions and afterwards the Master answered some questions from the audience about the Bahá'í teachings on Christ.[17] A brief report of this meeting was published in *The Christian Commonwealth*:

> ABDUL BAHA AND A UNIVERSAL RELIGION
> During his stay in Paris, Abdul Baha has visited Pastor Monnier's Theological Seminary and addressed an audience composed chiefly of professors, clergy, and theological students. One of the questions they asked him was with regard to the unification of religions.
> 'Is it possible and through what channels will it be realized?' Abdul Baha replied that the enmity and rivalry existing between religions is a thing of words. The followers of all religions believe in a reality the benefits of which are universal – which reality is a medium between God and man. The Jews call that reality Moses; the Christians, Christ; the Mussulman, Mohammed; the Buddhists, Buddha. When the devotees of religions, he said, look

beyond the name of their founder, whom they have never seen, to the one reality for which he stood, the day of unification will be in sight, and the realities of all the holy books will be revealed.

Abdul Baha is unable to accept the invitation of the International Congress of Religions to address the conference which is to be held in Paris in July, but he is sending a paper.[18]

This article was later published in Dutch in the Theosophist weekly magazine *Eenheid*.[19]

A few days after this meeting the liberal Protestant magazine *Evangile et Liberté* carried an article about the Bahá'í Faith by the pastor Paul Vergara (1883–1965). 'This serene and venerable figure makes a deep impression on all who approach him,' stated Vergara before summarizing some of the Bahá'í teachings.[20] This article was later echoed in *The Christian Commonwealth*.[21]

Article in *Le Petit Journal*

Le Petit Journal (Paris) was a daily newspaper close to the Fédération Republicaine, a conservative republican party. Its small size, its low price and its modern production system made this journal one of the most read newspapers in France, with a circulation of some 850,000 copies.[22] In 1884 the journal launched its Sunday *Supplement Illustré*, a pictorial supplement characterized by its full-color front and back pages. The issue of the *Supplement Illustré* of 4 May 1913 carried on its front page a full page color illustration depicting 'Abdu'l-Bahá preaching in a mosque with His hands raised and surrounded by an attentive group of men, some of them kneeling. The caption read, 'The New Prophet of Islam. Abdul Baha preaching peace and brotherhood in a Constantinople mosque.'

On its first page the magazine published an article about the Bahá'í Faith based on comments made by Abdon Buisson Effendi, a member of the Ottoman legation in Paris and founder and secretary general of the *Comité France-Orient*, an organization created in 1913 to foster commercial cultural relations between Europe and the Ottoman Empire. The text was preceded by the following editorial introduction:

This is a philosophy as beautiful and noble as optimism, tolerance and brotherhood. Alas! Our social reformers do not always practice them in our days. And it is curious to note that sometimes we find them less frequently among us than with those Muslims that the poorly informed West so readily accuses of fanaticism.

A man is in Europe travelling to preach this doctrine of serenity and kindness. He is of Persian origin and is called Abdul-Baha. He is the son and worthy successor of Baha-Ullah, prophet and founder of Bahaism, who about half a century ago, began to spread in the Muslim world the ideas of tolerance and brotherhood.

Baha-Ullah proclaimed that all men are brothers, that progress is the great law of the world and that 'the legal impurity of infidels was abolished'.

'All men', he said, 'are the drops of one sea, and the leaves of a same tree, all races are pure.' He didn't ask from men anything else than to have 'noble thoughts, sound morals and hygienic costumes'.

These beautiful doctrines have now crossed the borders of the Muslim world. Abdul-Baha, son of Baha-Ullah, has brought them throughout the universe. He is returning to Constantinople to carry out a work of progress and resignation.

Buisson's text continued with statements based on the false assumption that 'Abdu'l-Bahá was visiting the capital of the Ottoman Empire, and linked this visit with the recent loss by the Turks of the Balkans:

> The leader of the Bahaist movement . . . after having toured the capitals of the world and proclaimed recently, right here, his great design for a unity of religions, faith and love, has just arrived in Constantinople, where in the wake of peace, he has began to preach his good doctrine. Its dissemination can make his Muslim brothers, 'the resigned to God', to accept the consequences of a war which has so unfortunately turned against the Ottoman arms.

After reviewing some of the Bahá'í teachings in relation to Islam the author declared that 'anyone who has listened to him ['Abdu'l-Bahá] is forced to admit being subjugated and seized by the magic of his words and the clarity of his intellect that shines in the glow of his look.'[23]

Beatrice Irwin Meets 'Abdu'l-Bahá

Several American Bahá'ís traveled to Europe to visit the Master in Paris. One of them was Beatrice Irwin (1877–1956), who met Him on several occasions at the end of March 1913.

According to Sohrab, she shared with Him her project of writing articles on the Bahá'í Faith for an English periodical 'circulated in intellectual and spiritual circles of England'.[24] This project came to fruition when she published in the *Occult Review* (London) a six-page article introducing the Bahá'í Faith and recounting her meetings with 'Abdu'l-Bahá in Paris:

> Of Abdul-Baha, the present leader of the Cause, a great deal might be written, so full is the personality of the man. An interview recently granted me by him in Paris left upon my mind a profound impression. He sat in a small room, fragrant with hyacinths. His white turban, flowing green robes, spontaneous gestures, and above all the resonance of his voice, called up to my mind the freshness of spring and the impetuousness of mountain torrents. He spoke of the spiritual value of practical things, and of the message of the West to the East. He dwelt upon the necessity of bringing our educational advantages within reach of all oriental races, in the largest spirit, and devoid of mental prejudices of caste and creed.
>
> 'Civilisation is not stationary,' said Abdul-Baha. He showed, by historical analogy, how the tides of intellectual and spiritual development change in their courses, flowing now from East to West, now from West to East, and how in this process it is the *interchange* that is the essential factor, the vital consideration. It matters not where or when it is night or day, provided that night and day succeed and merge into one another. The glory of the West should lie in her practical message to the Oriental races, the glory of the East in her receptivity and gratitude for that message. The West would do well to pause and emulate this spiritual humility and faith, as the East must emulate the intellectual energy of the West. Here indeed were practical precepts for the Universalism of which Abdul-Baha is the representative, and in spite of the delicate imagery of his Persian address, interpreted for us by Mirza Sohrab, his thought was expressed with scientific force and precision. There

were no abstractions, no visionary transports, but there was the alert and joyous vitality of one anxious to share his happiness and his knowledge with his fellow-creatures . . .

During his travels Abdul-Baha has not only addressed public gatherings of various characters, social, religious and ethical, but his private apartments have been open daily to all inquirers, and he has answered their questions personally with untiring devotion. My first visit was paid at 9.30 a.m. and already others were there, before me, waiting to see him! My next call was at dusk, and again I found the ante-rooms full of eager faces.

On this occasion I asked for Abdul-Baha's opinions upon psychic development, which is so essential a feature of Hindu and Sufi philosophies. His reply was guarded, but on the whole he was not in favour of mystic experiments, as he pointed out that, in order to be valuable, such experiments must be profound, and that the practical conditions of life in the West did not usually afford the time and patience necessary to such researches. Again, it was the practical note that dominated the discourse of this Eastern seer, for he insisted that, at the present juncture, general spiritual development was more needed than individual psychic culture, and that those who could grasp and spread the Bahai teachings would be paving the way to conditions whose outcome will be the universal psychic unfoldment towards which humanity is tending.[25]

Echoes of 'Abdu'l-Bahá's Visit Outside France

As had occurred in 1911, the visit of 'Abdu'l-Bahá to France attracted some attention in England and the United States. On 26 February *The Christian Commonwealth* provided details about 'Abdu'l-Bahá's first weeks in France and mentioned His planned travels to Stuttgart, Budapest and Holland.[26] The article was later published in the Theosophist weekly magazine *Eenheid* in the Netherlands.[27]

At least one American newspaper published information about the second visit of 'Abdu'l-Bahá to France. On 2 March the *Chicago Sunday Tribune* carried an article by its Paris correspondent who resorted to sarcasm to summarize his impression of the Master. 'Besides being "a prophet of peace" Abdul looks much the keen business man of affairs,' stated the reporter. 'In spite of his years, which are sixty or more, and his forty years in a Turkish prison, he looks strong and wonderfully robust. His eyes are quite remarkable, for they are not the eyes of a religious enthusiast but rather as if they saw into people and things, sized them up, and rated them accordingly.'[28]

After 'Abdu'l-Bahá's departure from France *The Christian Commonwealth* published the following summary of His last activities in Paris and also mentioned that He was unable to visit the religious congress that was soon to be held in Paris (see next section):

ABDUL BAHA IN PARIS

To the great regret of the committee, Abdul Baha Abbas will be prevented from attending the congress. He returned here about the middle of May, after holding most successful meetings at Budapest, Vienna, Stuttgart, and other places. At Stuttgart there are now over 2,000 Bahaists. May 23 was the Master's sixty-ninth birthday, and also the anniversary of the proclamation of the Bab in 1844. The occasion was celebrated by a stirring address by Abdul Baha at the house of M. and Mme. Dreyfus in the Rue Greuze. M. Dreyfus – who, like his wife, is an accomplished Persian scholar – translated into French, and Mme. Bernard, an English lady, addressed a few words to the numerous English and American visitors present. Another meeting was held on Monday, 26th, at the house of Mr. Edwin Scott, the eminent American artist, whose views of Paris form, as usual, quite a feature in this year's Salon of the Societe Nationale. Abdul Baha retains a most pleasing recollection of his meeting in London. He thinks everybody should subscribe to THE CHRISTIAN COMMONWEALTH. After a short rest here he has proceeded to Egypt to join his family, and will then make a tour of the Holy Land, where the Bahaist movement has very many adherents.

C. H. H.[29]

The International Congress of Religious Progress

As mentioned above, during 'Abdu'l-Bahá's visit to the Theological Seminary of Pastor Monnier, He was invited to speak at the International Congress of Religious Progress which was to be held in Paris from 16 to 22 July. Owing to His planned travel to Egypt, 'Abdu'l-Bahá was unable to accept the invitation but sent instead a Tablet to the secretary of the Congress, the Boston liberal Christian Dr Charles W. Wendte,[30] which was read at one of the sessions.[31] Hippolyte Dreyfus participated in the program with a lecture on the Bahá'í Faith.[32]

Several journals mentioned the fact that 'Abdu'l-Bahá was expected to participate in the congress. In France these included the daily newspaper *Le Matin* (Paris), with a circulation of 647,000 copies,[33] *Le Temps*,[34] the *Revue Chrétienne*[35] and *Le Théosophe*.[36] Details were also published in North America[37], Australia[38] and Scotland.[39]

In England *The Christian Commonwealth* published on 16 July a portrait of 'Abdu'l-Bahá as well as portraits of other speakers[40] and a week later the same journal mentioned that 'Abdul Baha, who is now in Port Said, sent a cordial message to the International Congress at Paris. Since his arrival in Egypt a stream of pilgrims has been flowing from all parts of the Orient to welcome the leader of the Bahai movement. His health is well maintained, and he is as occupied as ever in delivering his message. We hope to publish next week a summary of his message to the Paris Congress.'[41] Portions of the letter addressed by 'Abdu'l-Bahá to the Congress were published on 30 July:

THE FOUNDATION OF SPIRITUAL UNION
ABDUL BAHA'S MESSAGE TO THE PARIS CONGRESS

As we stated last week, Abdul Baha who is at present in Egypt, was unable to be present at the International Congress in Paris, ill-health and weakness causing him to shrink from the journey. His message to Dr. C. W. Wendte is a lofty plea for the recognition of religion as the foundation of spiritual union between nations. Religion, wrote the leader of the Bahais, means the unity of the spirit, the union of thought, the ideal chain binding together the children of men. There are two kinds of civilisation, a natural and material order established for the physical world and a spiritual order which serves moral ends. The founders of natural civilisations are the scientists and philosophers; divine civilisation is established by the prophets of God, divine manifestations in the world of men. Religion is the basis of the spiritual civilisation. Natural civilisation is like unto the body, and is concerned with it; divine civilisation is like unto the spirit. A body without spirit is dead, though it may appear beautiful and comely. By religion we mean those necessary bonds which unify humanity. This is its essence. But a thousand times alas! the solid foundation has been abandoned and forgotten, and the leaders of religion have fabricated dogmas and ceremonials which are at complete variance with the essentials of religion. As these dogmas and ceremonies differ from each other they cause difference, and difference breeds strife, and strife ends in open war; blood is shed, the innocent are slaughtered, their homes are pillaged, their children become captives and orphans.

Thus religion, which was intended to be the cause of friendship, has become the cause of enmity; it was meant to be sweet honey, and has turned into bitter poison: it was meant to illumine the world, and it has spread confusion and gloom; it was meant to confer eternal life, and has become the fiendish instrument of death. So long as these dogmas are in the hands and these nets of deceit and hypocrisy are in the fingers religion will be a harmful agency in the modern world. They are superannuated, and must be given up. Free of tradition, we may investigate the real objects of divine religion; and since the foundation of religion is one, and that one is reality, and since reality is indivisible, and not subject to multiplicity, therefore true unity and amity between all religions will be instituted; the true religion of God will be unveiled in all its beauty and sublimity before the world. Your honourable congress must tear asunder the veils and remove these suffocating cerements; it must dispel these dark, impenetrable clouds that the Sun of reality may shine through. Praise be to God this is the century of science, this is the cycle of reality; mankind has acquired a glorious capability of realising the oneness of its life. This is the hope of this exiled one. From the throne of the Eternal I beg assistance for you and confirmation, so that you may be strengthened and enabled to accomplish a task which has been regarded from the beginning of the world as impossible and utopian. Upon you be greeting and praise![42]

29

CENTRAL EUROPE

As seen in previous chapters, on 1 March the Protestant journal *Evangile et Liberté* mentioned that 'Abdu'l-Bahá planned to visit Germany. This information was echoed in *The Christian Commonwealth* on 12 March.[1] However, it was not until 1 April 1913 that 'Abdu'l-Bahá left Paris to start a one month journey that took Him not only to Germany but also to present-day Hungary and Austria.

His first stage was Stuttgart, where the Bahá'í Faith had been established for less than a decade by Dr Edwin Fischer and Alma Knobloch, two Germans who had become Bahá'ís in the United States.

Probably to avoid opposition, 'Abdu'l-Bahá requested the German Bahá'ís not to publicize His visit in the press.[2] Thus references in periodicals related to His first sojourn in Stuttgart are rare and consist basically of news published in Esperanto journals about His meeting on 5 April with the local Esperantists (see chapter 33).[3] He nevertheless granted an interview to the editor of a monthly German magazine published in Switzerland who expressed his wish to write about the Bahá'í Faith in his journal.[4]

Arrival in Budapest: First Interviews

An engineer of Jewish origin, Leopold Stark (1866–1932) was probably the first Bahá'í in Hungary. He had been a Theosophist for a long time and during a nine month sojourn in London, around 1904, he became acquainted with a good number of British Theosophists, one of them being the Scottish born A. P. Cattanach, who at one time had presided over the Battersea Lodge. Cattanach became a Bahá'í around 1910 or 1911 and soon afterwards sent some Bahá'í literature to Stark. From their personal study of these documents Stark and his wife became Bahá'ís.[5]

On 25 February 1912 Stark delivered a lecture on the Bahá'í Faith at the Budapest Theosophical headquarters[6] and afterwards published an article in the journal of the Hungarian Theosophists.[7] As soon as he heard the news of the return of 'Abdu'l-Bahá to Europe, he corresponded with Ahmad Sohrab and invited the Master to Budapest. Through his efforts several societies in Budapest – including commercial, academic, Esperantist and Theosophist organizations – also sent invitations to 'Abdu'l-Bahá.[8] It was while in Stuttgart that 'Abdu'l-Bahá responded positively to the invitation and on the morning of 9 April He left Germany for Budapest.[9]

Stark was a prominent citizen in Budapest. As an electrical engineer he held various positions of responsibility in different corporations including the technical direction of the metropolitan electric company of Budapest. He was member and officer of various scientific and technical societies and the author of several scientific works. He had also been president of the Hungarian Theosophical Society from 1910 to 1911.[10] This social position allowed him to widely publicize the visit of 'Abdu'l-Bahá[11] and to encourage several societies in the city to arrange meetings for Him.

When the Master arrived in Budapest[12] many personalities gathered at Hotel Ritz – where He stayed during His sojourn in the city – to welcome Him.[13] Among them was Sandor Gieswein (1856–1923),[14] Catholic prelate and president of the Hungarian Esperanto Society; Dr Gyula Germanus (1884–1979),[15] a scholar of the Oriental Academy who officially greeted the Master in the name of all the societies and organizations represented in the party; Ignác Kúnos (1860–1945),[16] director of the Oriental Academy; the engineer Károly Zipernowsky (1853–1942);[17] Abdul Latif Effendi, the imam of the Hungarian Muslims, and many others.

Representatives of several journals were also among the welcoming party or visited the Master at the Hotel Ritz. Two newspaper photographers took shots of the Master and His entourage. These pictures were later published in the newspapers *Persi Tükor*,[18] *Budapest*,[19] *Tolnai Világlapja*,[20] *Uj Idök*[21] and *Az Érdekes Újság*.[22]

Vilma Balogh, a reporter with *Világ* ('The World') was among those who waited for the Master at the train station and later at Hotel Ritz. Her detailed account of His arrival is quite interesting and her comments about 'Abdu'l-Bahá sympathetic. However, she attributed to

'Abdu'l-Bahá statements that He could never have made, for instance, that His wife was dead, that one of His daughters was studying in Switzerland or that He had a son with a doctorate in law. As has been shown in previous chapters, sometimes reporters would attribute to 'Abdu'l-Bahá statements made by others or published in other journals. In this case it is probable that one of the Hungarian scholars who went to the Ritz to welcome the Master – probably Dr Ignác Kúnos, who is mentioned in the article – furnished the reporter with the poor information about the Bahá'í Faith and 'Abdu'l-Bahá published in the journal.

'He begins to talk in a wonderful voice, reflecting inner harmony. Words leave his lips with a plastic fineness,' stated Balogh. 'His gestures are noble, rare and intensive. It is easy to understand why seven million people enthusiastically trust in him and submit to his preaching.'[23]

A reporter with the *Pesti Napló* ('Journal of Pest'), a leading political daily journal with an estimated circulation of 45,000 copies,[24] published on 10 April his impressions of the arrival of 'Abdu'l-Bahá. Usually 'Abdu'l-Bahá's words were translated from Persian into English by Sohrab and then into Hungarian by Stark. The reporter with the *Pesti Napló*, however, was fortunate enough to be present at the same time as Dr Germanus, who translated into Hungarian from Arabic. While the general tone of the article is sympathetic, the fact that 'Abdu'l-Bahá stayed at the recently inaugurated Ritz and was accompanied by secretaries led this journalist to the wrong conclusion that 'Abdu'l-Bahá was a millionaire. The article also included a summary of the history of the Bahá'í Faith (not reproduced here):

THE BABI PROPHET
BY OUR OWN CORRESPONDENT

A great man has arrived in Budapest. He is neither an emperor, nor a prince, nor some famous writer. He is an 'apostle', the prophet of the unification of humankind, Abdul Baha, the teacher of Bahaism. For us, with minds saturated by materialism, it may look strange or even ridiculous that there is a man today who is wandering from town to town to seek salvation for his suffering fellow human beings by preaching love and human community. And still the facts provide a wonderful justification for the prophet. In America, England and on the continent, in countries where industrial production has reached the highest levels, there are millions who believe in this new manifestation and who find improvement in it.

The prophet was to be welcomed by a delegation at the Western railway station at 1.40 pm today but to our greatest astonishment he did not arrive.

As it turned out later, Abdul Beha arrived at the Eastern railway station and so the delegation drove to Hotel Ritz. The exotic guest was already there and had booked with his secretary a splendid four-room apartment. He can afford it since he is a multimillionaire. He was welcomed in English by Lipót Stark and Sándor Giesswein. Dr Germanus then greeted him in Arabic and this made the prophet's face light up.

'Aksan wa altaf kalámak!' 'Your words sound sweet and charming,' he said.

With the help of Professor Germanus I requested an interview from the prophet, a gentle looking, exceedingly agile and enthusiastic old gentleman. He said the following:

'Why should we hate and murder one another when we are all the creatures of the same God, of a creative God whose work is being ruined by wars?'

Asked whether he considers world peace possible he looked in our eyes for a second and then said with determination:

'The cause of war is ignorance. Peace will only be achieved through learning because science is not destructive. The national rivalry inciting peoples against one another will break under the knowledge of the people.'

Talking about women, he said:

'Although the role of women is different from that of men, they must have equal civil rights. Women are at least as much state supporting elements as men.'

At this point we were interrupted by a photographer who took a shot of the prophet. We walked aside but as soon as the camera clicked Abdul Baha continued to address his words to us:

'Our century is the century of inventions, the century of the solution of nature's phenomena. Without love this century is not perfect! . . .'[25]

The popular *A Nap* ('The Day'), an evening political journal supporting

Hungary's independence and with a circulation of some 90,000 copies, published the day after the arrival of the Master the following editorial which was probably written by Sándor Braun (1866–1920),[26] the newspaper's founder and editor. The text basically displayed a critique of Hungarian politics apropos of the visit of 'Abdu'l-Bahá:

> Well, it is not a bad thing that a man from the Orient is visiting us to teach us the most progressive, modern and harmonious ideals of the West. However, this wise man is bound to encounter a great deal of disappointment here, because this poor Persian believes that we have already reached the summit of human progress, and so he can only come here with high-flying, progressive teachings. On the contrary, this is still a feudal world, the ties to the land are still very strong and life is so full of pashas that one feels that not even under the Turks there have been so many pashas ruling us. If this poor Persian knew that he was entering into a country of prisoners, that the parliament of this prisoner-country has less freedom than the Tehran parliament has, I swear he would have not crossed Hungary's border . . .
>
> But, after all, he is here to proclaim his teachings. He could well take up the causes of general, equal and secret suffrage – to keep their logical order – he could well demand first the emancipation of men, because even if women are made equal to men, what worth would it be for emancipated women to enjoy equal rights with the slave men? . . .
>
> We would be pleased if the old wise man would take our good fame to the Orient and would not depart with the impression that it was a pity for us to leave Persia's neighbourhood about one and a half thousand years ago, because we are not that very far away from Asia even today.[27]

The same issue of *A Nap* carried the news of the arrival of 'Abdu'l-Bahá in Budapest in a short article introducing the Bahá'í Faith.[28] The *Budapesti Napló* (Journal of Budapest), a liberal daily newspaper with a circulation of 15,000 copies, published an article presenting the figure of 'Abdu'l-Bahá and some of the Bahá'í teachings. Some of the information on the Bahá'í Faith was provided by Dr Kúnos.[29]

A representative of the *Pesti Hírlap* (Gazette of Pest), an independent daily with a circulation of 60,000 copies, also visited the Master and interviewed Him. The next day the *Hírlap* carried one of the harshest articles published during the whole period of the travels of 'Abdu'l-Bahá. Under the title 'A Bahai Apostolnál' ('With the Bahá'í Apostle'), the article began by calling 'Abdu'l-Bahá insane and a lunatic. The author even stated that 'Abdu'l-Bahá's 'views on voluntary poverty are bound to remain hypotheses, since we know that Abdul Baha is the owner of huge pearl-fisheries that are worth millions.'

'It is only to be regretted that Baha came to us at the invitation of progressive societies since he brought nothing new or substantial to the Hungarian public', the article concluded.[30]

On 10 April 'Abdu'l-Bahá was interviewed by a reporter of *A Nap*. As mentioned, this newspaper had the day before already published two articles about the Master.

THE PROPHET SPEAKS TO BUDAPESTERS
WE HAVE THE RIGHT TO HAPPINESS AND IT IS OUR DUTY TO BE HAPPY

The number 3 is of cabballistic importance in the Orient, and Abdul Baha Abbas, the third prophet of the Bahai teachings, wears three caftans – a green, a black and a coffee brown one. Under the three caftans there is a faint yellow dolman and under the dolman and the white linen shirt there is the warm heart of the Oriental apostle. Indeed, the figure of Abdul Abbas arouses respect. He is tall, has a long white beard, mild but suggestive eyes and slightly lean hands, with which he draws beautiful gestures into the air whenever he speaks. Apart from that, he takes amazing poses and his movements show enthusiasm. And when he opens his wonderfully thin and red lips to speak, his old eyelids close and his parchment-like face gets spiritualized. He speaks in Persian and two of his aides take notes of what he says, because the old prophet always says something different and he is supposed to utter the new words at the inspiration of an inner, godly voice. It is interesting to feel that a gospel or a new testament is in the making here because the Bahai ideals have seven million followers already.

His secretary, Mirza Ahmad Sohrab, interprets the words of the Persian sage into English. Baha is acting like an apostle not only while delivering a lecture, he also preaches the ideals when he has one or two guests only. At times, he speaks in an arguing voice, as if he were answering someone. When he speaks about human wickedness and the cruelties of war, his voice gets slightly angry. Any time he changes his tone to stress his sentences he looks most interesting. On such occasions he is most impressive and creates the greatest illusions of his being a man from the Orient.

When we visited him at his apartment at the Hotel Ritz yesterday, he told us: Mankind has to be aware of its being homogeneous, because the very descent of man is uniform. There are no racial boundaries and there are no separate religions. Sexes have equal rights and equal duties. All of us are equally entitled to happiness and it is also our duty to be happy. God is great and wonderful. God builds and builds ceaselessly. And man must not destroy. People are ignorant, they do not recognize the real causes of the various phenomena and find joy in wars, cruelties and destruction. Therefore, ignorance has to be eliminated which in turn will make evil disappear.

The Bahai prophet said many other nice and godly things and then he stood up and stretched out his hands to bid farewell to us. He walked up to the window, opened it and stared at length at the glittering Danube River, flowing majestically. The spring sunshine rested upon him and the slight breeze from Buda blew around gently and tenderly.[31]

A reporter with the *Neues Pester Journal* (Budapest), a German journal with a circulation of 34,000 copies, also had an opportunity to see and interview 'Abdu'l-Bahá:

Abdul Baha Abbas received the writer of these lines in the afternoon in the 'Hotel Ritz', where he lives with his retinue in a row of elegantly furnished apartments. Abbas is travelling in the company of an interpreter, three secretaries and an Arabian servant. Since he is only able to speak Persian, the interview proceeds with the aid of an interpreter who has command of many European languages and a considerable level of fluency. The first impression that the visitor obtains of Baha Abbas is one of a broken, tired old man, and one wonders that this seventy-year-old man possesses the physical and moral strength to travel the world year-in year-out without intermission, and to preach the truth of his teachings with the enthusiasm and energy of a youth. A long, black silk caftan, a white silk turban and the long flowing snow-white beard have their desired effect. According to the ways of the Orientals he speaks with great animation in spite of his age by bestowing his words with emphasis through expressive gestures. We question him about the nature of his teachings, about Bahai, of which much still remains unknown in Europe. In the course of the interview, Baha Abbas forms a picture of his teachings, which is not at all fantastical or adventurous in itself. His teachings are directed towards promoting eternal peace to all spheres, namely that of religion. All differences which lead to strife among people must be set aside and one must strive towards the unity and equality of people, because this is the fundamental condition for thriving and democratic progress. He is an unconditional supporter of the equal rights of the sexes, in relation to the extension of voting rights to women, and he has already espoused these equal rights for many years in his homeland and in Turkey where he was persecuted due to his advanced ideas. Baha Abbas speaks in a compelling manner of the advantages of educating the sexes together; about religious intolerance, which he describes as one of the fundamental evils of human society; about his favourite idea, the creation of an international arbitration court, in which all nations of the earth would send their representatives. The first step to lead to the general peace is disarmament, though at present the international situation is such that one cannot even think of a restriction to armament at any time. Baha Abbas expresses himself in detail about the accusations raised against him by the Ottomans, who claim that he wanted to lay the foundation stone of a new faith; whoever maintains this does not understand his teachings; he has compiled his teachings from all religions and always focuses on securing eternal peace for humanity. His teaching may be summarised in these words: the religion of love.

In the course of the afternoon with Baha Abbas the Director of the Oriental Commercial Academy Dr Ignác Kúnos, Professor Dr Julius Germanus, Reichstag delegate Canon Dr Merzander Geißwein (representing the Budapest Feminist Association) and the Persian consulate secretary Eigel made speeches. The Persian prince Sirdar Urnam Singh, who lives in Budapest, lingered for a long time with the Persian guest. The lectures held on Friday were attended by countless members of the Feminist Association, the Peace Association and the Esperanto Society.³²

Apparently no reporter from the *Pester Lloyd* met 'Abdu'l-Bahá upon His arrival but the journal published on 10 April a general article about Him and the Bahá'í Faith.³³

Talk at the Old Parliament Building

According to Sohrab, the many articles published in the local press during the first days of 'Abdu'l-Bahá's visit in Budapest aroused the interest of the general public in the figure of the Master and on Friday, 11 April, many people visited the Ritz to have a chance to see Him.³⁴

A meeting convened jointly by the Oriental Academy, the Esperanto Society, the Theosophical Society and feminist and pacifist organizations was scheduled for that day at 7 p.m. at the Old Parliament Building, 8 Sándor St.

In the morning 'Abdu'l-Bahá received, among many other visitors, representatives of these organizations, including Dr Germanus. A note in the weekly *Kurir* mentioned that 'this morning, the prophet received various delegations, including the feminists, the students of the Oriental Academy and the Theosophical Society. All of them were delighted by the suggestive personality of the patriarch.'³⁵ The *Világ* similarly reported that 'this morning, a delegation of ten members of the Oriental Academy paid a visit of respect to the prophet Abdul Baha. In answer to a welcoming speech in Turkish, the prophet expressed his pleasure that in Budapest he has been able to know an institution which has set as its prime aim the fostering of relations between East and West.'³⁶

Some eight hundred people attended the event to listen to 'Abdu'l-Bahá. In the days before the meeting announcements were published in *Egyetértés*,³⁷ *Pesti Napló*³⁸ and *Pesti Tükor*.³⁹

When 'Abdu'l-Bahá entered the parliament hall the whole audience rose spontaneously to greet Him. In his role as president of the Hungarian Peace Society, the prelate Sandor Gieswein opened the meeting, welcoming the Master in glowing terms. 'Abdu'l-Bahá, who had to be interpreted by two translators, Sohrab and Dr Germanus, spoke on international peace, the equality of women and men and the need for an international language. His address was very well received by the audience and when the meeting was over many people approached the platform to see Him. Afterwards He received in a private room some of the people who wanted to express their gratitude for His talk.[40]

Several journals carried accounts of this meeting. *Budapest*, with a circulation of 45,000 copies, reported:

> Abdul Beha, this mystic evangelist of the 20th century, got here from the faraway treasure-rich Persia. He does not claim himself to be God's prophet, but still appears to follow the path of Jesus. He is a prophet of this world, which is enlightened although rotten in its morals. He is not riding on a donkey to preach the words of God, but rushes along on the Orient Express from one country to the other and rallies his believers from among the millions converting them to behaism, which means godly eternal love.
>
> No doubt, however, Abdul Beha is the child of the modern age and this is manifest in his teachings among other things. While voicing the sacred words of God, he often refers to modern ideals as well. In addition to eternal love and happiness, he wholeheartedly is a propagandist of the cause of world peace and, with more enthusiasm than even the suffragettes, he demands the right for women to vote and equality between men and women.
>
> The noble and unselfish work of this Persian sage is worthy of respect and deserves the great sympathy by which he has been welcomed on his world tour . . .
>
> The public who came to hear the prophet Abdul Beha filled to capacity the large hall of the Old Parliament. He has come to this country, fittingly called 'the country of hatred', to teach people to love each other. There was an unusually great interest in this aged and respectful apostle of peace, who was led into the auditorium by the papal prelate Sándor Giesswein and who was received by a huge applause from the public. Giesswein affectionately greeted this sage of the Orient, who, as he put it, is touring the world in the name of sacred idealism, holding high the olive branch of peace. He came to us to win followers to his sacred and noble ideals. Then, through an interpreter, he asked Abdul Beha to deliver his lecture which was translated into Hungarian by Professor Dr Gyula Germanus of the Oriental Academy.

Abdul Beha first expressed his thanks for the great respect extended to him by the people of Budapest and then he said he was grateful to God that he had found such a high grade of ideals in the West. He expressed his strong conviction that this century will mark the advent of equality and fraternity and that the hostility that has caused the decay of peoples would come to an end. There are two powers in man, he went on, the intellectual and the beastly powers and until now it has always been the beastly one which prevailed. World wars originate from the beastly instincts of man and these helped the spread of barbarism, wildness and crime in the world. So man should not despise animals just because they wish to tear each other apart, for that comes from the very nature of animals. If wolves would not tear lambs apart, they would starve to death, so beasts cannot be blamed for their violence and bloodlust. And still, man does not give mercy to wolves when he catches them, but kills them mercilessly, although the teeth of the wolves are shaped in a way that they are fit only for eating live animals and not plants. All these prove that man is more bloodthirsty than wolves, because man kills deliberately. And while the beasts kill one or two of their fellow creatures a day, in order to quench their hunger, man, created in the image of God, may well kill 100 men a day while at war. Ever since the beginning of the world, hostilities among men have always been great. Thousands of civilized towns were destroyed, whole countries were annihilated, but mankind has gained nothing. Wars have been going on for six thousand years among men and it is now time for general world peace to replace wars. Until now, people have destined the fruit of their tireless labour largely to military purposes, while in a state of world peace all the nations could take their rest and can work, peacefully, for noble aims.

The scholar said: God can find joy only if there is peace and therefore we do please God if we promote world peace. A means of achieving general peace is the creation of a world language, so that everybody could understand each other. If everyone would speak one and the same language then misunderstandings and discords will fade away . . . He expressed his confidence that the future will bring a uniform language which will link East and West. He said he was pleased to see that there was already such a language, the

Esperanto, and if that would spread all over the world, then it will bring general affection and friendship.

Then he spoke with great affection about women and praised them as the enthusiastic protectors of love and faith. Amidst great applause, he stated that in every country women have matured to enjoy equal voting rights with men. He said that if women would be granted the right of voting then there will be no more wars in the world. A tender mother, were this decision to depend on her, wouldn't allow her son to go and be slaughtered on the battleground. The mother, whose most beautiful being is her son, will prevent him from dying on the battlefield.

Equality between men and women is a prerequisite and promoter of general peace; until it is achieved the world would remain imperfect. The world consists of two parts, the sage argued; the worlds of women and men are bound to unite sooner or later in order to fulfil their common devotion. This world is like a bird; it has two wings, the man and the woman, but now the wings are unbalanced and thus it cannot soar towards love and happiness. The world cannot progress until man and woman become equal. Man's first educator is the woman, so if mothers are left in ignorance and oppression, their children cannot be perfect either. So, if we wish to live in a perfect world, we have to make women perfect and have to give them the right to vote.

He then talked about the horrors of the war in the Balkans and spoke with regret on the massacre of the population of those vast and fertile lands, on the destruction of so many towns and the annihilation of so much wealth. One hundred thousand people killed another one hundred thousand, and thousands of mothers and widows are mourning their children and husbands. Mankind would surely have stood up if animals would have carried out such cruelties. Animals have never organized armies in order to murder each other, and it is only man, the so-called superior being, who can murder without mercy.

This globe, he said, concluding his interesting lecture, is a single piece of land and thus the human race has to be one family, too. All the religions in the world have one basis, and this is love. Let us be religious, let us love each other and follow the words of God. Let us struggle for the good and against war in order to find happiness. The audience received the interesting lecture with enormous applause, after which Sándor Giesswein expressed his thanks to Abdul Beha, who blessed Hungary and wished happiness to the people of the capital.

S.H.[41]

Other newspapers published similar accounts. *Az Ujság* ('The Gazette'), a liberal journal with a circulation of 58,000 copies, also published a detailed report. *Világ* published a summary of the talk which, besides the information published in other journals, quoted some of 'Abdu'l-Bahá's comments on the subject of an international language: 'The example of the Arabs shows how people speaking different languages, Egyptian, Assyrian, Syrian, Chaldean, could merge into one nation.' The article also mentioned that the Master 'expressed his desire that Hungary should become the land from where the brotherhood and affection embracing all mankind should start out and fill the whole world'.[42]

The conservative and nationalist *Budapesti Hírlap*, with a circulation of 65,000 copies, published a positive account of the talk, which repeated most of the information published in other journals. Referring to the Bahá'í Faith as the 'the most significant modern ethic movement of the Orient', the journal quoted 'Abdu'l-Bahá as stating that 'attraction towards each other is a dominating law in the universe and also in nature' and that 'Europe is a huge arsenal and only a spark is enough to explode this tremendous treasury of cultural relics', a statement that, as shown earlier, He repeated several times during His travels in Egypt, North America and Europe. 'What would happen if mankind would try, at least for a century, to live in peace?' 'Abdu'l-Bahá is reported as having said, 'Should peace turn out to be harmful for the development of mankind, we could still go back to war.' The article concluded by stating that the 'lecture was received by the audience, who were mainly women, with great acknowledgement and Sandor Giesswein spoke warmly when he thanked Abdul Beha for his words.'[43]

The account in the *Neues Pester Journal* (Budapest) reported that 'the lecture, translated into English and Hungarian, was received with great applause'.[44]

Another German journal, the *Pester Lloyd*, which at the time had a circulation of 15,000 copies, reported:

It certainly took a while before a Persian sentence of Abdul Baha was translated into a Hungarian round of applause, because it had to be first translated by his secretary Mirza Ahmad Sohrab into English and then from English into the Hungarian. At the first point the pomegranate of the East still arrived tolerably fresh: during the second brief stretch it rather suffered from a loss in flavour, and the words were delivered in a rather flat way. The beautiful parallelisms, the luminous power of the imagery, the intimacy of the expression were there, and yet the remaining logical veins were too dry and transparent to compensate for the lost sensuous fullness. Therefore, all that remained to us was the grand head of the prophet's son, flowing with white hair, his otherworldly and changeable eyes that glimmered in foreign fires, his splendid oriental mien and manner of moving, his restless murmuring lips, his strange and mysterious voice that already speaks to the heart without being deciphered, his handshake, full of infinite character, warm and firm. He began with Adam and Eve, speaking of the animal and spiritual aspects of Man and the world, in order to flow with surprising swiftness to the trinity of Pacifism, Esperanto and Feminism. For six thousand years we have waged war; little good has come of it: let us then try a century of peace! Even if nothing comes of it, at least we always have time to return to the old barbarisms. Regarding Feminism, he made a poetic argument to those gathered: humanity is a bird and man and woman are its two wings; how could these pinions carry the bird to the spheres of heaven if one were lame or even simply weaker that the other? On this basis the Persian demanded voting rights for women, and resounding applause roared at him. Prelate Gießwein, who also welcomed him, thanked him for his remarkable congress with the various isms that span East and West in the name of human solidarity. Finally, we also saw Court Counsellor Professor Ignác Goldziher at the lectern, who must have been the most authoritative individual to judge the origins and the importance of the teachings recited.[45]

On 27 April the fortnightly *Erdekes Ujság* carried the same information published in other journals together with a picture of 'Abdu'l-Bahá accompanied by His secretaries and Mr Stark, and a portrait of Him alone.[46]

La Verda Standardo (Budapest), the official organ of the Hungarian Esperanto Society, mentioned that 'During the talk there was a welcome interruption when Mr Loränd's students from the Horánszky Street Middle School arrived en masse.'⁴⁷

In London, *The Christian Commonwealth* mentioned in a report about the celebration of local Bahá'ís of the Feast of Riḍván that 'During the meeting a letter was read from a friend in Budapest stating that Abdul Baha had arrived there on April 8, and has since addressed many gatherings. The public lecture he delivered was presided over by a Roman Catholic priest, president of the Hungarian Peace Society.'⁴⁸

Talk for the Turanian Society

The Turanian Society, also known as Société Asiatique de Budapest, was an institution created in 1910 by scholars and politicians who considered that the origin of the Hungarian people was in Central Asia. It had its own journal, the bi-monthly *Turán* (Budapest), and included in its membership eminent scholars like Germanus, Vámbéry and many other personalities who had met the Master during His sojourn in Budapest.

This society invited 'Abdu'l-Bahá to deliver an address in a special meeting arranged for Him at the emblematic building of the Hungarian National Museum on 14 April, at 6 p. m. Announcements of the meeting were published on the previous days in at least the *Budapesti Hírlap*⁴⁹ and the *Egyetértés*.⁵⁰ These reported that the title of the address was 'Peace among nations and religions' and that entrance was free of charge.

'Abdu'l-Bahá was introduced by Pairet Alajos (1866–1930),⁵¹ founder and vice-president of the Turanian Society, and editor of *Turán*. The Master opened His address by reviewing the history of the Turanian people and then presented some of the Bahá'í teachings. In the course of His talk He insisted again on the need for international peace.⁵² At the conclusion of the address Pairet Alajos expressed his wish that the text of 'Abdu'l-Bahá's talk be published in *Turán* in Hungarian, French and Turkish.⁵³

According to press reports, among the prominent citizens of Budapest who attended the meeting were the orientalist Ignácz Goldzieher (1850–1921),⁵⁴ who on 11 April received 'Abdu'l-Bahá at his home;

the journalist Gyula Pekár (1867–1937);⁵⁵ and the ethnographers Vikár Béla (1859–1945)⁵⁶ and Gyula Mészáros (1883–1957),⁵⁷ among others.

In the following days the local press reported this public talk. The similarities among different articles reveal that this news was probably distributed by agencies or derived from a press release by the Turanian Society. The account in the liberal *Magyar Nemzet* ('Hungarian Nation') is typical:

PEACE AMONG NATIONS AND RELIGIONS
At the invitation of the Turanian Society, Abdul Baha Abbas effendi, leader of the movement known as Bahaism, held a very interesting lecture under the title 'Peace among nations and religions'.

The great hall of the National Museum was filled to capacity by the audience and the public followed the poetic lecture of the Persian scholar and philosopher with great interest and appreciation. He delivered his lecture in Persian. His secretary translated his statements into English sentence by sentence, and the English translation was retranslated into Hungarian by Lipót Stark, director of the Municipal Electricity Company.

The lecture was introduced by Paikert Alajos, Vice-President of the Turanian Society, who paid tribute to the worldwide aims and aspirations of Bahaism and afterwards, amidst the enthusiastic applause of the audience, thanked Abdul Baha for the outstanding lecture.

Present at the occasion were the noted orientalist Ignácz Goldzieher, Gyula Pekár, Béla Vikár, Viktor Hagara, Károly Rónai, Dr Gyula Mészáros, Dr. Abdul Latif, the Turkish imam of Budapest, Sirday Radja, an Indian aristocrat currently staying in Hungary, Omer Feridun, a Turkish-Persian scholar, and a number of noted ladies.⁵⁸

Similar accounts were published in *Az Ujság*⁵⁹ and in *Budapest*.⁶⁰ The *Független Magyarország* ('Independent Hungary') published the following:

Abdul Baha Abbas Effendi, leader of the movement known as Bahaism, gave a very interesting address in the large auditorium of the National Museum under the title 'Peace among nations and religions'. In the course of his presentation he said that in ancient times Turán had been a populous and prosperous area and a centre of learning. This onetime paradise became a desert due to the dissension of the people and by the cruel wars between religions and races which deter permanent progress. Hatred and divisions among nations and religions is the main reason behind the slow progress and frequent setbacks of general culture and welfare.

He said that the Jewish, Christian, Mohammedan and Buddhist religions are basically identical. The Persian sage illustrated this point with several examples and arguments. He praised love, brotherhood and mutual support and condemned the insanity of wars. He repeatedly stated that women should be given equal rights with men, and in this regard he gave a variety of examples from the Jewish, Christian and Mohammedan traditions and from the history of Persia, his native land.

Abdul Baha's words, which evidenced his rhetorical skills and deep philosophy, were delivered in Persian. His Persian secretary translated his master's sentences word by word into English, and these were in turn translated into Hungarian by Lipót Stark, director of the municipal electric company.[61]

A very similar account in the *Pesti Hírlap* added that in 'the course of his presentation, the Persian scholar paid tribute to the worthy and important mission of the Turán Society'.[62] Other periodicals that published the same news in Budapest were the *Pester Lloyd* (Budapest),[63] the weekly *A Polgár* ('The Citizen')[64] and the weekly political and literary review *Ország-Világ* ('Country-World').[65] *Turán*, the organ of the Turánian Society, briefly mentioned the meeting.[66] In Prague, the *Národní Listy* ('National Journal') published this news in Czech.[67] 'Abdu'l-Bahá's talk was also the basis of an editorial published on 20 April 1913 in the religious magazine *Protestáns* (Budapest).[68]

A representative of the short-lived political journal *Pesti Tükör* personally attended the meeting at the National Museum and had a chance to interview the Master after His address, resulting in this article:

WHAT DOES AN ORIENTAL SAGE KNOW ABOUT US?
VISITING ABDUL BAHA ABBAS

As has been already reported, Abdul Baha Abbas, the wealthy Persian gentleman, is visiting our country. He is the founder and chief prophet of the philosophical movement – for it cannot be called a religion but rather perhaps a sect – of Bahaism, which is named after him. Yesterday with the help of an interpreter he gave a new lecture about his ideas and aims. A large number of people were present at his conference which was held at the great hall of the National Museum. When the prophet concluded his address he was cheered by the audience. As a sign of his contentment, he stroked his long, white and beautiful beard three times – this being apparently a custom in the East – and then, with an amiable smile, he retired into an adjoining hall with his attendants. As has been mentioned earlier, Abdul Baha Abbas is a very wealthy man, a grand seigneur who can afford the luxury of travelling with a retinue of six. The prophet conversed with the university professor and distinguished orientalist Goldzieher, and with Abdul Hlatin Effendi, the Turkish imam in Budapest. The conversation was all the more interesting because Hlatin Effendi and Canon Giesswein, who was also present, are both priests of positive religions and therefore can't agree in all respects with the apostle of Bahaism.

We wanted to find out how much the Oriental sage knew about us Hungarians. Dr Gyula Germanus, the learned professor of the Oriental Academy, was kind enough to introduce us and also to serve as an interpreter. Thus, we were able to naturally converse with him on Hungarian matters. To our surprise, Abdul Baha Abbas began to talk about the origin of the Hungarians, he called us Eastern relatives and, contrary to the supporters of the Finno-Ugrian theory, he believes Hungarians to be of Turkish-Tatar origin.

To the question as to whether any Hungarians follow his teachings, the prophet once again gave an unexpected answer via the interpreter. He said that many Hungarians who had to leave this country in 1849 emigrated to Persia, where they joined the followers of his – the prophet's – father: they settled down in Persia and their descendants are ardent followers of Bahaism to this day.

How does Your Excellency like Budapest? – I asked the prophet in the hope of receiving again an unusual answer, and so it was:

People are good – said the sage – life is wonderful and the sun is shining warmly. I enjoy being here, I think I shall spend a few more days here. I would like to visit the tomb of Gül Baba, I have heard that he was a good man, fond of roses. This was a long time ago, it's true. Today, people are more wicked than they used to be; right now by the Turkish border they are killing each other.

The Turks were once a mighty people. This city belonged to them and so did the castle on the other side where the prophet's flag fluttered from its pinnacles.

That which is seized by the sword shall perish by it – this was the sage's Koran-like remark. It was not very appropriate, however, since neither Pest, nor Buda have yet perished and much less by the sword.

Later, the prophet also spoke about how Hungarians – being an Oriental people acclimated to the West – were best suited for the reception and the spread of Bahaism. Being a polite and chivalrous nation, I do not doubt of the Persian sage's words. In my mind I could picture János Csernoch as a leading prophet of Bahaism, giving away the possessions of the primate among the poor. Then suddenly the Persian surprised with some strange questions.

– It is true that after the death of the present king, the Hungarians will break away from Austria?

I was not quite sure what to reply and said that these things do not come about so quickly and precisely. Afraid of the elder gentleman's further difficult questions I hurriedly concluded the conversation.[69]

According to Sohrab, the day after 'Abdu'l-Bahá's talk for the Turánian Society, He was interviewed by a reporter from *Az Est* (Budapest).[70]

Visit to Vienna

'Abdu'l-Bahá left Budapest on 18 April and proceeded to Vienna where He gave several public addresses and met a large number of visitors. Publicity in the press was, however, avoided. One reference to 'Abdu'l-Bahá's visit to the city appeared in an Esperanto journal (see chapter 33) and few days after His departure a local journal published a general article about Him and the Bahá'í teachings.[71] Sohrab mentions, however, that on 22 April 'Abdu'l-Bahá granted an interview to a representative of *Die Zeit* (Vienna).[72] Interestingly, Sohrab also mentions that when the Master visited the Turkish Ambassador in Vienna, He brought for the diplomat copies of the articles published in the

Asiatic Quarterly Review, *Christian Commonwealth*, *Woking Mirror*, and *The Palo Altan*.[73]

Return to Germany

'Abdu'l-Bahá returned to Stuttgart on 24 April and on this second visit to Germany the Master allowed some contact with the press.

Just a few days before His arrival, one evangelical journal, the *Evangelisches Gemeineblatt für Stuttgart*, published an article warning its readers against 'Abdu'l-Bahá:

> In the last few weeks, this local association has seen its prophet, the Persian Abdul Baha, in its midst, and the throng attending his gatherings was not inconsiderable.
>
> Wherein does the appeal of this new movement lie? No doubt to some extent in the mysterious aura which surrounds it. Its writings, which mostly have strange titles, are not published in the book trade, instead they go from hand to hand, circulated in particular by women; its gatherings are not listed in the newspaper, but filled by the personal promotional work of the followers; even the name with the exotic oriental sound adds to its prestige. Certainly, everything mysterious always has a particular appeal and in cases where some of our contemporaries have a strong need for religious delicacies, they assimilate and adopt anything that resembles religion.
>
> A second reason lies perhaps in the rich impact of Christian words and ideas. Bahai not only uses and interprets the words of Jesus, it also speaks of Jesus as the 'Son of God' and claims that the end is nigh, and that he is therefore a part of the true, perhaps the better character of the Christian faith. In reality, however, its position towards the Bible and towards Christianity is a thoroughly hostile one and therefore all the more dangerous because it completely breaks down the biblical truths under the guise of confirming them and communicates these truths by reinterpreting them to the contrary.
>
> Whoever would like to learn more about Bahá'í should start with the brochure published in 1912 by Röttger (Kassel) 'The New Religion of the False Christ' suggested by Richard Schäfer (price 60 S).[74]

The day after His arrival in Stuttgart, 'Abdu'l-Bahá delivered an address in one of the city's museums. The local press announced the meeting.⁷⁵ Owing to illness, however, 'Abdu'l-Bahá was unable to attend and asked a local Bahá'í to speak in His place. When His secretaries reached the museum and saw that more than fifteen hundred people had gathered to listen to Him, they returned hastily to 'Abdu'l-Bahá's hotel and informed Him of the circumstance. Despite His fatigue, 'Abdu'l-Bahá went to the meeting and gave the talk.⁷⁶ A reporter with a local journal, the liberal *Stuttgarter Neues Tagblatt*, published the following account the next day:

> A dignified old man with a long white beard, a high brow and the sharply cut noble eyes of a distinguished aristocratic Oriental, as one might think an Abraham or – one must forgive the configuration – a Hafiz – thus sat Abdul Baha yesterday evening in a fauteuil in the Bürgermuseum, bowed by the burden of his 70 years and the strains of a long journey, giving a brief speech to the countless listeners. The speech was translated into German via an interpreter. It had at first been doubtful whether he could appear in person, which is why one of his followers in Stuttgart spoke of the 'master' and his goals, until he himself came unexpectedly.
>
> Abdul Baha, a Persian, actually Abbas Effendi by name, is the son of Bahá'u'lláh, who he himself and his followers in Persia believe to be the 'returned' Christ. Unfortunately, he also died before the kingdom of his expectations had materialized, as did some of his predecessors in this rapture, and the son now has the task of spreading the teachings of the father. He did so yesterday in Stuttgart, in an overtly friendly form, although the two-fold translation, first into English and then into German, naturally hindered an immediate relationship between the speaker and the listener. He spoke of peace for the people, of the solidarity of all men, of the curse and the anti-godliness of war and was kind enough to give to the 'highly cultivated' Germany the hope that 'the light of peace' would spread from here. There were succinct sentences in Oriental stylization, filled by the human spirit of an experienced, warm-hearted Magi from the Orient.
>
> However, whether he is certain to find many followers among the civilized people of Western Europe is questionable. Certainly, the

Bahai movement has spread widely, even in Europe, the crystallization points being primarily health resorts and elegant salons. This is understandable, because everything exotic has a certain appeal. If one, however, contemplates the principles that were impressed on the visitors yesterday as 'the goals of the Bahai religion', one must then question whether the appeal can last. These sentences describe Bahai expressly as a 'religion', although its followers would rather only speak of a 'movement' which has the sole purpose of uniting the races and peoples and precipitating world peace. The principles show that the whole movement deals with a reform of Mohamadanism, in which the idealistic but ahistorical spirit of the age of enlightenment and protestant ethics is established. It is pleasing that there is a promising seed here for the renewal of Islam – but it remains to be seen what kind of mission these teachings should have in the Occident, whose cultural foundations for the large part already contain these 'new goals'. It is characteristic even in Europe that one clearly promotes the idea of harmony among people and world peace. Perhaps the impact of this mission then lies in the fact that these endeavors will strengthen those which existed in the European cultural world even before the appearance of Bahai. And then one may welcome the European journey of Abdul Baha, even if in thought one might reject him as a bringer of a higher religion.[77]

The conservative *Staatsanzeiger für Württemberg* (Württemberg State Gazette) published in its supplement of 30 April a further account of the meeting, in which some antipathy towards the Baháʾí Faith can be detected:

On Friday, in the hall of the Bürgermusem, the Bahai movement, which was introduced here two years ago from Persia via London, held a canvassing meeting. The present prophet of this school of thought, a 70 year old man called Abdul Baha (meaning Servant of the Glory) – the third prophet after the founder 'Báb' who appeared in 1844 – travelled to the gathering. After the opening discussions by the leader of the Stuttgart Association, in which Bahai was distinguished as an international peace movement, building itself up upon a blurred mixture of religions, the old man, who was clearly affected by the long journey, made his speech. To bring peace and friendship, so he remarked, was the duty of our enlightened century; in particular, an educated people such as the Germans should recognize this calling, which is both godly and human. National and religious differences are bridged by Bahai, and our century of scholarly education will also become the radiant age of peace. In spite of the necessary interpreting, the naïve warm-heartedness of the apostle of peace was evident; certainly, there had been no expression whatsoever of the real foundation for his delusions, as if his teachings, which even employed words used by Jesus, would bring something new and have practical meaning among Christian people. The considerable number of visitors was astounding; some were drawn there out of curiosity. However, it would be regrettable if superficial religious knowledge and flippancy were to lose the standard for substantive truths to such an extent that they would be supplanted by the worn-out expressions of fraternalism and humanity as offered in Bahá'í.[78]

Outside Germany, *The Christian Commonwealth* reported the following about 'Abdu'l-Bahá's two visits to Stuttgart:

ABDUL BAHA IN GERMANY.
With the consent of Abdul Baha Abbas a correspondent in Stuttgart sends us news of his recent visit to the Bahais of the Fatherland. Wherever he goes the holiness, the simplicity, that breathes from the personality of this great leader of men produces a deep impression, and lifts men nearer to God. 'The memory of these heavenly hours will linger in the souls of the friends throughout eternity,' writes our correspondent.

Abdul Baha, accompanied by his interpreter, Mirza Ahmad, and other members of his suite, reached Stuttgart Tuesday, April 1, and a week of public and private gatherings ensued. Wednesday, at the residence of Herr Herrigel, he received and talked with a large number of friends. Thursday he addressed a large audience at the Burger Museum. The hall could have been filled twice over; believers and friends came from far and near. Friday he met a company of children with their parents at Esslingen, graciously accepting from every child a tribute of flowers, and handing to each child a box of chocolates. At the close, waving his hand, the children gathered about him, and he engaged in prayer for them and their parents. Saturday, in view of his untiring efforts to bring about international peace, religion and language, Abdul Baha was welcomed by the Esperanto Club as a pioneer of the new age. April 8 Abdul Baha and his following left for Budapest. They also visited Vienna for a week, returning to Stuttgart April 24, en route for Paris. At a Unity meeting, at which tea was served, Abdul Baha bade farewell to the Bahais of Stuttgart, 'in his courtly Eastern fashion', leaving about 'a heavenly atmosphere', this concluding the return visit. He returned to Paris May 1.[79]

A few weeks later the same journal published the following comments made by 'Abdu'l-Bahá in Stuttgart:

I came from a distant land. I have travelled twenty thousand miles until I came to you in Stuttgart. Forty years I was a prisoner. I was young when I was put into prison, and my hair was white when the prison doors opened. After all these long years of the sufferings of prison life I willingly took upon myself all the hardships of a long journey. Now I am here in order to be united with you, in order to meet you. My purpose is that perchance you may illumine the world of humanity; that all men may unite in perfect love and friendship; that religious prejudices, national prejudices, race distinctions, all may be completely abandoned. The religions of to-day consist of dogmas. Because these dogmas differ from each other discord and even hatred is manifest. Religion must be the basis of all good fellowship. Think of the turmoil that to-day exists in the Balkans; how much blood is shed; how many thousands of mothers have lost their sons, how many children have become orphans, and how many buildings, villages, and cities have been destroyed! The Balkan States have become a volcano. All this ruin originates from the prejudices created by the different dogmas, called forth by superstitions and race prejudices.

The essence of the religion of God is love, and the Holy Books bear testimony to that, for the essence of the religion of God is the light of the world of humanity; but mankind to-day has forgotten what constitutes true religion.[80]

The day after His arrival in Stuttgart, 'Abdu'l-Bahá delivered an address in one of the city's museums. The local press announced the meeting.[75] Owing to illness, however, 'Abdu'l-Bahá was unable to attend and asked a local Bahá'í to speak in His place. When His secretaries reached the museum and saw that more than fifteen hundred people had gathered to listen to Him, they returned hastily to 'Abdu'l-Bahá's hotel and informed Him of the circumstance. Despite His fatigue, 'Abdu'l-Bahá went to the meeting and gave the talk.[76] A reporter with a local journal, the liberal *Stuttgarter Neues Tagblatt*, published the following account the next day:

> A dignified old man with a long white beard, a high brow and the sharply cut noble eyes of a distinguished aristocratic Oriental, as one might think an Abraham or – one must forgive the configuration – a Hafiz – thus sat Abdul Baha yesterday evening in a fauteuil in the Bürgermuseum, bowed by the burden of his 70 years and the strains of a long journey, giving a brief speech to the countless listeners. The speech was translated into German via an interpreter. It had at first been doubtful whether he could appear in person, which is why one of his followers in Stuttgart spoke of the 'master' and his goals, until he himself came unexpectedly.
>
> Abdul Baha, a Persian, actually Abbas Effendi by name, is the son of Bahá'u'lláh, who he himself and his followers in Persia believe to be the 'returned' Christ. Unfortunately, he also died before the kingdom of his expectations had materialized, as did some of his predecessors in this rapture, and the son now has the task of spreading the teachings of the father. He did so yesterday in Stuttgart, in an overtly friendly form, although the two-fold translation, first into English and then into German, naturally hindered an immediate relationship between the speaker and the listener. He spoke of peace for the people, of the solidarity of all men, of the curse and the anti-godliness of war and was kind enough to give to the 'highly cultivated' Germany the hope that 'the light of peace' would spread from here. There were succinct sentences in Oriental stylization, filled by the human spirit of an experienced, warm-hearted Magi from the Orient.
>
> However, whether he is certain to find many followers among the civilized people of Western Europe is questionable. Certainly, the

Bahai movement has spread widely, even in Europe, the crystallization points being primarily health resorts and elegant salons. This is understandable, because everything exotic has a certain appeal. If one, however, contemplates the principles that were impressed on the visitors yesterday as 'the goals of the Bahai religion', one must then question whether the appeal can last. These sentences describe Bahai expressly as a 'religion', although its followers would rather only speak of a 'movement' which has the sole purpose of uniting the races and peoples and precipitating world peace. The principles show that the whole movement deals with a reform of Mohamadanism, in which the idealistic but ahistorical spirit of the age of enlightenment and protestant ethics is established. It is pleasing that there is a promising seed here for the renewal of Islam – but it remains to be seen what kind of mission these teachings should have in the Occident, whose cultural foundations for the large part already contain these 'new goals'. It is characteristic even in Europe that one clearly promotes the idea of harmony among people and world peace. Perhaps the impact of this mission then lies in the fact that these endeavors will strengthen those which existed in the European cultural world even before the appearance of Bahai. And then one may welcome the European journey of Abdul Baha, even if in thought one might reject him as a bringer of a higher religion.[77]

The conservative *Staatsanzeiger für Württemberg* (Württemberg State Gazette) published in its supplement of 30 April a further account of the meeting, in which some antipathy towards the Bahá'í Faith can be detected:

On Friday, in the hall of the Bürgermusem, the Bahai movement, which was introduced here two years ago from Persia via London, held a canvassing meeting. The present prophet of this school of thought, a 70 year old man called Abdul Baha (meaning Servant of the Glory) – the third prophet after the founder 'Báb' who appeared in 1844 – travelled to the gathering. After the opening discussions by the leader of the Stuttgart Association, in which Bahai was distinguished as an international peace movement, building itself up upon a blurred mixture of religions, the old man, who was clearly affected by the long journey, made his speech. To bring peace and friendship, so he remarked, was the duty of our enlightened century; in particular, an educated people such as the Germans should recognize this calling, which is both godly and human. National and religious differences are bridged by Bahai, and our century of scholarly education will also become the radiant age of peace. In spite of the necessary interpreting, the naïve warm-heartedness of the apostle of peace was evident; certainly, there had been no expression whatsoever of the real foundation for his delusions, as if his teachings, which even employed words used by Jesus, would bring something new and have practical meaning among Christian people. The considerable number of visitors was astounding; some were drawn there out of curiosity. However, it would be regrettable if superficial religious knowledge and flippancy were to lose the standard for substantive truths to such an extent that they would be supplanted by the worn-out expressions of fraternalism and humanity as offered in Bahá'í.[78]

Outside Germany, *The Christian Commonwealth* reported the following about 'Abdu'l-Bahá's two visits to Stuttgart:

ABDUL BAHA IN GERMANY.
With the consent of Abdul Baha Abbas a correspondent in Stuttgart sends us news of his recent visit to the Bahais of the Fatherland. Wherever he goes the holiness, the simplicity, that breathes from the personality of this great leader of men produces a deep impression, and lifts men nearer to God. 'The memory of these heavenly hours will linger in the souls of the friends throughout eternity,' writes our correspondent.

Abdul Baha, accompanied by his interpreter, Mirza Ahmad, and other members of his suite, reached Stuttgart Tuesday, April 1, and a week of public and private gatherings ensued. Wednesday, at the residence of Herr Herrigel, he received and talked with a large number of friends. Thursday he addressed a large audience at the Burger Museum. The hall could have been filled twice over; believers and friends came from far and near. Friday he met a company of children with their parents at Esslingen, graciously accepting from every child a tribute of flowers, and handing to each child a box of chocolates. At the close, waving his hand, the children gathered about him, and he engaged in prayer for them and their parents. Saturday, in view of his untiring efforts to bring about international peace, religion and language, Abdul Baha was welcomed by the Esperanto Club as a pioneer of the new age. April 8 Abdul Baha and his following left for Budapest. They also visited Vienna for a week, returning to Stuttgart April 24, en route for Paris. At a Unity meeting, at which tea was served, Abdul Baha bade farewell to the Bahais of Stuttgart, 'in his courtly Eastern fashion', leaving about 'a heavenly atmosphere', this concluding the return visit. He returned to Paris May 1.[79]

A few weeks later the same journal published the following comments made by 'Abdu'l-Bahá in Stuttgart:

I came from a distant land. I have travelled twenty thousand miles until I came to you in Stuttgart. Forty years I was a prisoner. I was young when I was put into prison, and my hair was white when the prison doors opened. After all these long years of the sufferings of prison life I willingly took upon myself all the hardships of a long journey. Now I am here in order to be united with you, in order to meet you. My purpose is that perchance you may illumine the world of humanity; that all men may unite in perfect love and friendship; that religious prejudices, national prejudices, race distinctions, all may be completely abandoned. The religions of to-day consist of dogmas. Because these dogmas differ from each other discord and even hatred is manifest. Religion must be the basis of all good fellowship. Think of the turmoil that to-day exists in the Balkans; how much blood is shed; how many thousands of mothers have lost their sons, how many children have become orphans, and how many buildings, villages, and cities have been destroyed! The Balkan States have become a volcano. All this ruin originates from the prejudices created by the different dogmas, called forth by superstitions and race prejudices.

The essence of the religion of God is love, and the Holy Books bear testimony to that, for the essence of the religion of God is the light of the world of humanity; but mankind to-day has forgotten what constitutes true religion.[80]

30

THIRD VISIT TO EGYPT

'Abdu'l-Bahá left Paris on 12 June 1913 and proceeded to Marseille where on the following day He boarded the steamer *Himalaya* bound for Egypt. Four days later, 17 June, 'Abdu'l-Bahá reached Port Said.

The *Egyptian Gazette* gave the news of His arrival on 18 June and wrongly stated that He 'will proceed in a few days to Haifa, where he will join his family'.[1] Soon afterwards a correspondent with the same journal sent the following account, which was published on 27 June 1913:

> ABDUL BAHA IN EGYPT
> WONDERFUL SCENES AT PORT SAID
> EASTERN BAHAIS ASSEMBLED IN FORCE
> (FROM OUR SPECIAL CORRESPONDENT)
> Port Said, June 26
>
> During the past few days Port Said has been the scene of a wonderful gathering of Eastern followers of the new religion of which Abdul Baha is the head. After a long journey through Europe and America, where thousands of new converts have joined this new gospel of fraternity, peace, and interracial unity, he arrived here a few days ago in order to meet a number of Persian, Turkish and Russian adherents, who have come from the most out-of-the-way parts of the world to meet the venerable and beloved head of their faith. Many of these people have been waiting for months past in Syria in order to have the opportunity of greeting Abdul Baha.
>
> His Holiness is staying at a private house, which he has rented for a few months. He is too tired after his long journeying to come to Alexandria or Cairo, and hopes to repose for a short time at Port Said before he goes to Syria, where his presence is much needed owing to the enormous increase in the number of converts.

PRAYER-MEETINGS ON A ROOF

At Port Said the pilgrims have erected a huge tent on the roof of a native hotel and there they gather and sing hymns and praise to God, with touching devotion. Many of them are curiously dressed, in great lambskin hats and long divided skirts with enormous pleats. They are mostly converts to Bahaism from Islam, and Turkey, Persia and the Caucasus district are very fruitful fields for the missionary efforts of this beautiful new creed, which may eventually transform the Near East.

Thousands of believers have signed petitions for Abdul Baha to visit Burmah and India, for Bahaism is taking root among the Hindus and Buddhists.

I have had many talks with their Master at Port Said and find that he is most gratified with the results of his visit to the United States and Europe. In Vienna and Budapest special interest was shown in the tenets of his religion. Among one of his great sympathisers is Baroness von Suttner, the great peace propagandist, who won the Nobel Prize some years ago, the authoress of that celebrated work, 'Die Waffen Nieder'. In Budapest he was especially asked to preside and speak at a public meeting of Orientalists by Professor Germanius.

Abdul Baha is a great advocate of Esperanto and everywhere he is urging better international understandings through the medium of that universal language.[2]

While in Egypt the western press continued to publish articles about 'Abdu'l-Bahá's movements. Thus, for instance, on 6 August *The Christian Commonwealth* published the following report – probably by Thomas Atwood – about 'Abdu'l-Bahá's activities in Egypt:

ABDUL BAHA ABBAS IN EGYPT
(*From a correspondent*)

Friends of the Bahai movement – and who among progressive Christians does not heartily sympathise with the Cause? – will be interested to know that Abdul Baha has recently returned to Egypt after fifteen months' absence, during which he has visited the principal cities of the United States, England, France, Germany, and Austria, cheering and encouraging his many followers in those countries by his presence among them. His arduous work has somewhat told upon him, and after a few days spent at Port Said, where many Persian pilgrims who had been awaiting his arrival and many old friends met him, he proceeded to Ramleh (the pleasant suburb of Alexandria), where he has taken a house for the summer months. It was his original intention to go to his house at Haifa, where his family reside, but in the unsettled state of affairs in Syria he was advised to remain in Egypt for the present, and his family have joined him there.

Many enthusiastic Bahais, both Eastern and Western, are at the present time gathered together in Ramleh. Some of these would do well not to allow their zeal to outrun their discretion. They are too much bent on making converts, whereas the great feature of Bahaism is that it does not aim at being a sect, but the means of joining people of every religious creed in one great band of earnest workers in the cause of Brotherhood and Love. The Master is the first to deprecate attempts at proselytising, especially in this Mohammedan country . . . T.A.[3]

The article continued with a few paragraphs summarizing some of the Bahá'í teachings. The *Egyptian Gazette* reproduced portions of this article and included the following comments:

The Master's arrival at Port Said and his reception there has already been detailed in our columns. The 'Christian Commonwealth', which is the recognised organ of Liberal Christians of all denominations, has from time to time fully reported Abdul Baha's movements in the United States and Europe, and we are indebted to Mirza Ahmad Sohrab, his secretary and interpreter, for many interesting particulars of incidents that took place during the lengthened tour in the United States and Canada. Leaders of religions thought of every type joined in welcoming the Master and from such opposite poles as Roman Catholicism and Unitarianism he received both encouragement and support. The Roman Catholic leader at Montreal, a very conservative body, met him, though not publicly, while on the other hand he attended a monster celebration by the Unitarians at Boston, Mass., where the assembly of 5,000 people, nearly half of them Unitarian Ministers, rose to their feet by one common impulse as he appeared on the platform.

It is the intention of the Bahai leader to visit India in the autumn, where the movement has already made considerable progress. Mrs Besant, another apostle of peace, unity and concord, has been doing a great work in that country, but on different lines – those of Theology. There is ample room, Abdul Baba Abbas claims, in our Indian Empire for both.[4]

From Egypt 'Abdu'l-Bahá also maintained correspondence with the editors of various western journals such as *The Christian Commonwealth* and *Theosophy in Scotland* (see chapter 34). On 3 September *The Christian Commonwealth* carried a Tablet by 'Abdu'l-Bahá especially sent for publication in that journal. The translation was published together with the facsimile of the original Persian:

UNIVERSAL PEACE
BY ABDUL BAHA ABBAS

To the Editor of THE CHRISTIAN COMMONWEALTH, London, England

HE IS GOD!

O thou esteemed and kind friend!

After journeying throughout the United States of America, and the great capitals and metropolis of Europe, I have returned to the East. With the results of this journey I am most pleased and well satisfied – because I met noble people and associated with worthy souls, who are in reality the cause of honour and glory to the world of humanity. They were learned and wise, well informed with the realities of events and the well wishers of the human world, especially the advocates of universal peace.

In these days the world of humanity is afflicted with a chronic disease. It is one of bloodshed, the destruction of the divine edifice, the demolition of cities and villages, the slaughter of the noble youths of the world of humanity, children becoming orphans and women homeless and shelterless. What calamity is greater than this? What crime is more heinous than this? What disease is more dangerous than this? What folly is more direful than this? Consider that in former days there were only religious wars, but now there are racial and political wars fought at staggering expense and sacrifice. A thousand times alas for this ignorance, this bloodthirstiness and ferocity!

I became pleased with and grateful to the societies which are organised in the West for the promotion of universal peace, and with whose presidents, officers, and members I frequently conversed. I hope that the sphere of the activities of these societies may become from day to day enlarged; so that the lights of the higher ideals may illumine all regions, the oneness of the world of humanity be proclaimed in the East and in the West, and the world of humanity may attain to composure and well-being. These revered souls who are the servants of the world of humanity and the promoters of the cause of universal peace shall ere long shine like brilliant stars from the horizon of mankind, flooding the regions with their glorious lights.

In the past century freedom was proclaimed, and the foundation of liberty was laid in all the western countries. Praise be to God that the sun of justice shone forth and the darkness of despotism and tyranny disappeared.

Now in this radiant century in which the world of humanity is being matured it is assured that the flag of universal peace shall become unfurled and shall wave over all regions of the globe. This is the most great principle of Baha Allah, for the promotion of which all the Bahais are ready to sacrifice their possessions and their lives.

Notwithstanding my bodily weakness and infirmity, I have travelled East and West for the last three years. In every temple I cried out and before every audience I raised my voice for the enlistment of their sympathy. I declared the evils of war, and explained the benefits of universal peace. I elucidated the causes which lead to the honour and glory of the world of humanity, and told them of the ferocity and bloodthirstiness of the animal kingdom. I showed the defects of the world of nature and made an expedition of the means whereby the illumination of the world of humanity is fully realised. I unfolded and caused the appearance of the foundation of the divine religions, and proclaimed the teachings of His Holiness Baha'o'llah. I demonstrated the existence of God by irrefutable, rational proofs, and proved the validity of all the prophets of God.

I gave utterance to my inmost conviction that the reality of the religion of God is the cause of the life of the world of humanity; it is divine civilization and pure enlightenment.

By the explanation of all these principles my object has been no other than the promotion of universal peace. Praise be to God that I found hearing ears, observed seeing eyes, and discovered informed hearts. Therefore, I am well pleased with this journey.

But on the other hand the well-wishers of the world of humanity and the advocates of universal peace must make an extraordinary forward movement, organise important international congresses, and invite as delegates most progressive and influential souls from all parts of the world; so that through their wise counsels and deliberations this ideal of universal peace may leap out of the world of words into the arena of actuality and practical demonstration. It is true that this question is of paramount importance, and will not be realised easily. However, we must take hold of every means until the desired result is obtained.

Fifty years ago whosoever talked about universal peace was not only ridiculed but called a visionary and utopian. Now praise be to God that at this time it has assumed such importance that everyone acknowledges that this question of universal peace is the light and spirit of this age. But they state that the pathway to this much desired goal is obstructed by a number of not clearly defined stumbling-blocks, which, however, can be removed by intelligently and persistently educating public opinion.

I hope the noble leaders of the world of humanity who are the divine bestowals amongst the people, and the means of pacification amongst the nations, will arise with the utmost of effort and whole hearted resolution to extinguish this world-raging conflagration, especially now that the blood of innocent people is freely shed in the Balkan States, the lamentations and moaning of the orphans are reaching to the very gate of heaven, and the disconsolate cries and harrowing agonies of the mothers penetrate our souls with the irresistible force of human tragedy. Thus through the endeavours of these guardians of the rights of mankind the world of creation may enjoy the repose of conciliation, the banner of universal peace be unfurled, the tabernacle of the oneness of the world of humanity be pitched, all mankind be gathered under its protecting shade, and the shining star of the eternal felicity and happiness of the world of humanity may dawn with the utmost of brilliancy from the horizon of international comity, and the luminous orb of the spiritual brotherhood of all races and tongues may illumine that united gathering of humanity with the ineffable lights of God throughout countless ages and cycles.

(Signed) ABDUL BAHA ABBAS

Translated by Mirza Ahmad Sohrab, 19 July 1913, Port Said, Egypt[5]

Letter from Arminius Vámbéry

During 'Abdu'l-Bahá's visit to Budapest He met the renowned orientalist Arminius Vámbéry (1832–1913) on at least two occasions. Vámbéry was one of the most respected scholars in his main field, turcology, and also a well-known international author. One of his best-known works, *Travels in Central Asia* (1865), was an interesting account of his trip across Turkey, Central Asia and Persia, which was published in German, French, English and Spanish, among other languages, and briefly mentioned the Bábís in connection with the events in Shaykh Ṭabarsí. Besides this work, he also published several dictionaries as well as scholarly works.

The first private meeting between 'Abdu'l-Bahá and Vámbéry took place on 11 April 1913, when 'Abdu'l-Bahá visited the professor at his home for more than an hour and the two conversed in Turkish and Persian.[6] A second meeting of two hours was held on 14 April during the course of which Vámbéry expressed his desire to write a series of articles about the Bahá'í Faith.[7]

Once in Egypt, 'Abdu'l-Bahá wrote to Vámbéry and also sent him a carpet as a present. The old scholar, who died just a few months later on 15 September, replied in Persian to the Master with his now famous letter of appreciation.

A translation into English of this letter was prepared by Ahmad Sohrab and submitted by Jean Stannard to the *Egyptian Gazette* which published it on 24 September 1913. A copy was also sent to the *International Psychic Gazette* which published the letter in its September issue:

THE APOSTLE OF PEACE

In view of the death of that distinguished scholar and Orientalist, Arminius Vambery, I feel that the subjoined letter sent only a few weeks before his death to Abdul Baha (Abbas Effendi) becomes a historic document of world-wide interest and importance. This hitherto unpublished letter I am happily permitted to make public. Written in Persian, its exquisite diction and courtesy reveal how thoroughly this wonderful scholar inherently understood the heart of the religious East, and how fully he sympathised with all truly noble aims.

To many, Vambery was perhaps known only as a brilliant and indefatigable anthropologist and researcher into hidden origins; to others who know the infinite complexities of life and thought in the near East, he means a great deal more. His strenuously active life comprised more knowledge based on experience than is generally to be found in the career of three ordinary diplomats. His linguistic attainments were great, for he spoke and wrote over fifteen languages. Naturally his judgement on men and things was remarkable for its penetrative accuracy and shrewdness. For four years he worked as special adviser to Sultan Abdul Hamid. A particularly hard youth, fought in such bewildering surroundings as Turkey, Persia, and the Balkans, proved that he possessed unequalled opportunity for observation and study.

Many biographical sketches have appeared from time to time in European reviews, and now many more will surely be presented, but it may be doubted whether any will reveal the inner soul and high aspirations of this scholar at a ripe old age, as does the contents of the following communication. We seem to feel the glow of a flame that flashed out from one who had always searched to meet a great truth, and a supreme conviction that this glad experience had finally been accorded him, and that he was satisfied.

The meeting between Abdul Baha and Vambery took place in Buda Pesth last April, where the great Bahai Master met with an ovation from the scholars, Orientalists and social reformers. On the return of Abdul Baha to Egypt, he wrote to Vambery sending him a gift, and the following letter was the reply.

For the information of those who are unfamiliar with Eastern expressions we may add that the style is, in Islam, adopted only by the religiously learned and only to a supremely great teacher or leader.

'I forward this humble petition to the sanctified and holy

presence of Abdul Baha Abbas, who is the centre of knowledge, famous throughout the world, and loved by all mankind. O, thou noble friend, who art conferring guidance upon humanity, may my life be a ransom to thee!

'The loving epistle which you have condescended to write to this servant, and the rug which you have forwarded, came safely to hand. The time of the meeting with your Excellency, and the memory of the benediction of your presence, recurred to the memory of this servant, and I am longing for the time when I shall meet you again. Although I have travelled through many countries and cities of Islam, yet have I never met so lofty a character and so exalted a personage as your Excellency, and can bear witness that it is not possible to find such another. On this account, I am hoping that the ideals and accomplishments of your Excellency may be crowned with success and yield results under all conditions; because behind these ideals and deeds I easily discern the eternal welfare and prosperity of the world of humanity.

'This servant in order to gain first-hand information and experience, entered into the ranks of various religions, that is, outwardly, I became a Jew, Christian, Mohammedan and Zoroastrian. I discovered that the devotees of these various religions do nothing else but hate and anathematise each other, that all their religions have become the instruments of tyranny and oppression in the hands of rulers and governors, and that they are the causes of the destruction of the world of humanity.

'Considering those evil results, every person is forced by necessity to enlist himself on the side of your Excellency, and accept with joy the prospect of a basis of the religion of God, which is being founded through your efforts.

'I have seen the father of your Excellency from afar. I have realised the self-sacrifice and noble courage of his son, and I am lost in admiration.

'For the principles and aims of your Excellency, I express the utmost respect and devotion, and if God, the Most High, confers long life, I will be able to serve you under all conditions. I pray and supplicate this from the depths of my heart.

Your servant,
    VAMBERY[8]

Other Articles

Lua Getsinger was among the American Bahá'ís who visited 'Abdu'l-Bahá on His return to Egypt. She arrived in Port Said on 23 July. In the course of her meetings with the Master He asked her to travel to India to teach the Bahá'í Faith. Some of the instructions and encouraging words she received from 'Abdu'l-Bahá were written down by Ahmad Sohrab and published afterwards in the Bahá'í bulletin *Star of the West*.[9] The text was also reproduced in England in the *International Psychic Gazette*.[10]

As described in earlier chapters, during the course of His travels 'Abdu'l-Bahá met with several members of the New Thought Movement and also addressed meetings arranged by the New Thought organizations both in America and England. Some of their publications had published accounts on the Bahá'í Faith long before 'Abdu'l-Bahá's western travels.[11]

One of the leading figures in the New Thought movement in America was Annie Rix Militz (1856–1924). She became a member of Christian Science in 1891 and afterwards opened a sanctuary in Alameda and several Homes of Truth across California, in which New Thought practices and theories were taught. In 1911 she founded the magazine *Master Mind* and in 1913 she selected 50 people, including 'Abdu'l-Bahá, to be 'Honorable Subscribers' of the periodical. 'Abdu'l-Bahá's response to her invitation was published in the magazine on December 1913:

> *From Ramleh, Egypt, comes a letter in response to an offer to include that gracious prophet, Abdul Baha Abbas, in our Fifty Honorable Subscribers, and it gives me joy to share it with you, my readers. It is written in Persian, and a translation, kindly supplied by M. Ahmad Sohrab, accompanies it:*

To the Editor, The Master Mind
Mrs. Annie Rix Militz, Los Angeles, Calif.

He is God!
   O, thou respected soul!
   Thy letter was received. Likewise a copy of your blessed

Magazine. Praise be to God that thou art confirmed in this philanthropic ideal and thy aim is service to the world of humanity.

I hope that thou will become assisted in this undertaking and that all the articles published in its columns may be in conformity with science and reason. For whatever agrees with reason and science is acceptable, irrefutable, and a reality which cannot be controverted.

Likewise I supplicate towards the Kingdom of Abha and beg for thee complete success, the sublimity of the Kingdom, the heavenly illumination and the freedom of consciousness.

Because you have selected me one of your honorable subscribers I am very thankful and grateful. Upon thee be greetings and praise!
(Signed) ABDUL BAHA ABBAS,
Translated by M. Ahmad Sohrab, 12 September 1913, Ramleh, Egypt

May all the blessings with which I am blessed rest upon you, my beloved Readers.

Ever yours for the Whole Truth,
ANNIE RIX MILITZ[12]

In ensuing issues of *Master Mind*, Annie R. Militz included quotations from the writings of 'Abdu'l-Bahá.[13]

PART II

31

GENDER EQUALITY AND THE SUFFRAGE MOVEMENT

The question of the rights of women, and especially the demand for the extension of the franchise to women, was one of the most pressing social issues in Europe and North America at the time of the visits of the Master.

The woman suffrage movement began in the mid-19th century and reached its climax in the years between the turn of the century and the First World War. It was in the United Kingdom and the United States where the movement was most militant and had the greatest success in terms of social influence.

One of the first national suffrage organizations in the United Kingdom, the National Union of Women's Suffrage Societies (NUWSS), was founded in 1897 with the fusion of 17 suffragist groups. The work of the NUWSS focused on information campaigns demanding the vote for women which were addressed to the general public and especially to members of Parliament.

In 1903 some members of the NUWSS led by Emmeline (1858–1928) and Christabel Pankhurst (1880–1958) broke away to form their own organization, the Women's Social and Political Union (WSPU), which was characterized by the use of methods that sometimes included violence. Members of this group were labeled 'suffragettes' to differentiate them from the less militant suffragists.

The WSPU in turn suffered a split in 1907 when a group of women led by Charlotte Despard (1844–1939), among others, founded its own organization, the pacifist Women's Freedom League (WFL), which agreed to use tactics based on civil disobedience but refused to take part in violent campaigns.

Despite its internal divisions, the NUWSS remained the mainstream and largest suffrage organization in the United Kingdom.

During His visits to London, 'Abdu'l-Bahá met with members of the three organizations and some of these groups even organized meetings to hear the Master. Each organization also had its own publication. The NUWSS published *The Common Cause*, the WFL published *The Vote* and *The Suffragette* was the organ of WSPU. All three periodicals published references to the Faith and to 'Abdu'l-Bahá.

In the United States, the suffrage organizations were mostly grouped in the National American Woman Suffrage Association (NAWSA), which was formed in 1890 after the fusion of the American Woman Suffrage Association, founded in 1868, and the National Woman Suffrage Association, founded in 1869. Although the methods used in North America were generally more moderate than those employed by the suffragettes in the United Kingdom, in the early 20th century American suffragists with the help of their English colleagues began implementing some of the campaigning methods used by the most radical British organizations. 'Abdu'l-Bahá also had close contact with various suffragist organizations in North America and their leaders.

As has been seen in previous chapters, one of the questions repeatedly posed to 'Abdu'l-Bahá by the many reporters who interviewed Him in America was His position on woman suffrage and the feminist movement. As a consequence, many articles published in non-suffragist periodicals also stressed the fact that the Bahá'í Faith holds gender equality as one of its pivotal teachings.

First Visit to England, September 1911

During 'Abdu'l-Bahá's first visit to London a number of notable suffragists were received by Him. One of them was the famous feminist leader Emmeline Pethick-Lawrence (1867–1954), who was one of the founders of the Women's Social and Political Union (WSPU), editor of the *Votes for Women* magazine and a member of the Women's International League for Peace. Little has been recorded about this meeting, but a short reference to her meeting with 'Abdu'l-Bahá was included in an article written for the *New York Sun* by the Bahá'í writer Mary Hanford Ford:

> Abdul Baha is deeply interested in the modern movement for the advancement and enfranchisement of women. He teaches the

absolute equality of men and women –'the soul has no sex' – and deplores the seclusion of Oriental women as one of the mistakes which progressive civilization must soon set right. He had a lively conversation in England with Mrs Pethick Lawrence and asked her some pregnant questions as to her 'views'.

She suggested that our civilization is imperfect because men have been trying to fly with only one wing, and equal rights for women would give them the other. He surprised her by the smiling admission that perhaps the new wing would be the stronger! And then went off into an eloquent little homily upon the achievements of Zenobia, that hero woman of the past, at once a queen, a wife and the savior of her people.[1]

Just a few months after meeting 'Abdu'l-Bahá, Pethick-Lawrence was sentenced to nine months in prison because of her activities.

The presence of 'Abdu'l-Bahá in London also prompted the publication in some suffragist periodicals of articles dedicated to the Bahá'í Faith. The weekly organ of the National Union of Women's Suffrage Societies (NUWSS), *The Common Cause* (London), published in its issue of 21 September 1911 a lengthy article by Marguerite Norma-Smith, a full-time worker with NUWSS, about the life of Ṭáhirih, which closed with the following tribute:

> It was this woman's destiny to be the pioneer of woman's emancipation in the East. Kurret-ul-Aine was a great and noble soul who walked the pathway of renunciation, giving all of herself that others might be free, suffering imprisonment, persecution, death rather than be untrue to the Vision that was given to her.
>
> Her name is loved and honoured by thousands of women in the East. Her life, thought, and teaching has influenced consciously or unconsciously the men and women of many lands.
>
> Women in this country fighting for freedom should honour the memory of Kurret-ul-Aine, she who looked towards the same horizon which is our goal, and who dared greatly, in a land, and at a time, when to declare the divinity of woman equally with man, needed a courage and faith that makes many of us feel humble.[2]

An editorial note introducing the article, and probably penned by its editor, Helena Swanwick (1864–1939),[3] briefly mentioned 'Abdu'l-Bahá and affirmed that His visit to England 'is arousing wide-spread interest in the teaching of Bahaism'.[4]

After the publication of Norma-Smith's article on Ṭáhirih, Nina Boyle (1865–1943),[5] a member of the Women's Freedom League, addressed a letter to the editor of *The Common Cause* complaining about the excessive attention that in her opinion was being paid to 'Abdu'l-Bahá among suffragists:

> May I make a few remarks on the subject of Bahaism, which is beginning to occupy an all too prominent part in suffrage circles, owing to the elusive bait of 'equality of the sexes' dangled by the leaders. The work and the fate of the beautiful and devoted poet, Kurret ul Aine, must appeal to all women; and anything that will rouse Mahomedan women from their submission is undoubtedly to be welcomed; but that is no reason for raising Abbas Effendi to the position that many foolish enthusiasts in the West claim for him . . .

This letter continued with a series of accusations directed against the Bahá'ís in general and 'Abdu'l-Bahá in particular. Boyle stated that the Bahá'í religion was behind the political upheavals in Persia and affirmed that in 'Abdu'l-Bahá's house 'women do not feed at his own table, nor do they go out freely, nor are they unveiled'. These comments elicited three replies from three suffragists, one of them a Bahá'í.

The first of these appeared in the same issue of *The Common Cause*, and was probably written by Swanwick:

> We gladly print Miss Boyle's letter, but she appears to misunderstand our motive in publishing accounts of various movements such as Bahaism . . . The Women's Movement is world-wide. Suffragists are helped and inspired by the knowledge that this is so, and naturally interested in all its manifestations. We do not, however, anticipate that our readers will become Bahaists, from reading Miss Norma-Smith's article; nor do we know in what other movements they have become 'entangled'. But we strongly deprecate the attitude of mind which considers whether teaching comes from a man or a woman, or will receive it only from the latter.[6]

The second reply was written by the noted suffragist Agnes Maude Royden (1876–1956), who was a member of the executive committee of the NUWSS and was to be appointed editor of *The Common Cause* in the next year. During World War I she held the vice-presidency of the Women's International League for Peace and Freedom and became a preacher at the City Temple. Royden decided to visit 'Abdu'l-Bahá in order to ascertain the truth of the accusations made by Boyle and attended one of the meetings held at Cadogan Gardens. There she listened to one of 'Abdu'l-Bahá's talks and was able to interview Ethel Rosenberg. Royden's account of the meeting and her remarks about the accusations made by Boyle were published on 5 October in *The Common Cause*:

> The N.U. Press Secretary secured permission for me to visit Lady Blomfield's flat in Cadogan Gardens this morning and learn something of Bahaism at the fountain-head – for Abdul Baha Abbas himself was there, speaking to his disciples.
>
> Abbas Effendi had already begun his discourse when I arrived, his words being interpreted at intervals for the benefit of those who, like myself, knew no Persian. He was speaking of the revival in material progress which had recently taken place in India, under the British rule, and reminding us that progress to be real must be spiritual. He urged us all to pray that God's Holy Spirit might bring new life to India. We are all the servants of God, he said, and as such, His friends. It is only superstitions that have divided us.
>
> Abbas Effendi then went on to speak of the true meaning of 'Law'. Not only secular but Divine law should be taught, since on the possession of good laws depends the happiness and the progress of every people. 'There is not only the law of the sheep, but the law of the Shepherd. We in England do not realise this. Some even say there is no Shepherd! Yet it is He Who guides, guards, and pastures us.'
>
> We in the West, said the teacher, suppose that to be a 'law' which is passed by Commons and Lords, and signed by the Emperor. This is superficial. A law must be a real relation to the needs of the people. 'The Law is the true relation of things to one another according to their nature.' To make laws it is therefore necessary to understand the nature and relation of all things; but this is beyond

human power. God alone, therefore, is the true law-giver, Who understands all and has a remedy for all.

At this point Abbas Effendi ended his discourse and left us; but as he had not spoken on the points which have aroused controversy in your paper, I remained to talk the matter over with Miss Rosenberg, Hon. Secretary to the Bahai community in London.

Miss Rosenberg had stayed for eleven months in the household of Abdul Baha Abbas when he was in the Turkish prison-fortress of S. Jean d'Acre. She speaks therefore with first-hand knowledge when she says that the ladies of the household dine at his table, with his brothers, nephews, and guests. They are educated and cultured women, and if they take it in turns to 'housekeep', this is no more derogatory to them than it is to English ladies.

It must be remembered that Abbas Effendi has been since the age of seven a prisoner or an exile. At S. Jean d'Acre, a Turkish prison, in the midst of a Mahometan population, it would be impossible for the ladies of the household – the wife and daughters of Abbas Effendi – to receive foreign male visitors. They understand that the laws of the Bahai community have decreed the emancipation of Eastern women, and have often discussed the question of 'how' and 'when' with Miss Rosenberg herself. Monogamy is, of course, enforced. Education is held to be a debt from parents to their children, and if to educate all be quite impossible, then the daughters should (it is taught) be educated rather than the sons, since they are mothers of the race. In Burmah, where women have achieved a freedom and independence unique in the East, the Bahai women, who were brought up as Mahometans, follow the example of the Burmese, and attend public meetings of men and women. It is difficult for Western women to understand the revolution of ideas implied in this apparently simple act; but those who know the East will not underestimate it.

With regard to the charge that the Bahai movement is 'merely political agitation', it is one which will not be of so much interest to your readers as the teaching with regard to women. Since, however, the accusation has been made, it is only fair to state that the Bahai community in Persia has actually been in danger of massacre at the hands of revolutionaries, owing to their persistent refusal to take any part in political agitation at all. Abdul Abbas Effendi expressly forbade his followers (and this can be proved by documentary evidence) to take any part in the Persian revolution. The Bahai teaching is submission to the Government and laws of the country, and it is significant that an American gentleman, who spent a year visiting the Bahai communities in India, reported them to be alone in speaking well of the existing (British) Government.

The charge of 'political agitation' is, of course, the easiest of all jibes to hurl at a spiritual movement. It was on this unproven charge that the martyrs of 1852 perished – among them Kurret-ul-Aine. It was also on this that thousands of Christians were murdered centuries ago. But English women will not consent to judge or to condemn a movement which ever asserts itself to be one for sex-equality, without a first-hand knowledge of its writings and its works. A. Maude Royden[7]

The third reply to Boyle's letter came from the Bahá'í Elizabeth Herrick, a member of the radical WSPU, who in a letter addressed to the editors of *The Common Cause* stated:

Hindhead, Surrey, October 3, 1911

Mrs. Elizabeth Herrick sends us an interesting letter on the Bahai movement, from which we quote the following passages:– 'Many Bahai women are working in the different franchise movements, and at least one Persian man gladly carried a banner in the last great women's procession . . . I have it on the authority of Miss Marion E. Jack, who was a teacher of English in the household of Abbas Effendi for seven months, that the women do sit at meat with him, and go in and out as they choose, without asking anyone. If they go out veiled – well, it will not always be so. We are without votes – and that will not always be so. We do not dream of blaming our leaders for such a state of things.'[8]

Sadly for Nina Boyle, just two days after her letter was published another feminist weekly *The Vote* (London), organ of the Women's Freedom League – a publication to which Boyle was a regular contributor – gave more attention to the Bahá'í Faith and started publishing the story entitled *A Woman Apostle in Persia*, which was based on the life of Ṭáhirih. The author of the narrative was none other than the famous Charlotte Despard (1844–1939), the founder of the Women's Freedom League and editor of the magazine, who would meet 'Abdu'l-Bahá on several occasions. Despard divided her text into four chapters which were published in three installments.[9]

On 13 September *The Christian Commonwealth* published in its column 'From the Turret' an article about the life of Ṭáhirih signed by E.M.J. It appeared apropos some comments about female suffrage made in the Persian parliament and published in *The Times*. The bulk of the biographical information about Ṭáhirih was provided by Tudor Pole. Before describing Ṭáhirih's life the author inserted the following comments:

> Clearly the Sheikh Assadullah (a member of the Maslijs) does not believe in the equality of men and women, and he no doubt expressed the orthodox thought of Persia. But we have in London just now a visitor who represents one of the great radical revolutionary forces which not only Persia, but East and West have to reckon – the more powerful that it is a religious force. Abbas Effendi is the head of the great Bahai community, which has recognised that the ignorance of women holds the nations in darkness, and teaches that all girls should receive an education as good as that given to boys. Indeed, if there is not sufficient money to educate both the boys and girls of a family, the education of the girls must take precedence.
>
> This teaching is bearing fruit. Since the declaration of the Constitution five years ago, Persian women have been eagerly seeking education. Notwithstanding the strenuous opposition of the Mohammedan priests, scores of modern schools are being opened to which they flock. This summer the first Persian girl, a Bahai, Ghodsia Khanum, has left her own country in search of knowledge, and is now enrolled as a student at the Lewis Institute in Chicago.[10]

This article was afterwards mentioned in *The Common Cause*.[11]

Chicago: Address to the Federation of Women's Clubs

During His first visit to Chicago 'Abdu'l-Bahá addressed a gathering of local women's organizations held at the La Salle Hotel on Thursday, 2

May 1912 and organized by the Woman's Bahá'í Assembly of Chicago.

Several announcements of the event were published in advance. The *Record-Herald* announced, for instance, that as well as the Master, 'Dr McEwen, chairman of public health of the I.F.W.C, and Mrs Robert McCall, chairman of civics, would speak on their respective organizations.'[12] A similar announcement was published in the *Tribune*.[13] The announcement published in the *Examiner* stated that the program would consist of 'brief addresses given by representatives from different clubs on the subject of "Woman's place in the world of To-Day". Mme. Ragna Linne will sing and Miss Elena Moneak will give violin selections.'[14]

In His talk 'Abdu'l-Bahá spoke on the emancipation of women.[15] Representatives of the major Chicago newspapers were present at the meeting and wrote accounts of it. The report in the *Examiner* related that a thousand people were present at the meeting and gave the names of some of the speakers:

ABDUL BAHA TALKS TO CLUB WOMEN ON VOTE
PERSIAN PHILOSOPHER ADVOCATES FEMALE SUFFRAGE AS MEANS OF SOCIAL REFORM

Equal rights for all, regardless of sex, sanctity of the home, and observance of the Golden Rule were some of the suggestions offered by Abdul Baha Abbas, Persian reformer and philosopher, at a reception tendered him in the large ballroom of the Hotel La Salle yesterday afternoon by the Bahai Woman's Assembly of Illinois.

More than 1,000 men and women were present, representing all sections of Chicago and neighbouring cities. The reception was one of several social affairs in honor of Abdul Baha, and the themes of many speakers were along the lines of uplift for humanity.

DRESSED IN PERSIAN GARB

After reviewing conditions which prevail in European countries and what had been done to remedy them, he asked for the entire co-operation of all good citizens in making Chicago a better city.

'As for female suffrage,' he said, 'it is but right and just. There should be equal rights for all, regardless of sex. The woman does much for the uplift of the home and society. She can do far more if given the franchise, where her best efforts will enable her to make for better communities.'

Mrs. Fannie G. Lesch, president of the Bahai Woman's Assembly, presided.

Among the many speakers were Mrs. Minnie Starr Grainger, president Illinois Federation of Woman's Clubs; Mrs. Gertrude Blackwelder, Illinois Woman's Clubs; Mrs. F. A. Dow, Arche Club; Mrs. Callie P. Coon, Illinois Woman's Clubs; Mrs. George Colby, Kilo Association; Mrs. Esther Falkenstein, Falkenstein Settlement; Mrs. D. Harry Hammer, Chicago Woman's Club; Mrs. Celeste Parker Wooly, Social Economics; Mrs. Catherine Abbott, Business Woman's League; Mrs. Addie Andre; Mrs. Helen Beales, Peace Society; Mrs. P. Kochersperger, Theosophist Society; Mrs. Francis Squire Potter and Professor Henry Greener.[16]

The account appearing in the *Record-Herald* on 3 May reproduced some paragraphs of the notes of 'Abdu'l-Bahá's talk:

SUN AID TO SUFFRAGE
ABDUL-BAHA TELLS FEDERATION THAT SOL'S RAYS HAVE MANIFESTED EQUALITY OF WOMAN

Abdul-Baha, 'The Servant of God', asserted his belief in the equality of men and women before a meeting of the Federation of Women's Clubs at the Hotel La Salle yesterday afternoon. Speaking a sentence at a time, and then pausing for an interpretation to be made by his nephew, Dr. Ameen Fareed, he said in part:

'The functions of the sun are to reveal things mysterious. This is the century of light. The sun of reality has gloriously revealed itself toward mankind.

'One of the great things hidden in the realm of existence was the potential capability of womankind. Through the light of the sun of reality the capability of womankind has become manifest to the extent that the equality of man and woman is an established fact.

'In past ages woman was wronged and oppressed, and especially so in Asia, Africa and Australia. In some parts of Asia women were not considered a part of mankind. One tribe there for a long time held to the belief that women were a manifestation of Satan and that men were a manifestation of the Merciful One.

'At last the century of light arrived. In this age the reality of many things has been exposed. Among them is the well known fact that womankind is the equal of mankind.'[17]

On 5 May the *Inter-Ocean* offered a very similar account, according to which 'Abdu'l-Bahá 'was greeted with enthusiasm when he entered the large hall'. He was also reported as having stated that 'True progress will never be possible until after womankind and mankind are on an equal basis . . .'[18]

In a brief note the *Chicago Journal* reported that 'Abdul Baha Abbas, "great teacher" of the Bahaists, was swamped today with invitations to address clubs following his plan for feminine suffrage before 1,000 persons at Hotel La Salle. The meeting was held under the auspices of the Bahai Woman's Assembly of Illinois. "Female suffrage is just and right," said Abdul Baha Abbas.'[19]

On 5 May the *Examiner* published an account of the meeting outlining the impression 'Abdu'l-Bahá's words made on the audience:

ABDUL BAHA FOR SUFFRAGE
PERSIAN DECLARES MODERN CIVILIZATION DEMANDS EQUAL RIGHTS
Coming from a Mohammedan nation in which women are held in as great subjection as in any other part of the civilized world, Abdul Baha of Persia has succeeded in awakening Chicago club women to a new zeal for securing equal political rights with men. In his addresses to Chicago audiences the 'servant of ineffable splendor', leader of the worldwide Bahai movement, has emphasized his belief that woman is the equal of man and deserves to have all the civic privileges that he enjoys.

The preaching of this advanced doctrine by a product of Persian civilization was considered remarkable by the members of the Cook County Federation of Women's Clubs, who listened to an address by Abdul Baha at the Hotel La Salle. The speaker was conscious of the contrast between his preaching and the conditions back home in the land of the Shah; but even in Persia women are coming to their own, he held.[20]

The Woman Voter, the official organ of the New York State Suffrage Association, published in its June issue an article by W. P. Dodge in which large selections of 'Abdu'l-Bahá's talk at Hotel La Salle were reproduced.²¹

New York: International Peace and Woman Suffrage Meeting

On Monday 20 May, the New York State Suffrage Association arranged a public meeting for 'Abdu'l-Bahá at the Metropolitan Temple, Fourteenth Street and Seventh Avenue. The Republican congressman William Stiles Bennet (1870–1962) and the British suffragist Elizabeth Freeman (1876–1942) were also invited to participate in the event which had been announced previously in such newspapers as *The New York Times*,²² the *Daily Eagle*²³ and *The Evening Post*.²⁴

'Abdu'l-Bahá's address focused on the subject of the emancipation of women and on their role in establishing peace.²⁵ In the audience were reporters who afterwards wrote accounts of the meeting. The most detailed one appeared in the *New-York Tribune*:

SUFFRAGE TO END WAR
ABDUL BAHA SAYS WOMEN WILL RULE THE WORLD IN PEACE

BENNET TALKS POLITICS
THEN SLIP OF A GIRL, WHO BROKE WINDOWS WITH MRS. PANKHURST, SPEAKS FOR THE CAUSE

Woman suffrage had three advocates of widely contrasting personalities on the same platform last evening, when the Persian apostle of peace, Abdul Baha Abbas, Miss Elizabeth Freeman, the slip of a girl who has broken windows with Mrs. Pankhurst in London, and former Congressman William S. Bennet spoke at a meeting called by the Woman Suffrage party at the Metropolitan Temple. Mrs. E. Jean Nelson Penfield, the party chairman, presided.

Abdul Baha must have found 'votes for women' an inspiration, for he not only talked longer but gestured much more than he did when he spoke on peace at the recent reception to him at the Hotel Astor. And highly did the women – they were mostly women who heard him – appreciate it.

There was a lot of applause as the measured sentences came forth in Persian, to be translated by his dark haired nephew, and a regular ovation at the end – which he acknowledged by gravely rising and touching his forehead with his right hand five times.

Universal peace, said Abdul Baha, would never be realized except through universal suffrage. 'For the children,' he said, 'are educated by the mother, and it is most difficult for a mother to send to battle her dear ones, her offspring, reared by her, watched over by her through many laborious nights and days.

'Therefore, when womanhood takes part in the affairs of the world, war will cease. This is certain beyond all doubt.'

WOMEN NOT INFERIOR TO MEN

The white haired old Persian has no use for those persons who hold that women are inferior to men. The only trouble, he declared, was in their education.

'When their education is similar they will be the peers of men, and more,' he said. 'History has proved this, for have not certain women in past ages surpassed men?'

Then Abdul Baha gave long accounts of the achievements of Zenobia, Queen of Palmyra, and Cleopatra to illustrate his point.

'It is a great mistake,' he said, reverting to his belief that women are capable often of surpassing men, 'a great mistake to allow the education of women to be inferior to that of men, for do not the women educate the men? It is not the father who is the child's teacher; it is the mother, and if her education be defective, then, alas for humanity!

'To women belong the same rights as to men. Shall human beings, who possess thought, be less than the birds and beasts, among which the female has the same power as the male? No, as the human is not complete without the right hand and the left hand, so the world must have the male and the female equal and free.'

Mr. Bennet, who really didn't look as if he had lived the forty years for which, he says, he has believed in woman suffrage – but maybe he began in his cradle, for he said he got his politics on the woman question from his mother – tickled the audience immensely with stories of how ignorant men can be in politics.

MR. BENNET ON POLITICS

'They say women shouldn't vote because they don't know politics,' he exclaimed. 'Why, the day after I was elected to Congress I was walking down Broadway, feeling pretty good, and my nearest neighbour met me. "Say," he said, "why didn't you run in this contest?" Well, it developed that this man, living in my district, had voted for me without knowing I ran – voted the ticket and never looked at a name on it. What woman could beat that?'

Miss Freeman's speech dealt with some resolutions, read by Mrs. Penfield, asking better police protection for 'the mission workers, particularly Mrs. Rose Livingston, who rescues voting girls from cadets in Chinatown'. Mrs. Freeman has been speaking in that district herself.

'How do you like, you protected women,' she said in ringing tones, after touching on conditions there, 'how do you like to feel that women in this city of ours, many of them are so poorly paid for their work that they are forced to supplement their wages by going on the street?

'We must have suffrage to cope with this evil. Even the magistrates know that the suffragists stand to help women, for not long ago when a child was rescued from Chinatown and taken into court, the Judge said, "Take her to the suffragettes."'[26]

The *New York Times* also published an account of the meeting, quoting some of the words of the Master:

ABDUL BAHA TO SUFFRAGISTS
VOTES FOR WOMEN MUST PRECEDE WORLD PEACE, HE DECLARES

Abdul Baha Abbas, the apostle of international peace, talked to the members of the Woman Suffrage Party and their friends about peace and woman suffrage last night at a big meeting in the Metropolitan Temple, Seventh Avenue and Fourteenth Street. He spoke in his native language and, sentence by sentence, his words were translated by his nephew.

There is no difference in the physical or intellectual value of men and women, he said. It is only a difference of education which has made an apparent difference and there will never be universal peace, he added, until there is equal suffrage.

'If the educator is imperfect,' said Abdul Baha, as he was translated, 'the educated must also be imperfect – even man. The mother is the first educator of men. If the mother is imperfect, alas for the condition of men.'[27]

New York: The Minerva Club

A further meeting with New York women took place in a gathering of the Minerva Club,[28] a society created in 1898 as a literary and social club for women that held regular meetings at the Waldorf-Astoria on the first and third Monday of each month.[29]

This institution was chaired by a Bahá'í, Mary Stokes MacNutt, and thus its members had known of the Bahá'í Faith for several years. As early as 1905, when Mrs MacNutt returned from her pilgrimage to the Holy Land, the club had organized a meeting at which she shared with an audience of hundreds her experiences visiting 'Abdu'l-Bahá. An account of this meeting quoted her saying: 'I can't tell publicly of my trip to the East and of that gentle soul (Abdul Baha), a king in prison. But I have a message to you from him. One day I said to him, "Oh, I wish I could take your face back to the women of my country!" And he answered. "Take back my love; that is my face, and tell them to love and be kind to one another."' Her remarks were 'enthusiastically applauded'.[30]

The meeting for 'Abdu'l-Bahá was arranged at the Waldorf-Astoria Hotel on Monday, 25 November 1912. An announcement in the *Times* gave some details about the participants and the program.[31]

At least two journals reported this meeting. The *New-York Tribune* published a rather sarcastic account on 26 November:

MINERVAS HEAR A. BAHA
PERSIAN SAGE COMPLIMENTS ON THEIR 'RADIANT FACES'

PREACHES SEX EQUALITY
WINS APPLAUSE, LASTLY, BY PRAISING SUFFRAGISTS FOR FIGHTING FOR THE VOTE

Mrs. Mary Stokes MacNutt, president of Minerva, and Mr. MacNutt were a happy pair yesterday, for they got Abdul Baha, of Persia, to speak at the club's annual luncheon at the Waldorf-Astoria.

Abdul Baha didn't attend the eating part of the function, but he came afterward, looking as if he had on the same white turban and the same long gown that he wore when he landed here from Persia last April.

His face was just as peaceful as it was then, too, and he didn't seem the least bit touched by his seven months of America, though he told the women in energetic Persian, which was translated for them by his black bearded attendant, that everywhere he went in this country it was 'hurry, hurry, hurry'.

He made a great hit with the assembled Minervas because he called them 'a radiant faced assemblage' and told them that women were fully the equal of men where they weren't men's superiors,

'The only real difference between men and women,' he said, 'is that men's faces are covered with disagreeable growths of hair, while women's faces are clean and decent.

'And even that is true now only in Oriental countries, for I perceive that here in America gentlemen are doing away with that difference by shaving.' Here the white haired sage let his blue eyes twinkle a little, just to show that a seer could crack a joke.

'Women,' said Abdul Baha, 'to-day are proving their right to be the peer of men. In past ages they have been kept down. They have been forbidden education, but now the world is learning that the welfare of the body politic can be attained only by the co-operation of women on an equal plane with the men. Given the opportunity, they are showing that physically, intellectually, spiritually their capacity for attainment is the same as that of the men.

'In plant life, in the animal kingdom there is no assertion of superiority on the part of the male. How then is it possible for human beings, supposed to be the representatives of justice, mercy, generosity, equity, how is it possible for them to practice such injustice? It is not. The distinction between men and women is fast disappearing, God would not permit it.'

Lastly the aged seer brought out a round of applause by praising the courage women had shown in their fight for the vote.[32]

The *New York Press* published a brief note about the meeting which reported that 'Baha ended his address by saying the time had come when the influence of women was equal if not paramount to that of men, and that the progressive welfare of the body politic was impossible without the aid of women.'[33]

Further Comments in America

The Bahá'í position on gender equality was also the subject of several editorials and comments in American journals. The Socialist journal *Daily People* (New York), for instance, published in its issue of 15 April excerpts of what appears to be an interview with 'Abdu'l-Bahá:

> ABDUL BAHA FAVORS EQUAL SUFFRAGE
> Woman suffrage as a means of hastening the era of world-wide peace is one of the new doctrines advanced by Abdul Baha, the Persian philosopher and leader of the Bahai religion.
> 'When women are enfranchised and are given the opportunity to get the grasp on civic affairs which men now have, the question of world peace will be settled or become merely the question of a few years.' The gray-haired old man whose arrival has caused a stir among his followers in this country declared:
> 'Besides being less inclined to war than their brothers, women have the mother instinct to further prevent their precipitating war between any two countries. For this reason, if no other, I am heartily in favor of woman suffrage.'
> 'But don't you think that such a system would take the woman entirely out of the home?' he was asked. The kindly eyes sparkled a bit, as he answered: 'I don't think that would necessarily follow.'[34]

The *Philadelphia Telegraph* published an article on 22 April complaining about the success that the Bahá'í religion was having among women:

> OCCUPATION NOT OCCULTATION
> The Visit of the noted Persian teacher, Abdul Baha, for the purpose of lecturing throughout the United States on 'The Religion of Brotherhood and Peace', has started much discussion in cultured circles of this new international movement.
> We have noticed a growing tendency, especially among American women, to adopt the fads of Eastern occultism as a substitute for what religion they have. There are said to be over 3,000 Bahaists already in this country . . .
> Bahaism prohibits polygamy and concubinage as degrading to women; condemns mendicancy and asceticism; and advocates a

life of generosity to one's self and one's neighbor. For the rest, it is vaguely pantheistic and rapturously occult.

Why, may it be asked, in the name of common sense, should this program appeal to Americans and especially American women? They are in need of no such gospel. American women have all the protection they need and all the rights they have as yet asked for. Why go to Persia for a religion such as this? What those who will flutter over and fawn upon the dewy-eyed Abdul most need is not a sickly occultation but a spirited occupation to keep them from further neurotic absorption in crystal-gazing and weird psychopathic séances to which too many of them are already too much addicted.[35]

On May 12, the *Brooklyn Daily Eagle* also included the following article on the 'Bahais and Women' which was partly based on the interview granted by 'Abdu'l-Bahá to Wendell P. Dodge weeks earlier (see vol. 1, chapter 10):

The attitude of Bahais toward women is remarkable when one considers the Oriental beginning of this movement. In Persia, where women's faces are never seen save by their nearest relatives, the weaker sex played a heroic part in the early days of the Bahai Movement. They urged their husband and sons on to martyrdom, and paid the same penalty, and even worse for their religion.

One of the greatest leaders under the Bab was a woman, Kurrat Al Eyn, whose intellect, heroism, and charm of personality made her such a powerful advocate of her religion that she was put to death by the government. Upon one occasion, as she was addressing her brother coreligionists, she dropped her veil, which shocked even the progressive Persians so that one of them is said to have committed suicide rather than to look upon the light of day with eyes which had beheld such a sacrilege.

The Bahai Movement teaches the equality of the sexes, and moreover, urges education upon its followers as a sacred duty . . .

Abdul Baha, the present head of the sect, counsels all adherents to educate their children but if they cannot educate both the boys and the girls, to educate the girls, for they will be the mother of the coming generation. This is a radical idea for the East, but it is already taking effect there, for the Bahai women of Persia are eager for education, and a girls' school has already been founded in Teheran, the first of its kind, to serve as a model for future schools throughout the country.

The Bahais lay great stress upon the important position which women hold in this age. They acknowledge no difference in capacity between the sexes and banish the idea of woman's inferiority to man. Abdul Baha points out in one of his writings the fact that the females of many species of animals are stronger and more powerful than the male, and asserts that the chief cause of the mental and physical inequalities of the sexes is merely custom and training, which for ages past have moulded women into the idea of the weaker vessel.

As the Bahai movement predicts the dawning of a new age of world-peace and civilization, so it predicts that woman will play a large part in this evolution. The world in the past has been ruled by force, and man has dominated over woman by reason of his more forceful and aggressive qualities both of body and mind. But the scales are already shifting – force is losing its weight and mental alertness, intuition and the spiritual qualities of love, service, in which woman is strong, are gaining ascendancy. Hence, the new age will be an age less masculine, more permeated with the feminine ideals, or so to speak more exactly, it will be an age in which the masculine and feminine elements of civilization will be more properly balanced.

This is the general attitude of the Bahai Movement toward woman and from it many deductions may be drawn. One of these is the absolute equality of the sexes in the service to the cause, for the Bahais have no clergy or official hierarchy. Its believers and teachers are drawn equally from both sexes.[36]

Weeks later the same journal commented in its editorial section that 'Abdul Baha Abbas, Persian prophet, sees men and women again equal as they were in the Garden of Eden. Fashionably dressed Suffragettes may regard the prophet as a reactionary rather than a progressive.'[37] In Denver the *Post* published on 3 August a short editorial note stating that 'Abdul-Baha Abbas, the Persian prophet, says men and women will eventually be even as they were in the Garden of Eden. If Abdul

Baha has any followers in this country this declaration ought to get lots of votes for the women.'[38]

On 25 August the Boston *Herald* published an article reproducing some of the comments about woman made by 'Abdu'l-Bahá on board the *Cedric* upon His arrival in America.[39]

Second Visit to London

A few weeks before 'Abdu'l-Bahá's departure from America, London's *Standard* mentioned to its readers the fact that while in America He had met and spoken at different women's organizations and reported that 'The Bahai movement aims at the unification of religions and the establishment of universal peace. The latter cannot, in the opinion of Abdul Baha, be brought about without the enfranchisement of women.'[40]

On His second visit to London a meeting to hear 'Abdu'l-Bahá was arranged by the Women's Freedom League at the Essex Hall – the usual meeting place of the organization – on 2 January 1913. Ahmad Sohrab, who acted as interpreter for 'Abdu'l-Bahá, reports that over one thousand people gathered to hear the Master and that the hall and the gallery had to be used because no seats were left.

Charlotte Despard opened the meeting with some introductory remarks about 'Abdu'l-Bahá, in the course of which she stated that 'I prefer to call him a prophet rather than a teacher'. When 'Abdu'l-Bahá started to speak He was interrupted several times by bursts of applause and at the close of the meeting many people wanted to shake hands with Him.[41]

London journals, especially suffragist magazines, gave considerable attention to the event. In the days leading up to the meeting some periodicals published advertisements about it[42] and *The Vote*, the organ of the Women's Freedom League, published an announcement introducing the figure of 'Abdu'l-Bahá and Tahirih. 'With the great doctrines of the Fatherhood of God and the Brotherhood of Man, Bahaism preaches universal peace and equality of the sexes,' stated the announcement, 'we know that our readers will welcome this unexpected opportunity of hearing a great teacher from the East and make every possible effort to give him a fitting reception.'[43]

On 10 January *The Vote* published several references to the meeting

GENDER EQUALITY AND THE SUFFRAGE MOVEMENT

in different sections. The front page reproduced a large picture of the Master and in the editorial section Charlotte Despard described the meeting:

> It was a memorable occasion, which will leave its impress on all those who were present. Here we are not so much concerned with what was said then, or at other times, during the visit to London of this strange and beautiful human being who is called by his disciples 'the Servant of God', as with the spirit that, wherever he goes, seems to radiate from him.[44]

The same issue also included the following account of the meeting:

> The announcement that Abdul Baha would speak on the Equality of Men and Women at a meeting arranged by the Women's Freedom League, at the Essex Hall, on Thursday, January 2, attracted so large a gathering that not only was the Hall crowded to its utmost limits, but many had to be turned away. Mrs. Despard presided, and in an introductory speech welcomed the Prophet from the East with his great message of peace. She said that it was the false relations between men and women which had brought discord, and what all desired was that the discord should cease. She gave a brief outline of the Bahai movement, beginning with the coming of the Bab – The Gateway – who died a martyr's death, but his teaching lived, and the number of his followers grew in spite of persecutions, imprisonments, and martyrdoms. She spoke of the wonderful progress of the woman's movement in Persia, and especially of Qu'urut 'ul Ain and her remarkable influence on the emancipation of women, through her tragic life to a martyr's death. We can never forget, she said, the great spiritual force behind the woman's movement; it is moving throughout the world; knowing this, we go on with courage and hope.
>
> After the Master's address, Mrs. Holmes made a moving appeal for service in the woman's Cause; personal service and the service of money; the Suffrage movement, she said, was part of the great Divine plan for the regeneration of the world. Till the status of woman was raised it was impossible to complete the plan.
>
> Lady Bloomfield, in a short speech about the Bahai movement,

said she was glad to identify herself with her sisters working for freedom. She told how the message of Abdul Baha was not an essay written in a luxurious library; it was a cry of regeneration ringing out from behind prison walls. Now he had come out into the world with his message – peace, the banishment of religious differences, humanity not fighting against each other but against evil, and the equality of men and women. Mr. Sidley, in a sympathetic speech, said that none could fail to be impressed by the simplicity and sympathy of the Master after forty years of prison. All paid homage to his courage and fidelity of purpose and the Divine intention of his message.[45]

The Vote also published the full text of the talk. One interesting feature of this address is that it is probably the first occasion on which the memorable sentence attributed to Ṭáhirih, 'You may kill me as soon as you like, but you cannot stop the emancipation of women', is recorded.

AN EASTERN PROPHET'S MESSAGE
ABDUL BAHA SAYS: 'THERE IS NO DISTINCTION: MEN AND WOMEN ARE EQUAL'

A venerable figure, radiating brotherliness, despite long years of imprisonment, wearing a long brown robe and a white turban, which emphasized the keen, alert eyes, Abdul Baha greeted with evident pleasure the crowded audience which received him with reverent enthusiasm at the Women's Freedom League meeting, Essex Hall, on January 2. The leader of the Bahai Movement, speaking through a very able interpreter, said:–

This is a wonderful gathering, I hope its purposes and objects will be realised, demonstrating to mere man that men and women are equal. May it become an impetus to women in all parts of the world to greater achievements!

The world of humanity is like a bird with its two wings – one is male, the other female. Unless both wings are strong and impelled by some common force, the bird cannot fly heavenwards. According to the spirit of this age, women must advance and fulfil their mission in all departments of life, becoming equal to men. There is no difference between men and women. They must be on the same level as men and receive all their rights. This is my earnest prayer, and it is one of the fundamental principles of Baha Ullah.

GENDER EQUALITY AND THE SUFFRAGE MOVEMENT

Baha Ullah proclaimed that the world of humanity was one tree; all nations, peoples, religions, men and women constitute the branches, leaves, blossoms, fruit. In this one peerless tree there is no distinction of gender in God's sight. Whoever practises humanitarian work draws near to God, whether man or woman; there is no distinction.

As we study world phenomena we come to the conclusion that in the mineral and vegetable kingdoms there is no difference between male and female; in plant life there is no strife for suffrage; the vegetable kingdom has suffrage already. Likewise in the animal kingdom there is no quarrel and strife between male and female, although it is an inferior creation to man. The male never taunts the female with his superiority; both enjoy perfect equality. Why should man, who is endowed with great intelligence, who is made in the likeness of God, stoop so low as to permit such things? That he should ever dare to declare himself superior to woman is astonishing. He thinks himself as a creation to be above woman. He declares that at present women have not attained to his intellectual and artistic level; that they are intellectually weaker; their will power is less; so man must be superior.

Some scientists have declared that the brains of men are heavier when weighed than women's, and so science shows that men are superior. Yet when we look round us we see people with small heads, whose brains must weigh little, but they show the keenest intelligence and great powers of understanding; and others with big heads, whose brains must be heavy, and yet they are witless. Therefore the avoirdupois of the brain has nothing to do with intelligence or superiority.

When men bring forward the second proof of their superiority by saying that women have not achieved as much as men, they use poor arguments which leave history out of consideration. If they kept themselves more fully informed historically they would know that great women have lived and achieved great things in the past, and that there are many living and achieving great things to-day.

Let us turn for a moment to history, and we shall see what women have accomplished in humanitarian, charitable, religious, and administrative work. As regards political life there was the great and powerful Queen of Palmyra, Zenobia, whose dramatic history most people know. When the king, her husband, died, she showed such administrative capacity that the Roman Government appointed her his successor; she waged wars and gained great victories in Syria, she laid siege to Cairo and took it; but she also organised an efficient and just Government, and through her sagacious administration, wise deliberation, strict justice, and great hope for the advancement of the people under her rule, her new subjects unanimously accepted her as Queen, although she belonged to another nation. She built many cities, the remains of which are to be seen to-day; the many tourists from Europe and America who visit them are astonished at the signs of her power and wisdom. She became so powerful that she threw off the Roman yoke, and when the legions of Rome were marshalled against her she completely routed them, although her army was much smaller. Clad in a red mantle, wearing her crown, sword in hand, she charged at the head of her army; such dauntless courage was irresistible, and victory was complete.

Many other women have accomplished great things in the past, too many to be mentioned here to-night; they have administered justice, shown themselves powerful, resourceful, and courageous. These are historic facts. In the religious world it is the same. You find recorded in the Old Testament how all the conquests of the Israelitish nation were inspired by one woman; His Holiness Moses was not permitted to cross the Jordan after caring for the children of Israel in the wilderness forty years, but a woman led them to victory. Likewise during the Messianic dispensation, after the crucifixion of His Holiness Christ, the apostles were shaken in their faith; even Peter, the rock on which the Church was to be founded, had denied his Master three times; finally it was Mary Magdalene who strengthened them assuring them that the Christ ever lives, is changeless; His body was crucified, but He was the Word of God from the beginning to eternity. This fearless woman saved Christianity to shine everlastingly on the horizon of glory.

Amongst the women of our own time there is Qu'urat 'ul Ain, the daughter of a Mohammedan priest; at the time of the appearance of the Bab she showed such tremendous courage and power, that all who heard her were astonished. She threw aside her veil, despite the immemorial custom of the Persians, and although it is considered impolite to speak with men, this heroic woman carried on controversies with the wisest men, and in every meeting she vanquished them. The Persian Government took her prisoner, she was stoned in the streets, anathematised, exiled from town to town, threatened with death, but she never failed in her determination to work for the freedom of her sisters. She bore persecution and suffering with the greatest heroism; even in prison she gained converts. To a Persian Minister, in whose house she was imprisoned, she said: 'You may kill me as soon as you like, but you cannot stop the emancipation of women.' At last the end of her tragic life came; she was carried into a garden and strangled. She put on, however, her choicest robes as if she were going to join a bridal party. With such magnanimity and courage she gave her life, startling and thrilling all who saw her. She was truly a great heroine. To-day in Persia among the Bahais there are women who also show unflinching courage, and are endowed with great poetic insight; they are most eloquent, and speak before large gatherings of people.

Women must go on advancing; they must extend their knowledge of science, literature, history for the perfecting of humanity. Ere long more will receive their rights. Men will see women in earnest, bearing themselves with dignity, improving the civic and political life, opposed to warfare, demanding suffrage and equal opportunities. I expect to see you advance in all phases of life; then will your brows be crowned with the diadem of eternal Glory.

In giving his benediction at the close of the meeting, Abdul Baha said:–

O Thou Almighty, confirm the members of this Society; assist these souls present to arise and serve the world of humanity, to proclaim the oneness of the world of women, that they may become free from past prejudices and behold the countenance of God. O God, confer marvellous progress upon this Society; cause it to advance in all the virtues of humanity; illumine the hearts of all with the rays of Thy Kingdom; quicken their spirits with the breath of Thy Holy Spirit, and bestow the life of God. Give us Thy blessing so that men and women may have equal freedom; may they attain to equal rights so that even male and female may be entirely forgotten. May all unitedly and solemnly serve Thee and obtain the blessings of God. Give us Thy bounty, O Lord, so that all humanity, men and women, characterised by the image of God, may attain the supreme knowledge of

Thee, discover the foundation of all holiness, live and act in accordance with Divine teaching, unitedly and with one accord, their hearts cemented and spirits joyous till they see the world of heaven![46]

The Suffragette, the official organ of the Women's Social and Political Union, which was edited by Christabel Pankhurst (1880–1958), also published the talk of 'Abdu'l-Bahá's at Essex Hall, preceded by a short introduction to the Bahá'í Faith. Christabel was one of the founders of the WSPU and a noted suffragette. Her mother, Emmeline Pankhurst, one of the most influential feminists of the 20th century, met 'Abdu'l-Bahá on 19 January 1913 and in the course of the interview confided to Him that her daughter was so impressed with the talk that she decided to include its text in her magazine.[47] 'Abdu'l-Bahá already knew of this publication for on 12 January, Mary S. Allen (1878–1964), another member of the WSPU who later was among the founders and officers of the Women's Police Service, visited Hin and presented Him with a copy of the issue of *The Suffragette*.[48]

In its issue of 3 January, *Votes for Women* (London) also published a brief report of the address: 'His Excellency Abdul Baha, in the course of an address given at the Essex Hall last week, on "The Equality of Women", said that in Persia to-day women were showing dauntless courage in promoting their movement; they were proving their intelligence and their capacity with men in all that applied to science and art, and were attaining to the highest degrees in the colleges. Women had been the inspiration of religious movements, in ancient times, and in Persia the Bahai movement had had its martyr heroine, Kurartul Ayn, who had died to open the gate of the new life to her country-women.'[49]

The Socialist *Daily Herald*, with a circulation of some 50,000 copies, published the following account:

THE MAIMED WING
FAMOUS PERSIAN MYSTIC'S PLEA FOR WOMAN'S SUFFRAGE

Speaking at the Essex Hall last night, Abdul Baha, the well-known mystic – a 'master' who is reputed to have three million followers – likened modern humanity to a bird, its two wings being respectively man and woman. The bird cannot fly if one wing is maimed. The position of woman today is a crippled handicapped one, and this affects all humanity.

Abdul Baha drew a comparison also between men and the animal and vegetable kingdom. The vegetables knew no distinction of sex; in fact they enjoyed Suffrage. If the world of Nature was above the petty show of authority and superiority of one [illegible] over another, how much more ought men [illegible] be. Women have played a great part in the history of the world. Zenobia, Queen of Athens [*sic*], was instanced as an example of the administrative capacity of women. She brought her empire to such a height of efficiency and power, that she was enabled to fight and conquer the Roman army, the Queen of Empires. She herself led her army and drove the Romans back to the gates of Rome.

The state of women in Persia was rapidly improving, said Abdul Baha. They were showing their equality in all matters of intellect, attaining to the highest degrees in the colleges. It would not be long, he prophesied, before women would have the franchise.[50]

The account in *The Standard* (London) read:

WOMEN'S PROGRESS IN PERSIA
ADDRESS BY ABDUL BAHA

His Excellency Abdul Baha delivered an address at Essex Hall, Strand, on 'The Equality of Women'. There was a crowded attendance, the great proportion of the audience being women, largely composed of members of the Women's Freedom League (by whom the meeting had been called), while on the platform and in other parts of the hall where many Persians and natives from other parts of the East.

Mrs. Despard, president of the Women's Freedom League, in opening the proceedings, said that the women's movement had made tremendous strides in Persia, and when the women of England thoroughly realised that their movement did not belong to themselves alone, but that it was spreading and gaining great strength in the East, as well as in other parts of the world, she was certain they would go on with renewed courage and hope.

Speaking through an interpreter, Abdul Baha said their common object was to demonstrate that men and women were equal. That gathering, he hoped, would prove an impetus to women in all parts of the world, so that they might go on towards greater achievement and greater accomplishment. The world of humanity was compared to two wings of a bird, one wing the male and the other the female. As long as the two wings were not strengthened and reinforced by some common impetus and force the bird could not fly heavenward. Therefore it was in the spirit of this age that women must and should advance. They must go on and fulfil their mission in all departments of life, so that they might become equal to men and attain to the same level and have equal rights. In Persia to-day women were showing dauntless courage in promoting their movement; they were proving their intelligence and their advancement in all that applies to science and art, and were going rapidly forward. It was the same in other parts of the world, and to stop the emancipation of women was, he declared, impossible.

A vote of thanks was passed to Abdul Baha, and a collection realised a substantial sum.[51]

The *Manchester Guardian* gave the following particulars of the event:

THE BAHAI MOVEMENT
ABDUL BAHA ON THE EQUALITY OF THE SEXES

Essex Hall was filled with women last night when, at the invitation of the Women's Freedom League, Abdul Baha, the leader of the Bahai movement, which now has three million followers, set forth the Bahai teaching concerning the equality of the sexes. Since reaching England last month on his return from a long visit to America, the 'Master', as his disciples call him, has been kept busy addressing meetings, visiting churches and institutions, and receiving visitors representative of all modern progressive movement at the West End flat, where he is staying. He is a picturesque figure in his tawny robes and white turban, emblem of authority. His worn face is full of dignity and a wistful gentleness. He could not enter into political questions, said Mrs. Despard in her introduction, but as leader of a movement which recognised the equality of men and women, he came to bring inspiration and encouragement.

Humanity was a bird with two wide wings, said Abdul Baha, speaking in parables. But unless those wings were of equal strength and development, how could it fly heavenward? It was in accordance with the spirit of the age that woman should advance and fulfil her mission in all departments of life, that she should become equal with men and share his rights without any difference whatever. This was his earnest desire, and this was one of the fundamental principles of Bahaism. Men claimed superiority to women. He marvelled that they should dare to do so, or that they could sink so low as to permit present conditions of inequality to exist. History was full of stories of the great achievement of women. Women had been the inspiration of religious movements in ancient times, and in Persia the Bahai movement had had its martyr heroine, Kurratul Ayn, who had died to open the gate of the newer life to her countrywomen. To-day in Persia women were seizing every opportunity for education, and were making great advances in art, science, and history. It was his earnest prayer for the women of England that they should perfect themselves in every quality, and by sheer merit win the fullest recognition of their inherent rights.

Abdul Baha is shortly going north, and arrangements are being made for him to visit Manchester.[52]

The information that appeared on 8 January in the *Christian Commonwealth* was very similar to that appearing in other journals.[53] Over the next few days agencies distributed a shorter account – which appears to have been a press release – which was published in several newspapers inside and outside England, including in the suffragist magazine *The Common Cause*, *The Christian Science Monitor*, and even in journals in India and Australia.[54]

Jus Suffragii (Paris), the monthly organ of the International Woman Suffrage Alliance, also included a short review of 'Abdu'l-Bahá's address.[55]

* * *

The British pro-suffragist press continued publishing references to 'Abdu'l-Bahá weeks after His talk for the Women's Freedom League. On 15 January *The Christian Commonwealth* published a special section on the suffrage movement that included a series of short messages from noted thinkers in support of women's rights. Among the contributors there were religious leaders who had met 'Abdu'l-Bahá, such as Archdeacon Wilberforce and Rev. R. J. Campbell. On a visit to

'Abdu'l-Bahá on 12 January, Albert Dawson, the editor of *The Christian Commonwealth*, had also asked the Master to send a few lines for that section. The following was published as His message:

> In view of the impeding discussions in the House of Commons, we communicated with a number of representative men and women, and have received the following replies:–
>
> ### ABDUL BAHA
>
> The world of humanity has two wings: one wing is the male, the other the female. When both wings are strengthened alike the bird will be able to soar heavenward. When women are granted the same educational advantages as men, the same opportunities to serve mankind, the same prerogatives – when they have received the suffrage, humanity will receive a new power, and the human race will wing its flight toward the ideal summit of progress and perfection.[56]

A copy of this special edition of *The Christian Commonwealth* was sent to all the members of the House of Commons as well as to other notables in England, and probably many of them read 'Abdu'l-Bahá's note.

On 17 January, *The Suffragette* (London) informed its readers that Lady Blomfield was to give a talk on the Bahá'í Faith on 21 January at one of the meetings of London's New Constitutional Society for Woman Suffrage held at the house of its president, Mrs Cecil Chapman.[57]

It is also worth noting that just a few months after the departure of 'Abdu'l-Bahá from London, the *Fortnightly Review* published a literary work by Constance E. Maud based on the life of Ṭáhirih which appeared under the title 'The First Persian Feminist'. The text was introduced with the following comments:

> The present Woman's Movement is a tree grown now to such dimensions that its branches extend to the remotest lands where men and women live in any kind of ordered community. The roots strike deep into the very hearts of the mothers of the race, and spread beneath the surface of life, wide as the fruit-bearing branches overhead.
>
> But this tree has been of slow growth, so slow that the roots were already strong and ineradicable before even a green shoot appeared.

Unnoticed, unheeded, often trodden under foot, were these first shoots, but again and yet again the indomitable life in the roots put forth new growth and always with renewed vigour, until now, in every land, the women are awakening from their age-long sleep. Even in the most reactionary countries they are beginning to stir and shake off the apathy bred of hopeless centuries behind high walls, barred windows, and veils...

But this great awakening has, like all other onward and upward struggles of the race, claimed its sad toll of martyrs, and among these no name deserves to stand higher than that of Qurratu'l'Ain, the Persian woman.[58]

Carrie Chapman Catt

Among those suffragists who expressed interest in the Bahá'í religion was Carrie Chapman Catt (1859–1947). For many years she was the president of the National American Woman Suffrage Association (NAWSA). As such, she was a very well-known lecturer and writer, who also had some influence at the political level.

It was Catt's work at the international level, however, that secured for her a unique place in the history of the suffrage movement. She was one of the founders of the International Woman Suffrage Alliance, an organization that coordinated most of the national suffrage organizations of the world and which was founded in 1904 at the initiative of NAWSA. Catt held the presidency of this organization from its inception in 1904 until 1924. In this period she traveled extensively across the world, mobilizing women in different places and assisting in the establishment and consolidation of national suffrage organizations in several countries, including China.

In mid-June 1913 the International Woman Suffrage Alliance held its seventh congress in Budapest. The event gathered no less than 240 delegates representing 22 countries and the audience included the presidents of many national suffrage societies.[59] Among the speakers were several individuals who had met 'Abdu'l-Bahá during His journeys. These included Jane Addams (Chicago), Alexander Giesswein (Budapest), Maude Royden (London) and Rabbi Stephen S. Wise (New York).

On June 15, in her presidential address opening the congress and given in Budapest's Academy of Music, Catt reviewed the progress of the suffrage movement around the world and made special mention of the work for the advancement of women being conducted in different countries and territories of the East. In reviewing the case of Persia, Catt stated:

> What Theosophy and other sects are doing for Hinduism, the Bahais are doing for Mohammedanism. Its founder, Abdul Baha, called the Bab, came some sixty years ago in Persia, but he and his followers were cruelly persecuted, and many were put to death. What makes this sect of peculiar interest to us is that among his early disciples was a rare and gifted soul, Kurret ul Aine. What fateful coincidence of dates it was, that while American women in 1848 were founding the beginning of an organized suffrage movement, this Persian woman tore her veil from her face, and declared rebellion against all the tenets of Islam which relegated women to a position of subjection. Her eloquence encouraged the timid, and women followed her example. The priests came to put difficult questions, but she knew her Koran better than they, and she made converts by the scores. Her success was too great, the priests were alarmed, and they applied that world-old but vain check to the growth of truth – they put the teacher to death. A Bahai in Cairo told me that 20,000 men and women had given up their lives for this new faith, but it has followed the universal rule of truth under persecution, and has steadily marched on and on, until fully one-third of the people of Persia have espoused it.
>
> Doubtless the greatest influence of the Bahais has been upon Persia – there the memory of Kurret ul Aine is still fresh, for she kindled an undying hope in the hearts of the women of her country. Under the influence of the new movement, schools for boys and girls were established over all Persia, and the idea of self-government was rapidly growing in the minds of the people. Women, freed for a time from traditional custom, agitated and organized and even spoke in public. Emancipation for women and self-government for Persia seemed not far distant. In the movement women had become a mighty and a recognized power. Vasel el Rayiaith, another Bahai, in recognition of their services, introduced a woman suffrage Bill in the Persian Parliament . . .[60]

It is still not clear when and how Catt learned about the Bahá'í religion. When 'Abdu'l-Bahá was visiting North America, she was away traveling in the Middle East and the Indian sub-continent until November 1912. However, in mid-December 1911 she was in Egypt after having visited Syria and the Holy Land. It is possible that she met 'Abdu'l-Bahá soon after His return from France. In fact, in her address she mentions having met the Bahá'ís in Cairo.

Catt's address in Budapest was afterwards published in *The Suffragette* (London), where the members of the Women's Social and Political Union were able to read her interesting tribute to Ṭáhirih.[61] *The Common Cause* published in turn its own report of the congress, which was penned by Agnes Maude Royden and mentioned the fact that a message had been received from the Bahá'í women in Persia:

> A greeting came from Persia – 'What hath God wrought?' Mrs. Catt explained that the first telegraphic message ever sent was sent from Washington by a man, and received in Baltimore by a woman, and these were the words sent. And the day on which they were dispatched was also the birthday in Persia of the first Baba [*sic*] who preached the equality of men and women. In allusion to this fact, our Persian sisters sent this message to us. Their progressive movement, alas, has been stifled, as have all other movements for reform in that unhappy country, by outside interference. But it cannot die.[62]

Catt would mention Ṭáhirih again at the Biennial Convention of the General Federation of Women's Clubs which was held in Chicago in June 1914 and which attracted 3,200 delegates from all over the United States and near ten thousand visitors. Her speech was delivered on 12 June, under the title 'The World Progress of Women', and in it Catt assessed the global impact of the suffrage movement. At one point in her discourse she drew parallels between the lives of Ṭáhirih and Susan B. Anthony (1820–1906), one of the pioneers of the feminist movement in North America:

> Women are not in rebellion against men. They are in rebellion against worn-out traditions, and against superstitious relics of bygone ages. It is a battle between the men and women who have seen the vision and those who have not.

> It is a marvelous thing to see how this movement has come up among all people. Usually movements are confined to one people, but the woman movement is world-wide. Before there were steamships and telegraphs and railroads, two wonderful women were born, one an American prophetess – Susan B. Anthony, the other a Persian woman. One was born in the Christian west, the other in the heathen east. One came from among a people who had made their boasts of being the most generous to their women in the world. The other arose in the world's most conservative country.
>
> The Persian woman was of a noble family. In early youth there came to her a vision which made her arise, burst through the throng of traditions which had bound her and go out with a message of freedom, to take off the veil from the face of the women in Persia.
>
> She spoke to the people and the mob went away saying there was much truth in what she said. The priests sought to confuse her. She knew her Koran better than they. But in the fateful year 1848, while still in her youth, beauty and strength, she was struck down by an assassin in order that the movement for women might come to an end.
>
> The vision did not come to Susan B. Anthony until three years later, but when it came she followed it, and the vision was the same as that which had come to the Persian woman.[63]

In 1916 Catt chose a property in Washington to be rented by the National American Woman Suffrage Association and used as temporary headquarters in Washington of the Congressional Committee of the NAWSA and as the centre of various local suffrage organizations. Various members of the NAWSA would live there permanently.

The property was located at 1626 Rhode Island Avenue. It had served as the residence of the Minister of Belgium, the Ambassador of Japan, the Secretary of State Elihu Root – a relative of Martha Root – and other notable people. The neighbor on the opposite side of the avenue was Gifford Pinchot, whose summer residence in Milford was visited by 'Abdu'l-Bahá (see vol. 1, chapter 17). Its owner at the time was Alice Hemmick, the mother of Laura Dreyfus-Barney.

On 9 December 1916 the *Woman's Journal and Suffrage News* (Boston) reported the acquisition of the new facility for the NAWSA, and in the course of the report, the article mentioned a letter received by Mrs Walter McNab Miller, Vice-President of the NAWSA:

A curious coincidence with regards to the house was a letter received by Mrs. Walter McNab Miller last week, written by a friend who had no idea such a move was contemplated, informing her that Abdul-Baha Abbas, the famous Persian religious leader and mystic, has come out for increased rights for women in that far off land. Abbas slept in the new Suffrage House some years ago, the guest of Mr. and Mrs. Hemmick. Mrs. Hemmick says she has frequently discussed the question of the votes for women with the distinguished Persian, both here and in his native land.

The Woman's Peace Party came into being in this house, and Mrs. Hemmick, its owner, was first president.[64]

32

RACE UNITY

As seen in previous chapters, in many of His talks and interviews 'Abdu'l-Bahá touched on the subject of race unity.

Racial prejudice and the idea of racial supremacy were not only social problems in America but also the conceptual framework that legitimized the policies of the European colonial powers. They were also the nucleus of those ideologies which at the time of the travels of 'Abdu'l-Bahá were in their embryonic stage but which in less than three decades would lead Europe and eventually the whole world to an unprecedented disaster.

This chapter reviews some of the press accounts of addresses of 'Abdu'l-Bahá to organizations and meetings concerned with the issue of race unity.

The Universal Races Congress: London, 26–9 July 1911

The Universal Races Congress was organized with the aim of establishing a forum to 'discuss, in the light of science and the modern conscience, the general relations subsisting between the peoples of the West and those of the East, between so-called white and so-called coloured peoples, with a view to encouraging between them a fuller understanding, the most friendly feelings, and a heartier co-operation'.[1] It was based on the belief that racial prejudice was behind every conflict between nations and that overcoming racial prejudice was therefore an indispensable condition for the establishment of peace.

The Congress, which was held in the large hall of the University of London, brought together more than 2,100 participants, with 17 governments sending official delegates. It was presided over by Lord Weardale (Philip James Stanhope 1847–1923). The American writer and educator Felix Adler (1851–1933), who had conceived the event some years before, presided over the general committee of the

Congress. William Pember Reeves (1857–1932), at the time director of the London School of Economics and a former government minister from New Zealand, chaired the executive council. During the sessions over 60 papers by some of the most prominent thinkers, social leaders and politicians of the time were presented. Workshops and side events were also held in addition to the official meetings.

'Abdu'l-Bahá was invited by the organization to participate in one of the sessions scheduled for the Congress but He was unable to attend. Instead He sent a paper and a message of greeting which were read on His behalf.

On 17 March 1911 *The Times* of London announced the inclusion in the official program of 'His Excellency Abdul Baha Abbas (Abbas Effendi)' with a paper entitled 'The Bahai Movement' and scheduled for the morning of 27 July.[2]

Two days before the opening of the Congress the same journal wrongly reported that 'Abdul Baha Abbas, promoter of the Bahai movement in Persia, will present a paper which will deal with that movement.'[3] Other magazines in England such as *Light* (London)[4] and *The Christian Commonwealth* (London)[5] also anticipated the participation of 'Abdu'l-Bahá. Similar information was also published in Egypt[6] and France.[7]

The day before 'Abdu'l-Bahá's message was read, *The Christian Commonwealth* published a lengthy article by Wellesley Tudor Pole with his impressions of the Congress and announced that 'Abdul Baha, the present leader of the Bahai Movement, has sent a special letter of greeting to the Congress, and it will be read to-morrow (Thursday) at the morning session'.[8]

In its following issue, 2 August, *The Christian Commonwealth* published a second article by Tudor Pole which included the text of the greeting:

Great interest was aroused on Thursday during the discussion on Abdu'l Baha's letter to the congress, the full text of which follows:

'Alexandria, May 29, 1911
'To the President, First Universal Races Congress

'My Dear Friend: –Your letter of invitation has been received, and I am much obliged for it. It is my utmost desire to be present at such a gathering, for I am thoroughly confident that beneficial results shall surely follow these meetings, and that they will become the means of establishing friendship and love among the world's different races. Thus the basis of enmity may be destroyed and the tent of unity of the world of humanity be raised throughout all regions.

'I regret much that circumstances may prevent me from attending, but I will endeavor as much as lies in my power to attend. Failing to do so, pray excuse me.

'With a sincere heart I supplicate at the Divine Threshold that this congress may be successful in founding a noble institution which shall be permanent and everlasting; that it may ignite a candle from which a heavenly light shall beam and plant a tree whose fruit may be friendship, love and unity between all the children of men, so that conflict and warfare may be abolished, and patriotic, racial, religious and political prejudices become unknown. Peace should replace strife, enmity be superseded by love, estrangement annihilated, and unity established. Then what has been spoken of in the heavenly books will become well rooted in the hearts of all, and the glad tidings of the sacred writings be fulfilled. In conclusion I offer my utmost appreciation and respect to such a blessed congress.

'(Sig) ABBAS.'

The chairman, Mr. J. M. Robertson, MP, made sympathetic reference to the spiritual language in which the letter was couched, and his remarks were applauded.[9]

On 28 July, the day after 'Abdu'l-Bahá's message was read, the *Manchester Guardian* summarized the words of Dr Christian L. Lange,[10] who spoke at the same session, and reported some of the remarks made by him with regard to 'Abdu'l-Bahá's letter:

He took it that religions ought not to be discussed – (*hear, hear*), – but it could not be avoided – and he had no wish to do so – that the religion of the writer would tinge his views.

Therefore he thought Abdul Baha, of Persia, was quite right, in dealing with the Bahai movement, to say that they should approach the discussion with good feeling. He said they invited suggestions from other people, and particularly from Eastern races in pointing out in what respects our Western civilisation might gain from their own institutions. – (*Cheers*).¹¹

The Tablet sent as a paper for the Congress was included in the proceedings together with an introduction to the Bahá'í Faith penned by Tudor Pole.¹² In the United Kingdom, the *Westminster Review* published a review of the proceedings by Harold Berman in which the author quoted an excerpt of the Tablet of 'Abdu'l-Bahá.¹³ Rev. C. C. Martindale published a long review for the Catholic magazine *The Month*. Half of his article was dedicated to a discussion of the Bahá'í Faith (see chapter 36 below).¹⁴

Echoes of the Tablet also found their way into publications outside the United Kingdom. A. Piquet Chessel, a correspondent with the South African weekly *Indian Opinion* (Phoenix), reproduced in a report about the Congress portions of the communication sent by the Master as well as fragments of one of His writings:

> There is in existence to-day, mainly in Persia, but spreading throughout the East and the West, a remarkable movement known as the Bahai movement, drawing its adherence from members of all the great faiths of the world, a movement of a spiritual nature designed to promote Universal Brotherhood, founded upon the basis of that Universal Religion that underlies every religious system. The leader of the movement, Abdul Baha Abbas, addressed a letter to the Congress . . .
>
> Passive Resisters will be glad to hear the following from this great man:– 'The Quintessence of Truth is this: we must all become united and harmonised, in order to illumine this gloomy world; to abolish the foundations of hostility and of animosity from among mankind; to rejoice the inhabitants of the Universe with the Holy Fragrance of the Nature of the beauty of Abha; to enlighten the people of the East and of the West with the Light of True Guidance; to hoist the Tent of the Love of God and suffer each and all to enter under its protection; to bestow comfort and tranquillity on every one under the shade of the heavenly tree; to astonish the enemy by the manifestation of the utmost love; to make, of ravenous and bloodthirsty wolves, gazelles of the meadow of the Love of God; to administer the taste of non-resistance to the tyrant; to teach the

long-suffering and the resignation of martyrs to the murderer; to spread the signs of Oneness; to chant the praises of the Glorious Lord . . . to cry out in the ears of the children of the kingdom, verily the earth is illumined by the Light of its Lord! This is Reality! This is Guidance! This is Service!'[15]

In its previous issue, *Indian Opinion* had also mentioned the presence of Bahá'ís at the Congress.[16] It should be noted that this magazine was founded and directed by Mahatma Gandhi and thus it is certain that as early as 1911 he already knew and had read about the Bahá'í Faith.

Also in South Africa, *The Christian Express* (Lovedale) mentioned that 'A quaint and interesting communication to the Congress is a letter from the Persian prophet Abdu'l Baha, the present head of the Bahai movement. In Persia alone there are estimated to be at least two million Bahais.'[17]

In the United States, the *Journal of Race Development* published at Clark University (Worcester, MA) also mentioned the talk of 'Abdu'l-Bahá in its review of the Congress proceedings.[18] Its editor, George Hubbard Blakeslee, later met with 'Abdu'l-Bahá in Boston and invited Him to speak at Clark University (see vol. 1, chapter 16, pp. 325–6). In New York, the *Catholic World* also published a review of the proceedings in which the author dedicated several pages to commenting on the Bahá'í Faith in a rather critical tone (see chapter 36 below).[19]

In Europe, 'Abdu'l-Bahá's messages to the Congress were also briefly mentioned on two occasions in a Czech journal published in Prague[20] and in a French scholarly journal.[21]

* * *

As well as the paper of 'Abdu'l-Bahá, the Bahá'í participation during the Congress also hosted other activities. A few days before the opening of the event a series of lectures on the Bahá'í Faith was arranged to which delegates and the general public were invited. The following announcement outlined the whole program:

> In connection with the first Universal Races Congress, which will be held at the University of London, South Kensington, July 26–29, under the presidency of Lord Weardale, a series of lectures has been

arranged at the Passmore Edwards Settlement. These will take place at 8.30 p.m., on Tuesday, Wednesday, Thursday, and Friday, July 18–21. The first lecture is by Mrs. Stannard (lately from India and Egypt) on 'The Awakening of the East', Mr. B. S. Mosley (from Cairo) in the chair; the second, 'Personal Experiences of a Bahai', by Dr. Arastoo Hakim (of Teheran), Mr. Tarmadonul-Molk, and Mr. Sydney Sprague (of Cairo), chairman, Mr. Eric Hammond; the third by Mr. S. H. Leeder, on 'Arab Life and Religion from Personal Observations', chairman, the Right Hon. Ameer Ali Seyd, M.A.; and the fourth by Miss A. M. Buckton (the well-known authoress of 'Eagerheart') on 'The Relation of the Bahai Movement to Christianity', Mr. Ebenezer Howard presiding.[22]

On 26 July *The Christian Commonwealth* published a lengthy account of these meetings.[23] A week later the same periodical published the text of a talk about the Faith delivered during the Congress by Tammaddun'ul Mulk and also a summary of another talk by Sydney Sprague.[24] On 9 August, the same journal published an account signed by Jessie Phillips of a different Bahá'í meeting held at Caxton Hall, Westminster, on 1 August. The speakers – among them many delegates at the Congress – were invited to compare the Bahá'í Faith with other systems of thought. Some of those who took part in the program were Judge Henry Moseley from Egypt, who acted as chairman, Wellesley Tudor Pole, Hippolyte Dreyfus, Jean Stannard and Bishop Matthew.[25] The same issue contained a further report of the Congress by Tudor Pole in which no direct reference to the Bahá'í Faith was made but in which the author declared that 'Some of us believe that the all-wise Christ-Spirit has again come incarnate in our midst, and has lighted a new lamp in Persia that will someday illumine the whole world!'[26]

First Visit to Washington

In Washington 'Abdu'l-Bahá was invited to address a public meeting held at Howard University on 23 April 1912. The event had a special significance since Howard University, a black educational institution, was one of the country's foremost champions in the struggle for the emancipation of the black people in the United States. On the same day 'Abdu'l-Bahá addressed a regular meeting of the Bethel Literary and Historical Society which was held, as usual, at the Metropolitan African Methodist Episcopal Church in Washington.²⁷

The meeting at Howard University was announced in several articles published in local newspapers and attracted a large audience.²⁸ 'Abdu'l-Bahá spoke on the abolition of racial prejudice and the unity of mankind²⁹ and some accounts of the event were published in the local press. The *Washington Times*, for instance, reported that 'Abdul made two addresses yesterday, the first at Howard University, and the second at the Metropolitan A. M. E. Church. At Howard University an audience of about 1,000 persons crowded Rankin Chapel and listened to the Persian speaker expound the doctrine of the oneness of the human race.'³⁰ The account published in the *Star* stated that 'an audience of 1,000 persons crowded Rankin Chapel' and quoted some of 'Abdu'l-Baha's words.³¹

The Bee, a leading Washington black weekly, published some weeks after the address a brief note vividly describing the atmosphere and the reaction of the public during the meeting:

ABDUL BAHA
REVOLUTION IN RELIGIOUS WORSHIP

On Tuesday, April 23d, Abdul Baha, the venerable Persian, leader of the Baha movement, which has several millions of followers throughout the world, and is attracting considerable attention in Washington, addressed the students and faculty of Howard University. The occasion was impressive and most interesting, as in flowing Oriental robes this speaker gave his message. He was received with such fervor that the breathless silence during his address was followed by prolonged applause, causing him to bow his acknowledgments and give a second greeting.³²

In an interview for New York's *Independent* given in July, 'Abdu'l-Bahá referred to His visit to Howard University:

In Washington recently I addressed the students of Howard University – about fifteen hundred of them – and I told them that they must be very good to the white race of America. I told them that they must never forget to be grateful and thankful. I said to them: 'If you want to know really what great service the white race here has rendered to you, go to Africa and study the condition of your own race there.' But at the same time I said that the white people here must be very kind to those whom they have freed. The white people must treat those whom they have freed with justness and firmness, but also with perfect love. America's example in freeing the slaves has been a power for freedom everywhere. Because America freed her slaves, even at the cost of one of the bloodiest wars of modern times, other nations have felt themselves bound to free slaves. America's leadership in humanitarian and altruistic matters is generally acknowledged. Instead of robbing the weak, she helps them. The nations look to America to lead them in good works.[33]

When 'Abdu'l-Bahá departed from Washington, *The Bee* summarized the effect of His visit on the city and the general attitude of the Bahá'ís regarding the racial issue:

ABDUL BAHA ON RELIGIOUS UNITY

Abdul Baha Abbas, the leader of the Baha movement for the worldwide religion unity, has been in the city. Through the missionary work of Mrs. Christian D. Helmick (Mrs. A. C Barney that was), quite a colony of colored Bahaists has been developed in Washington, and these earnest disciples gave their patron saint an especially warm reception. On Tuesday evening the venerable prophet addressed a large audience at Metropolitan A. M. E. Church, in connection with the Bethel Literary Society. At noon Tuesday, the Abdul spoke to the students of Howard University. The principal advocate of the Bahai faith in this city is Mr. Louis C. Gregory, a brilliant young lawyer and government official, whose zeal in the work was so absorbing that he made a comprehensive tour of Egypt and the Holy Land to study at first hand the history and philosophy of this remarkable cult.

The Bahai belief is that universal peace can come only through the harmony of all religions, and that all religions are basically one. Its consistent espousal of the 'fatherhood of God and the brotherhood of man' is causing the new faith to find considerable favor among many of our leading people. Its white devotees, even in this prejudice-ridden community, refuse to draw the color line. The informal meetings held frequently in the fashionable mansions of the cultured society in Sheridan Circle, Dupont Circle, Connecticut and Massachusetts Avenues, have been open to Negroes on terms of absolute equality. The liberality of the Bahai faith is evidenced in the fact that one can be of any known religious denomination, and yet maintain good-standing as a disciple of Bahai.[34]

On 4 May the *Chicago Defender* offered to its readers a summary of 'Abdu'l-Bahá's activities in Washington, describing His visit to the capital as a 'triumphal march' over racial prejudices:

TO BREAK THE COLOR LINE
ABDUL BAHA, THE GREAT PERSIAN PHILOSOPHER AND TEACHER, AIMS TO UNITE THE PEOPLES OF ALL RACES AND CREEDS IN ONE GREAT BOND OF BROTHERHOOD

Washington DC. May – Abdul Baha (the servant of God), the great Persian philosopher and teacher, head of the Bahaists, will reach Chicago next Monday. He comes to bring hope to the colored people.

His visit to Washington has been a triumphal march. He has met and conquered Southern prejudices. He made addresses at Metropolitan A. M. E. church, at Howard University and at many of the white churches and halls and was listened to by many thousands of people of both races, who applauded his propaganda of the fatherhood of God and the brotherhood of man.

He was the guest of one of Washington's wealthiest women, one who moves in the most exclusive social circles at the capital, and yet her house has been thrown open to rich and poor and black and white. Southern people whose hearts were once filled with the most bitter prejudices against their brothers in black, have publicly acknowledged their change of heart and now they treat the colored people as brothers indeed.[35]

Among the color lines that 'Abdu'l-Bahá broke during His sojourn in America was that of interracial marriage. During their pilgrimage in Alexandria, Louis Gregory, a prominent Bahá'í and worker for the social rights of the black people, and Louisa Mathew, a Bahá'í from the United Kingdom, were encouraged by 'Abdu'l-Bahá to marry and they did so, coinciding with His presence in America. On 28 September, the *Chicago Defender* stated, 'Announcement is made of the engagement of

Mr. Louis G. Gregory of the Treasury Department, and Miss Louise Mathew, of Kent, England. Mr. Gregory is an ardent believer in the faith of Abdul Hamid [sic], leader of the Bahai cult, and so is Miss Mathew. They met abroad some months ago en route to Persia [sic], where they were making a closer study of the history of the Bahai religion, and the acquaintance and sympathetic interest quickly ripened into love. The marriage takes place this month. Mr. and Mrs. Gregory will make their home in Washington, after a brief tour of the east.'[36]

When 'Abdu'l-Bahá again visited Washington on His return from California, various black newspapers made the following statements about Him:

> ABDUL-BAHA COMING TO THE CAPITAL
> Washington DC, Nov. 8 (special). – Abdul Baha, the founder and chief exponent of the Bahai sect of religionists, is to pay this city another visit soon, coming on from Chicago. The local arrangements, as far as the colored adherents are concerned, are in the hands of Mr. L. G. Gregory. No color line is drawn, but Mr. Gregory will see to it that the colored brethren are kept informed of the meetings and ceremonies. Prof. and Mrs. G. W. Cook, of Howard University, Lieut. T. H. R. Clarke and Assistant Registrar C. F. Adams are enthusiastic believers in the cult, along with Mr. Gregory and many others of like prominence, and are of the opinion that the spirit of Bahaism will go far toward solving the race problem in this country, by obliterating it through the spread of the Fatherhood of God and the Brotherhood of Man.[37]

The Conference of the National Association for the Advancement of Colored People

The National Association for the Advancement of Colored People (NAACP) was founded in 1909 by a group of leading African-Americans and white liberals who endeavored to improve the conditions and defend the rights of the American black population. Among the founders and leading members of the association, which today has over half a million members, was the famous civil rights leader William DuBois (1868–1963) who was associated with the Bahá'í Faith through his wife Nina, who was a Bahá'í in New York.

In 1912 the NAACP held its fourth Annual Conference in Chicago. The opening session took place at Sinai Temple on the evening of Sunday, 28 April, and had an attendance of over a thousand people.

'Abdu'l-Bahá was invited to address the opening session and was also invited by Jane Addams (1860–1935), honorary chairman of the conference and the founder of Hull House, to a reception held there.[38] An article appearing simultaneously in *The Chicago Defender* and *The Broad Ax* (Chicago), which was probably released by the organizers, gave some general information about the conference and stressed the fact that 'Abdu'l-Bahá was to be present at some of its sessions:

> . . . One of the most striking features of the opening session of the conference, held at the new Sinai Temple on Sunday evening, will be the appearance of the venerable Abdul Baha, head of the Baha order, which is now spreading, with its tenets of brotherly love and inter-racial harmony, around the world. The Baha cult comes originally from Persia and embraces people of all religions and races, Christians, Mohammedans, Jews and others. It is said that Abdul Baha made a profound impression in London last year when he appeared at the great Universal Congress of Races.
>
> Abdul Baha insists that he is not seeking converts to a special religion but is merely preaching to the followers of all faiths, creeds and colors that they can, and should, live in harmony and mutual respect. He is strenuously opposed to race discrimination and oppression.
>
> Dressed in his picturesque robes and turban, Abdul Baha will appear for a few minutes at the Sunday night meeting and address the audience briefly. The other speakers that night will be Mr. Oswald Garrison Villard, editor of the New York Evening Post and the grandson of William Lloyd Garrison, the abolitionist; Dr. Emil G. Hirsch, and Prof. William Pickens of Talladega, Ala., one of the most eloquent colored speakers in the country. Miss Jane Addams will preside at that meeting.[39]

'Abdu'l-Bahá was also mentioned in announcements published in other journals.[40] The *Baltimore American*, for instance, mentioned that 'by his presence, ['Abdu'l-Bahá] will testify to the sympathy of the Persians in the cause of the Africans'.[41]

The original program for 'Abdu'l-Bahá, however, had to be changed since He arrived in Chicago on the evening of 29 April and thus His address at the opening session was moved to the closing session.

On 4 May the *Chicago Defender* published an account by Mildred Miller, one the participants at the conference, in which 'Abdu'l-Bahá was mentioned:

> The reception at Hull House was a very delightful and interesting affair. That wonderful teacher of peace and the brotherhood of man, Abdul Baha, of Persia, made his first appearance at Hull House.
>
> In both of his addresses at Hull House and Handel hall, Abdul Baha very eloquently showed the folly of discrimination on the account of the only point of difference between men, that of the color of the skin.
>
> A garden of flowers, all of one color, would be monotonous and by no means beautiful.
>
> The local committee deserves much credit, of course, for the arrangements for the comfort, etc., of the guests and attendants upon the N. A. A. C. P. conference, but yet when one looked at the ushers for the evenings at Handel hall one could not but think of Abdul Baha's garden with the one color and variety of flower.[42]

An editorial in the same issue thanking the conference speakers and the organizers briefly mentioned the Master.[43]

A report by Mary White Ovington (1865–1951), secretary and co-founder of the NAACP, was published in *The Survey* (New York) and contained a reference to the words of the Master in one of His talks: 'Following a reception Tuesday afternoon at Hull House Abdul Baha, the head of the Bahai movement, visited the delegates. In his brown robe and turban, with his white hair and beard, Abdul Baha is a noble figure. He spoke through his interpreter, and after describing the many things that unite the races, he showed that all that separated them was their color. And this was foolish prejudice, he said, since for all to be one color would be monotonous. The colors of the race were like the colors of the flowers in a garden. Who would wish to have white flowers only? God had made the garden beautiful by giving it flowers of many hues.'[44] This report was also briefly mentioned in the *Christian Register* (Boston).[45]

The Crisis (New York), the official publication of the NAACP, published in its May 1912 issue an article in its section 'Men of the Month' that was dedicated to the Master. It was presumably written by William DuBois, editor of the magazine, and as well as its references to 'Abdu'l-Bahá, it also contained a full page reproduction of one of the portraits taken of Him in Paris and a summary of the history of the Bahá'í Faith.

> ... The movement presents in many respects a striking parallel with the early growth of Christianity. Like Christianity, it began as a protest against the corruption of established, intolerant, unspiritual religion, and also like Christianity it drew on itself the most inhuman persecutions. The number of martyrs is estimated at about 10,000. They have been burned alive, beheaded, torn in pieces, hanged and tortured in all the ways official cruelty could devise. There has not been an instance of recantation. The records of the Bahais speak of the victims 'athirst' for the draught of martyrdom, and it is indeed true that they died with songs on their lips.
> ... At Abdul Baha's house in Acca all men are welcomed. Persian, African, Frenchman, American – they all meet as brothers before the master. He is the most generous and hospitable of men and all are welcome to his table. He follows literally the scriptural injunction to give his goods to the poor; the coat he wears is usually all he has.
> Naturally, he is interested in the question of race prejudice in this country, where he has so many disciples. Recently he sent this message to one of them, Mrs. M. L. Botay, who has sent it to The Crisis.
> 'Give Mrs. Botay my greetings and love and tell her she must greatly endeavor through the assistance of heaven to cast light among the colored people, so that they may become as our brothers, no blacks, no whites, both as one. By this means you shall free America from all prejudice. Because in the Kingdom of God all are the same, whether black or white. The greater the faith of either, the more acceptable is the Kingdom. A faithful colored believer is a child of the Kingdom, while a white unbeliever is deprived. God looks upon hearts, not upon colors. He looks upon qualities, not upon bodies.'[46]

In June 1912 *The Crisis* again mentioned 'Abdu'l-Bahá in a report of the conference:

... There were scattered throughout the sessions speeches of widely different character from those mentioned: The amusing and keenly epigrammatic oratory of Pickens, the calm sweet universalism of Abdul Baha and the interesting statement of Dr. Keating.

... The last night presented a scene which one would travel far to see. A Jewish rabbi presided; on the platform were Mrs. Emmons Blaine and Mrs. Cyrus McCormick, her mother; among the speakers were three striking personalities: the president of the Illinois Miners' Labor Union; a Southern white man; the head of a colored settlement and a cultivated colored woman who in quiet tones told of the dynamiting of her own home. As opening and climax to this remarkable gathering came a speech of Abdul Baha and a farewell from Julius Rosenwald. Small wonder that a thousand disappointed people were unable to get even standing room in the hall.[47]

The same issue also contained extracts of 'Abdu'l-Bahá's address at Handel Hall.[48] The talk at Hull House was published in the *Theosophic Messenger* (Chicago), in August 1912.[49]

Just a few weeks after the participation of 'Abdu'l-Bahá at the conference, the black journal *The Appeal* (St Paul, MN) published the following comments praising 'Abdu'l-Bahá's efforts for racial unity:

Abdul Baha, Abbas Effendi, oriental world leader and head of the Bahai Movement, has been received with great favor during his visit to this country. He has traveled as far West as Chicago and will tour the United States.

Abdul Baha brings the message of universal peace and amity. The basis of his religion, if it may be so called, is the abolition of the color line and the uniting of all men, regardless of creed or complexion, on a platform of common humanity.

Bahaism is a great improvement on the spurious Christianity which exists in the United States. Few Caucasian Christians even preach equality of mankind and a Caucasian Christian who practices the square deal in the treatment of his brother in black is a rare bird. With Bahaists, the Fatherhood of God, and the Brotherhood of Man is not only a theory but also a practice.[50]

33

AN INTERNATIONAL LANGUAGE

In several of His writings Bahá'u'lláh called the governments of the world to select 'a single language for the use of all on earth, and adopt ... a common script.'[1] According to the Bahá'í teachings, the establishment of an international auxiliary language is one of the requisites for the unfoldment of a new world order and the establishment of the Most Great Peace, and thus it was one of the subjects about which 'Abdu'l-Bahá spoke repeatedly in His public talks in the West.

During the lifetime of Bahá'u'lláh two plans to create a universal language were put into action. The first was the Volapük, which was constructed in 1879 by the Catholic priest Martin Schleyer (1831–1912), who claimed that God had inspired him in a dream with the idea of creating an international language. After some years of extraordinary growth, in which the Volapük movement spread across Europe with more than 250 clubs and 25 periodicals, dissensions within the movement diminished its original vigor until it virtually disappeared.

In 1887 a young Warsaw ophthalmologist of Jewish background, Ludwig L. Zamenhof (1859–1917), published a booklet describing the grammar of a language on which he had been working for ten years with the aim of fostering international peace by overcoming the linguistic barriers existing between the peoples of the world. The title of that work was *Lingvo Internacia* (International Language) and was signed with the pseudonym Doktoro Esperanto (Doctor Hopeful). The language he created was thenceforth known as Esperanto.

In 1905 the first International Esperanto Congress[2] was convened in France with delegates from more than 20 countries. By 1913 Esperantists around the world were able to maintain no less than 140 periodicals in 36 countries. As we shall see, in that year almost all Esperanto magazines carrying international news mentioned 'Abdu'l-Bahá.

American Esperantists

In mid-August 1910, a few weeks before the departure of 'Abdu'l-Bahá from Haifa for Egypt, the city of Washington hosted the sixth International Esperanto Congress. The occasion was of historical significance because for the first time such an important event for Esperantists was held on the American continent. While the number of participants was considerably lower than Congresses held in previous years – 350 participants against the 1,500 that had attended the previous Congresses in Barcelona (1909) and Dresden (1908) – it nevertheless attracted delegates from several countries and helped to promote Esperanto on American soil. Dr Zamenhof, who personally attended the Congress, received considerable attention from the press and was able to publicize Esperanto with much success.

Among the Bahá'ís attending the congress were Ali Kuli Khan, who acted as the official representative of the Kingdom of Persia, and Amin'u'lláh Faríd. The latter greeted the Congress on behalf of the Bahá'í community and shared Bahá'u'lláh's teachings regarding an international auxiliary language. A report of the Congress appeared in the *Amerika Esperantisto* (Chicago), the official organ of the Esperantists in the United States. It briefly mentioned Farid's participation stating: '[the Bahá'ís] say that the original Baha prophesied the coming of a universal language. This salutation, like that of the theosophists and others, was quite unofficial and outside the formal sessions of the congress, where religious and political topics were strictly taboo.'[3]

In a letter, 'Abdu'l-Bahá gave Farid exact instructions about his involvement at the Congress. This letter was published some months after the Congress in the *Amerika Esperantisto*:

Persia. – Abdul Baha, the present head of the Bahai movement, which seems to be rapidly growing in importance, has sent a communication to Dr. Ameen Fareed, who greeted the Sixth International Esperanto Congress on behalf of the Bahai movement, as follows (translation):

His Honor, Dr. Fareed –
Upon him be Baha-el-Abha! O servant of the Holy Threshold! You have written in regard to Esperanto and your speech before

the Congress. It was most appropriate and acceptable. If possible meet with Dr. Zamenhof and show him the Kitab-el-Akdas (Book of Laws) and translate the verse which concerns the Universal Language and tell him: This clear verse which was revealed forty-five years ago, will prove the cause of spreading your Universal Language in all the East. The Bahais shall consider the study of this language as an incumbent duty upon them, and it will be to them a religious duty. Therefore, men, women and children, all will acquire it.[4]

The article then continued quoting those passages of the Kitáb-i-Aqdas addressing the issue of an international language. 'Abdu'l-Bahá's letter was also printed in the *British Esperantist* (London)[5] in the 1912 volume of *Das Esperanto ein Kulturfaktor* (Leizpig), a yearly volume printed for the annual German Esperanto Congresses,[6] and in the Australian journal *Daily Herald* (Adelaide).[7] In France, the magazine *La Revuo* (Paris) also mentioned the participation of Faríd at the Congress as the representative of the 'bahai movement'.[8] The Bahá'ís were also mentioned in a report that appeared in the Bohemian Esperanto magazine *Rund um die Welt* (Prague).[9]

In the ensuing months other references to 'Abdu'l-Bahá were published in *Amerika Esperantisto*. As early as November 1911, for instance, while 'Abdu'l-Bahá was in Europe, the magazine carried information about the upcoming Second Annual Conference of the Persian–American Education Society and mentioned the fact that 'Abdu'l-Bahá was expected to participate in the program (see vol. 1, chapter 11, pp. 245–53). It should be noted that Edwin C. Reed, General Secretary of the Esperanto Association of North America, was one of the members of the Central Executive Board of the Persian–American Education Society and thus had frequent contact with the Bahá'ís. The article also carried the following information:

> The Persian–American Educational Society, with headquarters in Washington, D. C, recently received the news that several classes in Esperanto are about to organize in Persia. In the school of Tarbiat, at Teheran, a class for the study of the International Language is already established. In the cities of Tabriz and Urmiah, Persia, there is considerable interest and enthusiasm, and the Persian–American Educational Society is providing them with the necessary

textbooks. This is a very good beginning, and it is hoped that as Abdul Baha, the leader of the Bahai Revelation, has commanded his three million followers in Persia to study this language, many classes will be established in other cities before long.[10]

During His first visit to Washington, 'Abdu'l-Bahá conveyed a message to the American Esperantists through Joseph Hannen, one of the early American Bahá'ís and himself an Esperantist. This message, which years later was included in the volume *The Promulgation of Universal Peace*, was first published in the *Amerika Esperantisto*. Hannen prefaced the message with an introduction outlining the context in which it was delivered:

> On Thursday, April 23, Abdul Baha gave to the writer a special message to the Esperantists of America, and through them to the associated friends of the world. This message was dictated in the course of an exceedingly busy day, when the venerable leader of the Orient, whose friends and followers number thousands in the Occident, was seated in the Reception Room of Mrs. Parsons' home at 18th and R streets. The wonderful countenance of the 'Servant of God' – the meaning of his name, Abdul Baha – was aglow with enthusiasm as he delivered the following . . .[11]

This message was also published in the *British Esperantist* on January 1913.[12]

London Esperantists

In 1903 a group of Esperantists created the London Esperanto Club. This organization led in turn to the establishment in 1904 of the British Esperanto Association. One of the pioneers of Esperanto in London and its main financial supporter was William Stead, the editor of the *Review of Reviews* (London), who met 'Abdu'l-Bahá in 1911 (see chapter 35 below). The first president of the club was Felix Stone Moscheles (1833–1917).

Moscheles was the son of the pianist Ignaz Moscheles and himself a noted painter. A personal friend of Zamenhof, he was not only a leading Esperantist but also an ardent pacifist who eventually presided over the International Arbitration and Peace Association and was a member of the International Peace Bureau.

La Londona Esperantisto (London), the organ of the London Federation of Esperanto Groups, mentioned 'Abdu'l-Bahá as early as September 1911 in an article by T. Bayard Simmons about the First Universal Races Congress in which the author stated that 'not without interest for the Esperantist is the letter addressed to the delegates by Abdul Baha Abbas, the leader of the Bahai Movement, a movement which has always stood for the principle of an International Language.'[13]

During 'Abdu'l-Bahá's second visit to England, Moscheles invited Him to speak at his studio on 19 January 1913. The meeting started at 4 p.m. and many prominent people in London society were invited to hear the Master.[14] Lady Blomfield opened the session with a presentation on the origins of the Bahá'í Faith and afterwards Moscheles introduced 'Abdu'l-Bahá, who in His address spoke on the subject of peace and the need for a universal language as a means for its achievement.[15]

An account of the meeting was published in *The British Esperantist* in February 1913. The article mentions William Mann, who was a leading Esperantist and Theosophist, the assistant editor of *The British Esperantist* and the translator into Esperanto of a booklet by Sydney Sprague on the Bahá'í Faith.

> Abdul Baha on Peace and Esperanto.– On Sunday, January 19, a distinguished audience filled to overflowing Mr. Felix Moscheles' charming studio in Chelsea, to hear the famous Bahai leader discourse on the appropriate theme 'Peace and Esperanto'. Lady Blomfield, who presided, gave, by way of introduction, an eloquent account of the remarkable history and progress of the Bahai movement, which now has a numerous following both in the East and in the West. After a few words of welcome from Mr. Moscheles, Abdul Baha addressed the meeting in euphonious Persian, his remarks being skillfully translated sentence by sentence into English by Mr. Ahmad Sohrab.
>
> In his interesting address, of which we can here give only the main points, the speaker said that while last century was characterized by the note of liberty and the strengthening of the spirit of nationality, this century, which would be a still more remarkable

one, was to have as its characteristic the note of internationality and of the unification of the peoples of the world, in religion, science, art, commerce. The practical means to the realisation of this world-unity were now being established, and high in importance among such means were the Hague Tribunal of International Arbitration and the Auxiliary Language, Esperanto, which was to make possible this unification by giving channels for the free expression of the spirit of love and sympathy and co-operation between man and man the world over. Both of these, the international court and the international language, had been foretold fifty years ago by the great founder of the Bahai movement, Baha'o'llah, and both must inevitably be established and prevail. Mr. W. Mann expressed the gratitude of the Esperantists present for the speaker's advocacy of their language, advocacy which was all the more valued because the criticism was sometimes made, without real basis in fact, that Esperanto was unsuited for Eastern needs. Abbas Effendi, in reply, said that Zamenhof was worthy of all men's reverence and love for his great service in this work of world-unity, and that he, for his part, would make known and recommend Esperanto among the Bahais wherever he went.[16]

The news of this talk was also published in other journals in England[17] as well as in Australia[18] and France.[19]

Meeting with Edinburgh's Esperantists

The first public address of 'Abdu'l-Bahá in Scotland was delivered at a meeting organized in His honor by the Edinburgh Esperanto Society on 7 January 1913. This was not however the first contact that Edinburgh Esperantists had with the Bahá'í Faith, for on 6 November 1912 William M. Page, the secretary of the local Esperanto Society, had read a paper on the Bahá'í Faith to its members.[20]

The minutes of the Esperanto Society show that it was the Edinburgh Bahá'í Jane Whyte who suggested that a meeting with 'Abdu'l-Bahá be arranged. The idea was discussed and approved in a special session held by the council of the Society on 27 December 1912.[21]

'Abdu'l-Bahá's address to Esperantists was held at the Freemason's Hall at 8.15 p.m. and was preceded by a half hour recital performed by the famous blind organist and composer Alfred Hollins (1865–1942). Some eight hundred people attended the meeting, which was announced in local newspapers.²²

The Presbyterian leader and writer Dr John Kerman (1864–1929) presided over the meeting. In his opening words he offered a long and sympathetic introduction to the Bahá'í Faith. Andrew Wilson, of the British Esperanto Society, welcomed 'Abdu'l-Bahá on the platform on behalf of the organization. The Master then spoke on the need for an international language. His address and His encouraging words about Esperanto were highly welcomed by Esperantists. The scientist Patrick Geddes, at whose invitation 'Abdu'l-Bahá was to speak at another meeting the next day, closed the meeting with some further remarks about 'Abdu'l-Bahá and the Bahá'í Faith.

On the following day, 8 January, the Edinburgh newspapers the *Scotsman*, the *Evening Dispatch* and the *Evening News* published various accounts of the meeting, which included lengthy summaries of Dr Kerman's words and of 'Abdu'l-Bahá's address. The *Evening Dispatch*, moreover, included an article on the Bahá'í Faith which was based on Sydney Sprague's work *The Story of the Bahai Movement* (1908). In Glasgow, the *Herald* also published on 8 January an account of the meeting.²³

The account in the *Evening Dispatch* opened by stating that 'Considerable interest has been aroused in certain circles in Edinburgh over the visit of Abdul Baha, whose mission it is to explain the Bahai teaching to the Western world. Abdul Baha, who presents a striking figure in his loose Persian robes, opened his campaign in the city last night by addressing a crowded meeting of ladies and gentlemen in the Freemasons' Hall over which the Rev. Dr. Kerman presided.'²⁴ The *Scotsman* also indicated that 'Much public interest was taken in last night's meeting, the hall being crowded, and a large number of the audience standing throughout the proceedings.'²⁵ In the same vein, the *Evening News* indicated that 'The hall was crowded to the doors, and many people contented themselves with standing.' 'Abdu'l-Bahá was described as having 'the appearance of the patriarchs of Biblical days'.²⁶

The account in the *Evening News* also mentioned the fact that some in the audience expected 'Abdu'l-Bahá to speak about the Bahá'í Faith rather than of the need for an international language: 'In paying the best possible compliment to the Society, whose guest he was, Abdul

Baha, unwittingly disappointed the great majority of those who had come to hear him. They had hoped to hear from his lips some outline of the religion for whose sake he suffered 40 years of imprisonment at the hands of the Turks, but Abdul Baha devoted his remarks entirely to an appreciation of Esperanto as an auxiliary international language.'[27] It was in His second public address in Edinburgh, held on 8 January and arranged by the Outlook Tower Society, that 'Abdu'l-Bahá offered a detailed presentation on the Bahá'í Faith (see chapter 27 above).

The article in the *Scotsman* offered a lengthier summary of Dr Kelman's words. In his presentation he introduced for the audience the history and social doctrine of the Bahá'í Faith. His talk was, of course, given from the standpoint of a staunch Christian. However sympathetic and inclusive his words were, Kelman's presentation transmitted some of the misconceptions common among priests and missionaries, especially Presbyterian, who in their critiques of the Bahá'í Faith portrayed it as a mere copy of Christian morals and values (see chapter 36 below). He made clear to his hearers that for him Christ alone was the way for salvation and that he considered the Bahá'í Faith as just a new interpretation of Christ's teachings.

A portion of the article was later reproduced in *The Christian Commonwealth*.[28] The *Evening Dispatch* offered a similar account of Dr Kelman's words and the *Evening News* mentioned that Dr. Kelman stated that 'they who greeted Abdul Baha that evening did so as Christians' and that this comment was followed by applause.[29]

'Abdu'l-Bahá's address was also summarized in detail. The summary that appeared in the *Evening Dispatch* was followed by quotations from Bahá'u'lláh's Hidden Words:

> Abdul Baha, whom the audience greeted by rising from their seats, expressed his gratitude for the remarks of the previous speakers. The spread of the language of Esperanto was an evidence of the spirit of the age; and every movement in the world of humanity which brought in its train unity and accord was good, and every movement which created discord was evil. This century was a radiant one, owing to its many discoveries and inventions, but the greatest of all the undertakings was the unification of language, because it was more beneficial and productive of more brotherhood than any other undertaking of this age. Unity of language brought about

good fellowship, and was conducive of accord, besides bringing about the entire sweeping away of misunderstandings between the peoples of the world. Students from the East, coming to the West to study the sciences and discoveries of the West, had to devote at least four years of their precious time towards the acquisition of the language of the country before they could start on the special branch of study which it was their intention to follow. If, however, this auxiliary language formed part of the curriculum of all the schools, this difficulty would be obviated.

To-day, even if one were to study ten languages, he might yet desire to travel abroad, and he might be handicapped on account of not knowing the language of a particular country. He himself had studied many Oriental languages very profoundly, knowing Arabic more deeply than the Arabians themselves, and yet when he came to the West he had been obliged to bring with him a translator. (Laughter.) In short, to understand and to make oneself understood there must be an international language. His Holiness Baha'o'llah, 50 years ago, wrote a book, which was entitled the 'Most Holy Book', and in that book one of the fundamental principles of the Bahai revelation was that there must needs be the invention of a universal language. Therefore they were grateful that this Esperanto language had been created, and all the Bahais in the Orient had been commanded to study it very carefully. The unification of language would transform the world of humanity into one world; would do away with the present misunderstanding between the religions; and would bring the East and the West into a spirit of fellowship and love. (Applause.)

Professor Patrick Geddes then returned thanks to Abdul Baha on behalf of the meeting.[30]

The Scotsman gave a similar account and mentioned that after the meeting 'many of the audience availed themselves of the opportunity given to shake hands with the Bahai leader'.[31]

The account in the *Evening News* indicates that 'Abdu'l-Bahá's lecture was interrupted several times by applause and that the meeting was 'concluded with the singing of the Catholic and missionary psalm "All people that on earth do dwell"':

Abdul Baha, in returning thanks for the cordiality of his welcome, attributed it to the loftiness of aim and purity of intention on the part of the speakers. It showed how greatly and wonderfully this spirit was rushing forward, and it was evidence of the spread of Esperanto, and that was a source of universal happiness to all of them. (Applause.) The unification of language was more beneficial and productive of more brotherhood than any other undertaking of this age. The unity of language brought about good fellowship and won hearts. It meant the entire sweeping away of misunderstanding between the people. It caused the appearance of reality, and it established accord between all the men. Let them thank God that Esperanto had been created. (Applause). They had commanded all the Bahais in the Orient to study this language very carefully, and ere long it would be spread all over the East. (Applause.)

The significance of this was that the contending races, the warring nations, the inimical religions, would come together in the spirit of love and amity. The different nations would raise the standard of solidarity. This was the day-spring of the Millennium. (Applause.) The unification of language would bring together the East and the West in the spirit of fellowship and love. This auxiliary international language would gather together the various races in one tabernacle – as if the five continents of the world had become one continent. It would do away with ignorance and superstition. Let them hope for that day when even the boundaries of native languages would be swept away and the world might enjoy one language. What greater bounty was there than that? (Applause.)[32]

At least two editorials about the meeting were published on 8 January. The *Evening Dispatch* described it as remarkable, unique and significant:

> Dr Kelman described the meeting in the Freemasons' Hall last night as a remarkable one. It was very remarkable; it was unique, significant. Here we had a crowded, highly respectable, and representative gathering of Edinburgh people, presided over by one of the most prominent of the city ministers, and called together by the Esperanto Society to welcome a Persian prophet who has come to deliver a religious revelation to the British people. Abdul Baha, an aged and noble-looking man in Persian garb, with flowing grey

beard, massive brow, and large kindly eyes, paced to and fro on the platform, giving his message in short sentences to his Persian interpreter, who passed it on in excellent English to an attentive and sympathetic audience. Then, after others had spoken, the meeting joined in singing the 'Hundredth Psalm', not a line of which, be it noted, expresses any thought with which the teaching of Abdul Baha is out of harmony.

Doubtless many of the audience were disappointed with the Persian teacher's address; for, instead of propounding the Bahai revelation as probably they expected he would do, he confined himself to a simple and temperate exposition of the utility of Esperanto. But evidently Abdul Baha is a practical and prudent man. He may have been warned that Scottish people have strong ideas of their own in matters of religion, that he must walk warily, and that anything savouring of novelty must be presented to them gradually and cautiously. Still, his words were very effective and full of meaning. His mission is to teach the lesson of the oneness of humanity and to establish the brotherhood of man on earth here and now. To this end, he seeks to show, one of the first and most obvious steps is to foster the growth of a universal language by means of which men will be enabled to understand one another better and to make a common store of the knowledge which has been garnered by men of every clime and colour.

It is understood that at his second meeting this afternoon Abdul Baha will unfold the principles of the revelation, which has been espoused by millions of Orientals during his own ministry and that of his two predecessors. But there need be no alarm. There is nothing subversive in his doctrine. It contains nothing but what the best of men have taught for thousands of years, and what Christian nations have been endeavouring to realise for nearly twenty centuries. He is endeavouring to do what Foreign Secretaries, and Peace Conferences, and Ambassadorial Conversations have been striving to do – with cannon at their backs. He proclaims universal peace and calls upon the nations to settle their differences by a board of arbitration; he pleads for a broad spirit of friendship and tolerance to be shown to all the peoples of the earth. The means by which he proposes to reach that beneficent end Abdul Baha will himself explain. And as Western nations have not been conspicuously successful in their efforts in that direction, it would be well to listen attentively to what this Persian has to say. His coming is at least opportune, when Europe is full of armed men with murder in their eyes.[33]

A short editorial note in the *Evening News* expressed its author's disagreement with some of the statements of the Master: 'Abdul Baha expressed a belief, which is really touching, in the power of a common language to reconcile differences of religious opinion. Unhappily, the world's experience does not encourage that view. Europe had a common language, Latin, in the Middle Ages, but that did not hinder the tremendous disruption of the sixteenth century. That Esperanto will pave the way to a universal religion is a fancy doomed to disappointment.'[34]

On 11 January William M. Page sent to several Esperanto Societies across the world a report of the meeting as well as the translation into Esperanto of 'Abdu'l-Bahá's talk. As a consequence, the Master's words made a great impact on Esperantists. *The British Esperantist*, the official organ of the British Esperanto Association, published in its February issue the following report of the meeting:

SCOTLAND

Edinburgh.– The Edinburgh group has been able to carry through an important piece of propaganda work, not only for themselves, but for the Esperanto movement in the East. The society had the honour of being invited to make arrangements for a public meeting of Edinburgh citizens to greet Abdul Baha, the distinguished Persian reformer and mystic, and head of the Bahai movement. The meeting took place in the Freemasons' Hall, one of the finest halls in the city, on January 7, and 800 persons were present, many having to be content with standing room. Rev. Dr. Kelman presided, and Mr. Andrew Wilson and Prof. Patrick Geddes took part in the proceedings. While the audience was assembling, our *samideano*, Mr. Alfred Hollins, the world-famous recital organist, gave a selection on the beautiful new organ. Abdul Baha's speech, which was entirely on the subject of international language, has been translated into Esperanto, and is found in another column; but the important passage in it was: 'Let us thank the Lord because this Esperanto language is created. *We have commanded all the Bahais in the Orient to study this language very carefully, and ere long it will spread all over the East.'* The address was given in Persian, and was translated into English by Mirza Ahmad Sohrab, who has already some little acquaintance with Esperanto. The programme of the meeting contained a portrait of Abdul Baha, and the words of Dr. Zamenhof's 'Prego sub la Verda Standardo', with translation into English by Mr. W. M. Bassett. That Abdul Baha is in earnest in his desire to spread Esperanto in the East is evidenced by the fact that he has ordered 400 copies of the programme of the meeting to be sent to Persia, and has taken with him a supply of Esperanto books.[35]

As stated in the article, the same issue contained the full text of the talk translated into Esperanto:

Every movement in the world of humanity bringing on its back unity and accord is good; and every matter which creates discord and disharmony is evil. This century is a radiant century. Its discoveries are many. Its inventions are great. Its undertakings are multitudinous. On account of these great accomplishments, this century is superior to all other centuries. But the greatest undertaking is the unification of language, because it is more beneficial and productive of more pleasure than any other undertaking of this age. The unity of language brings about great fellowship between hearts. The union of language is the cause of the attainment of accord. It brings about the entire sweeping away of misunderstanding between the people; it establishes accord between all the children of men. It gives broader conceptions and greater vision to human minds, and to-day the greatest undertaking in the world of humanity is to understand and make yourself understood. Every individual member of the body politic, on account of the wide spread of an auxiliary international language, will be enabled to put himself in touch with the current events and ethical and scientific discoveries of the age. An auxiliary universal language will give us the key – or the master key – to the understanding of the secrets of the past ages. Through an international language every nation in the future will be enabled to pursue its scientific discoveries very easily and without any difficulty.

AN INTERNATIONAL LANGUAGE

It is well known to you that the Oriental people, young men coming to the West trying laboriously to study the discoveries of the West, for many years must work hard so that first they may study the language and then their special branch of learning. At the very least, they must give many years of their life to the study of the language of the country they go to; then they can start on the study of that special branch of science in which they are interested. For example, let us suppose that a young man from India or Persia or Turkestan or Arabia, desiring to study medicine, comes to this country; at the very least he must study the English language for four years, and nothing else; and then he may begin the study of medicine. But if this international auxiliary language were a part of the curriculum of education in all the schools, in his childhood he would study that language in his own country and then, no matter to which country he desired to go, he would be enabled to study his special branch of science very easily, without losing any years of his life.

To-day, even if each one of us studied languages, yet, if someone desired to travel abroad, he might be handicapped on account of not knowing the special language of a given country. I have studied the Oriental languages very profoundly, knowing the Arabic language more deeply than the Arabians themselves, having studied the Turkish language and the Persian in my own native land, and knowing other languages of the East, yet, when I came to the West, I was obliged to bring with myself a translator, and it is as if I know no language whatever. But if there were an international language, well, the Persian language of my own native land and the other one would have been sufficient to carry me along in all the countries of the world. Just think how the international language will facilitate communication between all nations of the world. Let it be said that half of our lives is spent in the acquirement of languages; for in this enlightened age every man must study languages, so that if he expects to travel to Asia and Africa and Europe he may be able to converse with the people; but by the time he has studied one language, there is another one to travel to. So you see that this life is spent in the acquirement of these languages, which are a handicap to international communication. Well, this international language will free man from all these problems. In short, to understand and make yourself understood, there must needs be an international instrument. The teacher and the student must know each other's language, so that the teacher may be able to impart his knowledge and the student acquire that knowledge. In the world of humanity there is no greater factor than to make yourself understood to your fellowmen, for civilisation itself, the progress of civilisation, depends upon this process. To acquire arts and sciences one must know how to speak, make himself understand and understood at the same time. So on this understanding and making yourself understood will depend the acquisition of sciences, and it will make men to comprehend all affairs of life; and this process of understanding and making yourself understood depends upon language. Therefore, if this auxiliary language is established, all the members of humanity will then be enabled to understand each other. As I speak now, an episode comes to my mind which happened in Bagdad. There were two friends who did not know each other's language. One of them got sick; the other one called upon him, but he could not express his sympathy, so by making a sign he asked him 'How are you?' By making another sign, the sick man answered 'I am almost dying', and the friend who called, thinking that he had told him that he was feeling much better, said, 'Thanks be to God.' By such incidents you realise that the best thing in this world is to be able to make yourself understood by your friends, and also to understand them, and there is nothing worse in this world than not to be able to convey your thoughts. But if there is this auxiliary language, all these difficulties will be removed.

Now, praise to God, this language of Esperanto is invented, and this is one of the special endowments of this brilliant century; this is one of the greatest undertakings of this great age. Up to this time the world of humanity has failed to bring about this invention. This unification of languages had never crossed the minds of the thinkers of the past ages, and in reality it was an impossibility in those times, because then there was no freedom in going and coming, and no travelling and no intercourse between the various countries. Now the means of communication and transport are greatly increased, therefore it is necessary and it is possible to bring about the use of this international language.

His Holiness Baha'u'llah fifty years ago wrote a book; that book is called 'The Most Holy Book', and in that book one of the fundamental principles of the Baha'i movement is that there must be the invention of an auxiliary language; and then he goes on to explain the benefits and profits that will accrue through such a medium. Now let us thank the Lord because this Esperanto language is created. Therefore we have commanded all the Baha'is in the Orient to study this language very carefully, and ere long it will spread all over the East. Therefore I request you also, non-Esperantists and fellow-Esperantists, to put your utmost exertion into the spread and promulgation of this language, because it will hasten that day, that millennial day, which has been prophesied by the past prophets and seers, that day in which, it is said, the wolf and lamb will drink from the same fount, the lion and the deer graze in the same meadow. The signification of this Holy Writ is that the contesting races, warring nations, inimical religions, will come to each other in the spirit of love and amity – then, the day-spring of that millennium and every means, every instrument which confers unity and amity upon the children of men, that is love and that is the spirit.

As we said, the greatest affair in this world is the reality of an auxiliary international language. The unification of language will transform the world of humanity into one world; the unification of language will do away with the misunderstandings between religions, and the unification of language will bring together the East and the West in the spirit of fellowship and love. The unification of language will change this world of many families into one family. This auxiliary international language will gather the various races under one cover, as if the five continents of the world had become one continent, because then they can convey their thoughts to each other. The international auxiliary language will do away with ignorance and superstition, for each child, no matter to which race or nation he may belong, will be able to pursue his studies in science and art, because at that time he will be called on to study only two languages – one his own native language, and one the international auxiliary language. Let us hope for that day, when even the boundaries of native languages will be swept away and the world may enjoy one language. What greater bounty is there than this? What more munificent welfare is there than this? Then the world of humanity will become the delectable paradise, just as it is said that in heaven there is one language. The material world will become the expression of the world of the inner. Then the discoveries will be unfolded; inventions will become multiple; sciences will advance by leaps and bounds; scientific agriculture will take a wider sphere of accomplishment, because at that time the nations will be able quickly to assimilate the thoughts which are expressed, and because all these thoughts will be expressed in that universal language. If this international language is a factor in the future, all the countries of the East will be enabled to acquire the sciences of the West in no time, because they will be able to read these books and comprehend their meaning; and the Western nations will be enabled to acquire the thoughts and ideas of the East, and through this they will be enabled to improve their condition. In short, on account of the establishment of this international language, the world of humanity will become another world; extraordinary progress will be attained. Take, for example, a family in which the various members speak each a different language; how difficult it is for them to convey their thoughts to each other, and how great and wonderful it is when they are able easily to understand each other's thoughts. For if they know each other's language, they will go on very rapidly; there is no doubt whatever about this. Therefore it is our hope that the Esperanto language will spread universally before long, that it may he promulgated in all the countries, so that all the people may live with each other in the spirit of amity and love.[36]

In London the *Vahan* also mentioned this talk in an article by Ralph Nicholson on Theosophy and Esperanto in which he stated that 'Abdu'l-Bahá 'has taken with him to Persia 200 pamphlets and books on Esperanto for distribution and has ordered an expert Persian teacher to come to England to learn Esperanto, in order to spread a knowledge of the language throughout Persia'.[37] A similar note was published in the *Esperanto Monthly* (London), a journal created by William Mann to teach Esperanto,[38] and in other journals.[39]

Outside the United Kingdom, 'Abdu'l-Bahá's address to Edinburgh Esperantists generated no fewer than 30 articles in Esperanto and general journals around the globe, many of them defining 'Abdu'l-Bahá's talk as 'a great triumph for Esperanto'. All these articles were based on William Page's report or the article that appeared in the *British Esperantist*.

In the Americas the news of 'Abdu'l-Bahá's address was published in Brazil,[40] Chile,[41] Cuba[42] and in the United States, where, as well as an article that appeared in the *Amerika Esperantisto*,[43] the news was also published in the *Idaho Falls Times*.[44]

In Europe the news was published in several countries and territories including Belgium,[45] Bohemia,[46] France,[47] Germany,[48] Hungary,[49] Italy,[50] Norway,[51] Poland,[52] Portugal,[53] Sweden[54] and Switzerland.[55] In Spain, where Esperanto had been introduced in some areas primarily by members of the army, 'Abdu'l-Bahá's talk was mentioned with sympathy by Lieutenant Román Ayza in the right wing army weekly *La Correspondencia Militar* (Madrid)[56] and in the conservative and Catholic *El Día de Madrid*.[57] The organ of the Spanish Esperantists, *La Suno Hispania* (Valencia),[58] and the organ of the Catalan region Esperantists, *Tutmonda Espero* (Barcelona),[59] also mentioned 'Abdu'l-Bahá.

La Ondo Esperanto (Moscow), the official organ of the Russian Esperantists, also carried in February 1913 the news of 'Abdu'l-Bahá's talk in Edinburgh.[60] The article prompted a letter to the editor by a Persian Esperantist writing from Tabríz who complained about what he considered to be an excessive propaganda for the Bahá'í Faith on the part of Esperantists. He also pointed out that Esperantists in Persia could face danger if in the eyes of the Persian public opinion the Bahá'í religion and the Esperanto movement were linked:

> In Issue 2 of 'La Ondo Esperanto' I read a letter about the speech by the famous Abdul Baha, who promised to inform all of his followers in the East about Esperanto and, at the same time, find a way for them to learn Esperanto. Undoubtedly Abdul Baha will be able to do that easily. I also believe that almost all Bahais will learn and fervently promote our language, but in my opinion, that kind of advertisement will be dangerous for our cause, if not in the whole Eastern world, at least in Persia. This is why:
>
> Four years ago when the first Esperantists in Persia started to promote Esperanto by word of mouth and in writing, various high-ranking people were already starting to murmur that 'Esperanto is the Bahais' official language. Esperanto is an enemy of Islam.' There are quite a lot of Bahais in Persia, but they cannot state openly that they are Abdul Baha's followers. Here the government, and sometimes even the general population, persecute Bahais, kill their

leaders and try by every means to hinder fervent promotion of this new idea. In my opinion it is even dangerous to publish such information. In Persia, if Abdul Baha's sympathy towards Esperanto were known, if it were known that Bahais were also Esperantists, then our cause would certainly be in unavoidable danger. It would not only hinder wider promotion, but would make stony ground of our fertile soil, where the seeds of our cause would be buried for a long time.

No Esperantist may forget that Esperanto has no link with national or religious questions. It follows that Bahais, as followers of the religious dogma, must learn Esperanto independently of the ideas of Abdul Baha, but as private individuals.

In summary, I would say that with Abdul Baha's help we will acquire many new recruits in the East, but at the same time, we will provoke the hostility and dislike of the whole Islamic world, for as long as there are Muslims on the earth.

In the 20th century, national and religious divisions between almost all peoples still run too deep. Our first responsibility is to not provoke similar feelings.

V. Sarkisjan[61]

This letter was reproduced in the French magazine *La Revuo* (Paris)[62] and was followed by an editorial – probably by Félicien Menu de Ménil – stating that despite the problems that might rise in Persia as a result of giving publicity to the Bahá'í Faith, the editor considered it necessary to inform his readers about it. Accordingly, over the year 1913 this magazine carried several articles about the Faith.

Sarkisjan's letter was also mentioned in the magazine *Progreso* (Paris), the official organ of the international union of the Ido movement, a schism inside the Esperanto movement. The author of the text agreed with Sarkisjan in that Esperanto should have 'no link with national or religious questions' and took the opportunity to direct a critique to Zamenhof, who had recently made public a statement outlining the principles of *Homaranismo*, a personal project for a universal religious movement with many similarities to the Bahá'í teachings. The author considered this action on the part of Zamenhof as a complete deviation from the principle of neutrality of the Esperanto movement. Months later the same text was reproduced in the Ido magazine *La Langue Auxiliare* (Verdun).[63]

The news about 'Abdu'l-Bahá was also published in the Japanese monthly *Orienta Azio* (Tokyo).⁶⁴ Several journals in Australia also mentioned the talk in Edinburgh.⁶⁵ In Egypt a correspondent with the *Egyptian Gazette* wrote that 'amongst the followers of Abdul Baha Abbas Esperanto is studied – indeed every one of his three million disciples has been ordered by him to take it up'.⁶⁶

The full text of the talk was also published in several journals. As mentioned earlier, an Esperanto translation was published in the *British Esperantist*.⁶⁷ It was later published in France in *La Revuo* (Paris)⁶⁸ and quoted in *Le Fraterniste* (Paris).⁶⁹ In Hungary it appeared in *La Verda Stanndardo* (Budapest)⁷⁰ and in Poland in the *Esperantysta Polski* (Warsaw).⁷¹ Portions were also published in Germany in the 1913 volume of *Das Esperanto ein Kulturfaktor* (Leizpig), which in that year was edited by Professor Paul G. Christaller, who met 'Abdu'l-Bahá in Stuttgart.⁷²

Interestingly, this talk was also published in languages other than Esperanto. In Britain, the *Hastings and St. Leonards Observer* published portions in English.⁷³ A Spanish translation of part of the talk appeared in *La Duj Stelo* (Santiago), the official organ of the Chilean Esperanto Society.⁷⁴ A translation into Russian was published in the *Volga Stelo* (Saratov)⁷⁵ and a German translation appeared in the *German-Austria Esperantisto* (Vienna), the official organ of the Austrian Esperantists.⁷⁶

The minutes of the Edinburgh Esperanto Society show that at their monthly meeting held in March 1913 the 'Secretary reported that he had received several congratulatory letters from abroad in connection with Abdu'l-Baha's speech'.⁷⁷ One of these messages was received from none other than Dr Zamenhof. Both the original message and an English translation were published in *The Christian Commonwealth*:

> Through a correspondent who sent him a report of the meeting in Edinburgh, at which Abdul Baha made his important declaration in respect to Esperanto . . . Dr. Zamenhof, the inventor of the language, has written from Warsaw: . . .
>
> Dear Sir, with true joy I received your letter of 13th January, and the programme of the reception of Abdul Baha. The person of Abdul Baha and his work I very much highly esteem; I see in him one of the greatest benefactors of mankind.– Yours, Zamenhof.⁷⁸

It is remarkable that in so short a time, and through 'Abdu'l-Bahá's influence, the Bahá'í Faith went from being considered taboo in an international Esperanto Congress to generating attention from Esperantists worldwide, even receiving a personal commendation from Dr Zamenhof.

Some months after 'Abdu'l-Bahá's talk, the British Esperanto Society arranged for the publication of the address. *The Christian Commonwealth* reported:

> The British Esperanto Association, London, has issued a reprint in Esperanto and English of the address in which Abdul Baha Abbas 'commanded' the Bahais to learn Esperanto. The price is 1½d. each, or 1s. per dozen, post free. This now famous address has evoked an extraordinary desire on the part of Bahais to learn Esperanto. It has appeared in all the principal Esperanto gazettes throughout the world, and has been alluded to in newspapers circulating in the East. Some American Bahais are working in Persia in the interests of the propaganda of Esperanto as well as Bahaism, and a grammar of Esperanto in Persia is in active preparation. Esperanto grammars in Arabic and Turkish are already in use among the Bahais.[79]

Second Visit to Paris

During 'Abdu'l-Bahá's second sojourn in France He was invited by the Paris Esperanto Society to be the guest of honor at the monthly banquet of the society, which on that occasion was held in the Hotel Moderne on 12 February 1913.

'Abdu'l-Bahá arrived around eight o'clock in the evening. After receiving Esperanto leaders in a separate room, the Master was conducted to the main hall where an audience of some two hundred people greeted him with applause as He sat at the table of honor facing all the guests. 'Abdu'l-Bahá was introduced by the president of the Paris Esperanto group, Carlo Bourlet,[80] who was also editor in chief of the magazine *La Revuo*. He read in Esperanto parts of 'Abdu'l-Bahá's address to Edinburgh Esperantists (the whole talk was published in the March issue of *La Revuo*) and expressed to 'Abdu'l-Bahá the gratitude of Esperantists for his words in favor of an international language and for having accepted the invitation of the Esperanto Society despite His poor health.[81]

One hour later, after dinner, 'Abdu'l-Bahá addressed the audience and His talk was translated from Persian into French by Hippolyte Dreyfus.[82] The number of participants was higher than the original estimates and included some Esperantists from abroad, for whom Dreyfus's translation was in turn translated into Esperanto. After 'Abdu'l-Bahá's talk Bourlet expressed his wish to cover the costs of the publication of an Esperanto instruction book for Persians.

In the ensuing weeks and months several articles about the Master's talk were published in different journals. The *Paris-Esperanto*, official organ of the Esperanto Federation of the Paris Region, published the following account of the meeting:

> The many dinner guests on 12 February had a very pleasant surprise. Abdul Baha, the great leader of the Bahais, kindly responded to the invitation of the Council and attended the dinner with Mr. Hippolyte Dreyfus, head of the French Baha'i community, Mrs. Dreyfus and two Persian secretaries. The importance of this event will be appreciated when it is considered that Baha'u'llah's religion, which originated in Persia fifty years ago, already has more than two million followers in its country of origin and is spreading with surprising rapidity in Europe and the United States.
>
> Despite his fatigue and poor health, the eminent patriarch gave us during the dinner an admirable speech in Persian, elegantly translated by M. Dreyfus, in the course of which he not only affirmed the absolute necessity of an international language, but again declared, as he did a month ago in Edinburgh, his faith in Esperanto. Abdul Baha orders his followers to learn our language. This can have incalculable consequences for the spread of Esperanto in Eastern countries.
>
> Needless to describe the enthusiasm with which his words were welcomed.
>
> We also had the pleasure to have among our guests several foreign Esperantists: Mr. and Mrs. Mabel Mackey, Melbourne (Australia), Mr. Sosnowsky, from Poland, and M. Lerber, a Swiss Esperantist who kindly gave us charming speeches in Esperanto.
>
> One last word. The announcement of the presence of Abdul Baha had caused an unusual increase of guests. At the last moment we had to double the number of tables, and therefore we could not

sit down at table till half past eight, and we were too close in a small room. All these difficulties would disappear if we took the trouble of notifying Mr. Chaussegros by postcard or [*illegible*], even at the last moment, that we intend to attend the dinner. We need to know the number of guests only two hours in advance in order to have everything as ready as possible.[83]

A further account was published in the *Amerika Esperantisto*:

> Abdul Baha, leader of the Bahai Movement, was the guest of honor at the February monthly dinner of the Paris Esperanto Group. About two hundred were present. In presenting him to the members, Prof. Bourlet, president of the group, said (translation): 'We are all pleased that you have been in favor of the Esperanto language and have commanded the Bahais to learn it. With your large following in the Orient the Esperanto language could be widely spread, and you have well said that a universal auxiliary language will be the greatest means of communication between the nations, and will remove from amongst us many of the present misunderstandings. We have different opinions and various thoughts, but in this age the ideals which we are silently working for – the oneness of humanity– are one. We are all working for the realization of that day.'
>
> After the banquet Abdul Baha gave an address on the great advantages to result from widespread use of the international language, pointing out its absolute necessity in the present day of international movements and international communication, and expressing his appreciation of Dr Zamenhof's work. 'All of us must be grateful and thank him for this noble effort,' he said, 'for in this way he has served his fellow-men well.' He also expressed the desire that Esperanto should in the near future be added to the curriculum all public schools.[84]

The *British Esperantist* carried similar information:

> On February 12 Abdul Baha was the guest of the evening at the monthly 'Dinner' of the Parisian Esperantists at the Moderne, when he once again spoke with warm approval of the value of an auxiliary language to international life. His speech, delivered in Persian, and

translated with remarkable skill sentence by sentence by Mons. H. Dreyfus, was received with great applause. In it he pointed out how 'in the Orient many peoples quite dissimilar in origin, customs and life have gone by the name of Arab since Arabian became their common language, although the majority of them are not Arabs at all. When Esperanto is spoken generally by Frenchmen, Englishmen, Germans, etc., they will all, as it were, belong to one new people comprising all the others.' The speaker also mentioned that he had sent for one of his followers to come specially from Persia to London to learn Esperanto thoroughly, in order that it might afterwards be taught generally to Bahais in the country. – A.H.[85]

'Abdu'l-Bahá's address was later published in different languages. In April 1913 *Paris-Esperanto* published a translation into French made by Dreyfus from the Persian stenographic notes taken by Ahmad Sohrab.[86]

In May 1913 *La Revuo* published an Esperanto rendering of the talk which was preceded by an introduction to the Bahá'í Faith.[87] The text was translated by Camille Chaigneau from Dreyfus's French translation. This international bi-monthly magazine was probably the most important Esperanto publication at the time and had a very large following among Esperantists all over the world. It was the only periodical to which Zamenhof contributed articles and translations and, in fact, his texts in *La Revuo* were one of his main sources of income.[88] In July and September 1913 *La Revuo* published further articles about the Bahá'í Faith.[89]

In its issue of March 1913 *La Movado* (Paris), the official bulletin of the French Society for the Promotion of Esperanto, also published its own Esperanto translation of portions of the talk, as well as a picture of the Master.[90]

Ahmad Sohrab prepared a translation into English of his own Persian notes of the address. This translation was published in April 1913 in the *International Psychic Gazette* (London) and was preceded by a short account of the meeting:

> His Excellency ABDUL BAHA addressed the Paris Esperanto group on February 12, 1913, at a banquet which was accorded him at the Hotel Moderne in that city. M. Bourlet, President of the Paris Esperanto Society, in introducing Abdul Baha, said that one of the

principles of the great world religion which he was promulgating, was the establishment of a universal language.

There was a deep silence as Abdul Baha rose but his remarks were punctuated by cheers as he walked up and down the banquet hall, stopping to emphasize with frequent gesture. He spoke in Arabic, M. Hippolyte Dreyfus of Paris interpreting into French. Here and there one noted that the French translation was undergoing still further interpretation by Esperantists for the benefit of neighbours who did not understand French but knew Esperanto: the occasion itself offering a noteworthy argument for the imminent need of a universal tongue.

ABDUL BAHA said: Human undertakings are divided into two kinds – universal and specific. The result of every universal effort is infinite, and the outcome of every specific effort is finite.

In this age, those human problems which create general interest are universal; their results are likewise universal for humanity has become interdependent. The international laws of to-day are of vast importance since international politics bring nations nearer to one another. It is a general axiom that in the world of human endeavour, every universal affair commands attention and its results and benefits are limitless. Therefore let us say that every universal cause is divine and every personal matter is human. The universal light for this planet is from the sun and the special electric ray which tonight illumines this banquet hall appears through the invention of man. In like manner the activities which are trying to establish solidarity between the nations and infuse the spirit of universalism in the hearts of the children of men are like unto divine rays from the sun of reality and the brightest ray is the coming of the universal language. Its achievement is the greatest virtue of the age, for such an instrument will remove misunderstandings from amongst the peoples of the earth and will cement their hearts together. This medium will enable each individual member of the human family to be informed of the scientific accomplishments of all his fellow men.

The basis of knowledge and the excellencies of endeavour in this world are to teach and to be taught. To acquire sciences, and to teach them in turn, depends upon language, and when the international auxiliary tongue becomes universal, it is easily conceivable that the acquisition of knowledge and instruction will likewise become universal.

No doubt you are aware that in the past ages a common language shared by various nations created a spirit of solidarity amongst them. For instance, 1,300 years ago there were many divergent nationalities in the Orient. There were Copts in Egypt, Syrians in Syria, Assyrians and Babylonians in Baghdad and along the River of Mesopotamia. There existed among these peoples rank hatred; but as they were gradually brought nearer through common protection and common interests, the Arabic language grew to be the means of intercommunication, and they became as one nation. They all speak Arabic to this day. In Syria, if you ask any one of them, he will say, 'I am an Arab', though in reality he is not – some are Greeks, other Jews, etc.

We say 'this man is a German, the other an Italian, a Frenchman, an Englishman,' etc. All belong to the great human family yet language is the barrier between them. The greatest working basis for bringing about unity and harmony amongst the nations is the teaching of a universal tongue. Writing on this subject fifty years ago, His Holiness Baha'u'llah said that complete union between the various sections of the world would remain an unrealized dream as long as an international language was not established.

Misunderstandings keep people from mutual association, and these misunderstandings will not be dispelled except through the medium of a common ground of communication. Every intelligent man will bear testimony to this.

The people of the Orient are not fully informed of the events in the West and the West cannot put itself into sympathetic touch with the East. Their thoughts are enclosed in a casket. The universal language will be the master key to open it. Western books will be translated into that language and the Easterner will be informed of the contents; likewise Eastern lore will become the property of the West. Thus also will those misunderstandings which exist between the different religions be dispersed. Religious prejudices play havoc among the peoples and bring about warfare and strife and it is impossible to remove them without a language in common.

I am an Oriental, and on this account I am shut out from your thoughts, and you likewise from mine. A mutual language will become the mightiest means toward universal progress, for it will cement the East and the West. It will make the world one home and become the divine impulse for human advancement. It will upraise the standard of oneness of the world of humanity, and make the earth a universal commonwealth. It will be the cause of love between the children of men and create good fellowship between the various creeds.

Praise be to God, that Dr. Zamenhof has constructed the Esperanto language. It has all the potential qualities of universal adoption. All of us must be grateful and thankful to him for his noble effort, for in this matter he has served his fellow men well. He has constructed a language which will bestow divine benefits on all peoples. With untiring effort and self-sacrifice on the part of its devotees it holds a promise of universal acceptance.

Therefore every one of us must study this language and make every effort to spread it so that each day it may receive a wider recognition, be accepted by all nations and governments of the world, and become a part of the curriculum in all the public schools. I hope that the business of the future conferences and congresses will be carried on in Esperanto.

In the future, two languages will be taught in the schools, one the native tongue, the other an international auxiliary language. Consider today how difficult is human communication. One may study fifty languages and travel through a country and still be at a loss. I myself speak several Oriental languages, but know no Western tongue. Had this universal language pervaded the globe, I should have studied it and you would have been directly informed of my thoughts and I of yours and a special friendship would have been established between us.

Please send some teachers to Persia, if you can, so that they may teach Esperanto to the young people. I have written asking some of them to come here to study it.

I hope that it will be promulgated very rapidly; then the world of humanity will find eternal peace; all the nations will associate with one another like mothers and sisters, fathers and brothers, and each individual member of the community will be fully informed of the thoughts of all.

I am extremely grateful to you and thank you for these lofty efforts, for you have gathered at this banquet to further this great end. Your hope is to render a mighty service to the world of humanity and for this exalted aim I congratulate you from the depths of my heart.[91]

The Peacemaker (Philadelphia) also published this talk[92] and years later it also appeared in the *Amerika Esperantisto*.[93]

A few weeks after 'Abdu'l-Bahá's visit to the Esperantists in Paris, the magazine *Le Fraterniste* (Paris), a periodical of the working class dedicated to both anarchist and Spiritualist subjects, mentioned 'Abdu'l-Bahá in two of its issues. Camille Chaigneau, who, as mentioned above, translated the Master's talk from French into Esperanto, was, as well as being an Esperantist, an active member of the Spiritualist circles and for this reason wrote a bilingual column in *Le Fraterniste* dedicated to Esperanto.

In his columns of 28 March and 4 April,[94] Chaigneau quoted from 'Abdu'l-Bahá's talks in Edinburgh and Paris, interspersing them with brief but sympathetic remarks. At the end of the second column Chaigneau stated that 'one can conclude therefore that the thought that guides Abdul Baha in his propaganda is that of a true promoter of fraternity'.

In Australia *The Advertiser* (Adelaide), published in 14 June in its section on Esperanto the news of 'Abdu'l-Bahá's address in Paris and quoted a few lines of His words.[95]

As mentioned in a preceding chapter, on 13 February, the day after His meeting with Esperantists, 'Abdu'l-Bahá was the guest of the Paris Theosophical Society. In the course of His address He made a reference to the Esperanto language which was reported in *Amerika Esperantisto*:

> The next evening Abdul Baha addressed the Theosophical Society of Paris, at 59 Ave de la Bourdonnais, and near the close of his address on this occasion he said (translation): 'We observe that today the means of unity are brought about. This in itself is an evidence that the divine confirmations are with us. One of the principles of the oneness of the world of humanity is the invention of the international auxiliary language, Esperanto. We observe that this language is spreading daily and its advocates are increasing. It is indubitable that the international auxiliary language will become instrumental

in wiping away the present misunderstandings, and each individual will be able to be informed of the thought of all humanity.'[96]

In October 1913 *Le Théosophe* (Paris) published an article about Esperanto in which its author mentioned that 'Recently the great idealist, Abdul Baha, announced in the course of a speech full of praise, that he has instructed his followers to learn Esperanto immediately and to teach it to their children. We hope, therefore, that our Theosophist brothers in all countries will soon dedicate some time to familiarizing themselves with this neutral instrument which is indispensable for that human brotherhood, pure and united, which has been the dream of the prophets of all the peoples and of all the ages.'[97]

On 15 February 'Abdu'l-Bahá received Professor Théophile Cart (1855–1931) of the 'École libre des sciences politiques,' who, after Zamenhof, was a key figure in the Esperanto movement and who was also the founder and editor in chief of the magazine *Lingvo Internacia* (Paris). He had been encouraged by some of his Persian students to visit 'Abdu'l-Bahá and he finally met Him at His residence in Rue St. Didier 30.

The March 1913 issue of *Lingvo Internacia* magazine carried fragments of Cart's interview with 'Abdu'l-Bahá:

On 15 February, at 4 pm, one of my Persian students from the School of Political Science was kind enough to escort me to Abdul Baha for a private conversation. He interpreted for us in a cheerful sitting room where, apart from us, several Persians were drinking glasses of tea, and for nearly an hour I was able to question the famous mystic about various topics and mainly about Esperanto. His answers were long and eloquent, but unfortunately, because of their very length, my young friend was obliged to summarize his words, not wanting, out of respect, to interrupt.

Though Abdul Baha is not young, he did not appear to be at all tired, at least during our conversation. He spoke clearly, loudly, good-humouredly, often laughing as he told anecdotes.
How, in your opinion, I asked him, *will an international language help to bring a shared peace?*

By simplifying international relations. When people know each other better, they will also understand each other more deeply. They will realise that, despite different clothing, people are the same and that our religions have much in common; the Mohammedans, for example, are much closer to the Christians than is generally believed. Because of language differences, we mostly notice the differences between our faiths, customs, desires, but when we have a second common language alongside our national languages, we will also see the true, essential similarities between us. In the East and North Africa, for example, common use of Arabic has largely done away with the previous suspicion and conflict that resulted mainly from linguistic diversity. The same will occur when all nations and races are able to use the same language.

Will people in the East learn Esperanto easily?

Yes. They learn English or French, so why should they have great difficulty in learning Esperanto, which is much easier?

Are you confident that Bahais will learn our language as you advise?

Yes. Of course, that will not be their central aim. However, because they understand the importance of a shared language in attaining our ideal, they will certainly obey my order joyfully and will work to promote Esperanto, not just in the East, but also in the United States of America, where we have many disciples.

Have you already met many Esperantists during your travels?

Yes. They greeted me very kindly in Edinburgh and two or three days ago here in Paris itself. I now intend to travel to Germany, where I shall probably also visit them. I get on very well with them.

Another issue: What should our position be in the light of unfair attacks? Should we remain silent or refute them?

We must simply speak the truth, but never attack and especially never ever seek personal vengeance. If someone were to kill my son, I should have no right to kill the criminal. It is the duty of society, not of the individual, to bring justice through punishment.

But if society remains indifferent?

We must wait peacefully. In the end, truth, good and justice will overcome and peace will triumph!

At these words I took my leave. Abdul Baha wished me goodbye, warmly thanking me for my kindness to his young compatriot because, although persecuted in his homeland, 'he loves it wholeheartedly'.[98]

As described in chapter 28 above, among those who visited 'Abdu'l-Bahá in Paris was Albert L. Caillet, president of the Société Unitive and editor and founder of the *Bulletin de la Société Unitive* which in March carried a long article about the Master and the Bahá'í Faith. In the same issue, Caillet announced to his readers plans for a new magazine which, under the title *Revue Universelle*, was expected to serve as an organ for various progressive movements including the Bahá'í Faith.[99] The *Revue Universelle* (*Universala Unuigo*) became a reality as a yearly publication edited by Nikolai Sheierman in Lubotin, Russia (now Ukraine).

The first article of the first issue of this periodical was dedicated to the Bahá'í Faith. Since the magazine was bilingual, the article, covering 11 pages, was printed in both Esperanto and Russian. It provided a lengthy, sympathetic and accurate introduction to the Bahá'í Faith. Among the works that the author – probably Sheierman himself – listed in the bibliography were two works in Russian: Atrpet's article 'Babizm i Bekhaizm' included in his *Imamat: Strana Poklonnikov Imamov* (1909); and a translation into Russian of Sydney Sprague's *The Story of the Bahai Movement* (1908), which was translated by A. Kovalev from the Esperanto translation of William Mann.[100] A preface to the magazine also briefly mentioned 'Abdu'l-Bahá.[101] The Swiss magazine *Bibliothéque universelle et Revue Suisse* (Lausanne) mentioned this article in a review of the first issue of the *Universala Unuigo*.[102]

It is interesting to mention that, in addition to these contacts, according to a report by Ahmad Sohrab on 22 March 1913 'the secretary of the Esperanto Society called on the Master and he told him that yesterday he delivered an address on the Bahai Movement in Esperanto language before a large gathering in Sorbonne University.'

Stuttgart, Budapest and Vienna

As discussed in chapter 29 above, during the month of April 1913 'Abdu'l-Bahá visited cities in Central Europe. In some of them He met with Esperantists and gave public talks for them. In Stuttgart, for instance, He was invited to speak to a meeting arranged by the local Esperanto group, 'Esperanto Stelo'. His arrival had been announced for some weeks with anticipation in at least one Esperanto journal, the *Svaba Esperantisto*, which on 31 January reported that 'it is expected that he ['Abdu'l-Bahá] will return to his home via Stuttgart in the near future'.[104]

The meeting was held at eight in the evening of 5 April and was chaired by the president of the society, Professor Paul Christaller, who introduced 'Abdu'l-Bahá with a long speech in German. 'Abdu'l-Bahá spoke on the need for a universal language and His words were translated into English by Sohrab and then into German by Mr Ekstein, a local Bahá'í.

On May 1913, *Germana Esperantisto* (Dresden), the official organ of the German Esperanto Society, briefly mentioned in its national news section that 'Abdul Baha, the Persian reformist, spoke at a meeting of the group on the relationship between Esperanto and the Bahá'í movement'.[105] On a different page of the same issue, the journal carried a longer report of the meeting:

> Abdul Baha, the leader of Bahaism, was invited by the 'Stutgarta Esperanto Stelo' (Stuttgart Esperanto Star), to speak on 5 April about the need for an international auxiliary language. Professor Christaller welcomed Mr Abdul Baha with the following words: Esperantism wants to unite languages, Bahaism, religions. Both aim to ennoble humankind. In the same way that we Esperantists do not want to do away with national languages, so the Bahaists do not want to do away with existing religions, but rather to draw attention to their common strands. We Esperantists are neutral in terms of politics and religion, and so we have invited Abdul Baha not because of the religious aspect of Bahaism but because of his interest in Esperanto. The evening perfectly illustrated the need for an auxiliary language as there was nearly a Babel-like language confusion. Abdul Baha spoke in Persian and two interpreters strove to interpret his words into English and then into German. He stated that:
>
> Unity is the guarantee of progress. Unity takes many forms: patriotism, for example, unites, but is insufficient for the whole of humankind. Language is a strong force for unity. History shows that at times language has already been a uniting force. In ancient times, the Egyptians, Chaldeans and Assyrians formed separate nations with separate languages. One language overcame the

others, namely today's Arabic language. Today, the inhabitants of those countries have the same name and feel united. This proves to us that language can link people. Much conflict between modern cultures results from misunderstanding due to language diversity. These misunderstandings will disappear as Esperanto spreads. This is why the founder of Bahaism, Baha Ollah, wanted to fix a common language. An international auxiliary language will certainly be fundamental and a great power towards uniting religions. I stand before you and yet I am completely unable to communicate my innermost feelings and ideas to you. If I knew Esperanto, and if Esperanto were already more widely spoken, I could speak to you without difficulty. For that reason, let us fight for the spread of Esperanto. Every universal matter is divine. The sun shines on all alike, so it is divine, similarly the rain. Every enterprise that aims to unite humankind is divine. Esperanto has divine origins and will raise high the banner of peace and fraternity.[106]

This report was later published in other Esperanto journals in Germany,[107] Bohemia,[108] Switzerland[109] and the United States.[110]

In Budapest, 'Abdu'l-Bahá was the guest of a meeting held in His honor which was organized by the Theosophical, Esperantist and Turanian societies. As mentioned in chapter 29, several journals published news about this meeting, one of them being the *La Verda Standardo* (Budapest), the official organ of the Hungarian Esperanto Society.[111]

The president of the Hungarian Esperanto Society was the Catholic prelate Sandor Gieswein. He personally welcomed 'Abdu'l-Bahá upon His arrival in Budapest, chaired one of the public meetings addressed by the Master and met with Him on different occasions.

One of the members of the Hungarian Theosophical Society wrote a letter to the *Espero Teozofia* (Paris), a Theosophist magazine written in Esperanto, in which he gave details about the visit of the Master to Budapest:

Mr Elemér Szikszay, in a very interesting letter which, due to lack of space we are unable to reproduce in its entirety, describes a talk given by 'Abdu'l-Bahá in Budapest. Here is an extract: 'The prophet-like elderly man spoke to us in simple words and his whole demeanor was that of a true, pure-hearted sage. It was regrettable that it was necessary to twice interpret his words, first from Persian into English and then from English into Hungarian; consequently much of the original value was lost. However, this was favorable in promoting our dear language: the audience was convinced of the curse of multilingualism and, in fact, applauded enthusiastically when the speaker arrived at the subject of the international language Esperanto.'[112]

The *Amerika Esperantisto* briefly mentioned that 'Abdul Baha visited Budapest during the last month and addressed the Esperantists of this city in the old Palace of Parliament. The event was arranged by the "Idealist Society", and the large audience was composed mostly of Esperantists, suffrage and peace advocates.'[113] A report on the Esperanto activities in Hungary, written by Paulo Balkányi, also appeared in *La Revuo* (Paris) and briefly mentioned the Master.[114]

In Vienna 'Abdu'l-Bahá touched on the subject of Esperanto on one of His two visits to the Theosophist headquarters in the city. A report of His visit to Vienna was published in the *German-Austria Esperantisto*:

> Abdul Baha, the leader of Bahaism, also visited Vienna during his tour of Europe. On the 23rd and 25th of April he spoke at the Adyar Theosophical Society about Baha'ism. Unfortunately, the Viennese Esperantists had not received sufficient notice about the arrival of the eminent pioneer of high cultural aims. For that reason, only Doctor Sós was able to greet him in the name of Esperanto and to give him a copy of La Movado (The Movement) which included his portrait and an article about his visit to Paris. Abdul Baha favours Esperanto and during his visits to London, Paris, Stuttgart, etc, he announced to Esperanto groups that he wishes to spread our dear language amongst his adherents in Persia, who now number more than two million people. Amongst other things, he noted that his father, Baha Ullah, the first prophet of Bahaism, was already emphasizing the need for a universal language, which alone could create solidarity and reciprocal friendship amongst people of all nations. His talk itself illustrated the usefulness of a common auxiliary language very well. Abdul Baha spoke in Persian; a Persian interpreter translated his words into English and a third gentleman from English into German. Because of this the whole thing was

very tiring and the talk lasted three times as long as it would have had a common language been used.

Following Baha's talk, Doctor Sós directed several words to the distinguished audience specifically about Esperanto and expressed the desire that all would soon also join our movement.[115]

The following month the same journal published the text of 'Abdu'l-Bahá's talk in Edinburgh.[116]

The Universal Esperantist Congress

From 24 to 31 of August 1913, the Esperanto movement held its world congress in Berne, Switzerland. A little over 1,200 delegates from all over the world attended the event at which the founder of the international language was also present.

A representative of *The Christian Commonwealth* participating in the congress interviewed Zamenhof for the magazine and among other questions asked him about his impressions of the Bahá'í Faith. This was his answer:

> I feel greatly interested in the Bahai movement as it is one of the great world movements which like our own is insisting upon the brotherhood of mankind and is calling on men to understand one another and to learn to love each other. The Bahais will understand the inner idea of Esperanto better than most people. That idea is on the basis of a neutral language to break down the walls which divide men and accustom them to see in their neighbour a man and a brother. I, therefore, think that when the Bahá'ís learn Esperanto, its inner idea will be a great moral force that will compel them to propagate it independently of their special beliefs. I have always found that the most zealous workers for Esperanto are those who appreciate its inner idea, and not those who see in it merely an instrument for material profit, although of course its commercial value is undoubted. Many people have doubted whether Esperanto would be accepted by Eastern peoples. I have never done so, and I feel certain the Bahais will carry the language into many places where ordinary European propagandists would never have gone.[117]

On the morning of Sunday 24 August, the first day of the Congress, church services were held before its formal opening. A report of the Congress in the *Amerika Esperantisto* underlined the interreligious character of the services and added that 'Esperanto softens not only national barriers, but also even religious, following the intention of Zamenhof. He and Abdul-Baha would rejoice on seeing the crowd of Congress members of all beliefs, who ran from the Synagogue to the Temple, from the Temple to the Church and filled them . . .'[118]

In the ensuing years and decades, Esperanto Congresses around the world, both national and international, would include in their programs sessions on the Bahá'í Faith, and some Esperanto magazines would even have permanent sections containing Bahá'í news. Bahá'ís in Persia, Europe and America founded and took an active role in many Esperanto groups and Bahá'í literature was translated into the international language. These close connections are best exemplified in the figure of Lidia Zamenhof (1904–42), daughter of the founder of the Esperanto movement, who eventually became a Bahá'í.[119]

It is impossible to provide here a comprehensive list of the many references to the Bahá'í Faith and to 'Abdu'l-Bahá that were published in Esperanto journals after the Master's return to Palestine. From some of these articles, however, it is apparent that 'Abdu'l-Bahá was well-remembered by Esperantists until the end of His life.[120]

34

THE THEOSOPHICAL SOCIETY

The Theosophical Society was founded in 1875 by Helena Blavatsky (1831–91), Henry Steel Olcott (1832–1907) and William Quan Judge (1851–96), as a syncretic philosophy with elements of Eastern religions, occultism, esotericism and mysticism. The nucleus of the Theosophical doctrines was developed mainly by Blavatsky but over the years it evolved, giving rise to several divisions inside the movement.

Believing that all religions have a common basis, 'the Secret Doctrine', Theosophy's view of religions appears similar to that of the Bahá'í Faith in some respects. It encourages the study of religions and has an open attitude towards religious diversity. Its hope for a 'universal brotherhood of humanity' is also similar to some Bahá'í concepts. These and other similarities in the aims and inclusivity of both movements may explain the close relations that existed between Bahá'ís and Theosophists during the time of 'Abdu'l-Bahá's travels and later.

In several countries there were strong links between the Bahá'í communities and Theosophical societies, and a good number of the early Bahá'ís of North America and some European countries came from the ranks of Theosophy, some keeping both identities for several years. During the early decades of the 20th century this close relationship also resulted in the publication of several articles about, and scores of references to, the Bahá'í Faith in Theosophical magazines.[1]

At the time of 'Abdu'l-Bahá's visits to the West this receptivity and openness to the Bahá'í Faith on the part of Theosophists was translated into several invitations to address Theosophical societies in England, Scotland, the United States, France, Austria and Hungary. Accounts of many of these meetings were published in both Theosophical and general periodicals.

First Visit to England

In 1911 London was one of the principal centers of Theosophy in the West. British-born Annie Besant (1847–1933)[2] was, from 1907, the president and world leader of the Theosophical Society. Her lectures and articles were quite popular in some social circles and received wide attention in some British periodicals. The Theosophical Society of England and Wales was, moreover, able to sustain simultaneously at least five major magazines plus other minor periodicals.

Besant mentioned the Bahá'í Faith as early as 27 June 1909 in a lecture delivered at St James's Hall, London, on the subject of the 'world teacher' expected by the Theosophists. She attempted to show how this messianic figure had been foretold in all the great religions as well as in various ancient traditions. In the course of her presentation, which was published in *The Christian Commonwealth*, Besant mentioned the Bahá'í Faith, stating that: 'The Bab, who declared the coming of a mighty one, followed by another, said to be yet greater than Himself, and yet a third, the Abbas Effendi of the present time, certainly a great spiritual teacher, but one who still declares that the mightiest is yet to come to bind together the Eastern and the Western world.'[3]

This friendly but wrong statement prompted a letter sent from Lebanon on 17 July 1909 and probably penned by Jean Stannard in which the author corrected Besant's statements and presented the figures of the Bahá'í Faith.[4]

Some members of the British Bahá'í community had established close contacts with Theosophy. Lady Blomfield, hostess of 'Abdu'l-Bahá in London, had been for some years one of its members before becoming a Bahá'í and personally knew its leaders. Alice Buckton gave at least one talk to the members of the Theosophical Society in Letchworth Garden City, a town with close connections with Bruce Wallace and hence with the family of Wellesley Tudor Pole. In her address, delivered on 16 July under the title of 'The Most Great Peace', she spoke of her recent visit to 'Abdu'l-Bahá in Egypt.[5] In early 1911 Ethel Rosenberg was invited to give a series of lectures on the Bahá'í Faith to Manchester Theosophists.[6]

On Monday, 9 January 1911 Tudor Pole gave a talk about 'Abdu'l-Bahá and the Bahá'í Faith to the Bath Theosophical Lodge.[7] In the summer of 1911 he was invited to participate in the third Theosophical summer school – held from 11 to 25 August – where he 'gave a most interesting account of his experiences in Persia in connection with the Bahais'.[8] Participants sent the following telegram to 'Abdu'l-Bahá: 'International Theosophical Summer School, in conference assembled, send through Mr. Tudor Pole fraternal greetings, and desire to unite with your work for universal racial understanding, peace, and fellowship.' 'Abdu'l-Bahá's reply read as follows: 'Greeting caused great happiness. Hope godly power will raise the tent of unity for the material and spiritual rest of mankind.'[9]

* * *

When 'Abdu'l-Bahá visited London in September 1911 He received several members of the Theosophical Society, including Annie Besant, who invited Him to speak at the London headquarters of the Society.

The Vahan (London), the official organ of the Theosophical Society in England and Wales and edited by its General Secretary James I. Wedgwood (1883–1951),[10] announced to its readers in its October issue that 'The great Bahaist Teacher, Abbas Effendi, has been in London during the month. The T. S. is to have the honour of entertaining him on September 30.'[11]

Annie Besant, who had just left for India, was not present but 'Abdu'l-Bahá was welcomed by the vice president of the Theosophical Society and chairman of the meeting, Alfred P. Sinnet,[12] who was a personal acquaintance of Lady Blomfield and who had previously visited 'Abdu'l-Bahá several times, and by James Wedgwood in his capacity as general secretary.

In His talk 'Abdu'l-Bahá introduced the Bahá'í Faith to His audience and outlined nine of its principles. Interestingly, and as was the case with other addresses in London, the talk had been written and translated before the meeting and its English rendering was read after 'Abdu'l-Bahá's address.[13]

The November issue of *The Vahan* carried a detailed account of the meeting written by Eva M. Martin, a regular contributor to *The Vahan* and other Theosophical magazines. 'So numerous were the members who wished to do him honour that not a few latecomers had to be turned away from the doors, because no available inch of space was left,' stated Martin.

Our President, having already set sail for India, was unable to welcome the honoured guest personally, but the Vice-President, Mr. Sinnett and the General Secretary were present to do the necessary honours. Mr. Sinnett introduced Abdul Baha in an interesting speech in which he gave an account of the Bahaist movement, and showed the special reason why Theosophists should welcome it.

Looking at the calm, beautiful face of the present leader of this great Bahaist movement, one seemed to understand how it was that this man and those who preceded him, had been able to inspire many thousands of people with such faith and courage that they willingly endured poverty, imprisonment, exile, even torture and death, rather than deny the light that had been shown to them. We know that even so lately as 1901, 170 persons suffered martyrdom at one time in the city of Yezd,[14] and the tale of mental and physical suffering endured there and elsewhere during the latter half of the nineteenth century will probably never be known in full.

Abdul Baha is the son of the great Persian teacher who was known as 'the Glory of God' – the one whose coming the Bab (or foreteller) prophesied far and wide throughout Persia, until in 1850 he was publicly shot to death in Tabriz for so doing. The present head of the movement calls himself 'the Servant of God', and has devoted his life to spreading the principles of Bahaism, which (he said) include universal brotherhood; the divine origin of all religions; peace; charity; industry; the emancipation of women; the equal education of boys and girls; purity of body and mind; kindness to animals; and many others whose accordance with the teachings of Theosophy is a cause for rejoicing rather than for wonder.

In his short speech the Abbas Effendi touched on many of these things, laying especial stress on the desire of the Bahais for universal peace, and for the establishment of a great board of arbitration which should settle all international disputes.

He spoke in a low soft Persian, which sounded strange in its Western setting; but Mr. Sinnett read a translation, prepared beforehand.

Then once more the Teacher rose, and speaking with greater animation, told of the great kindness shown to him in the West, of the eager search for truth which characterised the people, and of the mighty influence for good which one day might radiate from the great city of London. This and much else was given, with the aid of an interpreter; the meeting received his blessing, and after much handshaking, the guest of the day was carried away in a motor car.

One felt, in listening, that these two movements, Theosophy and Bahaism, so distinct and yet with so much in common, each having made a direct and irresistible appeal to so many hearts in both Eastern and Western countries, promised to show up, once and for all, the unnecessary pessimism of that saying of Kipling's which has been quoted and re-quoted *ad nauseam* as the 'last word' on the subject: 'For East is East and West is West, and never the twain shall meet.'

For those who were present saw the representatives of East and West meeting not only in their physical bodies, with expressions of friendship and good will, but meeting in thought, in sympathy, in aim, and in belief, to an extent which probably has never before been equalled. Undoubtedly much beauty was built up within the walls of our temporary building on that memorable afternoon. May there be much more to follow, until we all feel that, in the truest sense of the words, the ground on which it stands is 'holy ground', and that no thoughts save those of Truth, and Love, and Beauty, can there find an answering vibration.

Eva M. Martin[15]

This account was later published in the magazine *Sophia* (Madrid), organ of the Spanish Theosophical Society.[16] The same issue of *The Vahan* carried an editorial summarizing some of the results of 'Abdu'l-Bahá's visit to London and attributing them to the influence of the 'spiritual impulse' of Theosophy.[17]

This editorial was reproduced on 16 November in the French magazine *Le Théosophe* (Paris)[18] and was summarized in the December issue of *Sophia* (Madrid).[19]

In an article for *The Contemporary Review* (London), Harrold Johnson included the text of 'Abdu'l-Bahá's address delivered to London Theosophists. This talk was later included in the volume *'Abdu'l-Bahá in London*.[20]

* * *

After the departure of 'Abdu'l-Bahá from Europe, references about Him in relation to Theosophy continued to be published in British journals and magazines.

On 3 January 1912 a reader of *The Christian Commonwealth* stated, referring to 'Abdu'l-Bahá and the Bahá'í Faith, that 'It would be interesting to know what Mrs. Besant, in her new role of "John the Baptist" (to quote Dr. Horton), has to say as to this movement. Is this he that should come, or look we for another?'[21] On 10 April 1912, another reader enquired from the editors about the Bahá'í position on reincarnation and its relationship with Theosophy:

THEOSOPHY AND BAHAI TEACHING

Lieut. R.N. (Retired) writes:

'As a Theosophist who numbers many valued friends among Bahais, may I seek enlightenment on this question: How do the teachings of Baha'o'llah on reincarnation agree with those of Theosophy? My own idea is that they are identical. True, all Bahais I have talked with scoff at reincarnation as (they think) we understand it, and reiterate: "There is a return of qualities, not of entities." But is that not exactly what Theosophy teaches: The extinction of the personality, but the return of the individuality laden with acquired qualities?'[22]

A reader of *The Vahan* also asked about the relationship between Theosophy and the Bahá'í Faith. The question was answered by Annie Besant herself. While she didn't say that she was opposed to the Bahá'í Faith, she was straightforward in stating her disagreement with those Bahá'í teachings that posed a direct challenge to the Theosophist belief in the coming of a 'world teacher'. While most of Theosophists were awaiting the coming of that messianic figure and hoped that the young Krishnamurti would, after finishing his education and training, become that savior, Bahá'ís consider Bahá'u'lláh to be the fulfillment of all religious prophecies regarding the future coming of a great divine Messenger. This was untenable for some Theosophists.

Would you kindly ask Mrs. Besant to state the attitude of Theosophy towards Bahaism? Has the Bahaist movement originated from the

> *White Lodge?*²³ *Baha Ullah specifically states that it is useless to look for the advent of another great prophet and revealer after himself until at least another thousand years or more have elapsed. Is Abdul Baha a forerunner of the Christ, or considered so by Theosophists? Is it advisable for Theosophists to join the Bahaist movement?*
>
> Theosophy cannot be said to have any attitude, save that of sympathy, with all movements of a spiritual nature. Its attitude to Bahaism is the same as towards other religions. To my mind all spiritual movements are due to impulses from the one White Lodge; I know nothing special as to this one. I do not, of course, agree with the statement made above as by Baha Ullah; time will prove; we need not quarrel over it. Theosophists probably vary in the opinions they hold as to Abdul Baha, and no one has any right to commit them to any special view. There seems to be no object in Theosophists joining the Bahaist movement; in their own Society they have all that the Bahaists teach, and more, except the exclusive belief in one particular person. Every Theosophist is free to believe in him, but the T. S. can never be committed to belief in any one particular Teacher.²⁴

These statements by Besant were later reproduced in other Theosophical journals in America²⁵ and France.²⁶

During 'Abdu'l-Bahá's sojourn in America, Marguerite Pollard, secretary of the Cheltenham Lodge (England) and regular contributor to *The Theosophist* (Bombay), the international organ of the Theosophical Society,²⁷ wrote an interesting article on the Bahá'í Faith. Using an inclusivist and open tone, she expanded on the differences between the Bahá'í religion and the Theosophist philosophy. The article included quotations from the Bahá'í scriptures and some introductory notes. Regarding the Theosophical belief in the coming of a great teacher Pollard mentioned:

> The Bahais are saying that all these Prophecies refer to Baha'u'llah and that the Jewish and Muhammadan cycles mentioned in the sacred bocks, were completed in the year 1844, the year when the Bab began his work. But if, as is so widely expected, a great Teacher comes at no distant time, what will be the result? Will the world again have to witness the pitiable spectacle of jealousy and scorn

and hatred between the followers of the Masters who have come to bring peace upon earth?

Pollard also explored the question of reincarnation. While the Bahá'í Faith does not teach reincarnation and considers that, after death, human souls continue their evolution in spiritual worlds, Theosophy, on the contrary, adheres to the mainstream Hindu concept of reincarnation.

> Abbas Effendi considers the belief in reincarnation a 'puerile imagination'. This is the only point in which his teaching is at *variance* with the more important opinions, beliefs, or working hypotheses of Theosophists, and members of the great religions of India. But it seems as if the Bahai religion, as now presented, were more suited to the types of mind to be found in the Jewish, Muhammadan and Christian faiths than to the great communities of Buddhists and Hindus in China and India. All Theosophists, however, must wish the Bahais every success in their work of spreading religious unity throughout the world and of uniting all peoples in love and brotherhood . . .[28]

* * *

While not directly related with the travels of 'Abdu'l-Bahá it is nevertheless interesting to mention here an article published by Wellesley Tudor Pole who had himself been a Theosophist and who, as some of his works show, during his life retained some Theosophical concepts in his esoteric thought.

As mentioned above, many Theosophists believed in the imminent coming of a messianic figure. Annie Besant, who believed that her pupil Krishnamurti was that figure, established in 1911 the Order of the Star of the East (OSE), which was headed by Krishnamurti himself.

On 6 December 1911 Tudor Pole published in *The Christian Commonwealth* a two column article with the significant title 'The Star of the East' in which he presented the Bahá'í Faith and suggested that Bahá'u'lláh was the awaited messianic figure. No doubt these statements were actually addressed to Theosophists and posed a challenge for many of them.[29]

First Visit to France

The Theosophical Society of Paris invited 'Abdu'l-Bahá to speak at their headquarters at 59 Avenue de La Bourdonnais. The French Theosophical Society was probably the second largest in Europe after the Society of England and Wales and in 1911 produced four major magazines plus other periodicals.

As in England, French Theosophists maintained a close relationship with Bahá'ís. In 1908, for instance, Hippolyte Dreyfus was invited to speak to the Paris Theosophists. The text of his presentation on the Bahá'í Faith was published in the January 1908 issue of the *Annales Théosophiques*.[30]

'Abdu'l-Bahá addressed the Theosophists on 26 October. As in His address to London Theosophists, 'Abdu'l-Bahá gave in Paris a general introduction to the Bahá'í Faith and explained 11 of its principles.[31]

The *Bulletin Théosophique* (Paris) was the monthly organ of the Société Théosophique de France and was edited by its secretary general, Charles Blech (1855–1934). In its issue of November 1911 the Bulletin announced that 'The great Bahaist teacher, Abdou'l Baha, is spending several weeks in Paris. Members of the TS of France had the honor of receiving him at their headquarters on Thursday evening, October 26.'[32]

As mentioned earlier, Jean Lefranc, a reporter with *Le Temps* (Paris), was present at the meeting and soon afterwards included a short account of it in an article on 'Abdu'l-Bahá (see vol. 1, chapter 7, pp. 161–3).[33]

The fortnightly journal *Le Théosophe* published on 16 November a summary of the talk of 'the great Prophet of Bahaism'.[34]

The full text of the talk was included in the December 1911 issue of the quarterly journal *Annales Théosophiques* (Paris) and its publication was announced in *Le Théosophe* and in the *Bulletin Théosophique*.[35]

Besides the notes of the address of 'Abdu'l-Bahá, very similar to those included in *Talks by Abdul Baha Given in Paris* (1912), the text in *Annales* also carried the opening and closing remarks made by Charles Blech, who introduced 'Abdu'l-Bahá with the following words:

> Four years ago, in this room, M.D.B [Dreyfus] outlined for us the principal lines of Bahaism. Those attending the conference did not expect to have the honor to know and to receive at this place

Abd-ul-Baha, the great and respected prophet of that religious and moral awakening of Islam.

I am happy to greet him today on behalf of all of you and assure him of our respectful sympathy.

While Theosophists and Bahais differ in some points of doctrinal teaching, don't we have a common morality? Don't we have one goal – the unity of all religions, service to others and the brotherhood of man? And cannot we ignore these differences and consider only the common ideal that unites us and give us the strength and number to fight against materialism and irreligion, against superstition and ignorance?

A large number of us, Theosophists, have our eyes set on a star that has to rise soon to unite the religions and bring peace on earth; we have symbolized it with the foundation of the order of Star of the East. Our Bahai friends turn their attention to a star that disappeared over the horizon on 28 May 1892, and who represents for them the last manifestation of God on earth. But these two stars cannot be compared to those commonly called the morning star and evening star, which science has recognized to be only a single star, the planet Venus.

A few weeks ago our president, Annie Besant, received tonight's guest, Abdul Baha, at the headquarters of the Theosophical Society in London. A most cordial friendship has been established between the two leaders of our two great movements. Let us each remain loyal and faithful to his star but let us not forget that the stars are all dependent on the same spiritual Sun.[36]

Blech concluded the meeting stating that: 'The words of Abdul Baha are too good to allow myself to speak after them. I speak on behalf all of you in thanking him warmly for the lessons he has given us. We are pleased to see our movement associate with the great and wide movement of Bahaism; this fraternity will certainly be a great help to achieve the goal they both pursue.'[37]

After this expression of friendship, 'Abdu'l-Bahá briefly addressed the audience for a second time and closed the session with a prayer. The prayer was not included in the record of the meeting but the editors noted that 'the *mantras* had a profound and beneficial influence'.[38]

On 27 November the *Revue Théosophique Française* (Paris) published an account of the meeting which included a brief introduction about the history of the Bahá'í Faith. The author was probably Dominique A. Courmes (1843–1914),[39] editor of the magazine.

RECEPTION OF THE LEADER OF THE BABI MOVEMENT AT THE THEOSOPHICAL HEADQUARTERS IN PARIS

... Abbas Effendi is of medium height, dressed in Oriental fashion, his countenance is grave and benevolent, his voice is resonant. He speaks only Farsi and was translated for us by M. Dreyfus-Barney, the sympathetic Parisian propagandist who presented the doctrine of the Bab to us a few years ago. A good number of Theosophists gathered at the meeting on October 26 in our headquarters in the Avenue de La Bourdonnais. Our Secretary General gave a warm welcome to Abbas Effendi, who took the floor and began by saluting France and the Theosophists. Then, in rich and poetic language, he paid great respect to Truth which he compared to the sun that illuminates and vivifies, and which he recommended we revere above every other thing. In sum, he briefly but thoroughly presented the main points of the Babi doctrine, namely: the fundamental unity of religions; the unity of mankind – and hence brotherhood; that religion should be a bond of love; that there should be no contradiction between true religion and true science; that divisions due to one's background or beliefs are unfounded; that there must be an equitable distribution of the means of livelihood among all men; that there must be absolute equality among men before the law; that there must be a tribunal of arbitration to settle disputes among nations and to ensure universal peace; that religion should not mix with politics; that women must receive the same education as men; that the spirit of goodness must be spread everywhere.

That made a total of eleven excellent principles and then Abbas Effendi retired and left us with no opportunity to learn his ideas about the human soul itself, the evolution of man and the important question of reincarnation.

We are inclined to think that Babism is based only on general principles and in this case it has no analogies with the fundamentals of Theosophy and, therefore, is not as beneficial to humanity.[40]

The author regretted that 'Abdu'l-Bahá did not share 'his ideas regarding the human soul, the evolution of man' and reincarnation. These subjects were addressed by 'Abdu'l-Bahá in a second talk to the Paris Theosophists given in 1913 (see below).

On 16 December *Le Théosophe* published a further article about the visit of 'Abdu'l-Bahá that included some general information on the Bahá'í Faith. It was written by the director of the journal, Gaston Revel (1880–1939),[41] and included a portrait of 'Abdu'l-Bahá. Contrary to Courmes, Revel stressed in his article the points he saw in common between the Bahá'í Faith and Theosophy:

BAHAISM

The presence of the Persian prophet Abdul-Baha in Europe has produced such a favorable impression that we are naturally led to devote him a few lines. This is not a simple new sect, but a real and important embryonic Universal Religion the aspirations of which are not only high but also of a practical and immediate fulfillment . . .

He has the beautiful countenance of a patriarch, pure of heart, his words are sound and full of imagery. Abdul-Baha is also modest, and from this we understand that he is far from establishing himself as an all-powerful magician, he does not consider himself a wise man nor as the sole intermediary between God and men. He welcomes everyone with a good-natured friendliness, he does not speak until he is asked. In a word, he is a truly wise man and we are not surprised that he is so loved by his people . . .

'It is in everyday life that man must prove himself worthy of his religion,' said Abdul-Baha, 'work is good for people, to be tolerant to all religions of the world is to love God as he desires to be loved.' Profound words that all men should engrave in their memory . . . Bahaism and Theosophy have so many points in common that it would be impossible to list them all here . . . These similarities certainly explain why the conversation between our president Mrs. Annie Beasant and Abdul-Baha, was at once so interesting and so cordial.[42]

On His departure from France 'Abdu'l-Bahá made a short visit to Marseille. There he was invited to speak to the local branch of the Theosophical Society. A brief account of the meeting was published in the *Revue Théosophique Française* and stated that 'the Marseille branch received on December 6, at their headquarters, Abdul Baha, leader of the Bahais, who talked about materialism in his customary simple, clear and fair way, just as we observed in Paris.'[43]

In America

As was the case in England and France, 'Abdu'l-Bahá's presence in America aroused considerable interest in the Bahá'í Faith among Theosophists and several lodges invited Him to lecture. On 25 April 'Abdu'l-Bahá addressed a group of Theosophists at the home of Agnes Parsons in Washington.[44] A few days afterwards, 4 May, 'Abdu'l-Bahá addressed the Chicago branch of the Theosophical Society in a meeting convened at the Northwestern University Hall, Evanston.[45] A further meeting arranged by Chicago Theosophists was held on 14 September. On 30 May 'Abdu'l-Bahá addressed the New York Theosophists[46] and on 24 July He spoke to Boston Theosophists about the immortality of the soul.[47] In Malden, Massachusetts, 'Abdu'l-Bahá addressed another Theosophical branch on 27 August.[48] In California He was invited to speak on 11 October to San Francisco Theosophists in a meeting specially held at the Yosemite Hall in the recently built Native Sons' Building.[49] His last talk in America for the Theosophical Society was held in New York on 4 December.[50]

In April 1912, coinciding with the arrival of 'Abdu'l-Bahá in America, the *Theosophic Messenger*, official organ of American Section of the Theosophical Society, published a lengthy article written by Nellie H. Baldwin in which the Bahá'í Faith was introduced with impartiality.[51] In August the same journal published the text of 'Abdu'l-Bahá's address at Hull House, Chicago.

On 31 May the Brooklyn *Daily Star* published a short account of the meeting with New York Theosophists held on the previous day:

> Abdul Baha, the leader of the Bahai movement, spoke Thursday evening before a large audience at Theosophical Headquarters, Seventy-Ninth Street and Broadway, Manhattan. He spoke of the solidarity of the human race and the fundamental likeness of all religions, and urged his hearers to work for human brotherhood and universal peace. He said: 'There never was a time when the

spirit of humanity was more favorable to the inculcation of tolerance and mutual understanding'.⁵²

On 14 September 1912, 'Abdu'l-Bahá was invited by the American section of Theosophical Society to one of the sessions of its twenty-sixth national assembly which was held in Chicago. In his address He spoke on the human soul, the purpose of man's life and also introduced some of the Bahá'í principles.

In his report of the convention, Albert P. Warrington (1866–1939),⁵³ secretary general of the American Theosophical Society and editor of *The Theosophic Messenger*, mentioned 'Abdu'l-Bahá and stated that 'The lecture of his Holiness, Abdul-Baha, given at the social gathering, was enjoyed by everyone. What a charming Bhakti he is! His address was taken down in shorthand and will be duly published in *The Theosophic Messenger*. May he long live to carry on his noble work, and may it be our happy privilege to come into his pure and benign presence many times again. He is singularly fortunate in having his nephew, Dr. Fareed, as interpreter, for his attainment as a master of chaste and beautiful English is indeed high.'⁵⁴

As announced by Warrington, *The Theosophic Messenger* published the text of the talk in its December issue. According to a footnote the text was compiled from stenographic notes of Fareed's translation:

AN ADDRESS TO THE THEOSOPHICAL SOCIETY
By His Holiness, Abdul Baha

I have the utmost of happiness this afternoon to be present at this revered meeting – an assemblage of spiritual susceptibilities, an assemblage free from blind imitation, an assemblage trained in the investigation of reality. Therefore I am most happy and I shall never forget this session.

Man is possessed of three verities: first, that of animalism; second, the human reality; third, the reality of the Kingdom. The animal reality can only conceive of the animal world and this is, according to terminology, the animal mold. The second reality is the human reality, which constitutes intellectual perception and the capacity of conceiving every image freely present, the capacity to attain to the image of the Kingdom, and acquires the capacity to present simply the image of the animal. This may be termed the human mold. As to the third reality, which is the reality of the Kingdom, that is the reality representing the image and likeness of God, which is entitled the body of the Kingdom and is sometimes called the astral[55] mold or body.

According to the divine philosophers of the Orient, the statement is made that man is possessed of these three molds. One mold is the animal mold; the other is the human mold, which is capable of illumination and capable also of gloomy states. It is capable of the acquisition of virtue and likewise subject to all vices. The third mold is the mold of ideal perfection, and that is called the body of the Kingdom, the astral temple or mold. This is according to the terminology of the divine philosophers of the Orient.

Hence this makes it evident and manifest that if the animal dark mold should overcome the reality of manliness, then man is inferior to the animal even, and baser than the brute. For in the animal the astral temple does not obtain. In the animal the intellectual capacities are not present. Therefore if it remains in darkness the animal is quite excused, it is not responsible. But in man, who is possessed of the intellectual capacities and the mold of the Kingdom, who is possessed of the image and likeness of God – if these divine bestowals should remain latent and hidden, assuredly he is inferior to the animals because the divine bestowals have been laid waste. But if the forces of the Kingdom should overcome and the Temple of the Kingdom should become resplendent and the image and likeness of God become manifest in man, verily he is the noblest of creatures and the greatest of phenomena. Such an one is a radiant man; such an one is a merciful man; such an one is a beautiful man; such an one is verily the image and likeness of God.

The appearance of the manifestations of God and the appearance of the divine manifestations and the appearance of divine philosophers, all have been for the sole purpose of man becoming educated, that the animal realities may be transmuted into the realities of the kingdom, which shall become resplendent. Thus may man become freed from the world of defect and arrive at the highest state and apogee of perfection; may become saved from the bondage of nature; may become the manifestation of all merciful attributes. The activities of the holy, divine manifestations of God have been for no other purpose save that of education, and this is verily the terminal body, this is the perpetual effulgence, this is the glorious appearance unto time immemorial. Unto time without end this shall be a continual effulgence. The bounties of God have had no beginning and shall have no end, because the bounties of God are expressive of the sovereignty of God which is effective in its penetration throughout the phenomena in the world. The sovereignty of God is not, like the human reign of sovereignty, an accidental affair – at a time not existing, a new coming into being, and at a time terminating. That is human sovereignty. But the sovereignty of God has had no beginning and for it there is no end.

The names and attributes of God have ever been effective and will continue to be effective forevermore. Notwithstanding this, it is astounding that some thoughtless persons have conceived for the effulgence and bounties of God a beginning and likewise an ending. They would state, as it were, that the terminal body is subject to cessation and that divine effulgence may come to a sudden terminus, the everlasting bestowals be ended and names and attributes inactive and useless. This is ignorance. How is it possible for the Sun of Reality which was ever in the highest horizon of sanctity to set forever in its horizon? All spiritual beings and intellectual and ideal souls owe their growth and evolution to the Sun of Reality. Were the rays and the heat and the light of the Sun of Reality to cease, then the world of ideation and the souls of the spiritual world would become extinct. If for it there shall be no rising again, all expressions of life of the ether will become non-existent. No man would linger, no animal would linger, no vegetation, no trace of life would linger, because all phenomena are dependent for their nourishment and nutrition and education upon the light and heat of the Sun. If for the Sun there shall ever be a cessation of effulgence, all phenomena will become nonexistent and likewise the world of the reality of man. The world of minds and souls, the world of the spirit, all receive their education from the heat of the Sun of Reality. If the Sun of Reality sets not to rise again, its light will terminate; then surely the world of minds and spirits will have to come to an end too, and this is self-evident. But, in short, the effulgences of God have forever existed and will exist forevermore. The Sun of Reality has ever had its rising and will continue to have its Sun rise again. For the bounty of God there is never a terminus.

The effective penetration of the names and attributes of God will have no end. The Lordly effulgences have no terminus. Because the reality of divinity is infinite, therefore its bounties are infinite. To conceive of any ending for those bounties is utter ignorance. If is like conceiving a sun without light and heat or ray, and this is an impossibility and every wise man knows that such a conception is preposterous.

Among the effulgences of the Sun of Reality and the bounties of God, His Holiness Baha'o'llah appears on the Persian horizon, illuminating the Orient, giving forth teachings which are for the salvation of humanity, for the illumination of mankind, for the appearance of the virtues in the world of humanity, for the attainment of the perfections of the human world. These were the teachings founded by His Holiness, Baha'o'llah; and I here desire to emphasize those teachings for you, because some have asked, 'What has Baha'o'llah brought new? What new foundation has he laid?'

The first postulate is the Oneness of the world of humanity; that all mankind represents the servant of God the ALL-glorious; that the Lord has created them all; that He provides for all; that He educates all; that He protects all; and that He is kind and clement to all humanity, to all of His creations. If He did not have love for all then He would not have been kind. Now inasmuch as we see expressions of His kindness to all humanity, regardless of distinction, all mankind must be conceived of as being immersed in the sea of His mercy. And man must emulate the policy divine. He must love all humanity and he must see all humanity submerged in the ocean of God's mercy. At most, it is this: Some are weak; they must be strengthened. Some souls have weak perceptions; they must be trained, in order that their perceptions may become acute and keen. Some souls may be sick; they must be treated, in order that they may get well. Some are childlike; they must be educated, in order that they may attain to the state of maturity. But to all LOVE must be shown; to all kindness must be exercised. Baha'o'llah, addressing all humanity, says: 'We are all the leaves of one tree, the blossoms of one tree, the fruits of one tree, and that is the Tree of Humanity.' For all humanity is honored in its capacity to attain humanitarianism. Where do you find a foundation so broad and liberal? Is there a book which considers all the world of humanity as integral, proclaiming its Oneness? This is the foundation laid by Baha'o'llah.

Again, he states that every soul must independently investigate reality. He must not emulate or follow blindly the imitations of asserters. He must not give any importance to that sort of ignorance, for imitations are darkness, the cause of separations, the cause of contention amongst men, the cause of sedition or warfare amongst men, and therefore reality must be investigated. Thus may all mankind attain to the utmost of amity and fellowship. And these are the new institutes of Baha'o'llah.

Among the institutes or teachings of Baha'o'llah is this: That religion must prove a factor in the cause of unity and fellowship. It must bind together *all humanity*. Now if religion should become the cause of hatred and enmity, the cause of alienation among men, the separating of man from man, assuredly, he declares, irreligion is preferable to religion. For the purpose of religion is no other than love and amity. This is one of the special teachings of Baha'o'llah. In no books do you find it so expressed. Religion must conform to reason and science. If religion should prove contrary to reason and science it is not worthy of credence. It is superstition absolutely, and not worthy of man's acceptance, because then man cannot be inspired with confidence, he cannot be assured of it, for it has proven disagreeable and contrary to reason and the scientific postulates. What inspires the human heart with confidence? That wherein his reason can concur and science prove; therefore if religion should be contrary to reason and the scientific postulates, it is superstition and unworthy of man's credence.

Among the teachings of Baha'o'llah is the following: That religious prejudice, sectarianism, national prejudice, patriotic prejudice, political prejudice – all these forms of prejudice are the destroyers of the foundations of mankind and contrary to the good pleasure of God, because God has purposed that amongst men there shall be love and unity.

If history be consulted from its inception to the present time you will find that all the bloodshed amongst men, the laying waste of lands, etcetera, have been due to religious prejudice, racial prejudice, political prejudice, partisanship, or some political form of bias. Hence, it becomes evident that every prejudice is destructive as regards the foundations of men. Until these prejudices pass away the world of humanity will not find composure. All these prejudices are purely imaginary and superstitious.

Let us first regard religious prejudice. The foundations of the religions of God are one. The teachings of God are one. His Holiness, Abraham, was the head of reality, for the religion of God is ever reality. His Holiness, Moses, was the head of reality. His Holiness, Christ, was the founder of reality. His Holiness, Zoroaster, was the founder of reality. His Holiness, Buddha, was the founder of reality. His Holiness, Baha'o'llah, was the founder of reality. All the present religions are fundamentally one, and that is reality. Were it not for their reality they would have been false and would have passed away. Now, so long as the foundation of the divine religions is one, whence these prejudices? Wherefore should the religions hate each other? Why should the religions rise in opposition to each other? This is absolute ignorance. This is base human nature. For the foundation of the divine religions is one; there is no divergence or difference therein. Hence, religious prejudice is without grounds.

Now as to racial prejudice. All of us, after all, are the progeny of one parentage. We are all the children of Adam and we all belong to the same tribe. We are not divergent peoples. We are the variegated leaves, blossoms, flowers, and fruits of the same tree, and why in the world should we have alienation? Why should we call some Germanic, others Greek, others French, or some British? Why this separation, so long as all of us belong to the same tree, so long as we all belong to Adam's family? We are one tribe, one kind – humankind, mankind. Hence the prejudice of race is without a basis. What does German mean, English or French, Russian or Turk? All these are superstitious names. We are all human and we are all men belonging to the same race, the same lineage and progeny; thus racial prejudice is false.

As to the patriotic prejudice. God has created one centre, and it was destined to be the habitation of all mankind. Thus we all belong to the same Fatherland. But we have come to drawing imaginary lines, whereas God has not created those lines. Why such distinctions over boundary lines? It is one continent, the same earth – in reality, one home. Therefore, patriotic prejudice is without foundation.

Now consider political prejudice. The greatest policy imaginable is that of God, and we must emulate the policy of God. That is complete. Human policy, however accomplished it may be, cannot compare with the policy of God. Assuredly divine policy is transcendental, comprehending all policies. We must follow the policy established by God. But as to policies emanating from selfishness, no doubt such will be the cause of the destruction of the human world. Therefore all these prejudices, so destructive, must be laid aside. We must be freed from all these forms of bias and we must serve the world of humanity. This is amongst the special teachings of Baha'o'llah.

Furthermore, in the teachings of Baha'o'llah, as to the qualities of men and women, he declared years ago that man and woman are both human and are the creatures of one God; that in the estimation of God there is no distinction of gender. All were created after His image and likeness. All humanity is verily the image of God, whether male or female. You will find the genders male and female in all phenomena, in the animal world, in the vegetable kingdom. There is no distinction observed by the vegetable. For example, there are the male palm tree and the female palm tree; the male fig and the female fig tree; the male mulberry and the female mulberry – all the vegetables and trees you will find have gender, but amongst them there is no fight about prerogative. You will discover that amongst the animals the equality of male and female is observed; there is no difference; male and female in the utmost of amity live together. The females do not vaunt themselves over the males and the males do not vaunt themselves over the females. In the utmost of unity and accord they live together; and man should not be inferior to the animals, especially when the male and the female constitute the two wings of the human temple in the human world. One wing is represented by the male and the other by the female. If one wing remain weak, then weakness will handicap the other wing, and undoubtedly a bird cannot fly with unequal wings. But if both wings be equal in strength, then the flight of the bird will be lofty. Likewise in the world of humanity. When the male and female become perfect and co-equal in all their rights, both wings becoming strong, then the world of humanity will soar upward. This is the special teaching of Baha'o'llah.

Among the teachings of Baha'o'llah is the adjustment of the means of livelihood amongst men so that each individual member of the body politic may enjoy the utmost of comfort and welfare, but with perfect order accrued to the general social body; with a conservation of means but with a certain system of economics which he has detailed. According to that order and system, all the individual members of the body politic – that is to say, each individual member of the social body – in the utmost of comfort, in the utmost of ease will live, but the degrees and stations will also be conserved, because in the world of humanity order must prevail and degrees must be conserved; were the degrees to be destroyed, disorder would result. The world of humanity may be looked upon as an army. An army must have generals, must have the marshal, the sergeant, the captain, the corporal, likewise the infantry. All the army cannot be infantry or soldiers and all cannot be sergeants. There must needs be degrees. But the point of importance is that each individual member of the army enjoy the utmost ease and happiness. There are expressed instructions concerning this and these teachings of Baha'o'llah solve the difficulties which have come, problems of capitalism and of labor which will in the future be entirely erased. This is one of the specialties of the great teachings of Baha'o'llah.

Among the teachings of Baha'o'llah is this: That man is possessed of two natures. He is in need of two civilizations. One is the material civilization, which insures the perfect order of his physical welfare; and the other his spiritual life, or spiritual civilization, which is the divine civilization insuring happiness everlasting. As to the material civilization, the men of dignity on the earth are the founders, and man is in need of them. As to the divine civilization, the founders thereof are the manifestations holy and divine. Man cannot attain to happiness everlasting through the sole agency of material civilization. Just as he is in need of material civilization, likewise is he in need of spiritual civilization. The founders of the material type are the wise men of the earth. The founders of the spiritual divine civilization are the holy divine prophets. By material civilization only corporal happiness will come, but through the divine civilization the life eternal will attain, susceptibilities of the supernatural will attain, the divine perfection will become resplendent and the image and likeness of God will become a verity. Therefore man, however much he may advance in material civilization is nevertheless in need of spiritual or divine civilization and, without the latter, material civilization availeth not.

There are many other teachings which have been given by Baha'o'llah. Great are the foundations, which you have not found in any other book or in any other scripture.

I praise God that in America such meetings as this do obtain, held on a basis of brotherhood for humanity and based upon an appreciation of verities, founded in the investigation of realities. This revered assemblage in reality may be counted one of the greatest of world assemblages, comprehending the most delightful ethics of humanity wherein the attractions of the conscience are quite evident.

I am hoping that day by day such susceptibilities and feelings of the conscience may be continued; that the divine bounties may encompass all; that the spiritual effulgences may become resplendent; and that this revered assemblage may advance along all the degrees of human advancement, thus reaching the utmost of happiness on this plane. For all will I seek the eternal honor and glory, and I ask God that day by day the bestowals and useful service of this body may increase.[56]

Second Visit to England

On the afternoon of Saturday 14 December 1912, 'Abdu'l-Bahá spoke at the City of Liverpool Lodge, a local branch of the Theosophical Society created in 1895 with headquarters at 165 Oakfield Road. On the morning of the same day Mrs Armour, the president of the lodge (the secretary was C. A. Kinnish), was received by 'Abdu'l-Bahá at the Adelphi Hotel. In the afternoon she returned to take 'Abdu'l-Bahá in her car to the meeting arranged for him at eight.[57]

In His address 'Abdu'l-Bahá touched on the subject of religious unity and the purpose of religions. At a time when Jiddu Krishnamurti was being trained by Annie Besant and her followers to be the future 'world teacher', 'Abdu'l-Bahá exhorted His listeners to seek for the 'Sun of Truth', to search for One with an 'education marked with a divine power', 'superior to the laws governing human education' and not depending on 'human means for knowledge', someone who 'does not need the light from a human lamp nor yet from an astral body'.[58] In this direct way he invited His audience to search for Bahá'u'lláh.

On 16 December at least two accounts of the meeting were published in the local press. *The Liverpool Courier* published the following:

VISIT OF PERSIAN MYSTIC
ADDRESS TO THEOSOPHICAL SOCIETY

Abdul Baha, the Persian mystic, who sojourned in Liverpool over the week-end on his way from America to London, Paris, and thence to the Far East, addressed the Theosophical Society at their headquarters, on Saturday night, on 'The Search for Truth'. He remained seated, and spoke in Persian, M. Hippolyte Dreyfus (Paris) acting as interpreter.

Jews and Christians and Mohammedans, he said, followed the precepts of their fathers and refused to go forth and seek for themselves. Theosophists and Bahaies had abandoned all dogmas in their earnest search for truth. The tribes and nations of the world were seething with discontent because they were not seeking truth. Truth admitted of absolutely no division, and accepted neither limitations nor boundaries. All dogmas differed; hence the nations were opposed. The different dogmas made wars and strife. If it were not for these differences in religions there would be no wars. In Persia there were many tribes, governments and religions, but they cut down the barriers of dogma, became followers of Baha-u-llah, and were now as one. Jews, Christians, and Zoroastrians. &c, met to seek for truth, and so became united.

All the different religions of God that have risen on the face of the earth had one purpose – to educate man and to inform him with the spiritual, the luminous, the divine, so that he might partake of that divine spirit and find eternal life, show forth the virtues of mankind, and from a world of darkness enter a world of light. There was no other reality of meaning to the different religions. Their purpose was one, the teaching was one. Man might be said to have three natures. One was sunk in darkness, and he was a prisoner to his desires, for here he possessed the same qualities as the animals. The second nature might be called his human nature. This was the home of the mind and the soul. The third was his likeness to God, and this he possessed in proportion to the divine qualities he imparted – the breeze of the Holy Spirit, pure spirituality, luminosity. All the religions, prophets, and great teachers had no other purpose than to raise mankind from the animal to the divine nature. Their purpose was to free man and to make him an inhabiter of the realm of reality. For although the body of man was material, his reality was spiritual. He appealed to them to always hope that one day a Sun of Truth would rise and bring a dawn, whose light would destroy all the darkness of the human world, unite hearts and make souls happy, do away with contention and establish universal peace. Then would there be no divisions; all would be united and live as one family under the flag of unity and love; then would mankind be inspired with a new progress and show forth diverse virtues; a new spirit would be given to him, and the new world would be invested with a divine beauty. His hope was that they might do all in their power to help to invite to this earth God's greatest blessing in their search for truth.[59]

A shorter but very similar account was also published in the *Daily Post*.[60]

Among the visitors received by 'Abdu'l-Bahá in London on 23 December were Albert Dawson, editor of *The Christian Commonwealth*, and James Wedgwood, editor of *The Vahan*. Both of them asked 'Abdu'l-Bahá for a message for their publications and He acceded to their requests.

'Abdu'l-Bahá wrote a special message to *The Vahan* which was presented in the publication as a 'new year's greeting'. In introducing 'Abdu'l-Bahá's message Wedgwood stated:

> During his sojourn beneath 'the smoke-laden counterpane' of this great city of London, may his wisdom fall on rich soil in many hearts; may he long be spared to inspire the world with those great ideals for which Bahaists and Theosophists labour in common.[61]

The translation of 'Abdu'l-Bahá's message was prepared by Ahmad Sohrab on 24 December and was published with a facsimile of the original Persian and a picture of 'Abdu'l-Bahá. Copies of this message reached as far as Hungary. When, months later, the Master visited Budapest, members of the Theosophical Society requested Him to sign their copies of His portrait in *The Vahan*.[62]

As He did during His address to Liverpool Theosophists, 'Abdu'l-Bahá proclaimed in His message to the readers of *The Vahan* that 'the Sun of Reality' had dawned:

A NEW YEAR'S GREETING FROM ABDUL BAHA
ABDUL BAHA'S MESSAGE TO THE READERS OF THE 'VAHAN'
TRANSLATED BY MIRZA AHMAD SOHRAB

This Sun of the Ethereal Regions shines forth from the firmament. All the contingent beings grow and develop through its educative outpouring. Were it not for the heat and the effulgence of the sun, the geologic stratum of the globe would not have been formed: the precious mines would not have been brought into being, the dark soil would not have manifested the virtue of vegetation, the plant life would not have developed, the animal kingdom would not have enjoyed the instinctive powers, and the human world on this sphere of earth would not have existed.

All these generous gifts are through the outpouring of the rays of the sun, which is only one sign of the signs of the Omnipotence of His Highness the Almighty.

When the sun appears from the vernal equinox, the world of being is transformed into another world. Existence is clad with the emerald garment of verdancy, the trees produce leaves and blossoms, and yield fresh and luscious fruits. Warm blood circulates through the arteries and veins of every animate being, obtaining new life, and acquiring vitalising vigour and energy.

Likewise the Sun of Reality, which is the radiant luminary of the world of the spirits, souls, and minds; the effulgent Orb of the empire of the intellects and hearts, is the real Instructor of Humankind and causes the flourishing and maturity of the spirits, the unfoldment of the powers of intelligence, and the evolution of the virtues of the souls. For that Divine Sun there is also destined a rising and a setting vernal equinox, and autumnal equinox, equatorial line, and zodiacal signs.

It has been long since that Great Orb has set, the world of the minds, the souls, the spirits and the hearts has been steeped in darkness and gloom; the power of the ideal growth and development lost sight of; a visible inertia has attacked the world of thoughts; the susceptibilities of the hearts entirely forgotten, and the spiritual revelations have been discontinued.

Praise be to God! that again the Sun of Reality has dawned, flooding the earth with its glorious Light. All creation is now beginning to stir and awake. At every movement a new life is appearing and, day by day, wonderful traces of the spirit are being revealed. The sleepy ones must become awakened, and the negligent ones must become mindful. Now, in this day, may the blind ones, receive sight! The deaf ears become unstopped! The dumb tongues be unloosed, and the dead receive new life; so that the signs of the Favours of this Glorious Age may become manifest! May the happiness of the Most Great Day encircle all hearts! May the Splendours of Love illumine the soul and mind; so that the darkness of the infinite worlds of intellect and vision may be completely dispelled!

May your spirits be happy!

ABDUL BAHA[63]

This message was later published in German in *Adyar-Mitteilungen* (Leizpig), organ of the German Theosophists.[64] What was the reaction of Theosophists to this and other statements made by 'Abdu'l-Bahá is an interesting issue that needs more research. What is certain is that some Theosophists were not comfortable with the popularity and social sympathy that the Bahá'í Faith was gaining. *The Vahan* published in its February issue an editorial that illustrates well this reaction. In it Wedgwood, without losing a cordial tone when speaking of 'Abdu'l-Bahá and the Bahá'í Faith, presented the Bahá'í teachings as the antithesis of Theosophy and as a merely ethical doctrine inferior, in his view, to the more 'scientific' and more needed doctrines of Theosophy.[65]

Wedgwood's statements were later responded to by George Andree[66] in a lecture delivered at the Outlook Tower, Edinburgh, on 30 April 1913. Andree agreed with Wedgwood's simplistic definition of the Bahá'í Faith as an ethical doctrine and of Theosophy as a scientific one. But for Andree these characteristics made the Bahá'í Faith not the antithesis of Theosophy but its complement. 'These two world movements are designed to work in concert,' he declared, and expressed the view that both movements were furthering the same ends.[67]

* * *

A further meeting with Theosophists took place in early 1913. The writer Eric Hammond, author of *The Splendour of God* (1909) and one of the editors of *Abdul Baha in London* (1912), arranged a meeting for 'Abdu'l-Bahá with the members of the White Lodge in Wimbledon. The president and founder of this lodge was Daniel N. Dunlop (1868–1935),[68] a prominent member of the British Theosophical Society and the founder and editor of the monthly magazine *The Path* (London).

The meeting was held on 3 January, at the ground floor of Dunlop's residence in Sunnyside, Wimbledon, which was used as the headquarters of the lodge. 'Abdu'l-Bahá spoke, among other things, about the three realities coexisting in human beings – animal, rational and spiritual – and the nature of God and His relation with creation. Notes of this address were published in *The Path* on February 1913:

THE THREE REALITIES
ABDUL BAHA

How beautiful it is to organize such lovely gatherings that are not based upon the pursuit of the material principles of life! Such gatherings belong to the study and the investigation of spiritual facts . . . The Spiritual Power has gathered us together. Our aim is to discover the realities of phenomena. When we ponder over the reality of the microcosm, we discover that in the microcosm, or the literal man, there are deposited three realities. Man is endowed with an outward or physical reality. It belongs to the animal kingdom, because it has sprung out of the material world. This side of life, or this first reality, is darkness and gloom, because the world of matter is the world of darkness. This is the animalistic reality of man, which he has in common with all animals.

Man, however, enjoys a second or higher reality which is the intellectual reality that comprehends all phenomena, or is infinite as regards the phenomena. It is a governor victorious over the world of matter. It discovers and unfolds the realities of sentient beings; it 'explodes' the laws of Nature, because it is superior, above and beyond the laws of Nature from a physical standpoint.

When we ponder over the morphology of the human body we find that man, like any other animal, is subject to the laws of Nature. All creation is the captive of Nature; it cannot deviate one hair's breadth from the mandates of Nature. For example, the fire is circumscribed and limited within the boundaries of the laws of Nature, and it cannot surpass any laws laid down by Nature. This globe of ours is the captive of the postulates of Nature; it cannot deviate one hair's breadth from the laws of Nature. All the stellar bodies in this infinite universe, notwithstanding their colossal size, cannot deviate from the laws laid down for their coursings by Nature; they are the prisoners of Nature, they cannot go out of the circle or of the circumference which is allowed for their journeyings. The great shoreless sea is the prisoner of nature. The vegetable kingdom in its entirety is a captive of Nature. The animal kingdom is a captive of Nature. All this will show you that these phenomena cannot go beyond the limits set by nature. Likewise man, as far as his first reality or his physical life is concerned, is also a prisoner of nature.

But the reasonable or intellectual reality with which man is endowed enables him to transcend the laws of physical nature. For example, according to the laws of nature man is a denizen of the earth, he must walk upon the earth, and, because he is born on this globe, he belongs to this earthly life. This is a regulation of nature. But man, through his intellectual power, transcends this law of nature, discovers the science of aviation and flies in the air like a bird. He becomes like a fish and goes to the very depths of the seas. He builds a great fleet and sails over the seas. It is, therefore, an indubitable fact, that man is able to transcend the laws of nature; this intellectual reality of man predominates nature. Through it man is enabled to make a fruitless tree fruitful. He transforms the wild woods into fruitful orchards. He changes the plains of thistles and thorns into lovely meadows and rose gardens. Then there is the electrical energy which breaks the very mountains. Man through the application of intellectual force takes this electrical energy and makes it a captive within the incandescent lamp. According to the postulate of reason, his voice is a free agency. Man takes it and makes it a prisoner within a box – a phonograph. Man through this power is enabled again to communicate with the East and the West within a few minutes. Through this intellectual power, while he is in Europe he is able to discover America. This is an extraordinary power! He may live all his life in the East, and yet through this power may organize great affairs in the West. All these sciences that we enjoy were the hidden and recondite mysteries of nature, but man was enabled to discover these mysteries, and out of the plane of the unseen he brought them into the world of the seen. All the artistic accomplishments and undertakings which we have to-day were once the secrets of nature; man discovered them and brought them to the plane of visibility. In short, the exploration of the secrets of nature seem to be very numerous. Therefore, the citation of these facts will demonstrate to you that man is superior to nature. He is, in fact, its governor, although his physical reality is a captive of nature. It is then self-evident that in man there exists an intellectual reality which is superior to his physical reality.

There is, however, a third reality in man, that is the spiritual reality. Through that medium come spiritual revelations. This is a celestial power which is infinite as regards the intellectual as well as the physical realms. This power is conferred upon man through the breath of the Holy Spirit. It is an eternal reality, an indestructible reality, a reality which belongs to the divine kingdom. This celestial reality, or the third reality, delivers man from the material world. It is a power which enables man to escape from the world of nature.

This is proven from scientific as well as spiritual evidence. When we ponder and look over phenomena we observe that all have their origin in a single element. This single cellular element travels and has its coursings through all grades of existence. I wish you to ponder over this carefully. This single element has been in the realm of the mineral kingdom. While staying in the mineral kingdom it has had its coursings and transformations through myriads of images and forms.

Having completed its travellings through the mineral kingdom it has ascended to the vegetable kingdom and in this kingdom it has had again its travellings and transformations through myriads of images; sometimes it has been a grain, again it was in the form of a leaf, anon it was a flower or an animal, a tree, or a blossom! Then it attains to the stage of fruition and is a fruit. This single primordial element has had its transformations through these infinite forms and images. Again in the human kingdom it has its transferences and coursings through multitudes of forms. In short, this reality or this single primordial atom has had its numerous travellings through every stage of life, and in every stage or form it was endowed with a special and peculiar virtue. Therefore the great and divine philosophers have had an epigram as follows: 'All things are involved in all things.' Every single phenomenon has enjoyed the postulates of God, and in every form of these infinite electrons it has had its perfections of virtue. This, I hope, is evident and clear to you. This flower once upon a time was the soil; the animal eats it; it ascends to the animal kingdom. Man eats the body of the animal, and there you have the ascension into the human kingdom, because all phenomena are the eaters and the eaten. This breath we inspire, is it not true that there are many thousands of infinitesimal microbes in it, each one of these microbes going into the make-up of our composition? And this will show you that the lower forms of life can be transmuted into the higher realms of existence. Therefore, every primordial atom of these atoms, singly and indivisibly, has had its coursings throughout all sentient creation, going constantly into the make-up and aggregation of elements. Thus you have the conservation of energy and the infinity of phenomena, the indestructibility of phenomena, changeless and immutable, because life cannot become annihilated. The utmost is this: that the form, the outward image, throughout these changes and transformations is dissolved. The realities of all phenomena are immutable and unchangeable. Extinction or mortality is nothing but the transformation of pictures and images, but the reality back of these images is eternal. And every reality of the realities of life is one of the bounties of God. Some people believe that the divinity of God had a beginning. Therefore with this principle they have limited the downpour of the bounties of God. For example, they think that there was a time when man did not live, and that there will be a time in the future when the race of man will be destroyed; that there was a time when this globe did not exist. Such a theory circumscribes the power of God, for how can we understand the divinity of God but through the manifestation of his qualities? How can we understand the fire? Through its physical heat, through its flame? Were not heat and flame in this fire, naturally we could not say that the fire existed. The illumination of the lamp is through electrical energy, and if we believe that there was a time in this world when this electrical energy was not in existence, then that is equal to the statement that there was no life at all. Or, to take another example, the sun; let us say that there was a time when the sun was not endowed with rays and heat. That is equal to saying that there was no sun, because the very existence of the sun is demonstrated through its heat and rays. If there was a time when God did not manifest his qualities, then there was no God, because the attributes of God presuppose the creation of phenomena. For example, we say God is the Creator. A creator must of necessity create. We say God is the provider. The provider must have someone to provide for. We say God is omniscient. Then omniscient knowledge is the second degree of omniscience. Therefore, as long as God has been God there has been creation, there have been the creatures. God has no beginning and His creation has no ending, for the postulate of God is never failing. The effulgence of God cannot be suspended. The sovereignty of God cannot be interrupted. If we conceive a beginning for the world of creation, then we have conceived for the dominion and sovereignty of God a beginning, which is a false theory. In reality His sovereignty is without beginning and without ending. Can we ever dream or conceive of a King without subjects? Without an army, without a kingdom? Is it possible? No. A king is in need of a kingdom; he is in need of an army; a king is in need of wealth. Now as long as the Kingdom of God, the sovereignty of God, is immemorial, the creation of this world throughout infinity is presupposed. When we look at the reality of the subject we will see that the bounties of God are infinite, without beginning and without ending. The greatest bounties of God in this phenomenal world are his manifestations. This is the greatest postulate. These manifestations are the sum of the reality. Therefore, for the appearance of the *whole* of the divine manifestations of God there has been no beginning, and for the appearance of the *whole* of the divine manifestations of God in the future, there is no ending whatsoever, because God is infinite and His grace cannot be limited at all. And if we ever dare to circumscribe His grace within certain limited spheres, then we have as a necessity circumscribed the reality of divinity which is all-powerful. Therefore the perfect man ever beholds the rays of the sun, he ever expects the coming of the effulgence of God, he ever gazes at the grace and bounties of God, he ever ponders over the omnipotent God, and he knows of a certainty that the reality of divinity is not finite, His names and His attributes are not finite, His graces and bounties are not limited and the coming of the manifestations of God are not circumscribed. This fact is self-evident and manifest.

Those people who have hearkened to the teachings of Baha-Ullah – Hindus, Mohammedans, Christians, Zoroastrians, Buddhists, Jews – such people have discarded their past rancour and are associating with the utmost love and unity. Take my example and see with what degree of love I am associating with you to-night, loving you with all my heart and soul. In the same way all those people are living together, with the utmost accord and unity, to such an extent that they are ready to sacrifice their possessions and lives for each other; and to such an extent has the transformation been wrought, that they are ever self-sacrificing for each other. Were you to enter into any gathering in the Orient, it would be very hard for you to discover who is a Christian and who is a Jew, or who is a Zoroastrian; for they are just like so many flames which have become one big flame. (Applause.) All these different faiths are merging into one great Faith.[69]

* * *

Months later, while 'Abdu'l-Bahá was in Paris, Daniel Dunlop invited the Master to participate at the Fifth Theosophist International Summer School, which was held in Peebles, Scotland, at the end of July 1913. 'Abdu'l-Bahá could not accept the invitation owing to His return to Egypt but instead sent a letter to Dunlop, who acted as the secretary of the Summer School, in which He encouraged the participants to work for universal peace. This letter was published in the *International Psychic Gazette* (London):

HE IS GOD! Beloved and Respectful friends,

Your letter of invitation received indicated that the Fifth International Summer School will be held in Scotland. On this account I was made very happy, but I regret my inability to present myself as I am on the eve of departure for the Orient. However, if my physical body is not present in that illumined gathering, my heart and spirit will be in your midst. I will ever keep it in my memory and pray to God that that revered Congress may become confirmed in rendering a most great service to this radiant century.

Every century holds the solution of a predominant problem. Although there may be many problems, yet one looms large and becomes the most important of all. In the past century the most important question that occupied the minds of men was the establishment of political freedom, and this aim was more or less spread broadcast.

But in this luminous century, the greatest aim of the world of humanity is Universal Peace, which must be founded, so that the realm of creation may obtain composure, and the East and the West which include in their arms the five continents of the globe may embrace each other, and mankind rest beneath the Tabernacle of the Oneness of the world of humanity, with the Flag of the Universal Peace waving over all the regions. So long as this question has not become the light of the assemblages of the world, eternal prosperity shall not be obtained and estrangement will not be changed into good-fellowship.

I hope that the members of your Congress will become the vanguard of this heavenly army, conquering every region through their irresistible force.

According to the incontrovertible teachings of Baha-u-llah, and his irrefutable commands, the Bahais must interest themselves and be ever ready to give up even their lives in the furtherance of all international problems which are the fruits of good intention, and based upon the principle of the Oneness of the world of humanity, especially the question of Universal Peace. They are ever ready and prepared to serve. Unquestionably, up to this time, more than 20,000 people have hastened toward the arena of martyrdom for the promotion of these teachings of Baha-u-llah. They have sacrificed their possessions, wealth and lives.

All the great movements have advanced through altruism, selflessness and self-sacrifice, more than through the interchange of public opinions. It is my hope that all of us with the greatest power may arise to serve this most important cause, and thus become the true servants of the world's welfare.

You have observed that the greatest forces of the civilised nations are spent in the accumulation of the means of warfare. Under these sad conditions, how can we expect that Peace and reconciliation will be realised. Strive ye with all your hearts and souls, so that these colossal resources may be expended in that which would be conducive to secure general well-being and prosperity. May they become the means of life, and not the power of destruction to the edifice of man. May they confer fellowship upon the hearts and not create hatred and enmity through illusory ideas.

This is the hope of the well-wishers of the world of humanity. I hope that we may become assisted and confirmed therein.

I present my highest considerations of respect to the revered members of your noble Congress.

(Signed) ABDUL BAHA ABBAS

Translated by Mirza Ahmad Sohrab[70]

Visit to Edinburgh

One of the public addresses of 'Abdu'l-Bahá during His sojourn in Edinburgh was delivered on 9 January 1913 at a meeting convened by the Scottish Theosophical Society.

Scotland's section of the Theosophical Society was formed in 1910. The same year Scottish Theosophists launched their own organ, *Theosophy in Scotland* (Edinburgh), which continued until 1923. In 1911 a property was bought at 28 Great King Street, Edinburgh, as headquarters for the Scottish section of the Theosophical Society and as a meeting place for the local lodge, Orpheus. David Graham Pole (1877–1952),[71] who also acted as editor of *Theosophy in Scotland*, was the first secretary general of the society.

Articles published in *Theosophy in Scotland* from 1911 to 1913 reveal a great interest among Scottish Theosophists in the Bahá'í Faith and 'Abdu'l-Bahá. On May 1911, the magazine carried a lengthy article presenting the Bahá'í Faith which also shows that Scottish Theosophists had expected Tudor Pole to give a lecture for them about his visit to 'Abdu'l-Bahá in Egypt. 'Shall we not then fervently hope and pray for the swift spread of a movement of such a truly fraternal character as this,' stated the article, 'and look forward to the day when the hope of the Theosophist and of the Bahai shall be realised, and the unity and peace of the whole world shall be an accomplished fact.'[72]

When on September 1911 'Abdu'l-Bahá visited London, Graham Pole traveled from Edinburgh to meet Him. On October 1911 *Theosophy in Scotland* published this editorial:

The Leader of the great Bahai movement which is making such gigantic strides in the direction of Brotherhood all over the world has during the past month visited England for the first time. He seems to be a man of great spirituality and there is no doubt of his being a great power for good and for the healing of the nations. 'The Servant of God' is surely a fit title for such an one and it is the only title he claims or asks; 'The Master' is the title his followers give him. He simply radiates with Peace and Goodwill. To him and the great movement for which he stands we extend the right hand of fellowship wishing them most heartily godspeed.[73]

The same issue, which also contained two quotations from the Bahá'í writings, included an account by Graham Pole, offering some details about his visit to 'Abdu'l-Bahá in London:

ABDUL-BAHA (ABBAS EFFENDI)

Many of our members during the past month have had the opportunity of meeting Abdul-Baha, or, as he is better known to many, Abbas Effendi, the head of the great worldwide Bahai movement. The history of that great movement was very briefly sketched in our May issue, and it is sufficient here to state, that in addition to three million adherents in Persia, there are some twelve million more scattered over the face of the globe.

I had the privilege of being received by Abdul-Baha, and it is impossible to come near him without recognising that at least here is a very great and good man. He is sixty-seven years of age, very venerable and kindly in appearance, with the keen eye of a man in his prime. His reception was most courteous and hearty, and the breadth of his view is all-embracing. Theosophy, Freemasonry and all such kindred movements he welcomes as endeavours towards the realisation of the Universal Brotherhood of humanity. He sees in all religions some expression of the Divine, and he realises and teaches that behind all diversity there is Unity.

It is surely a hopeful sign of the times that on Sunday, 10th September, he spoke in the City Temple, London, on the invitation of the Rev. R. J. Campbell, while on Sunday, 17th September, he addressed a large congregation in St. John's, Westminster, at the request of Archdeacon Wilberforce.

'Abdul Baha' simply means 'The Servant of God', and that is all he claims for himself. Certainly it is a title no one would deny him, for the spirit of Christ permeates him, and one feels that it is good to be near him. I asked him if he would care to send any message to the members of the Theosophical Society in Scotland. He very willingly assented, and after I had written it down to the dictation of the interpreter, he signed it.

Surely the movement which acknowledges Abdul Baha as its leader – a movement which stands for Unity and Brotherhood – is one with which we should as far as possible join hands. Let us study their literature as far as it is available for us, help them where we can in the great cause of breaking barriers between different nations, creeds, castes and colours, realising as the Master (the title by which Abdul Baha is known to his followers) says, that a garden needs not only one colour or one kind of flower, but all kinds and varieties to make it perfect.

I was fortunate in meeting Abdul Baha again on each of the following three days I was in London, and count myself privileged to have been permitted to come in close contact with one whose presence and conversation give strength to carry on the daily round and common task.[74]

Graham Pole's version of 'Abdu'l-Bahá's message to Theosophists read:

To the Members of the Theosophical Society in Scotland.

Give my most friendly greetings to all the Theosophists. You all in reality have arisen to help humanity because you are freeing yourselves from superstition and you are casting ignorance far from your minds. You wish the welfare of mankind, and this object is a mighty one. Every man that in this day rises to save his brothers is nearing the threshold of God, for all the manifestations and prophets of God have striven to bring about unity among men, and they have worked for harmony. The foundation of the Divine teaching is this unity and harmony. Moses strove for unity among men; the Christ did all to promote this understanding, and Mohammed also proclaimed the necessity of this union. The Buddha also worked for the same great goal. The Gospel and the Koran and the Holy Writings are the basis for this unity. The foundation of the religions of

God is one; the faith of God is one and that is to bring between men love and understanding; and Baha'u'llah has renewed the teachings of the prophets and of the manifestations and has again proclaimed on what foundation the religion of God is established. He is bringing together again different nations, and he has been able to unite together antagonistic sects. The spirit of Baha'u'llah is bringing all the members and all the organs of the body of humanity to a complete understanding. As you are members of this body of humanity striving to bring about the accomplishment of this great aim, I pray God to assist you. ABBAS[75]

In November 1911 the journal published a photograph of 'Abdu'l-Bahá and reported that it had been 'specially sent by Abdul Baha for publication in our magazine'.[76]

Scottish Theosophists also wanted to support the publication of the volumes of 'Abdu'l-Bahá's talks in England and France. A note appeared on April 1912 in *Theosophy in Scotland* mentioning that 'a proposal has been made that a fund should be opened for the publication of the London and Paris addresses given by Abdu'l-Bahá. Any subscriptions sent to the Editor for this purpose will be acknowledged and forwarded to the proper quarter.'[77]

'Abdu'l-Bahá's address to Scottish Theosophists on 9 January 1913, was announced some days in advance in the local press.[78] The address was scheduled for 8 p.m. at the headquarters of the society and admission tickets were sold for half a shilling. *Theosophy in Scotland* also announced in its January 1913 issue that 'We are sure that many of our members will be most anxious to meet one of so great influence in the world, and we hope that he may be able to visit and perhaps address us at Headquarters. To come into such a presence is in itself a benediction.'[79]

Graham Pole visited the Master on the day of His arrival in Edinburgh, 7 January, as one of the guests of a dinner held in His honor.[80] On the day of the address 'Abdu'l-Bahá visited the headquarters of the Theosophical Society around 7:00 p. m. and met privately and had interviews with some of its members. After His address, 'Abdu'l-Bahá stayed at the headquarters and had dinner with some Theosophists, who asked Him to write a dedication in their guest book and to sign some Bahá'í books and pictures of Him. Later in the evening Graham Pole accompanied 'Abdu'l-Bahá in a car ride to Mrs Whyte's residence.

Sohrab wrote about Graham Pole, saying that 'The General Secretary was the happiest man on the face of the earth! He is a young man, full of enthusiasm, brimming over with hope and optimism.'[81]

In His address 'Abdu'l-Bahá spoke on the immortality of the soul and on progressive revelation.[82] Accounts of the meeting were published in *The Scotsman*[83] and in the *Evening Dispatch*.[84] In February *Theosophy in Scotland* published the text of the talk:

ADDRESS TO THE THEOSOPHICAL SOCIETY IN SCOTLAND
BY ABDUL BAHA
(From the interpretation by Mirza Ahmad Sohrab)

It gives me very great pleasure to be with you this evening and to take part in your delightful gathering, for you Theosophists – praise be to God! – are always independent investigators of reality, released from mere imitation of the customs of your forebears and ancestors. Your purpose in life is to achieve and welcome the knowledge of reality, no matter from what region the light may dawn. The religions of to-day are all captives in the claws of custom and of blind dogma, for the absolute reality and dominant truth which prompted the foundation of these very religions in the past are entirely forgotten, and certain blind observances of ritual and sacerdotal mummeries have crept in which are in entire opposition to the fundamental principles of Divine religion. True religion, which comes from God, is founded for the purpose of illuminating the world of humanity, and for the emancipation of the human race. It establishes a complete fellowship between all hearts, and unfolds before our vision the Kingdom of Heaven. But – a thousand times, alas! – religions so founded have become the cause of contention and mutual strife, and to-day they are constantly waging war against each other. There is even bloodshed among their representatives, who engage in strife, ransack each others' possessions, and destroy each others' homes. What makes them do all these things? They do them because they are prisoners of blind dogma.

As an illustration, take anyone you meet. You ask him to what religion he belongs. He says he is a Jew. 'Why art thou a Jew?' 'Because my father was a Jew, and my ancestors were Jews. That is why I follow in their footsteps.' Another man is a Mussulman.

'Why art thou a Mussulman?' 'My father was one, and my forebears also.' And if you put this query to the devotees of other religions they will give you the same answer. And indeed if you go through the whole category of the present-day religions you will find that in all of them numbers are following blindly; and that it is a case of 'the blind leading the blind'. But, if you inquire, you will find they have never investigated the reality; for if they had done so they would all have become unanimous and would work in harmony. If reality is one, then it is not subject to division; and this absolute reality is the foundation of all religions.

The Theosophical Society has freed itself from such blind imitation of what was thought and done in the past; and, soaring up toward the heaven of reality, is ever trying to investigate the deeper truths which underlie all religions. Therefore I am very happy.

As we look upon this world – the Macrocosm – and upon all that goes to make up man – the Microcosm – what do we find? We find that every organism is composed of single primordial atoms, and has come into existence through the interaction of the elective affinities inherent in them. Its existence is a scientific fact. Every given atom of these myriads of atoms has passed through multitudinous forms, and in every form it has manifested a particular virtue or power.

For example, looking upon this flower, there is no doubt that it is composed of single atoms, simple elements. There was a time when the various substances composing it were all in the Mineral Kingdom, and during that period they underwent many transformations. Having completed their course in the Mineral Kingdom, these atoms ascended to the Vegetable Kingdom, and they will go on, maybe for many hundreds of years, continuing their journey through experiences in this vegetable life. One day this, which is now a chrysanthemum, may become a rose; another day it may form part of a carnation. Another day it may enter into the composition of a tree. In short, each indestructible atom goes on journeying, first through the Mineral Kingdom, and then through successive stages of the Vegetable World. This is a fact in harmony with the laws of Biology.

Now this atom having run its course through the Vegetable Kingdom ascends next into the Animal Kingdom, where again it has its varied experiences. Having finished these, it enters the realm of humanity, and travels through its many and varied stages. In short, this primordial atom has undergone transformations through all the kingdoms and sub-kingdoms of life, and, in consequence of these experiences, it manifests in a certain form and possesses a particular virtue or power.

It is one of the philosophic epigrams of the East that everything is included in the All. Therefore every man during this multitude of transformations is gradually learning to know the many aspects of that All, and in every transformation has the opportunity of acquiring a fresh virtue, so that man may become a compendium of all the virtues of creation. This is an exposition of a divine mystery.

Philosophic man, or the inner man, is indestructible. He is ever existent. For the immortality of the soul is a fact not to be denied. The spirit is everlasting; it is illimitable. The rational proof of the immortality of the soul is as follows:– Man enjoys two realities – two verities (or aspects of Truth). The first aspect of this human verity is *material*; and the second aspect is *spiritual*. The aspect which is material is subject to non-existence. But the ideal aspect of man, which is the spirit, is indestructible. What does mortality or death mean? It means transference from one body to another body. Thus, to take again the illustration of this flower. This flower, you may say, is doomed to death. It is dying. Why? Because it is losing its present form and is returning to its original constitution, which is mineral; but there is ever a conservation of energy lasting through all creation; so that even the material constituents which make up this flower never die, but are constantly transformed. Thus, when grass is eaten by an animal, you may say that the grass is dead. But the real fact is that it has only lost its vegetable form and become absorbed into the animal kingdom; and through this process animal life is made possible; the plant has never been lost. So that we may say of annihilation that it is a process of transference from one form to another; but the elements are indestructible. That is all that is meant by annihilation. Thus it is with the body of man, his material form that you see before you. The spirit leaving the body means that this temporal body, having done its duty, will return to its original constituents and become part of the earth; but it still has an existence.

So that death simply means a step beyond the present conditions of life; in this way the material body of man may go through many forms and changes, and die and again be born, because it is used constantly in the making of various new forms and shapes. At the same moment one body cannot occupy the same space as another. It may only occupy one space. Take, for example, any given body – say a triangle. As long as it is triangular it cannot become a square, nor can it become a hexagon. It cannot become any other geometrical figure; for if it becomes a hexagon it cannot remain a triangle. One body can only be one shape at one time. So two forms cannot become part of one body at the same time. But even as you are sitting here, your soul or mind or spirit, by whatever name you may call it, contains all these various forms. At this very moment you can conceive of a triangle, a square, a hexagon, or any geometrical shape all at the same instant. Just at this time in your mind, in your spirit, you may call up anything. There they are, these forms, existing simultaneously, without having to be broken, and to replace one another in succession. They are all present in your spirit. In this way all forms exist in the spirit. There is no need of breaking one form so that the spirit may enjoy another form. The spirit is independent of these forms, and at the same time it can hold all these forms. Therefore this is scientific proof that the spirit is eternal. Why do we enjoy the immortal spirit? It can never be transformed from one shape into another. It is able to contain all the shapes and forms in the world. This is self-evident. The spirit enjoys immortal life. Another piece of evidence:– This physical body of man once in a while is subject to sickness. At other times it gets well. Sometimes the body grows fat and at other times it grows the opposite way – all lean – so that the body goes through very various conditions: but the spirit is ever the same. If the body grows lean the spirit does not grow lean, and if a man enjoys three hundred pounds avoirdupois, his spirit does not weigh three hundred pounds. Therefore this Divine and heavenly Absolute Reality, which is in man, is not subject to transformation or change. If one hand is cut off and the other arm is cut off, and the lower limbs are cut off, you will see that the man is going on living all the time, and his spirit is not mutilated. He is exactly the same man. The eternal spirit in him is undying. Third proof:– What is death? Death means the losing of sensations or susceptibilities.

While in a state of sleep man's body lacks all sensation. His eyes do not see. His ears do not hear. The power of smell does not act. All the senses are in a state of quiescence. The power of touch is not present. Alt the senses are at rest. They are asleep. Yet notwithstanding all this the man travels. He journeys, he dreams. His spirit sees, and his tongue speaks. In that very state of quiescence he is endowed with all his faculties. Now if man was made only of this material flesh he would not have these various conscious experiences while in the state of dream. This likewise demonstrates the fact that in the inner reality of man there is a second deeper reality by which everything is surrounded. Therefore it is another evidence that in man God has hidden a second reality, which second reality is entirely free from all the fatalities of life, ever going forward, never retrogressing; and this will show you that man enjoys this immortal and everlasting spirit.

The fourth proof:— While speaking you use the word 'I'. 'I went there.' 'I came here.' Who is this 'I' that speaks within you? It can look out and see its own body. It is evidently the ego within (*cogito ergo sum*). Therefore there is a second indestructible reality in man.

The fifth proof:— When you want to undertake a great thing you retire within the chamber of your own thought and wonder 'will it be profitable?' Ought I to do this? What will be the results of this? '*Who is the consultant within you?*' That consultant is the spirit. You consult with it and you get the proper opinion: and if the spirit dictates 'Go on and do it' you will go on and do it; and if it dictates 'No, it is not profitable,' you will not dare to do it. And this state is constantly working in man, and it is a proof in regard to the immortality of the soul. That inner reality is the rider and your body is the charger. The body is like unto this glass, and the spirit within you is like unto the light which illumines the glass. Although this glass be broken, the light will not be broken. Although the bulb containing the electric light goes through the process of dissolution, the light is not destroyed. It remains latent as electric energy; and another glass will come and take the place of its predecessor, and you will again have the light shining through it.

Man has had all this journeying through the various grades, and he is travelling still, and will travel, until in the end he will reach a destination which is superior to this physical life. That is called the state of perfection; but he is constantly breaking these glasses, and purifying them, making for himself, by degrees, a purer and purer vehicle, until it becomes perfectly transparent. At one time this glass that is here before us was in the course of vitrification in the mineral kingdom; and in the same way there was a time when the constituents of our material body were in the vegetable kingdom, and at another time they were a part of animal life. Now they have come together so as to form the human body. Therefore, although the glass be shattered, the light of the spirit of the true Reality will ever shine; and this is another proof. It is not a traditional proof – not a matter of belief and theory. It belongs to the philosophy of the Kingdom, and it is unanswerable.

To take another line of argument, the world of existence, the world of manifestation, by itself and in itself, cannot enjoy perpetuity. No, the phenomenal world, or world of existence, has, rather, the capacity for receiving bounties and outpourings. There is a Reality which is central. The world of existence has emanated or issued from that central Reality. As this material globe of ours – which in itself is not luminous – is vivified by rays emanating from the phenomenal sun – for the sun is a star – so the spiritual ray issues from this stupendous centre of life, and immediately all are illumined thereby.

The greatest Divine outpouring is the appearance of Divine Masters in this world. These Divine and Heavenly verities consist of one central verity. But they have diverse dawning places; just as this electric light here is always the same light, although it shines through various glasses. One day it shines through this glass, another day this glass is extinct and it will shine through the second glass. A third day it shines through a third glass – you can have many glasses – but the energy which gives the light is the same without any difference. The light is indivisible. It is one light, and although these Heavenly Divine Masters, as far as their personalities are concerned, are different, as regards their inner nature they enjoy one central realm, and that one central realm emanates from the central spiritual sun. There are many mirrors from which the sun is reflected. Yet the sun is one. This is an astronomical question. For example:– Here on the map you have 12 rays issuing forth from the central body. As you look you see that there is one centre and one stellar body; but this stellar body is capable of transmitting many

many rays of light to all parts. One light gives forth these 12 rays. Similarly one sun, the phenomenal sun, dawns at one time from the celestial sign of Capricorn; at another time it shines from the sign of Leo; at another time it will appear from the sign of Aries. It will shine from one point in spring, and again from another point in winter; but the sun is the same sun, and the ray is the same ray, although it passes through many signs. When the sun dawns from any particular sign its heat is of a certain intensity. Similarly, there are differences in these divine manifestations, or 'Masters'; but in reality they all show forth the one central Truth. Man must never look at the dawning points. He must ever look upward and see the sun. He must be an adorer of the sun, no matter from what point it appears. He must recognise the light, no matter through which glass it has been admitted. For light is illimitable, and man must attain to that state of divine perception. He must never limit himself to any one system. There are many mirrors reflecting the light; but though all these mirrors should be shattered, the light would remain. So long as we are seeking the light, and turning our attention constantly toward it, we shall love the light, no matter from which globe it may be shining.

And now I have made you quite tired.[85]

'Abdu'l-Bahá's prayer at the end of the meeting was also reproduced in the same issue:

> Oh, Thou Almighty God! Illumine our minds. May the eyes of the blind be opened and the ears of the deaf unstopped. Arouse the hearts that are dead. Quicken the souls that are fast asleep. Deliver us from every tribulation. Suffer us to attain to Thine infinite Kingdom. Oh, Lord, confer upon us Thy bounty so that we may attain to Thy knowledge. May we be lovers of Thy beauty, no matter in which human temple it may appear. May we become the adorers of the sun of Thy reality, no matter from which dawning-place it may shine forth. May we be the seekers of sweet fragrance, no matter from which rose it is diffused. Oh, Lord, deliver us from the material world and lead us on to Thine Eternal Kingdom, so that we may walk in Thy pathway, seek after Thy holy places, and in the consecration of the elect may we witness the transfiguration of

Thy bounteous Truth. Thou art generous. Thou art compassionate. Thou art Omnipotent. Thou art Omniscient.[86]

Some months after His sojourn in Scotland, 'Abdu'l-Bahá sent from Paris a letter to Graham Pole which mentions that He had received some magazines, probably *Theosophy in Scotland*:

> To His Honour Mr D. Graham Pole, upon him be Baha-o-llah, El-Abha
> Edinburgh, Scotland
>
> He is God!
>
> O thou revered Friend!
>   Thy letter was received. Its contents indicated that that illumined lady soared toward the Kingdom of the Merciful. Alas! that such a light which was shining in your Society has become extinguished, but it has become radiant in the Lamp of the Kingdom. She has obtained the Eternal Light. Therefore be ye not sad!
>   The Magazines which you forwarded were received. I am most grateful to you for this Service. I will pray in thy behalf and beg for thee Divine Confirmation so that in Scotland thou mayest upraise the Banner of the Oneness of the World of humanity through the Assistance of Baha-o-llah and become the promoter of the heavenly Teachings which are the Spirit of this Age! May you always see His Holiness Baha-o-llah as your helper and assistant.
>   Convey longing greeting to all the friends!
>   Upon thee be Baha-El Abha!
>   Abdul Baha Abbas[87]

'Abdu'l-Bahá ordered that some of the articles published in *Theosophy in Scotland* be translated into Persian and sent to various Bahá'í communities.[88] The magazine continued publishing articles on the Bahá'í Faith. On June 1913, the magazine reported that Alice Buckton and a certain Mr. Andre, the Vice President of the Letchworth lodge, had delivered four lectures on the Bahá'í Faith and that they were holding weekly meetings for those interested in learning more.[89] The same issue contained a review of Myron H. Phelps's *Abbas Effendi: His*

Life and Teachings.⁹⁰ In the ensuing months a series of articles signed as 'I.M.' offered the readers of *Theosophy in Scotland* the Bahá'í perspective on certain subjects.⁹¹ In September the magazine published a Gaelic translation of a passage from the Bahá'í writings.⁹²

Graham Pole continued to send 'Abdu'l-Bahá articles published in his magazine. The Master sent in early July 1913 from Port Said a second letter to Graham Pole, in which He touched upon subjects such as the need for divine civilization, human nature and his spiritual powers. It was published in the October issue of *Theosophy in Scotland* together with a facsimile of the original and a picture of 'Abdu'l-Bahá. In introducing these documents the magazine mentioned that 'a meeting for the study of the teachings of this religion of Brotherhood is held in Edinburgh every Tuesday at 8 p.m. at Woodburn, Canaan Lane.'⁹³

A LETTER FROM ABDUL BAHA
To the Secretary of the Theosophical Society and the Editor of *Theosophy in Scotland*, Mr. Graham Pole, Edinburgh, Scotland; upon him be Bahaollah El Abha!

'HE IS GOD'

My dear, respectful friend,

Your letters written to Mirza Ahmad were received, and I, too, perused them. Their contents imparted happiness, for they indicated the loftiness of thy aim and the goodness of thy intention. The articles which you have already published in *Theosophy in Scotland* show the catholicity of thy vision and the range of thy sympathy. A wise thinker and a scholarly writer pens such articles, the influence of which may be far-reaching, the effects of which eternal, and the results of which universal – so that all mankind may turn their faces towards the kingdom of the Merciful and the celestial emanations may shine and gleam from the reality of man like unto radiant lamps. To-day the human world is in need of the heavenly teachings which are the very spirit of this age and the light of this century. The physical and material civilization has made extraordinary advancement, but the Divine civilization is totally forgotten, while in reality Divine civilization is like unto the light and material civilization is like unto the lamp. This lamp without that light is dark. Therefore we must strive in order that the heavenly Light may shine within the human glass, the world of morality may become illumined, and the infinite excellences which are as the adornments of the reality of humanity may shine forth like unto a transcendent luminary. The world of nature is an arena which belongs to the animal kingdom. When you look upon any kind of animal or bird you observe that the bounties of the material world are prepared for its enjoyment to the utmost perfection, which bounties are not so easily accessible or readily obtained by man. For example, imagine the happy estate of a sweet-singing nightingale with the most delicate taste and artistic temperament it has built its nest upon the loftiest branch of a noble tree which has grown on the summit of a mountain. In reality this nest is superior to and more beautiful than the palaces of kings. The air is of the utmost purity; the surrounding scenery most ravishing; the sweeping panorama very entrancing; the cooling water most sweet; all the mountains clad in luxuriant verdancy and rich colours; and all the harvests gathered on the plain and in the farms are as the wealth of this bird. In the immensity of its freedom it can fly from mountain to mountain, and it can eat from any harvest it chooses. It toils not neither does it spin; it entertains no thought and no plan for tomorrow; it has no sorrow, no disappointment, no regret, and no pessimism. In its own nest it lives with the utmost happiness and joy, and now and then it breaks forth in rapturous songs of gladness. Therefore it has become proven that the bounties of the material world have their greatest display in and for the animal kingdom. On the other hand imagine the difficulties of poor man! Now he is a wanderer and anon he is sick. To-day he is weak and to-morrow he is a captive. This month he is poverty-stricken and indigent and next month he is threatened with danger. Day and night he is striving and laboring till he gains a mouthful of bread to satisfy his hunger. Consequently from this comparison you can easily observe the vast chasm of difference which exists between human life and animal life. It is now established that the bounties of the world of nature are more completely manifested upon the arena of the animal kingdom. Although man does not enjoy a perfect share and an inexhaustible portion of these material bounties, yet in the divine world he is the manifestation of the infinite Bestowals, the lamp for the irradiation of the Light of Reality, the transparent mirror for the polarization of Celestial Beauty, the channel for the out-flowing of the heavenly Graces, the dawning-point for the emanation of the effulgences of divinity, and the possessor of a holy, transcendental Power which surrounds all the created phenomena. That is the mystical reason why man alone is enabled to discover the existence of other entities, governing the natural world and bringing the secrets of nature out of the plane of invisibility upon the plane of visibility. He dominates the despotism of nature. He controls the laws of nature. Now he becomes a bird and flies in the air; again he builds an iron horse and gallops over the seas; and then he transforms himself into a fish and dives deep beneath the ocean. In short, man alone is powerful to unravel all the secret and hidden mysteries of nature and display their marvellous results before our eyes. Consequently we may call him the controller of the laws of nature and the manipulator of its intricacies. This holy Power is a particular gift to man. Through this holy Power he is distinguished above the animals. Inasmuch as he possesses such a transcendent Power he must become the manifestation of Divine Civilization; the dawning-place of the lights of Eternity; the spreader of the heavenly virtues; the promulgator of the Teachings of God; a servant of the world of morality – stirring the souls into cheerfulness through the spiritual Glad-tidings, freeing the spirits from helplessness and conferring upon them the Hope of Eternal Life! This is the honour of the world of humanity! This is the perfection of mankind. This is the Everlasting Welfare!

(Sgd.) ABDUL BAHA ABBAS[94]

A few weeks afterwards Graham Pole wrote to 'Abdu'l-Bahá from India and mentioned to Him the work being done by Annie Besant. In His reply, dated 29 August, 'Abdu'l-Bahá mentioned Annie Besant. Portions of this letter were afterwards published in *Theosophy in Scotland*:

> . . . The ideal of Mrs. Besant, truly, I say, is very lofty. She is working and labouring most valiantly, and her utmost hope is to render a service to the world of humanity and be the means of the establishment of good-fellowship and love between all the communities of

the earth. At all times I am praying in her behalf so that the confirmation of the Kingdom may surround her, and that she may sow the seeds of service in pure productive soil; that she may gather many, many harvests; then the heavenly benediction will be gained, the outpouring of the Holy Spirit be realised, and her services, troubles, and hardships be crowned with eternal results. I desire this station for her.[95]

Second Visit to France

On 25 January 1913 'Abdu'l-Bahá received the president of the Theosophical Society who invited Him to address its members on Thursday, 13 February, 1913, at eight o'clock in the evening, as part of a regular weekly meeting of the Society. According to Sohrab, many people attended the lecture and 'Abdu'l-Bahá was introduced by the president of the society in lofty language. In His address, 'Abdu'l-Bahá touched upon subjects and concepts similar to those expounded in His talks addressed to the Theosophists of Wimbledon and Edinburgh.[96]

French notes of this address were published in *Le Théosophe* on 1 March.[97] Ahmad Sohrab rendered the text into English based on his own notes of 'Abdu'l-Bahá's words in Persian. This translation was published in *Theosophy in Scotland* on May 1913:

ADDRESS BY ABDUL BAHA TO THE THEOSOPHICAL SOCIETY IN PARIS

When we look upon the world of genesis we observe that all forms of creation are endowed with life.

It was a theory held by the ancient men of learning that the mineral kingdom lacks life, but according to anatomical investigations carried on by physiologists on one hand and biologists on the other hand it has been discovered that the mineral kingdom has life. Our contemporary thinkers prove this matter by certain irrefutable deductions and evidences. Herein we will summarise them. As a premise to our discussion let us say that, in accord with scientific proofs and biological discoveries, all forms of phenomena have life, but their life and their energy is in keeping with their degree of environment and adaptation.

Life as an attribute of growth is manifest in the mineral kingdom, but its manifestation is very minute. Likewise life can be seen in the vegetable kingdom as an increasing power of growth, but compared to the animal kingdom it lacks instinct. This latter quality is more powerfully manifested in the vegetable than in the mineral kingdom; and when we study the animal kingdom we observe that the power of life is expressing itself through more capable media, showing manifold attributes. Ascending to the human kingdom, we observe that life, or what is figuratively called Spirit, is manifesting itself in the utmost power and transcendency. The more man perseveres along the path of progress the greater will be the manifestation of life. The child when born to the mother manifests more of this element of life than while in her matrix. The display of the forces of life upon the arena of existence cannot be compared to the dark and narrow world in which the babe lived for nine months. And when life attains to the summit of maturity its manifestations will be along many lines, and cover many fields.

From this you can understand that this essence of Spirit manifests itself to a greater extent in the human world than in the mineral, vegetable, and animal kingdoms. Therefore Spirit in the human world is the discoverer of the realities of phenomena. All the inventions which are made, all the sciences which are discovered, all the mysteries of nature which are brought to light, come through the power of this Spirit of life. While living in the Orient man organises affairs in the Occident. While living on the earth he discovers the heavenly constellations.

All these things will show you that the Spirit of life is omnipotent, especially if it comes into communication with God and becomes the recipient of the eternal Light. Then it will be an effulgence of the radiance of the Sun of Reality.

This state is the greatest of all the states. In this connection the spirit of man is akin to a mirror, and the Sun of Reality is reflected in it. Then it becomes the collective centre of all the virtues. Its emanation is the bestowal of one of the bestowals of the Divine. Its perfections are the manifold Splendours of the infinite Luminary. Its sanctity is from the highest summit of heavenly holiness. This state is the state of inspiration; it is called the state of the Divine Grace. It signifies that the rays of the Sun of Reality are resplendent in the mirror, and the virtues of the Sun of Reality are reflected therein. This is the last degree of human perfection, for the attainment of which all the thinkers and philosophers have longed and dreamed; it is the Mystery of Mysteries, and the Light of Lights. Therein the Spirit becomes eternal, self-subsistent, age-abiding, absolute, incomparable.

When we look upon the world of creation from another standpoint we observe that every given phenomenon is the result of the composition of many single atoms. In other words, these indivisible atoms through the law of affiliation have adhered together, and a being steps into the world of creation. Every single atom of these aggregate atoms has its myriad transferences through the infinite grades of life.

This is a self-evident proposition. It is not a mere theory; it has been proved by science that all phenomena are the resultant factors of the composition of individual atoms. Every single atom of these atoms has its coursings through all the kingdoms of life.

For instance, the atom which has gone into the composition of man was at one time in the mineral kingdom. It passed through all the degrees of the mineral kingdom, appearing under various forms and images, manifesting a peculiar property in each form or image. Then it ascended to the vegetable kingdom, again going through many experiences and adorned with a certain attribute in each experience. After this it entered the animal kingdom; it was incarnated throughout multitudes of animal forms, and in each form it showed evidence of distinct qualities. Finally it stepped into the human kingdom, travelling throughout endless forms of the world of humanity and in each form showing forth a particular character.

As the forms of phenomena are infinite, therefore the transference of this primordial atom throughout the degrees of the world of creation, embodying various images, is infinite. Consequently all phenomena are embodied in each separate phenomenon.

Consider what a transcendent unity exists, that from this standpoint every atom of the atoms of life, is the expression of all life. This is the harmony which underlies all creation. This is the law and order in the world of existence. What wonderful symmetry! What heavenly co-ordination! What divine union! Every phenomenon of creation is a bounty of the Divine, therefore the Divine bounties are each infinite, unlimited and illimitable.

Look upward through this immeasurable space and watch the

majestic order of these colossal spheres. These luminous orbs are numberless. Behind our solar system there are many stellar systems. You may extend your vision beyond the fixed stars, and again you shall behold many spheres of light.

In brief, the creation of the Almighty is beyond the grasp of the intellect. Consider how this creative bounty of God is unlimited and not subject to suspension; then how much greater is the spiritual bounty of God!

While the physical bounty of the world of creation is infinite, how is it possible to circumscribe the spiritual bounty which is the basis of Divine creation. It is proven that the spiritual world is greater than the physical world; the physical world is nonexistent in comparison to the spiritual world.

Reflect that every human being is limited through his physical body, but his spirit is unlimited. The body of man may travel for a few miles and then be fatigued, but the spirit may travel throughout all the immensity of space. While walking on the earth, man may grasp in thought the motion of the heavenly bodies, and define their courses.

This will demonstrate to you how much greater man is in spirit than his physical environment. Although the Divine grace, whether physical or spiritual, is unlimited, yet some ignorant souls through selfish desire limit the outpouring of the heavenly grace. How thoughtless they are! They say that the age of this world is, for example, 10,000 years; by this they mean that the descent of the Divine grace has been only 10,000 years in duration, while in reality the Divine grace is infinite. We cannot state reasonably that the world is 10,000,000 or 100,000 or 100,000,000 years old.

The Divine grace has ever descended upon man. The world of creation has had no beginning, and will have no end, because it is the arena upon which the attributes and qualities of the Spirit are being manifested. Can we limit God and His power? In the same manner we cannot limit virtues and perfections.

Just as the Reality underlying Humanity is unlimited, likewise His grace and bounties are unlimited. The greatest Divine bounty is the appearance of the holy heavenly Manifestations of God. How can we ever limit and circumscribe this bestowal while in reality it is the greatest of the spiritual gifts?

If the scientists have proven that a molecule is an aggregate of myriads of atoms, and the atom in turn is the result of infinite electrons, how then can the sun be limited? If the drop is infinite in its particles, how much more the sea? If the material world is infinite with regard to its manifestations of life, can the spiritual world become finite? Therefore the gifts of God which are the appearances of the holy Divine Manifestations, have ever been in the past, and will ever be in the future.

Where was Adam when God was exercising His Divinity? Where was this petty infinitesimal world of ours when God was bestowing His bounties upon this infinite universe? Can we ever limit the bestowal of God? If we limit the Divine bestowal then it is equal to limiting God Himself.

The world of humanity has ever been in a state of anticipation for the coming of the holy Divine Manifestations. Each religion expected the coming of the Promised One, and longingly prayed for the dawn of the Sun of Reality. A thousand times, alas! When He appeared they remained heedless, and did not turn their faces towards Him. Pitiful indeed is their condition. They were praying for the dawn of the glorious Sun of Reality, but when it appeared from the eastern horizon they cried clamorously 'Where is the sun? We do not see it.'

For instance, the Israelitish nation expected the coming of the Messiah. Day and night they were praying in the Temple, lamenting and bemoaning in the Holy of Holies, saying, 'O God, send to us the Messiah, our Deliverer and Redeemer.' Thus they were hoping for the arrival of their Promised One. But when His Holiness the Christ appeared they turned away from Him. When the Orb of Reality dawned they could not see it, for their eyes were covered with the veils of superstition and dogma; they did not become the recipients of that bestowal, they did not hearken to the call of God, they did not drink from the chalice of love, they did not behold the rays of the Sun of Reality. It is now nearly 2000 years since their Messiah appeared, and still they are waiting!

Consequently let our eyes be always open, the windows of our minds flung wide, so that when the holy Divine Manifestations appear we may not become deprived of their bounty by the veils of dogmas; so that when the heavenly Herald shouts the Word of God we may not he deaf; so that when the holy perfumes of the paradise of the Almighty are diffused our nostrils may not be afflicted as by a cold. Then we will be enabled to inhale the holy fragrance, to behold the Divine splendours, to hearken to the voice of God, and to be regenerated with the new spirit. Then our life will he renewed, we shall enjoy eternal existence, we shall be quickened with the breath of the Holy Spirit and become informed of the mysteries of creation. Then we will be inspired to upraise the standard of the oneness of the world of humanity, we shall take a portion from the Divine grace, and we shall become illumined with the rays of the heavenly Luminary. Then the world of humanity will mirror forth the attributes of the Kingdom, and the human race will become like unto a sea; each individual composing the body politic will be considered as one wave of this sea. As we look at the sea it is the sea of God; as we look upon the waves they are the souls of humanity. The sun is one, the rays emanating from it are one, and they are shining upon all beings. When we look upon the light it is one light, but when we look upon the phenomena they are numerous.

This century is the century of the oneness of the world of humanity, this century is the century of love, this century is the century of universal peace. This is the century of the dawn of the Sun of Reality, this century will see the establishment of the Kingdom of God upon earth; therefore let us take every means so that the federation of the world may be organised, and that we may become benefited by the infinite bounties of God. We observe that to-day the means of unity are brought about. This in itself is an evidence that the Divine confirmations are with us. One of the principles of the oneness of the world of humanity is the invention of the international auxiliary language Esperanto. We observe that this language is spreading daily, and its advocates are increasing; it is indubitable that the international auxiliary language will become instrumental in wiping away the present misunderstanding, and each individual will be able to be informed of the thought of all humanity. Therefore we must all strive to spread amongst our fellow-men this language. This international auxiliary language will be an introduction to the establishment of the oneness of the world of humanity. The greatest efforts must be displayed in this direction.[98]

The *Revue Théosophique* briefly mentioned the meetings in its issue of 27 March[99] and published a summary of Wedgwood's editorial in the February issue of *The Vahan*.[100] Three months later the same journal mentioned the publication in *Theosophy in Scotland* of Sohrab's translation of 'Abdu'l-Bahá's talk to Theosophists in Paris.[101]

35

SPIRITUALISM AND ESOTERICISM

The mid-19th century saw the birth in New York of the Spiritualist movement. Three sisters from Hydesville – Margaret, Kate and Leah Fox – declared in 1848 that two of them had the capability of communicating with the dead. In ensuing years Cora Scott, Achsa Sprague and many others put forward similar claims and soon the United States was filled with individuals touring the country and demonstrating their supposed psychic faculties.

The movement was especially appealing to members of Christian reform movements and grew rapidly. In the United Kingdom and the United States, spiritualism spread mostly among the middle and upper classes, while in continental Europe it found a fertile soil among radical socialists and anarchist workers who saw in spiritualism a counterbalance to established religion.

The spiritualist movement was probably at its apex when 'Abdu'l-Bahá visited the West. By that time it had also become rather heterodox and included in its areas of interest various esoteric sciences other than the mere communication with the dead. It also sustained its own periodicals and organs. As we shall see, 'Abdu'l-Bahá was mentioned in many of them.

Interestingly, several early Bahá'ís in the West had close contacts with the spiritualist movement at the time that 'Abdu'l-Bahá visited Europe and North America. Such was the case, for instance, of Wellesley Tudor Pole and Arthur Cuthbert. It was probably thanks to these links that many prominent spiritualists had the chance of visiting and interviewing the Master.

First Visit to London

On His first visit to London 'Abdu'l-Bahá received Felicia Rudolphina Scatcherd (1862–1927),[1] a leading British spiritualist who was editor of and contributor to various spiritualist journals and the author of several books on spiritualism and parapsychology. As seen in chapter 8, Felicia was also a friend of Platon Drakoulès, leader of the Greek Socialist Party of which she was eventually appointed vice president. She also held close political contacts with the Turkish Committee of Union and Progress.

Two years after her meeting with 'Abdu'l-Bahá she recounted in an article for the *International Psychic Gazette* (London) how she first came into contact with the Bahá'í Faith and later with 'Abdu'l-Bahá:

> When Abdul Baha first came to England, I refused all invitations to visit him. I had met those who had made pilgrimages to his prison-home in Akka, and they talked so much about 'the Blessed Perfection' and 'the Manifested Splendour' that, though interested in what seemed a useful enough form of hero-worship for those to whom it appealed, I had no desire to see Abbas Effendi for myself.
>
> Yet from the first moment that I heard of the Bahai movement I recognised its value, and in London and Paris promoted its interests whenever the occasion occurred.
>
> One day in February, 1907, I met that earnest Bahai, Mr. Arthur Cuthbert. He introduced his companion, Mr. Sydney Sprague, as one who had come from America to spread the Bahai teaching. Mr. Sprague had been some time in England, but progress had been slow, and he was slightly disheartened.
>
> I took my card from my pocket, and giving it to Mr. Sprague, said: 'Tell the Editor of the *Review of Reviews* I want him to interview you. If he does this, and becomes your friend, you will have all the impetus you need.'
>
> That one page interview in the March number of the *Review of Reviews* for 1907, written by Mr. W. T. Stead, still seems to me one of the clearest summaries of the Bahai teachings.
>
> From time to time I attended a Bahai assembly, but remained as aloof from its influence as ever. In European Turkey where it was most needed it made little progress. I had pointed out to Ahmed

Riza, then President of the Turkish Chamber, and others, how grievous it was for their country that the Young Turk Reformers were mainly Positivists or Atheists, and suggested the initiation of a movement that should attempt to bring out the spiritual truths of Islam while dropping the accretions of the ages. But these avowed Atheists only began to attend the orthodox services in their mosques, and the people despised them yet more heartily for this sorry farce. So I had only made matters worse. I was somewhat indignant that the drawing rooms of London, Paris and New York were coquetting with this newer faith, instead of endeavouring to spread it among the peoples whence it had sprung, who were in sore need of its enlightenment.

Then in the spring of 1911, a dear friend compelled me to accompany her to a reception of Abdul Baha, then, as now, the guest of Lady Blomfield, of 97, Cadogan Square. The submissive sweetness with which the venerable man received the homage of his followers affected me strongly. I wondered whether, like the gifted Heinrich Heine, he ever shrank from the burden of an enforced role of divinity. And an impulse seized me to see him in converse with an intellectual and spiritual peer. But when I cast about to find such a one, I realised the true greatness of the man in whose presence I found myself. I did not go forward with the rest to greet him on this first occasion. I stood at the door busy with my thoughts. And as if he knew these thoughts, as he passed out, he gave me a playful slap on the arm, as one would administer reproof to a wilful child, and his eyes danced with merriment.

Again and again I have noticed evidence of his awareness of the mental states of those around him. And I am assured that this keen intuition has been observed in his correspondence. Those whom he has never seen have been amazed to receive, from the Prophet in Akka, correct perceptions of conditions pertaining to them in America.[2]

Scatcherd's article continued with an account of her meeting with 'Abdu'l-Bahá in Egypt, where she traveled in early 1912 with Dr Plato Drakoules and his wife, as well as the text of a letter from 'Abdu'l-Bahá sent in May 1911 to the Bahá'ís in London (see chapter 8).

The Review of Reviews mentioned this article in February 1913.[3] The whole article was later published as a booklet under the title *A Wise Man from the East* (1914).

As mentioned above, Scatcherd was a close friend of the famous editor William Thomas Stead (1849–1912), her mentor in the world of journalism, and encouraged him to visit 'Abdu'l-Bahá. In a brief account included in the same article she described Stead's meeting with the Master:

> Then it occurred to me that Mr. Stead was the person I wished to see in converse with the teacher from the East. During that memorable meeting I gained much insight into the characters of these two remarkable men. Abbas Effendi was delighted when he learned that, from its inception, the *Review of Reviews* had been already a pulpit from which the leading tenets of Bahaism had been vigorously enunciated.[4]

Stead started his career as a journalist writing for and later editing the *Northern Echo* (Darlington). In 1880 he joined the *Pall Mall Gazette* (London) and in 1883 was appointed its editor. As a Christian nonconformist, he used his journals to denounce social injustice and in 1883 started a campaign against child prostitution and slavery that involved the investigation of real cases. For this research he was eventually sentenced to a few months in prison but was nevertheless successful in his campaign, Parliament approving a Bill raising the age of consent from 13 to 16 years in 1885. In 1890 he left the *Pall Mall Gazette* and founded the famous *Review of Reviews* (London) from which he also continued to defend the causes of justice and international peace. Apart from his better known persona as a journalist and pacifist, Stead was also an Esperantist and a spiritualist.

In 1912 Stead was invited to attend a meeting in New York arranged by President William Taft. He traveled to America on board the *Titanic* thus tragically becoming one of the most famous among the long list of casualties of that disaster.

Before meeting 'Abdu'l-Bahá, Stead had mentioned the Bahá'í Faith several times in his *Review of Reviews*. In July 1896 he reviewed an article by J. D. Rees on 'The Bab and Babeeism' which had appeared in the *Nineteenth Century Magazine* (London).[5] In March 1907 the magazine published the interview with Sydney Sprague mentioned above by Scatcherd,[6] as well as a review of an article by Sprague which appeared in the *Theosophical Review* (London).[7] A month afterwards Stead included in his magazine a lengthy article about the Bahá'í Faith which also incorporated the text of 'Abdu'l-Bahá's letter to Jane Whyte of Edinburgh known as the 'Seven Candles of Unity'. The article opened with the following comments:

> The interview which I published last month with a disciple of the Behaist Messiah has attracted such widespread attention that I think it may be worthwhile supplementing it by further particulars which I have received from devout Christians who have been touched by the deep spiritual life of the Behaists. It has been specially impressed upon me that no mistake could be greater than for Christian missionaries of whatever Church to antagonise the Behaists. They are really Persian Quakers, and a concordat between them and the Christian world ought not to be difficult to arrange . . .
>
> Mr. Rendell Harris, now President of the Free Church Federation, being a Friend, ought surely to get into communication with Abbas Effendi without delay. For this man, Abbas, seems to have the root of the matter in him, and the Behaist faith to be one that worketh miracles.[8]

In June 1911 Stead published a review of Ethel Stevens's article on 'Abdu'l-Bahá[9] (see chapter 3 above) and in April 1912 – soon before Stead's death – the magazine also mentioned Constance Maud's article on the Master published in the *Fortnightly Review* (see chapter 6 above).[10]

The feminist writer Constance Maud was present during the meeting between 'Abdu'l-Bahá and Stead. In later years she described that moment in one of her books:

> 'I have preached Bahai doctrine, but I have added to it a truth which Baha Ullah failed to give the world,' said W. T. Stead eagerly, and blissfully regardless of the somewhat delicate ground on which he was venturing in his walking boots.
>
> 'What truth is that?' inquired Abdul Baha, alert, and, it must be admitted, somewhat surprised.

'The truth of actual present communication between dwellers on earth and our loved ones who have passed on to the other side.'

Abdul Baha replied that he taught and believed absolutely and literally in the communion of saints, but to teach the expediency of seeking communication in séances he regarded as unwise.

'You make no provision, then, for the poor doubting Thomases,' rejoined Mr. Stead, 'those longing for evidence, for proof, for consolation. Julia's Bureau, dedicated to St. Thomas, opens a way for this sad and numerous company to belief in God, the soul, and immortality.'

Abdul Baha, with infinite gentleness, explained that in his opinion the average man needed all his energies concentrated on an actively holy life, and a danger lay in emphasising too much the unseen world around him, though he himself was vividly conscious of the reality of the Unseen, and knew as an experienced fact that 'all religions are based on inspiration from the Unseen'.

'You have this personal experience,' W. T. Stead took him up quickly, 'but see how, like the priest of all ages, you would keep the pearl of great price in your own hands, instead of giving it freely to all the people. To the poor you allow no access to truth except through certain prescribed channels.'

'Meat is for strong men, not babes,' replied Abdul Baha. 'Christ said there were many things He could tell, "but ye cannot bear them now".'

The wise old eyes regarded his accuser with sympathy and affection. There were things, perhaps, aspects of truth he had attained, which few of his own hearers could have borne. You cannot pour more wine into a goblet than it will hold. But it was not for himself that W. T. Stead had taken up the cudgels, and this Abdul Baha felt instinctively, recognising in his visitor one whose very reason of being was love for his fellow men. He nodded his head in quick understanding as Stead explained that he himself had never been a Thomas; with him it was a case of adding knowledge to faith. But with many better men than he it was the reverse. They were unable to believe in any truth until it had been evidentially demonstrated; knowledge must precede faith, hence the value of spiritualism and all psychic research. A great feature in the Founder of Christianity was His recognition of the necessity of providing for these seekers after truth.

He gave them miracles; He showed them materialised spirit forms after the change called death, His own and others, Moses and Elias.

Abdul Baha listened with absorbed interest, without, however, letting go of his point, i.e. the danger of seeking your spiritual nourishment in psychic experiences rather than a holy life.[11]

* * *

The weekly magazine *Light* (London), 'A journal of psychical, occult and mystical research' created in 1881, was the official organ of the London Spiritualist Alliance and was edited at the time by E. W. Wallis (1848–1914). As described in chapter 4, months before the arrival of the Master in the United Kingdom, *Light* carried an account of a talk by Wellesley Tudor Pole on the Bahá'í Faith and his experience of meeting the Master in Egypt; it also mentioned 'Abdu'l-Bahá among the participants of the Universal Races Congress.[12] In an editorial published on 23 September, the same day as the Master's departure from London, this magazine published the following comments:

> Several years ago Mr. Wake Cook,[13] in one of his admirable lectures to the London Spiritualist Alliance, told the Members and Associates the remarkable story of the Bahaist movement that had sprung up in Persia and was spreading rapidly in the East. The present leader, Abdul Baha, who is on a brief visit to London, has been explaining that Bahaism does not ask any man to abandon his faith, but to live it to the utmost, and to show that behind all systems and creeds there is but one religion, that of love and truth and goodness, and one God. Bahaists, he said, believe in equality in the treatment of men, and in the equality of men and women.
>
> Abdul Baha is an old man of medium height. His face is strong and venerable. He has kindly looking eyes, and beneath his white beard a smiling mouth. He denies being a prophet, and makes no claim to supernormal powers. He is 'A servant of God', and believes that the foundation of divine religion is one and cannot be changed; but that there are seasons in the religious life of the peoples of the earth, and that there are signs everywhere of an awakening; a spiritual springtime has come again. We agree. Bahaism and Spiritualism

are at one so far as we can judge. Every personality and every movement that makes appeal to what is best, purest, and noblest in mankind has our fraternal sympathy and good-will.[14]

During the second visit of 'Abdu'l-Bahá to London this magazine continued to publish references to the Bahá'í Faith and also reviewed two books about 'Abdu'l-Bahá (see appendix 3).

First Visit to Paris

'Abdu'l-Bahá's second public address in France was delivered on Thursday, 9 November 1911, in a reception for Him organized by the 'Alliance Spiritualiste', a spiritualist organization with a social agenda. The meeting was held at the Saint Germain Atheneum – a theatre and cultural centre located at 21 rue de Vieux Colombier – and the occasion caught the attention of several journals in Paris, which sent their reporters to cover the meeting.

The reception was announced on 7 November in the *Excelsior*[15] and on 9 November in *Le Figaro*.[16] The meeting was advertised as 'an exposition of the principles of Bahaism'.

'Abdu'l-Bahá was warmly introduced by Mme. Jeanne Beauchamps, president and founder of the institution. Then Louis Le Leu, secretary general of the Alliance, gave a short introduction to the Bahá'í Faith. 'Abdu'l-Bahá's words focused on the subject of the spiritual nature of man and the unfoldment of a new civilization.[17]

At least two photographers were present at the meeting and took snapshots showing 'Abdu'l-Bahá seated and surrounded by several people. One of these pictures was published in the *Excelsior* (Paris),[18] which was a daily illustrated journal, and the other in *Le Petite République* (Paris), which had a daily circulation at the time of some 67,000 copies.

One of the newspapermen present at the reception was Edouard de Vorney, reporter with *Le Siècle* (Paris), a moderate leftist and anticlerical journal with a circulation of just 5,000 copies. According to his own statements, after the meeting he had the opportunity of interviewing 'Abdu'l-Bahá, but the section of his article dedicated to the interview (not reproduced here) seems to be a summary of statements contained in Dreyfus's *Essai sur le Bahaisme* and of interviews with Bahá'ís, rather than an actual interview with 'Abdu'l-Bahá. His account of the public meeting was published on 10 November on the front page of *Le Siècle*:

BAHAISM IN FRANCE
RECEPTION IN PARIS WITH ABDUL BAHA ABBAS
INTERVIEW WITH THE GREAT PROPHET

There are modern religions like there are men; there are some whose name you will never know, who will disappear without leaving a trace. This, however, is not the case with Bahaism, or the Universal Religion. Founded some fifty years ago it is now extending its influence over the five continents of the world and has, apparently, millions of followers.

Yesterday afternoon, the French Spiritualist Alliance received with great ceremony, in the salon of the Athenée Saint Germain, Abdul Baha Abbas, the son of Baha Ullah, founder of the Universal Religion.

At 2:30, an ordinary electric bell announced the arrival of the apostle. After a few moments of waiting, the curtain rose slowly, as if in regret.

Then this strange scene presented itself before our eyes: Like the setting of a comedy (the always-present living room with gilded ceilings and a marble fireplace made of cardboard) under the bright and intense lights of the spotlights, were gathered around a table covered with the traditional green baize an old man –with a white hair and beard, an aquiline nose, wrapped in a brown robe and wearing a broad, tall snow white turban – who seemed to be in discussion, in the most serious and scholarly manner, with a group of gentlemen.

This is Abdul Baha Abbas accompanied by the board of the Spiritualist Alliance.

In the room there is a long tremor when the leader of Bahaism rises to give an explanation of the principles of the new religion.

Bahaism has as its principles liberty, justice, love and kindness. We must all seek the truth because it leads to the discovery of the spirit, which we perceive by its signs and which manifests itself to us both through the senses and without them. By connecting with these divine stirrings humanity will become one single being. With divine justice, peace will reign on earth and the human race will be unified. After having said this, Abdul-Baha Abbas began to pray. So it concluded.

Before retiring, the prophet blessed his audience, obligingly posed for the photographers and then entered his carriage.[19]

A reporter with the moderate Socialist daily newspaper *La Petite Republique* (Paris), which had a circulation of 47,000 copies,[20] was also among the audience. His account, which also included some historical information about the Bahá'í Faith, included one of the pictures of 'Abdu'l-Bahá taken at the meeting:

> The son and successor of the Splendour of God is a majestic and white-haired old man; a white turban on his head; his hands in the large pockets of a yellow caftan, in a nasal voice he spoke very noble and edifying phrases that a translator in a black coat interpreted one by one with great precision.
>
> The precepts of Baha-Abbas are beauty itself, not to mention the charm of the images and parables, they are as clear and resounding as crystal; we perceive through them, and in them, even more. In them the ear takes a delicate pleasure, and the soul a true sweetness. You feel overcome before the vision of a 'Divine Jerusalem, made not of mortar, stone and wood', a completely spiritual city where there will be peace amongst men. It is true that all the prophets foretold as much, and that Wells promises it to us after his comet has purified our atmosphere. But a singular charm positively emanates from this Abdul-Baha, and his forty listeners were more wrapped in it, rather than, perhaps, conquered by it . . .[21]

Émile Berr (1855–1923),[22] editor of the *Supplement Littéraire* of *Figaro*, was also present at the meeting and wrote the following account which, while not very sympathetic, nevertheless offered some interesting details:

A PROPHET

It should be unnecessary to explain who Abdu'l-Baha Abbas is, since all the well-informed Parisians must know this old man, the sovereign pontiff of the 'Universal' Religion, founded by his father. He has arrived from England, where he had a great success, after having visited Egypt. He has already been residing in Paris for one month, and *Le Figaro* told his story a few days after his arrival . . .

Yesterday, at 2:30, the Spiritualist Alliance received him at the Athénée Saint Germain. The invitation said:

'Reception for Abdul Baha Abbas, son of Baha'u'llah, founder of the Universal Religion, and talk by him on the principles of the Baha'i Faith, of which he is the leader.'

In Paris they say 'There are people everywhere.' It is true, even at three in the afternoon, to hear an old man relate in Persian the principles of a universal religion. The room of l'Athénée was packed. Some mature gentlemen, many ladies, and among the ladies, Englishwomen and Americans in great number. England and America are the countries where the competition among churches does not create fear, where every new religion is welcome.

Yesterday the prophet received from friends and members of the Spiritualist Alliance – especially from its leaders – the most cordial welcome; and the audience that listened to him was reverent and tenderly attentive.

He is a great old man of the purely oriental variety; a white-haired old man. For his long hair is white; his long beard is also white, white like the tunic covered by a beige coat. He has deep and kind eyes, delicate hands that he gently pushes into his pockets while talking.

He advanced, without awkwardness, onto the little scene at the Athénée escorted by two of his compatriots in costume, and the apparition of these outfits against the gilded framed curtain made one think of anything other than the presentation of a new religion. But there was silence. Around the master sat the distinguished founder of the Alliance and her principal collaborators. Noble words and welcomes were pronounced and then the prophet arose.

He does not know a word of French. But by his side he had the most devoted of his interpreters, a young Parisian lawyer who went to live in Akka to get to know Abdul Baha Abbas, and who is today one of the most fervent Bahais amongst us.

While the lecturers from the Spiritualist Alliance were speaking, M. Dreyfus-Barney leaned towards the prophet and translated for him in a low voice the words he could not understand. Now, he was translating aloud, into French, the words of the Master.

At the risk of making the Bahais indignant, we dare give our humble opinion: what the Master says is not very new.

Standing, hands in pockets, at once noble and familiar, he paces, and, with a guttural and singing voice, mumbles things in his beard. He says a short phrase in Persian, and once the sentence is complete, a bit of French falls upon our ears. We hear, 'The spirit is everything . . . the body is nothing. Matter will perish . . . spirit will not. Life is one . . . and men are as waves of a sea animated by a single law. The soul is free . . . it is light . . . light does not need the lamp; the lamp needs the light. As such, the body needs the soul, the soul does not need the body.' etc.

And so it goes, very slowly, for about half an hour. No one makes a sound. Finally the Master stopped. He says he's praying for us. And on the edge of the stage, there he is, perfectly still, eyes closed, hands open and turned up horizontally. And the voice of the old man rose, very sweetly, hesitatingly, to chant . . . Abdul-Baha Abbas, in this posture, is very handsome, venerable. But all the same, there were a few of us in the room who would have really liked to know just what is Bahaism; why it seems this religion is necessary; and how and by what means it will adapt itself, practically, to the others, without interference, to become the 'universal religion', something like the Esperanto of Faith? That was not explained to us. And it is probable that we will never know. It's annoying, because we came to Vieux-Colombier to learn this.[23]

The conservative, royalist and Catholic *Le Gaulois* (Paris), with a circulation of some 30,000 copies, carried on 26 November an editorial by Albert Flament in which he sharply criticized the influence that the Oriental world was having on the domestic life and customs of the French people. In his long discourse, Flament mentioned the talk delivered by 'Abdu'l-Bahá on 9 November: 'Abdul Baha Abbas's translator repeated very short sentences which are by no means new ideas: love, charity, resignation. But these turbaned patriarchs, with their lack of gestures, their deep voices and their dark, veiled eyes, have a strange gift to persuade even the deaf.'[24]

A brief note of only a few lines was also published in the fortnightly *La Renaissance Contemporaine* (Paris), mentioning only the fact that the audience needed a translator because 'Abdu'l-Bahá's talk was in Persian.[25]

On January 1912 the organ of the 'Alliance Spiritualiste' published the proceedings of the meeting. The text included notes of 'Abdu'l-Bahá's talks as well as the opening and closing remarks by members of the Alliance.[26]

North America

In New York 'Abdu'l-Bahá was interviewed by Wilbur Juvenal Colville (1859–1917), an Englishman who, from the age of 14 claimed to be able to communicate with the dead and traveled extensively in England, the United States and Australia working as a medium. He was also the author of several books and eventually established himself in the United States, where he also practiced alternative medicine.

Colville was a contributor to *The Occult Review* (London) from 1907. This monthly magazine, 'devoted to the investigation of supernormal phenomena and the study of psychological problems', was established in 1905 by the aristocrat Ralph Shirley (1865–1946). Shirley was also director of William Rader & Son, a publishing company specializing in occultism and esotericism. The *Occult Review* was published in two editions, one British and one American.

On August 1912 the magazine carried an article by Colville describing his meeting with 'Abdu'l-Bahá and introducing the Bahá'í Faith (the latter not reproduced here):

ABDUL BAHA ABBAS – THE PROPHET AND HIS TEACHINGS
BY W. J. COLVILLE

As so very much interest centres at present in the person, work, and teachings of this renowned man, who is at present in America, conducting many public meetings and giving interviews to innumerable persons representing almost all phases of thought and activity, the present moment seems specially opportune for giving publicity to an interview kindly granted to the present writer in New York City, June 18, 1912.

I was much impressed with the quiet dignity and extreme graciousness of speech and bearing which characterize this truly remarkable man, whose venerable appearance and cordial manner prove singularly attractive. The house in which Abdul Baha, with his staff, was residing was a comfortable but by no means ostentatious residence, charmingly situated in one of the most pleasant and accessible of the residential districts in New York.

No less than in England has Abdul Baha Abbas been sought after and appreciated on the other side of the Atlantic, and it is extremely interesting and instructive to watch the constant procession of visitors who attend with reverential interest upon all that falls from the lips of this teacher, whose utterances, given mellifluously in pure Persian, are immediately translated into excellent English by his nephew, Dr. Ameen U. Fareed. Asking for definite information from headquarters concerning the exact position taken by Abdul Baha himself regarding his mission, and wishing to be able to state publicly on his own authority what the doctrines actually are which he is so earnestly and industriously teaching in the various countries he visits, I was graciously favoured with a detailed statement from his own lips, and furnished with writing material that I might instantly transcribe his words as quickly as they were translated by the interpreter. Though I may not have succeeded in giving the translation verbatim, I feel certain that I have grasped all the salient features, and that what follows is not an inaccurate statement of what was actually uttered in my hearing and reported on the spot by invitation of the speaker and his representatives . . .

Universal Peace is the one supreme end which Abdul Baha has in view, and all that he proposes is for the furtherance of that one grand result. It may well be asked by honest inquirers what position his followers assign to him, and there has been much controversy on this point. For myself, and as the result of my personal interview, I have not much to say further than that his friends and sympathizers evidently regard him as a great authority on all ethical matters, and they read his tablets, as they listen to his words, with decided reverence.

In America this international teaching is becoming widely popular, and the distinguished prophet has been most cordially welcomed into many liberal Christian pulpits. It is certainly a sign of advancing religious unity that he is invited (as on Sunday, June 9) to occupy, in the conservative city of Philadelphia, the pulpit of one of the Unitarian churches in the morning and to address a large congregation of Baptists in the evening. The personality of Abdul Baha is quietly imposing; there is a natural grace and dignity about him which proves far more impressive than any stately pomp of circumstance, and we can well understand, at least if we are at all sensitive to human atmospheres or auras, that a spiritual effluence proceeding from him and encircling him, draws and holds many who do not know precisely what it is that attracts them and keeps them loyal to his standard.

Taking my own stand simply as a fearless truthseeker, I gladly confess myself as very favourably impressed with the body of doctrine enunciated and with the evident sincerity of its venerable teacher. Whatever differences may have arisen, or may yet arise, concerning Abdul Baha's real position among the spiritual enlighteners of our planet, it seems certain that he is faithfully doing his utmost to unify and not to further subdivide. It must be rather a matter of temperament than of doctrine when different persons agreeing thoroughly on main essentials take varying views of the actual status of some illumined individual. I cannot do other than endorse all the inspired and inspiring teaching which I heard fall from the lips of this sincere and holy man. If his followers abide by the sublime verities he enunciates and resolve to carry his sublime exhortations into actual practice in daily living, we shall all have great cause to rejoice that Abdul Baha Abbas has been among us, for he is indeed a teacher of practical righteousness in feeling, thought and action.[27]

This article was briefly mentioned in the *Review of Reviews* on August 1912.[28] *The Occult Review* continued publishing articles on the Bahá'í Faith during the lifetime of 'Abdu'l-Bahá.[29]

Second Visit to London

On 2 January 'Abdu'l-Bahá was visited by John Lewis, editor of the *International Psychic Gazette*, a recently-launched periodical which served as the organ of the International Club for Psychical Research.[30] Lewis was accompanied by C. W. Child, a palm reader who wrote the book *Scientific Palmistry*, and by Arthur Cuthbert, who, as well as a Bahá'í was a spiritualist and regular contributor to the *International Psychic Gazette*.

According to Sohrab, Lewis had met 'Abdu'l-Bahá for the first time in Egypt. Scatcherd, however, indicates that it was she who introduced Lewis to 'Abdu'l-Bahá in London:

I wished Mr. Lewis to see Abbas Effendi for himself. And Lady Blomfield kindly arranged an interview for us on the 2nd of January.

Mr. Child, the well-known palmist, also accompanied us. I longed, in the interests of science, to get impressions of those marvellous hands, should Abdul Baha not object.

Mr. Lewis put questions on reincarnation, the immaculate conception, etc. In answering the latter question, Abdul Baha finished with one of his quaint observations, to the effect that to those who accepted the creation of the first man without any human parent, it should not be difficult to accept the birth of a being with one human parent only!

His answer about reincarnation was very interesting. In the *Contemporary Review* last year, an article appeared by that able writer, Constance Maud, in which the Master's views on the subject are given at length.

Then delicious tea was served in Persian fashion. It made me feel I was back in Egypt, and I dared again to make a request. The kind and eloquent interpreter (Mirza Ahmad Sohrab) explained my wish, and Abdul Baha submitted to the process of having an impression of his hands taken, with the utmost graciousness and good-will, and signed the four imprints, which I hope will appear in next month's *Gazette*, with Mr. Child's delineation.

'Now, Mr. Editor, what are your impressions of this Teacher from the East?'

Here is what he thought. I quote him without his permission, and he will have to let it stand or fill up the gap it leaves:–

He is the positive strong man, the father, the pioneer, the leader, the man of dogged determination and perseverance; combined with the negative gentle man, the mother, the shepherd, the man of patience and sympathy, intuitive and spiritual, teaching by symbols and parables, rather than by logical appeals to the intellect. He is the mystic and the initiate who has received his divine illumination in the silence and the solitudes, and whose greatest difficulty in life will probably be to find in this mundane world, audiences to understand and appreciate his mystical inspirations.[31]

As mentioned by Scatcherd, Lewis asked 'Abdu'l-Bahá several questions and also told Him that he intended to publish articles about the Bahá'í

Faith in his magazine. The questions put by Lewis were about the Bahá'í position on reincarnation (a doctrine admitted by Theosophists but not by spiritualists), the immaculate conception and the coming of a new revelation (again, a doctrine postulated by Theosophists).[32] Incomplete notes of 'Abdu'l-Bahá's answer on the question of reincarnation appeared in the February issue of the *International Psychic Gazette*.[33]

When C. W. Child asked 'Abdu'l-Bahá to be allowed to read His palms the Master consented, saying, 'All right.'[34] Child believed that he was capable of defining the personality of any person by interpreting the lines and forms in their hands. To this end he had contacted several celebrities and from time to time he would publish their psychological profiles obtained in this way.

Child had brought with him four sheets of paper. In the bathroom of Lady Blomfield's apartment he used charcoal to impregnate the sheets and afterwards requested 'Abdu'l-Bahá to impress His hands on them obtaining two copies of each hand which were in turn signed by the Master.[35] The very detailed and lengthy explanations of Child on 'Abdu'l-Bahá's hands appeared in the February issue of the *International Psychic Gazette* and were accompanied by pictures of the impressions of His hands. Child concluded his 'forensic' report stating that 'Taking these wonderful hands as a whole, they reveal a rare and magnanimous personality, unswerving devotion to the calls and claims of humanity, and an implicit trust and obedience to "the vision and the faculty divine".'

THE HANDS OF ABDUL BAHA

From the moment that Abdul Baha landed in England, I was eager to take an impression of his hands to add to my extensive collection of celebrities. Thanks to the kindly services of Miss Scatcherd, my wish was gratified on the second day of the present year. The venerable apostle and teacher readily placed his hands at my disposal, and gave every possible assistance. He evinced considerable interest, and was most sympathetic and patient.

The first thing that impressed me about his hands was their healthy, fresh appearance. They seemed to suggest placidity and spirituality. Although small and narrow, they are admirably developed, and are characterised by their softness, flexibility, fineness of texture, and the magnificent sweep of the shapely thumbs. These characteristics speak eloquently of idealism and inspiration, love and aptitude for study, cosmopolitanism and versatility, excessive refinement, great impressionability and sensitiveness, as well as genuine human sympathy and philanthropy. The owner of such delicate and beautiful hands could not possibly evade life and its responsibilities, but would be urged irresistibly and insistently on to take a full, active, and real part in alleviating the sorrows and afflictions of humanity. At the same time he would be ever teaching, persuading and enlightening man how most effectively to overcome the ills and inconsistencies of life, and become radiant, happy, and useful beings, meet for the Master's service.

Let us first of all compare and analyse the thumbs. These it will be noted differ slightly, the thumb on the right hand being more flexible. As I have explained on other occasions, the importance and intrinsic value of the thumb can never be overstated. It most faithfully reveals the individual's capacity to exercise self-control and to master circumstances, his ability to govern, reason, and to mould his destiny according to his will. The thumbs are abnormally long, splendidly proportioned and attest the possession of a vigorous, healthy and masterful will, singling its owner out as a law unto himself, and the absolute arbiter of his own fate. The greater firmness of the left thumb may be interpreted as an indication of his having exercised great tenacity and pertinacity until the inner spiritual forces were awakened and called into active and consistent service. It also shows fidelity to principle and knowledge of self-unfoldment, ensuring a more gentle persuasive, tolerant and sympathetic attitude, whereby the mission and purpose of his life might be successfully and completely fulfilled. In the right thumb we have the suggestion of gracious and tender solicitation for the well-being of humanity, and determination never to doubt the intrinsic good inherent in every individual, making an all-conquering appeal to that, and that alone. It reveals the positive, yet gentle man, ever bent upon the faithful discharge of his myriad duties, and the perfecting of his own life. In untiring and devoted service is his happiness and reward.

A careful study of his fingers yields most interesting and instructive information. These represent mind or the spiritual self. It is rather singular that the second phalanges should be longest, the first or nail portions, which I should certainly have expected to have been in excess of the rest, being the shortest, excepting that of the fourth or little finger. As I have already pointed out, the pronounced refinement, delicacy, pink colour and flexibility of the hand, together with the length and curving of the line of head, naturally led me to expect very long first (nail) phalanges. Now, why this apparent contradiction? Well, there is no contradiction; for the more we study nature, the more she causes us to marvel at the various symbols she employs, whereby to express herself in her own way. The method adopted here is both ingenious and illuminating, confirming the truth of the assertion that 'those who seek shall find'.

It is not for Abdul Baha to live entirely in a world of his own creation, and to give himself up wholly to the vagaries and romances of the mind.

Rather, on the contrary, his role is that of the practical mystic – an apparent contradiction – and this sublime and unique forte calls for exceptional method of expression. This being so, note the squareness of the second phalanges, and the attenuation of the third or lower ones. Here we have striking testimony to the subject's wealth of worldly wisdom and common sense, with no yearning for the acquisition of material things. Hence the first short phalanges bear witness to intuition and inspiration, rather than to great intellectual force, while the remarkable development of the second reveals the practical wise utilitarian and counsellor, who must be true to life, and know how to apply great truths in a world of men largely given over to mammon and self-aggrandisement. The narrowing of the third, in conjunction with the strong, majestic second (middle) finger, and the sloping line of head, bespeaks dislike of convention, love of solitude, and rare ability to penetrate and understand spiritual things.

I have shown that Abdul Baha possesses an invincible will, as evidenced by his thumbs. Attention to the placing, position, and formation of his first, index finger, will immediately disclose the fervent religious leader, and a man of extraordinary charm and purity of heart. Observation of the third, with its broader finger-tip and shorter length, will carry some idea of his rare artistic talent, love of beauty and sunshine, a silent reverent nature – student and one who knows not vanity. The peculiar setting and moulding of the fourth, little finger, bespeaks desire for rest, dislike of hustle, great patience and one who is a slow, earnest and thoughtful speaker, weighing well his words and choosing them with the utmost care and precision. There will be no extravagance, and no attempt whatever to trifle with language, which he will appreciate as the greatest blessing bestowed upon man. All must be simple, pure and 'done as ever in the great taskmaster's eye'.

The remarkable difference in the formation and development of the fingers of both hands afford an excellent example of the recluse and seer, combined with the genial, sympathetic and humane-hearted teacher and friend, to whom duty is a privilege and self surrender to the highest, a consecration and a joy.

I will now take the mounts and compare them. In both hands they are all noticeably full, those of Mars and Venus being the strongest. Now these give excellent insight into the real character and disposition, inasmuch as the latter indicates sympathy, grace, love of harmony and melody, geniality and vivacity, while the former denotes extraordinary powers of resistance, endurance, fearlessness and the 'do-or-die' spirit. In combination with the beautiful quadrangle (wide even space between the lines of heart and head) it bespeaks one who has the courage of his convictions, who is steadfast, far-seeing, and possesses a triumphant temperament that prohibits doubt and failure and bestows an understanding mind. This is further emphasised by the clear, deep, drooping line of head, which in addition, reveals the poet and mystic.

I may point out here that a good quadrangle, if not excessively lined and poorly coloured, is an infallible indication of sincerity and genuineness, denoting nobility of character and catholicity of thought. The mounts of Jupiter, Saturn, Apollo and Mercury partake of the qualities of their respective fingers, and these we have already alluded to. It now remains to examine the mount of the Moon. This, it will be seen, is quite in harmony with the others, showing normal development, thus denoting healthy imagination, ingenuity, and, with other indications, talent for musical composition. The firm and even development of the mounts testify to untiring and unsparing efforts to live up to ideals, and to the cultivation and development of natural gifts.

We now come to the markings. Take first the line of heart. This traces its way across the hand beneath the fingers. Its exceptional length, beautiful branchings, depth and clearness, reveal a most lovable, unselfish, and delightful nature. The line of head, running parallel, is also remarkable for its depth, clearness, and gentle slope. Such a head line asserts that its possessor must follow his natural bent at all hazards, quite irrespective of profit or loss. The line of life is not particularly strong, and shows that health will depend largely upon self. The several fine lines under the little finger testify to medical power, and in combination with the full mount of Venus and excellent quadrangle reveals the natural healer. The many ascending lines upon the palms evidences a very eventful, useful life, the numerous cross lines – denoting obstacles and hardships consequent upon an unfavourable environment and lack of scope. It shows unmistakably that the working and warring of the personality with circumstances has been incessant and relentless. The markings on the left hand are much more auspicious than those on the right, and go to emphasise what we have just said.

Taking these wonderful hands as a whole, they reveal a rare and magnanimous personality, unswerving devotion to the calls and claims of humanity, and an implicit trust and obedience to 'the vision and the faculty divine'.

Had it been possible to take a print of Abdul Baha's hands at frequent intervals throughout his life, we should have had an infallible record of difficulties successfully overcome and victories won, the lines on his hands, especially those on the right, having undoubtedly undergone many changes. Mr. W. T. Stead, writing in my autograph book on February 27th, 1911, emphasised this point as follows: – 'If every man had his hand printed by a palmist every birthday, he would have a valuable series of documents ready for his biographer.'[36]

This interpretation of 'Abdu'l-Bahá's hands was reprinted as part of a booklet prepared by Child under the title *Hands of Famous Men: Their Significance* (1913) which was advertized on least on two occasions in the *Review of Reviews*. From Paris the secretaries of 'Abdu'l-Bahá sent several packages containing copies of the *International Psychic Gazette* to Bahá'í communities in America and the East.[37]

In the ensuing months Lewis included in his magazine many other articles about the Bahá'í Faith.[38]

* * *

A few weeks after the departure of 'Abdu'l-Bahá from London the magazine *Light* published a short note entitled 'Abdul Baha on Karma', which reproduced a portion of Phelps's *Abbas Effendi* dealing with the question of reincarnation.[39]

Second Visit to Paris

As shown previously, on His first visit to Paris 'Abdu'l-Bahá was invited to address the Alliance Spiritualiste. On His return to France, He was again invited by the Alliance to address its members at a general meeting held on Friday, 21 February 1913, at 14 Rue de Trévise, at the time the headquarters of the Paris YMCA. The meeting was arranged through the Bahá'í Madame d'Ange d'Astre.[40]

The *Alliance Spiritualiste* (Paris), the organ of the society, published in April 1913 the proceedings of the society's general meeting which included 'Abdu'l-Bahá's address as well as the words of the officers of the Alliance who introduced him. The article opened with the comments of Albert Jounet (1863–1923), vice president of the Alliance Spiritualiste:

> On his return from America, where he has luminously spread his doctrine of conciliation and universality, Abdul Baba Abbas was received with joy by the A. S. which in 1911 had had the great pleasure of welcoming and hearing him.
>
> In the Young Men's Christian Union hall, rue de Trévise, gathered the enthusiasts of Unity and Love, those who, despite recent bloodshed, the threat of greater conflicts and the revival of separatist illusions and hatred, live in their thoughts in the One Humankind of the future and the One Humankind of the eternal divine world. It was a moment of light and sympathy in the middle of the dark flight of passing and fratricide . . .[41]

Jeanne Beauchamps, the president of the society, welcomed 'Abdu'l-Bahá with an address on the need for unity and love, which she concluded stating, 'At this meeting Abdul Baha represents the spiritual force of the Orient. All the spiritualists of the occident are hoping the universal mind may bring about this law of love which alone can unite the Orient and the Occident.'[42]

Louis Le Leu, secretary general of the Alliance Spiritualiste, welcomed 'Abdu'l-Bahá with words about peace and 'Abdu'l-Bahá Himself:

> In the month of November 1911 the Master, Abdul Baha, during his first trip to Paris accepted the invitation of the A. S. and we all have kept the loving memory of that beautiful meeting.
>
> And now, Master, after a year of great work in the United States and in many large cities of Europe, work which was crowned by success, recalling our first brotherly reception, you accept to be with us again.
>
> We thank you deeply for, as you know, the AS is pursuing an ideal, which, while respecting all forms of thought and all modes of belief, intends to bring together, through study and a reasoned knowledge of things, the scattered rays of truth to their natural centre . . .
>
> Like us, Abdul Baha, you are working for the realization of that sublime work and, like us, you know that if the light comes from the Orient, it is also written that the soul of the Occident will be the throne of that light. Your presence among us is a living symbol of this great effort of the elite of all races towards the accomplishment of the radiant promises of unity.[43]

Then 'Abdu'l-Bahá delivered His address in which He spoke about international peace and the unity of the peoples of the world. His words were probably translated into French by Dreyfus. The notes of the translation were published in *Alliance Spiritualiste* as part of the proceedings of the meeting.[44] Ahmad Sohrab took his own notes of the Persian words of 'Abdu'l-Bahá. These were published on May 1913 in the *International Psychic Gazette*:

> When we glance with the eye of insight over the world of phenomena, we observe that every movement which establishes unity and amity brings in its train life. On the other hand, every cause which originates differences and enmity carries death in its wake.
>
> Every philanthropic movement which has been established in the world of creation has been brought into existence through love and unity. Every cause which has produced ruin and devastation has been born through hostility and differences. Therefore we must constantly strive to discover a cause whereby amity and unity will result in the human world.

To-day there are many causes which bring about more or less unity. The first, which creates love and affection, is the family bond. The second is the patriotic bond. The third is the racial bond. And the fourth is the political bond.

All these, although useful in their own limited spheres, are not potent enough to bring about the unification of the human race. Have we not learnt often, with much sorrow, that there has been a quarrel between the members of a family or the inhabitants of one land, or the denizens of various states, or the individuals of different nations?

The greatest cause which will establish permanent amity and unity in the world is the potency of the Spirit. For we all know that spirit is a ruler over the cupidities of the body. If the people are resuscitated through one spirit, there is not a trace of doubt that the greatest bond of union and harmony will be established amongst them.

In every age there have been various ties which bound the people together, but the greatest tie of all ages, the unbreakable tie which bound the hearts together, was the tie of religion. Religion has been the means of uniting contending nations and harmonising warring tribes. At the time of Christ, there were many nations who were thirsting for one another's blood, carrying fire and sword into each other's countries. They were the Romans, the Greeks, Chaldeans, Assyrians, Egyptians, and Syrians. It was impossible to unite these conflicting tribes and peoples. But when the power of religion came into action, it swept away all these barriers and cemented these nations together who for ages had been fighting against one another.

By the word religion, I do not mean the present dogmatic and theological imitations, but I mean the readjustment of the moral life of humanity, without which it is impossible to establish harmony and concord, for war, conflict, friction and strife are the results of the deterioration of morality, and the corruption of character. Once the morality of the world of humanity is beautified and adorned with praiseworthy virtues, there will be an end to war.

The tribes and nations who are in a state of savagery are in constant warfare with one another, such as the tribes of Peninsular Arabia and Central Africa. These barbarous communities ever wage war with one another, for their moral world is dark. On the other hand, as morality has reached to a higher level of perfection in Western countries, war is not carried on with the same deadly rancour. It is more or less temporary. Many reforms are introduced, such as care of the wounded, non-molestation of the noncombatants, and observation of certain international laws, which are entirely unknown to the savage tribes.

These facts show that there must needs be a great power in these days whereby nations are united and agreed. There is no greater power than the principle of the oneness of humanity. This principle must be proclaimed and put into practice, so that all the nations and religions may again remember the long-forgotten lesson that they are all the progeny of one person, and the denizens of one land. Are they not breathing one air? Is not the same sun shining upon them? Are they not the sheep of one flock? Is not God the universal Shepherd? Is He not kind to all of us?

Let us banish all phantasmal thoughts then from our minds, and there will not remain the geographic distinctions of East and West, North and South, European and American, English and German, Persian and French.

When we ponder over the creation of this infinite universe, we realise that this globe of ours is the smallest of all. Each one of these stupendous bodies, these colossal planets, revolving in yonder immeasurable space, the infinite blue canopy of God, is a thousand times greater than our small earth. Therefore, although to our eyes this globe is very spacious, when we look upon it with a divine eye, it is reduced to the tiniest atom. This small globe is not worthy of division. Is it not one home, one native land? Is not all humanity one race?

How short-sighted are we if we try to divide a room into the eastern and western corners. The geographical division of this world is exactly the same. Through our ignorance and lack of understanding, we divide this common home, we divide the members of this family into various races; we divide religion into different sects; and then with these suppositional divisions we wage war against one another; we shed one another's blood; and we pillage one another's possessions.

Were we given the vision of human brotherhood, we should not engage in warfare. If one person kills another he is called murderer, and the civil authority will bring him before the law and imprison him, but if he kills 100,000 people in a battlefield, he will be hailed as a conqueror. If a person steals one franc, he will be branded as a thief, but if he pillages a whole country he will be acclaimed a great hero. How ignorant is humanity!

From a physiological standpoint, men are not created like carnivorous animals, like lions. Their teeth are not made for meat-eating. All the parts and members of the human body are created for love and good fellowship, and the prosperity of the world depends upon the practice of these virtues.

Through long custom, savagery and blood-thirstiness are kneaded into the very being of man. There must needs be some tremendous force then to upraise the standard of eternal friendship between nations. It must come through self-sacrifice and consecrated service.

When the Eastern Countries were engaged in cataclysmic wars and the shedding of blood, His Holiness Baha-u-llah, like unto a glorious sun, shone forth from the Eastern horizon. In the midst of the contentions and clashing rivalries of the Oriental peoples he boldly proclaimed the doctrine of the oneness of the world of humanity. Numerous souls who had the courage of their convictions clustered around his banner.

In order to promote universal peace and the confederation of the nations they were ever ready to give up their possessions and their lives. His Holiness, Baha-u-llah, suffered imprisonment, exile, and incarceration for fifty years. Under the chains he raised his voice and summoned all the people to come under the tent of Unity. More than 20,000 people hastened to the arena of sacrifice, and while singing the songs of joy they were martyred by the hands of the executioners. The governments of the East arose with great determination to exterminate this cause. They held councils and said, 'We must uproot the tree of this community; let us abolish the foundation of this palace of universal peace which these people desire to found; we want to carry conquest to other countries, we desire to make other nations captive, we wish to extend the boundary of our dominions, we want to defend our countries. How are we going to do all these things except through militarism, and as Baha-u-llah's aim is to prevent war, let us destroy him, and his followers, so that his ideas may not become wide-spread.'

The Bahais are most self-sacrificing in this path; they have proved it by their deeds; they are neither visionaries nor Utopians. With the greatest power and strength they have arisen to serve their fellow-men. Through their marvellous power they have established amity between the various nations and religions, and they are working incessantly day and night. To-day, in the Orient, those souls who have accepted the teachings of Baha-u-llah, from amongst the various sects, religions, and nations, are cemented together with the power of affinity and love. Were you to enter any of the Bahai assemblies in the Orient you would behold the Mussulmans, Buddhists, Jews, Christians, and Zoroastrians, all associating together with such a spirit of affinity and brotherhood, that no one can differentiate them, one from another.

Consequently, you observe that these souls have reached the highest state of self-sacrifice. If occasion arises, all that they possess will be sacrificed, in order to unfurl the banner of the solidarity of the human race, over the regions of the East and West, that all differences may be annulled, and all people, from one end of the earth to the other, may sing in one accord, the song of life and peace, that it may be borne on the wings of light, up to the throne of God, there to be blended with the hallelujah of the heavenly angels. Thus heaven and earth may be harmonised with the golden strains of divine music.

The domestic animals live amongst each other in the greatest peace and harmony, and never fight. If you bring together sheep from various countries, from France, Persia, America, not one would say I am a Persian sheep, or an American sheep. Let us at least live together as these domestic animals do. Again, if you collect in one room doves from Asia, Europe, Africa, America and Australia, cooingly they will love one another. Man, who is endowed with intelligence, must not be less than these creatures.

The world of existence is like unto an orchard, and humanity is like unto the trees. All these trees are planted in the same orchard, they are reared through the heat of one sun, watered with one rain. We must be the cause of the adornment of each other in this orchard.

The world of humanity is like unto a rose-garden, and the various races, tongues and peoples are like unto the various flowers.

Were you to enter a rose-garden you would observe that the variety of flowers adds to the charm and beauty of the scene, so that variety enhances unity. Why should we not look upon the human world with this rose-coloured vision?

If the various races do not associate with one another, then how can we ever expect the realisation of that far-off dream of the millennium?

In short, I hope that as this century is a radiant century, and as this age is a merciful age, the world of humanity will be united, and the standard of the solidarity of the human race be hoisted in Paris, for Paris is a centre of refined civilisation; it has advanced greatly along the path of science; it is like unto a lamp, and the light within this lamp shall be the realisation of oneness in the world of humanity. I hope this light may shed its benign rays into all regions.

I request that each one of you may work for this great cause, and hold fast to every means so that blood-thirstiness may be abandoned, and the horizons of the world may become illumined by the rays of divine humanity, and the East and the West may become enlightened with the light of its Lord.[45]

Finally, Albert Jounet closed the meeting with a long talk in which he briefly mentioned 'Abdu'l-Bahá, saying that 'One of the great consolations of this world is that there is a human presence who you can see living the love of men and the love of God.'

On 26 February the president of the Alliance Spiritualiste visited the Master at His temporary residence at 30 Rue St. Didier and they held a long interview. 'Abdu'l-Bahá spoke to a quite pessimistic Jeanne Beauchamps on the need to promote love and unity and encouraged her not to feel impotent in this endeavor for, regardless of the small number of the defenders of peace and love, their efforts were always confirmed by God. As He had done in His talk to the spiritualists, He emphasized to Beauchamps that only one common faith could bring humankind together.[46]

The Case of Frank Decker

Frank Decker was a spiritist of Syrian background living in New York who became a rather famous medium in the years preceding the Second World War. He allegedly was able not only to contact the souls of the departed ones but also to materialize them. In this state the contacted souls would speak and even touch the surprised people attending Decker's seances. The list of illustrious spirits who 'appeared' in his studio ranged from Pythagoras to Omar Khayyam and all of them were able to speak fluent English. Despite the fact that it was proved on various occasions that Decker's purported powers were just a fraud and the result of the display and action of complex tricks, he nevertheless had a large following and many clients ready to pay him for his supposed intermediation with the other world.

In 1936 another spiritist, Edwin F. Bowers, wrote a book in defense of spiritualism in which, in an attempt to prove the veracity of the phenomenon, he described many of Decker's seances. At two points in the book Bowers affirms that Decker used to 'materialize' the spirit of 'Abdu'l-Bahá. The first of the two quotations below is Bowers' own testimony of one of these supposed visits:

> The spirit of the great Persian prophet and master, Abdul Baha, was materialized on several occasions. He gave us his blessing in Arabic, after which he discoursed learnedly in English on matters connected with psychic development.
>
> This great spirit also materialized – apparently in full form. I could feel his thoroughly developed hands as they took me by the arms to lead me around the room. Also, I distinctly felt his shoulders and chest, as he happened to press against me in guiding my course.[47]

The second description of a 'materialization' of 'Abdu'l-Bahá came from a certain Elizabeth B. Darwin, who left the place as a convinced spiritualist:

> I stood reverently, and listened to an invocation in Arabic by the great Persian Master, Abdul Baha, and felt his hand upon my head. I bowed in awe and deep humility while I received his blessing, delivered this time in English. And I heard the stertorous breathing of Frank Decker, lying back in his chair in a deep trance, during all this time. I am still amazed with the wonder of it all.[48]

The interest of these comments relies not merely in the fact that they show that Decker probably met 'Abdu'l-Bahá during His sojourn in North America but also reveals the way in which 'Abdu'l-Bahá was still remembered by the public in the 1930s.

36

OPPOSITION

Generally speaking, in the 19th century Christian missionaries in Persia and the Middle East had expressed some sympathy towards the Bahá'ís, as among them they found people with an open, tolerant and inclusive attitude towards Christians who were ready to converse with the missionaries. Some westerners even came to regard the movement as a form of Christianity that would be useful and conducive to the success of missions among Muslims. Over time, however, in some cases this sympathy was transformed into hostility as the Bahá'í Faith – in contrast to the limited success of the Christian missions – steadily progressed among Muslims, Jews and Zoroastrians in Persia and began to spread among Christians in the West.

It is not surprising, therefore, that when 'Abdu'l-Bahá visited Europe and North America some missionaries openly expressed their opposition to the Bahá'í Faith and tried to stem the popularity and celebrity that the Bahá'í Faith was gaining as a result of 'Abdu'l-Bahá's presence in Christian lands. Some members of the clergy wrote articles against 'Abdu'l-Bahá and others used their pulpits to oppose Him.

The attacks made from the Christian ranks used a variety of arguments. One common accusation in all of them was, however, that the Bahá'í teachings were not original and that its doctrines could be found in Christianity.[1] This statement shows that those who expressed it had a lack of knowledge or simply a disregard for some of the basic Bahá'í theological doctrines – such as its concept of the Manifestations of God or its definition of God – and its social principles – such as the need for an international tribunal, an international language, universal education, gender equality and so on – which are not present in any other religion and which 'Abdu'l-Bahá emphasized many times in His talks. Eventually, 'Abdu'l-Bahá instructed Mírzá Abu'l-Faḍl-i-Gulpáygání to write a treatise rebutting the attacks by Christian ministers and missionaries, which was published in Chicago under the title *The Brilliant Proof* (1912).

As we shall see, 'Abdu'l-Bahá was also attacked by the Covenant-breakers, the supporters of His half-brother Mírzá Muḥammad 'Alí, who, in his thirst to undermine the authority over the Bahá'í community bestowed upon the Master by Bahá'u'lláh Himself, had used a relative in America as an agent of disinformation.

Finally, some opposition also came from the more radical ranks of the socialist movement.

All these attacks, however, had few repercussions in the press and represent a minuscule proportion of the total number of articles that were written about 'Abdu'l-Bahá and the Bahá'í Faith at the time.

Missionaries in Persia

The arrival of 'Abdu'l-Bahá in London in 1911 and the way in which He was received by Rev. Reginald Campbell and Archdeacon Wilberforce raised objections on the part of some Christian missionaries. As early as 27 September the evangelistic weekly *The Christian* (London) expressed in plain words that the Bahá'í Faith was a problem for missions:

> . . . no other attitude is possible to Evangelical Christians than that of antagonism to this modern innovation. Bahaism would mean an end to Christian missions; and we, who believe that our Lord is the unique Son of God, the peerless Man, the only Saviour, must look to Him for brotherhood and peace.[2]

One of the first to attack 'Abdu'l-Bahá after His arrival in the West was Peter Z. Easton (1846–1916), an American Presbyterian missionary in Persia who met 'Abdu'l-Bahá in London in 1911 and afterwards wrote two articles against the Bahá'í Faith. The first appeared in *The English Churchman* (London) on 28 September 1911. This magazine had already mentioned the Bahá'í Faith in a previous issue in an editorial apropos of the visit of 'Abdu'l-Bahá to the City Temple. 'The Rev. R. J. Campbell, who has been very quiet of late, has just discovered in Bahaism "one of the most remarkable religious movements of this or any age",' stated the article, which defined the Bahá'í Faith as 'but one of a number of Pantheistic sects' and which, following Easton, also stated that 'there are things in its [Bahá'í] history which gravely discredit it'.[3]

Easton's article started with a short account of his own visit to 'Abdu'l-Bahá, in which both communicated in Tartar Turkish, and was followed by a summary of his views on the Bahá'í Faith. Following Gobineau's *Les Religions et Philosophies dans l'Asie Centrale* (1865) – a book with a considerable section on the Bábí religion which, while sympathetic and well-intended, was highly inaccurate – the missionary stated that the Bahá'í Faith 'is a pantheistic, not a Christian, nor even a Mohammedan movement'. The article then continued with a series of attacks against Bahá'u'lláh in which the author basically used the arguments put forward by the followers of Mírzá Yaḥyá to discredit Him and which had been published in previous years by Edward G. Browne. Thus, Easton accused Bahá'u'lláh of usurping the leadership of Yaḥyá and of being responsible for the assassination of some of Yaḥyá's followers in 'Akká. To these he added the accusation of blasphemy for allowing His followers to address Him with titles such as 'The Lord of the Vineyard'. 'In short,' concluded Easton in his section on Bahá'u'lláh, 'he was a moral and spiritual monster, who exalted himself against all that is called God or that is worshipped. To become a Bahai means to put this anti-Christ in the place of the God and Father of our Lord Jesus Christ. This is what the people of Great Britain are now invited to do. But, it may be objected, it is impossible to believe that such a demon in human form could exist, and, even if this were possible, a system so awful, so abominable would find no adherents. To this I reply that this is what has happened over and over and over again in the history of Persia and other Oriental lands.'[4]

Easton published a further article for *Evangelical Christendom* (London) in which he developed the idea that the Bahá'í Faith is a pantheistic religion, directed further attacks at Bahá'u'lláh, whom he defined as 'worse than Barabbas – betrayer, assassin, and blasphemer – a worthy successor of that long line of Persian antichrists' and regretted that Archdeacon Wilberforce had invited 'Abdu'l-Bahá to speak at his church. 'The Archdeacon must choose whom he will serve,' stated Easton, 'whether the God and Father of our Lord Jesus Christ or the Antichrist, Baha.' The missionary's animosity led him as far as stating with regard to the killing of thousands of Bábís and Bahá'ís that 'there is no need of wasting any sympathy on the suffering of the Babis'.⁵

Easton continued making the same sort of attacks in America. A representative of *The Sun* (New York) interviewed him just a few days after the arrival of 'Abdu'l-Bahá in the United States. In summarizing his ideas about the Bahá'í Faith, Easton plainly stated that the movement had to be opposed: 'I am firmly convinced that strong utterances should be made to awaken American Christians to the truth of Abdul Baha's propaganda. Bahaism is not Christian, it is not Mohammedan; on the contrary, it is essentially anti-Christian and anti-Mohammedan . . . I greatly fear that this cult of Bahaism may find fruitful ground in the United States, and I am anxious to raise my voice and urge Christians to crush it in its infancy'.⁶ The article also reproduced large portions of his article in *The English Churchman*.

This interview prompted a reporter with the *Washington Herald*, who was present at the talk of 'Abdu'l-Bahá held in Washington's Metropolitan Methodist Church, to question the Master about the statements made by the missionary. On 25 April, the *Herald* quoted 'Abdu'l-Bahá as stating regarding pantheism that 'like the mirror reflects the warmth and the rays of the sun, so does Christ reflect the love of God'.⁷ This was probably part of a longer answer along the lines of the arguments He used in some of His writings to explain the impossibility of pantheism.

Following this article in the *Herald*, H. P. Hoar, a reader signing as the president of the Oriental University, addressed a letter to the editor trying to defend the Bahá'í Faith. Regarding the accusation of pantheism, the letter stated that 'Bahais do not put any man in the place of God, nor do they believe in the dangerous orthodox trinity dogma . . .' Responding to Easton's call to 'crush' the Bahá'í Faith, Hoar stated that 'true Christians are true Bahais, whether they call themselves Bahais or not . . . To everyone who gets in touch with this irresistible world-movement of Bahaism the spirit of the Lord Christ becomes more powerful because of the nonsectarian universality it breathes . . . To call upon Christians to arraign themselves against Bahaism means to do so without the authorization of Christ, and in opposition to his principle of unity through love.' The letter concluded by stating that 'what the world needs and Bahaism endeavors to aid in is getting away from superstition, fear, anthropomorphism and ecclesiastical system-building, and the acceptance of the Fatherhood of God and the Brotherhood of Men, i.e., of all men, not only those of our own narrow circle, so that, finally God may be all-in-all.'⁸

Among the missionaries to Persia who wrote articles about the Bahá'í Faith was the Presbyterian William Ambrose Shedd (1876–1918), son of the missionary John Haskell Shedd (1833–95), who had himself mentioned the 'Bábís' in several of his articles.⁹

In 1911 Shedd wrote an article – too long to reproduce here – for *The Missionary Review of the World* (New York) dealing with the Bahá'í Faith in fair and neutral terms and summarizing its history and teachings. The purpose of this article was, however, to show that in some theological points the Bahá'í Faith was in direct conflict with Christianity.¹⁰ Shedd's article was later reprinted in *Evangelical Christendom* (London).¹¹

On 7 December, the *British Weekly* (London) carried a letter to the editor from Shedd in which the missionary made the following comments apropos the visit of 'Abdu'l-Bahá to London:

> Dear Sir, – The wide publicity and favourable introduction given last summer in London to Abdul Baha and the religion of Bahaism leads me to ask the privilege for a word in your columns. If Bahaism is presented to the public on its own merits as a new effort to meet the spiritual needs of man, the Christian missionary is the last man to object to its having a sympathetic hearing but if it is presented as an equivalent of Christianity or even as an approach to Christianity, it is time to protest. It claims to be the unification of all religious belief, and to offer to this age the form of religion most needed. This it claims to do by abolishing all ritual and all dogma. But the fact is that it presents both ritual and dogma of its own, as may easily be seen by reading a scientific account of it (e.g., the articles on Babi in the *Encyclopaedia Britannica* and in *Hastings Encyclopaedia of Religion and Ethics*).
>
> Not only in its origin is it Mohammedan but also in its acceptance of Mohammed as one of the Great Prophets. Indeed, it goes beyond the Koran in declaring that Mohammed was sinless, and was a Manifestation of God. No honour is given by it to Christ which is not given to Mohammed and to Baha Ullah, and it regards Christianity as a superseded revelation. It removes God farther from human life than does Mohammedanism, knows nothing of

an immanent Spirit, and denies the need of any salvation other than enlightenment. The doubtless charming personality of Abdul Baha, the many Christian ideals accepted by Bahaism, and the possible services it may render (not has rendered) in the Orient are not called in question; but it comes to the West not in order to learn, but to offer the leadership of another in the place of Jesus Christ.[12]

Thus while keeping a correctness in the tone and avoiding direct confrontation, Shedd tried to portray the Bahá'í Faith as an offshoot of Islam and again reiterated some of the doctrinal points in which Bahá'í teachings contradict Christian dogmas. This letter was later reprinted in *Evangelical Christendom* (London)[13] and in the French magazine *Le Christianisme* (Paris).[14]

In September 1912 *The Missionary Review of the World* (New York) carried a letter from Robert McEwen Labaree (1867–1952) – son of the missionary Benjamin Labaree who decades before had mentioned the Bábís in some of his correspondence and writings – complaining about the welcome that was given to 'Abdu'l-Bahá in London and in America by Campbell and Grant:

> I cannot tell you how troubled I have been to find in enlightened America so many people interested in, and I might almost say fascinated with, Abdul Beha and his teaching, and to learn that clergymen of as much poise and of as high standing as Dr. C. have been lending him their pulpits. I wish that I had some way of convincing these good people that Behaism as preached in America is very different from the Behaism of Persia; that in the East it is essentially Mohammedan in its emphasis on the externals of religion as well as in its standards of morals; and that its talk on love and universal peace and the Fatherhood of God and brotherhood of man is largely assumed for Western consumption. The Abdul Beha is an Oriental and like most Orientals, he has the chameleon's power of changing his color to suit his environment.
>
> But the thing to which I would most like to call the attention of men like Dr. C- and R- C-, is the harm that they are doing in thus entertaining and advertising these wolves in sheep's clothing. I am sure that they are hurting people here at home where there is now all too much of religious unrest. For example, I happened to

dine the other Sunday at a house where there was a young lady of unusually good intelligence. The question of Abbas Effendi and his teaching came up, and she insisted that there must be something to him, or such sane men as Dr. C- would never have let him speak in their churches. Of course, she had much more reason to trust Dr. C-'s saneness than mine, and so anything that I could say was unavailing to prove to her that Behaism has nothing whatever to offer to Christianity.

But I am sure that the chief harm of such mistaken hospitality is the effect that it has on the mission field. The Behaists of Persia are everywhere proclaiming that there are a million followers of the Beha in America and that they are increasing in numbers continually. Last year after Abdul Beha's visit to England and the cordial reception he met with by such men as Canon Wilberforce and Reginald Campbell, the Behaists in our region immediately began to tell of it and point to it as proof that the West was all ready to accept the new faith. It seemed to me that we missionaries were receiving a stab in our backs by those who ought to have been the first to hold up our hands.[15]

In July 1912 the Presbyterian monthly *Woman's Work* (New York) published a letter by Bessie Allen, a missionary in Persia, also complaining about the example set by Campbell and hoping that 'everything possible will be done to keep him ['Abdu'l-Bahá] out of American pulpits and college chapels'.[16] In January 1913 the missionary magazine *The East and West* (London) published a more than 20-page article on the Bahá'í religion penned by a missionary in Persia, Walter A. Rice. Rice criticized the Bahá'í conception of progressive revelation, the doctrine of the Manifestation of God and, like his contemporaries, considered that Bahá'í theology was eminently pantheistic.[17]

Months later a correspondent for the missionary magazine *The Moslem World* (London) blamed Christians for attracting 'Abdu'l-Bahá to the West:

Abdul Baha, knowing men and religious movements well, believes that Christian countries need his message about the evils of war, the emancipation of women, the power of brotherly love, even as Moslem countries do . . . disobedience to Christian teaching in

Christian lands has called to this man to come and speak to Christian men of the things in which they have wandered from the way of Christ.[18]

Attacks from the Episcopal and the Methodist Episcopal Churches

Easton's interview with the New York *Sun* and the questions posed by the *Washington Herald* to 'Abdu'l-Bahá were not two isolated episodes but appear to have been part of a concerted campaign to discredit Him upon His arrival to America.

As shown in chapter 10, 'Abdu'l-Bahá's first public address in America, delivered at the Church of the Ascension in New York on 14 April 1912, aroused some opposition among the members of the church, who protested that a non-Christian had been invited to address the parish from the pulpit in a Sunday service. This episode was to have important repercussions outside New York as well, as can be gathered from an article in the *Baltimore News* which reported that 'Abdul Baha, who preached in an Episcopal church in New York the Sunday after Easter, will not occupy an Episcopalian pulpit when he comes to Baltimore', adding that 'Bishop Murray said today that Baha will not preach in any church in the Maryland Diocese'.[19]

Weeks later the Episcopal magazine *Living Church* (Milwaukee) carried a harsh editorial on the Bahá'í Faith in which its author – probably the editor of the magazine, Frederic Cook Morehouse (1868–1930) – stated that 'the hysterical curiosity about Abdul Baha, the real Persian, who has been travelling across the continent with some silly Americans and English in his train, is little worthy of intelligent people . . . Christianity is the one and only Universal Religion, if it is true. If it is not true it is a marvellously daring and august imposture. But believing it is true, Christians do not admit that it requires to be completed or enriched . . .'[20]

In Washington, some local Episcopal and Methodist Episcopal churches launched simultaneous attacks on 'Abdu'l-Bahá. On Sunday 28 April, coinciding with the Master's presence in Washington, two Methodist pastors, Rev. James S. Montgomery of the Memorial Methodist Episcopal Church in Washington and Rev. James Gray of the Hamline Methodist Episcopal Church, devoted their sermons to preaching against 'Abdu'l-Bahá. An announcement of Montgomery's service stated that he 'will speak on "The Popular Appetite". This subject will be applied to the teachings of Baha and the sensation he is causing, the speed craze, and numerous phases of the instability of religious and social life.'[21]

On Monday 29 April the *Washington Herald* gave full coverage to both sermons. Gray, who was by far the harsher in his attack on 'Abdu'l-Bahá, followed in his sermon all the arguments employed by Easton and represented the Bahá'í Faith as essentially anti-Christian, even polygamist, and 'Abdu'l-Bahá was accused of concealing the real tenets of the Bahá'í religion. He reportedly accused 'Abdu'l-Bahá of being 'mentally deficient or mentally dishonest' as 'either false or a fool' and 'incompetent to teach men'. Montgomery used a softer tone but his arguments were basically the same.[22]

A further account of Montgomery's sermon was published in *The Washington Post* in an article which began: 'The Rev. Dr. James S. Montgomery led the congregation of the Metropolitan Memorial . . . in a plea that Abdul be made to see the error of his teachings, and go back to the sands of Persia with a broader vision.' Montgomery was also reported as having stated that 'I do hope that a sojourn in this country will cause him to see the light, and that he will return to his Eastern home a greater man. The incarnation of Jesus Christ, the keystone of our holy faith, is unknown to the teachings of Abdul. This is to deny the foundation stone on which Christianity must rest for its glory and for its perpetuity. It would be well if some of those who have listened to Abdul's lectures would take the role of teacher themselves, and convert to Christ this remarkable priest of the "universal cult".'[23]

Soon after the departure of 'Abdu'l-Bahá from Washington, Ernest Smith of the St Thomas Episcopal Church also devoted a Sunday service to speaking against 'Abdu'l-Bahá in his sermon entitled 'Mohammedanism and its Persian Cult – Bahaism'. The *Evening Star* published the following account of Smith's words:

> 'A gentleman from Persia', Dr. Ernest Smith said, 'has been travelling through the United States and has lately been here in the capacity of a missionary to declare to us the things which belong to our place. For this, he is worthy of all honor. Doubtless he is a sincere and high-minded man, who is profoundly convinced both of the truth and the importance of his message. Perhaps it is a little

unfortunate that the country he comes from is in its decadence, both politically and morally.

'According to Herodotus, the Persians devoted a third of their educational curriculum to training their children to speak the truth, but today scarcely an individual can be found willing to tell the truth unless he has something to gain by it.

'On examination it turns out that this missionary is simply a Mohammedan. He therefore believes in the Koran, with its polygamy and its sensual paradise, and that Mohammed is superior to Christ. He is not, however, an orthodox Mohammedan. Few if any of the Persians are. Their saint worship and sacerdotalism and use of bhang and opium are abhorred at Mecca. He represents a sort of Oxford movement known as Bahaism in the Mohammedan Church – a cult which commenced some thirty or forty years ago – the good in it probably inspired by Christian missionaries to the Persians.

'Testing this Persian missionary's teachings by results and, comparing them with the results of Christ's teaching as manifested in Christianity's hospitals, houses of mercy, homes, orphanages and higher ideals generally, and withal sweeter, nobler, more inspiring ideals of God, we do not know whether to admire more the splendid faith of this Persian in his creed or to pity more his colossal ignorance.

'"By their fruits ye shall know them." Therefore we cannot encourage this high-minded, earnest, conscientious Persian, who at great self-sacrifice has left his own country and kith and kin to teach us. Doing so, we would be traitors to Christ, whom we dare not compare, but may contrast, with the Arabian prophet, of whom it has been said that whether he be priest, hero, sage or impostor, "Allah only knows." Because of these things the only Godspeed we can bid him is a Godspeed back to his own country.'[24]

On 27 May the *Baltimore Star* summarized the attacks directed at 'Abdu'l-Bahá from Washington, noting the fact that 'Ministers of every Christian creed are banding together to fight the invaders' and that 'even the most rabid of his critics impute to him none other than the most sincere motives though many of the clergy are of the opinion that he has come to the wrong land to teach his faith'. 'With all the imperturbability of the Oriental,' stated the article regarding 'Abdu'l-Bahá, 'he says nothing in answer to these attacks.'[25]

Months later the *Washington Post* reported that the Rev. George F. Dudley, of the St. Stephens Episcopal Church in Columbia Heights, who had been one of the speakers at the Convention of the Orient-Occident Unity held in Washington, in the course of one of his sermons 'made a strong defense of Christianity against Bahaism'.[26]

Finally, on November 1912, the *Christian Advocate* (Nashville), journal of the Methodist Episcopal Church, carried an article by William Thomas McElroy[27] about the Bahá'í Faith in which, after summarizing its teachings, he stated that 'there is much in Bahaism that is good. There is much that is preposterous as well. There is also much that is quite harmless. But there is nothing in it, so far as we can see, that would induce a member of any of the recognized branches of the Church of God to become its adherent.'[28]

Further Attacks in America

Just a few days before 'Abdu'l-Bahá's arrival in America, the religious journalist William T. Ellis who, as mentioned in chapter 4, had met 'Abdu'l-Bahá in Egypt, wrote a new article dedicated to the Master which was signed 'The Religious Rambler'. In describing 'Abdu'l-Bahá, Ellis stated He 'has a commanding personality and a face radiant with spirituality', adding that 'nobody questions Abbas Effendi's sincerity; he clearly does not belong with the religious charlatans who infest this country'. Regarding 'Abdu'l-Bahá coming to America, Ellis reported that it was 'arousing certain missionary leaders to active protest against what they declare to be the specious and misleading teachings of this new faith, which some devotees are proclaiming as the final religion of the world'. In his analysis of the Bahá'í Faith the journalist expressed his view that 'stripped to the bone, Bahaism is but Moslemachism' and that 'it is truer to the ideals of Islam than those of any other faith, except for this radical departure of tolerance'. Ellis also regretted that 'Behaism brushes aside all the claims of Christianity, and classes it with Buddhism and African devil-worship' and that for Bahá'ís 'Jesus is only one in a long line of prophets, most of them unknown, of whom the head of the Behaists is the latest'.[29]

On 30 May 1912 Ellis published in the Presbyterian magazine *The*

Continent (Chicago) a third article about the Bahá'í Faith. It reproduced some portions of his first article about 'Abdu'l-Baha, this time describing Him as 'a stately Persian, good to look upon his strong, shining face, with the hawklike eyes and General Booth nose'. Despite the considerable attention paid by the press to 'Abdu'l-Bahá, Ellis further declared that 'the Titanic disaster, and a presidential campaign that would be the better for the infusion of a few Bahaist principles, have crowded the new teacher out of the newspapers'. Regarding the Bahá'í Faith he expressed the view that 'it sets up no high exactions of duty; it is as nebulous as the morning mist'.[30] The rest of the article tried to convince the reader of the unoriginality of the Bahá'í Faith.[31] An editorial in the same issue declared that Ellis's article pointed out 'the essential inwardness of the fallacy of Bahaism'.

This article in *The Continent* was the basis of a column by the reporter and former Baptist priest William O. Lovett which was published in the *Grand Rapids Evening Press* on 20 June 1912. In the course of the article – basically a summary of Ellis's – Lovett mentioned one local minister, the Rev. A. W. Wishart, whom he described as liberal, joining 'with the rest in asserting that Abdul Baha's teaching is a late imitation of that of Jesus'. Perhaps influenced by the articles penned by Easton, Lovett also defined the Bahá'í teachings as pantheistic.[32]

After the publication of this article the pastor of the Holland Unitarian Church in Grand Rapids, Bernard Anthony Van Sluyters, who had probably met 'Abdu'l-Bahá at the Unitarian Annual Festival held in May in Boston, delivered a sermon defending the Bahá'í Faith.[33] Lovett included in his column transcriptions of parts of Van Sluyters's sermon and from these it can be concluded that the Unitarian minister offered an extensive presentation of the Bahá'í Faith. Lovett referred to Van Sluyters as 'a staunch defender and advocate in Grand Rapids' of 'Abdu'l-Bahá and reproduced portions of his sermon, including the following statements:

> This certainly is a message for the times, it is a pity that it has to come to us Christians from Persia. It is humiliating and arouses our prejudice and religious hatred. All that is good in the preaching of Abdul Baha is contained in the teaching of Jesus; his doctrine of love to God and love to man is a statement of universal religion that cannot be improved. But Christians have not been true

to the religion of Jesus. Hair splitting formalism and creeds, church hatreds, social injustice and industrialism cry to heaven for vengeance, wars and race hatred are pronounced in Christian lands, it may be that Christianity is a failure, but in reality the religion of Jesus has never yet been tried.

In Bahaism some things seem fanciful and partake of distinctly eastern flavor, but the great principle of the movement is sound—justice, righteousness, blessedness, brotherhood. Some Christian preachers proclaim the same tidings, but one more earnest prophet can do no harm.[34]

Months later the Grand Rapids local Women's Missionary Social Union convened a meeting at the Park Congregational Church to hear several missionaries bound for the East. The main speaker was Frances B. Patterson who was invited to speak against Mormonism. According to a report that appeared in the *Grand Rapids Evening Press*, other speakers included a certain Rev. D. Dykstra[35], destined for Arabia and who 'in an address warned Americans against the "refined Mohammedanism" of the new cult of Abdul Baha, now being introduced in this country'.[36]

The Unitarian magazine *Unity* (Chicago), published on 6 June a comment on Ellis's article, also listing some of the subjects on which 'Abdu'l-Bahá spoke at the Lake Mohonk Conference, stating that these are 'worthy of study and deserving of repetition, no matter by whom declared or by whom claimed'.[37]

In Canada the Rev. E. I. Hart of the Dominion Square Methodist Church devoted his dominical service of 8 September 1912 to a sermon about 'Abdu'l-Bahá. An account of the service appeared in the *Montreal Daily Witness*, which quoted Hart as repeating what other priests had said in the United States:

> I do not find a single truth in it [the Bahá'í Faith] that Christianity had not taught or is not teaching to-day. Long before this Eastern movement was heard of in Canada we had been teaching and practicing them. There is not a feature of their social reform propaganda but has been and is being championed by men and women within the Christian Church.[38]

Small cults like the Koreshan Unity also opposed 'Abdu'l-Bahá. Just as some Christian clergy tried to convince the public that anything presented by 'Abdu'l-Bahá was already contained in the Bible, Koreshans claimed that anything good in the Bahá'í Faith was already present in the writings of their founder, Cyrus R. Teed (1839–1908), Koresh.[39]

The Catholic Church

The Catholic hierarchy received 'Abdu'l-Bahá with some indifference. During His travels apparently no Catholic church invited Him to speak and very few Catholic priests are reported as having met Him personally.

Nevertheless, some comments about Abdu'l-Bahá were published in Catholic journals. London's *The Month* carried in October 1911 a lengthy article by the Rev. C. C. Martindale about the Universal Races Congress. Its author had been present at some Bahá'í meetings and devoted half of the text to a neutral presentation of the Bahá'í Faith. Martindale called upon his church to study the Bahá'í Faith and 'where she recognizes herself or her ideals in it, she will spring forward eagerly to lay hold of those good elements, lest they be lost, and will work with them towards perfection. Where she sees perversion, ignorance, lacunae, monstrous growths, her heart will bleed for the endangered souls. The only attitude she cannot take is that of indifference.'

Martindale recognized that in issues like the status of women the Bahá'í Faith was effecting a transformation in the East and suggested that 'Justly may the Church ask of her missionaries closely and with sympathy and equity to examine these phenomena.' At the same time, and like other Christians before him, Martindale expressed his view that anything good in the Bahá'í Faith had a Christian origin. Thus, when summarizing some of the Bahá'í teachings he states that 'these are Christian ideals, claimed by Christianity as in some sense at least her property; introduced by her; propagated, explained, and to be realized by her.' He then concluded his article with the following comments about the spread of the Bahá'í Faith:

> For good or ill, truth or falsehood, God has been involved. Men and women of all colours and castes, races and creeds, are praying to Him to bring to pass exactly what He has declared, through

Jesus Christ, it is His will should come to pass. What attitude are the believers in Jesus Christ, then, to take to this phenomenon? At least we must exult at the thought that it is the Church's office to be the universal pacificator, the eternal mother; and here are symptoms of a world-wide wish for peace (though we are not blind to the chaos and the war), and here are men eager to hold their fellows, and be held, for brothers. That it is her mission not alone to be intrinsically One (for that she never can cease to be), but, to unify; and here are East and West . . . That it is her mission to be the Church of no one country, colour, race, period, civilization, 'mentality', but in her catholicity to include and unify all modes of which humanity is possible.[40]

The proceedings of the Universal Races Congress were also reviewed in an article that appeared in the *Catholic World* (New York) in July 1912. Its author devoted the final pages of the article to a presentation of the Bahá'í Faith. While he considered the Bahá'í presence in the program as a positive aspect of the Congress and described some of its teachings as 'noble and generous', he also emphasized those Bahá'í teachings which, in his view, were contrary to the Catholic dogmas:

> But when we come to the definite teachings, precepts, ceremony, and ritual of Baba'u'llah the lustre grows dim. It is good to forbid war, suicide, injustice of all kinds; it is excellent to teach and practice the charity of universal brotherhood, but what does all this avail when dogma is rejected, and pantheism preached? The Bahai religion inculcates prayer, and what is prayer without sacrifice and sacramentals, those essential visible bonds uniting man to the invisible, of the life of the soul by grace. Without these, mysticism, on which Babism lays such stress, is a delusion. Bahai repudiates priesthood and sacrifice; the solitary life of monk and nun is banned, and marriage is enjoined upon all as the highest estate of man. Moreover Babism denies of course the divinity of Our Lord, and teaches that Christ was only a type of the greatest of the world prophets, and with His Sacred Name it links those of Moses and Buddha, nay, Baba'u'llah himself and Abdu'l Baba the dweller on Mount Carmel.

The author also regretted the fact that while 'the Universal Races Congress deemed its discussion incomplete without a reverent consideration for the words of the oriental stranger from Mount Carmel', at the same time 'We do not read the name of the great solitary of the Vatican in the papers of the Congress, nor does his scheme find place in the volume of Inter-Racial Problems...'[41]

In California the *San Francisco Monitor*, a Catholic weekly journal with a circulation of 22,000 copies, carried on 5 October an editorial – probably by Charles Phillips – about the approaching visit of 'Abdu'l-Bahá to California. The author cautioned his readers:

> We foresee that the daily papers are about to give this city a fearful dose of 'fashionable religion'. Baha is coming to town: Baha, founder of the very latest of popular cults; prophet, seer, and several other heathenish things that tickle the fancy of the giggle-minded. We give due warning. The local press will soon be flooded with the doings, the sayings, the thinkings, the breathings of Baha. Be prepared for the deluge!

The author then warned:

> The harm in Bahaism and all such so-called 'religions' is first of all, this: They deny the divinity of Jesus Christ the Second Person of the Blessed Trinity. They draw Him down to the level of a mere good man, a kindly philosopher. Surely that is harm enough! For once the divinity of Christ is denied... then what is left? To deny Christ's divinity is to call Him a liar and throw all His teachings to the winds. To virtue and moral safety then, good night!

The editorial closed requesting its readers to 'Keep away from Baha, no matter how beautifully his "gentle teachings" may be exploited during his visit to San Francisco. Don't go near him. Stay at home and say the Rosary instead.'[42]

Days later, after the *San Francisco Call* had mentioned in one of its articles that many women were visiting 'Abdu'l-Bahá,[43] a further reference to Him was made in the editorial of the *Monitor*: 'I told you so, Baha... has made the flurry we predicted among our local giggle-minded... Of course there were no Catholic women among those who went to sit at the feet of the Baha. If only those deluded dames who did go would give one-half the time they spend on such foolishness to a pursuit of the Truth at their very hand, how much happier they would be!'⁴⁴

Socialists and Communists

Minor opposition to 'Abdu'l-Bahá also arose from socialist circles. In the course of His talks 'Abdu'l-Bahá would sometimes outline how economy and labor should be organized in the future. His scheme, which implied the existence of private property and private capital investment, was simply unacceptable for communists, as were also His comments on social organization.

In London the *New Age* magazine, a socialist literary journal directed and edited by Alfred Richard Orage (1873–1934) published on 21 September the following comment about the arrival of 'Abdu'l-Bahá in England:

> Seeds of strange religions are wafted from time to time on to our shores. But fortunately or unfortunately they do not find the soil in us in which to flourish . . . The latest to land in public is Bahaism, of which, indeed, many of us have heard in private these many years. 'Baha'u'llah's counsels', we are told, 'are faithfully carried out . . . A Bahai must have a trade, an art, or a profession . . . he must take part in some work for the benefit of the community.' From this we forecast less success in England for Bahaism than for Christian Science, let us say, that makes no such demands of the idle rich.⁴⁵

Years later a regular contributor to *New Age* visited 'Abdu'l-Bahá in Haifa. He was the young German Carl Erich Bechhöfer (1894–1949) – sometimes signing his articles as Charles Brookfarmer – who from 1911 had been traveling the world. A communist, a supporter of the war and of the Russian revolution, he visited 'Abdu'l-Bahá on 8 February 1914, and interviewed Him on economic matters. Of course, the answers of the Master to the questions put by Bechhöfer – very similar to the contents of His talk to the socialists in Montreal (see chapter 19) – did not please him and the long article that ensued, which was published on 26 February 1914, was highly satiric and irreverent in its tone.⁴⁶

Another contributor to the *New Age* magazine was a certain Abdul

Mutaqim who in 1915 had read the Bahá'í pamphlet produced in Montreal, *Abdul Baha on War and Peace*. In the course of the article Abdul Mutaqim quoted extensively from a Tablet of 'Abdu'l-Bahá written at the beginning of the World War (see chapter 38) and used this text to direct a critique to the Master's teaching on Peace. 'Abbâs Efendi seems not to perceive that . . . deeds – i.e. violence – are needed to effect a change . . . Where evil becomes dominant, as in Europe at the present day, it will be overcome eventually by evil – that is, violence. Words, conferences, courts of arbitration, will not end it. The remedy which Abdul Bahâ prescribes comes evidently from a wrong diagnosis.' 'What use in crying "Peace!" There is no peace', concluded Mutaqim. 'The choice before mankind is war and war – war for the liberation of humanity, or war for the amusement of the apes.'[47]

This article prompted Eric Hammond to write a letter to the editor to 'protest amiably' at Mutaqim's comments in the course of which he summarized the life of 'Abdu'l-Bahá and some of His teachings and stated that 'Abdul Muntaqim writes without apparent desire to comprehend, and extends little grace to one who has borne a life-long sorrow for the religion of peace. It is easy to gird at a presentation of that religion because of Eastern imagery and Oriental manner of expression. "War must cease," says Abdul Baha, and Abdul Muntaqim smiles. Yet all the civilised world is using those very words, and the struggling nations proclaim the fact that they "war against war". The last sentence of the article gives the writer away.'[48]

Hammond's letter prompted Bechhöfer, now signing with his real name, to attack 'Abdu'l-Bahá again in a letter sent from Russia in which he mentioned his interview with Him in Haifa. Referring to his alter ego, the young journalist stated that 'I also know Abdul Baha personally and respect neither him nor the movement he represents, and, if I remember rightly, Mr. Charles Brookfarmer also personally interviewed Abdul Baha; from his report I imagine that he, too, was not much impressed by him and the movement he represents. To begin with, Abdul Baha is no more a prophet than my little finger, and his father, from whom he inherits the goodwill of the business, was as little spiritual as my big toe.' Regarding 'Abdu'l-Bahá repeated admonitions about the war in Europe, Bechhöfer stated that 'I can say this, that the old boy is very clever at anticipating questions, a gift which, considering his long life in captivity, does him infinite credit. But it is all he has to make an impression with, for he has neither common sense nor ideas.'[49] It was probably these negative comments about 'Abdu'l-Bahá that prompted the artist Wyndham Lewis to dedicate to Him a 'blast' in the first issue of the very short-lived 'Vorticist' magazine he edited.[50]

The *Daily Citizen* was a short-lived socialist journal published in London and Manchester. On 2 January 1913 a curious editorial attacking 'Abdu'l-Bahá was published in the pages of its Manchester edition:

> SWEET RELIGION.
> Socialism of a sort is the fashion in the West End just now. Of course it is not called Socialism. That name is just a little vulgar; Bahaism sounds so much more distinguished. The prophet of the cult, a Persian named Abdul Baha, after bleating, that is to say beating, against the bars of a Turkish fortress for 40 years is now having a great time. He is one of the star turns of Society. Among other things, he has contrived a new decalogue. It is a most proper decalogue, because no sins are mentioned in it. The Baha world is too well behaved to make that necessary. All the decalogue lays down are aims, charming aims to which the most fastidious can't take exception. One of them is the 'readjustment of the economic condition of Society (with a swell 'S'), justice and fairness to all, but the classes not to be disturbed'."This does not mean the classes in Bahaism. It refers to the select who are opposed to the unselect – or the masses. What could be more comforting and grateful? You become a Bahaist, and sleep with the feeling that your luxuries and unearned increments are now insured.'[51]

The publication of this editorial prompted one of the readers of the journal, who identified himself as a socialist and as a Bahá'í, to address the following letter to the editor:

> SOUL OF BAHAISM
>
> To the Editor of 'The Daily Citizen'
>
> Sir,– As a fellow Socialist and ardent Bahai, I wish to protest against an article which imparted the impression that the Bahai religion was for the exclusive few. It was the brotherhood note in the Bahai movement that first interested me.

As a Socialist I find that it gives a soul to Socialism. Abdul Baha preaches brotherhood from the spiritual standpoint. He says that we should 'look upon each member of the human family either as a father or sister or mother or brother'. There is a dominant note of solidarity in this world-movement which is a relief from that over accentuated individualism which has crept into some of the Christian teachings. The Bahai answer to the question, 'What shall I do to be saved?' would be 'Serve your brother'.' 'Be as one soul in many bodies.'

It is a religion of deeds, not words. There is no ritual. The temples, of which there are several in the Orient, none as yet in this country, but one to be erected at Chicago, in America, are centres of activity. Around the central hall are built a hospice for travellers, a house for homeless children, cripples, etc. Into the central or worshipping hall all are invited to enter, with equal privilege, each for himself to find here the meeting of his spirit with the spirit of the infinite and loving Father, and hence in peace to depart to serve his brother.

London. CITIZEN ADMIRER[52]

Second Visit to England

On 'Abdu'l-Bahá's return to England, He received further attacks in the press. This time they did not come from priests or missionaries but from Christian layman.

This was especially the case in Edinburgh where after 'Abdu'l-Bahá's successful and widely publicized visit some local newspapers published letters – probably written by one single individual – attacking Him and the Bahá'í Faith.

On 8 January the *Evening Dispatch* published a letter to the editor from a reader who considered the Bahá'í teachings to be a menace to the efforts of missionaries. 'Consider,' stated the correspondent, 'what it must mean to accept the tenets of Bahaism and "not antagonise or denounce any religion". It means that all missionary effort to preach the Gospel according to the Scriptures must cease.'[53] This letter was responded to by another reader signing as 'a Bahai Christian' who tried to clarify the Bahá'í position on the unity of religions[54] and by a 'London reader' who wrote a letter reiterating the points already touched upon by 'Bahai Christian'.[55]

On 13 January the *Evening Dispatch* carried a letter by Benjamin McCall Barbour (1865–1943) who was a preacher of the King James Bible Believers, a sect that considered this 1611 translation of the Bible as an infallible text and as the sole valid translation of the New Testament. In this letter the Bahá'í Faith was presented again as detrimental for Christian missions and as 'antagonistic to the most sacred fundamental facts of the Christian faith and subversive of the teachings of the Word of God'. The parallels of this letter with the one that appeared on 8 January – where a text by Barbour on the Bahá'í Faith was quoted – suggest that its author was Barbour himself or one of his fellows.

A further letter by Barbour appeared on 13 January in the *Scotsman*.[56] Employing a tone and contents similar to the other articles, an unsigned letter was published on 11 January in the *Evening News* in which the author stated, 'Suffice it to say that it is surely evident to anyone with even the most superficial knowledge of Scripture, that there is not a fundamental doctrine of the Word of God in which this so-called "gospel" is not a negation.' 'And yet,' wrote the author with regret, 'this is what ministers in Scotland, who owe their positions to a profession of loyalty to God and His Word, are apparently itching to preach.'[57]

It is apparent therefore that while the Edinburgh press published several letters against the Bahá'í Faith, they did not come from the general ranks of the churches and religious leaders who had invited 'Abdu'l-Bahá to speak but from an independent preacher or members of his circle, which consisted of some 30 people.

On 11 January, a farewell reception in honor of 'Abdu'l-Bahá was held at Caxton Hall, London, and a few days later *The Christian Commonwealth* published an article describing the meeting in glowing terms (see chapter 26).[58] This article prompted the renowned Anglican writer Gilbert Keith Chesterton (1874–1936) to write a one-column article for the *Daily News and Leader* (London) expressing his disapproval at the tone employed in the magazine and with the contents of some of 'Abdu'l-Bahá's published utterances. 'With all respect for that eminent Persian's idealism,' stated Chesterton, 'I cannot say that the fragments of his utterance I have read were electrifying' and added that 'his style might be improved by a slight infusion of . . . Bernard Shaw'. The writer then discussed the subject of the unity of religions. Chesterton agreed with there being a common moral basis for all individuals but considered unity among religions impossible owing to their diverse ontological concepts. 'I will admit without hesitation that there is an original and universal revelation of right in the human conscience everywhere, and I will admit . . . that we could all profess these moral ideals while holding all kinds of theories about the plan and system of the universe.' Chesterton gave the example of the Balkans to prove that sometimes what religions have in common is not some positive value but, for instance, the value of war. Thus, Chesterton would say, the unification of religions could lead to paradoxical situations.[59]

This article was answered on the pages of *The Christian Commonwealth*:

> We know Mr. G. K. Chesterton as a fearless and ardent supporter of that section of the Christian Church to which he belongs. We know him as an ever-ready wit, and as a thinker who possesses that rare gift of turning things upside down in order to show their significance more plainly. He is brilliantly clever and versatile, but he is not always successful when he writes on the subject of religion. We find ourselves unable to believe that he takes himself quite seriously, and we certainly cannot always take him seriously. In the 'Daily News' last Saturday he devoted a column of pointed criticism to the movement which is largely associated with the name of Abdul Baha, and incidentally ridiculed the title which we gave to our account of the proceedings at the Caxton Hall on the occasion of Abdul Baha's farewell. It has not, apparently, occurred to Mr. Chesterton that a farewell may be joyous. When the leader of the Bahais was released from prison, in which he had spent many long years, he was almost unknown in Europe and America. Now, as he leaves England and returns Eastward, he and those who have come under the spell of his personality may well rejoice in what he has been able to accomplish. But Mr. Chesterton's jibe at our heading (referred to in our 'Table Talk') is not so important as his remarks on the subject of the unity of religions. Mr. Chesterton is quite right in supposing that a supporter of the Bahai ideal would not accept the relevancy of any references to the apparent agreement between adherents of different religions on such matters as the moral value of war. Because Balkan Christians and Turks agree (supposing that they do agree) that military adventure and military

glory are things always lawful and often laudable in a religious man, it certainly does not follow that this common conception is one on which 'unifiers' would or could concentrate. We may remind Mr. Chesterton that, even among us, there are those who still uphold the military ideal and give it the blessing of religious ritual; yet undoubtedly the Christian sentiment is flowing strongly against war and in favour of brotherhood and peace amongst the nations. As Mr. Chesterton supposes, we reply to his strictures by pointing to a larger unity founded on moral ideals such as justice, purity, and love. Now comes our chief quarrel with Mr. Chesterton. We can all join in worshipping a God of Love. It is pointless to remark that a Roman in Caesar's time would have understood us to mean Cupid. Mr. Chesterton is surely aware that conceptions change in content from age to age! We are not asking Romans in the time of Caesar to worship a God of Love, but men living in a century which sees the world drawn together by stronger bonds that represent and at the same time strengthen the forces that unite men. Need we ask Mr. Chesterton to look up Green's 'Prolegomena to Ethics', and apply what is there said of 'courage', of 'chastity','of 'love'? Or perhaps he will read the following words of Abdul Baha and then tell us whether he finds the dilemma quite so clearly defined: 'Remove from amongst yourselves racial, patriotic, religious, sectional, political, commercial, industrial, and agricultural prejudices, so that you may become freed from all human restrictions and become the founders of the structure of the unity of the world of humanity. All the countries are one country; all the nations are the children of one Father. The struggle for existence among the ferocious wolves has become the cause of all the differences and strifes; otherwise the expanse of the world is spacious and the Table of the Bounties of the Almighty is spread in all regions.'[60]

Another response to Chesterton's comments came from the socialist politician Henry Snell (1865–1944), who was a member of the South Place Ethical Society. Writing in *The Ethical World*, Snell lamented the orthodoxy of Chesterton. 'This passionate disbelief of Mr. Chesterton in the unifying power of moral idealism is perhaps the most characteristic product of an age of futile creeds,' stated Snell, who added that 'the world appears to be made up of people who live in mental prisons of their own constructing, and who simply deny that any sweeter air exists than that in which they have been accustomed to live.'[61] In later years Snell was elected to the House of Commons and in 1931 was given the title Baron Snell.

Attacks by Covenant-breakers

In 1904 Shu'á'u'lláh, son of Muḥammad-'Alí, was sent to the United States to take over the small band of followers that his father and Ibrahim Kheiralla still had in Kenosha. His mission was to extend to the North American territory the campaign of opposition and calumny that his father was already perpetrating in the Holy Land and which eventually led 'Abdu'l-Bahá to prison and almost cost Him His life.

Taking advantage of the enormous attention that the American media was giving to the visit of 'Abdu'l-Bahá, Shu'á'u'lláh presented himself to the press as His nephew and circulated an open letter which was distributed in Chicago by his group of supporters in Kenosha and in California by himself. In it, in an apparently friendly and cordial tone, he requested that a public meeting be called at which 'Abdu'l-Bahá and himself could discuss the 'differences' between his father and the Master. This meeting had to be conducted in English, and a representative of Associated Press had to be present. The agenda of the proposed meeting, which was organized in ten points, was in itself a summary of the attacks and manipulations used by the Covenant-breakers to discredit 'Abdu'l-Bahá.[62]

Chicago's *Examiner* was probably the first newspaper to publish some of the allegations of Shu'á'u'lláh. Its representative asked 'Abdu'l-Bahá about the accusations made by Shu'á'u'lláh – who apparently had set the date of the meeting for 18 June – and noted that 'Abdul Baha . . . showed no anxiety yesterday when asked concerning the ten questions he is expected to answer at the forthcoming peace conference of the faith in this city.' The article also summarized some portions of the open letter.[63] So did the Chicago *Sunday Tribune* on 12 May.[64]

In a move for further publicity, Kheiralla, signing as 'Representative of Mohammed Ali Bahai', sent a letter to the Kenosha *Evening News* stating that 'to our regret, His Excellency ignored till the present the open letter sent to him by his nephew. Also, his followers reported to us that he will never appoint a conference nor attend its meetings.'

The letter continued, "therefore we beg of you, to publish this report that all those concerned might know through your esteemed paper for a recent certainty if His Excellency is willing to fulfill his promise and attend the conference or not.' The same article also included the version of the facts from Bernard M. Jacobsen, a Kenosha Bahá'í:

> Secretary Jacobsen of the National Bahaist movement is in Kenosha today and speaking for Abdul Baha, he has declared that should he return to Chicago after his visit to the western part of the country he will be very glad to meet with any of the people who are believers in the faith and that he feels certain that all differences can be adjusted in a manner that will establish unity and harmony. Mr. Jacobsen, however, does not regard the questions that have been asked Abdul Baha as pertinent to the well being of the organization and he claims that the faction led by Dr. Kheiralla has failed utterly to show that there is any reason for a public debate of the questions raised on account of the fact that all of these may be answered by a strict interpretation of the addresses of Abdul Baha.[65]

A similar episode took place when 'Abdu'l-Bahá visited California. Shu'á'u'lláh personally approached some newspapers in San Francisco with a second open letter which was very similar to the first but which included a preamble in which Shu'á'u'lláh went so far in the manipulation of the facts as to state that Muḥammad 'Alí was 'chosen by God, in "The Book of My Covenant", to occupy the same position you are now occupying'. Apparently only the *San Francisco Call*[66] and the *Los Angeles Examiner*,[67] a newspaper with a circulation of 65,700 copies, published his letter. In an article entitled 'Bahai Leader a Stoic', the *San Francisco Call* mentioned on 14 October that 'Abdul Baha Abbas . . . disclaimed yesterday even to consider the written charges that his nephew brought against him. They are unworthy, he said, of the slightest consideration . . . The venerable teacher explained briefly his attitude toward such allegations, and at the same time disclaimed all spiritual relationship with his brother, Mohamed Ali, and the nephew who made the accusations.'[68]

PART III

37

RETURN TO HAIFA

On Tuesday, 2 December 1913 'Abdu'l-Bahá sailed from Alexandria, reaching Haifa on 5 December and concluding one of the most glorious periods in His ministry and in the annals of the Bahá'í Faith. The West had known first hand a unique figure in religious history, one who by His character and outstanding qualities had left an indelible impression on the lives of thousands and who had won the sympathies of many more.

By the comments recorded by His followers, it is apparent that 'Abdu'l-Bahá had expressed His wish to visit India. However, the outbreak of the Great War that He had anticipated so many times in His public addresses in Europe and North America made this wish impossible. Instead, there lay ahead years in which renewed dangers threatened the life of 'Abdu'l-Bahá.

In the interim between the return of the Master to the Holy Land and the war there were some months of relative tranquility in which the pilgrimages of eastern and western Bahá'ís were resumed and in which travelers would still be able to call on Him. Simultaneously, some western journals continued to pay attention to the movements of the Master.

As early as 14 January 1914 *The Christian Commonwealth* wrote a note about the arrival of 'Abdu'l-Bahá in Haifa:

> Abdul Baha Abbas has returned to Akka. His daughter writes to an English friend that he is very happy to be home again with his family and friends. He has been so extremely busy seeing people and attending to his vast correspondence that he has scarcely had a moment's rest since his return. The poor of Akka are overjoyed to have the 'Master' in their midst again.[1]

Among the western visitors in Haifa was the writer Maude M. Holbach. She had visited Palestine in 1912 when 'Abdu'l-Bahá was in America and gathered information about Him 'from an Englishman living in Palestine and knowing him personally' which she later included in her book *Bible Ways in Bible Lands* (1912).[2] Months later she met 'Abdu'l-Bahá personally in New York and later in Europe, eventually becoming a Bahá'í. In Paris she requested permission from 'Abdu'l-Bahá to visit Him in the Holy Land to gather information for a book she was planning to write on the Bahá'í Faith.[3] The permission was given and she and her husband spent the winter of 1914–15 in Haifa. The interesting account of how she encountered the Master was published in a lengthy article about the Bahá'í Faith written in Haifa and appearing in the prestigious monthly magazine *The Nineteenth Century and After*:[4]

> It was at the conclusion of his American tour that it was my privilege and happiness to meet Abdul Baha. Nearly three years ago, when visiting Haifa and Acre to study the ground of the Crusades, I first heard of the Oriental teacher – and turned a deaf ear! For the time that I should recognise his greatness was not yet! An English resident of Haifa at that period spoke of him as a modern Elijah who had founded a second School of the Prophets on Mount Carmel. Someone else in Jerusalem told me that I should write about the Bahai Movement if I wanted a new subject, but 'I went my unremembering way', smiling with English superiority at the statement that Americans were coming to sit at the feet of the new prophet! A year later at Oxford I found, when reading in the Bodleian Library, a book which opened my eyes to the beauty of the Bahai teaching, but much had happened in the year – some study of comparative religions, and particularly of Christian Science, with its message, 'Man is not material, he is spiritual,' and of the power of universal love to heal both mind and body, had prepared me for it.
>
> A few months later, in a London drawing-room, I found a portrait of Abdul Baha and recognised it immediately, though I had never seen any portrait of him, by the intuition that comes to some of us in certain crises of life. My hostess [Lady Blomfield], who had been the first to welcome 'the Master' to England, coming into the room immediately afterwards, I eagerly questioned her, and learned that I was standing in the first room Abdul Baha had entered on

reaching England, and in the house that had been his English home.

In the following October (1912) I went, consequently upon the outbreak of the Balkan War, on a hastily organised lecturing tour to America, entirely ignorant that Abdul Baha was still in the United States, for a letter inquiring as to his movements had been lost, and in a rush of engagements and preparations I had not given the matter any more thought. Again the hand of Fate led me. By a remarkable coincidence, within a few days of landing I learned that Abdul Baha was in New York and would leave very shortly for England, and that a farewell banquet to him, given by the Bahais of America, who had come from far and near, was even then taking place. This time nothing, I resolved, should prevent me meeting the great man of whom I had heard so much. An exchange of telephone messages with the Great Northern Hotel, where the banquet was taking place, a hasty toilet, a rush through the brilliantly lit streets of New York at a taxi's topmost speed, and I entered a banqueting room where three to four hundred guests were already seated, and saw beyond the long table an upper table at which a venerable figure in Oriental robes was standing, surrounded by a group of more Orientals (among whom I afterwards found was the Persian Charge d'Affaires from Washington), and addressing the guests in a strange tongue which was translated sentence by sentence into poetic English. I can remember nothing of what he said except that this was a feast differing from all other feasts because it was a feast of love – and divine! Room was made for me, the stranger and late-comer, with true Bahai courtesy, at one of the principal tables, where I could have the best view of the guest of the evening. Later Abdul Baha walked slowly round the banqueting-hall followed by his interpreter, stopping from time to time to give a short address and laying his hands in blessing on the head of every guest. Probably I was the only one present who was not a Bahai, and I am well aware I displayed my ignorance of the movement in my conversation, for a New York business man who was my table neighbour seemed surprised by my remarks, while I was vastly impressed by his simple downright 'straight talk' (to use an Americanism) of the practical value of Bahai principles in business life, in promoting harmony with his workmen of various nationalities, because he now regarded them all as brothers instead of, as formerly, Greeks, Armenians, and 'niggers'.

Wonderful days followed, in which I had the privilege of conversing alone (through an interpreter who somehow effaced himself completely, and seemed but a living mouthpiece) with the unique personage who impressed those who came within his influence more and more deeply as they became more imbued with his spirit, as well as of being present at his interviews with men and women of various attainments and mental stature, to each of whom he suited himself and by all of whom he was evidently regarded with the deepest veneration. The most interesting of the interviews at which I was privileged to be present were, I think, that which took place when the Secretary of the New York Peace Society [William H. Short] called to bid him 'Good-bye' and discussed the International Peace Question; and a private interview to which I accompanied the wife of a diplomat, an American who had lived much in the East and heard of the Persian prophet through her great friend, a high Turkish official, Prince Oslan, having come under the spell of his spiritual personality and being changed, to use her own words, 'from a brilliant worldling to a spiritually minded man'.

Abdul Baha does not preach – he prefers to teach. Although at the request of the Theosophical and other Societies he addressed some large public meetings, his usual 'talks' are much more informal. It was his custom in America to receive callers from 9 o'clock till noon, and during these hours his ante-room was always thronged with those who desired to meet or consult him, waiting for their turn; and then to come into the general reception room, shake hands with all present, and give a short address of general interest. I have often felt that it is not so much his words as his spirit which carry conviction, and this spirit is reflected among his followers to such a degree that to find oneself at a Bahai assembly, whether in New York or Chicago, London or Paris or Stuttgart (the centre of the movement in Germany), is everywhere to find oneself among friends animated by a real spirit of mutual help and brotherhood . . .

It has been erroneously stated by some ill-informed or ill-disposed people that the object of Abdul Baha's journey to America was to obtain money from the 'friends' there (the term used by the Quakers has been very fittingly adopted by the Bahais, with whom they have many points of similarity); so far from true is this that Abdul Baha returned the 30,000 dollars collected and sent as a voluntary offering of love for the expenses of his tour, with a message that it should be used for the poor of America, and everywhere he went he gave liberally to charitable institutions, besides privately relieving individual cases of want.

His departure from New York was a remarkable sight, for Bahais had come to that city from far and near, some even from California, to bid him farewell, and when the great modern liner left her moorings the pier was black with people whose eyes were centred on the patriarchal figure with the long grey beard and snowy turban, who looked the embodiment of the Old Testament prophets and presented so remarkable a contrast to his modern surroundings. Few among the onlookers were unmoved, many women were openly weeping, and I saw men whose eyes were dim, while those of Abdul Baha's Persian followers who were left behind were unrestrained in their grief!

'Isn't it sad he is going?' said someone as the great ship slowly moved out to sea. 'Ah! but how glad for those he is going to!' was the reply from one who knew how eagerly people were waiting to welcome Abdul Baha in England and Scotland, as well as in Paris.[5]

Of her meeting with 'Abdu'l-Bahá in Paris, Holbach wrote:

It was my privilege to be in Paris on the 23rd of May last year and to visit and congratulate Abdul Baha very early in the morning, when he and his entourage were drinking their Persian tea after the morning prayer at sunrise, and before the long stream of callers of all nations arrived to do him homage. Well do I remember that May morning – the peace of its early hours, the cordiality of the Master's welcome, the spirituality of the atmosphere. I saw him again later in the day; his rooms were filled with the floral offerings of his friends from Orient and Occident; Persian officials rubbed shoulders with distinguished Frenchmen, Christians with Jews and Mohammedans. America was largely represented . . .[6]

The article then continued summarizing 'Abdu'l-Bahá's travels in Europe and also reproduced Vambéry's letter to 'Abdu'l-Bahá, of which Holbach stated that 'it was my privilege to see the original and hear Abdul Baha read it aloud'.[7]

While in Haifa Holbach wrote several articles on 'Abdu'l-Bahá for *The Christian Commonwealth* reporting some of His movements and offering important historical data for that period. After her return to Europe, the journal continued publishing information about the Master supplied by other correspondents, especially Ahmad Sohrab.

Holbach's first letter appeared on 21 January and gave some details about 'Abdu'l-Bahá's arrival in the Holy Land:

> Those who were privileged to meet the Bahai Teacher during his visits to Europe and America will be interested to know that this venerable man, whose long journeyings in the Western World were of such consummate interest to those who had watched the movement from the time that he was a political prisoner in the Turkish penal settlement of Acre, has, after nearly two and a half years of absence, returned to his home on Mount Carmel, where he was eagerly awaited, not only by his own family and the Bahai communities of Haifa and Acre, but by over 80 pilgrims from Persia, many of whom have come hither at the cost of years of self-denial to await the return of their revered leader to the Holy Land. The talked-of journey to India is for a time indefinitely postponed, for Abdul Baha's health has suffered from his strenuous life in the Western World and he is not equal at present to the strain of another extensive tour, though since he reached Haifa he has suffered less from insomnia than in Egypt. Mr. and Mrs. Gelzinger, who have done such splendid work in spreading the Bahai gospel of peace in America, sailed last month from Port Said for India, and Mrs. Stannard, who has gained much experience of dealing with Orientals in Cairo, has followed them there.[8]

On 8 January, Holbach sent a further letter to *The Christian Commonwealth* giving details about the last days in Haifa of a group of Persian pilgrims:

> I write this by a window that looks across an orange garden to the slopes of Mount Carmel, which rises almost abruptly beyond the red-roofed houses of the German colony. The 'Mount of God' is but a hill in comparison with the mighty Alps, yet how great is its fascination, how beautiful it appears now in the moonlight! From

time immemorial it has been the home of the prophets. The latest of them, Abdul Baha, dwells here to-day, and the simple Germans who left their native land to await the second coming of their Lord upon this mountain are his neighbours! In my ears is the sound of the sea, for the blue Mediterranean laps the shores of Carmel, and across the bay Acre gleams white in the moonlight. 'The greatest Prison' it was called when Baha'o'llah dwelt there, a prisoner in a penal city. But a blessing surely rests upon it now, for the sun seems ever to shine there when the sea and sky are grey. The soil upon which its houses are built has been many times soaked in blood. Christian and Saracen massacred one another there in turn. Many prisoners have languished there since Napoleon's pride was humbled by his failure to take 'the petty town' which yet he designated 'the key to the East'.

Since his return from Europe five weeks ago Abdul Baha has more than once visited Acre and remained some time, visiting old friends who knew him in the days of his imprisonment. During one of his visits there he sent for the American Bahais who are making a pilgrimage to the Holy Land, that with him they might visit the tomb of Baha'o'llah. Another day the Persian pilgrims were sent for, of whom a contingent have now returned to their native land. They left yesterday, on their long journey to Hamadan, the old capital of Persia, proceeding first by train to Damascus, thence to Aleppo, and from there by carriage and on horseback, the journey occupying three weeks. All those who have left are Jews!

It was my privilege to be present at two farewell gatherings given in their honour, which I shall never forget. At the first the men assembled at the Tomb of the Bab which occupies a commanding position on the slope of Mount Carmel, and is a striking object from my window soon after dawn, when the rays of the rising sun illumine it. The tomb is surrounded by a garden on a terrace on the mountain side, and the building has several chambers. In the largest of these about fifty to sixty Bahais were assembled on the occasion to which I refer – Jews, Zoroastrians, Mohammedans, and Christians – to listen to an address by Abdul Baha. While the Master was speaking tea was served by the giver of the feast. Then all proceeded to an inner chamber, which in turn led to the tomb proper, and here the Tablets were chanted by one of the pilgrims, a very learned Mullah and great orator. The reverence of the Oriental Bahais for their leader must be witnessed to be understood. When Abdul Baha came down the mountain side clad in his flowing robe and white turban, and followed by his disciples from far and near, the scene was truly Biblical.

Next day the women pilgrims met at the home of Rouhah Khanoum (one of Abdul Baha's daughters, who has lately returned from Europe and is known personally to many who are interested in the movement in London and Paris), and bid a touching 'Good-bye' to their fellow-believers.

'We are so glad to know you, and we are going back to tell our sisters in Persia about you,' one said to me. How much those few words meant, for every pilgrim who comes here, whether man or woman, represents numbers of Bahais in his or her native land. A small Pilgrims' Home for Women, such as already exists for men (thanks to the generosity of Mirza Jaffir Shirazi, a Russian Bahai from Turkestan), is very greatly needed. At present the twenty to thirty women pilgrims have been accommodated in Abdul Baha's own household. The Men's Pilgrims' House occupies a beautiful site adjoining the tomb of the Bab on Mount Carmel. Here Bahais from all parts of the Orient meet and spend memorable days within sight of the home of their beloved leader, and go thence bearing his message of the unity of the human race all over the Eastern world.

It will interest all readers of *The Christian Commonwealth* to know in what esteem this paper is held by the Oriental Bahais and how carefully they have preserved the 'Bahai' edition of March 27, 1912. One is shown by its proud possessor, Aga Mohammed Hassan, each sheet framed and the whole preserved for future generations in a box of most costly wood.

I will close with Abdul Baha's Message to the pilgrims at the Tomb of Baha'o'llah on Christmas Day, which is likewise his message to the Bahai world: –

'It is part of the Divine Wisdom that I should keep silent for a time! All that was required of me, that is to raise my voice in the churches, synagogues, conventions, and meetings, calling the attention of the people to the Kingdom of God and the appearance of Baha'o'llah, praise be to God through the confirmation of the Blessed Perfection is accomplished. Now it is the turn of the believers of God. Now I am ever expecting to hear the sweet voice of the friends raised and the watchword, Ye Baha el Abha, reaching to the ear of the heart and spirit. Those souls who have become subservient to the will of God as manifested in the life and teachings of Baha'o'llah must know of a certainty that they attract unto themselves heavenly confirmation and assistance. Now, existence upon the Sacred Threshold is the magnet whereby aid is attracted. The more the believers humble themselves at the Divine Threshold (the Bahai expression for the throne of God), the more powerful and universal will be the descent of the Holy Spirit of New Dedication upon them. The more they strive to teach souls the greater will be their power of sanctification and attraction.

'To-day divine powers reinforce the souls who are spreading the cause of God. Whoever walks upon this highway is confirmed; those who appear now dried plants will be changed into fruitful trees. God's blessing will rest upon all who enlist in the service. They are the flowers of the garden of Abha – they must breathe forth their fragrance! . . . They are the trees planted by the sacred hand of Baha'o'llah in the orchard of the Kingdom. He hath watered you with the rivers of his knowledge and hath protected you from winds and storms.

'I hope that each one of you may become a tree laden with delicious fruits for the healing of the nations!'[9]

A letter dated 19 January reported that correspondence had been received in the Holy Land giving details about the plans for the building of the Bahá'í House of Worship in Chicago and about the progress of the Bahá'í Faith in Persia.[10] Six days later Holbach reported the passing of Mírzá Abu'l-Faḍl-i-Gulpáygání and quoted 'Abdu'l-Bahá saying that 'He had my perfect confidence. When enemies attacked the cause I referred them to him.'[11]

On 7 February a further letter told of pilgrims coming from Russia and Persia.[12] On 25 March the journal published a letter about the House of Worship in Ishqabad. Describing the interreligious character of its dedication, the author quoted 'Abdu'l-Bahá as saying, 'Praise be to God that Baha'o'llah has broken the barriers of religious prejudice. He has commanded all the Bahais to consort with those of other religions and nationality with the utmost love and kindness and fellowship. They are all the fruits of one tree and the leaves of one branch . . . We must make religion the cause of love and affiliation, and not the means of controversy and strife. Praise be to God that we are all the children of the Kingdom.'[13] The same issue carried an account of the celebration of the feast of Naw-Rúz in London.[14] 'Abdu'l-Bahá had sent a Tablet to the Bahá'ís of London which was read at this meeting and published in *The International Psychic Gazette* (London):

> ABDUL BAHA'S TABLET ADDRESSED TO THE BAHAIS IN LONDON, WHO HAD SENT HIM A NEW YEAR'S GREETING ON MAR. 21, 1914.
> Through Mirza Yuhanna Dawud, London, to the Friends of God, and the Maidservants of the Merciful One. He is God!
>
> O shining Bahais! Your New Year's greeting brought infinite joy and fragrance, and became the cause of our daily rejoicing and gladness. Thanks be to God! that in that city which is often dark because of cloud, mist, and smoke, such bright candles (as you) are glowing, whose emanating light is God's guidance, and whose influencing warmth is as the burning Fire of the Love of God. Thus your social gathering on the Great Feast is like unto a Mother who will in future beget many Heavenly Feasts, so that all eyes may be amazed as to what effulgence the true Sun of the East has shed on the West. How it has changed the Occidentals into Orientals, and illumined the Western Horizon with the Luminary of the East! Then in thanksgiving for this great gift, favour and grace, rejoice ye and be exceeding glad, and engage ye in praising and sanctifying the Lord of Hosts.
>
> Hearken to the song of the Highest Concourse, and by the melody of Abha's Kingdom, lift ye up the cry of Ya Baha'ul-Abha! So that Abdul Baha and all the Eastern Bahais may give themselves to praise of the Loving Lord, and cry aloud: Most Pure and Holy is the Lord, Who has changed the West into the East with lights of Guidance! Upon ye all be the Glory of the Most Glorious One![15]

Among the visitors who called on 'Abdu'l-Bahá in this period was Howard Sweetser Bliss (1860–1920), the president of the American College in Beirut. A letter dated 28 February reported some of the words of the Master during the meeting with the missionary:

> The much-respected president of the American College at Beirut

has just been on a visit in Haifa, and a very interesting conversation took place when he called upon Abdul Baha. The subject was liberalism in religious education, with special reference to members of different religions praying in each other's places of worship.

'The American College at Beirut,' said Abdul Baha, 'is carrying on a sacred mission of enlightenment, and every lover of real culture and civilisation must wish it great success. Years ago, when the college was in its infancy, some bigoted Mohammedans complained bitterly of the religious education insisted on and especially that students were asked to attend the Sunday services in the church.

'I told these grumblers that their views were based upon ignorant prejudice, as no harm could be done to the Mohammedan students by attending a Christian church or learning about the Christian religion, but, on the other hand, it would benefit them to be informed as to the contents of the Old and New Testament. I said: A church is a house of prayer! Let them enter therein and worship God! What wrong is there in this? Students attending the services in a church glorify God. I have no doubt that much good will be accomplished and misunderstandings removed if Mussulmans attend Christian churches with reverence in their hearts and sincerity in their souls, and likewise Christians may go to the Mohammedan mosques and magnify the Creator of the Universe. Is it not written in the Holy Scriptures, "My house shall be called of all nations the house of prayer?" All these houses of different names – church, mosque, synagogue, pagoda, temple – are no other than houses of prayer. What is there in a name? Man must attach his heart to God and not to a building. He must love to hear the name of God, no matter from what lips. When I was in Tiberias my house was near the synagogue. When the Jews gathered there, at midnight and sang 'Hallelujah' I would get up and listen to them and in my heart pray with them. When a man's life is a life of eternal quest after God he will worship him no matter where he may be. I pray to God in the mosque, in the church, or the synagogue in the same spirit. In all of them I am in his presence.'[16]

The Rev. A. Briggs, an American minister, also visited 'Abdu'l-Bahá on those dates. The account of the meeting, inserted in a letter explaining the Bahá'í position on Christianity, was published on 8 April:

An American minister who has been on a tour round the world inspecting the missions, and is visiting Palestine on his homeward way, called on Abdul Baha recently and asked him, apropos of the Bahai teaching on the fundamental oneness of religions, 'How long will it be before the members of the different religious communities accept this teaching?' 'I hope,' said Abdul Baha, 'it may be in this twentieth century.' The minister further asked: 'Which of the greatest religions of the world is nearest to the ideal of universal brotherhood?' and was told, 'There are prepared souls in every religion. To-day God is working in all the churches, instructing many souls in celestial brotherhood. These souls are related by invisible and spiritual ties, and are being ripened by the Holy Spirit.'[17]

Further information about this meeting was published on 17 June.[18]

On 15 April, *The Christian Commonwealth* published more news about 'Abdu'l-Bahá, summarizing various letters received from Haifa:

A delightful picture of Abdul Baha is impressed on the mind by the letters that pass regularly from a Bahai at Haifa, Palestine, to the 'believers' in the United States. Abdul Baha is now very well, and very happy at being among those who love him so devotedly. The district round Mount Carmel is beautiful at all times, and in the early months of the year doubly glorious on account of the flowers. The letters speak of the almond trees aglow with white and pink blossom, of the roses, and of the sunshine. Abdul Baha walks much in his garden, and he delights to receive the pilgrims there. 'All morning,' says one of the letters, '"the Beloved" was walking in the garden with the Persian Consul from Acca. Now and then, as a number of the pilgrims passed by the door, he would ask them to come in. The sun was brightly shining on the roses, hyacinths, carnations, violets, and anemones. Chairs were brought out and "the Beloved" sat among the rose-beds. He was very beautiful and radiant, diffusing all around the tender fragrances of the Spirit.' Children the great teacher loves as well as flowers, and when they visit him he sends for 'bon-bons' and they sit upon his knee. The days are spent in writing letters (tablets they are called) to the Bahais in different parts of the world, and in receiving and teaching visitors and pilgrims who flock to Haifa in large numbers.

Many have come long distances. The last letter to hand tells how an old believer, Mohammed, from Kerman, had just arrived. He had been four months on the way. 'He was weeping like a child when his feet touched the ground of the garden of "the Beloved".' Frequent visits are paid to the tomb of Baha'o'llah, the founder of Bahaism, when Abdul Baha himself conducts the service ('recites the visiting tablet'). He takes his meals with one or two guests only, sitting on the floor, at a round table, raised about a foot from the ground. The letters abound with stories of his charity. The teaching of Baha'o'llah, he tells his followers, is that we must show our affection to all people. We must not look at their evil deeds; we must not consider their race, their religion, or their nationality. We must do our utmost to help everyone.[19]

Further information was published on 22 April:

Mirza Mahoud, one of the Bahais attached to the Bahai settlement at Haifa, is writing in Persian an account of Abdul Baha's visit to the Occident. He has completed the first volume, covering the period spent in America, and handed it to his master for his perusal. The next volume will deal with the European tour. Other volumes are contemplated, containing Abdul Baha's addresses and translations of many newspaper articles.

A Roman Catholic priest in Acca has been opposing the Bahai cause and calumniating those who stand for it. Undeterred by this enmity, Abdul Baha contributed a sum of money to the Roman Catholic institution in that place. When someone near him remonstrated, he replied, 'We are commanded by Baha'o'llah to assist all communities, without the exclusion of any. We do not consider their deeds; we never lose sight of the fact that men are all the children of God, and their wants must be relieved without the distinction of race or religion.'

Abdul Baha's relations with the high dignitaries resident in Haifa representative of other religions are most friendly. On a recent visit to Dr. Coles, head of the English Hospital, a missionary institution, Dr. Coles related how during Abdul Baha's absence in America he had received many inquiries about him from strangers who knew that he had lived in Syria for many years. 'You know well what kind of answers I wrote,' said Dr. Coles. 'I know, I know,' replied "the Beloved", 'you would have written naught else but the truth. During my journeys in the West I wished for your presence not seldom, for many evil reports were put in circulation by my enemies there.'[20]

A letter by Holbach on Indian Bahá'í pilgrims arriving in Haifa was published on 29 April, in which she also described 'Abdu'l-Bahá:

> Abdul Baha is now visiting Acre and living in the house of Baha'o'llah, close to the prison where he was brought as a child with his saintly father, and the seventy Persian exiles who were banished with their leader to the Turkish penal settlement forty-six years ago.
>
> It is wonderful to see the venerable figure of the revered Bahai leader passing through the narrow streets of this ancient town, where he lived for forty years as a political prisoner, and to note the deep respect with which he is saluted by the Turkish officials and the officers of the garrison from the Governor downwards, who visit him constantly and listen with the deepest attention to his words. 'The master' does not teach in Syria as he did in the West, but he goes about doing good, and Mohammedans and Christians alike share his benefactions. From sunrise often till midnight he works, in spite of broken health, never sparing himself if there is a wrong to be righted or a suffering to be relieved. To Christians who regard Abdul Baha with impartial and sympathetic eyes, this wonderful selfless life cannot fail to recall that life whose tragic termination on Calvary the whole Christian world recalls to-day.[21]

A letter published on 13 May reported that news had been received in Haifa of the martyrdom of Bahá'ís in Persia.[22] An article appeared on 27 May reporting that 'Abdu'l-Bahá's health has much improved since his return to Syria, and he can now dispatch without physical weariness the ever-increasing volume of his correspondence', and added that He 'has two small grandsons, Moneeh Effendi and Hossein Effendi, between six and eight years old. They frequently accompany him on his drives.'[23]

A letter dated 18 May reported that 'Abdul Baha is now sojourning near Tiberias on the Lake of Galilee and taking the hot baths that have been famous since the time of the Romans. He is also taking a much-needed rest at this quiet spot, and to ensure that his correspondence for the present is not forwarded.'[24]

Among the pilgrims who visited 'Abdu'l-Bahá in Haifa were two Persian Bahá'ís who had been traveling through India teaching the Bahá'í Faith and who brought with them to the Holy Land a petition from the Indian Bahá'ís inviting the Master to visit them. The following report appearing on 24 June mentions their visit:

> Abdul Baha was in the act of dictating tablets for the Persian believers when Mr. Shirazi and Mr. Vakil were announced. The former was dressed in a long, flowing cashmere shawl coat, and looked very picturesque. Abdul Baha, looking up from a letter which he held in his hand, beamed at him a heavenly smile and welcome. 'I have been looking forward to this meeting,' he said. 'I longed always for thy visit. Praise be to God that this is realised. Do not think that because I am not writing to everyone I do not know their material and spiritual conditions. I know. Truly I say, thou art sincere and steadfast in the cause. The trip that thou didst make through India was for the sake of the cause of God. Rest thou assured that the reward of that journey will be great.'
>
> Mr. Shirazi and Mr. Vakil, as well as a petition they brought with them, expressed the hope that Abdul Baha would visit India. 'India must become prepared,' he said. 'A centre of magnetic power must be created there in order to attract me. If such a centre of attraction comes into being, I might come.'[25]

A further article published on 15 July described the way the Master mediated in a religious dispute between two Muslims:

> The controversies that are going on in our Western world with regard to religion have their parallels in the Eastern world, and especially in Mohammedanism. For example, there are two sects in the Mohammedan world, the one holding that the words of the Koran are 'uncreated and eternal', the other one believing that the words are 'created and finite'. Between these two contradictory schools of thought various battles are waged, and many books are written upon this subject. The Sheiks, representing these schools and denominations, come to Abdul Baha to argue with and question him and he

has to answer them in detail; otherwise they would go away and spread the report that he had been unable to answer them. His task is a very difficult one, for as a letter to hand from Haifa says, 'the answer must be given in such a manner as to establish a conciliation between these two schools holding such extreme views, and at the same time reality must be expressed.'

At a recent conversation with the Sheiks, which lasted from eight in the morning till six in the evening, Abdul Baha met this particular controversy, which is only our own familiar controversy with regard to the nature of the inspiration of the Bible, in this way. By quoting to the Sheiks verses from the Koran he established the fact that there are three kinds of words: Finite words, having no permanent effect in shaping the destiny of mankind, or reforming the people; creational words, such as the laws of the prophets, which are changed from dispensation to dispensation according to the exigencies of the time; and, lastly, spiritual words, the ethical and moral teachings of the manifestations of God. These are unchangeable, because the spirit behind these words is the Spirit of God, and therefore eternal. Therefore, said Abdul Baha, when one school states that the words of God are 'uncreated and eternal' they are right, because they mean the spiritual words, and when the other school asserts that the words of God are 'created and finite' they are right; they are thinking of the 'finite words' and the 'creational words', which change in value and meaning.[26]

On 22 July *The Christian Commonwealth* carried a picture sent by Holbach of 'Abdu'l-Bahá surrounded by a group of Eastern pilgrims in front of the Mansion of Bahjí.[27] The same issue carried another story about pilgrims visiting the Master:

> An incident rich in meaning occurred the other day when the pilgrims were visiting Abdul Baha at Acca. There were about forty present, sitting on the floor, and one of the Zoroastrian believers approached his master, and according to the Eastern custom, was about to kiss his feet. Abdul Baha restrained him and explained his reason to his disciples in the talk that followed. Kissing the hands, the feet, kneeling and bowing are strictly forbidden in the Bahai Dispensation, he said. These are archaic customs of the religious

East, and the nucleus of the New Humanity must throw away these swaddling clothes. The teachers of religions have awed and forced the simple, innocent people into these spurious customs, but these outward manners are injurious to the nobility and majestic grandeur of the soul. They pollute the minds, degrade the loftiness of characters, and debase the beauty of human nature. Hearts must be united, souls affiliated with each other, all mankind must turn their faces to spiritual susceptibilities and concentrate upon the facts of consciousness. The Mohammedan Sheiks and Ulemas, while walking in the streets, always had their hands out of the sleeves of their Abas, ready to be kissed by the crowd. How harmful this is! The deed which is conducive to humility, meekness, submissiveness is acceptable to God, but the action which in the least degree connotes the existence of pride, self projection, is human, and not accepted by the Lord of mankind.[28]

On 30 September *The Christian Commonwealth* published comments attributed to 'Abdu'l-Bahá regarding an article published in that journal months before:

A letter from Palestine tells us that Abdul Baha has been much interested in the article 'The Challenge to the Ministry', which appeared in *The Christian Commonwealth* of May 13. It was read aloud to him as he walked along the shore of the Sea of Galilee and as he continued his walk he commented on it thus: 'These are the harbingers of the coming of the spiritual spring-time; the fore-shadowing of the appearance of the Kingdom of God; the certain promises for the dawn of the Sun of Reality and the struggling voices that are ushering in the era of human and celestial brotherhood. Discarding all the accumulated dogmas and pagan rituals of the last ages, we must return to the fountain head of the teachings of Christ. This is the only way. A whole-hearted surrender of our will to the will of God, a degree of self-sacrifice as manifested in the lives of the saints and the martyrs, a spiritual enthusiasm and attraction capable of disregarding all the world's hardships and persecutions, a complete self-surrender to the influx of the Holy Spirit, and a holy dedication of one's entire forces to the service of humanity will establish the Kingdom of God in the hearts of all men.'[29]

On 30 June, Hans Springer, a young Esperantist from Stuttgart who was touring the world, visited 'Abdu'l-Bahá in Haifa. A short account of this meeting was also published in *The Christian Commonwealth* on 7 October.[30] A few weeks afterwards the following letter, probably from Ahmad Sohrab, about the daily correspondence of the Master was published:

> Hundreds of letters come to Abdul Baha from all parts of the world, especially from Europe and America, writes a correspondent in Haifa. In many cases they contain the most natural and spontaneous outpourings of the heart; throbbing cries for more spiritual light and wisdom, and the need of the guidance of the Holy Spirit. Touching the human plane, the range of personal wishes and individual aspirations is as infinite as the mind of man is able to conceive. Here is a letter from an expectant mother; she asks for a name for her unborn child. Another person desires to move from her present apartment, and she would like to know if Abdul Baha approves. A young man has quarrelled with his sweetheart, and he wonders if Abdul Baha's spiritual power is strong enough to bring about the much-longed-for reconciliation. Unexpected events have estranged a man from his wife, and false pride has separated them; he is repining in loneliness; will not the Beloved bring back into their lives the sweet harmony of the first few months of their ideal courtship and the first few years of their blissful married life? A man has invented a trans-Atlantic airship; will not Abdul Baha inspire the heart of a capitalist to assist him financially in the construction of this aircraft? Amongst other interesting things are the children's letters, so full of affectionate simplicity, sweetness, directness, and beautiful trust. I have in my hand a lovely letter written to Abdul Baha by a ten-year-old girl, Kathleen Hillis, from Los Angeles. Abdul Baha laughed over it and dictated a tablet for her this afternoon. On the envelope of Miss 'Kathleen's' letter the following line was written, probably by her mother, 'From a beautiful white rosebud of California to the full-blown White Rose of Persia'.[31]

* * *

The North American Bahá'ís Mason Remey and George Latimer made a brief visit to Haifa in October 1914. Notes by Latimer of 'Abdu'l-Bahá's interpretation of one of Bahá'u'lláh's Hidden Words were published on 6 January 1915 in *The Christian Commonwealth*:

> An American pilgrim, Mr. Latimer, who recently visited Abdul Baha, asked him the interpretation of a verse of 'The Hidden Words', which, he said, was being quoted by a certain sect in America to prove that they are 'Manifestations of God'. The verse and Abdul Baha's interpretation are interesting in relation to recent European controversies as to Immanence and Transcendence. The English rendering of the Arabic verse is: 'Oh Son of Spirit! I have created thee rich: Why dost thou make thyself poor? Noble have I made thee: Why dost thou degrade thyself? From the clay of Love I have kneaded thee: Why seekest thou another? Turn thy sight unto thyself, that thou mayest find me standing within thee, Powerful, Mighty and Supreme.' Abdul Baha explained the verse in this way. There are two kinds of 'standing within'. The first is like the 'standing' or containing of water in an earthen bowl. This is not true as applied to the human relation with God. The essence of' God is not a body like water to be contained within the body of an earthen bowl – man. There is another 'standing within', that of the sun in a clean mirror. The verse should be interpreted from that standpoint. 'Purify thy heart that it may become like a transparent mirror. Then thou shall find me standing, within thee, Powerful, Mighty. Supreme.' This, Abdul Baha said, was the right interpretation, because it gave to God transcendence of station, while on the other hand, the mirror having been polished, reflects the rays of the sun.[32]

Three Tablets of 'Abdu'l-Bahá

As well as reporting 'Abdu'l-Bahá's movements and circumstances in Haifa, the British press published some of His correspondence.

On 31 December 1913, for instance, exactly one year after 'Abdu'l-Bahá's talk at Oxford University (see chapter 26), *The Christian Commonwealth* published portions of a Tablet addressed to Thomas K. Cheyne, who had been Abdu'l-Bahá's host on that occasion, and who was a Bahá'í and a member of the editorial board of *The Christian Commonwealth*:

Dr. T. K. Cheyne, Oxford, has received from Abdul Baha a letter, from which we are permitted to quote the following: – 'O thou, my spiritual philosopher! Thy letter was received. In reality its contents were eloquent, for it was an evidence of thy literary fairness and of thy investigation of Reality . . . There were many Doctors amongst the Jews, but they were all earthly, but St. Paul became heavenly because he could fly upwards. In his own time no one duly recognised him; nay, rather, he spent his days amidst difficulties and contempt. Afterwards it became known that he was not an earthly bird, he was a Celestial one; he was not a natural philosopher but a divine philosopher. It is likewise my hope that in the future the East and the West may become conscious that thou wert a divine philosopher and a herald to the Kingdom . . . Thy respected wife in reality deserves the utmost consideration . . . Praise be to God that she is also thy co-worker and co-partner in the perfection of the Kingdom.[33]

On October 1910 the General Convention of the Protestant Episcopal Church approved the project of launching world ecumenical conferences for Christian churches. The idea soon received the support of religious leaders of different Christian denominations and plans were made to convene the first of these events. However, owing to the war and the slowness of the preparations, the first of these conferences was not held until 1927. In the meantime, the organizers of the conference met regularly and issued publications related to the preparations. From time to time the press would also publish news about these arrangements. On 1 February 1914 'Abdu'l-Bahá sent a Tablet to the editor of *The Christian Commonwealth* regarding this Christian conference. He suggested that a congress for all religions of the world should be arranged at which differences and disunity could be resolved:

> I have read in *The Christian Commonwealth* that there is a proposal to hold a World's Conference of Faith and Order, at which representative delegates of all Christian denominations will be present. This news gave me great joy and satisfaction, inasmuch as every movement which tends to bring about even the partial unity of the world of humanity is praiseworthy and commendable. However, if it were possible to bring about the realisation of a World Conference

of Religions it would yield infinitely greater results to the human race. For every human movement is derived from specific policies and conventions; on the other hand, every divine movement is an effulgence of the Holy Spirit of God. Consequently, it will be more profitable if the scholars and thinkers, the wise men of to-day and the philosophers undertake the organisation of a Universal Congress of the Religions of the World. This is the greatest, most urgent and pressing need of the day. For this period is the period of light, this cycle is the cycle of scientific discovery; this time is the time of reality. Through the wise deliberations of the members of such an august assembly the religions of the world might abandon all doctrines which are mere dogma and tradition and retain only that which is absolute and fundamental. In this manner they shall discover that the object of all the religions of the past has been none other than the inculcation of reality and absolute reality is never susceptible of multiplication or division. The Middle Ages were the ages of obscurity, those who sought to investigate truth groped in the dark, doubted and hesitated to go forward; the nations held blindly to tradition! Praise be to God, that in this cycle the great Sun of Reality has dawned, flooding the horizon of the world with its radiant light! Consequently it is most necessary to bring about such a representative assembly, that they may strive with might and main to lay the foundations of the oneness of the world of humanity, to relinquish tradition and dogma, and promulgate the fundamental principles and cardinal doctrines of the great religions of the world.

The cardinal principle of the religion of God is love. Divine love will bring about the promulgation of divine order. Divine order is no other than the consolidation of all the mighty, beneficial forces of the world of humanity – that is, justice, affiliation, brotherhood, the fostering of culture, the reconciliation of religion with science, true philanthropy, universal peace and conciliation, and the illumination of the human race. All the members of the world of humanity are the sheep of God. He is the Universal Shepherd; he is kind and compassionate to every one of his flock. This is the divine order, unquestionably the divine order is more comprehensive and universal than that of man!

I am exceedingly pleased with the broad policy initiated and maintained by *The Christian Commonwealth*, for that liberal organ is free from all prejudice, and the Editor thereof is a promoter of the ideals of the oneness of humanity.[34]

Six days after this Tablet was written, Holbach wrote to the same journal that 'News has just reached here from India that a World Congress of Religions is being arranged by the Theists to be held in India next year. It is a remarkable coincidence that the suggestion of the need and benefits that would accrue from such a congress were set forth in Abdul Baha's message to *The Christian Commonwealth* last week.'[35]

As seen in earlier chapters, as a result of 'Abdu'l-Bahá's visits to the West, various Unitarian ministers took the initiative to dedicate their Sunday sermons to presenting the Bahá'í religion to their parishes and even deciding to use their Sunday school classes for the study of its teachings. Among the British ministers who took this step was Rev. Christopher J. Street (1855–1931), also a Unitarian, who was in charge of the Upper Chapel in Sheffield and had close links with the Free Religious Association.

In early 1914 he received a Tablet from 'Abdu'l-Bahá praising his efforts and encouraging him to deepen his knowledge of the Bahá'í Faith. This Tablet was afterwards reproduced in a local journal:

> At the evening service at Upper Chapel, Sheffield, yesterday, the Rev. C. J. Street, who has several times preached on Bahaism and its succession of great teachers, read an interesting 'Tablet', which has just been sent to him by Abdul Baha, the prophet of a beautiful world-faith, who is now again in Haifa, in Syria, after his long and exhausting tour in Europe, America and Africa. Addressing the Rev. C. J. Street, M.A., LL.B., as 'thou respected heavenly doctor', the Bahai prophet says:
>
>> 'Praise be to God that the call of the kingdom reached thy ears, and thou didst become informed with the principles of his Holiness Baha-Allah. Unquestionably day by day thou wilt add to thy knowledge of this subject. If possible thou mayst ask from London or America the translations of some of the Tablets of his Holiness Baha-Allah.
>>
>> To-day all the inhabitants of the world are submerged in

the darkness of dogmas and religious, sectarian, racial and political prejudices; peradventure, God willing, thou mayst become a brilliant star, and cause the disappearance of these darkenesses from those parts; so that the Light of Divine Love may illumine those regions and the Flag of the Oneness of the World of Humanity be upraised. Upon thee be greeting and praise.

(Signed) ABDUL BAHA ABBAS'[36]

Interview with Archie Bell

Archie Bell (1877–1943), a regular correspondent for the *Plain Dealer* (Cleveland), traveled through the Holy Land in mid-1914 and met 'Abdu'l-Bahá in Tiberias on 9 June. He was accompanied by the photographer and later film producer Edward Manuel Newman (1870–1953). In the course of their travels they contributed a series of articles and pictures for the *Plain Dealer*. Their first reference to 'Abdu'l-Bahá was published on 11 August 1914:

> I went to Acre, chiefly because I thought I would find there a prisoner of Turkey whom I wished very much to see. Abbas Effendi, the Persian head of the Bahai movement, or the Babists and Babites, as they are called in America. Chance favoured me and I found him elsewhere, but in Acre I was informed that he had been released after a confinement of something like forty years, and being a free man he had immediately left Acre, which seems to be a city at the end of the world, an unhealthful city, owing to its position by a big marsh from which malarial odors constantly rise, and a city to which the former Sultan of Turkey, Abdul Hamid, condemned all his political suspects, religious leaders and the men of action whom he wanted to be watched day and night.[37]

Bell finally met the Master in Tiberias and was able to interview Him on two occasions. The account of the first of the interviews appeared on 18 August and included a picture by Newman showing 'Abdu'l-Bahá on the balcony of His residence in Tiberias, the Casa Nova Hospice, with Archie Bell:

ALONG HOLY BYPATHS – XXIX
By Archie Bell.

TIBERIAS, July 8. – It seemed a most fitting climax to my experiences in Palestine, for I was starting in two days for the great Arabian wilderness and merely lingered around the Sea of Galilee because it is a beautiful place, made doubly so by its associations with the life of Jesus Christ, who spent so much of his life there. Thus, if I would have imagined some splendid ending to this pilgrimage and tour I could not have wished for better than happened near Tiberias on the shores of the lake where Jesus taught and gave to his disciples their message which was to be carried to the corners of the earth.

For here I met another prophet, one who during his lifetime has millions of zealous followers, and one whom his followers believe has fully as much scriptural prophecy to fortify his claims to leadership among men as did the man of Nazareth. Like Jesus Christ he has been persecuted and has suffered on account of his preaching. Like Jesus Christ he has come to the Sea of Galilee and he walks up and down its holy shores, preaching and teaching his disciples, who follow him as he walks and talks. Already much myth and legend is springing up around him, for he is the holiest man of the East, despised by many, cursed by the fanatical followers of other religions, and loved by believers in him with a love that becomes devotion itself.

GREAT PERSONALITY.

One day on the sands of Galilee I met Abbas Effendi, as he is known in Palestine and Persia, or Abdul Baha, as he is better known in America. He is the recognized head of the Bahai movement, as he said he preferred to have his religion known, or the Babists and Babites as they are, popularly called. Abbas Effendi, a patriarch and prophet from Persia, is a person of tremendous magnetism. You 'feel' him when he approaches you. Irrespective of his religious teachings the wise men of the earth who have met him have considered him one of the wisest who lives. And he has met the distinguished men of all nations. They have visited him in his prison home at Acre, as they visited Tolstoy at his farm in Russia. Men like William J. Bryan have made it a part of their pilgrimage of Palestine to call upon him and pay their respects. Wise doctors from Europe have called upon him to discuss philosophy, as it is taught in the East, and they have found that he has absorbed all the philosophies of the European continent, knows practically all about all the religions of the world, and is able to discuss each with its leaders, while to everyone who meets him he speaks, not of the error of other men's ways, but graphically and poignantly explains to every man how his religion is but a part of that great universal religion which he himself preaches and believes is soon to cover the world.

A SKETCH PORTRAIT.

Without a doubt he is the most impressive person in appearance I have ever seen. He has long white hair, a long snowy beard, his face is of a dusty whiteness and he dresses in white robes and wears a white turban. When I first met him he was walking along alone, but he was closely followed by his secretary and interpreter and three or four of his Persian followers, who like himself are exiled from their native land. No doubt I stared at him, for he had a commanding presence. His carriage was majestic and I felt instinctively that he was a person of Importance.

A FRIENDLY GREETING.

But as I stared, he kindly saluted me and murmured a friendly greeting in Persian, which I did not understand. Instinctively, I raised my hat to him. He has a compelling personality which radiates something that commands respect and I wondered who he was.

THE DRAGOMAN'S SALUTE.

With me at the time was my dragoman, who seeing what I did, looked in the direction of the one we were passing and quickly, with oriental politeness, he held his hand to his forehead and remained stock still until the old gentleman had passed.

'That is Abbas Effendi,' he said to me, 'the prisoner from Acre. I wonder how he happens to be walking along the shores of the Sea of Galilee.'

'Abbas Effendi,' I repeated, 'the man for whom I inquired at Acre. I must speak to him.' But the dragoman was dumb and powerless, as the Persian language is not one of his accomplishments.

Then I addressed one of his followers in English, and as chance would have it, I spoke to his interpreter, a Persian gentleman who had been for ten years attached to the Persian legation at Washington. Certainly he would present me. There was no hesitation, as he quickly took me to the side of his master, bowed profoundly and introduced me. The old man held out his hand and touched mine. 'I am pleased,' he said, 'very pleased to meet one from far away America. I am very glad, when you have come to these foreign countries to learn and observe, that you may go back to your own country knowing more of the world than you could know if you remained in one country. I am glad that I have met you in this hallowed and beautiful place, the Sea of Galilee's shores. I trust that your visit here will be pleasant, and that you will continue your journey and return to your home in safety.'

There seemed to be finality to his words. It seemed that my 'interview', which I craved, was over, for the old man started along, after raising his hand to his forehead as a sign of farewell. So I pressed the interpreter to request another interview for me, at a more convenient time, perhaps, when I could talk to the wise man and learn something of his teachings.

'Abbas Effendi will be pleased if you will call upon him at his home up there at three o'clock this afternoon,' said the interpreter, as he pointed to a little white house near the lake, with an overhanging balcony that had a view over the whole extent of the sea.

Thus ended my first meeting. Fortunately for me there were three others. Together we walked slowly along the sands and together we sat on his little balcony near sunset and I heard of that great new religion which is to reconcile the whole world. He told me of his millions of followers in Persia (the English officials fifteen years ago estimated the number as between three and four millions in Persia alone) and he told me of the thousands who are flocking to his banner in India, but he seemed to me even more interested in his message to Europe and America. 'Particularly America,' he said, 'for there is the new country, one that is not weighed down by superstitions and prejudices which are so difficult to overcome. America is a receptive country, capable of seeing and hearing and believing.'

And while Abbas Effendi himself did not care to give any figures, because he said that there was no way of knowing the exact truth, his interpreter told me that they were of the opinion that there were about fifty thousand converts to the Bahai movement in America, their strongholds being in Chicago, Boston and Washington. At Chicago he had heard the Babists had purchased a large tract of land just outside of the city and would soon erect a church. In Europe many churches had been built and Abbas Effendi was recently pleased to learn that in the Caucasus a million-dollar structure had recently been completed by his people, and had naturally become the finest structure devoted to the cult in the world, because in Persia, where numbers are greater, the people are poor and up until this time are obliged to meet in central halls and rooms.[38]

The article then continued with a brief summary of the lives of the Báb, Bahá'u'lláh and 'Abdu'l-Bahá. The next installment of Bell's account was published on the following day, 19 August:

Before I saw Abbas Effendi the second time I had quite a lengthy interview with his secretary and close friend, Mirza Ahmad Sohrab, the brilliant young Persian, who is devoted to the head of the Babists and spends his entire life in his company. He admitted to me that a close record is being kept of everything of importance that is uttered by the 'Renovator of the Worlds', as he is known to his followers. Abbas Effendi has written much, but it is not from his writings so much as from what he says that his disciples gain that faith which is prompting them to undergo persecutions and sufferings for the sake of the new movement.

Abbas Effendi is a dynamo of energy. He was born in 1844 and is therefore an old man. His life as a prisoner, for he has been closely confined for forty years, might have left him a physical wreck; but instead of that he seems to have undergone an almost superhuman recuperation. He rises early in the morning, receives visitors of all nationalities and creeds during the day, often attends the services of the Jews in the synagogue, goes to prayer with the Moslems in their mosques, and attends Christian churches. He carries on a correspondence with his followers in all parts of the world and directs any number of momentous affairs; but his secretary tells me that after the affairs of his busy day are over he will often call him, assure him that he is not weary and will either read, dictate or talk until far into the hours of the night. He knows not fatigue, but attendance upon him often wearies the younger men, who should be stronger.

THE PROPHET'S BEVERAGE.

The first time I called upon him in his temporary home, overlooking the Sea of Galilee, he arose to greet me and then motioned me to be seated as he called to a servant to bring me a glass of tea. 'Perhaps you do not like tea,' he said, 'but this is Persian tea and there is a difference. I assure you that this is worth drinking.'

A BRISK OLD MAN.

When I inquired as to his health, he assured me that he had not felt so strong for many years. Instead of undermining his constitution, his long imprisonment at Acre seems to have had the opposite effect. All of the latent energy of his young manhood seems to have been stored up for the present. He said he had no complaints to make. His life had been nothing but one succession of troubles. He had been an exile, as his father had been before him. But he spoke of these things in a soft and gentle voice.

WHY DOES ONE COME?

'Why,' he asked, 'why is it that you come to see me? You say you write for an American newspaper. People of the world care to hear more about the successful and beloved men of the world, so why do you not speak to them? I am an outcast among men, for I have been until now a political prisoner – and I am the son of a prisoner.'

SIMPLY A MESSAGE.

But he did not exactly mean what he said, because he willingly talked of himself and of his religion and kindly replied to my many questions, many of which he must have answered many times. Over and again he said that his was not a new religion. 'Bahaism is simply a message,' he would repeat, 'its prophecies are readily explained by all religions. We strongly forbid all leadership, hence the Bahais remain unorganized and make no proselytes, but teach that each person shall live the highest within his own religion and among his neighbors, until his life tells silently that he is a Bahai.'

UNIVERSAL BROTHERHOOD.

Briefly summed up, however, and robbed of the beautiful rhetoric in which Abbas Effendi is able to clothe his sentences – I wished afterward that I had received his permission to jot down what he said in shorthand – he is preaching a universal religion which includes about every known creed of the well known religions. His aim seems to reconcile everything. He preaches equal suffrage to men and women. He would have a universal language and told me that he believed Esperanto would do, after a few changes had been made in the present system. He has lectured one evening before a meeting of Socialists and agreed with them in many essentials. The next night it happened that he lectured before a large audience in a room next to their cathedral. He agrees with the Moslems and discusses at length with them the teachings of their prophets in whom he believes. He accepts Jesus Christ as the Son of God and an inspired prophet. He believes in almost everything that is taught by orthodox Jews. He believes that Buddha was an inspired prophet. The same honor is given to Confucius, while he has a strong leaning toward Zoroaster.

Oh, this man can discourse learnedly upon the philosophy of Herbert Spencer, Kant and Schopenhauer. Also he can speak learnedly of those eastern philosophers of whom we of the west have never even heard the names.

I asked him if he included Christian Science in his apparently all-reaching and all-embracing religion.

'I find gems of truth in what she said,' he replied, 'and these things I include and accept. But there are many exaggerations in what she taught. I say to you, if you have a mental ailment, it can be cured by thought. If you have a physical ailment or a broken bone, I would say to you "quickly send for a doctor". Earthly trouble can be cured only by earthly means and has not to do with God.'

'Is the day of miracles over, or will other miracles occur in the future?'

'You mean, I take it, things which we believe at present to be contrary to natural law?' I replied in the affirmative.

'To that question, I shall only reply, I believe that everything is possible; with God at any time.'

Then as if wishing to turn the conversation to other subjects, he said in polite oriental fashion: 'It is beautiful to be young and free, so you may travel around the world and see the beautiful things of the earth.'

And I recalled on that last day, when I saw him, that he said the same thing. As I came down to the beach to take a little boat that carried me across the Sea of Galilee where I took a train for the south, he came to bid me farewell and repeated the same words, as he raised his hands slightly and added: 'You will have a safe voyage across the great sea that takes you to your home. It is beautiful to be young and free to go where you will.' And lifting up his white robe, he turned and walked along the sand, which seems to have a fascination for him, followed by three or four of his disciples.

'There may be a light in a room, but it merely sheds light in that room,' he said. 'There may be many lights, with colored bulbs of various hues and shades. But the source of all those lights is the same – and there must be sources; it is the dynamo that is hidden from sight. So it is with all the religions. They sparkle here and there in various colors – but there is but one source for them all, just one light and that is God. Self-seeking preachers and teachers have wandered far from that Real Light. And it is that Light that we now seek in the real truth. Men have wandered far from the teachings of Christ, Buddha, the Jewish prophets and all of the others. Ours is not a new religion, it is the very old one; we desire to unite all forms in their original purity.'

Then I spoke of his persecutions.

'What is it for one man to suffer?' he asked. 'It is as nothing. If one man may enjoy little comfort on earth and at the same time be leading many men to see the Light – ah, that is the thing!'

He said that his religion should have no paid ministers. He teaches and he expects those whom he teaches to do likewise without money. They should perform this service in addition to whatever else they do in life . . .

And that, in a nutshell, was what gained from my interview with Abbas Effendi himself. He beliefs that Christ taught 'love thy neighbor as thyself'. He believes that Mohammedans, Jews, Buddhists and Zoroastrians were taught to believe the same thing, and that not one of them are doing as they were taught. Thus he would become the great 'renovator' or conciliator. He would bring all men together in a spirit of brotherly love – and he would raise the status of women – particularly in the east, so that they might have an equal standing with males.

And as Queen Victoria wrote to his father in 1869: 'If this is of God, it will stand; and if not, there is no harm done.'[39]

These articles were later included in Bell's *The Spell of the Holy Land* (1915) together with a different picture of 'Abdu'l-Bahá from the one published in the *Plain Dealer*.

A Talk on the Soul

In London *The International Psychic Gazette* published notes of 'Abdu'l-Bahá's talks in Haifa. In July 1914 the magazine published one and a half pages of notes of a talk on the soul attributed to 'Abdu'l-Bahá:

> IN HAIFA, *February*, 1914.
> Thou hast asked concerning the spirit and its immortality after its departure. Know thou that at the time of its translation it ascends and ascends until it reaches the presence of God, clothed in a temple (body) which will not become subject to the changes wrought by ages and cycles, nor by the contingencies of the world, nor the emanations thereof. It will continue to exist through the eternality of the Kingdom of God – its sovereignty, its dominion, its potency. From it will appear the signs of God and His qualities, the Providence of God and His Bestowal. Verily the pen is unable to move in a befitting manner in explaining this truth – its exaltation and loftiness. The Hand of Mercy shall cause it to enter into men's minds, though it cannot be grasped through any explanation, nor be described by those means which are available in the world.
>
> Blessed is the spirit which abandons the body previously sanctified and freed from the doubts of the nations. Verily, it moves in the atmosphere of the Will of its Lord, and it enters into the Supreme Paradise. It is welcomed by the angels (lit. countenances) of the Herdouss, the Most High. It associates with the Prophets of God, and His chosen ones, and it converses with them, and relates to them those events which have happened to it in the Path of God, the Lord of both worlds.

Were one to become informed of that which is pre-ordained for the spirit in the worlds of God, the Lord of the Throne and the Earth, he would become immediately enkindled with the fire of yearning for this impregnable, exalted, holy Abha (glorious) state of being.

The Prophets and the Messengers have come in order to guide mankind to the straight path of the True One. Their aim has been no other than the education of the people, so that at the time of death they may depart to the Supreme Friend, with perfect sanctification, purification and severance. I declare that the Prophets are causative of the improvements and the progress of the nations. They are the leaven of existence and the greatest means for the appearance of sciences and arts in this world.

> I died from the mineral and became a plant, I died from the plant and re-appeared in an animal;
>
> I died from the animal and became a man.
>
> Wherefore then should I fear? When did I grow less by dying?
>
> Next, must I die from the man
>
> That I may grow the wings of angels.
>
> From the angel too must I seek advance;
>
> Once more shall I wing my way above the angels.
>
> And I shall become that which entereth not the imagination.
>
> Then let me now become naught – naught,
>
> For the harp string crieth unto me –
>
> Verily unto Him do we return, When all things perish, save His Face.

THE SOUL

As to the question concerning the soul, know thou, verily, that 'soul' is a term applied to numerous realities, according to the exigencies of these following relations in regard to development in the world of existence: –

(1) In the mineral kingdom, soul is called 'latent force', silently working for the disintegration of the substance of the mineral.

(2) In the vegetable kingdom it is called 'virtue augmentative', or the power of growth, which attracts and absorbs the delicate materials of inorganic substance found in the mineral kingdom of matter, and transforms them into the condition of growth. Thus the inorganic substance found in the mineral kingdom becomes growing vegetable life through the effect of the word of God. This vegetable soul, i.e., 'virtue augmentative', or power of growth, is a quality which is produced by the admixture of elements, and appears in accidental organisms, of which contingency is an essential attribute.

(3) In the animal kingdom it is called 'sense perceptions' (or instinct). This soul term, as applied to the animal kingdom, is also a natural quality resulting from the mixture of the elements, and it appears from their mingling and combination, for it is a quality which results from the composition of bodies (organisms), and is dispersed at their decomposition. From this we are to understand that the animal soul is not endowed with the capacity of attaining immortality, as the life force is dispersed at the decomposition of the animal tissues.

All these things up to this point are a contingent reality, and are not a divine reality. But a contingent reality, which is perpetuated by the fullness of existence, will then suffer no corruption, and will thus become a divine reality, for the accidental reality is only distinguished from the existent reality by its subjection to corruption, For transformation is an essential necessity to every contingent reality, and this is what the Mature Wisdom has deemed advisable.

(4) In the human, worldly soul signifies the 'rational being, or mind'. This has a potential existence before its appearance in

human life. It is like unto the existence of a tree within the seed. The existence of the tree within the seed is potential; but when the seed is sown and watered, the signs thereof, its roots and branches, and all of its different qualities, appear. Likewise, the 'rational soul' has a potential existence before its appearance in the human body, and through the mixture of elements and a wonderful combination, according to the natural order, law, conception, and birth, it appears with its identity.

Be it known that to know the reality or essence of the soul of man is impossible, for, in order to know a thing, one must comprehend it, and since a thing cannot comprehend itself, to know one's self in substance or essence is impossible. As the comprehender cannot be the comprehended, man cannot know himself in reality or essence. In order to obtain knowledge of any reality, or soul of man, the student must study the manifestations, qualities, names, and characteristics of man. This much can be stated, that the reality of man is a pure and unknown essence constituting a depository, emanating from the Light of the Ancient Entity – God. This essence or soul of man, because of its innate purity, and its connection with the unseen Ancient Entity, is old as regards time, but new as regards individuality. This connection is similar to that of the ray to the sun – the effect to the primal cause. Otherwise, the thing that is generated, or the creature, has no connection with or relation to its Generator or its Creator.

Since the pure essence, whose identity is unknown, possesses the virtues of the worlds of matter and of the Kingdom, it has two sides – first, the material and physical; second, the mental and spiritual – which are attributes not found as qualities of matter. It is the same reality which is given different names, according to the different conditions wherein it becomes manifest. Because of its attachment to matter and the phenomenal world, when it governs the physical functions of the body, it is called the human soul. When it manifests itself as the thinker, the comprehender, it is called the mind. And when it soars into the atmosphere of God, and travels in the spiritual world, it becomes designated as spirit.

There are two sides to man. One is divine, the other worldly; one is luminous, the other dark; one is angelic, the other diabolic. Man is equal to the animals in all sensuous conditions, for all animal characteristics exist in him. Likewise, divine and satanic qualities are contained in man: knowledge and ignorance; guidance and error; truth and falsehood; generosity and avarice; valour and timidity; inclination towards God and tendency towards satan. Chastity and purity; corruption and vileness; economy and avidity; good and evil; all are contained in man.

If the angelic side becomes more powerful, and the divine power and brightness surround man, then the second birth takes place, and eternal life is found at this point. Man becomes then the noblest among creatures. On the other hand, if sensuous qualities surround, and if terrestrial darkness and sensuous passions predominate, if they meet in man only the worldly feelings, if they find him a captive of evil qualities and fallen into everlasting death, then such a man is the basest and most abject among all creatures. In such a man, divine power does not exist. An animal is not considered unjust and evil because of its cruelty and injustice, for it is not endowed, as is man, with divine qualities; but if man falls into the same evil condition, it is evident that he has permitted his ungodly attributes to overcome the divine qualities with which he was endowed. This shows the baseness and meanness that exist in human nature.

DIVINE TEACHINGS

There are two general and principal classes of divine teachings. One is spiritual, and pertains to the moralities. This is the fundamental basis of the divine law, unchangeable and unalterable, which has been reiterated and renewed in the cycle of every prophet. Its commands refer to justice, truthfulness, compassion, faith, love of God, self-devotion, self-sacrifice, steadfastness, including all divine and merciful attributes. This is the unchanging and unmoving law of God.

The second class of divine teachings is material and deals with behaviour, such as divorce, the commandments, the way of worshipping. All these conditions have changed in the cycle of every prophet. The character of divine sovereignty has no change or transformation, but the organisation and administration change continually. This is why Jesus Christ said: – 'I came not to destroy the law, but to fulfil it.' At the same time there are conditions that are changeable.

Spoken by Abdul Baha.[40]

38

THE WAR YEARS

After years of tensions between European powers, the 'spark' predicted by 'Abdu'l-Bahá in some of His talks that would precipitate a great war on the continent was ignited on 24 June 1914, when Archduke Franz Ferdinand, the heir to the Austrian throne, was assassinated in Sarajevo, Serbia. On 28 July Austria declared war on Serbia and consequently Russia, a long-time ally of Serbia, mobilized its troops. Germany, an ally of the Austro-Hungarian Empire, declared war on Russia, and France, obligated by its pacts with Russia, in turn declared war on Germany. In only a few months the war had extended to the whole world, involving almost all the major powers of the globe and their colonies.

The Ottoman Empire entered the war in support of Germany and Austro-Hungary and opened hostilities with the British in November 1914. Syria became a strategic region through which the Ottoman Empire would sent troops to the Egyptian front and through which eventually the allied troops stationed in Egypt would counterattack and march on their advance to the north. The population of the area suffered greatly from the ruthlessness of the Ottoman troops, and the famines and epidemics caused by the shortage of foods and goods ravaged the whole region.

'Abdu'l-Bahá's Prophecies about the War

Some newspapers in the West did not fail to call the attention of their readers to the fact that during 'Abdu'l-Bahá's travels in Europe and North America He had predicted in emphatic terms that a great war was near.

William T. Ellis who, as will be remembered, met the Master in Egypt in early 1911 and afterwards wrote about Him in a series of unsympathetic articles, mentioned 'Abdu'l-Bahá in a syndicated column that appeared soon after the outbreak the war. He declared that, 'A few years ago over in Alexandria in Egypt, Abbas Effendi, the head of the Behaists, told me as we talked of the possibilities of world peace, that he expected a great world war which would overwhelm humanity. Then, having in this bitter school learned the lesson of the waste and cost and needlessness of the anachronism of war, the world would enter upon the long-dreamed era of universal peace. That prophecy is also the judgment of most trained observers of international conditions. The Bosnian student whose mad pistol slaughtered the heir to a throne has suddenly called all mankind to school, to learn the lesson of peace and brotherhood, written in letters of blood and fire.'[1]

In Tasmania a contributor to *The Combat* (Hobart) mentioned 'Abdu'l-Bahá's predictions in His talks in the West[2] and in France the *Bulletin Théosophique* (Paris) reprinted under the title 'Prophetic Words pronounced by Abdul Baha' a portion of one of the Master's talks in Paris in which He spoke about the war.[3]

News about 'Abdu'l-Bahá

From time to time newspapers in the West published news about 'Abdu'l-Bahá's welfare during the war.

In England, *The Christian Commonwealth* kept its readers regularly informed about Him. Soon after war broke out a letter sent from Haifa reported some of 'Abdu'l-Bahá's comments on the conflict:

A CALL TO PEACE FROM THE HOLY LAND
ABDUL BAHA ON THE WAR

On August 3 Abdul Baha Abbas gave an address on the situation in Europe to a number of Persian students and Bahai pilgrims on Mount Carmel. He mentioned that when in America addressing Peace Societies, he foretold the consequences of armed peace in Europe, and pleaded for a different policy. He pointed out that both the conqueror and the conquered are losers by war. 'Racial difference', he continued, 'is an optical illusion. It is a figment of imagination, yet how deep-seated and powerful is its influence. All mankind have descended from one stock and are the children of one Father. Although this is the reality, it exercises little influence upon the minds of large numbers of people. Hatred and animosity destroy the basis of the structure of humanity, while love and amity are conducive to the well-being and prosperity of mankind. Kings and rulers, politicians and statesmen, remain in safety and send innocent men to the battlefield to tear each other to pieces.' Why, asked Abdul Baha, do not the disputants agree to arbitration? A Universal Court of Arbitration should resolve all the disagreements and contentions that arise between the nations of the world. He concluded: 'Man! it is better for thee to hide thy head under the earth! Thou hast crimsoned the ground with the blood of thy brothers! Thy hand is stained with their blood! Thou hast slaughtered and butchered God's own children! Thou hast destroyed the living temples of the Spirit! Thou hast trampled under thy feet the rights of man! Thou hast snuffed out the burning lamps of life and truth. It is strange, passing strange, that notwithstanding all these violations of the Divine law thou art yet wantonly boasting and exalting thyself above all mankind!'[4]

On 9 September the same periodical carried a very interesting account of a conversation between 'Abdu'l-Bahá and a German diplomat only a few weeks before the start of the war:

WAR AND PEACE
ADDRESS BY ABDUL BAHA

Abdul Baha followed the address, an account of which we published, Sept. 2, with another on the same theme. The room at Haifa in which he spoke was crowded with pilgrims, students, and friends. At times he was very animated and even passionate.

He mentioned that a few days previously he discussed with the German Consul the ominous signs of the European War, which had not then broken out. The Consul contended that a nation must go on increasing its military and naval expenditure if it desires to protect its growing commercial and national interests from the attacks of its equally powerful and expanding neighbours and rivals: that the greater the military equipment the more was the nation assured of making progress and developing its resources. Other Germans and members of other nationalities who were present all agreed with the Consul. Abdul Baha urged that if the power of love and peace became predominant its effects would be greater than those of hate and war. 'In the world of existence there is no power as efficacious and as penetrative as the power of love. Military power coerces and compels men into obedience through unnatural resort to force and violation, but mankind yield happily and willingly to the power of love.' If nations would use their resources in spreading love amongst mankind, in strengthening the ties of interdependence between nations and governments, and in establishing fellowship and affinity between the races, how different would be the result!

The German Consul and others raised objections to Abdul Baha's ideas, but he insisted that neither the conqueror nor the conquered would benefit by the present conflict. He reminded them that the nations who were now seeking to destroy each other belong to one race and profess the same religion, and earnestly pleaded for the cessation of strife amongst the children of one Father.[5]

As the war progressed the correspondence with the Master and the visits of pilgrims to Haifa had to be restricted. 'Abdu'l-Bahá also told the Bahá'ís in the area to move to the Druze village of Abú Sinán where they would be safe from the bombardment of the coast. These occurrences were reported on 18 November in an article that also described the progress of the Bahá'í Faith in Japan:

> The last news to hand from the Bahai headquarters says that Abdul Baha is at Acca, in excellent health, and working assiduously. Owing to the disturbed state of the country a refuge has been found for the members of his family and the Bahai community in a village two hours from Acca. Until further notice letters should be addressed, 'c.o. Ahmed Yazdi, Port Said', and not sent direct to Haifa or Acca. Copies of current periodicals may also be sent to Mirza Ahmad Sohrab at the same address. As a result of the war Abdul Baha will not be receiving any further pilgrims until the spring. It is possible that there may be some delay and interruption in the receipt of news from Haifa and Acca, as the French, Austrian and Russian post offices are closed and all letters must go through the Turkish post office.[6]

On 4 October 1914 'Abdu'l-Bahá sent a letter to the Bahá'ís in England about the world war. In this letter He summarized the efforts He had made during His travels in the West to help the establishment of universal peace and called upon citizens and world leaders to stop the war. *The Christian Commonwealth* published this document on 9 December 1914:

THE VOICE OF UNIVERSAL PEACE
BY ABDUL BAHA

After the declaration of the Constitutional Regime, in Turkey, in 1908, by the members of the Committee of Union and Progress, this prisoner of forty years was released, and journeyed for three years (1910–1913) throughout Europe and America. Notwithstanding my advanced age, with a resonant voice I delivered detailed addresses before large conventions and in historical churches. I enumerated all those principles contained in the tablets and teachings of Baha'o'llah concerning War and Peace.

About fifty years ago Baha'o'llah proclaimed certain teachings and raised the song of Universal Peace. In numerous tablets and sundry epistles he foretold in most explicit language the present cataclysmic events; stating that the world of humanity is facing the most portentous danger, and asserting categorically that the realisation of universal war is unfortunately inevitable and unavoidable. For these combustible materials which are stored in the infernal arsenals of Europe will explode by contact with one spark. Amongst other things, the Balkans will become a volcano and the map of Europe will be changed. For these and similar reasons Baha'o'llah invited the world of humanity to Universal Peace. He wrote a number of epistles to kings and rulers, and in those epistles he explained the destructive evils of war and dwelt on the solid benefits and nobler influences of Universal Peace. War saps the foundations of humanity. Killing is an unpardonable crime against God, for man is an edifice built by the hand of the Almighty. Peace is life incarnate; war is death personified. Peace is the Divine Spirit; war is a Satanic suggestion. Peace is the light of the world. War is Stygian darkness and Cimmerian gloom. All the great prophets, ancient philosophers, and heavenly books have been the harbingers of peace and monitors against war and discord. This is the Divine foundation. This is the celestial outpouring. This is the basis of all the religions of God.

In short, before all the meetings in the West I cried out:– 'O ye thinkers of the world; O ye philosophers of the Occident; O ye scholars and sages of the earth! A threatening black cloud is behind, which ere long shall envelop the horizon of humanity; an impetuous tempest is ahead, which shall shatter to splinters the ships of the lives of mankind, and a turbulent, furious torrent shall soon drown the countries and nations of Europe. Awake ye! Awake ye! Become ye mindful! Become ye mindful! Thus in the spirit of co-operation may we all arise with the utmost magnanimity, and through the favour and providence of God hold aloft the flag of the oneness of humanity, promote the essentials of Universal Peace, and deliver the inhabitants of the world from this most great danger.'

While travelling in Europe and America I met altruistic and sanctified souls who were my confidants and associates concerning the question of Universal Peace, and who agreed with me and joined their voices with mine regarding the principle of the oneness of the world of humanity; but alas! they were very few! The leaders of public opinion and great statesmen believed that the massing of huge armies and the annual increase of military forces ensured peace and amity amongst nations. At that time I explained that this theory was based on a false conception; for it was an inevitable certainty that these serried ranks and disciplined armies would be rushed one day into the heat of the battlefield, and these inflammable materials would unquestionably be exploded, the explosion being through one tiny spark. Then a world-conflagration would be witnessed, the lurid flames of which would redden all the horizons. Because the sphere of their thoughts was contracted and their intellectual eyes blind, they could not acknowledge the above explanation. From the beginning of the Balkan Confederation a number of important personages enquired of me whether this Balkan War was the expected Universal War, but it was answered: It will be terminated in Universal War!

In brief, the point to make clear is this: Baha'o'llah nearly fifty years ago warned the nations against the occurrence of this 'most great danger'. Although the evils of war were evident and manifest to the sages and scholars, they are now made clear and plain to all the people. No sane person can at this time deny the fact that war is the most dreadful calamity in the world of humanity, that war destroys this divine foundation, that war is the cause of external death, that war is conducive to the destruction of populous, progressive cities, that war is the world-consuming fire, and that war is the most ruinous catastrophe and the most deplorable adversity.

Cries and lamentations are raised from every part to the Supreme Being: the moanings and shriekings have sent a mighty reverberation through the world; the civilised countries are being overthrown; eyes are shedding tears because of the weeping of the fatherless children; hearts are burning and being consumed by piercing sobbings and uncontrollable bewailings of helpless wandering women: the spirits of hopeless mothers are torn by hopeless grief and endless sorrows, and the nerve-racking sighs and the just complaints of the fathers ascend to the throne of the Almighty.

Ah me! The world of creation is totally deprived of its normal rest: the clash of arms and the sound of murderous guns and cannon are being heard like the roaring of thunder across the heavenly track, and explosive materials have changed the battlefields into yawning graveyards, burying for eternity the dead corpses of thousands upon thousands of youth – the flower of many countries, who would have been the evolving factors in the civilisation of the future. The results of this crime against humanity can never be adequately described by pen or by tongue!

O ye governments of the world! Be ye pitiful toward mankind! O ye nations of the earth, behold ye the battlefields of slaughter and carnage! O ye sages of humanity, investigate sympathetically the conditions of the oppressed: O ye philosophers of the West, study profoundly the causes that led to this gigantic, unparalleled struggle! O ye wise leaders of the globe, reflect deeply, so that ye may find an antidote for the suppression of this chronic, devastating disease! O ye individuals of humanity, find means for the stoppage of this wholesale murder and bloodshed! Now is the true time; now is the opportune time! Arise, make an effort, and unfurl the flag of Universal Peace, and dam the irresistible fury of the raging torrent which is wreaking havoc and ruin everywhere.

Although this captive has been in the prison of despotism for forty years, yet he has never been so sad and stricken with regret and grief as in these days. My spirit is aflame and burning; my heart is broken, mournful, heavy, and despondent; my eyes are weeping and my soul is on fire! Oh! I am so bowed down, so sorrowful!

O people, weep and cry, lament and bemoan your fate! Then, hasten ye, hasten ye; perchance ye may become able to extinguish with the water of the new-born Ideals of spiritual Democracy and celestial Freedom this many-flamed, world-consuming fire, and through your heaven-inspired resolution you may usher in the golden era of international solidarity and world confederation.

O Kind God, hearken to the cry of these helpless nations! O Pure Lord, show thy pity to these orphaned children! O Incomparable Almighty, stop this destructive torrent! O Creator of the world and the inhabitants thereof, cause the extinction of this burning fire! O Listener to our cries, come to the rescue of the orphans! O Ideal Comforter, console the mothers whose hearts are torn and whose souls are filled with the blood of irremediable loss! O Clement and Merciful, grant the blessing of thy grace to the weeping eyes and burning hearts of the fathers! Restore calmness to the surging tempests, and change this world-encircling war into peace and conciliation.

Verily Thou art the Omnipotent and the Powerful, and verily Thou art the Seeing and the Hearing![7]

One week after the publication of this letter *The Christian Commonwealth* reported that 'A message from Haifa, Syria, to all Bahais, says that in these black days they must impress upon the mind of every person that peace is the sole remedy for all these terrible diseases. "In the time of peace all nations have been preparing for war. In the time of war let all men of good will prepare for peace." This is the burden of the message of Abdul Baha, and it is hoped everyone will follow it.'[8]

On 30 December *The Christian Commonwealth* reported that 'Abdu'l-Bahá had visited Ramleh for a few days and wrongly stated that He 'has taken up his abode at Port Said'.[9] On 17 February the journal corrected this information, stating that the Master had not left Haifa. The report included portions of a letter by Jean Stannard about conditions in the Holy Land:

Abdul Baha is still in Syria working with that deep love and wisdom which marks all his actions when the great needs of humanity and the poor dependents on his help claim his attention. All communication has long been broken between Turkish ports and the outside world. Now and then, after innumerable difficulties, an emissary has been got through to him, taking what money is possible for the relief of his family and others. Had it not been for the great influence possessed by Abdul Baha over the Turkish leaders the Bahais would have suffered not only the loss of all their homes and loved ones, but possibly the desecration of some of their holiest spots. Abdul Baha has been the means of keeping many forces in hand and the channel for helping countless numbers of starved and terrified families. His own people are scattered in various villages for better safety, and the conditions in Syria generally are terrible.[10]

On 24 February the journal published a summary of a letter of Munavvar Khánum sent to a Bahá'í in England:

> A well-known Bahai resident in London has received a letter from the daughter of Abdul Baha, Monover Khanum. The letter is dated January 4, 1915, and reached Port Said by special messenger, all regular communications being interrupted. From Port Said it was posted to London. Monover Khanum writes that her father and family are all living in a small village some three hours' journey inland from Akka. Abdul Baha spends the greater part of his time at Akka, and his health is unusually good. The conditions in Syria are quite indescribable; the inhabitants are fleeing inland from all the villages and coast towns, as they are in terror that these places will be bombarded by the English and French warships, and it is almost impossible to reassure them, but Abdul Baha is a great consolation and help to all these poor, frightened, helpless people. The only means of communication with the rest of the world is by means of an Italian steamer which very occasionally touches at Haifa.[11]

An interesting summary of a letter by Edward Getsinger offered some details about the way in which 'Abdu'l-Bahá assisted the population of Haifa by securing food for those in need:

> Prof. E. C. Getsinger sends particulars of a visit he has just paid to Abdul Baha at Haifa, undertaken at the instigation of the American

Bahais and friends who had been some months without news. His letter is dated Naples, February 15, the eve of his sailing for Washington, and confirms the news we gave last week from Abdul Baha's daughter, Monover Khanum. Mr. Getsinger says that he arrived in Haifa, January 26, after considerable difficulties with martial law at various ports. He saw Abdul Baha daily for a week and found him in better health than at any time during the seventeen years that he has known him, and this despite the fact that war conditions have placed most unusual burdens upon him in the care of the wives and children, whose bread-winners are at the Front. He provides flour and a few other necessaries by issuing tickets to each member of a family at specified times, and the tickets are exchanged by the shopkeeper for packets of rations. One such dole supplied 200 ticket-holders, not a man among them. Whatever men are in the locality and in need, whatever be their nationality, are given work in building roads, and paid a sufficient sum daily for their immediate necessities from the public funds. The measures the Turkish Government has taken in prohibiting the export of flour and foodstuffs, and even forbidding their sale to another city, has husbanded stores, and bread has never been so cheap as now. Mr. Getsinger asked Abdul Baha if he thought of attending the Bahai Congress at the Panama Exhibition. We shall give his reply, and other particulars, next week.[12]

Further information provided by Getsinger was published on 10 March:

Mr. E. C. Getsinger, some particulars of whose recent visit to Haifa we gave last week, tells us further that Abdul Baha travels back and forth between Acca and Haifa and the various villages surrounding these places, in rain and storm, and personally knows the needs of each particular group or family. Considerable sickness prevails among the people, and medical care is provided as well as food. Mr. Getsinger dined with Abdul Baha, and the staple food of the meal, the principal one of the day, consisted of bread and cheese. He discovered that even this was a special repast served in his honour, as in order that the needy may receive all possible assistance Abdul Baha is living with the utmost simplicity. Mr. Getsinger having apprised Abdul Baha of the endeavour of American friends to send food and relief to the poor of Haifa, he promptly said: 'No. I will look after my poor myself, in America there are plenty of poor: let the friends look after them. Besides, all such efforts would complicate matters with the military authorities.' 'I asked him,' says Mr. Getsinger, 'if he thought of attending the International Bahai Congress at San Francisco. To this he replied, as if it was quite an impossible question, "And what would become of the poor? I never would leave them. The Congress does not require my presence."'[13]

Fragments of the correspondence of another traveler were published on 31 March:

> E. S., a traveller just back from Akka, writes from Paris: 'In these days when nearly all communication is cut off between Syria and Europe, a few lines about Abdul Baha may be welcome to those interested in him. The great upholder of peace is in perfect, health, and in his presence there is calm. In the early days of the war nearly all the little Persian colony of Haifa and Akka left for Deuses, a village in the hills five miles back of Akka. The discomforts there are many, but no one seems to mind, and the days when Abdul Baha arrives for a rest from the harrowing scenes of distress in Haifa and Akka are days of rejoicing. These days, however, are scarce, for Abdul Baha finds it hard to be away for long from those poor souls of every class and denomination who call upon him at all hours of the day and night for assistance of every kind.'[14]

Further information by the same correspondent was published on 12 May:

> E. S., a traveller who has just returned from Akka, sends us from Paris tidings of Abdul Baha. 'The place where I have seen him happiest is in Akka . . . In spite of its beauty, as it rests a white city on the sea, even in its best days it is the most desolate of places, with its ruined walls, prison, crumbling houses, and dark narrow streets little better than alleys, but now, with its deserted streets, closed shops, and moral atmosphere of agony and distress occasioned by the Turkish Government's absolute disregard of the comfort and safety of her subjects, I know of no more depressing place to sit and

face danger. It seems, however, to be Abdul Baha's favourite abode. Here he lives on the edge of the sea, in a house damp and chill from the sea breezes, with a broken-hearted woman and a wee motherless child as its sole inmates,[15] in perfect calm, beauty, strength, and spiritual happiness. His is the room where Baha o'llah, his father, lived imprisoned for nine years, and all the house, so poor otherwise, is full of the spiritual power which sustained this persecuted family for so many years; outwardly dark and destitute, but inwardly illumined with that light which lighteth the whole world.'

A letter, dated April 17, from a correspondent in Cairo, states that all Syrian ports are now closed, and no news is coming through, but that the last tidings of Abdul Baha and his household were good.[16]

On 26 May, it was reported: 'Miss E. J. Rosenberg writes that she has received good news of Abdul Baha from M. Ahmed Yazdi, Persian Consul at Port Said. Under the date May 1 he writes: "Four or five days ago one of the students from the Beyrout College returned from Haifa and gave us glad tidings of the good health and safety of our beloved master."'[17] Further details were published on 9 June: 'A letter from Egypt, dated May 4, states that with very great difficulty a young Persian Bahai student managed to leave Haifa by one of the last Italian steamers to touch there. He says that Abdul Baha is well, and much more cheerful than he was some months ago. He adds that rice, sugar, and petroleum are now unobtainable in Syria, and that the Turks try to loot everything.'[18] On 22 September, *The Christian Commonwealth* summarized information that had been published in *Star of the West*[19] and on 20 October it published information sent by Lua Getsinger 'who spent the summer with Abdul Baha and his family, and only took her departure because it seemed not unlikely that America would be drawn into the war, and in that case, Abdul Baha doubted of his ability to protect her. The condition of Syria is pitiable – a blockade without, and Turkish crimes within. Food and fuel are almost exhausted, and winter looms ahead.'[20] Portions of her letter were reproduced on 27 October:

From Mrs. L. M. Getsinger, who was an inmate of Abdul Baha's household from December 3, 1914, until August 30, 1915, we have received the following dated Cairo, Egypt, October 8, 1915: – 'Unique conditions made this most remarkable man – about whom poets sing and college professors write books – appear "the shadow of a great rock" in that weary land. He was everything to all, whether Mohammedan, Christian, Jew, or Bahai. When death robbed a home, or the war, exacting its human toll, left a house unprotected and desolate, he was seen in the role of comforter. During cannonades, which caused the frightened inhabitants to flee into the mountains, he was the good shepherd. "My place is there before those guns now striking such terror into the hearts of the people. They are afraid, I must gather them; they are hopeless, I must assure them; they are helpless, I must receive them," he said on the occasion of the first bombardment which destroyed the R.R. bridge near the ancient town of Acca, and before the firing ceased he was ready to start out on this divine errand gathering the affrighted scattered flock from the hillsides and plains as he went from Abou Senan, comforting, soothing, and leading them back to the shelter of their own forsaken homes. He was "a treasurer to the poor", giving as long as there was anything to give, dividing his bread with the starving, who clustered and cried about his door. And he was a father to the fatherless, whose never-failing function was the hope of all aching hearts.'[21]

Further portions of Getsinger's letter were published on 3 November:

During the last bombardment which occurred early in August, Abdul Baha sat unmoved, watching it from a window; his sad patient face wearing the expression of one who knows what needs must be, all the reasons why, and calmly awaits a destined end, which may include the sacrifice of himself. Some months previously he had said: 'I have been in great danger and am still like one sitting under a suspended sword ready to fall at a moment's notice. For myself I do not even think, because I am ready to embrace any sacrifice and yearn for the cup of martyrdom, but I am obliged to think of those whom I must leave; their helplessness so cries out to me – before I go – that for their sakes I hope to be spared yet a little while. Still I am prepared and submissive to the will of God.' What an echo to the words of Jesus, 'Not my will, but thine be done!'

> When the locusts came and were devouring everything, many sought him asking him to pray that they would go away: 'Why?' he answered. 'They are the soldiers of God! They are only doing well that for which they were created; and in this respect are much better than human beings, who disobey all of God's commands. In my garden they are my welcome guests, let them eat that they may finish their work!'
>
> Thus surrounded by misery resulting from famine, encircled by sorrows beyond pen portrayal, encompassed by enemies who plot his downfall and seek his life, he lives, and knows, and smiles.²²

A further note published on 12 January 1916 – probably based on a letter by Lua Getsinger sent on 31 September 1915 – stated that 'Though Abdul Baha at Haifa is cut off from news of his friends in Europe and America, some letters from Haifa have reached America. It appears that the post and the pilgrims, once a chief feature of the life of Haifa, are greatly missed. Abdul Baha is now entirely occupied in dealing with the distress and misery in Syria caused by the war, and aggravated by a plague of locusts.'²³

Weeks later the journal published the following information, provided by a British soldier:

> The latest news of Abdul Baha has reached this country through an English officer interned in Syria as a prisoner of war. Abdul Baha and his family are now virtually prisoners again in Turkish lands, and are not allowed beyond five miles of Acca. The food supply is extremely short, especially rice, but Abdul Baha's health is said to be fairly good, and he is accomplishing wonderful work in cheering up his followers and in looking after the poor and distressed population in Acca, Haifa, and the surrounding districts.²⁴

In August and November *The Christian Commonwealth* quoted portions of the correspondence received in America from Ahmad Sohrab and published previously in *Star of the West*.²⁵ On 17 January 1917 an article on the severe famine in the Holy Land mentioned that 'The latest news of Abdul Baha which has reached us is that he is well and is living at Bahjee with his sister Monnavar Khanom [sic] and one of his granddaughters.'²⁶ Other short notes – often based on letters by

Ahmad Sohrab published in *Star of the West* – were published in the ensuing weeks and months relating that 'Abdu'l-Bahá was well.[27]

In November 1917 a letter from 'Abdu'l-Bahá reached England and was read at a meeting commemorating the anniversary of the birth of Bahá'u'lláh.[28] The text of this Tablet was published afterwards in *The Christian Commonwealth*:

> *The following letter, dated August 20, contains the latest news of Abdul Baha. The messenger, who bore it on foot from Palestine, took forty-five days to reach Teheran, and thence the letter was transmitted by post to England.*
>
> Oh your Honour Amin,– What though the doors be shut, the roads and the ways barred, and the usual means of communication be no longer existing, yet the streams of union and nearness of heart flow on without ceasing in the ecstasy of Spiritual Communion.
>
> Even though the Mirrors and the Lights be far apart, yet there is no severance, for the union, by the rays and bounties of reflection, remains ever firm and unfailing.
>
> The Bahais (the followers of the Light of God) ought to show forth such determination and steadfastness in all their works, that the world of humanity may greatly marvel, exclaiming, 'Behold what firmness and uprightness, what strength and vigour are theirs!'
>
> By night and by day the thoughts of this servant are verily filled with fragrant spiritual remembrance of the friends, and his constant and fervent prayer to His Holiness the Merciful is that He will so greatly bless them with the infinite Confirmations of the Holy Spirit that every drop (of water) may surge like the sea and every atom be made to shine visibly in the Light of the Sun! This can only come to pass through the Grace of God the Beloved.
>
> Convey to all the friends, one by one, from me the utmost of longing (to see them).
>
> (Signed) Abdul Baha Abbas
>
> Praise be to God that, with the aid and favour of His Holiness the Almighty, (our) days are passed in the best of health on Mount Carmel, at the house of his honour Aga Abbas Ghuli.
>
> Because of the inquiries by the friends as to the health and safety of the Bahais of this place, and because of the (customary) means of communication being severed, his honour Hadji Ramazan has

been sent (with this tablet), since he only at this time is able to undertake the journey. – (Signed) Abdul Baha Abbas.

Translated by Lotfullah S. Hakim, London[29]

Tablet to Andrew Carnegie

As seen in chapter 27, while in Edinburgh 'Abdu'l-Bahá wrote a Tablet for the American philanthropist, pacifist and businessman Andrew Carnegie, which was reproduced in some newspapers. 'Abdu'l-Bahá also sent a letter from Egypt to the Persian Consul General in New York, H. H. Topakyan, in which Carnegie was again mentioned.[30]

From Haifa 'Abdu'l-Bahá sent a second Tablet to Carnegie encouraging him in his efforts towards world peace and reminding him that after the conclusion of the war he would need to redouble his efforts. The New York *Sun* published this letter on 29 August 1915:

> PERSIAN PEACE CRY, SENT TO CARNEGIE
> ABDUL BAHA ABBAS, PHILOSOPHER AND PACIFIST, HAS WORDS OF
> PRAISE
>
> LAIRD GETS NEW TITLES
>
> Behold! Abdul Baha Abbas communes with 'the noble personage, his Excellency Mr. Andrew Carnegie! May God assist him! He is God!' All the way from Abdul Baha's home at Mount Carmel, Haifa, Syria, comes the following epistle to Mr. Carnegie, translated by Mirza Ahmad Sohrab:
>
>> 'Oh, thou Illustrious soul! Oh, thou the great pillar of the Palace of Universal Peace! I write thee this epistle for truly I say thou art the lover of the world of humanity and one of the founders of universal peace. To-day the most great service to the Kingdom of God is the promotion of the principle of the unification of mankind and the establishment of universal peace.
>>
>> 'Rest thou assured that through the confirmations of the Holy Spirit thou wilt become confirmed and assisted in the accomplishment of this most resplendent service, and in this mortal world thou shall lay the foundation of an immortal

and everlasting edifice, and in end thou wilt sit upon the throne of the incorruptible Glory in the Kingdom of God.

THE HARBINGER OF LIFE

'All the leaders and statesmen of Europe are thinking on the plans of war and the annihilation of the mansion of humanity, but thou art thinking on the plan of peace and love and the strengthening of the human world. They are the heralds of death, thou are the harbinger of life. The foundations of their mansions are unstable and wavery and the turrets of their palaces are tottering and crumbling, but the basis of thy structure is firm and unmovable.

'The world of humanity is facing in the future most portentous danger and supreme calamity. The continent of Europe has become like unto a gunpowder magazine and arsenal under which are hidden combustible materials of a most inflammatory nature. Its combustion will be dependent upon a sudden and unexpected enkindlement of one tiny spark which shall envelop the whole earth with a worldwide conflagration, causing the total collapse of European civilization through the furious, wild raging fiery tongues of war.

'Therefore, O ye well wisher of the world of humanity, endeavor ye by day and by night so that these inflammable materials may not come in touch with the burning fire of racial antipathy and hatred. To-day the life of mankind and their attainment to everlasting glory depend on their display of effort and exertion in accordance with the principles of His Holiness Baha Ollah.

COLUMNS OF EARTH SHAKE

'Now all that has been predicted has come to pass, and the lurid flames of this war have emblazoned the horizon of the East and West, causing a reverberating social earthquake through the columns of the earth. After this war the workers for the cause of universal peace will increase day by day and the pacifist party will array its force, displaying greater activity with better advantage and in the end gaining a permanent triumph and eternal victory over all the other parties,

'The realization of this matter is incontestable and irrefutable. Therefore, erelong a vast and unlimited field will be opened before your view for the display of your powers and energies. You must promote this glorious intention with the heavenly power and the confirmation of the Holy Spirit. I am praying in thy behalf that thou mayest pitch a pavilion and unfurl a flag in the world of peace, love and eternal life.

'I beg you to accept the considerations of my highest and deepest respect.'

Abdul Baha Abbas is a Persian philosopher and teacher, head of Bahaistic sect founded by Mohammed Ali in 1844. Abdul visited this country in 1912 and made many speeches here on peace and service to mankind. His epistle to Mr. Carnegie was sent through Mr. H. H. Topakyan, Consul General of Persia.[31]

This letter was afterwards reproduced or mentioned in other newspapers in America[32] and England.[33]

Rumors of Danger to the Life of 'Abdu'l-Bahá

From April 1915 the Ottoman Empire began the systematic repression of its Armenian citizens and the pages of the western press started to carry accounts of the many horrors perpetrated against them.

In this context, on 29 August 1915, 'Abdu'l-Bahá left Haifa for Nazareth. In a letter from Lua Getsinger sent from Port Said she is reported as having stated that He left 'to meet a serious situation and his goodbye to us was heartbreaking'.[34] H. H. Topakyan, the Persian Consul General to the United States, himself an Armenian who had lost relatives in Smyrna and Caesarea, was informed of this situation through Juliet Thompson.

In an interview for the *Christian Science Monitor* (Boston) reporting the massacres of Armenians, Topakyan mentioned the case of 'Abdu'l-Bahá, assuming that He had been taken by force to Nazareth by Turkish troops. Afterwards the newspaper reported in a lengthy article on its front page that 'word has been received of the spiriting away by the Turks of Abdul Baha Abbas, head of the Bahaists, from his headquarters at Mt Carmel, in Syria, and the fear is expressed that he has met the same fate that hundreds of thousands of Armenians have met at the hands of authorities centered at Constantinople'. It quoted Topakyan saying that 'the leader of the Bahaists was forcibly taken away, together with followers – numbering possibly between 15 and a score – and hurried off to Nazareth, where, it is thought, they have all met the same fate that the Turks have been dealing out to others since their entry into the war.'³⁵ In the editorial column of the same issue, it was stated that 'The world will learn, with amazement, this morning, that this gentle old man ['Abdu'l-Bahá], whose sole crime, for a whole lifetime, has been his desire to do good, has been dragged by soldiers, with his whole household from his Syrian retreat, and that his fate is entirely unknown.'³⁶

The news was, however, wrong. 'Abdu'l-Bahá had moved to Nazareth and then temporarily to Tiberias but had returned to Haifa after the summer. A report published in *The Christian Commonwealth* may contain the correct version:

> News concerning the welfare of Abdul Baha, the Persian mystic and teacher, has been, since the outbreak of war, very difficult to obtain. Information reached his followers that the Turkish government had, for reasons of safety, transferred him and his family to Tiberias. The latest report to hand is that he has now been reinstated at Haifa. Among the surrounding districts, so sorely stricken by famine and disease, his influence is very great. From Acca he wrote:– Though I have been in the prison of despotism for forty years, yet never have I been so sad and stricken with regret and grief as in these days. My spirit is aflame and burning – my heart is broken, my soul is on fire.'³⁷

Although the information published in *The Christian Science Monitor* was baseless, it was later reproduced in various newspapers.³⁸ It was also echoed in England, when in a parliamentary debate in the House of Commons the Liberal Party MP for Durham, Aneurin Williams (1859–1924), mentioned the Master in the course of a speech on the Armenian question, saying that 'Abd-ul-Baha Abbas, the greatest religious teacher of his time, who represented a wider religion embracing Muhammadism and other religions, a man who had spent his life in doing good, was violently taken from his home in Mount Carmel to Nazareth'.³⁹

On 29 October the *Monitor* corrected its report and quoted a letter to Howard Colby Ives from Ahmad Sohrab in which the latter stated that 'Abdu'l-Bahá 'has sent word to me that he is well, and that all the followers who had to go to Nazareth are well and that we are all now on our way to Tiberias'.[40] This information was again reproduced in other newspapers.[41]

On 26 November, *The Christian Science Monitor* reported the return of 'Abdu'l-Bahá to Haifa and quoted parts of a letter addressed to Juliet Thompson:

> The first direct word that has come to Bahaists in this country from their leader, Abdul Baha Abbas, within a year, has just been received by Miss Julia Thompson, head of the Bahaists in New York. Miss Thompson informs The Christian Science Monitor that Abdul Baha is now once more back at his headquarters in Haifa; Syria. Some weeks ago it was reported that the venerable Bahaist leader had been spirited away to Nazareth by the Turks and gravest fears were then entertained for his safety.
>
> Whatever difficulty the Bahaists in Syria might have had with the Turks has apparently been settled, since Abdul Baha has ordered his secretary and interpreter, Ahmad Sohrab, to return at once to the United States to perform certain duties for the cult. Ahmad Sohrab left Washington three years ago to go to Haifa as the personal assistant of Abdul Baha.
>
> Abdul Baha writes to Miss Thompson: 'We are now all under the divine protection of God, for which God be praised. All the news you have forwarded to us out here has been the means of imparting to us great gladness. We pray to God that he may terminate this war and open the doors of communication.'
>
> Abdul Baha explained that he had not communicated with his American adherents for so long a time because 'I did not wish to burden the censor with my letters, which had to be opened by him.' The opinion of Bahaists, however, is that there were other reasons which Abdul Baha has not seen fit to communicate at the present time.
>
> Abdul Baha, who himself was a prisoner for many years, owing to his religious beliefs and teachings, takes occasion in his communication to wish Thomas Mott Osborne, warden of Sing Sing prison, success in his reform plans at the penitentiary.
>
> 'I will pray for Mr. Osborne,' he says, 'and hope his educational

reforms in the prison may lead to a marked decrease in crime and lawlessness, and, that through his humane treatment of prisoners he may regenerate them, changing their hearts of flesh and sin into hearts of spirit, purity and manly courage. Mr. Osborne in doing this is doing a great service to humanity.'[42]

The Liberation of Haifa

On Monday 23 September 1918 the British troops under the command of General Allenby took control of Haifa and immediately secured protection for 'Abdu'l-Bahá, who now was free again.

On 17 October the British Bureau of Information released the news of the liberation of 'Abdu'l-Bahá and this was published in several newspapers in America:

> The British Bureau of Information announced yesterday the receipt of a cable message from London saying that British troops have discovered Abdul Baha at Haifa.
>
> Abdul Baha a Persian 'prophet' is head of the Bahai religious cult with members in all parts of the world. In 1912 he visited the United States, speaking in churches in various cities and addressing a convention of the Persian–American Education Society in Washington.
>
> The London message says that Abdul Baha had with him at his retreat at Haifa, which is at the foot of Mount Carmel, in Palestine, 'a small following of devoted Persian adherents, and it is reported his health his good. He is being well cared for by the British soldiers, who have always been inclined to treat such personalities with good humored respect.'[43]

On 17 November the *Pittsburgh Gazette Times* published an article with interesting information provided by the American Bahá'í Elinor Hiscox regarding contacts with 'Abdu'l-Bahá in the first weeks after the taking of Haifa. The information given by Hiscox, which probably reached the journal through Martha Root, was largely based on letters received from Wellesley Tudor Pole, at the time a major serving in the British Army, who from his military post in Egypt made crucial efforts to secure protection for 'Abdu'l-Bahá.[44] The article concluded by reminding its readers that 'Abdu'l-Bahá visited Pittsburgh, and quoted from one of His addresses in the city (not reproduced here):

ABDUL BAHA IS SAFE, WRITES FOLLOWER
HEAD OF NEW RELIGIOUS MOVEMENT PROTECTED IN PERSIA BY BRITISH
VISITED PITTSBURGH

Miss Elinor Hiscox, an American woman in Cairo, Egypt, a friend of Miss Martha L. Root, former Pittsburgh newspaper woman, writes of Abdul Baha, the living center of the covenant of the Bahai cause. Miss Hiscox first quotes a short letter she has just received from Capt. W. Tudor Pole, an English officer:

> I have returned from the front. Abdul Baha is well and is being fully protected and looked after by the British military authorities. I arranged for funds and relief stores to reach him and shall go to Haifa directly I can get away. I cabled London; please inform the Cairo friends.
>
> Miss Hiscox in another letter this week to a Wall Street Bahai in New York, writes:
>
> ... Capt. Tudor Pole has sent $1,000 to Abdul Baha and ordered food sent. He has also written to him that any time he would like to leave Haifa and come to Egypt, Capt. Pole will make all necessary arrangements to have him brought here. He has sent a friend and junior officer, whom I also know, and who is much interested in the Bahai teachings, to remain permanently at the military office at Haifa: he will see Abdul Baha frequently and look for his welfare and comfort. Mirza Mohamed Taki, one of the old Persian Bahais of Cairo, has sent $250, and many of us have sent letters through Capt. Tudor Pole to Abdul Baha.

Yesterday a second letter came from Miss Hiscox saying that Capt. Tudor Pole has just received a message from Col. Storres, now military governor of Jerusalem, who has just returned from a trip to Haifa, where he saw Abdul Baha and gave him the money from Capt. Tudor Pole. Abdul Baha is very well and all the family has food – not luxuries of course – but they have not suffered in that part of the country for necessary food. Abdul Baha said he did not need the money for himself, but he accepted it to give it to the poor. He sent greetings and love to all. He wishes to remain in Haifa for the present.

Before the war Col. Storres was Oriental secretary at the British residency in Cairo. He studied Arabic for a long time with a Bahai, Hussein Rouhy, who has traveled in America, and the Colonel saw a great deal of Abdul Baha when the latter was in Egypt en route to Haifa after his visit to America in 1912.

Soon after writing to Elinor Hiscox, Wellesley Tudor Pole traveled to Palestine and met 'Abdu'l-Bahá again after six years. On 18 December 1918 the *Palestine News*, the weekly newspaper of the Egyptian Expeditionary Force of the British Army in Palestine, carried a lengthy article by Tudor Pole in which he related his visit to 'Abdu'l-Bahá:

When I recently visited the 'Master', he was standing at the top waiting to greet me with that sweet smile and cheery welcome for which he is famous. For 74 long years Abdu'l Baha has lived in the midst of tragedy and hardship, yet nothing has robbed or can rob him of his cheery optimism, spiritual insight and keen sense of humour. His voice was as strong as ever, his eyes clear, his steps virile; his hair and beard are, if possible, more silver-white than before. He is delighted to welcome the change of regime, but I could detect a tragic note, for if the British occupation had taken place ten years ago, he would still have been young enough to travel throughout the Near and the Middle East, spreading the great tidings of his father's mission. Bahai proselytising has never been allowed by Abdu'l Baha in the Turkish Empire and now the 'Master' is too old to stray far from his home on Mount Carmel.

After lunch, Abdu'l Baha drove me out to the Garden Tomb of Baha'u'llah about two miles from the city. His love and reverence for his father are unbounded. He approached the Tomb in complete silence, praying with bent head; a wonderfully venerable figure in his white turban and flowing grey robe.

We took tea in the pilgrim-house adjoining the Tomb and Abdu'l Baha told many stories about Baha'u'llah, his superhuman endurance and his wonderful teaching. When we returned to Acca, the

Persian colony, consisting of perhaps 5 persons, had assembled, and we sat round the room listening to Abdu'l Baha's thrilling account of incidents in his life.

As I drove off on my return to Haifa, I caught a glimpse of the 'Master', staff in hand, wending his way through the Acca slums on his way to attend the local Peace Celebrations. Seen in his own Eastern surroundings, he stands out a majestic figure: simple, humble, inspired; a fitting Chief for a movement that may be destined to affect the religious and social future of the world.[45]

The next issue of the *Palestine News* carried a letter on the Bahá'í Faith by Major Roland Raven-Hart, perhaps the junior officer sent by Tudor Pole to Haifa to see after 'Abdu'l-Bahá, who made the following comments on the Esperanto language and the Bahá'í Faith:

The writer of the article on 'Abdul Baha' in the P.N. of December 19th. might have added a further proof of the long-sightedness of this teacher. Not only did he continually work towards the unity of nations, but, realizing that without comprehension there can be no union, he has repeatedly advised his followers to learn Esperanto, as the only workable language for use in intercourse between people of one language and those of another. The 'Hidden Words' and the older books of the teachings of the Bahai movement have been translated into Esperanto, and Bahais throughout the world correspond in that language. In fact, it is difficult to conceive of any world-movement using any medium but Esperanto for its literature, correspondence, or conferences, except from ignorance of the possibilities opened up by that medium.

Those interested in the Bahai movement would do well to get the above translation (Kasitaj Vortoj in Esperanto) from the British Esperanto Association, 1 Art Street, W.C. 1, at the cost of 4d., together with 'The Esperanto Manual' and the 'Edinburgh Pocket Dictionary', costing 2/6 together. The translation was made by a Bahai missionary in London, direct from Persian into Esperanto, and is a more true reproduction of the sense of the original than can be obtained in any comparatively inflexible national language – it is certainly an improvement on the other versions I have seen.[46]

After his return to England, Tudor Pole was interviewed by a representative of *The Christian Commonwealth*. In the course of the conversation, which dealt mostly with the conditions in Palestine, Tudor Pole mentioned 'Abdu'l-Bahá:

> Changing the subject, Major Tudor Pole spoke of Abdul Baha, who, after being a prisoner in the hands of the Turks, was overlooked and left behind at Haifa when they hurriedly evacuated the place, taking with them many of the inhabitants. He is now, under the British regime, taking his rightful place as a social and religious leader, and many are looking to him to solve the problems arising between Moslem and Christian sects. 'The night before Haifa fell,' said Major Tudor Pole, 'Abdul Baha called his friends together to his house on Mount Carmel and told them, as the shells passed overhead, that there was no cause for fear, that no damage would be done, and that Haifa and Acre would be taken without bloodshed. As a matter of fact, our shells passed over the houses and fell into the waters of the Bay of Acre, and our troops occupied Haifa and Acre practically without opposition.
>
> 'I should like to place on record, on behalf of Abdul Baha's friends in England and America, our gratitude to Mr. Balfour, who, in his official capacity, took the trouble to cable to General Allenby instructions that full protection should be given to Abdul Baha. When our forces arrived in Haifa General Allenby called upon Abdul Baha and expressed, on behalf of H.M. Government, their desire for his welfare . . . Representatives of all ranks of the Army, including the Indian and the West Indian regiments, on hearing of this prophet of Mount Carmel, have taken the opportunity of visiting him.'[47]

On 15 January 1919, *The Christian Commonwealth* published portions of a letter by Ahmad Sohrab giving details of the activities of the Master after His liberation:

> A letter from Haifa, dated December 2 1918, and signed by M. Ahmad Sohrab, who was a member of the party which accompanied Abdul Baha to Europe and America and has been with him in Palestine throughout the war, brings us good news of the beloved leader of the Bahais.

'The sudden and unexpected attack and capture of Haifa by the victorious British Army, under the leadership of General Allenby,' our correspondent writes, 'sent, an electric wave of joy through all parts of Syria, set at liberty hundreds of thousands of men, and opened the doors of correspondence and communication with our friends abroad. Abdul Baha, after four years of silence, was pleased again to meet and speak with men who understand his ideas and respect his convictions. English officers of all ranks – major-generals, brigadier-generals, colonels, majors, captains, lieutenants, as well as non-commissioned officers and privates – have called on him, drank tea with him, and listened reverently to his words of wisdom. The military Governors of Acca and Haifa have often met him, the former being his guest at dinner. Once about eight members of the Australian Flying Corps, who have their aerodrome at the foot of Mount Carmel, were his guests all day in Bahje, near Acre. They visited the tomb of Baha'o'llah, listened to the lecture of Abdul Baha on the history of the cause and its principles, and left in the evening in their large auto, with glad hearts and beaming faces. They were overwhelmed with the extreme kindness and attention of Abdul Baha. Surely they will never forget what they heard and saw, and will write home to their friends about their unique experiences. During the past two months Abdul Baha has been pleasantly occupied with these visits, and they have given him a great deal of joy . . .[48]

In its next issue the same journal continued with Sohrab's letter:

There have been great rejoicings at Haifa to celebrate the ending of the war, and Abdul Baha has entered fully into the Peace celebrations inaugurated by the military authorities. Early in December he was invited to assist at a meeting of the different religious heads of Haifa to institute a relief work for the poor, and a few days later to address a final word of prayer at an immense public gathering to celebrate the end of the war. He is in splendid health and spirits and appears to contemplate a visit to America probably via England.

We gave some extracts last week from a letter (dated December 2), from M. Ahmad Sohrab, who is with Abdul Baha at Haifa. M. Sohrab writes further: –

'Since the beginning of war Abdul Baha has been subjected to manifold trials and difficulties, but through them all his invincible spirit shone forth with greater brilliancy, his trust in God was a source of comfort for others, and his good humour saved all of us from a bitter pessimism which was too prevalent at the time. He was ever ready to help the distressed and the needy; often He would deprive himself and his own family of the necessities of life, that the hungry might be fed and the naked be clothed. With unconquerable determination and wonderful resourcefulness, he was divinely assisted to protect and keep alive the almost 300 members of the Persian Bahai Colony in Haifa and Acca. For three years he spent months in Tiberias and Adassayah, supervising extensive works of agriculture, and procuring wheat, corn and other food stuffs for our maintenance, and to distribute among the starving Mohamedan and Christian families. Were it not for his pre-vision and ceaseless activity none of us would have survived. For two years all the harvests were eaten by armies of locusts. At times like dark clouds they covered the sky for hours. This, coupled with the unprecedented extortions and looting of the Turkish officials and the extensive buying of foodstuffs by the Germans to be shipped to the "Fatherland" in a time of scarcity, brought famine. In Lebanon alone more than 100.000 people died from starvation. Thousands lived for a few days on the peelings of oranges and bananas, the skin of watermelons and the grass of the country, and then died with no one to mourn them or bury their corpses. It became a usual sight to find each morning the dead bodies of young girls and children along the public thoroughfare. People looked at them and passed by. Alas! All feelings of pity, sympathy and humanity are dead in us. At the sight of suffering children and dying old men and women, we stand like Egyptian mummies, like degenerate grinning donkeys!'[49]

In the summer of 1919, a reporter with the London *Times* was able to meet 'Abdu'l-Bahá in Haifa. He afterwards wrote an article which was published on 17 September and which was basically a summary of the history and teachings of the Bahá'í Faith.[50] This article was later reproduced in other newspapers.[51]

Meanwhile, American agencies distributed some notes on 'Abdu'l-Bahá. One of them stated that He 'is reported to be alive and in good

health' and added that 'reports of Abdul's death were unfounded'.⁵²
In January 1919 a further note released by agencies stated that 'With
the breaking of the Turkish power in Palestine another religious cult
has been liberated from persecution, that of Bahaism, or Babism' and
summarized for its readers some of the Bahá'í teachings and the life of
'Abdu'l-Bahá.⁵³

Resuming Correspondence with the World

The end of the war also allowed Bahá'ís and friends of 'Abdu'l-Bahá to
communicate with Him again.

Among the Master's correspondents was the former governor of
New York, William Sulzer (1863–1941),⁵⁴ who wrote to 'Abdu'l-Bahá
regarding the establishment of the League of Nations. 'Abdu'l-Bahá's
reply, dated 18 June 1919 and translated by Dr Zia Bagdadi, was published in the *New York World*:

> To the Honorable William Sulzer, ex-Governor, New York,
> Greetings:
>
> O thou, who art the well-wisher of humanity, felicitations!
>   Your epistle concerning the League of Nations has been received
> and read with great joy.
>   I am hopeful that the members of the League of Nations, especially President Woodrow Wilson, the well-wisher of the world,
> shall be confirmed in this: that in accordance with the teachings
> of Baha'o'llah there shall soon be established a Great Tribunal,
> the members of which shall be composed of the best men and women
> from all the Governments of the earth. This Great Tribunal must be
> the guarantor of universal peace.
>   The present is the beginning of the dawn of universal peace. The
> hope of the world is this: that the sun of universal peace may rise
> with a supremacy that shall entirely dispel the darkness of war and
> its infamous disgrace.
>   The question of universal peace is one of the principles of the
> teachings of Baha'o'llah. These teachings have other principles
> that make them complete, such as: The investigation of truth and
> reality and the abandonment of old superstitions; the oneness of

humanity; unity and religious amity; that religion must be the cause of concord; that all religions must conform with science and reason; that there must be no religious, racial or national prejudices; that there must be a oneness of language, that is, the adoption of a universal auxiliary language, so that every mind shall know two languages – one the national tongue and the other the universal language; that there must be a solution to social problems and economic questions based on justice to all; that there must be equality of the rights of women and men; that righteousness and justice must prevail, and that there must be education and freedom for all the sons and daughters of Mother Earth.

With the efforts of your President the matter of universal peace has come forth as expounded in the League of Nations.

Through the favor of the True One, and by the Word of God, I pray the League of Nations shall soon become a fact; that universal peace shall thenceforth be established; that then the brotherhood of man shall be recognized, and that your honor and the people of your country may continue a manifestation of their confirmation.

Praise be to God. Love and benediction.

Abdul Baha Abbas[55]

* * *

During the brief period that elapsed between the liberation of Haifa and the passing of 'Abdu'l-Bahá, many westerners traveling in Palestine attempted to meet Him. One of them was the famous suffragist Millicent Garrett Fawcett (1847–1929), who at the time of 'Abdu'l-Bahá's two visits to England was the president of the National Union of Women's Suffrage Societies, the largest suffrage organization in the United Kingdom, which published in its official organ, *The Common Cause*, several references to the Bahá'í religion (see chapter 31 above). In the spring of 1921 Fawcett visited Haifa and 'Akká, where she planned to meet 'Abdu'l-Bahá. She even carried an introduction letter with her. Unfortunately, 'Abdu'l-Bahá was in Tiberias and Fawcett was unable to meet Him. Nevertheless, she mentioned Him in the memoirs of her travels, in which she recounted that 'Abdu'l-Bahá 'was resident in Haifa at the time of the bombardment. He assembled his followers about him and told them to have no fear, that not a hair of their head would be touched: he was quite right, the shells were fired but fell harmlessly into the Bay of Acre.'⁵⁶

Jo Goudsmit, from the Netherlands, was luckier: not only was she able to meet 'Abdu'l-Bahá but she also corresponded with Him. In one of her various letters to the *Nieuwe Rotterdamsche Courant* (Rotterdam) narrating her impressions of the Holy Land the author gave an interesting account of her meeting with 'Abdu'l-Bahá:

ABDUL BAHA AND HIS TEACHINGS
(Private correspondence)

Tiberias, March 14

Of the many strange personalities one finds in Palestine, one of the most interesting and genial is Abdul Baha or Abbas Effendi, the name by which everyone in Palestine knows him.

I heard about this Prophet's son a long time ago; people had suggested that I should make a point of visiting him and told me about the work of the preachers of Baha'ism, who have been preaching world peace for over 70 years, and who want to unite the various religions into a single one. When my travels took me to Haifa, I requested an audience with Abbas Effendi, who was most willing to consent. An audience, that is what one should really call a visit with this man, who is treated by his many followers and admirers with royal honours. Abbas Effendi lives in one of the most beautiful villas in Haifa, surrounded by a lovely garden full of roses and flowering plants. We were led into a large and luxurious room, where Abbas Effendi soon joined us.

He is a venerable elderly gentleman, 76 years old, with white hair and a long white beard. He was wearing a grey robe, a white belt around his waist, a long brown coat, and a white turban. As customary in the east he was squatting on a cushion in the window sill while talking to us. He was interested to know what we wanted to find out from him. When I told him that I would like to write about him and his teachings in a Dutch newspaper, he was very happy because, he said, we don't have any followers in Holland yet and we are not well known there. Abbas Effendi speaks only eastern languages, Persian, Turkish and Arabic; however he has a secretary who is always around and translates his words into English.

It is very difficult to get Abbas Effendi to talk about himself but when he talks about his father, who was the actual prophet and founder of Baha'ism and whose faithful follower he is, his eyes lighten up, the old body rises up with youthful energy, the words flow from his lips, and one understands how this man can awaken enthusiasm and inspire thousands of people.

I asked him about the new religion founded by his father.

He answered that his father did not really create a new religion but a Baha'i organisation. It gets its name from the prophet Bahaullah, his father. For the last six thousand years, he continued, there has been intolerance and strife between the various religions, as well as fanaticism, hate, and political friction between peoples and countries.

Particularly in the east the situation is dark and confused. Bahaullah appeared in the east like the rising sun and illuminated the eastern darkness with his rays. He preached that people should not blindly follow the teachings of their forefathers but must search for the truth in all things themselves. Seventy years ago he began preaching a general religion in Tehran in Persia, a religion that unites all the fundamental principles of the different religions into one. The basic principles of this religion are:

1. Independent search for the truth, that is, one should refrain from blindly following others.

2. The unity of humankind; all people are lambs of God and God is the loving shepherd. He is kind to all of His lambs, He created, nurtured, and protected them all, this a sign of His love.

This is God's plan and we must follow God's plan because, no matter how perfect human plans may seem, it can never be compared to God's work. Therefore we must reject racism, religious and political prejudice, in order to be able to follow God's plan. Prejudice destroys humankind's happiness.

3. Religion should be a cause for harmony for humankind. If religion creates enmity and hatred, it would be better if religion did not exist.

4. Religion must be in agreement with science and common sense. If religion is not in agreement with science and common sense, it does not satisfy our conscience.

5. Equality between the sexes, because humankind has two wings, man and woman. If either one is weaker than the other, the bird cannot fly. If both wings have equal strength, the bird can fly, therefore if both do not have equal strength, humankind cannot flourish.

6. Peace throughout; a court must be established, depending on the size of the population each country must choose 2 or 3 members, who are the best, both in competence and character. These persons must be chosen by the parliaments of countries and this choice must be ratified by the people, the ministers, and the rulers of the country, so that these members are the true representatives of the entire country. All together they will form an international court of arbitration that will settle all international disagreements. The decisions of this court must be sufficient. If a country does not comply with these decisions, the whole world will turn against this country and force it to obey.

7. There must be a general language, that is, one language will be chosen from existing languages or a new language must be created that is spoken everywhere and becomes the general language. Since we need diversity, the individual languages must also be preserved.

A general language will encourage mutual relationships.

There are many other principles but the ones mentioned here are the most important.

How will these principles be implemented, I asked him.

These principles will be implemented with God's will. Currently they are spread out around the world, in Europe, America, Japan, Australia, India, Persia, etc.

Are there any priests?

All Baha'is are people who disseminate these principles by personal contact.

Do you have any religious rituals?

No, we only have some prayers in various languages, and sometimes we gather at my father's grave in Haifa.

How many members does your organisation have?

We have four to five million members around the world. Sometimes we have meetings; at a congress that we hope to organise soon we will have to decide whether we will adopt one of the existing languages as the world language or create a new language.

To my question if the organisation allows its members to marry more than one woman, the answer was: No, unless in rare exceptions, for example in the case of insanity.

Is there any class of people, for example young intellectuals, the lower class, or wealthy people, who are especially interested?

No, we have followers among all classes of the population. Everyone can adhere to his own religion, but still sympathise with our ideals and help disseminate them.

After our interview, Abbas Effendi, with innate courtesy, asked us to have tea with him and he led us, still accompanied by his secretary, to a large, simple room. The number of chairs made me think that we were in a kind of meeting room. The fine china, the fragrant tea, very rare in Palestine, the graceful way in which pastries and tea were served by an Arabic servant, made me assume a refined, luxurious household.

After tea I asked the secretary if the Master, as he is called, would tell us something of his personal life, since with great modesty he had avoided speaking of himself. The genial old man seemed to be a bit tired, so I was not surprised that he said he would like to put this off for another time. Subsequently we said a friendly goodbye to the Master, after he had given me a signed portrait as I had requested.

I did not expect to see him again soon and would have been hesitant to again take up the time of this interesting old man, if fate had not decided otherwise. On a beautiful spring morning we left Haifa to spend a week in Tiberias, on the shore of the scenic lake Kineret. Right away on the train we saw our old friend again, he was reclining in the corner of a compartment and was accompanied by a few servants and his secretary, who surrounded him with attention. All together we took the road from the station in Samakh to the boat that would ferry us across the lake to Tiberias. The beautiful scenery made us forget the discomfort of the boat which was little more than a barge. Abbas Effendi, too, wrapped in his luxurious travel blankets, enjoyed the clear spring sun on the friendly blue lake. He recognised us right away and greeted us with a friendly 'Good Morning', one of the few English expressions he knew. We shared the same destination and arrived together in the comfortable hotel in Tiberias, with its beautiful view of the lake and the mountains. Like an old acquaintance he was greeted there warmly and with a certain reverence. I intended to learn more about him in the next few days. This was not difficult, because on his own initiative he sent me an invitation to come and talk to him. Thus I found myself a few evenings ago sitting opposite him in the quiet, simple hotel room and he asked me, in his turn, about my plans and my expectations of the future of Palestine. He was now also willing to tell me a little more about his past and particularly that of his respected father.

Abbas Effendi's father, the prophet Bahaullah, began his career in Tehran, where the Persian government and the Muslim clergy did everything they could to oppose him because they considered his principles to be revolutionary. Bahaullah was the son of a Persian minister and from a very wealthy and prominent family. When he would not stop disseminating his principles, he was thrown in an underground prison, all his goods, houses, land, country estates, and property were confiscated; he was 28 years old at the time. This first time he spent four years in jail, he was accused of revolutionary acts against the government. His friends did everything they could to free him and before long they succeeded but he was banned from Persia. Then he went to Baghdad. His teachings spread quickly and the number of his followers increased. In Persia, where the movement gained momentum, they suffered from persecution. Soon thereafter the Persian Government asked that the Turkish government ban him from Baghdad, in order to separate the Baha'is from their leaders and so he was sent to Constantinople, from there to Adrianople, and finally to Akka in Palestine. He was banned in this way four times but he never thought of giving up his work. His friends helped him by smuggling from his prison cell letters and news to kings and other high officials, asking them repeatedly to do their utmost to help ensure world peace. This was fifty years ago; the letters have been published. In these letters he points out that the current politics were dangerous and he urged them to create a general peace court, in which all countries would be represented, to settle international disagreements. He also predicted the future; he addressed the German Emperor, for example, with the following words: 'Do not pride yourself on your fame, don't forget that Napoleon was greater than you; and how did he end? Take him as an example, help promote eternal peace. Berlin is now at the pinnacle of its fame but I already hear the laments of a crying Berlin.' In similar fashion he addressed the sultan of Turkey and predicted the return of the Jews to Palestine.

After living in exile in Akka for twenty-five years, alternately as an exile and as a prisoner in jail, he died, seventy-five years old and, no matter how much he had suffered, his determination was never broken. After his death his son continued his father's work, he had lived through it all with him and had always followed him into exile and imprisonment. He always lived in foreign countries and spent forty years in exile or in prison. Fifteen years after his father's death, revolution broke out in Turkey. After the constitution of Young Turks was established, by then 68 years old, he was released.

Abbas Effendi went to Egypt, Europe, and America and spent four years of his life traveling to disseminate his teachings. When the Balkan war began he returned to Palestine. The movement now has four to five million followers. His spirit unbroken after the long years of suffering, full of enthusiasm for his teachings which he treasures above all else, respected and loved by followers and outsiders alike, Abbas Effendi spends the remainder of his life spreading his teachings in word and in writing. He works from morning till night, answers letters from countries around the world, receives visits, and gives audiences.

May this friendly, idealistic old man, who has suffered so much for his ideas and ideals, have a happy twilight of his life. If there were many of these energetic personalities in the world such as Abbas Effendi and his father, what now appears to remain an illusion for many years to come and probably forever, might be possible: peace on earth and love between all peoples.[57]

Once this article was published, its author sent a copy to 'Abdu'l-Bahá, who in turn answered with a missive which was published in the same journal on 13 August 1921:

> At the conclusion of this article is a small sample of how easterners think and feel differently from what we are used to in Europe and how people treat each other in different ways. The following is the translation of a letter I received some time ago from my friend Abbas Effendi (son of the prophet and founder of Baha'ism), after

I had sent him the article that I recently published in the N.R.C. about him and his teachings:

Greetings and praise to you.

He is God (in coloured print) Oh, you, the truth-seeking traveler. Praise God that you reached Palestine, the Holy Country, the place of the association of only holy prophets, and have been able to continue to pursue your search, informing yourself, as is your duty, about the culture and people in Palestine. You searched for the truth, you met me and were completely open and honest in your dealings with me. I explained to you some of the principles of His Holiness Bahaullah. This is a token of my greatest love.

From Jerusalem you sent an article to one of the Dutch newspapers. This article was published and disseminated; you can be sure that this article will be of great importance in the future. It will be printed and publicised over and over again. Consequently, your name and fame will be revered at gatherings and meetings.

I pray for you, that you will be supported and blessed by everyone. Finally, I profess to you my deepest respect.
ABDUL BAHA ABBAS[58]

The Knighthood

During the war years 'Abdu'l-Bahá's efforts to secure food and to cover the basic needs of the population of Haifa and 'Akká were crucial for saving the lives of many. After the war His mediation and intervention in the affairs of Haifa were also crucial in preventing hostilities and establishing security in a city composed of diverse religious and national parties which supported different sides during the war but now were confronted with the challenge of re-establishing normal relations. 'One of Allenby's first acts,' mentioned a traveler in Palestine while discussing the difficult social conditions in the region, 'was to consult and afterward to decorate with an honor, the venerable Abdul Baha, "Servant of God", at whose house on Mount Carmel the professors of all religions are made equally welcome . . . The house of Abdul Baha was as an oasis of toleration amid a wilderness of intolerance. And it is only upon the lines which he laid down that Palestine can be governed.'[59]

In recognition of these services rendered by 'Abdu'l-Bahá to the population of Palestine, the British government made Him a Knight Commander of the Order of the British Empire, which attracts the title of 'Sir'.[60] A brief note of 'Abdu'l-Bahá's knighthood was published on 15 January 1920 in the Parisian magazine *L'Asie Arabe*. The same note mentioned that Hassan bey Checry, president of the municipality of Haifa, had also been knighted.[61]

39

THE PASSING OF 'ABDU'L-BAHÁ

First News

In the early hours of Monday 28 November 1921, 'Abdu'l-Bahá passed away in His home in Haifa.[1] News of His death was soon wired across the world and several articles were published in His honor bearing testimony to the esteem in which 'Abdu'l-Bahá was held in all corners of the world.

The London *Times* was the first journal in the West to publish the news. A correspondent in Haifa wired on 28 November that 'Abdul Baha Abbas el Bahai, the leader of the Bahai cult, died here today'. The article included information about the origins of the Bahá'í Faith and biographical notes about the Master. It closed by stating that 'Abdul Baha barely escaped being crucified by the Turks during their evacuation of Palestine. The British authorities recognized his position of influence, and it was at Lord Allenby's suggestion that he was knighted last year. He leaves no successor as head of Bahaism. The affairs of the movement will be directed by a council of 12. Abdul' Baha's grandson, Shoghi Rabbani, is at present studying at Oxford.'[2] This article was used by news agencies and was the basis of further articles published in other newspapers in the United Kingdom.[3] In the United States the Associated Press released a note based on this article which was published in many newspapers[4] and even reached Canada,[5] Cuba[6] and Japan.[7]

Some journals added information of their own to the information received by agencies. The *New York Times* recalled the fact that 'Abdu'l-Bahá had visited America in 1912 and that He 'was received not only by the societies of Bahaism, which had gradually grown up here, but also by several universities, notably Leland Stanford University, whose guest he was for several days'. The same article also mentioned that 'during the worldwide debate over the League of Nations his messages from Mount Carmel were frequent and eloquent in favor of the League. He also believed in the equality of sexes.'[8] The *Chicago Daily Tribune* also mentioned that 'Abdu'l-Bahá 'was in Chicago in 1912, the guest of the large congregation here. On May 1 he dedicated the site at the Sheridan Road bridge in Wilmette where the Bahaists now are building a temple . . .'[9]

Further Articles

As the days passed, several editorials and opinion articles about 'Abdu'l-Bahá appeared in the world's press. In America on 2 December the *New-York Tribune* published an editorial about 'Abdu'l-Bahá which consisted of an introduction to the Bahá'í Faith. It opened by declaring that 'A prophet, as his followers believe, and the son of a prophet, was Abdul Baha, who is now at rest with all prophetic souls bygone. He lived to see a remarkable expansion of the quietist cult of which he was the head. The Bahai temple, the nine sided architectural marvel that is to rise on the shore of Lake Michigan, will bear witness to the appeal of the blending of religions to thousands in the workaday New World.'[10]

Another editorial about the passing of 'Abdu'l-Bahá was published on the same day in the *Boston Herald*. In a solemn tone the article opened with the following words: 'The spirit has passed from the home of the Persian prophet on Mount Carmel, and heads are reverently bowed in every country because of the departure of Abdul Baha.'[11]

Also on 2 December the *Standard Union* (Brooklyn) published a picture of 'Abdu'l-Bahá released by the Underwood Agency.[12]

A satirical comment published in some journals stated apropos of the passing of the Master that 'Abbas multiplied its followers into hundreds of thousands by his "clairvoyance". He predicted the world war, with accuracy, three times. So did England's military and naval experts.'[13]

The *Evening Telegram* (New York) published on 4 December the following article, which included a portrait of 'Abdu'l-Bahá:

THE PASSING OF 'ABDU'L-BAHÁ

PROPHET OF WORLD PEACE CLAIMED BY DEATH AS ARMS PARLEY VINDICATES CULT
ABDUL BAHA'S CAREER ENDED JUST AT MOMENT WHEN UNIVERSE RECOGNIZES HIS PRINCIPLES

MOURNED IN ALL COUNTRIES
TENS OF THOUSANDS NOW FOLLOWERS — MIGHTY TEMPLE IN CHICAGO NEARING COMPLETION

Eleven years before the first peace tribunal convened at The Hague, in the latter days of the nineteenth century, a venerable Eastern prophet raised his voice and foretold the coming of a day when leaders of nations would hold a conference whose object would be universal peace – when limitation of armament would be effected, and the building of warships cease – when science devoted to the creation of destructive weapons should be turned to constructive creations for the good of mankind.

In cryptic language the prophet told of the disbanding of all armies, other than a mere soldiery to maintain internal order; and described in detail the lifting of the burden of taxation to maintain armament from the necks of the peoples all over the world.

While the Disarmament Conference in Washington was making great strides toward the fulfillment of this prophecy, the ancient and venerable wearily turned on his side in his Far Eastern home last Monday and died. But before the death mask had set his face in immobility, a smile of peace and good will stole over his face. Thus passed Abdul Baha, prophet and son of the founder of Bahaism, the 'universal religion'.

FOLLOWERS BY THOUSANDS

In all countries of the world today can be found mourners of the prophet Abdul Baha. Due to his personal visiting of many of the countries, including America in 1912, his gospel was received with open arms by gropers for the light and his followers now number tens of thousands.

Churches of all denominations in New York City and Chicago were thrown open to him, for, unlike the leaders of many cults, he preached not the errors of present religions but their sameness and the fact that they should all be united as one, inasmuch as they were founded on the same theory – the sovereignty of an Almighty God. Jews and Christians, Mohammedans and Buddhists, Zoroastrians and Spiritualists, Theosophists and Freemasons, all were urged by the prophet to recognize the universality of their religions and to worship in peace and harmony together.

The world was amazed at the doctrine, for the cult prior to the arrival the prophet in this country had been known to only a few thousand followers. Yet Abdul Baha was the son of the founder of a religion which has prospered in spite of persecution since its inception in Persia in the year 1834.

Today, in Chicago, the crypt of a mighty temple dedicated to Bahaism is nearing completion. Massive as to architecture, with a strange intermingling of Byzantine, Gothic and Renaissance in its decoration, its most beautiful feature lies in the adornment of its great dome, on which will appear the symbol of every religion in the world today. Three hundred thousand dollars has been expended in the erection of the temple so far, and a campaign for funds for its completion will be started in January when the National Board of Consultation meets there.

It is the first nine-sided temple to be erected. The 'nine' is significant, inasmuch as it is one of the symbols of Bahaism. Its significance is perfection, inasmuch as nine is the highest arithmetical unit. Its architecture, too, is significant of the desire for the union of all nations in the world.

WORLD PEACE PROPHESIED

Abdul Baha is dead, His life of persecution at the hands of the Mohammedans, which included years in close confinement, is over. But his works live on and his prophecy of universal peace, almost thirty years old, handed down to the public . . .

The growth of Bahaism is unique in its correspondence to the growth of other religions. It thrived under persecution. It had its martyrs and its traitors. The Sea of Galilee saw the prophet of Bahaism at its side for meditation, while the wilderness where the Nazarene fasted witnessed the seclusion of its founder for many years . . .

Preaching his doctrines, Abbas Effendi, the prophet of love, who became Abdul Baha (the servant of Baha) took up his father's work.

In 1912 he came to America to spread his doctrine. He also visited European countries. His followers grew in number, to the consternation of the Mohammedans. Then came the war, and Abdul Baha became a strict prisoner in his home in Haifa, Syria. Prior to the war the Turks had imprisoned him there and excluded all visitors but his work went on. When General Allenby loosed the captive chains in the land he went to Abdul Baha for advice. Then came Zionists, intent on guidance for their entrance into Palestine. The venerable old prophet no more was the captive martyr. He was rather the leader to whom all looked for guidance. Aged, yet with calm and keen intellect, he lived the final three years of his life in peace and plenty.

But it was through suffering that the prophet expected to accomplish his mission.

'Consider the candle how it weeps its life away drop by drop that it may shed its light', is one of his much quoted sayings.[14]

The *Wyoming State Tribune* (Cheyenne) related the following anecdote about 'Abdu'l-Bahá in an editorial:

A Cheyenne man relates that a serious-minded middle aged woman once came to his office and introduced herself as a representative of the Bahai movement and wished to organize a class here. With a great deal of dignity and reverence she said, 'Are you familiar with the Bahai movement?' Much to her consternation and surprise the man replied – 'Well, I know the prophet.' 'You mean Abdul Baha?' She rejoined. 'Yes, madam.' And then she was sure that he was making light of her cause. She seemed to think it sacrilegious that he should claim acquaintanceship with the Syrian Leader.

Yet it was literally true, as ten years before Abdul Baha Abbas during one of his world pilgrimages, had visited the United States, and this man had happened to attend a general gathering with Abdul and was fortunate enough to stand in the hand-to-hand circle with the prophet when he blessed those present.

It will be interesting to observe in the future if the Bahai Cult will long survive its great leader.[15]

The black journal *The Appeal* (St Paul) published another editorial that referred to 'Abdu'l-Bahá as 'one of the greatest men of the day'. After a presentation of the Bahá'í Faith, the article stated that 'there are many thousands of colored people in the United States who have left orthodox Christianity and have become Bahaists because of the hypocrisy of the so-called Christians on the color question'.[16]

Another black newspaper, the *Chicago Defender*, published the following editorial on 10 December:

> The news of the death of the magnetic leader of the Bahai movement will come as a great shock, not only to the followers who knew and loved this prophet and his teachings but to admirers everywhere . . .
>
> The philosophy of the Bahai movement has always appealed to us for there is little question but that if we could look forward with any confidence to a really universal religion which would transcend race and creeds, especially creeds, we would be freed from most of the ills from which we suffer at present. This movement is the only one to our knowledge which has among its followers those who actually practice what they preach when it comes to this question of race and class. We have never been able to discover a trace of race or class prejudice among the followers of Abdul Baha. We have joined them at worship and visited with them in their homes. From the point of view of tolerance, religious or otherwise, and for sweetness of character, we commend you to the true Bahai. May they prosper and increase in strength and numbers! We shall mourn the departure of their prophet and look forward to the rise of his successor to show this old world what man can do, if he will, to free himself of those trappings of the devil – hate and prejudice, and their twins – bigotry and intolerance.[17]

On 31 December, the *Defender* published a letter by Louis Gregory in which he expressed himself 'deeply touched by your recent article about Abdul Baha' and described his impressions of Him.[18]

On 9 December the *Jewish Criterion* (Pittsburgh) published an editorial by Charles H. Joseph stating that the religion

> . . . had been largely misunderstood and misinterpreted as is usually the case when the Occidental attempts to develop an intelligent contact with the spiritual ideas of the East. One cannot but consider

with respect the fundamental thought of Bahaism that it is the root of all constructive religions before they became corrupted by theology, dogma and politics. Now I am not saying that Bahaism is that root but I am in sympathy with that thought of a root or original truth that one day all religious peoples of the world may return to . . .[19]

On 18 December the *Kalamazoo Gazette* reported that 'when, on the first day of December, the papers carried the news of the death of Abdul Baha, many people were attracted by the beautifully gentle portrait of the ancient Persian and have wondered where they could learn something concerning the teaching of this venerable sage' and recommended the reading of Horace Holley's *Bahai: The Spirit of the Age* (1921).[20] Other journals also recommended the reading of this book.[21]

The Unitarian *Christian Register* (Boston) stated in a note that appeared on 12 January 1922 that 'the Christian world must mourn the passing of this teacher of the reconciliation of all religions, whose lofty moral beauty and profound spirituality was commented on with enthusiasm by those who came in contact with him'.[22]

Associated Press distributed a further article by a correspondent in Jerusalem who introduced the Bahá'í Faith and mentioned that 'His funeral assumed an international aspect at which were present many notables representing many countries. Sir Herbert Samuel, High Commissioner of Palestine, was in the procession'.[23]

This news was also published in some Mexican newspapers.[24]

The Independent (New York), a magazine that in 1912 had published several articles on the Bahá'í Faith, published Frederic Dean's reminiscences of 'Abdu'l-Bahá:

> ABDUL BAHA, whose death was chronicled in the press the other day, was more than a personality – he was an inspiration; an idealist, whose self-devotion breathed new life into dying creeds. His gospel appealed with equal force to Christians, Moslems, and Jews; to Buddhists and Hindus, Shintoists and Parsis. His idealism was to many a manifestation of the very source of life, light, and love. He came at a time when the soul's craving for hope and faith was – seemingly – unappeased by any one of the many organized and acknowledged religions.

I first met the teacher in an up-town church. I had been sent by my paper to report the sermon. The speaker's likeness to my own father was so startling, that, immediately after the service, I entered the anteroom and told him of the remarkable resemblance. Very quietly he answered: 'I am your father and you are my son. Come and dine with me.' Another engagement prevented, but I asked if I might take breakfast with him the following morning. 'Come,' he said. I went, and after that first meeting followed others. We walked in his garden, and, as we walked, we talked. I told him of his peculiar attraction to me on account of my own outlook on life; that I came from Southern Asia and that I was a Buddhist – a Buddhist-Christian. 'So am I,' replied the teacher. 'I am also a Confucian-Christian and a Brahmin-Christian; a Jewish and a Mohammedan-Christian. I am a brother to all who love truth – truth in whatsoever garb they choose to clothe it.'

We talked of many things – of the beginnings of religion – of animism and ancestor worship, of the mysticism of Indian philosophy, of Hellenic culture, and of the coming of the Buddha, of the Christ and of Mohammed. He instructed me in the religion of his own home country – went back to the time when Persia attained her unequalled prosperity under the Sassanide dynasty, in the second century after the coming of the Christ . . .

No leader of men could be more simple in his tastes or more naive in his expression of them. On the last day that I saw him he gave me his rose – he always had a freshly picked rose on his table – and kissed me on both cheeks (as was his wont). As he left me at the door he said, 'You may be waylaid on your way out. The people who are good enough to come to see me think of me and speak of me as something especially holy and set apart. But do not mind them. Think of me as your loving father and not as some divine thing to be adored.' In the reception room I was immediately surrounded by the patient watchers, who scrambled for the rose as for some sacred relic.

Those who met him carried away a nameless something that made life's pleasures brighter.[25]

Other articles about 'Abdu'l-Bahá were also published in the *American Review of Reviews*,[26] the *Outlook*[27] and the *Youth's Companion*.[28] In the early weeks of 1922 local newspapers reported or announced some of the services held in honor of 'Abdu'l-Bahá in the United States.[29] The passing of 'Abdu'l-Bahá was also recorded in the necrologies for the year 1921 that appeared in many newspapers. One of these was compiled by Edward W. Pickard and distributed by the Western Newspaper Union (Chicago).[30]

In England the *Morning Post* described 'Abdu'l-Bahá as 'resembling St. Francis of Assisi in charity, in kindness, and in an indomitable determination for true service to humanity. He enjoined his followers never to speak unkindly about another, even though that other be their enemy.'[31]

On 2 December the *Daily Mirror* and the *Daily Sketch*[32] published a picture of 'Abdu'l-Bahá. The caption in the *Mirror* recalled that 'he came to London in 1911 as missionary of his Asiatic faith, his venerable appearance attracting much attention'.[33] On 7 December the *Manchester Guardian* published a lengthy article about the Bahá'í Faith and the life of 'Abdu'l-Bahá entitled 'The Prophet of Acre'. In dealing with His visit to England the article stated that 'in 1911 he was one of the successes in London. One received invitations to hear him in public and meet him in private. He knew no English and his message, conveyed through an interpreter sounded thin. But no one who saw him could deny the power and beauty of the personal presence.'[34]

Another article about the passing of 'Abdu'l-Bahá appeared in the *Pall Mall Gazette* (London) on 19 December and presented the Bahá'í Faith. 'The death just announced of Sir Abdul Baha Abbas', opened the article, 'removes from the world's stage a man who, by his large following in all quarters of the globe, was held to be no less than a supernatural being.'[35]

'The Spiritualist magazine *Light* (London) reported on 3 December: 'Major Tudor Pole informs us that he has learned by cablegram, from Palestine of the decease of Abdul Baha Abbas . . .'[36]

The *Children's Newspaper*, a magazine which, as its title indicates, was addressed to children and which was edited by Arthur Mee, carried on 14 January 1922 an article about 'Abdu'l-Bahá and the Bahá'í Faith, which among other things stated:

> One of the little paragraphs in the papers of late has announced the death of Abdul Baha in Syria. It is an interesting piece of news, for Abdul Baha was the greatest apostle of a famous religion in the East . . .

One of the greatest problems of the future is how the changing world can get on with the devoted but stubborn, narrow, warlike Mohammedan faith. At least we all ought to know about it. Particularly we ought to know that today inside Mohammedanism there is a reform movement quietly going on, headed by men who claim, as is the custom with the East, to be prophets. It is perhaps only as a grain of mustard-seed, but it is one of the grains that may grow and astonish the world, as Christianity did, almost before the world is aware. The religion is called Babiism.[37]

In France *Le Temps* gave on 9 December the news of the passing of 'Abdu'l-Bahá and stated that 'some ten years ago Abdul Beha sojourned in Paris and expounded his charitable word in social circles'.[38] The following day the same journal carried an article by Jean Lefranc – who had written about 'Abdu'l-Bahá during His visits to Paris – in which he recalled his impressions of the Master:

Bahaism is in fact the religion of charity and simplicity . . . When I heard Abdul Baha I was convinced that he was a venerable old man. He took my hands and told me that the press is one of the great powers of the world and that he had proclaimed this truth in his books. Under his white turban, his eyes reflected intelligence and goodness. He was a like a father, affectionate, and simple. His power, it seemed to me, stemmed from the fact that he knew how to love all peoples and how to receive their love.[39]

On 9 December the *Journal des Débats* also published an article about the passing of 'Abdu'l-Bahá which stated that 'the loss of the teacher of St. John of Acre will be most keenly felt by all his followers and above all by those who had the privilege of his acquaintance. The Theosophists of Paris, especially, will never lose the remembrance of the venerable old man who visited them in 1911.'[40] This comment was later echoed in the *Egyptian Gazette*.[41]

In Switzerland, on 6 December 1921, the *Gazette de Lausanne* published accounts similar to those published by other newspapers.[42] In Austria, the *Neues Wiener Journal* also reported the passing of 'Abdu'l-Bahá in an article based on what had been published previously in *Le Temps*.[43]

THE PASSING OF 'ABDU'L-BAHÁ

In Alexandria, the *Egyptian Gazette* published on 30 November an article about the passing of 'Abdu'l-Bahá which also included a lengthy introduction to the Bahá'í Faith. It began with a cablegram sent from Jerusalem on 28 November reporting that 'Sir Abd-el-Baha Abbas Off. K.B.E. died last night at Haifa. The High Commissioner is leaving Jerusalem to-night to attend the funeral.' 'The death of Abdul Baha', continued the article, 'will be received with great regret in Egypt for, after the Turkish revolution and the downfall of Abdul Hami, he was enabled to leave Acre and came to Egypt. For some time he settled at Ramleh, having taken a flat close to the tramway halt at Seffer, where he used to receive his many visitors. We used often to see him, and published interviews with him in the "Egyptian Gazette". Few had a more impressive personality or exercised a greater charm that did this remarkable Persian.'[44]

In Cairo the *Sphinx* published on 17 December an article about 'Abdu'l-Bahá by the Bahá'í Jean Stannard.[45]

In India the *Bombay Chronicle* published a picture of 'Abdu'l-Bahá on 1 January 1922.[46] Coinciding with the Second All-India Bahá'í Convention, the *Times of India* (Bombay) published an editorial article about 'Abdu'l-Bahá which introduced the Bahá'í Faith and made the following remarks about the Master:

> In more normal times than the present the death of Abdu'l Baha, which was sorrowfully referred to at the Bahai Conference in Bombay, would have stirred the feelings of many who, without belonging to the Baha'i brotherhood, sympathize with its tenets and admire the life work of those who rounded it. As it is, we have learned almost by chance of this great religious leader's death, but that fact need not prevent us from turning aside from polities and the turmoil of current events to consider what this man did and what he aimed at . . .
>
> At his funeral last month on Mt. Carmel, which was attended by the British governor of Jerusalem, many nations paid a last tribute to the man whom all had honored and respected. It is not for us now to judge whether the purity, the mysticism, and the exalted ideals of the Bahai Movement will continue unchanged after the loss of the great leader, or to speculate on whether the Bahai Movement will some day become a force in the world as great as or greater than

Christianity or Islam. But we would pay a tribute to the memory of a man who was a great teacher and a great missionary, who wielded a vast influence for good, and who, if he was destined to see many of his ideals seemingly shattered in the world war, remained true to his convictions and to his belief in the possibility of a reign of peace and love and who far more effectively than Tolstoy showed the West that religion is a vital force that can never be disregarded.[47]

In Japan, the *Japan Advertiser* (Tokyo) announced on 7 January 1922 that 'a memorial service for His Holiness Abdul Baha will be held at 2 o'clock this afternoon at the Unitarian Church, Shikoku-macht, Mita. All who are interested in the services are invited to attend.'[48] The following day the same journal carried a picture of 'Abdu'l-Bahá and reported His passing.[49]

Esperantists also lamented the passing of 'Abdu'l-Bahá. A short note in the *British Esperantist* (London) stated that 'although we can not claim him as a practising Esperantist we lost a good friend when he died', adding that 'he lived, worked, suffered for human brotherhood and universal peace, and his teaching will not pass away'.[50] A few months later, *Esperanto* (Geneva), the official organ of the Universal Esperanto Association edited by Edmon Privat, also reported the passing of 'Abdu'l-Bahá, offering some biographical notes about Him and underlining His often-reiterated comments favoring the adoption of a universal language. 'Esperantists can see in the noble teachings of Bahaism', concluded the article, 'the realization of their ideal of unity and brotherhood.'[51]

The Funeral

The day after His passing, 'Abdu'l-Bahá was buried in a chamber of the Shrine of the Báb. The procession of the casket and the funeral were followed by thousands of inhabitants from Haifa and its vicinity and by a number of civil and religious authorities in Palestine.

The first account of the funeral appeared on 2 December in a two-page article published in the *Palestine Weekly* which introduced the Bahá'í Faith and reported:

(November 28th) Abbas Effendi the leader of the Bahaist movement, died here to-day.

THE PASSING OF 'ABDU'L-BAHÁ

(November 29th) The funeral of Abbas Effendi took place to-day. The procession from his house to the special cemetery on the way to Mount Carmel began at nine this morning, and continued till twelve. Thousands of people joined in the procession, and among them the High Commissioner and Mr. Storrs of Jerusalem. The funeral was carried out with marked simplicity. On the deceased's coffin there was nothing but a single wreath of flowers. At the graveside many men of many faiths joined in the mourning.[52]

A further account appeared in the *Egyptian Gazette* on 5 December and was based on a letter sent by a correspondent in Haifa on 29 November:

The death of Sir Abdul Baha Abbas, usually known as Abbas Effendi, early yesterday, Nov. 28, came as a great surprise to us all, as up till the day preceding it his picturesque figure had been seen about the town as usual. The burial took place to-day, and proved a very impressive ceremony, showing in what deep respect he was held by all classes and creeds.

There has probably never before been such a funeral in Haifa. A vast concourse of people went in procession from the town residence to the slopes of Mount Carmel where at the tomb of the Bab, the founder of the sect, his body now reposes. It is computed that 5,000 people were present, including leading Moslem and Christian celebrities, as well as Jewish and Druse; and at the tomb, ovations were made by a variety of speakers representing the different religions of the country, one by the Mufti being specially imposing. All bore testimony to the nobility of character of the dead leader, and to the lofty principles of the creed of which he was the first exponent. The British administration was represented by H. E. the High Commissioner in person, and by the Governors of Haifa and Jerusalem amongst others.

Abbas was knighted by King George last year, presumably for his support, through his followers there, of the British effort during the late war to preserve law and order in Persia. He was also known throughout the dark days of the Turkish military occupation of Haifa as a generous friend of the poor and destitute.[53]

One local journal in Haifa, *Al-Narif* (*The Bugle*), a weekly founded in 1911 which was owned by the Greek Orthodox Elia Zakka and directed by Soheil Zakka, published on 6 December a very detailed account of the funeral that filled almost the whole issue and which was later published in the Bahá'í magazine *Star of the West*.[54]

During the funeral, representatives of different religions and local dignitaries paid tribute to 'Abdu'l-Bahá in a series of speeches in which, in glowing terms, they expressed their admiration for Him. *Al-Narif* published the notes of most of the speeches, which were also published in *Star of the West*.[55]

On 6 January 1922, 40 days after the passing of 'Abdu'l-Bahá, a memorial meeting was held in Haifa in His honor. Over six hundred people attended the meeting at which again various civil and religious representatives paid their homage to the figure of the Master. Again, *Al-Narif* published a complete account in its issue of 17 January.[56]

The Succession

The Will and Testament of 'Abdu'l-Bahá was not read publicly until early January 1922 and it was not until 16 January that the American Bahá'ís received official communication that Shoghi Effendi had been appointed by 'Abdu'l-Bahá as Guardian of the Bahá'í Faith.[57] In the meantime there was some speculation about the future leadership of the Bahá'í community. Some thought that the Universal House of Justice would be immediately elected and this might be the origin of some news items in the press stating that a Bahá'í 'council' of twelve or nineteen members was to direct the affairs of the Bahá'í community after the passing of 'Abdu'l-Bahá.

In the meantime, the enemies of 'Abdu'l-Bahá did not spare a moment in their attempts to usurp the leadership of the Bahá'í community. A series of articles was published in Arabic journals in Egypt stating that Muḥammad-'Alí was to be 'Abdu'l-Bahá's successor.[58] In America, Shu'á'u'lláh, Muḥammad-'Alí's son, was able to circulate in some journals a picture of his father, the caption of which falsely stated that he had 'been chosen successor of the late Abdul Baha as head of the century old Bahai movement'.[59]

Finally, some journals announced that Shoghi Effendi had been appointed 'Abdu'l-Bahá's successor as head of the Bahá'í community.

The *Chicago Daily Tribune*, for instance, published a picture of him with the caption 'New Bahai Leader'[60] and other newspapers reported that 'the will of Abdul Baha names as "Guardian of the Cause and Head of the House of Justice" his grandson, Shoghi Effendi'.[61]

The Sign of God

Immediately after receiving a cable from Haifa reporting the passing of 'Abdu'l-Bahá, Wellesley Tudor Pole called Shoghi Effendi to his office, where he received the news of the death of his beloved grandfather. Owing to problems with his passport, he was not able to leave for Haifa until 16 December.

A few days before the passing of the Master, Shoghi Effendi was interviewed by Jessie A. Middleton, a correspondent with the *Egyptian Gazette* who was probably acquainted with Tudor Pole. The interview focused on the international progress of the Bahá'í community. Neither the journalist, nor Shoghi Effendi himself, could imagine that in a few weeks he would receive the surprising news of his appointment in the Will and Testament of 'Abdu'l-Bahá as Guardian of the Bahá'í Faith.

> Shoghi Rabbani, the young Persian scholar who is translating the Epistles of Baha'o'llah, the great founder and revealer of this religious teaching, has now returned to Haifa, but before his departure from England, and immediately before the passing of his grandfather Abdul Baha, I was able to obtain an interview with him, through the kindness of a mutual friend, and to glean some particulars of the extraordinary spread of the movement, which now has members in all parts of the world. The Bahai cause, briefly, has been described as 'the essence of all the Highest ideals of this century' and it embraces all religions in its circle. 'The Bahais believe this is the beginning of that Golden Age upon earth, the age of universal peace and love when, as Christ foretold, men shall come from the east and from the west, and from the north and from the south, and shall sit down in the kingdom of God.'
>
> Shoghi Rabbani has a most interesting personality. Unlike the typical Oriental he is very active – quick in his speech, movements and gestures. He is fired with great enthusiasm for the cause, to which he intends to devote his life. He speaks English fluently and

when he is on the subject which interests him most converses eloquently and well. He is extremely courteous and appreciative of the slightest service, has very pleasant manners and a bright cheery smile.

'I am the great grandson of Baha'o'llah,' said Shoghi Rabbani, 'and I was educated at the University of Beyrout in Syria. After graduating I acted for two years as interpreter to Abdul Baha on Mount Carmel, and translated his Epistles and Letters which have been sent to his friends all over the world. The Master, however, thought my English was not good enough for me to translate adequately the Epistles of his father Baha'o'llah ('The Light of the World') so he sent me to Balliol College, Oxford in the hope that I should acquire such command of the English language as would enable me to translate the Epistles forcibly and effectively, so that their truths could be revealed to the crowned heads of Europe and distributed all over the world. I have, up to the present with three others, translated some passages from the Epistles and intend to devote myself to other portions still untranslated.

'The Bahai movement has spread rapidly throughout the world and attracted the attention of the greatest scholars and savants of the day. It is not so much a new religion but a unifying of what is best in all existing religions, and has brotherhood and universal peace as two of its chief objects. It is a religion without priests, ceremonies or public prayers yet it has its Temples wherein its followers meet to worship God. Representatives of all creeds have met together in the first Bahai Temple erected in the city of Ishgabad in Turkestan which, before the war, formed part of the Tsar's Russian Empire. The foundations of a second Bahai Temple have just been laid in Chicago and soon, the Master says, the foundations of a third will be laid at Teheran, the capital of Persia and the native city of Baha'o'llah.

'The Bahai Movement at present possesses no fewer than four newspapers of its own in the East and West. The first "The Star of the West", was founded fifteen years ago in the U.S.A. The second, "Khwishid-i-Khawar" ('Sun of the East') was founded in Turkestan during the war. The third organ "Al Bisharat" ('Glad Tidings') was first published in India, after the Armistice, in Persian and Arabic, and is edited and directed by the Bahai Parsee Community in the

Bombay Presidency. The English section is contributed to and edited by Hindus, Persians, Parsees and Burmese. The fourth organ has been established in Japan since the war, and is the organ of the Bahai community in that country. There are Bahai centers in Tokio, Yokohama and various other Japanese cities. Bahai meetings were established before the war in Hawaii and Honolulu and Bahaism in the U.S.A. is keeping in constant touch with Japan and the intervening islands.

'Various Bahais, both men and women, have started for Japan, devoting time and energy to spreading the cause in that country so that to-day one finds in the capital of the great Eastern Island Empire spiritual assemblies designed to promote the Bahai Movement. The members are almost exclusively Japanese and the Bahai writings have been translated into their language from Esperanto. The proceedings of the Assemblies are invariably carried on in the Japanese tongue. The movement in Japan is making great headway among the poor and the blind and supplications have already been sent to the Master by young blind Japanese who have become interested in his teachings.

'The movement is just beginning to be known in Eastern China and Indo-China and Bahai books have already been placed in the Canton Library. Some of the Persian friends settled in Shanghai and Canton are co-operating with native Bahais in the advancement of the Cause in that city.

'In the U.S.A. during the war American Bahais – two women – started from Alaska and went as far North, as possible, living among the Eskimos and distributing a great amount of literature, while a little later another American woman travelled from the States to Central Africa (*sic*), crossed the Andes and distributed various pamphlets in five or six languages, addressed meetings and published articles. Recently, again, an American woman Bahai telegraphed to the Master asking his authorisation to proceed to South Africa, where she has been doing very good work among the Colonists in Johannesburg and Capetown.

'Since the war American friends in large numbers – growing larger and larger still – have sent various representatives to the newly born States of Central Europe. A Yugo-Slav Bahai who had attended the annual Bahai Convention in New York a few years previously and there, for the first time, he heard the principles of the movement from various speakers, was so impressed that he sent an appeal to the 'Master' asking leave to start for Yugoslavia and establish a centre there. In Italy an American woman has established Bahai centres. Switzerland has for years been the home of zealous Bahai friends who have never spared any effort to bring the cause to the notice of Professors of the Universities of Lausanne, Geneva and Lucerne. Naturally the greatest headway of all has been made in Persia itself where the number of Bahais amounts to about ten thousand.'[62]

APPENDIX 1

WRITINGS AND TALKS OF 'ABDU'L-BAHÁ PUBLISHED IN GENERAL PERIODICALS[1]

Writings, Prayers and Letters

April 1907 *The Review of Reviews* (London) published an article by William T. Stead on the Bahá'í Faith ('The Persian Messiah,' p. 393) which included 'Abdu'l-Bahá's Tablet sent to the Scottish Bahá'í Jane Whyte known as 'The Seven Candles of Unity'.

July 1909 *The Bible Review* (Applegate, CA), monthly organ of the Esoteric Fraternity in California, published a Tablet of 'Abdu'l-Bahá addressed to Benedict Peeke, son of the Bahá'í Margaret B. Peeke.

28 December 1910 *The Christian Commonwealth* (London) printed a short letter of 'Abdu'l-Bahá dated 30 November 1910, sent from Ramleh, Egypt, and addressed to the editor. With the letter was enclosed a selection from the writings of Bahá'u'lláh.

January 1911 *The Amerika Esperantisto* (Chicago) published a letter from 'Abdu'l-Bahá to Faríd on the need for an international language. This letter was later published in the *British Esperantist* on December 1911 and in the 1912 volume of *Das Esperanto ein Kulturfaktor* (Leizpig).

5 May 1911 *The Friend* (London) published two letters of 'Abdu'l-Bahá, sent from Egypt, in response to two letters by British Quakers. One of these letters was later published in the *T.P.'s Weekly* (London) on 4 August 1911.

26 July 1911 *The Christian Commonwealth* printed a letter dated 29 May 1911 sent by 'Abdu'l-Bahá to the president of the Universal Races Congress. Presumably this letter accompanied the text of the paper sent to the Congress.

27 July 1911 The paper sent by 'Abdu'l-Bahá to the Universal Races Congress was printed in the same year as part of the proceedings (*Papers on InterRacial Problems Communicated to the First Universal Races Congress*, pp. 156–7). Portions of it were quoted afterwards in various periodicals.

30 August 1911 *The Christian Commonwealth* published a telegram of 'Abdu'l-Bahá sent from Thonon-les-Bains in response to a telegram sent by Albert Dawson, editor of the magazine, greeting Him on His arrival in Europe.

13 September 1911 *The Christian Commonwealth* printed on p. 850 a facsimile and the translation of 'Abdu'l-Bahá's note written in the pulpit Bible at City Temple.

20 September 1911 *The Christian Commonwealth* reproduced on p. 884 a telegram from 'Abdu'l-Bahá to the National Brotherhood Movement and read during one of its sessions on 19 September.

20 September 1911 *The Christian Commonwealth* reproduced on p. 871 the image of a letter of 'Abdu'l-Bahá addressed to the publication. An English summary of the text was also published.

February 1912 *The Advocate of Peace* published portions of a letter to H.C. Philips, secretary of the Lake Mohonk Conference. This letter was translated by Ahmad Sohrab on 22 August.

August 1912 'Abdu'l-Bahá's message read at the International Congress of Moral Education held in The Hague from 22 to 27 August 1912 was published in *Mémoires sur L'Éducation Morale* (1912).

28 August 1912 *The Christian Commonwealth* published a letter from 'Abdu'l-Bahá to its editor, Albert Dawson.

1 November 1912 *The Palo Altan* published a letter from 'Abdu'l-Bahá to its editor, Henry Walter Simkins.

23 December 1912 At the request of James Wedgwood, editor of *The Vahan* (London), 'Abdu'l-Bahá wrote a message for its readers which was published in January 1913, p. 118.

January 1913 A letter sent in May 1911 by 'Abdu'l-Bahá to the Bahá'ís of London was included in an article by Felicia Scatcherd published in the *International Psychic Gazette* ('A Wise Man from the East', p. 158).

1 January 1913 *The Christian Commonwealth* published a translation of a letter from 'Abdu'l-Bahá to the Bahá'ís of the world. The translation was published together with a facsimile of the original text in Persian.

9 February 1913 *The New York Times* published the translation of a letter from 'Abdu'l-Bahá to Andrew Carnegie dated 10 January 1913 and written in Scotland, together with the text of the enclosing letter to H. H. Topakyan, Persian Consul in New York. Both letters were also reproduced in other journals.

April 1913 The *International Psychic Gazette* (London) published a collection of letters from 'Abdu'l-Bahá to the American Bahá'í Louise R. Waite which included the following items: a letter dated 1902 translated by A. Faríd; a letter dated 1909, translated by A. Faríd; a letter dated 1910, translated by A. Faríd; two letters dated 1912 translated by Ahmad Sohrab. See 'The Bahai Nightingale', p. 263.

April 1913 *The Asiatic Quarterly Review* (London) published a message by 'Abdu'l-Bahá to the editor, see pp. 225–36. Ahmad Sohrab's translation was accompanied by a facsimile of the original Persian.

June 1913 A letter to Daniel N. Dunlop, secretary of the Fifth Theosophical Summer School, held in Peebles, Scotland, was published in 'Abdul Baha on Universal Peace', *International Psychic Gazette* (London), August 1913, p. 5.

5 July 1913 'Abdu'l-Bahá wrote a message for David Graham Pole, secretary-general of the Scotland section of the Theosophical Society, which was published as 'Letter from Abdul Baha', in *Theosophy in Scotland* (Edinburgh), October 1913, pp. 83–4.

7 July 1913 'Abdu'l-Bahá wrote a letter for Albert Dawson, editor of *The Christian Commonwealth* (London), which was translated by Ahmad Sohrab on 19 July, and published in *The Christian Commonwealth* on 3 September 1913, p. 838, under the title 'Universal Peace'.

30 July 1913 *The Christian Commonwealth* (London) published portions of the letter sent by 'Abdu'l-Bahá to the sixth International Congress of Religious Progress held in Paris from 16 to 22 July 1913.

29 August 1913 Letter from 'Abdu'l-Bahá to David Graham Pole, published in *Theosophy in Scotland* (Edinburgh), February 1914, p. 143.

December 1913 The magazine *The Master Mind* (Los Angeles) published a letter from 'Abdu'l-Bahá to its editor, Annie Rix Militz.

25 February 1914 *The Christian Commonwealth* published a letter from 'Abdu'l-Bahá to the editor about the need for a Universal Congress of Religions.

June 1914 The *International Psychic Gazette* published a letter from 'Abdu'l-Bahá to the Bahá'ís of London on the occasion of the Bahá'í Naw-Rúz.

9 December 1914 A Tablet on the world war was published in *The Christian Commonwealth*. It is presumably dated 4 October 1914.

25 August 1915 The *New York Sun* published the translation of 'Abdu'l-Bahá's second letter to Andrew Carnegie.

8 December 1917 A letter dated 20 August and translated by L. Hakím was published in *The Christian Commonwealth*.

6 October 1919 The World (New York) published a letter dated 18

June 1919 from 'Abdu'l-Bahá to former New York Governor William Sulzer. The letter was translated by Dr Zia Bagdadi.

13 August 1920 The *Nieuwe Rotterdamsche Courant* published a letter from 'Abdu'l-Bahá to one of its reporters.

Public Talks

10 September 1911 'Abdu'l-Bahá's talk at the City Temple (London) was published in *The Christian Commonwealth* in September 1913, p. 850. A few weeks later at least two American newspapers also published the talk: *Los Angeles Times* (1 October 1911, p. 21, col. 3), and the *Buffalo Express* (8 October 1911, p. 5, col. 4).

September 1911 'Abdu'l-Bahá dictated to Graham Pole a message to Scotland's Theosophists which was published in *Theosophy in Scotland* (Edinburgh), October 1911, p. 81.

30 September 1911 'Abdu'l-Bahá's talk at the headquarters of the Theosophical Society (London) was published in March 1912 in *The Contemporary Review* (London) as part of Harrold Johnson's article 'Bahaism: The Birth of a World Religion'.

9 November 1911 A French translation of 'Abdu'l-Bahá's talk in Paris to a meeting of the Alliance Spiritualiste was published in the organ of the society, the *Alliance Spiritualiste*, in January 1912.

23 April 1912 'Abdu'l-Bahá dictated to Joseph Hannen a message to Esperantists which was published in June 1912 in *The Amerika Esperantisto* (Chicago) and in January 1913 in the *British Esperantist* (London).

30 April 1912 'Abdu'l-Bahá's address in Hull House during the Fourth Annual Conference of the National Association for the Advancement of Colored People was published in the *Theosophic Messenger* (Chicago), August 1912 (13:2), pp. 654–5.

30 April 1912 'Abdu'l-Bahá's address in Handal Hall at the final session of the Fourth Annual Conference of the National Association for the

Advancement of the Colored People was published in *The Crisis*, June 1912 (4:2), p. 88.

2 May 1912 Large portions of 'Abdu'l-Bahá address to the Federation of Women's Clubs (Chicago) were published in 'Abdul Baha and Woman's Suffrage', *The Woman Voter* (New York), June 1912.

12 May 1912 'Abdu'l-Bahá's address in the Unity Church, Montclair, was published in *The Montclair Times* (Montclair, NJ) on 18 May 1912 and was reprinted again on 8 June 1912.

15 May 1912 'Abdu'l-Bahá's address at the second session of the Lake Mohonk Conference on International Arbitration was published in the organization's annual report.

24 May 1912 'Abdu'l-Bahá's talk at a meeting of the Free Religious Association was published in the *Proceedings at the Forty–Fifth Annual Meeting* (1912), pp. 86–90.

1 June 1912 Portions of 'Abdu'l-Bahá's talk in Fanwood, New Jersey, were published in a local newspaper.

2 June 1912 The answer to one of the questions put to 'Abdu'l-Bahá after His address at the Church of the Ascension in New York was reproduced in December 1912 in the *Theosophic Messenger* (Los Angeles).

16 June 1912 'Abdu'l-Bahá's talk delivered in the Central Congregational Church of Brooklyn was reproduced in *The Brooklyn Daily Eagle* on the following day and in the *Washington County Post* (Cambridge, NY) some weeks afterwards.

19 July 1912 'Abdu'l-Bahá addressed a message to *The Independent* (New York) summarizing the purpose of His travels and the teachings of the Bahá'í Faith which was published on 12 September.

10 September 1912 'Abdu'l-Bahá delivered an address at the Hotel Iroquois, Buffalo, which was quoted on the following day in several local newspapers. *The Buffalo Express* published notes of almost all the address.

14 September 1912 'Abdu'l-Bahá's address at the twenty-sixth national assembly of the American section of Theosophical Society was published in the *Theosophic Messenger* (Los Angeles), December 1912, pp. 153–9.

8 October 1912 'Abdu'l-Bahá's talk at Stanford University, or selections from it, based on notes taken by Bijou Straun, was published in the following journals:

> 'Persian Indicts the Futility of War', *Daily Palo Alto*, 8 October 1912, pp. 1 and 3.
> 'Palo Alto Hears Abbas Effendi', *Palo Alto Times*, 9 October 1912, p. 1, col. 3.
> 'Palo Alto Hears Abbas Effendi', *Palo Altan*, 11 October 1912, p. 7, col. 1.
> 'Abdul Baha Speaks at Stanford University', *Palo Alto Times*, 11 October 1912, p. 7.
> 'Abdul Baha Speaks at Stanford University', *Palo Altan*, 18 October 1912, p. 6.
> 'To the World of Science', *Palo Altan*, 1 November 1912, p. 1.

8 October 1912 An article based on notes taken by Bijou Straun of 'Abdu'l-Bahá's talk at the First Unitarian Church of Palo Alto was published in 'Message to the Church', *Palo Altan*, 1 November 1912, p. 4.

12 October 1912 An article based on notes taken by Bijou Straun of 'Abdu'l-Bahá's address at Temple Emanu-El (San Francisco) was published as 'Message to the Jews' in a special edition of *The Palo Altan* published on 1 November 1912 (p. 3, col. 1). In England, *The Christian Commonwealth* published the talk as 'The Fundamental Unity of All Religions' on 1 January 1913 (pp. 263–4, col. 2).

4 November 1912 'Abdu'l-Bahá's talk at Cincinnati was published in the *Times-Star* on 6 November.

6 November 1912 'Abdu'l-Bahá's talk at the Church of Our Father, Washington DC, was published in the *Washington Evening Star* on 24 November.

15 December 1912 'Abdu'l-Bahá's address at Pembroke Chapel (Liverpool) was published in *Plain Truth*, the magazine of Pembroke Chapel. The text was edited by the Bahá'í Elizabeth Herrick from notes taken by Mr. J. Stiles.

20 December 1912 'Abdu'l-Bahá's address at the Westminster Palace Hotel was published by *The Christian Commonwealth* (London) on 1 January 1913. The text also included a transcript of the closing prayer recited by 'Abdu'l-Bahá for the Balkans.

25 December 1912 'Abdu'l-Bahá's address at the Salvation Army Shelter (London) was published in *The Christian Commonwealth* (London) on 1 January 1913.

31 January 1912 On 22 January 1913 *The Christian Commonwealth* (London) published a translation of 'Abdu'l-Bahá's talk at Manchester College, Oxford. A photograph of the original Persian text used for the translation was also printed in the same issue. Paraphrases of the same address had already been published in the *Oxford Chronicle*, 3 January 1913, and in the *Oxford Times*, 4 January 1913.

1 January 1913 'Abdu'l-Bahá's talk at the Cosmos Club was published in the *International Psychic Gazette* (London) in March 1913, p. 220.

2 January 1913 'Abdu'l-Bahá's talk at a meeting arranged by the Women's Freedom League at Essex Hall on 2 January 1913 was published in *The Suffragette* (London) and in *The Vote* (London) on 10 January 1913.

3 January 1913 'Abdu'l-Bahá's address to the Theosophical White Lodge in Wimbledon was published in 'The Three Realities', *The Path* (London), February 1913, pp. 285–90,

7 January 1913 'Abdu'l-Bahá's talk at a meeting organized by the Edinburgh Esperanto Society and held at the Freemason's Hall appeared in a number of newspapers. An Esperanto translation appeared in the *British Esperantist* (London) in February 1913. It was also published in March 1913 in *La Revuo* (Paris), *La Verda Standardo* (Budapest) and *Esperantysta Polski* (Warsaw). Parts of it were quoted in the 1913 volume of *Das Esperanto ein Kulturfaktor* (Leizpig) and in *Le Fraterniste* (Paris) on 4 April 1913. A translation into Russian was published in the *Volga Stelo* (Saratov) in March 1913. A Spanish translation appeared in *La Duj Stelo* (Santiago de Chile) in May 1913. A German translation appeared in the German–Austria *Esperantisto* (Vienna) in June 1913.

8 January 1913 'Abdu'l-Bahá's talk at a meeting arranged by the Outlook Tower Committee at the Rainy Hall (Edinburgh) was reproduced in part in *The Scotsman* (Edinburgh) on 9 January 1913.

9 January 1913 'Abdu'l-Bahá's talk at the headquarters of the Scotland section of the Theosophical Society was published in *Theosophy in Scotland* (Edinburgh), February 1912, pp. 167–70.

15 January 1913 'Abdu'l-Bahá's address at the Clifton Guest House (Bristol) was published in *The Clifton Chronicle and Directory* on 22 January 1913.

17 January 1913 Summaries of 'Abdu'l-Bahá's talk at the Woking Mosque were published in the *Woking News and Mail*, the *Surrey Times* (Guildford) and *The Surrey Herald and Middlesex News* (Chertsey). On 22 January *The Christian Commonwealth* published notes of the prayer recited by the Master after His address.

12 February 1913 'Abdu'l-Bahá's talk at Hôtel Moderne to Paris' Esperantists was partially reproduced in Esperanto in March 1913 in *La Movado* (Paris). A different Esperanto translation of the whole talk prepared by Camille Chaigneau appeared in *La Revuo* (Paris) in May 1913. A French translation by Hippolyte Dreyfus made from the Persian was published in April 1913 in *Paris-Esperanto*. An English translation from the Persian was published in April 1913 in the *International Psychic Gazette* (London) and in the *Amerika Esperantisto* (West Newton, MA) in November 1918.

13 February 1913 Notes from the French translation of 'Abdu'l-Bahá's talk at the headquarters of the Theosophical Society in Paris were published in 'Société Théosophique de France: Causerie par Abdou'l Baha',

Le Théosophe (Paris), 1 March 1913. An English translation by Ahmad Sohrab from his Persian notes was published in *Theosophy in Scotland* (Edinburgh), May 1913, p. 5.

21 February 1913 A French translation of 'Abdu'l-Bahá's talk in Paris to a meeting of the Alliance Spiritualiste was published in the organ of the society, the *Alliance Spiritualiste*, in April 1913, pp. 102–4. An English translation prepared by Ahmad Sohrab from his own notes of the talk was published in May 1913 in 'Abdul Baha on Universal Peace', *International Psychic Gazette* (London), pp. 299–300.

Addenda

From 22 March 1914, *The Washington Post* started to publish in its Sunday religious section passages from the writings and utterances of 'Abdu'l-Bahá. The quotations usually ran to the length of half a column or more.

Most of these texts were submitted by Aseyeh Allen of Washington, who selected chapters from *Some Answered Questions* and passages from *The Mysterious Forces of Civilization, Abdul Baha in London, Talks Given in Paris* and sometimes from letters of 'Abdu'l-Bahá and correspondence by Ahmad Sohrab published previously in *Star of the West*.

The newspaper continued to publish this little Bahá'í section until February 1917. During this time at least 136 articles were published.

A similar section appeared during the year 1916 in the black journal *Chicago Defender*. The present author has 15 of these articles but in all probability many more were published.

APPENDIX 2
PHOTOGRAPHS AND ILLUSTRATIONS

The press published many illustrations of 'Abdu'l-Bahá during His lifetime and many of these were produced by those who were not Bahá'ís. During the period of His travels, for instance, agencies such as the Associated Press, Harris & Ewing, and Underwood and Underwood released images of Him.

Exhaustive research needs to be done to properly catalogue and trace the origins of all these images. The following survey may be useful as a starting point:

8 September 1911 The *Daily Sketch* (London) published a photograph of 'Abdu'l-Bahá entering a building accompanied by some of his attendants. This picture was supplied by the London News Agency and also appeared a few days afterwards in *The Observer* (London).

October 1911 Pictures of 'Abdu'l-Bahá were taken at Boissons et Taponier studio in Paris. Some of these photographs appeared in the press. One of them was published on 16 December 1911 in *Le Théosophe* (Paris).

9 November 1911 'Abdu'l-Bahá gave a talk in Paris for the Alliance Spiritualiste. At least two photographers attended the meeting and took shots of 'Abdu'l-Bahá surrounded by Bahá'ís and participants at the meeting. Two of these pictures were published on 10 November in the daily pictorial journal *Excelsior* (Paris) and in *Le Petite République* (Paris).

12 April 1912 *The Evening World* (New York) published a drawing of 'Abdu'l-Bahá depicting Him seated on a sofa. The illustration also included a small portrait of some of His attendants.

26 April 1912 *The Washington Post* published a picture of 'Abdu'l-Bahá taken in the capital by the Harris & Ewing agency.

April 1912 In late April, just a few days after the departure of 'Abdu'l-Bahá from New York, the Bain News Service distributed across the United States a portrait of 'Abdu'l-Bahá which was afterwards published in several newspapers. Its caption briefly summarized some biographical facts about the Master.

5 May 1912 A long article in the *New York Tribune* by Kate Karew contained various drawings of 'Abdu'l-Bahá made by this famous caricaturist.

7 May 1912 The *Cleveland Leader* published a picture of the Master taken during His visit to the city. A picture of two of His attendants was also published.

7 May 1912 *The Plain Dealer* (Cleveland) published three pictures of 'Abdu'l-Bahá taken during His visit to the city.

7 May 1912 The *Cleveland Press* published two drawings of 'Abdu'l-Bahá.

16 May 1912 The American Press Association released a picture of the Bahá'í delegation at the Lake Mohonk conference. The picture included 'Abdu'l-Bahá and Edward C. Getsinger, Lua Getsinger, Amín Faríd, Ahmad Sohrab, Mírzá Varqá, Siyyid Assad'u'lláh and Dr Zia Bagdadí. The same agency simultaneously released a portrait of 'Abdu'l-Bahá also taken at Lake Mohonk.

23 May 1912 The *Boston Herald* carried a drawing representing 'Abdu'l-Bahá while delivering His address at the Unitarian Festival.

24 May 1912 The *Boston Traveler* carried a picture of 'Abdu'l-Bahá leaving His hotel.

10 June 1912 *The Philadelphia Press* published two pictures of the Master specially taken by the journal. One of them shows 'Abdu'l-Bahá seated and the other one shows Him surrounded by three of His attendants.

7 July 1912 *The Sun* (New York) published a portrait of 'Abdu'l-Bahá taken by Gertrude Käsebier.

1 November 1912 The *Palo Altan* published a photograph of 'Abdu'l-Bahá with the Unitarian minister Clarence Reed.

2 January 1913 C. W. Child, a hand interpreter, visited 'Abdu'l-Bahá at Cadogan Gardens and asked to interpret His hands. 'Abdu'l-Bahá gave His permission and impressions of His hands were taken at that time. These were published in February 1913 in *The International Psychic Gazette*.

17 January 1913 Pictures of the visit of 'Abdu'l-Bahá to the Woking Mosque were taken by A. Wildman at the request of the *Asiatic Quarterly Review*. One of the pictures was published in this magazine, which was the organ of the Oriental Institute, and in *The Surrey Herald and Middlesex News* (Chertsey).

9 February 1913 *The New York Times* published a photograph of 'Abdu'l-Bahá with the Persian Consul in New York, Hayozoun Hohannes Topakyan.

9 April 1913 On 'Abdu'l-Bahá's arrival in Budapest, two local photographers visited Him at the Ritz and took some pictures of Him. These were published in such journals as the *Persi Tükor*, the *Budapest*, the *Tolnai Világlapja*, the *Uj Idök* and the *Az Érdekes Újság*.

4 May 1913 The *Supplément Illustré of Le Petit Journal* (Paris) carried on its front page a full page color illustration depicting 'Abdu'l-Bahá preaching in a Constantinople mosque with His hands raised and surrounded by an attentive group of men, some of them kneeling.

12 November 1913 *The Bulletin of Photography* (Philadelphia) published on p. 625 a picture of 'Abdu'l-Bahá taken by Gertrude Käsebier.

December 1913 *The Camera* (Philadelphia) published on p. 721 a picture of 'Abdu'l-Bahá taken by Gertrude Käsebier.

July 1914 The *Bulletin de la Société Française de Photographie* reported that it had received the negative of a color picture of 'Abdu'l-Bahá as a donation to its archive.

22 July 1914 *The Christian Commonwealth* published a picture of 'Abdu'l-Bahá taken by Maude Holbach in front of the Mansion of Bahjí and surrounded by a group of pilgrims.

18 August 1914 *The Plain Dealer* (Cleveland) published a photograph by E. M. Newman showing 'Abdu'l-Bahá, accompanied by Archie Bell, on the balcony of the Casa Nova Hostel in Tiberias.

APPENDIX 3
BOOK REVIEWS

Several works by or about 'Abdu'l-Bahá were published during His lifetime and some of them were reviewed in the press. The first edition of Phelps's book on the Master received considerable publicity in some leading journals (see vol. 1, chapter 1, pp. 10–13). This appendix surveys reviews of other titles.

Some Answered Questions

During one of her pilgrimages Laura Clifford Barney took extensive notes of the answers she received to the many questions she put to 'Abdu'l-Bahá on different subjects. These notes were afterwards reviewed by 'Abdu'l-Bahá, who authorized their publication. In France these notes appeared in book form in 1908 under the title *Les Leçons de Saint Jean d'Acre* (E. Leroux, Paris) and received several positive reviews.

In France, the eminent orientalist Clément Huart (1854–1926), who had written several references to the Bábís and the Bahá'ís in his many articles and books, wrote a review for the *Revue du Monde Mussulman* (Paris) in which, after summarizing its contents, stated that 'The few indications we have given will so far, we hope, instill the desire to read the book. There is in it much more precision and clarity than in the works of Baha himself, which have been rendered into French by the zeal and effort of M. H. Dreyfus. We cannot look to the East without desiring to know the movement of the spirit which has stirred Persia since now sixty years and can propagate it to the rest of Muslim world . . .'[1]

The philosopher Jean Lucien Arréat (1841–1922) also wrote a review for the *Revue Philosophique de la France* (Paris) in which he stated that 'Abd-ul-Béha appears in his conversations as a man of broad and wide spirit, informed of our philosophy and our science, professing optimistic views on the future of our species, but applying in his treatment of issues a little of the old methods and processes of reasoning whether to explain the scriptures or to solve the great problems of religion and metaphysics . . . This publication offers, in short, a serious interest in the religious and political history of our time.'[2]

The January issue of the *Revue de l'Histoire des Religions* (Paris) carried a three-page review by the French Arabist Edouard Móntet, who offered a description of the five parts of the book and, despite regretting what he considered a lack of organization in the notes taken by Barney, stated that 'One cannot deny Abd-Ullah's breadth of mind, extensive knowledge, and the attraction exerted by his personal empathy.'[3]

Several announcements were also published by the general press, in newspapers such the *Journal des Débats*,[4] *New York Herald* (European Edition),[5] *Mercure de France*,[6] *La Revue*,[7] *Revue Critique*[8] and *Polybiblion*.[9]

The first English edition of *Some Answered Questions* was published in London, also in 1908, and soon afterwards received a number of press reviews.

The *Scotsman* (Edinburgh) published a review of the book on 5 March 1908, which outlined its contents and concluded by stating, 'They form little discourses which, while they must seem to Western readers to reflect ideas already elaborately worked out in many older systems of positive religion, are always eloquent, impressive, and characterised by genuine spiritual insight.'[10] A few weeks later, the *Morning Post* (London) also published a review of the book which was prefaced by an introduction to the history and teachings of the Bahá'í Faith.[11]

The Review of Reviews (London) published in April 1908 a further review in which the author declared that *Some Answered Questions* 'is a book ministers of religion might study and preach from with advantage'.[12] A review in the socialist magazine *New Age* (London) recommended the book 'to any who is interested in the newest of Eastern Theologies'.[13]

In the United States the *Washington Herald* wrote about the genesis and purpose of the book in an article that appeared on 28 April 1909.[14] References also appeared in the *Springfield Republican*.[15] A review in *The Outlook* (New York) said of the Bahá'í Faith that 'it is strenuously ethical and humanitarian' and 'generally catholic in religious sympathy'.[16]

Abdul Baha in London

After the first visit of 'Abdu'l-Bahá to England, a compilation – probably prepared by Eric Hammond – was published which included some of 'Abdu'l-Bahá's talks in London as well as notes of private conversations and journal articles.

On 1 August 1912 the Theosophist magazine *The Vahan* (London) published the following comments on the book:

> This little book is one which should not only be bought but read again and again. The teaching of Abdul Baha, who of course preaches the doctrine of Bahai, is almost identical as far as it goes with that of Theosophy since it strives for the reconciliation of all beliefs and for universal Brotherhood. But what strikes one most in this stranger from the East is his wide charity and his utter freedom from any sort of bigotry or exclusive dogma. Of dogma indeed he has none; to quote his own words, 'A Bahai denies no religion; he accepts the Truth in all, and would die to uphold it.'[17]

On 31 August 1912 the magazine *Light* also published a review of the work. It did not comment much about the book but contained some quotations from it.[18] In October 1912 *Theosophy in Scotland* published another review, that read, in part:

> Lovers of the 'Servant of God' who have not been able to meet him during his visit may almost make good their loss in the intimate picture of his gentle and strong nature which his conversations here afford. But apart from the valuable impression which is given of a patriarchal and amiable personality, we have his utterances on a great number of important questions, all the answers being full of his own serenity and unassuming certainty. The truly unsectarian basis of the Bahai movement is seen in his statement – illustrated with oriental quaintness – that 'it makes no difference whether you have ever heard of Baha'u'llah or not, the man who lives the life according to the teachings of Baha'u'llah is already a Bahai. On the

other hand a man may call himself a Bahai for fifty years and if he does not live the life he is not a Bahai . . .'

An excellent photograph of the teacher appears as frontispiece, and the get-up is pleasing.

All who are interested in the Bahai movement will find the book indispensable.[19]

Talks by Abdul Baha Given in Paris

In 1912 the first English edition of Lady Blomfield's compilation of the talks delivered by 'Abdu'l-Bahá in Paris in 1911 was published simultaneously in England by the Unity Press (Sheen, Surrey) and in the United States by the Bahai Publishing Society (Chicago). The volume was re-edited three more times during the lifetime of 'Abdu'l-Bahá (1915, 1916 and 1920) and in later decades subsequent editions were published in America as *The Wisdom of Abdul Baha* (1924) and in England as *Paris Talks* (1951). *Theosophy in Scotland* published the following review in August 1912:

> A man who numbers his followers by the million must in our day claim our respect, but when the same man is noted for the Christ-like qualities of his character and for his inspired utterances our respect must border upon veneration.
>
> To the four anonymous translators of these 'Talks' we owe a debt of gratitude. Their work has been one of pure love, and the knowledge that their efforts have made the sayings of Abdul Baha available to all English-reading nations is their reward; and we feel sure that many of our readers, on seeing this notice, will take the opportunity of procuring a copy of this volume in order to study the teachings of the present great leader of the Bahais. R. L. C.[20]

Both *Abdu'l-Bahá in London* and *Talks by Abdul Baha Given in Paris* were the subjects of an interesting review that appeared in *The Christian Commonwealth* on 19 June 1912:

> Those especially who followed with an intense interest and sympathy, and many with a whole-hearted devotion, Abdul Baha's memorable visits to London and Paris from the beginning of September to the

end of December last year will welcome these two volumes, the material for which has been gathered together by reverent hands from notes taken of his familiar talks and public addresses. Abdul Baha was accessible at all hours to those eager to learn of him, and answered their questioning with a wondrous insight, and sympathy, evidencing a remarkable power of adjustment to the most diverse attitudes of mind, and thereby demonstrating his own fundamental unity with his fellow-men.

It is a severe test for any teacher to have his casual utterances thus exposed to the full glare of day, and Abdul Baha well stands the test. Throughout these two volumes an even level of utterance is maintained, revealing one of the purest spirits who has trod this earth, full of love to his kind, and of an utter transparency and self-devotion to the highest. When we bear in mind, too, that he had never before addressed a public audience, had never before been photographed, was to a large extent an entire stranger to the social life and thought of Western Europe, could scarcely speak a word of English, we marvel that he should have been able so deeply to understand our needs and to go so far to meet them. Nevertheless, his utterances are still rather those of a little child, one of those of whom Christ spoke, and the language would hardly have been differently couched in Cairo, Acca, or Ispahan. Herein are revealed at the same time both the weakness and the strength of this movement. Have we of Western Europe remained or are we capable of becoming child-like enough to receive the message?

Of the two volumes the London one brings us more vitally into touch with the man himself. We feel here a warm, loving, gentle, pure, gracious spirit moving in our midst and sanctifying us. We have graphic descriptions of actual meetings in which he took part, actual contacts with men and women. To a considerable extent Abdul Baha did touch the currents of English life. In Paris he seems to have been a stranger. In London he preached in the City Temple and blessed the congregation from the steps of the altar in Archdeacon Wilberforce's church. In Paris Pastor Wagner's church alone seems to have admitted him. The portraits of 'the Master' which look upon us on opening each of these books – the one taken in London, the other in Paris – seem to convey the difference in atmosphere and the difference in the master's attitude. The face in the London portrait is serene and hopeful; that in the Paris one is anxious and almost bewildered.

The two volumes will serve admirably as an introduction to a movement destined, I believe, to have a great future in the East, and to exercise a deep though more indirect influence upon religious developments in the West. Its gospel is the unity of mankind and the unity of religions, a gospel testified to by the blood of countless of its martyrs. Portions of its Scriptures, especially in 'Hidden Words', may rank with the best devotional literature. To 'Hidden Words' and to such an account of the movement as Mr. Eric Hammond furnishes us with in his 'Splendour of God' readers will proceed after having read these volumes. They will find in this movement the water of life.

H. J.[21]

In January 1916 the *Occult Review* carried an article by Arthur Edward Waite (1857–1942), a regular contributor to the magazine, reviewing the book:

> When we are in a position to estimate certain final values in respect of the Bahai movement – possibly in two or three generations – that which will remain among us as permanent in importance and interest will include the personality, personal work and history of Abdul Baha, rather than anything that has been said or written by him. There is scarcely a page in this little volume which does not win us by its kindness, simplicity and utter sincerity. There is scarcely a page which contains a new thought or an utterance from a new standpoint. One is hearing the familiar parlance of all our altruistic synods and societies for amelioration and freedom in religious belief. I am by no means stating this in a spirit of condemnation; I am scarcely offering criticism. All of us who are dedicated to the true things, and who write ourselves down in humility as *servi servorum Dei*, cannot only take the utterances into our hearts, but every word having the seal of truth herein is written in our hearts already. They are the commonplaces of eternal life. They have been said and written among us a thousand times. But if there and here – very rarely – it happens that there is something which does not engage our sympathy and command concurrence, this is because

the venerable speaker has in the haste of a moment taken either some false step in mere logic or has offered an opinion for which the warrants seem wanting. It is good on any calculation to have the present memorial of Abdul Baha's visit to the western world. He has earned admiration and affection wherever he has been; and if we miss in his translated utterances the word which makes all things new, I am very sure that this volume – for all who can accept its messages – will do yeoman service towards the reign of peace on earth and universal good will.[22]

APPENDIX 4

INVITATIONS TO 'ABDU'L-BAHÁ

The number of invitations to visit different cities in North America received by 'Abdu'l-Bahá was so great that despite His efforts it was impossible to accept all the requests. Thanks to the announcements published in local journals it is possible to know the names of some of the places where an opportunity to receive the Master was sought but where He could not, in the end, travel.

In Syracuse, for instance, the *Herald* stated on 11 May that a 'church [First Universalist Church] is attempting to complete arrangements with Abdul Baha Abbas, patriarch and prophet and the supreme head of the new Bahai religion, to deliver a lecture in this city in the near future', and added that 'Dr. F. W. Betts has received assurance from Abbas' friends in New York city that there is a possibility of his delivering a lecture in this city.'[1] In New London (Connecticut) the *Telegraph* announced to its readers that on Sunday, June 23 'Abdu'l-Bahá would speak in the First Church of Christ (Christian Scientist).[2]

Another city that expected the visit of 'Abdu'l-Bahá was Portland, Oregon. The Bahá'ís in the area were very active in publicizing the arrival of the Master in the United States. The *Sunday Oregonian* (Portland) published in its issue of 28 April two articles about 'Abdu'l-Bahá and the Bahá'í Faith. One of them consisted of a portrait of Him and a short article about His arrival. 'He makes no distinction among creeds and races,' stated the article.[3] The second, a much longer article, was published under the title of 'The Bahais' and quoted some of the words of 'Abdu'l-Bahá spoken at All Souls Church, New York, and summarized the history and teachings of the Bahá'í Faith.[4] On 22 May the *Oregonian* reviewed the book *The Universal Principles of the Bahai Movement*[5] and a few weeks later the journal stated:

> . . . some time ago *The Oregonian* published an article on the Bahais

which endeavored to give a fair and appreciative account of that interesting denomination. By reading the article fifteen persons, whose names a friend has given us, were induced to write to the Bahai headquarters for more particulars. This fact is mentioned not only because we take a kindly interest in Abdul Baha and his disciples, but also because it shows that *The Oregonian* is read with serious attention by thoughtful persons who wish to keep in touch with the Ideas of the day.[6]

In June the Portland Bahá'ís invited Hippolyte Dreyfus to lecture on 'Abdu'l-Bahá[7] and weeks later Eunice Hoffman, a Bahá'í from Washington, was invited to speak about her impressions of the Master's visit to the capital and 'referred to the power and charm of the man who has succeeded in influencing all classes with his plea for a universal religion'.[8] On 1 September the *Oregonian* published another lengthy article about 'Abdu'l-Bahá in which the possibility of His visit to Portland was mentioned.[9]

An article appearing on 16 August in the *Telegram* offered more detailed information about a possible visit of 'Abdu'l-Bahá to Portland. It included a presentation about the Bahá'í Faith, a portrait of the Master and the following interview with a local Bahá'í:

> Local followers of Abdul Baha, the Persian mystic and leader of the new Universal religion, are agog over the news that he will in all probability spend a few days in this city during the coming month – an event that has been prayed for and eagerly sought ever since he arrived on American shores months ago.
>
> In Portland there are between 200 and 300 followers of Bahaism and the number has been steadily growing during the past few months, since a central publication bureau has been established in Chicago and a medium established through which news of the leader's movements could be obtained and his messages translated and conveyed through the press. Each Sunday night meetings are held on the sixth floor of Eilers Hall, and here are discussed the 'tablets' issued from time to time in the interest of the movement and study made of the articles of faith as promulgated by Abdul Baha Abbas . . .
>
> Several Portland Baha followers journeyed this spring to Chicago in order to sit at the feet of the Persian leader. They returned

profoundly impressed with his personality and the strength of his message. Among these was Mrs. J. W. Latimer, who declares he is without doubt the superman on the earth, that his wisdom, his wonderful spirituality, the sublimity of his message, his power to satisfy each soul's needs has never been equaled since the coming of Jesus Christ.

'I had a personal interview with Abdul Baha while in Chicago,' said Mrs. Latimer, 'and the experience is one which I shall never forget as long as I live. Never have I been in the presence of so majestic, so sublime a personality. He radiates peace, joy, majesty. Intuitively he answers the questions that come crowding to one's mind, and no one leaves him unsatisfied or doubting. The effect is indescribable, and was experienced by hundreds who came out of curiosity and intending to scoff, but "remained to pray". All day long he was besieged by people who clamored to have a moment's interview with him, and all through the day and into the night he dispensed comfort and gave hope to those who came.

'He is patriarchal in appearance, with pure white hair and beard and piercing wonderful eyes, now blue, now black with their intensity. He wears upon his head an Oriental turban and is garbed in a flowing robe, sometime of white, sometime black or natural undyed wools. His chief characteristic is his modesty, his humility. He will not permit his followers to call him "master" or any title that will set him above them, and declares he is to be known simply as "the servant of the people".'

Mrs. Latimer and other followers predict Portland will be stirred to the depths with the coming of the teacher.[10]

The *Portland Journal* published on 29 August another article summarizing the history and basic tenets of the Bahá'í Faith together with the following comments about His expected arrival:

Abdul Baha Abbas, the Persian head of the Bahais of the world, is expected to visit Portland soon. He has been in America since April last and has been received with unusual respect and esteem, not only by the followers of his teaching but also by churches of many denominations, institutions of learning, peace organizations and societies of various kinds . . .

Preparations are under way to receive the famous Persian upon his arrival in Portland in a manner befitting his dignity and great learning. A public reception will be arranged and he will probably be invited to speak in a number of the leading churches of the city and deliver addresses before the students of the local educational institutions . . .

He is now in Montreal, and purposes to visit the western coast in the near future. Friends of the Bahai cause in Spokane, Seattle and Portland hope, and have strong reason to expect that he will visit these places in the near future. Should he come to Portland he will doubtless be sought by all those who hope for the peace of the world and desire the real and active brotherhood.[11]

On 29 September the *Oregonian* announced that 'Abdul Baha will reach Portland Wednesday or Thursday of this week. Definite announcement will be made later. There will be a meeting tonight at 609 Eiler's building.'[12] On 4 October, however, the same newspaper stated that 'Abdul Baha will remain in San Francisco for three weeks or a month. His admirers have taken a house there for him with the intention of making him prolong his stay, so that in all probability Portland people will not have an opportunity of seeing this remarkable personality for some time.'[13] On 13 October the *Portland Journal* reported that 'Members of the Bahai Assembly are greatly encouraged over the receipt of a message Saturday morning, stating that definite assurance of the coming of Abdul Bahai, "the Apostle of Peace", would be received soon. Local members of the brotherhood believe that the Persian philosopher will be here next week.'[14] Finally, on the following day the *Portland Telegram* reported that Portland Bahá'ís had received word that 'Abdu'l-Bahá definitively 'will not visit Portland. Word has been received here today from San Francisco saying that the noted seer would leave there immediately for his native country owing to the present critical conditions there. Followers of his doctrines in this city have been making plans for giving their leader a hearty greeting, and today's news comes as a severe disappointment.'[15]

With this change in plans, the Bahá'ís of Portland decided to visit the Master in San Francisco. The *Oregonian* reported that 'More than a dozen Portland persons are on their way to San Francisco to meet Abdul Baha, the noted Persian leader of the universal peace movement, who probably will not be able to visit Portland before starting on his way to the Orient. Mrs. E. R. Rabb, Mrs. J. C. Fitch, Mrs. Hare, Mrs. Harmon, Professor J. Da Langesi and D. R. Suton left yesterday afternoon on the steamer *Rose City*; Mrs. Katherine O'Reilly, Mrs. J. W. Latimer and Mrs. D. T. Hunt and son left last night on the Shasta Limited and others will leave today. They will convey greetings from his followers in this city. When Abdul Baha was in Chicago, the Portland Bahai Assembly had a florist in that city deliver him a bouquet. Recently they received, in return, a box of candy with Abdul Baha's blessing.'[16]

The arrangements made by the local Bahá'ís in preparation for the possible visit of 'Abdu'l-Bahá aroused some opposition in Portland. The *Telegram* reported that 'not a single invitation from any church or Christian body has been extended to him and not a platform or pulpit placed at his disposal' and added that 'Portland pastors on being approached have either declared that he was an "impostor", a "poseur", or an "unsafe man". Some have even gone further and declared him to be a "dangerous man".'[17] These statements prompted a reply from Perry J. Green, minister of the New Thought Movement in Portland, who addressed the following letter to the editor:

A PULPIT FOR ABDUL BAHA

PORTLAND, Oct. 10 – (To the editor of The Telegram) – In your paper today I notice an account of the refusal of churches and societies to offer Abdul Baha their platforms. As minister of the Temple of Truth I wish to make a partial correction of this statement, by saying to your readers that as soon as we heard of Abdul Baha's coming to Portland we hurried as fast as we could to offer him our platform, believing that he has a great message of truth for the unbiased and fearless seekers of truth. We are not afraid of any teacher. If we haven't the truth, we want it bad enough to run the risk of getting it from a man who has nothing in his heart but universal love and good will for all people and religions. If we have the truth, our people could not be led astray by the reasonings of any teacher. It is not churchanity with us, but Christianity in its original essence that we aim to express and give to the world. The church at large in refusing their platforms to such a noble man as Abdul Baha only confess their weakness, through fear that their people are not able to discriminate between truth and untruth. Surely the prophecy is being fulfilled that 'judgment must begin at the (so-called) house of God'. This is manifest by the apparent disgust of the multitudes for the orthodox clergy, and their manifest absence in their congregations. Heartily and lovingly do we welcome Abdul Baha to our platform, ready to receive with grateful hearts any good he may have to give us that we do not already possess. Thanking you for the permission to correct the public mind with regard to our society, the Temple of Truth.[18]

'Abdu'l-Bahá was also invited to visit Seattle. As early as 16 September the *Seattle Times* reported that in a Sunday service sermon on religious unity, the Rev. Sydney Strong of the Queen Anne Congregational Church had announced to his parish the visit of 'Abdu'l-Bahá to the city and said of the Bahá'í teachings that 'All these things are signs of God's glorious presence; signs of the growing unity between men of good will'.[19] On 30 April the editorial page of the *Seattle Daily Times* also included a few comments about the arrival of 'Abdu'l-Bahá in America.[20] Another Seattle pastor, Rev. J. D. O. Powers of the Boylston Unitarian Church, was also reported as having briefly mentioned 'Abdu'l-Bahá during a sermon delivered on 29 September.[21] A few weeks later the same journal furnished its readers with further details about a possible visit of 'Abdu'l-Bahá to Seattle and quoted a local Bahá'í, Dr Claude F. Lathrop, as saying that 'we have wired him our invitation, but it is impossible to lay any plans for him in advance'.[22]

APPENDIX 5

THE CHRISTIAN COMMONWEALTH

The western journal that paid by far the greatest attention to the figure of 'Abdu'l-Bahá was *The Christian Commonwealth* (London).

This weekly magazine, appearing every Wednesday, was founded in 1881 as the voice of Liberal Christians from any denomination. During the ministry of Reginald Campbell at the City Temple (1903–15) the magazine became the semi-official organ of the League of Liberal Christian Thought and Social Service, popularly known as the Liberal Christian League, and the voice of the supporters of Campbell's 'New Theology'. The magazine had subscribers not only in England but also in the United States and Canada, South Africa, Australia and New Zealand, and in several European countries.

Its editor from August 1901 was Albert Dawson (1866–1930) who before holding that position had been staff member of the magazine for some years. Dawson was a close associate of the Congregationalist Rev. Joseph Parker (1830–1902), the founder of the City Temple. Dawson acted as Parker's personal secretary during Parker's lifetime[1] and was afterwards appointed as honorary secretary of the City Temple.

Dawson had the honor of being the first journalist in the West to interview 'Abdu'l-Bahá. For some years previously his magazine had carried a few pieces about the Bahá'í Faith but it was not until the visit of Tudor Pole with 'Abdu'l-Bahá in Egypt that *The Christian Commonwealth* started to publish references to the Bahá'í Faith with some regularity.[2]

The presence of the Master in London and His personal meetings with Dawson deeply strengthened the relationship between the periodical and the Bahá'í community to the extent that it started to serve as an unofficial Bahá'í bulletin for the British Bahá'ís. Writing to Albert Windust, at the time editor of the American Bahá'í magazine *Star of the West*, Tudor Pole reported that 'Bahai News is being published as often as seems wise in the "Christian Commonwealth" . . . On the whole we think it better to utilize a journal already existing for this purpose rather to found a separate journal . . .'[3]

The following note, which appeared in *The Christian Commonwealth* just a few days after the first meeting between 'Abdu'l-Bahá and Dawson, shows the extent to which Dawson was disposed to collaborate with the Bahá'ís and specially with the Master:

> We find there is widespread and growing interest in the Bahai movement and its leaders. We shall continue to devote attention to this wonderful manifestation of the Spirit of God. It was Abdul Baha's own suggestion that the facsimile message from himself, referred to above, should appear in *The Christian Commonwealth*, and by his kindness the first sitting he gave to a photographer was for this journal. We hoped to reproduce the portrait this week, but in order to obtain the best possible results we have deferred publication until next week. We think we can now legitimately claim Abdul Baha as a contributor to this journal; indeed, we see no reason why he should not join our editorial board. We may add that many copies of this and subsequent issues of *The Christian Commonwealth* will be circulated in Persia and other Eastern countries. Thus the paper is serving as a link and a channel between East and West, and divers religious faiths that are all aspects of the one religion – facets of the diamond of Truth.[4]

'Abdu'l-Bahá did become a contributor to the magazine for, as has been shown, many letters and messages of 'Abdu'l-Bahá appeared in the pages of *The Christian Commonwealth*, and some of these were expressly written for the magazine and its editor.

The Christian Commonwealth published two special Bahá'í issues. The first was an edition for America that included some of the articles that appeared during 'Abdu'l-Bahá's first sojourn in England plus articles introducing the Bahá'í Faith. It was published to coincide with His arrival in the western hemisphere and had a print run of 10,000 copies. In a letter from 'Abdu'l-Bahá to Dawson He thanked him for this service:

> On account of the ten thousand copies of [the Bahá'í edition of] *The Christian Commonwealth* that you have published the utmost

gratefulness and thankfulness was obtained. This praiseworthy deed of yours will never be forgotten by the Bahais, and you are very honoured and beloved in my estimation. I hope that this honour from you will remain everlasting and it is assured that it will remain eternal. May God be your protector![5]

The second Bahá'í issue was a special supplement published on 1 January 1913. The issue of 20 September 1911, also had an extensive Bahá'í content.

At some point during 'Abdu'l-Bahá's travels in America, Dawson contacted the Washington Bahá'í Joseph Hannen and requested that a Bahá'í be appointed to be a correspondent for his magazine. When 'Abdu'l-Bahá was informed of this He wrote the following letter to Hannen:

O thou my heavenly friend!

The letter which was written to you by the Editor of the Christian Commonwealth was perused. It is better that you be the Correspondent of this Journal, and spread it everywhere. This person (Mr. Albert Dawson) is a very excellent man, and showed us great love while we were in London. Therefore, the American Bahais must exercise toward him much respect. You correspond with him and send him the enclosed Tablet.

Show this Tablet that I write to you to all the Bahais, so that those friends who are able may subscribe to his paper.

Upon thee be Baha El BEHA!

Simultaneously, He sent the following message to Dawson:

To his honor Mr. Albert Dawson, Upon him be Baha'u'llah El-ABHA,
London, England

O thou beloved friend!

The letter which thou hast written to Mr. Hannen was read. I became very grateful and thankful to you. We have appointed Mr. Hannen to be your Correspondent, and we are hopeful in the Divine Favors to confirm and assist you in all the affairs.

It is my expectation to be in London before long, and then I shall find you there.

Upon thee be Baha El- BEHA![6]

In early 1913 the Master sent a Persian carpet to Dawson as a token of His gratitude for his important services to the Bahá'í Faith. The next day the editor penned the following letter to Luṭfu'lláh Ḥakím, through whom he had received the present, which perfectly summarizes the impression that 'Abdu'l-Bahá had left on him:

Dear Mr. Hakim!

I received a great and delightful surprise when I came to the office this afternoon and found your note with the lovely Persian rug, so generously presented to me by His Excellency, Abdul Baha Abbas. May I ask you to convey to him my very sincere thanks. I value the gift, not only on account of its beauty and usefulness, but also because of the donor and the good feeling which it represents. I am sure I shall not be misunderstood, when I say that our hearts go out toward the Master, not only by the reason of the lofty teachings which he brings and the authority with which he conveys it, but also because of his gracious personality, his warm-heartedness and his really wonderful thoughtfulness and attention to detail. My varied journalistic career has brought me into touch with many interesting personalities but I can honestly say that there is no experience that I shall look back upon with more pleasure and satisfaction than meeting Abdul Baha Abbas and being in some way associated with the great movement of which he is the head.

I am yours sincerely
(sig.) Albert Dawson[7]

After the return of 'Abdu'l-Bahá to the East the magazine continued to carry references to the Bahá'í Faith in almost all its issues until its disappearance. These included short announcements, articles about the activities of the British Bahá'ís, news about the international progress of the Bahá'í Faith, quotations from the Bahá'í writings, reviews of Bahá'í books and articles, short translations of Bahá'í writings into Esperanto, etc. But, above all, the magazine was characterized by its meticulous coverage of the activities of the Master not only in Europe and America[8] but also, as has been shown, after His return to Haifa and during the dark years of the world war.

The post-war financial situation, the decay of the movement that was started by Campbell, who had withdrawn from it, and the devastating blow that the war caused to the hopes of many former idealistic men and women who now were turned into skeptics, decreased considerably the influence of the magazine. Eventually its ownership changed and after its issue of 24 August 1919, *The Christian Commonwealth* became the *New Commonwealth*. With fewer pages and a smaller size, the magazine increased considerably its general and political contents to the detriment of religious information in an attempt to reach a wider readership. Dawson was replaced as editor by Frederick Thoresby and was appointed instead as business manager.

Interestingly, the new magazine carried in its second issue an article on the Bahá'í Faith.[9] Perhaps this was a last effort by Dawson to make 'Abdu'l-Bahá and the Bahá'í teachings known to the general public.[10]

APPENDIX 6

ARTS AND ARTISTS

During the lifetime of 'Abdu'l-Bahá many artists felt impelled to represent Him in their works, and the period of His travels was especially prolific in the production of art specimens related to His person.

As seen in the chapters of this book, 'Abdu'l-Bahá was the object of a number of poems and was photographed in Washington, New York, London and Paris by some of the most important studios of the time and by famous photographers such as Gertrude Käsebier.

He was also sought after by many portraitists. In the United States, for instance, His portrait was painted by Khalil Gibran, among others. In Egypt another portrait was made by the Greek painter Thalia Karavia (see vol. 1, chapter 8). In Budapest He gave three sittings to the renowned Hungarian artist Robert Nadler, who was also the president of the Theosophical Society in the area. One sculptor, the Spanish-born Antonio del Villar, who met 'Abdu'l-Bahá in New York, produced a bust of Him for a Bahá'í conference in Panama in 1946.

In some cases, the production of these art works had repercussions in the press. Such was the case of Gertrude Atherton's *Julia France and her Times* (1912), in which the author, a best-selling suffragist writer, used 'Abdu'l-Bahá as one of the characters in her novel. Many of the reviews of this book mentioned Him.[1]

In the United States, two artists – Theodore Spicer-Simon and Louis Potter – designed medallions bearing the profile of 'Abdu'l-Bahá. The design by Potter was commissioned by the Circle of Friends of the Medallion, which was based in New York. The medallion dedicated to 'Abdu'l-Bahá was the seventh issued by this organization and the last ever made by the artist, who died soon afterwards in an accident in Seattle. Some specialized periodicals published the image of the medallion. In describing it, the artist Réne T. Quélin affirmed that it was 'an excellent example of medallic portraiture, delineating this most estimable man, whose life is devoted to promoting peace and good will among all men'.[2] Spicer-Simon's medallion was exhibited in January 1919 at the Art Institute of Chicago.[3]

Frances Souley Campbell (1860–?) developed her career as an artist in California. She became famous thanks to her drawings of prominent people of her time using the silver-point technique. Among those who gave her sittings were presidents Theodore Roosevelt, William Taft and Woodrow Wilson. In the summer of 1912 she traveled to New York, where she decided to draw 'Abdu'l-Bahá's portrait. The Bahá'í-inspired magazine *Reality* recounts how she first became interested in drawing Him:

> The first time Miss Campbell ever saw Abdul Baha, she sat in his audience as he spoke, and presently taking out her drawing pad, began to draw the vivid illumined countenance at which she gazed. Is it singular that she caught reality, the light of the spirit? Her drawing will always remain a marvellous poetic interpretation of the Messenger of God. The portrait has become one of the great series of interpretative portraits of distinguished men and women, the creation of which gives Miss Campbell a unique place in the world of Art, where she has had no rival.[4]

In her diary notes, Juliet Thompson very briefly mentions, as part of her personal story, how she composed her own portrait of Him during one of the meetings between Campbell and 'Abdu'l-Bahá:

> The Beloved Master's portrait is finished. He sat for me six times, but I really did it in the three half hours He had promised me; for the sixth time, when He posed in His own room on the top floor, I didn't put on a single stroke. I was looking at the portrait wondering what I could find to do, when He suddenly rose from his chair and said: 'It is finished.' The fifth time He sat, Miss Souley-Campbell came in with a drawing she had done from a photograph to ask if He would sign it for her and if she might add a few touches from life. This meant that He had to change His pose, so of course I couldn't paint that day.[5]

Apparently, Campbell drew at least two portraits of 'Abdu'l-Bahá. The

American Art News magazine (New York) published a picture of one of these portraits and described her work, stating that 'In her sketch of the venerable prophet, Abdul Baha, the world leader of the Bahai movement – you see the touch of unfailing sympathy so pronounced in the life and work of this "Great Peace Advocator" and promulgator.'[6] On 31 August 1913 the New York *Sun* also published the portrait and affirmed that 'In the picture of the Persian prophet Abdul Baha, the head of the Bahai movement, the Bahaists feel the profound and perfect sympathies which distinguished his career and endear him to their hearts. There is that also in his face which bespeaks the tragedy of many years passed behind prison bars when he taught his turnkeys and made them converts to the faith of his father.'[7]

In 1922 the portraits were exhibited in New York along with other of Campbell's works. Among those who visited the exhibit was Windsor P. Daggett, a speech teacher who was interested in the production and collection of voice records. In his column for the famous musical magazine *The Billboard* (New York), Dagget described his visit to Campbell's exhibition and her comments on her work of 'Abdu'l-Bahá:

> The voice portrait hangs on the wall. The other afternoon I was visiting the Gallerie Intime on Fifth Avenue to see F. Soule Campbell's silver-point drawings and reproductions. Miss Campbell's portraits are familiar to the general public. Her head of Mary Baker Eddy is in every Christian Science home. Her official portrait of Woodrow Wilson for the Wilson Foundation adds to her long list of American statesmen. Her portrait of Sarah Bernhardt adds to her list of foreign celebrities. I was admiring two portraits of Abdul Baha, and discussing my choice of one in preference to the other, when Miss Campbell quietly remarked: 'I heard his voice and that started the picture.'
>
> Miss Campbell knew nothing about my collection of voices. 'Please repeat that remark,' said I.
>
> 'I heard his voice,' repeated the artist, 'and that started the picture. That gave me the key. In that rhythm I completed the portrait.'
>
> I stood somewhat amazed at the remark, perhaps looking incredulous, when Elizabeth L. Holt joined in the conversation. (I mention her because she is interested in American speech.) 'No

artist can explain technique,' enjoined Miss Holt. I tried no further to unravel the mystery of portrait making. But I had this much to salt down. Miss Campbell's portrait evolved from a voice. The voice was the key to character and it evolved a face. I have hung my inscribed copy of Abdul Baha on the wall. It is my voice portrait.[8]

Yet another artist who exhibited her work portraying 'Abdu'l-Bahá was Elizabeth Fisher Washington (1871–1953), a skilled and prolific miniaturist. In 1915 the Pennsylvania Academy of the Fine Arts (Philadelphia) hosted the twelfth Annual Exhibition of Water-Colors, Pastels and Black and White work. Washington was among the artists invited to present their work and she chose for the occasion a portrait of 'Abdu'l-Bahá which, according to a report 'was an admirable study of oriental character quite in keeping with the subject'.[9]

These are only a few examples of the way in which the art world received the figure of 'Abdu'l-Bahá. Much research needs to be done in this field, not only to ascertain the exact number of art works produced in His honor and to contextualize them, but also to find and rescue many of them from their unknown locations.

BIBLIOGRAPHY

Books

'Abdu'l-Bahá. *Majmú'i-yi-Khaṭábát-i-Haḍrat-i-'Abdu'l-Bahá* (Collected Letters of 'Abdu'lBahá), vol. 1. Iran National Bahá'í Archives.
— *Paris Talks*. London: Bahá'í Publishing Trust, 1967.
— *The Promulgation of Universal Peace*. Wilmette, IL: Bahá'í Publishing Trust, 1982.
— *Selections from the Writings of 'Abdu'l-Bahá*. Haifa: Bahá'í World Centre, 1978.
— *Some Answered Questions*. Haifa: Bahá'í World Centre, 2015.
— *Tablets of Abdul-Baha Abbas*, vol 2. Chicago: Bahá'í Publishing Society, 1915.

Abdul Baha on Divine Philosophy. Boston: The Tudor Press, 1918.

'Abdu'l-Bahá in London. London: Bahá'í Publishing Trust, 1982.

Atherton, Gertrude Franklin Horn. *Julia France and Her Times*. New York: Macmillan, 1912.

Bahai Scriptures. New York: Brentano's, 1923.

The Bahá'í World. vols. 1–12, 1925–54. rpt. Wilmette, IL: Bahá'í Publishing Trust, 1980.

Bahá'u'lláh. *The Kitáb-i-Aqdas*. Haifa: Bahá'í World Centre, 1992.

Balyuzi, H. M. *'Abdu'l-Bahá: The Centre of the Covenant of Bahá'u'lláh*. Oxford: George Ronald, 2nd ed. with minor corr. 1987.

Bell, Archie. *The Spell of the Holy Land*. Boston: Page, 1915.

Besant, Annie. *The Changing World and Lectures to Theosophical Students*. London: The Theosophical Publishing Society, 1910.

Blomfield, (Lady) Sara L. *The Chosen Highway*. Oxford: George Ronald, 2007.

Bowers, Edwin F. *Spiritualism's Challenge*. New York: National Library Press, 1936.

Buckton, A. M. [Alice Mary]. *Eager Heart: A Christmas Mystery Play*. New York: Chappell, 1910.

Caillet, Albert Louis. *Manuel Bibliographique des sciences Psychiques et Occultes*. Paris: L. Dorbon, 1912.

Catt, Carrie Chapman. *Address of the President at the Seventh Congress of the International Woman Suffrage Alliance*. London: International Woman Suffrage Alliance, 1913.

Child, C.W. *Hands of Famous Men: Their Significance*. London: Collins, 1913.

Complete Works of Pir-o-Murshid Inayat Khan, Journal and Anecdotes. Available online at http://wahiduddin.net/mv2/bio/Journal_1.htm (accessed 7 May 2018).

Dawson, Albert. *Joseph Parker: His Life and Ministry; Minister of the City Temple, London*. Boston: The Pilgrim Press, 1901.

Fenge, Gerry. *The Two Worlds of Wellesley Tudor Pole*. Everett, WA: Lorian Press, 2010.

Géza, Buzinkay. *Kis magyar sajtótörténet*. Budapest: Kiadó, 1993.

Goldzieher, Ignácz. *Vorlesungen über den Islam*. Heidelberg: C. Winter, 1910.

Hammond, Eric. *The Splendour of God*. New York: E.P. Dutton, 1909.

Harper, Ida Huster. *History of the Woman Suffrage*, vol. 6. New York: J.J. Little and Ives, 1920.

Heller, Wendy. *Lidia: The Life of Lidia Zamenhof, Daughter of Esperanto*. Oxford: G. Ronald, 1985.

Herrick, Elizabeth. *Unity Triumphant: The Call of the Kingdom*. London: Kegan, Paul, Trench, Trubner, 1923.

Holbach, Maude M. *Bible Ways in Bible Lands: An Impression of Palestine*. London : Kegan Paul Trench Trubner, 1912.

The Holy Bible. Authorised King James Version. London: The Gideons, International, 1957.

Korzhenkov, Aleksander. *Zamenhof: The Life, Works and Ideas of the Author of Esperanto*. New York: Mondial, 2010.

Lederer, György. "Abdu'l-Bahá in Budapest', Smith (ed.), *Bahá'ís in the West*. Los Angeles: Kalimát Press, 2004, pp. 109–26.

Ledermann, Richard (ed.). 'Abdul Baha Abbas'. *Das Esperanto ein Kulturfaktor. Festschrift anläßlich des 7 deutschen EsperantoKongresses*: Danzig: vom 27. Juli bis 1. August 1912, vol. 3. Leizpig, 1913.

— 'Persische Sprache'. *Das Esperanto ein Kulturfaktor: Festschrift anlässlich des 8 Deutschen Esperanto-Kongresses*, vol. 3. Stuttgart (Leizpig), 1913

MacKillop, Ian D. *The British Ethical Societies*. Cambridge: Cambridge University Press, 1986.

Maḥmúd-i-Zarqání. *Maḥmúd's Diary*. Oxford: George Ronald, 1998.

Maud, Constance. *Sparks Among the Stubble*. London: Allan, 1924.

Momen, Moojan. *The Bábí and Bahá'í Religions, 1844–1944. Some Contemporary Western Accounts*. Oxford: George Ronald, 1981.

The Passing of 'Abdu'l-Baha: A Compilation. Los Angeles: Kalimat Press, 1991.

Phelps, Myron. *Abbas Effendi: His Life and Teachings*. New York: G. P. Putman's and Son, 1903, 2nd rev. ed. 1912.

Pole, Major David Graham. *I Refer to India*. Adyar, India: Dr Annie Besant at Adyar, 1929.
— *India in Transition*. London: Hogarth Press, 1932.

Portland Reliefs and Medals by T. Spicer-Simon. Catalogue of the exhibition of January 1919 at the Art Institute of Chicago.

Rice, Walter A. 'Bahaism from the Christian Standpoint', *The East and the West*. London), 1913.

Shoghi Effendi. *God Passes By*. Wilmette, IL: Bahá'í Publishing Trust, rev. ed. 1995.
— *The Passing of 'Abdu'l-Bahá*. With Lady Blomfield. Stuttgart: Heppeler, 1922.

Smith, Peter (ed.). *Bahá'ís in the West*. Los Angeles: Kalimát Press, 2004.

Sohrab, Ahmad. *Abdul Baha in Egypt*. New York: New History Foundation, 1929.
— Correspondence with Harriet Magee from 5 December 1912 to 12 June 1913. US National Bahá'í Archives.

Spiller, Gustav (ed.). *Papers on Inter-Racial Problems Communicated to the First Universal Races Congress*. London: Universal Races Congress, 1911.

Star of the West. rpt. Oxford: George Ronald, 1984.

Stevens, E. S. *The Mountain of God*. London: Mills and Boon, 1911.

Stocker, Richard Dimsdale. *The Time Spirit*. London: E. Macdonald, 1913.

Thompson, Juliet. *'Abdu'l-Bahá: The Centre of the Covenant*. Wilmette, Il.: Bahá'í Publishing Trust, 1948.
— *Abdul Baha's First Days in America*. East Aurora, N.Y.: The Roycrofters, n.d.
— *The Diary of Juliet Thompson*. Los Angeles: Kalimát Press, 1995.

Townshend, George. *'Abdu'l-Bahá: The Master*. Oxford: George Ronald, 1987.

Travaux du 6e Congrès International Du Progrès Religieux. Paris: Librarie Fischbacher, 1913.

Tudor Pole, Wellesley. *The Silent Road*. London: C. W. Daniel, 1960.
— *Writting on the Ground*. London: Neville Spearman, 1968.

Weinberg, Robert. *Ethel Jenner Rosenberg*. Oxford: George Ronald, 1995.

Whittingham, George Napier. *The Home of Fadeless Splendour: Or, The Diary of a Pilgrimage to Palestine*. London: Hutchinson, 1928.

Newspapers, Journals and Periodicals

A Nap (Budapest)
A Polgár (Budapest)
Aberdeen Daily News (South Dakota)
Aberdeen Journal
Aberdeen Weekly News
Adiromdack Record Elizabethtown Post
   (Au Sable Forks, NY)
Advertiser (Adelaide)
Adyar-Mitteilungen (Leizpig)
African World (London)
The Afro-American (Baltimore)
Albert City Appeal (Iowa)
Alliance Spiritualiste (Paris)
Alton Democrat (IL)
Alton Evening Telegraph (IL)
Altoona Herald (Iowa)
The American (Baltimore)
American Art News (New York)
American Israelite (Cincinnati)
American Review of Reviews (New York)
Amerika Esperantisto (Chicago)
Anaconda Standard (Montana)
Anita Tribune (Iowa)
Annales Théosophiques (Paris)
The Appeal (St Paul, MN)
Army and Navy Gazette (London)
Arts and Decoration (New York)
Asiatic Quarterly Review (London)
L'Asie Arabe (Paris)
Atlantic News Telegraph (IA)
Attica Ledger and Tribune (Indiana)
Auburn Citizen (New York)
Auckland Star (Auckland, NZ)
Augusta Chronicle
Az Érdekes Újság (Budapest)
Az Ujság (Budapest)

al-Badr (Qadian, India)
Bahá'í Magazine
Bahá'í Studies Review
Ballston Spa Daily Journal (NY)
Baltimore American
Baltimore News

Bath Chronicle and Weekly Gazette
Bavara Esperantisto
Beatrice Daily Sun (Nebraska)
The Bee (Washington)
Belga Esperantisto (Antwerp)
Bexhill-on-Sea Observer
Bibliothéque universelle et Revue Suisse
   (Lausanne)
Billboard (New York)
Bismarck Tribune (North Dakota)
The Blast (London)
Bode Bugle (Iowa)
Bombay Chronicle
Bombay Courier (Bombay)
Bombay Times and Journal of Commerce
   (Bombay)
Boonville Standard (Indiana)
Boston Daily Globe
Boston Herald
Bow Island Review (Alberta)
Bradford Era (Pennsylvania)
Brazila Esperantisto (Rio de Janeiro)
Bridgeport Telegram (CT)
British Esperantist (London)
British Weekly (London)
Broad Ax (Chicago)
Brooklyn Daily Eagle (New York)
Budapest
Budapesti Hírlap
Budapesti Napló
Buffalo Evening News
Bulletin de l'Education de la Jeunese
Bulletin mensuel de la Société Unitive
   (Paris)
Bulletin Théosophique (Paris)

Cannelton Telephone (IN)
Casopis Ceskych Esperantistu (Prague)
Casper Daily Tribune (Casper, WY)
Cass City Chronicle (Cass City, MI)
Catholic World (New York)
El Católico (Madrid)
Charleroi Mail (PA)

Chehalis Bee-Nuget (WA)
Cheltenham Chronicle
Chicago Daily Tribune
Chicago Defender
Chicago Examiner
Chicago Journal
Chicago Sunday Tribune
Chicago Tribune
Children's Newspaper (London)
The Christian (London)
Christian Advocate (Nashville, TN)
The Christian Commonwealth (London)
Christian Express (Lovedale, South Africa)
The Christian Observer (Louisville, KY)
Christian Register (Boston)
Christian Science Monitor (Boston)
Christian World (London)
Le Christianisme au XX siècle (Paris)
Chronicle (Shellbrook, Saskatchewan)
Chronicle Telegram (Elvira, OH)
The Churchman (New York)
Citizen (Gloucester)
Claresholm Review (Alberta)
Clifton Chronicle and Directory (Bristol)
Clifton Free Press (Bristol)
Clifton Society (Bristol)
Club Women (New York)
The Common Cause (London)
Congregationalist and Christian World (Boston)
Contemporary Review (London)
The Continent (Chicago)
La Correspondencia Militar (Madrid)
Coshocton Tribune (Ohio)
Creede Candle (CO)
The Crisis (New York)
Cuba Esperantista (La Habana)

Daily Chronicle (London)
Daily Citizen (Manchester)
Daily Herald (Adelaide)
Daily Herald (London)
Daily Kenneber Journal (Augusta, ME)
Daily Mail (London)
Daily News (London)
Daily News (Perth)

Daily News and Leader (London)
Daily Northwestern (Oshkosh, WI)
Daily People (New York)
Daily Post (Liverpool)
Daily Sketch (London)
Daily Star (Brooklyn)
Daily Statesman (Austin, TX)
Daily Telegraph (London)
Dallas Morning News
Danville Republican (IN)
Darlington Herald (IN)
Deaver Sentinel (Big Horn, WY)
Denver Post
Derry Journal (Londonderry)
El Día de Madrid
Diario de la Marina (Havana, Cuba)
Dispatch Democrat (Ukiah, CA)
La Duj Stelo (Santiago de Chile)
Dundee Courier (Angus)

East and West (London)
Eau Clear Leader (WI)
Eenheid (Netherlands)
Egyetértés (Budapest)
Egyptian Gazette (Alexandria, Egypt)
Elgin Echo (IA)
Empress Express (Alberta)
English Churchman and St James's Chronicle (London)
Erdekes Ujság (Budapest)
Esperanto (Geneva)
L'Esperanto (Milan)
Esperanto Monthly (London)
Esperantysta Polski (Warsaw)
La Espero (Stockholm)
Espero Teozofia (Paris)
Ethical World (London)
Evangelical Christendom (London)
Evangelisches Gemeineblatt für Stuttgart
Evangile et Liberté (Paris)
Evening American (Chicago)
Evening Dispatch (Edinburgh)
Evening Express (Liverpool)
Evening News (Edinburgh)
Evening News (Kenosha, WI)
Evening Post (New York)
Evening Post (Wellington)

Evening Press (Grand Rapids, MI)
Evening Public Ledger (Philadelphia)
Evening Standard and St James Gazette (London)
Evening Star (Washington)
Evening Telegram (New York)
Evening Telegraph (Dundee)
Everywoman (San Francisco)
Excelsior (Paris)

Le Figaro (Paris)
Flaming Sword (Estero, FL)
Le Fraterniste (Paris)
Freeman (Indianapolis)
The Friend (London)
Fortnightly Review (London)
Független Magyarország (Budapest)

Galveston Daily News (TX)
Le Gaulois (Paris)
Gazette de Lausanne
German-Austria Esperantisto (Vienna)
Germana Esperantisto (Dresden)
Gil Blas (Paris)
Glasgow Herald
Goshen County Journal (Torrington, WY)
Grand Rapids Press (MI)

Hamilton Daily News (OH)
Hamilton Evening Journal (OH)
Hartford Courant (CT)
Hastings and St Leonards Observer (London)
Helena Independent (MT)
Herald (New Orleans)
Herald Dispatch (Utica, NY)
Herald of Gospel Liberty (Dayton, OH)
Hertfordshire and Cambridgeshire Reporter
Hobart Daily Republican (OK)
Homiletic Review (New York)
Horfield and Bishopston Record

Idaho Daily Statesman (Boise)
Idaho Falls Times
Idaho Statesman (Boise)
Ignacio Chieftain (Ignacio, CO)
Illustrated Buffalo Express

Illustrated London News (London)
Illustrated News (London)
Independent (New York)
Indian Opinion (Phoenix, South Africa)
Indianapolis Star
International Psychic Gazette
International Studio (New York)
Iola Register (KS)
Irish Times (Dublin)
Itala Esperantisto (Genoa)

Japan Advertiser (Tokyo)
Jewish Criterion (Pittsburgh)
Joplin Globe (Missouri)
Journal de Constantinople (Istanbul)
Journal des Débats (Paris)
Journal of Race Development (Worcester, MA)
Jus Suffragii (London)
Jus Suffragii (Paris)

Kalamazoo Gazette (Michigan)
Kansas City Star
Kingsport Times (Tennessee)
Kingston Daily Freeman (NY)
Kokoma Daily Tribune (IN)
La Kulturo (Prague)
Kurir (Budapest)

La Langue Auxiliare (Verdun)
Lexington Herald (KY)
Light (London)
Lima News (Ohio)
Lingvo Internacia (Paris)
Liverpool Courier
Liverpool Daily Post and Mercury
Living Church (Milwaukee)
Logansport Daily Tribune (Logansport)
Logansport Morning Press (IN)
London Budget
La Londona Esperantisto (London)
Londonderry Sentinel (London)
Los Angeles Examiner
Los Angeles Times
Le Lotus Bleu (Revue Théosophique Française; Paris)
Lytton Star (Iowa)

Magyar Nemzet (Budapest)
Mail (Drumheller, Alberta)
Manchester Guardian (England)
Manitoba Free Press (Winnipeg)
Manitowoc Herald-News (WI)
Marble Rock Journal (IA)
Marshall News-Statesman (MI)
La Marto (Haida)
Master Mind (Los Angeles)
Le Matin (Paris)
Mercure de France (Paris)
Mercury (Hobart, Australia)
Miami Herald
Mind (New York)
Missionary Review of the World (New York)
Monda Posto (Zurich)
Le Monde Espérantiste (Paris)
Month (London)
Montour Fall Free Press (NY)
Montour Falls (New York)
Montreal Daily Witness
Morning Herald (London)
Morning Oregonian (Portland)
Morning Post (London)
Moslem World (London)
Mountain Democrat (Placerville, CA)
La Movado (Paris)
Moville Mail (IA)
Mysteria (Paris)

Al-Narif (Haifa)
Národní Listy (Prague)
Nautilus
Near East (London)
Nebraska State Journal (Lincoln)
Neosho Times (Missouri)
Neues Pester Journal (Budapest)
Neues Wiener Journal
New Age (London)
New Commonwealth (London)
New York Evening Post
New York Herald (Paris)
New York Press
New York Sun
New York Times
New-York Tribune

New York World
Newark Advocate (OH)
News-Sentinel (Fort Wayne, IN)
Niagara Falls Gazette (New York)
Nieuwe Rotterdamsche Courant (Rotterdam)
Nineteenth Century (London)
Nineteenth Century and After (London)
North American Review (Boston)
Norvega Esperantisto (Oslo)
Nottingham Daily Express
Numismatist (Federalsburg, MD)
Nunda News (NY)

Oakland Tribune
The Occult Review (London)
Olean Evening Herald (New York)
Orienta Azio (Tokyo)
Ország-Világ (Budapest)
Otago Daily Times
Ovens and Murray Advertiser (Beechworth)
Outlook (New York)
Oxford Chronicle
Oxford Times

Palestine News
Palestine Weekly
Pall Mall Gazette (London)
Paris Esperanto
Park Record (UT)
The Path (London)
Pattsburgh Sentinel (New York)
Peacemaker (Philadelphia)
Pester Lloyd (Budapest)
Pesti Hírlap (Budapest)
Pesti Napló (Budapest)
Pesti Tükor (Budapest)
Le Petit Journal (Paris)
Phelps Citizen (NY)
Philadelphia Inquirer
Philadelphia Telegraph
Pinedale Roundup (WY)
Plain Dealer (Cleveland, OH)
Plain Truth (Liverpool)
Plattsburgh Sentinel (New York)
Pocahontas County Sun (Laurens, IA)

Pola Esperantisto [Esperantysta Polski]
  (Warsaw)
Polybiblion (Paris)
Portland Journal
Portland Telegram
Portugala Revuo (Lisbon)
Prager Tagblatt (Prague)
Progreso (Paris)
Protestáns (Budapest)
La Publicidad (Barcelona)

Quarterly Record of Higher Thought Work
  (London)

Racine Daily Journal (WI)
Racine Journal-News (WI)
Le Radical (Paris)
Reality
Record Gazette (Bedford, PA)
Record-Herald (Chicago)
The Register (Adelaide, Australia)
La Renaissance Contemporaine (Paris)
Republican (Gillete, WY)
Review of Reviews (London)
La Revista del Yucatán (Mérida)
Le Revue (Paris)
Revue Chrétienne (Paris)
La Revue Critique (Paris)
Revue d'études ethnographiques et sociologiques (Paris)
Revue de l'Histoire des Religions (Paris)
Revue du Monde Mussulman (Paris)
Revue de l'Orient, d'Algérie et des Colonies (Paris)
Revue Philosophique de la France (Paris)
Revue Théosophique (Paris)
Revue Théosophique Française (Le Lotus Bleu; Paris)
La Revuo (Paris)
Rivers Gazette (Manitoba)
Roland Record (Iowa)
Rund um die Welt (Prague)
Ruthven Free Press (Iowa)

Salem Democrat (Indiana)
San Antonio Evening News (Texas)
San Francisco Call
San Francisco Chronicle
San Francisco Monitor
San Jose Mercury Herald (California)
Savannah Tribune (Savannah, GA)
Scots Pictorial (Glasgow)
The Scotsman (Edinburgh)
Seattle Daily Times
Sheffield Daily Telegraph
Sheridan Post (Sheridan, WY)
Le Siècle (Paris)
Sind Gazette (Karachi)
Sonne der Warheit Organ des Deustschen Bahá'í-Bundes
Sophia (Madrid)
Sphinx (Cairo)
Springfield Republican (MA)
Staatsanzeiger für Württemberg (Stuttgart)
Standard (London)
Standard Union (Brooklyn)
Star (Baltimore)
Starke County Democrat (Knox, IN)
Straits Times (Singapore)
Stuttgarter Neues Tagblatt
Suffolk and Essex Press (Sudbury)
The Suffragette (London)
The Sun (Baltimore)
Sunday Independent (Dublin)
Sunday Oregonian (Portland, OR)
Surrey Herald and Middlesex News (Chertsey)
Surrey Times and County Express (Guildford)
Survey (New York)
La Svaba Esperantisto (Schussenried)
Svisa Espero (Zurich)
Syracuse Herald (Syracuse, NY)

Telegraph (Brisbane)
Telegraph (New London, CT)
Le Temps (Paris)
Teozófia (Budapest)
Teplitz-Schönauer Anzeiger (Teplice)
Le Théosophe (Paris)
Theosophic Messenger (Chicago)
Theosophic Messenger (Los Angeles)
Theosophical Forum (New York)

Theosophical Quarterly (New York)
Theosophical Review (London)
The Theosophist (Bombay)
Theosophy in Scotland (Edinburgh)
Timaru Herald
The Times (London)
Times of India (Bombay)
Tolnai Világlapja (Budapest)
Toronto World
Troy Times (Troy, NY)
Turán (Budapest)
Tutmonda Espero (Barcelona)
Twin Falls Daily Times (ID)
Tyrone Daily Herald (PA)

Uj Idök (Budapest)
Unitarian Advance (New York)
Unity (Chicago)
L'Univers Israélite (Paris)
El Universal (Mexico City)
Universala Unuigo (Lubotin)
Unuig-Informoj (Danzig)
Utica Morning Telegram (Utica, NY)

Vahan (London)
Van Wert Daily Bulletin (Ohio)
La Verda Standardo (Budapest)
La Vie (Paris)
Világ (Budapest)
Voile d'Isis (Paris)
Volga Stelo (Saratov)
The Vote (London)
Votes for Women (London)

Wanatah Mirror (IN)
Washington Herald
Washington Post
Washington Star (Washington DC)
Washington Times
Waterloo Times-Tribune (IA)
Waterville Times (NH)
The Week (Brisbane)
Weekly Scotsman (Edinburgh)
West Australian (Perth)
West Gippsland Gazette (Warragul, Australia)
Western Daily Press (Bristol)
Westminster Review (London)
Weston County Gazette (Upton, WY)
Wichita Daily Times (TX)
Williamsport Pioneer (IN)
Woking News and Mail
Woking Observer
Woman Voter (New York)
Woman's Journal (Boston)
Woman's Journal and Suffrage News (London)
Woman's Leader and the Common Cause (London)
Woman's Work (New York)
World (New York)
World's Work (Garden City)
Wyoming State Journal (Cheyenne)

Youth's Companion (Boston)

NOTES AND REFERENCES

'Abdu'l-Bahá
1. Shoghi Effendi, *God Passes By*, p. 242.

Introduction
1. Numbers 23:23.
2. *Bombay Times and Journal of Commerce*, 12 Apr. 1845, p. 246, col. 2; 'Epitome of News – Foreign and Domestic'; *Illustrated London News*, 19 Apr. 1845.
3. *Bombay Courier*, 19 Sept. 1845. The first known journal in the West to publish this news was 'Persia', *Times* (London), 1 Nov. 1845, p. 5, col. 4.
4. See *Journal de Constantinople*, 24 June 1848, p. 1, col. 5.
5. See, for instance, *Journal de Constantinople*, 29 Mar. 1849, p. 1, col. 2, n.t.; 'Persia', *Daily News* (London), 23 Apr. 1849, p. 5, col. 4; *Revue de l'Orient, d'Algérie et des Colonies* (Paris), Apr. 1849, vol. 5, p. 264.
6. See, for instance, *Morning Herald* (London), 2 July 1850, p. 5, col. 2; *El Católico* (Madrid), 24 Oct. 1850, p. 171, col. 2; *La Presse* (Paris), 18 Oct. 1850, p. 2, col. 4.
7. The Persian–American Educational Society hired the services of Henry Romeike's clipping bureau and collected many of the references to the Master published in the American press during His visit to the United States. This collection comprises some three hundred items and is now preserved in the US Bahá'í National Archives.
8. *Star of the West*, 23 Nov. 1914 (5:14), p. 213.

A Note from the Publisher
1. 'Epitome of News – Foreign and Domestic', *Illustrated London News*, 19 Apr. 1845.
2. 'Persia', *Times* (London), 1 Nov. 1845, p. 5, col. 4.

26 Second Visit to England
1. Sohrab to Hannen, 2 Dec. 1912 (Hannen-Knobloch family papers, B9, US Bahá'í National Archives).
2. 'Abd-ul-Baha', *Manchester Guardian*, 13 Dec. 1912, p. 10, col. 4.
3. 'Return to England of Abdul Baha', *London Budget*, 8 Dec. 1912, p. 1, col. 4.
4. 'Abdul Baha', *Evening Standard and St James Gazette* (London), 11 Dec. 1912.

5. 'Prophet of Peace', *Evening Express* (Liverpool), 13 Dec. 1912, p. 3, col. 4.
6. 'Persian Mystic', ibid. p. 5, col. 6.
7. See, for instance: 'News of the Day', *Derry Journal*, 16 Dec. 1912, p. 6, col. 1; 'Abdul Baha. Prophet of Peace', *Londonderry Sentinel* (London), 17 Dec. 1912, p. 3, col. 2; 'Forty Years in Prison', *Nottingham Daily Express*, 17 Dec. 1912. Outside the United Kingdom, see also 'Abdul Baha', *Straits Times* (Singapore), 15 Jan. 1913, p. 2, col. 3.
8. *Christian Commonwealth*, 11 Dec. 1912, p. 206.
9. For the details about the arrival see Fraser, 'Abdul-Baha's Arrival in England' in *Star of the West*, 19 Jan. 1913, p. 2, and Sohrab, Letter to Harriet Magee, 13 Dec. 1912, p. 2. Sohrab mentions that when 'Abdu'l-Bahá left the *Celtic* 'The Captain, the stewards, the sailors, the passengers, the maids, all of them came to the Master and expressed their pleasure and happiness. One of the maids told Him she had never seen any person on the steamer who has been as kind and as generous as the Master was to all of them.'
10. 'News of the Day', *Liverpool Daily Post and Mercury*, 14 Dec.1912, p. 6, col. 5.
11. ibid. p. 8, col. 5.
12. 'Peace Prophet', *Evening Express* (Liverpool), 14 Dec. 1912, p. 4, col. 3.
13. Sohrab, Letter to Harriet Magee, 15 Dec. 1912, p. 12.
14. ibid. p. 13.
15. For an account of the visit of 'Abdu'l-Bahá to the Pembroke Church see also Isabel Fraser, 'Abdul-Baha Addresses Pembroke Chapel', *Star of the West*, 19 Jan. 1913 (3:17), pp. 4–5. The article includes notes of some portions of the talk.
16. 'A World Religion and Universal Peace', *Plain Truth* (Liverpool), Jan. 1913, pp. 4–10. Later published in Herrick, *Unity Triumphant* (1923), pp. 87–95.
17. Sohrab, Letter to Harriet Magee, 19 Jan. 1913.
18. 'Arrival in England', *Christian Commonwealth* (London), 1 Jan. 1913, p. 261, col. 4.
19. According to Ahmad Sohrab, the Master and His companions left the hotel at 9:00 a.m. and walked to the Lime Street train station. The companions of the Master were Hippolyte Dreyfus, Ahmad Yazdi, Isabel Fraser, Elizabeth Herrick and Sohrab himself. The party left the train at Euston station. Sohrab, Letter to Harriet Magee, 16 Dec. 1912.
20. 'Abdul Baha in London', *Christian Commonwealth* (London), 18 Dec. 1912, p. 221, col. 4. For another announcement see *Light* (London), 28 Dec. 1912, p. 620.
21. Philip Stanhope, first Baron of Weardale, was a Liberal politician who had been a member of the House of Commons. He was a philanthropist and pacifist and became president of the Inter-Parliamentary Union and of the Save the Children Fund.
22. Sir Thomas Barclay was a Liberal politician and an authority in international law who was deputy chair of the International Law Association. He had been involved in the negotiations leading to the Entente cordiale and on ten occasions was nominated for the Nobel Peace Prize for promoting international arbitration.
23. For details about this meeting, see Sohrab, Letter to Harriet Magee, 20 Dec. 1912.

24. 'Abdul Baha's Return', *Christian Commonwealth* (London), 25 Dec. 1912, p. 239, col. 2.
25. *Christian Commonwealth* (London), 1 Jan. 1913, pp. 262–3. Isabel Fraser, 'Abdul Baha in London', *Star of the West*, 19 Jan. 193, pp. 9–10.
26. Sohrab, Letter to Harriet Magee, 21 Dec. 1912.
27. 'Abdul Baha Witnesses Mystery Play', *Christian Commonwealth* (London), 1 Jan. 1913, p. 254, col. 3.
28. Sohrab, Letter to Harriet Magee, 22 Dec. 1912.
29. This special issue was introduced in the following way: 'To Bahais and Others. In view of the world-wide interest in the Bahai movement, and the numerous requests that have reached us to publish addresses recently delivered by Abdul Baha Abbas, we have decided to add four pages to our next issue. We shall give the address on the Fundamental Unity of Religious Thought, delivered by Abdul Baha in the Jewish Synagogue, San Francisco, last October. This utterance shows how the founders of the great religions in Palestine and Arabia had the same essential message to deliver, the venerable speaker's references to the relations between Judaism and Christianity having a great significance not only for the Jews but the wider Christian public. We shall also publish a fuller account of the speech delivered by Abdul Baha at the reception given in his honour at the Westminster Palace Hotel last Friday, a brief report of which appears on page 239. In addition there will be a tablet from the Head of the Bahais, a facsimile of the Persian character being accompanied by a translation. What is in our judgment the most successful photograph of Abdul Baha will also be reproduced.' *Christian Commonwealth* (London), 25 Dec. 1912, p. 237, col. 4.
30. 'Towards Spiritual Unity', *Christian Commonwealth* (London), 1 Jan. 1913, p. 252, col. 3.
31. 'Abdul Baha in England', *Christian Commonwealth* (London), 1 Jan. 1913, p. 261. The photograph that accompanied the article was taken in 1911 at Boissonnas and Taponier studio in Paris. In the same edition it was announced that 'Abdul Baha Abbas can be seen by appointment during his stay in London. Communications should be addressed to the Secretary, Abdul Baha Abbas, 97, Cadogan Gardens. S.W.'
32. 'A Prophet of Peace', *Evening Post* (Wellington), 8 Mar. 1913, p. 12, col. 4; 'Prophet of Peace', *Timaru Herald*, 17 Mar. 1913, p. 11.
33. See Sohrab, Letter to Harriet Magee, 25 Dec. 1912, p. 3.
34. Isabel Fraser, 'Christmas Day with Abdul Baha in London', *Everywoman* (San Francisco), Dec. 1915, pp. 2–3.
35. 'Abdul Baha at a Salvation Army Shelter', *Christian Commonwealth* (London), 1 Jan. 1913, pp. 247–8.
36. 'Words of Wisdom', *Suffolk and Essex Press* (Sudbury), 26 Mar. 1913.
37. 'A New Sect', *Standard* (London), 27 Dec. 1912, p. 9, col. 7.
38. Sohrab, Letter to Harriet Magee, 29 Dec. 1912.
39. 'The Gospel of Bahaism', *Standard* (London), 30 Dec. 1912, p. 4, col. 3.
40. 'The Gospel of Bahaism', *West Australian* (Perth), 12 Feb. 1912, p. 8, col. 3; 'The Gospel of Bahaism', 21 Feb. 1913, p. 24, col. 1.
41. *Times* (London), 28 Dec. 1912, p. 8, col. 1, n.t.
42. 'Abdul Baha at the King's Weigh House', *Christian Commonwealth* (London),

1 Jan. 1913, p. 254, col. 3. Parts of this report were published in New Zealand; see 'Sunday Circle', *Otago Daily Times*, 15 Feb. 1913, p. 7.
43. 'Abdul Baha at the King's Weigh House', *Christian World* (London), 2 Jan. 1913, p. 3, col. 4.
44. Thomas Kelly Cheyne, who at the time was a Bahá'í, was an eminent biblical scholar and author of a large body of books and articles on the Old Testament. He was especially distinguished for his critical translations of some of the books of the Old Testament and his work as editor of the *Encyclopaedia Biblica* (1899–1903). His wife, Elizabeth Gibson Cheyne (1869–1931), was a poet and author of several works.
45. Sohrab, Letter to Harriet Magee, 31 Jan. 1913, pp. 5–7. For another account of the meeting of 'Abdu'l-Bahá with the Cheynes see Blomfield, *Chosen Highway*, p. 169.
46. John Estlin Carpenter was a scholar in biblical criticism and in comparative religion as well as a Unitarian minister.
47. 'Abdul Baha in Oxford', *Oxford Chronicle*, 3 Jan. 1913.
48. 'Aspects of Natural and Divine Philosophy', *Oxford Times*, 4 Jan. 1913, p. 4, col. 7.
49. 'Abdul Baha's Address', *Christian Commonwealth* (London), 22 Jan. 1913, pp. i–ii. According to the *Oxford Chronicle* the comments made by Carpenter were followed by applause from the public.
50. Sohrab, Letter to Harriet Magee, 18 Jan. 1913.
51. 'Abdul Baha's Address', *Christian Commonwealth* (London), 22 Jan. 1913, pp. i–ii.
52. 'The Union of Religions', *Christian Commonwealth* (London), 29 Jan. 1913, pp. 324–5.
53. 'Abdul Baha's Message to Bahais All Over the World', *Christian Commonwealth* (London), 1 Jan. 1913, p. 263, col. 1. This Tablet was later published in *Star of the West*, see 'Message to Bahais Throughout the World from Abdul-Baha', *Star of the West*, 21 Mar. 1913 (4:1), p. 3.
54. See Sohrab, Letter to Harriet Magee, 2 Jan. 1913, pp. 7–8.
55. 'Abdul Baha's Address to Cosmos Club', *International Psychic Gazette*, Mar. 1913 (8:1), p. 220. The editorial in the same issue stated: 'We print in this issue a report of His Excellency Abdul Baha's address to the London Cosmos Society, which will be appreciated by his many disciples. The Master delivered three wonderful addresses before the Alliance Spiritualiste, the Theosophical Society and the Esperanto Banquet in Paris, and these, through the courtesy of M. Ahmed Sohrab, his able interpreter, we hope to reproduce in early numbers of the *Gazette*. He claims that in these utterances will be found rich contributions to modern-world thought. M. Sohrab also promises us occasional articles on the progress of the Bahai religion and ideals throughout the world.' The text of the talk to the Alliance Spiritualiste is reproduced in chapter 35 below.
56. For details of this address see Sohrab, Letter to Harriet Magee, 12 Jan. 1913. For the text of the talk see 'Abdu'l-Bahá, *Paris Talks*, pp. 174–6.
57. 'Abdul Baha at Westminster Meeting', *Friend* (London), 24 Jan. 1913, p. 61.
58. 'Abdul Baha at Westminster Meeting', *Friend* (London), 31 Jan. 1913, p. 77.
59. ibid. p. 78.

60. *Friend* (London), 11 Apr. 1913, p. 238.
61. *Christian Commonwealth* (London), 15 Jan. 1913, p. 292, col. 3.
62. ibid. The address was briefly advertised as 'Abdul Baha and Dr Alexander Whyte', *Christian Commonwealth*, 8 Jan. 1913, p. 273, col. 4.
63. ibid.
64. Sohrab, Letter to Harriet Magee, 15 Jan. 1913.
65. 'Turks' Prisoner for 40 Years', *Daily Chronicle* (London), Western Edition, 17 Jan. 1913, p. 1.
66. 'Items of Local News', *Western Daily Press* (Bristol), 17 Jan. 1913, p. 5, col. 8.
67. 'Abdul Baha', *Clifton Chronicle and Directory* (Bristol), 22 Jan. 1913. An account of this talk together with its transcription appears in *Star of the West*, see Fraser, 'Abdul-Baha at Clifton, England', 21 Mar. 1913 (4:1), pp. 4–6. Fraser's version of the talk is almost identical to the text published in *The Clifton Chronicle* except for a closing paragraph that is not present in the latter.
68. 'Clifton Society Talk', *Clifton Society* (Bristol), 16 Jan. 1913, p. 8, col. 1.
69. *Western Daily Press* (Bristol), 20 Jan. 1913, p. 5, col. 8.
70. 'Clifton Society Talk', *Clifton Society* (Bristol), 23 Jan. 1913, p. 8, col. 3.
71. 'Local Happenings', *Clifton Free Press* (Bristol), 17 Jan. 1913, p. 3, col. 4; 'Notes and News', *Horfield and Bishopston Record*, p. 3, col. 3.
72. 'The Eleven Principles of Baha'o'llah', *Christian Commonwealth* (London), 29 Jan. 1913, p. 319, col. 3.
73. *Manchester Guardian*, 17 Jan. 1913, p. 16, col. 5.
74. 'Far and Near', *Daily Mail*, 17 Jan. 1913, p. 3, col. 7.
75. For more details about the visit of the Master to Woking see Sohrab, Letter to Harriet Magee, 17 Jan. 1913.
76. *Woking News and Mail*, 24 Jan. 1913, p. 6, col. 3; 'Novel Scenes at the Mosque', *Surrey Times and County Express* (Guildford), 24 Jan. 1913, p. 2, col. 7.
77. 'The True Basis of All Religions', *Surrey Herald and Middlesex News* (Chertsey), 24 Jan. 1913, p. 5, col. 1. The picture was taken by the *Asiatic Quarterly Review* and published with its permission.
78. 'Abdul Baha at the Mosque', *Woking Observer*, 22 Jan. 1913, p. 1, col. 3.
79. 'In an Oriental Mosque', *Christian Commonwealth*, 22 Jan. 1913, p. 2, col. 3.
80. ibid.
81. 'London Day by Day', *Daily Telegraph* (London), 18 Jan. 1913, p. 13, col. 4.
82. 'Correspondence, Notes and News', *Asiatic Quarterly Review* (Woking), Apr. 1913 (1:2).
83. *Badr* (Qadian, India), 20 Mar. 1913, pp. 9–11. Available from http://www.wokingmuslim.org/history/kh-mosque-second.htm. Last accessed 9 Mar. 2011.
84. 'Abdul Baha', *Daily Herald* (London), 18 Jan. 1913, p. 3, col. 4.
85. 'Abdul Baha's Visit to the Doré Gallery', *Quarterly Record of Higher Thought Work* (London), Feb. 1913, p. 2.
86. *Christian Commonwealth* (London), 22 Jan. 1913, p. 2, col. 3.
87. Sohrab, Letter to Harriet Magee, 9 Mar. 1913, p. 11.
88. 'On the Importance of Divine Civilization', *Asiatic Quarterly Review* (London), Apr. 1913 (1:2), pp. 225–36. The original Persian of the text up to the section 'On Material and Spiritual Education' can also be found in 'Abdu'l-Bahá, *Majmu'ih-i-Khatábát-i-Hadrat-i-'Abdu'l-Bahá*, vol. 3, pp. 30–2.

89. W. F. Rean, 'A Great Persian', *Daily Herald* (London), 21 Jan. 1913, p. 6, col. 3.
90. *Christian Commonwealth*, 15 Jan. 1913.
91. 'Abdul Baha's Movements', *Christian Commonwealth*, 22 Jan. 1913, p. 310, col. 1.
92. 'Current Comments', *Near East* (London), 24 Jan. 1913, p. 332, col. 3.
93. 'De Londres a Paris', *Gil Blas* (Paris), 24 Jan. 1913, p. 4, col. 1.
94. 'Abdul Baha to his friends', *Christian Commonwealth* (London), 23 Apr. 1913, p. 531, col. 2.
95. For the Ethical Movement in Britain see MacKillop, *British Ethical Societies*.
96. 'Arrangements for Lectures, &c.', *Friend* (London), 1 Dec. 1911, p. 790.
97. R. Dimsdale Stocker, 'Abdul Baha: An Impression', *Ethical World* (London), 15 Oct. 1911, pp. 148–9.
98. Stocker, *Time Spirit*, pp. 65–7.

27 Edinburgh

1. Sohrab, Letter to Harriet Magee, 10 Jan. 1913.
2. ibid. 13 Jan. 1913.
3. *Christian Commonwealth* (London), 1 Jan. 1913, p. 254, col. 3.
4. 'Abdul Baha and Dr Alexander Whyte', *Christian Commonwealth* on 8 Jan. 1913, p. 273, col. 4.
5. 'A New Religious Movement', *Evening Dispatch* (Edinburgh), 3 Jan. 1913, p. 4. The *Evening Dispatch* (Edinburgh) was a Unionist daily newspaper established in 1886 by the proprietors of *The Scotsman*.
6. 'Abdul Baha in Edinburgh', *Evening News* (Edinburgh), 3 Jan. 1913, p. 4, col. 4. The picture that accompanied the article was a portrait taken at Lafayette studios. The *Evening News* was an independent newspaper established in 1873. It merged with the *Dispatch* in 1963.
7. 'Abdul Baha to Visit Edinburgh', *Glasgow Herald*, 3 Jan. 1913, p. 8, col. 5. The *Herald* was an independent newspaper established in 1783. Its editor in 1913 was Frederick Harcourt Kitchin (1867–1932).
8. 'Abdul Baha to visit Edinburgh', *Evening Telegraph* (Dundee), 3 Jan. 1913, p. 4, col. 3.
9. 'A New World Teacher', *Evening Dispatch* (Edinburgh), 7 Jan. 1913.
10. 'Abdul Baha', *Evening Dispatch* (Edinburgh), 8 Jan. 1913.
11. See for instance 'International Amity', *Scotsman* (Edinburgh), 4 Jan. 1913, p. 1; 'Abdul Baha', 7 Jan. 1913, p. 1; 'Outlook Tower', 8 Jan. 1913, p. 1.
12. 'Abdul Baha in Edinburgh', *Scotsman* (Edinburgh), 9 Jan. 1913, p. 11. A short note was also published on page 6 of the same issue: 'Abdul Baha, the Persian Reformer, expounded the principles of the new International religion of Baha Ullah, of which he is now the chief exponent, to a well-attended meeting in the Rainy Hall, Edinburgh.' This news was repeated in *The Continent* (Chicago), 20 Feb. 1913, p. 245.
13. 'Abdul Baha in Edinburgh', *Glasgow Herald*, 9 Jan. 1913, p. 8, col. 3.
14. 'Universal Brotherhood of Man', *Dundee Courier* (Angus), 9 Jan. 1913, p. 5, col. p. 3.
15. *Evening News* (Edinburgh), 9 Jan. 1912, p. 4, col. 2.
16. See 'Notes After a Visit to Sir Abdul-Baha (Abbas Effendi)', *Star of the West*, 13 July 1921 (12:7), pp. 136–7.

17. See *Star of the West*, 21 Mar. 1921 (12:1), p. 25.
18. The interview was probably given on 7 January since on that day Ahmad mentions in his diary that a 'newspaper man interviewed our Beloved on some points of the Cause'.
19. In his varied career as a journalist Ion Smeaton Munro had been correspondent and art critic for the *Glasgow Herald* and correspondent in Italy for the *Morning Post*. He was appointed editor of the *Scots Pictorial* in 1911 and was author of two works about Italian history and politics.
20. *Scots Pictorial* (Glasgow), 18 Jan. 1913, p. 335. The lines summarizing the history of the Bahá'í Faith have been omitted.
21. 'A New World Teacher', *Weekly Scotsman* (Edinburgh), 11 Jan. 1913, p. 6, col. 6.
22. 'From Scotland', *Christian World* (London), 9 Jan. 1913, p. 13, col. 3.
23. 'Abdul Baha and Personal Immortality', *Christian Commonwealth* (London), 15 Jan. 1913, p. 291, col. 4. This article was the basis of at least two articles about the meeting which appeared in New Zealand, see 'Sunday Circle', *Otago Daily Times*, 1 Mar. 1913, p. 7; 'Religious World', *Auckland Star*, 29 Mar. 1913, p. 14.
24. 'Abdul Baha in Edinburgh', ibid. p. 296, col. 1.
25. 'Abdul Baha's Visit to Edinburgh', ibid. col. 2.
26. 'Bahai Leader', *Daily Herald* (London), 16 Jan. 1913, p. 6, col. 3.
27. *British Weekly* (London), 16 Jan. 1913, p. 485, col. 5.
28. *Manitoba Free Press* (Winnipeg), 10 Feb. 1913, p. 2, col. 3, n. t.
29. 'The Advance', *Herald of Gospel Liberty* (Dayton, OH), 16 Oct. 1913, p. 1078.
30. *Continent* (Chicago), 30 Feb. 1913, p. 245.
31. See *Maḥmúd's Diary*, 387.
32. *Star of the West*, 13 July 1912, p. 5.
33. 'Wealth', *North American Review* (Boston), June 1889 (148:391), pp. 653–65.
34. The original of this letter is held in the archives of the Carnegie Mellon University. The English translation was prepared by Sohrab and indicates that the letter and the translation were composed in Edinburgh. The address in the translation, however, is 97 Cadogan Gardens. Thus the letter was written in Edinburgh but sent with its translation from London.
35. See Sohrab, Letter to Harriet Magee, 10 Jan. 1913.
36. *New York Times*, 9 Feb. 1913, p. 12c. For a better translation of the letter to Carnegie see *Selections from the Writings of 'Abdu'l-Bahá*, no. 79.
37. 'Abdul Baha', *Dallas Morning News*, 18 Feb. 1913.
38. 'Bahaism in Edinburgh', *Christian Commonwealth* (London), 23 Apr. 1913, p. 531, col. 2. For the program see also 'Outlook Tower Edinburgh', *Scotsman* (Edinburgh), 26 Apr. 1913, p. 1, col.1.
39. 'Woman and the Universal Note', *Christian Commonwealth* (London), 30 Apr. 1913, p. 545, col. 1. See also an account in 'Outlook Tower Lectures'. *Scotsman* (Edinburgh), 28 Apr. 1913, p. 6, col. 5.
40. 'The Bahai Movement and Peace', *Christian Commonwealth* (London), 7 May 1913, p. 429, col. 4. For another account see also 'The Bahai Movement', *Scotsman* (Edinburgh), 29 Apr. 1913, p. 6.
41. ibid.
42. 'Queen Victoria's Message to Abdul Baha', *Christian Commonwealth* (London),

14 May 1913, p. 578, col. 2. For another account see also 'The Bahai Movement in Edinburgh', *Scotsman* (Edinburgh), 30 Apr. 1913, p. 8, col. 5.
43. 'The Bahai Movement in Edinburgh', *Scotsman* (Edinburgh), 1 May 1913, p. 6, col. 5.
44. 'Bahai Meetings', *Theosophy in Scotland* (Edinburgh), June 1913, p. 25.
45. 'The Most Great Peace', *Christian Commonwealth* (London), 28 May 1913, p. 370, col. 1; 'The Most Great Peace', 4 June 1913, p. 625, col. 2; 'Bahai Teachings in Practice', 18 June 1913, p. 654, col. 3; 'Self-Culture in Bahaism', 16 July 1913, p. 723, col. 4. The article on 18 June included the following note: 'Meetings for the reading and study of the Bahai teaching are held at 3.30 every Sunday at 'Woodburn', 54, Canaan Lane, Morningside, Edinburgh. Any information will be gladly supplied by Miss J. M. Anderson, 29, Marchmont Road, Edinburgh.'

28 Second and Third Visits to Paris

1. 'De Londres à Paris', Smartset, *Gil Blas* (Paris), 24 Jan. 1913, p. 4, col. 1. See chapter 26 above for portions of this article.
2. 'Persian Mystic in Paris', *New York Herald* (Paris), 10 Feb. 1913, p. 4, col. 5. I thank Jan Jasion for kindly sharing this reference with me.
3. Alice R. Beede, 'Glimpse of Abdul-Baha in Paris', *Star of the West*, 27 Feb. 1912 (2:18), pp. 6–7, 12.
4. 'Abdul Baha in Paris', *Christian Commonwealth* (London), 12 Feb. 1913, pp. 355–6. Some passages of the article are identical to the account published by Alice Beede one year earlier; see previous note.
5. 'Abdul Baha in Paris', *Eenheid*, 22 Feb. 1913. I am grateful to Jan Jasion for kindly sharing with me this and other articles that appeared in *Eenheid*.
6. Albert Louis Caillet was a civil engineer by profession with interests in esotericism and occultism. He was author of several works, among them the three-volume *Manuel Bibliographique des sciences Psychiques et Occultes* (1912). He was editor of *Bulletin mensuel*.
7. From 1914 the Société Unitive was part of the International New Thought Alliance.
8. Ustad Inayat Khan was born into a family of musicians in Barida, India, and soon acquired fame as a prodigy of classical Indian music. However, his interest in mysticism and spirituality led him to become a Sufi teacher, an occupation by which he is better known. He traveled extensively, performing and lecturing on Sufism. In 1914 he founded the Sufi Order of the West, which exists today as the Inayati Order.
9. See Sohrab, Letter to Harriet Magee, 6 Feb. 1913, p. 16.
10. See *Complete Works of Pir-o-Murshid Inayat Khan, Journal and Anecdotes*. Available online at http://wahiduddin.net/mv2/bio/Journal_1.htm (last accessed 18 Aug. 2015). In his memoirs Inayat Khan also mentions that he met Lady Blomfield in Geneva in 1920.
11. 'Bahaism', *Bulletin mensuel de la Société Unitive* (Paris), Feb. 1913, pp. 58–61 (translated by Elham Simmons).
12. ibid. p. 34.
13. ibid. p. 53. See chapter 33.

14. *International Psychic Gazette* (London), Sept. 1913, p. 39. This article was later reproduced in Fraser's *Abdul Baha on Divine Philosophy* (1918), pp. 75–6.
15. See Sohrab, Letter to Harriet Magee, 29 May 1913, pp. 3–5.
16. Henri Monnier was consecrated as a pastor in 1895 and was the pastor of the Church of l'Etoile from 1897 until 1932. He combined this task with the directorship of the Theological Seminary where he also taught classes. In 1932 he was appointed dean of the Faculty of Theology. He had also been vice president of the French Protestant Federation.
17. For notes of the meeting see 'Abdul-Baha Answers Many Questions Asked by Theologians of Paris', *Star of the West*, 28 Apr. 1913 (4:3), pp. 51–5. This was reprinted in Fraser's *Abdul Baha on Divine Philosophy* (1918). See also 'Abdu'l-Bahá, *Majmu'ih-i-Khatábát-i-Hadrat-i-'Abdu'l-Bahá*, vol. 3, pp. 61–7. For a revised translation of the Persian notes of the meeting see Seena Fazel (ed.), "Abdu'l-Bahá on Christ and Christianity: An interview with Pasteur Monnier on the relationship between the Bahá'í Faith and Christianity, Paris' in *Bahá'í Studies Review*, vol. 3.1 (1993).
18. 'Abdul Baha and a Universal Religion', *Christian Commonwealth* (London), 5 Mar. 1913, p. 414, col. 2.
19. 'Abdul Baha en een Universeele Codsdienst', *Eenheid*, 29 Mar. 1913.
20. 'Un Prophéte', *Evangile et Liberté* (Paris), 1 Mar. 1913. I thank Jan Jasion for kindly sharing this document with me.
21. 'Abdul Baha Going to Germany', *Christian Commonwealth* (London), 12 Mar. 1913, p. 429, col. 4.
22. Data for November 1912. In 1909 the journal claimed in its advertisements a circulation of its supplement of 1,900,000 copies.
23. 'Le Noveau Prophète de l'Islam', *Le Petit Journal* (Paris), 4 May 1913, p. 138, col. 1. A few weeks after the publication of this article, the journal *Le Radical* (Paris), published a short text with general information about 'Abdu'l-Bahá based on an article published in *La Vie*. See 'Un Nouveau Prophete: Abdul-Baha', *Le Radical* (Paris), 10 June 1913, p. 4, col. 3.
24. See Sohrab, Letter to Harriet Magee, 23 Mar. 1913, p. 10.
25. Beatrice Irwin, 'The Bahai Movement', *Occult Review* (London), Nov. 1913, pp. 280–6.
26. 'Abdul Baha in Paris', *Christian Commonwealth* (London), 27 Mar. 1913.
27. 'Abdul Baha in Parijs', *Eenheid*, 15 Mar. 1913.
28. 'Bahaism Seizes Paris', *Chicago Sunday Tribune*, 2 Mar. 1913, p. 11h, col. 5.
29. 'Parisinian notes', *Christian Commonwealth* (London), 11 June 1913, p. 634, col. 4. Sohrab mentions that on 23 May the Master received a correspondent of *The Christian Commonwealth*. See Sohrab, Letter to Harriet Magee, 23 May 1913, p. 6.
30. Charles William Wendte (1844–1931) was a Unitarian minister who from 1900 to 1920 was the general secretary of the International Council of Liberal Religious Thinkers and Workers and was also the president of the Free Religious Association (1910–14).
31. For the Persian text of this message see *Star of the West* (4:16), 31 Dec. 1913, pp. 1–2 (Persian section) and *Makátíb-i-'Abdu'l-Bahá*, vol. 1, pp. 224–5. For an English translation see *Abdul Baha on Divine Philosophy*, pp. 159–64 and

Sohrab's *Abdul Baha in Egypt*, pp. 19–23.
32. His presentation was on Friday, 18 July 1913, at a session starting at 4 p.m. The text of his paper is available as an appendix in *Travaux du 6e Congrès International Du Progrès Religieux*, Paris, 1913.
33. 'M. Boutroux l'Illustre Philosophe va présider un congrès religieux', *Le Matin* (Paris), 30 June 1913, p. 1, col. 4. The circulation data provided is for November 1912.
34. 'Le Congrès du Progrès Religieux', *Le Temps* (Paris), 1 July 1913, p. 3, col. 5.
35. *Revue Chrétienne* (Paris), July 1913, pp. 812 and 904c (photograph).
36. 'M. Boutroux', *Le Théosophe* (Paris), 1 July 1913, p. 46.
37. 'Congress of Religious Liberals Meets in Paris Next Month', *Washington Post*, 22 June 1913, p. 10, col. 1; 'International Congress of Religious Liberals', *Unitarian Advance* (New York), July 1913, p. 352; 'Science-Religion Debate', *New York Times*, 6 July 1913; 'Science-Religion Congress', *Sun* (Baltimore), 6 July 1913, p. 8, col. 2; 'Science-Religion Debate', *American Israelite* (Cincinnati), 7 July 1913, p. 7, col. 3; 'Congress of Creeds in Line with Science', *Toronto World*, 10 July 1913; 'Calls Congress of All Creeds', *Los Angeles Times*, 13 July 1913, p. 1, col. 7; 'Philosophers to Hold an Important Session', *San Francisco Chronicle*, 24 Aug. 1913.
38. 'Science–Religion Debate', *Daily News* (Perth), 6 Oct. 1913, p. 4, col. 6.
39. 'Religion in Paris', *Dundee Courier*, 23 July 1913, p. 4, col. 4.
40. *Christian Commonwealth* (London), 16 July 1913, cover. Caption on p. 710.
41. 'Abdul Baha's movements', *Christian Commonwealth* (London), 23 July 1913, p. 738, col. 2.
42. 'The Foundation of Spiritual Unity', *Christian Commonwealth* (London), 30 July 1913, p. 748, col. 4.

29 Central Europe

1. 'The Bahai Movement and Peace', *Christian Commonwealth* (London), 7 May 1913, p. 562, col. 2.
2. See Sohrab, Letter to Harriet Magee, 12 Feb. 1913, pp. 5–6.
3. ibid. 5 Apr. 1913, p. 2.
4. ibid. p. 10.
5. ibid. 15 Apr. 1913, pp. 5–7.
6. A report of this lecture was published as 'Hirek', in *Teozófia* (Budapest), Mar. 1912 (1:3), p. 71.
7. 'A Behái Mozgalomról', *Teozófia* (Budapest), Apr. 1912 (1:4), pp. 76–83.
8. These invitations were received in Paris on 10 Feb. 1913. See Sohrab, Letter to Harriet Magee, p. 18 for that date.
9. Previously E. C. Moore, cousin of the American Bahá'í Dr Susan Moody and a businessman in Budapest, had visited the Master in Paris on 29 March and asked Him whether He would visit Budapest. 'Abdu'l-Bahá 'did not give a definitive answer'. See Sohrab, Letter to Harriet Magee 29 Mar. 1913, pp. 7, 9–10.
10. His successor as president of the Theosophical Society was Robert Nadler, 1858–1938, a prominent Hungarian artist who during the visit of the Master to Budapest painted a portrait Him.

11. In Stuttgart 'Abdu'l-Bahá received a telegram from Stark stating that the local press was already publishing several articles announcing His arrival in the city. See Sohrab, Letter to Harriet Magee, 8 Apr. 1913, p. 7.
12. For published works in English about the sojourn of 'Abdu'l-Bahá in Budapest see the German Bahá'í bulletin *Sonne der Warheirt Organ des Deustschen Bahá'í-Bundes* in which various issues published in 1924 carried a bilingual account made from notes by Herringel and from the diaries of Maḥmúd. See also Martha Root's, 'Abdu'l-Baha's Visit to Budapest' in the *Bahá'í Magazine* (24:3), June 1933, pp. 84–9 and György Lederer's "Abdu'l-Bahá in Budapest' in *Bahá'ís in the West* (2004), pp. 109–26.
13. When Ahmad Sohrab telegramed from Stuttgart giving the details of the arrival of the Master in Budapest he did not give the correct details about the train He was to take. The welcoming committee in Budapest went to the wrong station to greet the Master and, unable to find Him there, went straight to Hotel Ritz.
14. Sándor Gieswein was the papal prelate from 1909 and was later a member of the Hungarian parliament. He was a very progressive intellectual who joined the Hungarian Peace Society, over which he presided, and the feminist movement. From 1911 he was the president of the Hungarian Esperanto Society and also a board member of the International Catholic Society. He was the author of several books and articles on theology and politics.
15. Dr Gyula Germanus, a scholar of Jewish background, was professor of Arabic and Islamic Studies. At the time of the visit of 'Abdu'l-Bahá he was a pupil of Arminus Vámbéry and had just returned from a three year assignment at the Oriental Department of the British Museum. Eventually he became a member of the Hungarian parliament, a member of the Hungarian Academy of Sciences and a scholar of world renown.
16. Ignác Kúnos was a famous Hungarian scholar of Jewish origin who specialized in Turkish studies and philology.
17. Károly Zipernowsky was an eminent Hungarian electrical engineer of Jewish origin who together with two other collaborators was the inventor of the alternating current transformer.
18. 'A próféta', *Pesti Tükor* (Budapest), 11 Apr. 1913, p. 6, col. 2.
19. 'A Szeretet Prófétája', *Budapest*, 12 Apr. 1913, pp. 7–8.
20. *Tolnai Világlapja* (Budapest), 20 Apr. 1913, p. 8 (n.t.).
21. *Uj Idök* (Budapest), 20 Apr. 1913, p. 438 (n.t.).
22. *Az Érdekes Újság* (Budapest), 27 Apr. 1913, p. 3.
23. Vilma Balogh, 'Egy érdekes próféta', *Világ* (Budapest), 10 Apr. 1913, pp. 7–8.
24. Circulation data for this and other journals is for 1910. Information extracted from Buzinkay Géza, *Kis magyar sajtótörténet* (1993).
25. 'A Bábí Próféta', *Pesti Napló* (Budapest), 10 Apr. 1913, p. 10.
26. Alexander (Sándor) Braun was a journalist of Jewish origin. He started his career in the *Pesti Napló*, becoming its editor in 1894. Later he also edited the *Budapesti Naplót* until he founded *A Nap* in 1905. His modern methods in journalism and his political activism made him a popular figure.
27. 'Effendi', *A Nap* (Budapest), 10 Apr. 1913, p. 1, col. 1.
28. 'Megjött a Keleti Bölcs', ibid. p. 5.
29. 'Perzsa apostol Budapesten', *Budapesti Napló*, 10 Apr. 1913, p. 5.

30. 'A Bahai Apostolnál', *Pesti Hírlap* (Budapest), 10 Apr. 1913, pp. 7–8.
31. 'Pestieknek Beszel a Próféta', *A Nap* (Budapest), 11 Apr. 1913, p. 5, col. 1.
32. 'Ein Persischer Celehter in Budapest', *Neues Pester Journal* (Budapest), 10 Apr. 1913.
33. 'Der Bahaismus', *Pester Lloyd* (Budapest), 10 Apr. 1913, p. 7, col. 1. This was the basis of another article about 'Abdu'l-Bahá and the Bahá'í Faith which appeared in Bohemia; see 'Der Bahaismus', *Prager Tagblatt* (Prague), 13 Apr. 1913, p. 4, col. 3.
34. Sohrab, Letter to Harriet Magee, 11 Apr. 1913, p. 2.
35. 'A Próféta Igéri', *Kurir* (Budapest), 12 Apr. 1913, p. 3. This article was published the day after the events it reported.
36. 'Abdul Abbas, Clőadása', *Világ* (Budapest), 12 Apr. 1913, p. 15.
37. 'Perzsa tudós Budpesten' ('Persian Scholar in Budapest'), *Egyetértés* (Budapest), 10 Apr. 1913, p. 12. This journal had a circulation in 1910 of 38,000 copies.
38. 'A Bábí Próféta', *Pesti Napló* (Budapest) 10 Apr. 1913, p. 10.
39. *Pesti Tükor* (Budapest), 11 Apr. 1913, p. 6, n.t. Included a picture of the Master.
40. 'Abdul Bahá, a próféta', *Az Ujság* (Budapest), 12 Apr. 1913, p. 7, col. 2.
41. 'A Szeretet prófétája', *Budapest*, 12 Apr. 1913, pp. 7–8.
42. 'Abdul Abbas, Clőadása', *Világ* (Budapest), 12 Apr. 1913, p. 15.
43. *Budapesti Hírlap*, 12 Apr. 1913, p. 9, col. 1 (n.t.).
44. 'Abdul Baha Abbas über den Bahasmus', *Neues Pester Journal* (Budapest), 12 Apr. 1913, p. 6.
45. 'Abbas Efendi in Budapest', *Pester Lloyd* (Budapest), 12 Apr. 1913, p. 6, col. 1.
46. *Erdekes Ujság* (Budapest), 27 Apr. 1913, p. 3, n. t.
47. 'Hungarlanda Kroniko', *La Verda Standardo* (Budapest), May 1913 (8:5), p. 79. Translated from Esperanto by Heather Eason.
48. 'A Bahai Feast', *Christian Commonwealth*, 30 Apr. 1913, p. 543, col. 2.
49. 'Turáni Társaság', *Budapesti Hírlap*, 13 Apr. 1913, p. 17.
50. 'Tudomány és Irodalum', *Egyetértés* (Budapest), 13 Apr. 1913, p. 16.
51. Pairet Alajos was an agronomist who held various positions in the public service, including Chargé d'Affaires in Washington. In 1908 he was appointed Secretary-General of the Hungarian Society of Economics. He was also appointed director of Hungary's National Museum of Agriculture. Alajos met 'Abdu'l-Bahá again during a visit on 16 April and expressed his desire to promote the Bahá'í teachings in Hungary.
52. For notes of this talk see 'Abdu'l-Bahá, *Majmu'ih-i-Khatábát-i-Hadrat-i-'Abdu'l-Bahá*, vol. 3, pp. 95–100.
53. Sohrab, Letter to Harriet Magee, 14 Apr. 1913, p. 11. Some sections of the magazine were trilingual. The present author has consulted different volumes of this periodical and has been unable to find the text of the address.
54. Ignácz Goldzieher was a figure of world renown in the field of Islamic Studies. He was the author of several works and mentioned the Bahá'í Faith in *Vorlesungen über den Islam* (1910) and in various articles.
55. Gyula Pekár was a journalist, lawyer and politician. He was a member of the Hungarian Academy of Sciences and was officer of various cultural and literary societies including the Turanian Society. In 1919 he was appointed Secretary of State for Public Education and was eventually appointed minister without portfolio. He was also the author of several books.

56. Vikár Béla was also a member of the Academy of Sciences and of the Hungarian Esperanto Society. As an ethnographer he specialized in Finland and was the translator of several Finnish works into various European languages.
57. Gyula Mészáros was a turcologist.
58. 'A Nemzetek és a vallások közti béke', *Magyar Nemzet* (Budapest), 16 Apr. 1913, p. 7.
59. 'A Nemzetek és a vallások közti béke', *Az Ujság* (Budapest), 16 Apr. 1913, p. 14.
60. 'A Nemzetek és a vallások közti béke', *Budapest*, 16 Apr. 1913, p. 9.
61. 'A Nemzetek és a vallások közti béke', *Független Magyarország* (Budapest), 16 Apr. 1913, p. 7.
62. 'A Nemzetek és a vallások közti béke', *Pesti Hírlap* (Budapest), 16 Apr. 1913, p. 8.
63. 'Der Persische Prophet Abdul Baha', *Pester Lloyd* (Budapest), 16 Apr. 1913, p. 7, col. 2.
64. 'Perzsa tudós a nemzetek és vallások békéjéről', *A Polgár* (Budapest), 16 Apr. 1913, p. 5.
65. *Ország-Világ* (Budapest), 20 Apr. 1913, p. 417, n.t.
66. 'Turáni előadások', *Turán* (Budapest) 1913, no. 2, p. 111.
67. 'Perský Prorok Abdul Baha', *Národní Listy* (Prague), 17 Apr. 1913, p. 1, col. 2.
68. 'A baháizmus missziója', *Protestáns* (Budapest), 20 Apr. 1913, pp. 244–5.
69. 'Mit tud Rólunk egy Keleti Bölcs', *Pesti Tükör* (Budapest), 14 Apr. 1913, pp. 5–6. Hungary became independent from Austria five years after this interview.
70. Sohrab, Letter to Harriet Magee, 15 Apr. 1913, p. 16. The present author has consulted different issues of this periodical and has been unable to find this interview.
71. 'Der Prophet des Babismus', *Neues Wiener Journal*, 3 May 1913, p. 7, col. 1.
72. Sohrab, Letter to Harriet Magee, 22 Apr. 1913, p. 2. The present author has consulted different issues of this periodical and has been unable to find this interview.
73. Sohrab, Letter to Harriet Magee, 20 Apr. 1913, p. 25.
74. 'Die Neue Religion', *Evangelisches Gemeineblatt für Stuttgart*, 20 Apr. 1913. Translation by Rhoda Lane.
75. One of these announcements was published in *Stuttgarter Neues Tagblatt*, 24 Apr. 1913.
76. Sohrab, Letter to Harriet Magee, 25 Apr. 1913, pp. 14–15.
77. 'Abdul Baha', *Stuttgarter Neues Tagblatt*, 26 Apr. 1913. Translation by Rhoda Lane.
78. *Staatsanzeiger für Württemberg* (Stuttgart), 30 Apr. 1913, n. t. Translation by Rhoda Lane.
79. 'Abdul Baha in Germany', *Christian Commonwealth* (London), 21 May 1913, p. 593, col. 3.
80. 'Forty Years a Prisoner', *Christian Commonwealth* (London), 25 June 1913, p. 663, col. 2. Previously published as 'Abdul-Baha at Stuttgart', in *Star in the West*, 17 May 1913 (4:4), p. 68. Notes by Margarethe Doering translated by Charles Ioas.

30 Third Visit to Egypt

1. 'Personal and Social', *Egyptian Gazette* (Alexandria), 18 June 1913, p. 3, col. 1. The same information was published in 'Personalia', *African World* (London), 28 June 1913, p. 437, col. 3.
2. 'Abdul Baha in Egypt', *Egyptian Gazette* (Alexandria), 27 June 1913, p. 3, col. 4.
3. 'Abdul Baha Abbas in Egypt', *Christian Commonwealth* (London), 6 Aug. 1913, p. 767, col. 4.
4. 'Abdul Baha Abbas: Return to Ramleh of Persian Reformer', *Egyptian Gazette* (Alexandria), 19 Aug. 1913, p. 5, col. 6.
5. 'Universal Peace', *Christian Commonwealth* (London), 3 Sept. 1913, p. 838.
6. See Sohrab, Letter to Harriet Magee, 11 Apr. 1913, p. 21.
7. See ibid. 14 Apr. 1913, p. 8.
8. 'Professor Vambery and the Bahai Religion', *Egyptian Gazette* (Alexandria), 24 Sept. 1913, p. 4, col. 4; also in *International Psychic Gazette* (London), Oct. 1913, p. 81. Reprinted in *Star of the West*, 19 Jan. 1913 (4:17), p. 284. See also Ahmad Sohrab, *Abdul Baha in Egypt* (1929), pp. 284–6.
9. 'The Lofty Summit of Unchanging Purpose', *Star of the West*, 16 Oct. 1913 (4:12), pp. 208, 210.
10. 'The Lofty Summit of Unchanging Purpose', *International Psychic Gazette* (London), Jan. 1914, p. 169.
11. See for instance Arthur Pillsbury Dodge, 'The Bahá'í Revelation', in *Mind* (New York), Feb. 1905, pp. 126–44.
12. 'Egypt', *Master Mind* (Los Angeles), Dec. 1913, p. 116.
13. See, for instance, the volume for 1915, pp. 74, 133 and 142.

31 Gender Equality and the Suffrage Movement

1. 'Abdul Baha, Head of New Religion, Coming Here', *New York Sun*, 17 Mar. 1912, p. 2, part 4. The article was also published as 'A Gentle Oriental Here', in the *Kansas City Star*, 27 Mar. 1912, p. 8b, col. 1. The article included a portrait taken in Paris. Mary Hanford Ford included the same information in an article published years later as 'The Economic Teaching of Abdul Baha', in *Star of the West*, see issue of 21 Mar. 1917 (8:1), pp. 1–7 and 11–16.
2. 'Bahaism and the Woman Movement', *Common Cause* (London), 21 Sept. 1911 (3:128), pp. 410–11.
3. Helena Swanwick was editor of the journal from the founding of the magazine. She was also an ardent pacifist to the point of resigning as editor of *The Common Cause* when the NUWSS refused to condemn the participation of the United Kingdom in World War I. Later she became a member of the pacifist organization Union of Democratic Control.
4. 'Bahaism and the Women's Movement', *Common Cause* (London), 21 Sept. 1911 (3:128), p. 406.
5. Nina Boyle established the first women's voluntary police force in 1914. At the time of writing this letter she was also the president of the Johannesburg Women's Enfranchisement League.
6. 'Bahaism', *Common Cause* (London), 28 Sept. 1911 (3:129), p. 432.
7. 'Abdul Baha Abbas in London', *Common Cause* (London), 5 Oct. 1911 (3:130), p. 442.

8. 'Letters to the Editor', *Common Cause* (London), 12 Oct. 1911 (3:131), p. 466.
9. 'A Woman Apostle in Persia', *Vote* (London), 20 Sept. 1911, pp. 280–1; 7 Oct 1911, p. 291, 14 Oct. 1911, pp. 304–5.
10. 'From the Turret', *Christian Commonwealth* (London), 13 Sept. 1911, p. 860.
11. See note 3 above and Emily M. Leaf, 'Press Department', *Common Cause* (London), 21 Sept. 1911, p. 412.
12. *Record-Herald* (Chicago), 28 Apr. 1912, n.t. See also *Record-Herald* (Chicago), 2 May 1912, n.t.
13. 'Baha Will Talk on Suffrage', *Chicago Tribune*, 2 May 1912.
14. *Chicago Examiner* (Chicago), 28 Apr. 1912, p. 23, col. 1, n.t.
15. See 'Abdu'l-Bahá, *Promulgation*, pp. 74–7.
16. 'Abdul Baha Talks to Club Women on Vote', *Chicago Examiner*, 3 May 1912, p. 2, col. 4.
17. 'Sun Aid to Suffrage', *Record-Herald* (Chicago), 3 May 1912.
18. 'Persian Purist Urges Ballot for Women', *Inter-Ocean* (Chicago), 5 May 1912.
19. *Chicago Journal*, 5 May 1912.
20. *Chicago Examiner*, 5 May 1912, p. 3, col. 2.
21. 'Abdul Baha and Woman's Suffrage', *Woman Voter* (New York), June 1912 (3:5).
22. 'Peddle Tea for Suffrage', *New York Times*, 12 May 1912, p. 10, col. 2.
23. 'In the Women's Clubs', *Brooklyn Daily Eagle* (New York), 18 May 1912, p. 4, col. 2.
24. 'With Suffrage Workers', *Evening Post* (New York), 17 May 1912, p. 4, col. 4.
25. For the text of the talk see 'Abdu'l-Bahá, *Promulgation*, pp. 133–7, and *Star of the West*, 1 Aug. 1912 (3:8), pp. 15, 18–20.
26. 'Suffrage to End War', *New-York Tribune*, 21 May 1912, p. 9, col. 3.
27. 'Abdul Baha to Suffragists', *New York Times*, 21 May 1912, p. 14, col. 3.
28. Maḥmúd refers to the club as the 'Women's Club of New York', see *Maḥmúd's Diary*, p. 409.
29. See *Club Women* (New York), 1907.
30. 'Club Honors its President', *New York Press*, 5 May 1905, p. 7, col. 4.
31. *New York Times*, 24 Nov. 1912, p. 3c, col. 4, n.t.
32. 'Minervas Hear A. Baha', *New-York Tribune*, 26 Nov. 1912, p. 11, col. 3. The same article was reproduced as 'Minervas Hear One Abdul Baha', in the *Syracuse Herald* (Syracuse, NY), 29 Nov. 1912, p. 7, col. 6.
33. 'Women's Press Club Holds Installation of Officers', *New York Press*, 1 Dec. 1912, p. 2, col. 6.
34. 'For the Socialist Woman', *Daily People* (New York), 15 Apr. 1912, p. 3, col. 6.
35. 'Occupation not Occultation', *Philadelphia Telegraph*, 22 Apr. 1912.
36. 'The Bahais and Women', *Brooklyn Daily Eagle*, 12 May 1912, p. 9b, col. 4.
37. 'Personal and Impersonal', *Brooklyn Daily Eagle*, 15 July 1912, p. 6, col. 4.
38. *Denver Post*, 3 Aug. 1912, n. t.
39. *Boston Herald*, 25 Aug. 1912, n. t.
40. 'From East and West', *Standard* (London), 18 Oct. 1912, p. 11, col. 4.
41. Sohrab, Letter to Harriet Magee, 2 Jan. 1913, p. 11.
42. See for instance, 'Women's Freedom League', *Standard* (London), 30 Dec. 1912, p. 12, col. 1; 'Women's Freedom League', *Standard* (London), 31 Dec. 1912, p. 12, col. 1; 'Women's Freedom League', *Standard* (London), 1 Jan. 1913, p. 12,

col. 1; 'Women's Freedom League', *Standard* (London), 2 Jan. 1913, p. 3, col. 1, and 'To-day', col. 3.; 'Women's Freedom League', *Christian Commonwealth* (London), 1 Jan. 1913, p. 252, col. 3; 'Women's Freedom League', *Daily Herald* (London), 2 Jan. 1913, p. 2, col. 3.

43. 'The Equality of Woman', *Vote* (London), 3 Jan. 1913 (7:167), p. 168. Another announcement was published in the section 'Headquarters notes', p. 159 and read: 'Meeting at Essex Hall: Come yourself and bring as many friends as possible to hear Abdul Baha speak on "The Equality of Women", Thursday evening, Jan. 2, 8 p.m.' See also in the same issue, 'Forthcoming events: W.F.L.', p. 170, p. 1.
44. 'Towards Unity', *Vote* (London), 10 Jan. 1913 (7:168), p. 180.
45. ibid. p. 182.
46. ibid. p. 181.
47. 'The Equality of Women', *Suffragette* (London), 10 Jan. 1913 (1:13), p. 185. The text does not include the opening remarks of 'Abdu'l-Bahá nor the closing prayers. There are minor differences in the texts published in *The Suffragette* and *The Vote* but the substance of the talk is the same. See Sohrab, Letter to Harriet Magee, 19 Jan. 1913.
48. Sohrab, Letter to Harriet Magee, 12 Jan. 1913, pp. 3–4.
49. 'A Girdle Round about the Earth', *Votes for Women* (London), 3 Jan. 1913 (6:252), p. 222. Paradoxically the same issue contained an advertisement for the previous day's event. See 'Classified Advertisements', p. 212, col. 1.
50. 'The Maimed Wing', *Daily Herald* (London), 3 Jan. 1913, p. 5, col. 2.
51. 'Women's Progress in Persia', *Standard* (London), 4 Jan. 1913, p. 13, col. 5.
52. 'The Bahai Movement', *Manchester Guardian*, 3 Jan. 1913, p. 14, col. 6.
53. 'The Equality of Man and Woman', *Christian Commonwealth* (London), 8 Jan. 1913, p. 267.
54. See, for instance, 'Flying Heavenward', *Daily News and Leader* (London), 3 Jan. 1913, p. 2, col. 4; *Sunday Independent* (Dublin), 5 Jan. 1913, p. 3; *Register* (Adelaide, Australia), 21 Feb. 1912, p. 8, col. 8; 'Flying Heavenward', *West Gippsland Gazette* (Warragul, Australia), 25 Mar. 1913, p. 6, col. 2; 'Flying Heavenward', *Times of India* (Bombay), 24 Jan. 1913, p. 11. See also 'A Persian Simile', *Common Cause* (London), 10 Jan. 1913 (4:196), p. 684; 'Abdul Baha Praises Women', *Christian Science Monitor* (Boston), 31 Jan. 1913, p. 9, col. 4.
55. 'Compte Rendu de la Women's Freedom League', *Jus Sufragii* (Paris), 25 Jan. 1913, p. 95. I thank Jan Jasion for pointing me to this reference. Also published in *Jus Suffragii* (London), July 1913, pp. 44–5.
56. 'Fiat Justitia', *Christian Commonwealth* (London), 15 Jan. 1913, p. 283, col. 4. On 17 Jan. 1913, announcements of this special issue mentioning 'Abdu'l-Bahá as one of the contributors were published in *The Common Cause* (p. 706) and *The Vote* (p. 193).
57. 'Reports of other Societies', *Suffragette* (London), 17 Jan. 1913, p. 211.
58. 'The First Persian Feminist', *Fortnightly Review* (London), June 1913 (93:558), pp. 1175–82. This article was advertised in 'In the Magazines', *Woman's Journal* (Boston), 5 July 1913, p. 5, col. 2.
59. For a report of this congress see Ida Huster Harper, *History of Woman Suffrage*, vol. 6, pp. 847–59. There is a reference to the Persian Bahá'ís on page 852.

60. Catt, *Address of the President at the Seventh Congress of the International Woman Suffrage Alliance* (1913), pp. 9–10.
61. Catt, 'Our Cause is One', *Suffragette* (London), 4 July 1913, p. 637.
62. Royden, 'The International Congress', *Common Cause* (London), 27 June 1913, p. 188.
63. 'Equal Suffrage is to be discussed at the Biennial', *Christian Science Monitor* (Boston), 13 June 1913, p. 4, cols. 4–5. See also, 'Important Suffrage Address', *Daily Statesman* (Austin, TX), 13 Sep. 1913, p. 1, col. 2; 'Mrs. Catt's Speech to the General Federation of Women's Clubs in Chicago', *Jus Suffragii* (London), 1 July 1913, p. 136.
64. 'Spacious Washington House', *Woman's Journal and Suffrage News* (London), 9 Dec. 1916, p. 395, col. 2.

32 Race Unity

1. Gustav Spiller (ed.), *Papers on Inter-Racial Problems Communicated to the First Universal Races Congress* (1911), p. v.
2. 'Universal Race Congress', *Times* (London), 17 Mar. 1911, p. 7, col. 4.
3. 'The Universal Races Congress', *Times* (London), 24 July 1911, p. 4, col. 4.
4. 'A Universal Races Congress', *Light* (London), 29 Apr. 1911, p. 198, col. 2.
5. 'Table Talk', *Christian Commonwealth* (London), 10 May 1911, p. 562, col. 1; 'Table Talk', *Christian Commonwealth* (London), 28 June 1911, p. 681, col. 4. See also 'An Easter Visitor', *Sheffield Daily Telegraph*, 6 July 1911, p. 6, col. 5; 'Babism', *Citizen* (Gloucester), 6 July 1911, p. 4, col. 3.
6. 'Abbas Effendi', *Egyptian Gazette* (Alexandria), 27 Mar. 1911, p. 3, col. 3.
7. 'Congrès des Races', *L'Univers Israélite* (Paris), July 1911, p. 626.
8. 'The Races Congress and its Message', *Christian Commonwealth* (London), 26 July 1911, p. 738.
9. 'The Universal Races Congress', *Christian Commonwealth* (London), 2 Aug. 1911, pp. 753–4. Also published in *Star of the West*, 20 Aug. 1911 (2:9), p. 3. The Tablet was also published in German as 'Tablet von Abdul Baha', in *Bavara Esperantisto*, 10 Jan. 1914 (2:1), p. 5. I thank Frederic Jean for kindly sharing with me the reference in this Esperantist magazine.
10. Christian Louis Lange (1869–1938) was a Norwegian pacifist. At the time of the Races Congress he was a member of the Second Hague Conference and General Secretary of the Inter-Parliamentary Union. In 1921 he was awarded the Nobel Peace Prize.
11. 'Races Congress', *Manchester Guardian*, 28 July 1911, p. 6, col. 2.
12. Gustav Spiller (ed.). *Papers on Inter-Racial Problems Communicated to the First Universal Races Congress*, pp. 156–7. Also published in *Star of the West*, 20 Aug. 1911 (2:8), pp. 5–6. For the Persian text of the paper see *Star of the West*, 7 Feb. 1912 (2:17), pp. 8–10 (Persian section), and 'Abdu'l-Bahá, *Majmú'i-yi-Khaṭábát-i-Ḥaḍrat-i-'Abdu'l-Bahá*, vol. 1 (1921), pp. 35–43. A comparison of the Persian text with the English shows that the latter was heavily summarized and that many passages in the original were not included in the translation. For full English translations of the original Persian see *Selections from the Writings of 'Abdu'l-Bahá*, no. 225 (from 'when thou traversest the regions' to 'united and agreed in perfect harmony') and no. 1. The volume with the proceedings

of the Universal Races Congress was released on 25 July 1911. Gustav Spiller was in possession of the original Persian manuscript and, after the publication of the proceedings, delivered it to the London Bahá'ís; see letters from Arthur Cuthbert to Albert Windust, 26 Aug. 1911 (Albert Windust papers, box 13, US National Bahá'í Archives) and to Ahmad Sohrab, 16 Sept. 1911, (Ahmad Sohrab correspondence, box 2, US National Bahá'í Archives).

13. *Westminster Review* (London), July 1912 (178:1), p. 50. The paragraph reproduced was the one beginning with 'The Congress is one . . .'
14. Rev. C. C. Martindale, 'Inter-Racial Problems', *Month* (London), Oct. 1911, pp. 353–63.
15. 'The First Universal Races Congress', *Indian Opinion* (Phoenix, South Africa), 9 Sept. 1911, pp. 350–1. The paragraph quoted is 'The Blessed One, Baha'u'llah . . . to the misguided and the oppressed'. The other Tablet quoted was addressed to the New York Board of Council in 1907. The whole text can be found in *Tablets of Abdul Baha Abbas*, vol. 2, pp. 429–33.
16. See 'The First Universal Races Congress', *Indian Opinion* (Phoenix, South Africa), 2 Sept. 1911, p. 340.
17. 'The First Universal Races Congress, V', *Christian Express* (Lovedale, South Africa), 1 Feb. 1912, pp. 19–20.
18. 'Notes and Reviews', *Journal of Race Development* (Worcester, MA), Apr. 1912, p. 494.
19. W.P.S., 'The Problem of Universal Peace', *Catholic World* (New York), July 1912 (95:568), pp. 516–26. For a brief reference to 'Abdu'l-Bahá's message in another American Catholic periodical see 'Notes on Recent Books', *Homiletic Review* (New York), Jan. 1912, p. 82.
20. See *Národní Listy* (Prague), 16 Aug. 1911, p. 3, col. 1; and 'První vseobecny svetobý sjezd národu', 13 Sept. 1911, p. 4, col. 1.
21. 'Analyses et notices', *Revue d'études ethnographiques et sociologiques* (Paris), May 1912, p. 246.
22. 'Universal Races Congress', *Christian Commonwealth* (London), 12 July 1911, p. 714, col. 1. For another British journal mentioning 'Abdu'l-Bahá's message; see 'An Eastern Visitor', *Sheffield Daily Telegraph*, 6 July 1911, p. 5, col. 5.
23. *Christian Commonwealth* (London), 26 July 1911, p. 738.
24. See *Christian Commonwealth* (London), 2 Aug. 1911, p. 754. Parts of this article were also published as 'An Oshkosh Man Experience', in *Daily Northwestern* (Oshkosh, WI), 19 Aug. 1911, p. 3, col. 3.
25. 'Bahaism: In Relation to Orthodoxy, Theosophy, and the Woman's Movement', *Christian Commonwealth* (London), 9 Aug. 1911, p. 779, col. 2. In a letter from Arthur Cuthbert to Albert Windust dated 2 August 1911 it is reported that Sir Richard Stapley was also one of the speakers (see Albert Windust papers, box 13, US National Bahá'í Archives).
26. 'International Consciousness', *Christian Commonwealth* (London), 9 Aug. 1911, p. 779, col. 1.
27. See 'Abdu'l-Bahá, *Promulgation*, pp. 49–52. The Bethel Literary Society, which at the time was presided over by the Bahá'í Louis Gregory, had in the past been the platform for several public lectures on the Bahá'í Faith; see, for instance, *Bee* (Washington), 2 Apr. 1910, in which a talk by Lua Getsinger, Fannie Knobloch,

Joseph Hannen and Faríd on 'The Race Problem in the Light of the Bahai Revelation' was announced. The account of this talk was published in the same journal on 9 April 1910. *The Bee* on 30 March 1912 announced the visit of the Master to Washington, stating that 'His coming to America is looked forward to with much interest, and his appearance at Bethel Literary will doubtless cause an unusual meeting.'

28. 'Abdul Baha to Remain in City Most of the Week', *Evening Star* (Washington), 22 Apr. 1912; 'Abdul Baha Makes Sightseeing Trip over the Capital', *Washington Times*, 22 Apr. 1912; 'Baha Will Address Students', *Washington Herald*, 23 Apr. 1912, p. 3, col. 3.
29. See 'Abdu'l-Bahá, *Promulgation*, pp. 44–6, *Star of the West*, 28 Apr. 1912 (3:3), pp. 14–15. For the Persian notes see 'Abdu'l-Bahá, *Majmu'ih-i-Khatábát-i-Hadrat-i-'Abdu'l-Bahá*, vol. 2, pp. 39–43.
30. 'Persian Savant to Give Last Lecture', *Washington Times*, 26 Apr. 1912, p. 14, col. 2.
31. 'Abdul Baha to give last lecture Friday', *Washington Star* (Washington DC), 24 Apr.1912. The same was published a few days later as 'Bahai Leader at Howard University', in the *Afro-American* (Baltimore), 27 Apr. 1912, p. 1, col. 5. The words attributed to 'Abdu'l-Bahá in this article coincide with those published a few days later in *Star of the West*, see 'Abdul Baha in Washington' by Joseph H. Hannen, 28 Apr. 1912 (3:3), pp. 14–15.
32. *Bee* (Washington), 25 May 1912.
33. 'America and World Peace', *Independent* (New York), 12 Sept. 1912 (73:3328), pp. 606–8. For the full text of the interview see vol. 1, chapter 17, pp. 387–91.
34. *Bee* (Washington), 27 Apr. 1912, p. 1, col. 5 (includes picture of 'Abdu'l-Bahá).
35. *Chicago Defender*, 4 May 1912, p. 5, col. 1.
36. *Chicago Defender*, 28 Sept. 1912, p. 4, col. 4, n.t.
37. *Chicago Defender*, 9 Nov. 1912, p. 1, col. 3. Also published as 'Abdul Baha Coming to the Capital', in *Freeman* (Indianapolis), 9 Nov. 1911, p. 1, col. 2.
38. 'Prophet Abdul Baha Here', *Chicago Examiner*, 1 May 1912.
39. Text from 'Chicago Ministers to Denounce Lynching', *Chicago Defender*, 20 Apr. 1912, p. 1, col. 3. Also published as 'Meeting of the National Association for the Advancement of Colored People', in *Broad Ax* (Chicago), 20 Apr. 1912, p. 1, col. 1. Five paragraphs with general information about the conference have been omitted here.
40. 'Leader of Persian Bahai to Talk Here', *Evening American* (Chicago), 24 Apr. 1912; 'Final Plans for Fourth Meeting N.A.A.C.P.', *Chicago Defender*, 27 Apr. 1912, p. 1, col. 6; 'The Meeting of the National Association', *Broad Ax* (Chicago), 27 Apr. 1912, p. 1, col. 5.
41. 'Persian Interested in African Cause', *American* (Baltimore), 28 Apr. 1912.
42. 'Speakers Encourage and Tell of Advance', *Chicago Defender*, 4 May 1912, p. 1, col. 7.
43. 'The First Step for the Equality of Man', ibid. p. 2, col. 4.
44. 'The Negro in America: Today and Tomorrow', *Survey* (New York), 18 May 1912 (28:7), p. 319.
45. 'Brevities', *Christian Register* (Boston), 13 June 1912, p. 562. For a further reference to the participation of 'Abdu'l-Bahá in the program of the event in

a Unitarian periodical see 'More Friends for the Negro', *Unity* (Chicago), 9 May 1912, p. 156, a report by the writer and Unitarian minister Celia Parker Woolley (1848–1918).
46. 'Men of the Month', *Crisis* (New York), May 1912 (4:1), pp. 14–16. The text was reproduced in other newspapers, for example as 'A Persian Teacher', in the *Savannah Tribune* (Savannah, GA), 11 May 1912, p. 1, col. 2.
47. 'The Fourth Annual Conference', *Crisis* (New York), June 1912 (4:2), p. 80.
48. ibid. p. 88. Same text as Supplement, 'Wisdom-Talks of Abdul Baha', in *Star of the West*, 17 May 1912 (3:4), pp. 10–11.
49. 'Without Distinction of Colour', *Theosophic Messenger* (Los Angeles), Aug. 1912, pp. 654–5. Same text as Supplement, 'Wisdom-Talks of Abdul Baha', *Star of the West*, 17 May 1912 (3:4), p. 5.
50. 'The Coming of Abdul Baha', *Appeal* (St Paul, MN), 11 May 1912, p. 2, col. 2. Also published on 18 May 1912, 25 May 1912 and 15 June 1912.

33 An International Language
1. Bahá'u'lláh, *Kitáb-i-Aqdas*, para. 189.
2. Held from 14 to 20 August 1905.
3. *Amerika Esperantisto* (Chicago), Nov. 1910 (8:4), p. 97.
4. 'Kroniko', *Amerika Esperantisto* (Chicago), Jan. 1911 (8:6), p. 140.
5. 'Esperanto and the Bahais', *British Esperantist* (London), Dec. 1911 (7:84), p. 234.
6. Richard Ledermann (ed.), 'Abdul Baha Abbas', *Das Esperanto ein Kulturfaktor. Festschrift anläßlich des 7 deutschen Esperanto-Kongresses: Danzig, Zoppot: vom 27. Juli bis 1. August 1912* (Leizpig), 1913, vol. 3, p. 195.
7. 'Esperanto Notes', *Daily Herald* (Adelaide), 16 Mar. 1912, p. 13, col. 3.
8. *La Revuo* (Paris), Oct. 1910, p. 80. I would like to thank Pedro Armindo for kindly sharing with me this reference.
9. 'Esperanto-Kongresse', *Rund um die Welt* (Prague), Oct. 1910, p. 229.
10. 'Kroniko, Persia', *Amerika Esperantisto* (Chicago), Nov. 1911 (10:4), p. 12.
11. 'A Message from Abdul Baha', *Amerika Esperantisto* (Chicago), June 1912 (11:5), pp. 19–20. The text was published later in *Star of the West*, 7 Feb. 1921 (11:18), p. 304 and in 'Abdu'l-Bahá, *Promulgation*, pp. 60–1.
12. 'A Message from Abdul Baha', *British Esperantist* (London), Jan. 1913 (9:97), pp. 18–19.
13. 'The First Universal Races' Congress', *La Londona Esperantisto* (London), Sept. 1911 (no. 25).
14. Sohrab, Letter to Harriet Magee, 19 January 1913, p. 11.
15. For the text of this talk see Herrick, *Unity Triumphant*, pp. 123–7.
16. *British Esperantist* (London), Feb. 1913 (9:98), p. 24.
17. 'Esperanto Corner', *Cheltenham Chronicle*, 8 Mar. 1913, p. 8, col. 5.
18. 'Esperanto Notes', *Advertiser* (Adelaide), 5 Apr. 1913, p. 16, col. 3.
19. 'Granda Britujo', *Le Monde Espérantiste* (Paris), Feb. 1913 (6:2), p. 19.
20. 'Scotland', *British Esperantist* (London), Dec. 1912 (8:96), p. 226. Also mentioned in 'Eksterlanda Kroniko', *Belga Esperantisto* (Antwerp), Feb. 1913 (5:4), p. 87.
21. Minutes of the meeting of the Council of the Edinburgh Esperanto Society,

27 Dec. 1912. The minutes also show that Mrs Whyte was asked to share the expenses of the meeting in case there was a deficit after selling the tickets. I thank David Merrick for kindly sharing with me transcripts of the references to 'Abdu'l-Bahá in the minutes of the Society.
22. 'Abdul Baha', *Scotsman* (Edinburgh), 7 Jan. 1913, p. 1.
23. 'Edinburgh Esperantists: A Persian Reformer', *Glasgow Herald*, 8 Jan. 1913, p. 10, col. 8.
24. 'Abdul Baha', *Evening Dispatch* (Edinburgh), 8 Jan. 1913.
25. 'Abdul Baha in Edinburgh', *Scotsman* (Edinburgh), 8 Jan. 1913, p. 10, col. 4.
26. 'Esperanto and International Amity', *Evening News* (Edinburgh), 8 Jan. 1913, p. 7, col. 4.
27. ibid.
28. 'Dr. Kelman on Bahai Teaching', *Christian Commonwealth* (London), 22 Jan. 1913, p. 2, col. 4.
29. 'Esperanto and International Amity', *Evening News* (Edinburgh), 8 Jan. 1913, p. 7, col. 4.
30. 'Abdul Baha', *Evening Dispatch* (Edinburgh), 8 Jan. 1913.
31. 'Abdul Baha in Edinburgh', *Scotsman* (Edinburgh), 8 Jan. 1913, p. 10, col. 4.
32. 'Esperanto and International Amity', *Evening News* (Edinburgh), 8 Jan. 1913, p. 7, col. 4.
33. 'Abdul Baha in Edinburgh', *Evening Dispatch* (Edinburgh), 8 Jan. 1913.
34. *Evening News* (Edinburgh), 8 Jan. 1913, p. 4, col. 1.
35. *British Esperantist* (London), Feb. 1913 (9:98), p. 25. A shorter note appeared also on the cover of the same issue, see 'From the Esperanto Watch Tower'.
36. ibid. pp. 35–6. Also published in *Star of the West*, 9 Apr. 1913 (4:2), pp. 34–6 and in *Bahá'í Scriptures* (1923), p. 338.
37. 'Esperanto', *Vahan* (London), 1 July 1913, p. 279.
38. *Esperanto Monthly* (London), Feb. 1913, p. 1.
39. See for instance, 'Universal Brotherhood. A World Language', *Bexhill-on-sea Observer*, 17 May 1913, p. 4, col. 4.
40. 'Diversajoj', *Brazila Esperantisto* (Rio de Janeiro), Mar.–Apr. 1913, p. 4 and ibid. 'Inglaterra', p. 7.
41. *La Duj Stelo* (Santiago de Chile), 1 May 1913 (3:27), pp. 9–10.
42. 'El Esperanto en el Mundo', *Cuba Esperantista* (La Habana), Feb.–Mar. 1913 (4:2–3), p. 8.
43. 'Unique Meeting in Edinburgh', *Amerika Esperantisto* (Washington), Feb. 1913 (13:1), p. 2. The article also quoted in English some lines from the Esperanto translation of 'Abdu'l-Bahá's address.
44. 'Esperanto Notes', *Idaho Falls Times*, 4 Mar. 1913, p. 2, col. 4.
45. 'Eksterlanda Kroniko', *Belga Esperantisto* (Antwerp), Feb. 1913 (5:4), p. 87.
46. 'Skotlando', *La Marto* (Haida), Feb. 1913, p. 23; 'Esperanto do Pravlasti Indoevropanu', *La Kulturo* (Prague), Mar. 1913 (2:3), p. 22; 'Skotlando', *Casopis Ceskych Esperantistu* (Prague), Mar. 1913 (7:3), p. 48.
47. Carlo Bourlet, 'Babilado', *La Revuo* (Paris), Feb. 1913, pp. 277–8 and also Feb. 1913 [supplement], p. 128; 'Abdul Baha kaj Esperanto', *La Movado* (Paris), Mar. 1913 (5:38), p. 32; 'Skotlando', *Le Monde Espérantiste* (Paris), Jan. 1913 (6:1), p. 5; 'Esperanto', *Le Fraterniste* (Paris), 28 Mar. 1913, p. 4.

48. 'Grossbritanien', *Germana Esperantisto* (Dresden), Mar. 1913 (10:3), p. 3; 'Esperanto im Orient', *La Svaba Esperantisto* (Schussenried), 31 Jan. 1913 (1:2), p. 12.
49. 'Tutmonda Kroniko', *La Verda Standardo* (Budapest), Mar. 1913 (8:3), p. 46.
50. 'Movimiento Esperantista Internazionale', *Itala Esperantisto* (Genoa), Mar. 1913 (3:3), p. 5; 'Cronaca Esperantista, *L'Esperanto* (Milan), 10 Apr. 1913 (1:7), p. 55.
51. 'Esperanto i Utlandet', *Norvega Esperantisto* (Oslo), June 1913 (5:3), pp. 22–3.
52. 'La nova sukceso', *Pola Esperantisto [Esperantysta Polski]* (Warsaw), Feb. 1913 (8:2), p. 25.
53. 'Gran-Bretanha', *Portugala Revuo* (Lisbon), Apr. 1913 (2:4), p. 45.
54. 'Jorden Runt', *La Espero* (Stockholm), Apr. 1913, p. 4.
55. 'Aus der Esperanto-Bewegung', *Monda Posto* (Zurich), 25 Mar. 1913 (8:3), p. 20; 'Diversajoj', *Esperanto* (Geneva), 20 Feb. 1913 (9:3), p. 42.
56. Román Ayza, 'Notas Esperantistas', *La Correspondencia Militar* (Madrid), 2 July 1913, p. 2, col. 4.
57. Román Ayza, 'Notas Esperantistas', *El Día de Madrid*, 4 July 1913, p. 3, col. 2.
58. *La Suno Hispania* (Valencia), Mar. 1913 (8:81), p. 36.
59. 'Eksterlanda Movado', *Tutmonda Espero* (Barcelona), Feb. 1913, pp. 21–2.
60. 'Grava Sukceso', *La Ondo Esperanto* (Moscow), Feb. 1913, (5:2), pp. 31–2.
61. 'Dangero Propagandmanisto', *La Ondo Esperanto* (Moscow), May 1913, (5:5), p. 87. Translated from Esperanto by Heather Eason.
62. 'Nota de la Redakcio', *La Revuo* (Paris), July 1913, pp. 504–5.
63. 'Danjeroza propagando', *Progreso* (Paris), July 1913, p. 308; 'Danjeroza propagando', *La Langue Auxiliare* (Verdun), Nov. 1913, p. 137.
64. 'El Skotlando', *Orienta Azio* (Tokyo), Apr. 1913 (11:18), pp. 19–21.
65. 'New World Teacher', *Telegraph* (Brisbane), 20 Feb. 1913, p. 3, col. 3; 'Esperanto and Peace', *West Australian* (Perth), 24 Mar. 1913, p. 6, col. 5; 'New World Teacher', *The Week* (Brisbane), 28 Feb. 1913, p. 17, col. 5; 'Esperanto Notes', *Advertiser* (Adelaide), 5 Apr. 1913, p. 16, col. 1; *Ovens and Murray Advertiser* (Beechworth), 31 May 1913, p. 4, col. 3.
66. 'Esperanto', *Egyptian Gazette* (Alexandria), 12 Dec. 1913, p. 5, col. 4.
67. 'Parolo de Abdul Baha pri Internacia Lingvuo', *British Esperantist* (London), Feb. 1913 (9:98), p. 35. An extract in Esperanto and English was later reprinted in 'Esperanto', *Hastings and St. Leonards Observer* (London), 19 Apr. 1913, p. 3, col. 8.
68. 'Parolo de Abdul Baha pri Internacia Lingvuo', *La Revuo* (Paris), Mar. 1913, pp. 322–5.
69. 'Esperanto', *Le Fraterniste* (Paris), 4 Apr. 1913, p. 4.
70. 'Parolo de Abdul Baha pri Internacia Lingvuo', *La Verda Standardo* (Budapest), Mar. 1913 (8:3), p. 35.
71. 'Parolo de Abdul Baha pri Internacia Lingvuo', *Pola Esperantisto [Esperantysta Polski]* (Warsaw), Mar. 1913 (8:3), pp. 39–41.
72. 'Persische Sprache', *Das Esperanto ein Kulturfaktor: Festschrift anlässlich des 8 Deutschen Esperanto-Kongresses: Stuttgart* (Leizpig), 1913 (vol. 3), p. 95.
73. 'Esperanto', *Hastings and St Leonards Observer* (Hastings), 19 April 1913, p. 3, col. 8.
74. *La Duj Stelo* (Santiago de Chile), 1 May 1913 (3:27), pp. 9–10. The text was accompanied by a picture of the Master.

75. 'Rech ob mezhdunarodnom jazyke', *Volga Stelo* (Saratov), Feb.–Mar. 1913 (2:2–3), pp. 28–30. I would like to thank Frederic Auret for bringing this document to my attention.
76. 'Bahismus und Esperantismus', *German-Austria Esperantisto* (Vienna), June 1913 (7:6), pp. 41–2.
77. Minutes of the monthly meeting of the Edinburgh Esperanto Society, 7 Mar. 1913.
78. 'Dro Zamenhof and Abdul Baha', *Christian Commonwealth* (London), 29 Jan. 1913.
79. 'Abdul Baha and Esperanto', *Christian Commonwealth* (London), 14 May 1913, p. 577, col. 3. On May 11 the Esperantist John Thornton gave an address for the Bexhill Brotherhood in which he briefly mentioned 'Abdu'l-Bahá. See 'Universal Brotherhood', *Bexhill-on-the-sea Observer*, 17 May 1913, p. 4, col. 4.
80. Charles Émile Ernest Bourlet (1866–1913), known as Carlo Bourlet, was an eminent French mathematician who combined his career as researcher, university teacher and writer with the promotion of Esperanto. He was the founder in 1906 of the magazine *La Revuo* (Paris) and its editor in chief until his passing (Félicien Menu de Ménil was its editor). He also founded a large number of Esperantist societies in France and launched the Esperanto Floral Games, a literary contest which was first observed at the International Esperanto Congress held in Barcelona in 1909. He was also the mediator between Zamenhof and the publishing company Librairie Hachette which from 1901 up to the passing of Bourlet published most of Zamenhof's books as well as the magazine *La Revuo*.
81. For details see Sohrab, Letter to Harriet Magee, 12 Feb. 1912, pp. 1–4.
82. For the Persian notes of this talk see 'Abdu'l-Bahá, *Majmu'ih-i-Khatábát-i-Hadrat-i-'Abdu'l-Bahá*, vol. 3, pp. 93–5.
83. 'Nos fêtes', *Paris Esperanto*, Mar. 1913, p. 1, col. 5. I thank Frederic Auret for bringing this document to my attention.
84. 'Abdul Baha the Guest of Paris Esperantists', *Amerika Esperantisto* (Washington), Apr. 1913 (13:3), pp. 3–4.
85. 'Abdul Baha and Esperanto', *British Esperantist* (London), Apr. 1913 (9:100), p. 63.
86. 'Allocution d'Abdul Baha', *Paris Esperanto*, April 1913, p. 1, col. 3.
87. 'Bahaia Penso', *La Revuo* (Paris), May 1913, pp. 415–20. This article was mentioned in 'Esperanto i Utlandet', *Norvega Esperantisto* (Oslo), June 1913 (5:3), pp. 22–3.
88. For details about the relationship between Zamenhof, Bourlet and the Librairie Hachette, see Aleksander Korzhenkov, *Zamenhof: The Life, Works and Ideas of the Author of Esperanto* (2010), pp. 53–4.
89. See 'Bahaia Penso', *La Revuo* (Paris), July 1913, pp. 503–5, and 'Bahaia Penso', September 1913, pp. 32–4.
90. 'Abdul Baha kaj Esperanto', *La Movado* (Paris), Mar. 1913 (5:35), p. 2, col. 2.
91. 'Abdul Baha on the Value of a Universal Language', *International Psychic Gazette* (London), Apr. 1913 (1:9), pp. 250–1. Later also published in *Star of the West*, 9 Apr. 1913 (4:2), pp. 36–7 and in Isabel Fraser's compilation *Abdul Baha on Divine Philosophy* (1916) in a slightly different version. For a reference to the

publication of the talk in the *International Psychic Gazette* see *The Occult Review* (London), May 1913, p. 296.
92. 'Abdul Baha on Universal Peace', *Peacemaker* (Philadelphia), Nov.–Dec. 1913 (31:11–12), pp. 82–5. This magazine received the text of the talk from Isabel Fraser.
93. 'A Voice from the Orient', *Ameriko Esperantisto* (West Newton, MA), Nov. 1918 (23:3), pp. 9–10.
94. 'Esperanto', *Le Fraterniste* (Paris), 28 Mar. 1913, p. 4; 'Esperanto', *Le Fraterniste* (Paris), 4 Apr, 1913, p. 4.
95. 'Esperanto Notes', *Advertiser* (Adelaide), 14 June 1913, p. 16, col. 3.
96. 'Abdul Baha the Guest of Paris Esperantists', *Amerika Esperantisto* (Washington), Apr. 1913 (13:3), pp. 3–4.
97. L.L.H., 'L'Espéranto', *Le Théosophe* (Paris), 1 Oct. 1913, p. 2, col. 2.
98. 'Unu Vizito al Abdul Baha', *Lingvo Internacia* (Paris), Mar. 1913 (18:3), pp. 105–7. Translated from Esperanto by Heather Eason.
99. *Bulletin Mensuel de la Société Unitive* (Paris), Feb. 1913, p. 53. See chapter 30.
100. 'Nova Religia Movado', *Universala Unuigo* (Lubotin), 1913, pp. 1–11.
101. ibid. pp. iv, vii.
102. 'Chronique Russe', *Bibliothéque universelle et Revue Suisse* (Lausanne), Oct. 1913 (72:214), p. 214. I would like to thank Jan Jasion for kindly bringing this document to my attention.
103. Sohrab, Letter to Harriet Magee, 22 Mar. 1913, p. 5.
104. 'Esperanto im Orient,' *La Svaba Esperantisto* (Schussenried), 31 Jan. 1913 (1:2), p. 12.
105. 'Stuttgart', *Germana Esperantisto* (Dresden), May 1913 (10:5), p. 69.
106. 'Abdul Baha en Stuttgart'. ibid. p. 72. Translated from Esperanto by Heather Eason.
107. 'Abdul Baha en Stuttgart', *Unuig-Informoj* (Danzig), May 1913, pp. 1–2; 'Stuttgart', *La Svaba Esperantisto* (Schussenried), 1 May 1913 (1:8), p. 55; 'Stuttgart', *Bavara Esperanto* (Augsburg), May 1913, p. 55 (I am grateful to Frederic Audret for kindly sharing this document); 'Persische Sprache', *Das Esperanto ein Kulturfaktor. Festschrift anlässlich des 8 Deutschen Esperanto-Kongresses: Stuttgart* (Leizpig), 1913, (vol. 3), p. 95.
108. 'Stuttgart', *Rund um die Welt* (Prague), May 1913 (4:5), pp. 107 and 113.
109. 'Stuttgart', *Svisa Espero* (Zurich), May 1913.
110. 'Foreign News', *Ameriko Esperantisto* (West Newton, MA), June 1913 (13:5), p. 6.
111. 'Hungarlanda Kroniko', *La Verda Standardo* (Budapest), May 1913 (8:5), p. 79. Translated from Esperanto by Heather Eason.
112. 'Diversajoj', *Espero Teozofia* (Paris), May 1913, p. 8. Translated from Esperanto by Heather Eason.
113. 'Foreign News', *Ameriko Esperantisto* (West Newton, MA), June 1913 (13:5), p. 4. For a further reference to 'Abdu'l-Bahá in connection with Esperanto during His second visit to Europe see also 'El la Malnova Mondo', Aug. 1913, p. 6.
114. 'El Hungarujo', *La Revuo* (Paris), May 1913 [supplement], p. 171.
115. 'Abdul Baha', *German-Austria Esperantisto* (Vienna), May 1913 (7:5), p. 38. Translated from Esperanto by Heather Eason.

116. See note 74: 'Bahismus und Esperantismus', *German-Austria Esperantisto* (Vienna), June 1913 (7:6), pp. 41–2.
117. 'The Strife of Tongues', *Christian Commonwealth* (London), 3 Sep. 1913, p. 826, col. 1. The same page contains a letter from 'Abdu'l-Bahá to a group of Bahá'í Esperantists in America.
118. 'Sunday – The Church Services; The Formal Opening', *Amerika Esperantisto* (West Newton, MA), Oct. 1913, p. 5.
119. See Heller, *Lidia: The Life of Lidia Zamenhof, Daughter of Esperanto*.
120. In June 1913 the *Amerika Esperantisto* reported that an Esperanto manual was being translated 'by a young Bahai who knows several languages', see 'Foreign News', June 1913 (13:5), p. 6. The same magazine reported that the Persian–American Educational Society was helping in the establishment of Esperanto groups in Persia, see 'Esperanto en Persujo', Feb. 1914 (15:1). This report was published again in Poland (see 'Esperanto en Persujo', *Pola Esperantisto* (Warsaw), Apr. 1914, p. 56), and Switzerland ('Tra la Gazetaro', *Esperanto* (Zurich), p. 79). On January 1918, 'Abdu'l-Bahá was again mentioned in *Amerika Esperantisto* in an article about Green Acre, see 'Why are you coming to Green Acre?', pp. 1–3. Green Acre was the venue for the tenth National Congress of the American Esperantists. The report of this Congress again mentioned 'Abdu'l-Bahá, see July–Aug. 1918 (22:6), p. 5. On page 13 of the same issue a brief note of a Bahá'í meeting was also published, see 'Esperantists at Bahai Gathering'. Joseph Hannen's address on Esperanto at the Bahá'í Congress held at Boston in May 1917 was reproduced in the *Amerika Esperantisto*, Oct. 1918 (23:2), pp. 4–6. On February 1919 the same journal published two Tablets by 'Abdu'l-Bahá to the American Bahá'ís translated into Esperanto by Martha Root, see 'Leteroj al Amerikaj Bahaanoj, 1906 kaj 1913', p. 9. In 1920 a report of the twelfth International Esperanto Congress, which was held in the Hague and which was the first since the start of the World War, mentioned that a missive from 'Abdu'l-Bahá was read at the first formal session of the Congress, see 'Dek-Dua Universala Kongreso de Esperanto', June 1920 (26:3), p. 3.

On March 1914, the *British Esperantist* reproduced a letter by Ahmad Sohrab sent from Egypt to a Bahá'í Esperantist, see 'A letter from Abdul Baha', p. 51. The same issue contained a report on the progress of the Esperanto movement in which 'Abdu'l-Bahá was again mentioned, see 'Esperanto in the East', p. 54. Similar information was published in 'Our Esperanto Corner', *Cheltenham Chronicle*, 25 Apr. 1914, p. 8, col. 1. Further comments on 'Abdu'l-Bahá and the Bahá'í Faith appeared in the *British Esperantist* in October 1916, see 'Persujo', p. 105, and 'Chicago', p. 106. The magazine *Esperanto* (Geneva), the official organ of the Universal Esperanto Society, published both articles in 1916, see 'Esperanto kaj Bahaistoj', 5 November 1916 (8:11), p. 127. One month later it also published an article by Agnes Alexander on the Bahá'í House of Worship in Chicago, see 'Nova centro de la Bahajanoj,' 5 December 1916 (8:12), p. 137.

In a review of the progress of the Esperanto movement in the year 1913, Dr Beiger briefly mentioned 'Abdu'l-Bahá in connection with His instruction that Bahá'ís should learn Esperanto. See 'Rückblick auf das Jahr 1913', *Germana Esperantisto* (Dresden), Jan. 1914, p. 21. Similar information was published in the German-language Bohemian journal *Teplitz-Schönauer Anzeiger* (Teplice), 23 Mar. 1914, p. 8.

In November 1921 a Tablet of 'Abdu'l-Bahá addressed to a group of contacts of Martha Root, probably from Brazil, was published in Esperanto by Agnes Alexander, see 'Abdul Baha kaj Unueco de la Mondo', *Esperanto* (Geneva), Nov. 1921, pp. 187–8.

William Page of the Edinburgh Esperanto Society continued his contacts with the Bahá'ís. One article by him was published as 'The League of Nations and Esperanto' in the Bahá'í-inspired magazine *Reality* (New York), January 1921, pp. 26–8.

34 The Theosophical Society

1. See, for instance, 'The Babis of Persia' in *The Theosophist* (Bombay), Jan. 1893, pp. 203–6 which was partially reprinted in 'Les Babis' in *Voile d'Isis* (Paris) 6 May 1896, p. 1. See also the articles published by Myron H. Phelps under the title 'The One Religion' in the *Theosophical Forum* (New York), Aug. 1904, pp. 69–80; Feb. 1905, pp. 187–92; *Theosophical Quarterly* (New York) 1905–6, pp. 224–33, 302–10 and 391–7. See also Sydney Sprague's 'Bahaism or a Universal Religion' in *Theosophical Review* (London), Jan. 1907, pp. 410–19 and Feb. 1907, pp. 495–502. These articles prompted a letter to the editor from R.H.R. Skeeles, Mar. 1907, p. 78, and Sprague's response appeared in April 1907, pp. 183–4. The same journal published the following articles: '*Some Answered Questions* (review)', May 1908, p. 78; Francis Sedlak, 'Abdu'l Baha & Reincarnation', July 1908, p. 417; Arthur Cuthbert, 'Bahai Philosophy & Reincarnation', Nov. 1908, pp. 252–9. In France an essay by H. Dreyfus, 'Le Béhaïsme', was published in *Annales Théosophiques* (Paris), 1908, no. 1, pp. 25–46. In Spain the politician Rafael Urbano published 'Babismo y Behaismo' in *Sophia* (Madrid), January 1908, pp. 3–15. In March 1912 the same journal published a review of Dreyfus's *Essai sur le Behaisme*, see 'El Behaismo', pp. 156–61. In the United States, see also the article 'The Bahai Revelation' by Harriet Tooker Felix in *Theosophic Messenger* (Chicago), June 1910, pp. 523–5.

2. Annie Besant joined the Theosophical Society in 1890 and from that time became one of its principal promoters and lecturers. For a period her house was used as the headquarters of the British Theosophical Society. In 1907 she was elected president of the Society. She founded several Theosophical lodges and assisted in the creation of various educational centers in India. She was author of over 150 books and a greater number of articles. As a Theosophist she firmly expected the coming of a 'world teacher'. In 1909 she came to the belief that Krishnamurti, a 14-year-old Indian boy, was to be this messianic figure and brought him under her tutelage. In later years Krishnamurti denied being such a figure.

3. 'The Coming Christ', *Christian Commonwealth* (London), 30 June, 1909, p. 691, col. 2. See also Annie Besant, *The Changing World and Lectures to Theosophical Students*, p. 150.

4. *Christian Commonwealth* (London), 11 Aug. 1909, p. 788, col. 2. The same page in the same issue included a review of Eric Hammond's *The Splendour of God*, under the title 'A Living Prophet'.

5. 'Town and district news', *Hertfordshire and Cambridgeshire Reporter*, 22 July 1910, p. 8, col. 1. According to the same report, on the following day Buckton gave a public talk in Letchworth Garden City's Howard Hall under the title 'The Comforter'.
6. Weinberg, *Ethel Jenner Rosenberg*, p. 120.
7. 'Bath Theosophical Society', *Bath Chronicle and Weekly Gazette*, 12 Jan. 1911, p. 7, col. 5.
8. 'The Summer School', *Vahan* (London), 1 Oct. 1911, p. 46. Tudor Pole also attended the fourth and fifth summer schools. A list of speakers at the fourth summer school also included other people who had been in close contact with 'Abdu'l-Bahá, such as Sir Richard Stapley, Dunlop and Patrick Geddes.
9. 'News Items', *Star of the West*, 8 September 1911 (2:9), p. 7.
10. James Ingall Wedgwood had been an Anglican until in 1907 when he became a Theosophist and as a result was expelled from his church. He held the position of general secretary of the Theosophical Society in England and Wales from 1911 to 1913 when he joined the Old Catholic Church of Great Britain. Eventually, and for various reasons including his involvement with the Theosophical Society, he was also expelled from this congregation. Eventually he founded, together with C. W. Leadbeater, also a Theosophist, the Liberal Catholic Church.
11. 'Theosophical Society in England and Wales', *Vahan* (London), 1 Oct. 1911, p. 50.
12. Alfred Percy Sinnet (1840–1921) was a journalist who began his career on *The Globe* (London). Later he moved to China to be the editor of the *Hong Kong Daily Press* then returned to London where he was appointed chief redactor of the *Standard*. In 1872 he moved to India where he was the editor of the *Allahabad Pioneer*. In India he met Blavatsky and joined the Theosophical Society. He held the position of vice president and in different periods acted as president of both the Theosophical Society and the London Theosophical Lodge.
13. For the translation of this talk see *'Abdu'l-Bahá in London*, pp. 27–30. For Persian notes see *Star of the West*, 18 February 1912, pp. 15–16 (Persian section) and 'Abdu'l-Bahá. *Majmu'ih-i-Khatábát-i-Hadrat-i-'Abdu'l-Bahá*, vol. 1, pp. 29–34.
14. A reference to the persecution of Bahá'ís of Yazd and its surrounding area in 1903.
15. 'The Visit of Abdul Baha', *Vahan* (London), 1 Nov. 1911, pp. 65–6.
16. 'La Visita de Abdul Baha', *Sophia* (Madrid), Dec. 1911, pp. 814–16.
17. 'Theosophical Society in England and Wales', *Vahan* (London), 1 Nov. 1911, p. 72.
18. 'Abdul-Baha à Londres', *Le Théosophe* (Paris), 16 Nov. 1911, p. 2, col. 2.
19. 'Por las Revistas', *Sophia* (Madrid), Dec. 1911, pp. 819–20.
20. 'Bahaism: The Birth of a World Religion', *Contemporary Review* (London), Mar. 1912, pp. 394, 401–2.
21. 'The Bahai Movement', *Christian Commonwealth* (London), 3 Jan. 1912, p. 230, col. 4.
22. 'Theosophy and Bahai Teaching', *Christian Commonwealth* (London), 10 Apr. 1912, p. 458, col. 4.
23. Theosophists believe in a concourse of immortal and powerful beings, the White Lodge, who select certain humans to instruct the world on spiritual issues.

24. 'Questions', *Vahan* (London), 1 June 1912, pp. 258–9.
25. *Theosophic Messenger* (Los Angeles), Sept. 1912, p. 732.
26. *Revue Théosophique* (Paris), 27 Aug. 1912, p. 199.
27. This journal was founded in 1879 by Blavatsky. Its subtitle defined the magazine as 'A Monthly Journal Devoted to Oriental Philosophy, Art, Literature and Occultism: Embracing Mesmerism, Spiritualism, and Other Secret Sciences'.
28. 'The Bahai Movement and Theosophy', *Theosophist* (Bombay), Sept. 1912, pp. 822–8.
29. 'The Star in the East', *Christian Commonwealth*, 6 Dec. 1911, p. 154.
30. 'Le Béhaïsme', *Annales Théosophiques* (Paris), 1908, no. 1, pp. 25–46.
31. For the text of this address see *Paris Talks*, pp. 127–34.
32. 'Informations', *Bulletin Théosophique* (Paris), Nov. 1911, p. 156.
33. Jean Lefranc, 'Le bahaïsme et son prophète', *Le Temps* (Paris), 3 Nov. 1911, p. 4, col. 2.
34. 'Discours d'Abdoul-Baha', *Le Théosophe* (Paris), 16 Nov. 1911, p. 1.
35. 'Informations', *Bulletin Théosophique* (Paris), Dec. 1911, p. 79.
36. 'Discours de Abd-Oul-Baha à la Société Théosophique', *Annales Théosophiques* (Paris), 1911, no. 4, pp. 213–20.
37. ibid. p. 219.
38. ibid. p. 220.
39. Dominique Albert Courmes was an officer in the French navy. He joined Theosophy in 1880 and in 1895 became editor of *Le Lotus Bleu*, also known as *Revue Théosophique Française*.
40. *Revue Théosophique Française* (Paris), 27 Nov. 1911, pp. 320–2.
41. Gaston Revel was the founder and director of *Le Théosophe* and also editor of *Annales Théosophiques*, the *Bulletin de l'Education de la Jeunese*, and, from 1914, of the *Lotus Bleu*. He was also a prolific lecturer as well as author and translator of several books on Theosophy.
42. 'Le Béhaïsme', *Le Théosophe* (Paris), 16 Dec. 1911, p. 32. The article included a photograph of 'Abdu'l-Bahá taken at Boissonas et Taponier studio.
43. *Revue Théosophique Française* (Paris), 27 Jan. 1912, p. 385.
44. See ' Abdu'l-Bahá, *Promulgation*, pp. 58–60 and *Star of the West*, 28 Apr. 1912 (3:3), pp. 22–3.
45. See ' Abdu'l-Bahá, *Promulgation*, pp. 87–91.
46. See ' Abdu'l-Bahá, *Promulgation*, pp. 156–60 and *Star of the West*, 28 Apr. 1913 (4:3), pp. 55–8.
47. See ' Abdu'l-Bahá, *Promulgation*, pp. 239–43.
48. See ibid. pp. 284–9.
49. At 414–30 Mason Street, San Francisco.
50. See ' Abdu'l-Bahá, *Promulgation*, pp. 462–8 and *Star of the West*, 1 Aug. 1916 (7:8), pp. 69–71, 74–6.
51. 'Abdul Baha Abbas Visits America', *Theosophic Messenger* (Chicago), Apr. 1912, pp. 410–11. The article included a portrait of 'Abdu'l-Bahá.
52. 'Brotherhood of the Human Race', *Daily Star* (Brooklyn), 31 May 1912, p. 8, col. 7.
53. Albert Powell Warrington was a lawyer by profession who in 1912 founded the Krotona colony, a settlement for Theosophists. The same year he became

secretary general of the American section of the Theosophical Society and the editor of the *Theosophic Messenger*, which changed its location from Chicago to Los Angeles.
54. 'The Convention', *Theosophic Messenger* (Los Angeles), Nov. 1912, p. 78.
55. Footnote in the original: 'Astral is herein used in the sense of spiritual.'
56. *Theosophic Messenger* (Los Angeles), Dec. 1912, pp. 153–9.
57. See Sohrab, Letter to Harriet Magee, 14 Dec. 1912. For an account of the visit of 'Abdu'l-Bahá to the Liverpool Lodge and a transcript of the talk see the account of Isabel Fraser, 'Address of Abdu'l-Baha before the Theosophical Society, Liverpool, England', *Star of the West*, 19 Jan. 1913 (3:17), pp. 3–4.
58. For notes of this talk see Isabel Fraser, 'The Search for Truth', *Star of the West*, 19 Jan. 1913 (3:17), p. 3.
59. 'Visit of Persian Mystic', *Liverpool Courier*, 16 Dec. 1912.
60. 'Persian Mystic's Dream', *Daily Post* (Liverpool), 16 Dec. 1912, p. 10, col. 4.
61. *Vahan* (London), January 1913, p. 119, col. 2.
62. Sohrab, Letter to Harriet Magee, 12 April 1913, p. 7.
63. ibid. p. 118, col. 2.
64. 'Ein Neujahrsgruss von Abdul Baha', *Adyar-Mitteilungen* (Leizpig), Jan.–Feb. 1913 (1:4/5).
65. 'Thoughts by the Way', *Vahan* (London), Feb. 1913, pp. 137–8.
66. Perhaps the 'Mr. Andre' mentioned in *Theosophy of Scotland* who was the vice president of the Letchworth lodge and who with Alice Buckton lectured on the Bahá'í Faith on several occasions after the visit of 'Abdu'l-Bahá to Edinburgh. See section on Edinburgh in this chapter.
67. *International Psychic Gazette* (London), June 1913, p. 325.
68. Daniel Nicolas Dunlop started his professional career as an employee of the Westinghouse Electrical Company. He founded the British Electrical and Allied Manufacturers Association (1911), the World Energy Council – later World Power Conference – the Electrical Research Association and the Electrical Development Association. He had joined Theosophy in Ireland and soon became one of its principal adherents. He wrote several articles on Theosophy and in 1910 launched the magazine *The Path*. He also founded various Theosophical lodges and was the organizer of the summer schools held by British Theosophists. In 1922 Dunlop abandoned Theosophy to join Rudolf Steiner's Anthroposophism.
69. 'The Three Realities', *Path* (London), Feb. 1913, pp. 285–90. This article was read to 'Abdu'l-Bahá while He was in Paris; see Sohrab, Letter to Harriet Magee, 9 Feb. 1913, p. 16. For a review, see *The Occult Review* (London), Mar. 1913, p. 177.
70. 'Abdul Baha on Universal Peace', *International Psychic Gazette* (London), Aug. 1913, p. 5.
71. Major David Graham Pole, a solicitor by profession, was one of the leading members of the Scottish Theosophical Society. He also joined the Territorial Army and fought in WWI. From 1929 to 1931 he was a Member of Parliament as a South Derbyshire representative for the Labour party. He was author of *I Refer to India* (1929) and *India in Transition* (1932).
72. 'The Bahai Movement', *Theosophy in Scotland* (Edinburgh), May 1911, pp. 4–6. The article was signed with the pseudonym 'Adhem'. I thank David Merrick

for kindly sharing with me copies of references to the Bahá'í Faith in this publication. For a reference to this article see 'Theosophy in Scotland', *Occult Review* (London), June 1911, p. 360. The same issue contains a review of Eric Hammond's *The Splendour of God* on pp. 363–4.
73. *Theosophy in Scotland* (Edinburgh), Oct. 1911, p. 77.
74. ibid. p. 78.
75. ibid. p. 79. For the Persian notes of this message see 'Abdu'l-Bahá. *Majmu'ih-i-Khatábát-i-Hadrat-i-'Abdu'l-Bahá*, vol. 1, pp. 18–19. For a reference to this message see *The Occult Review* (London), Nov. 1911, p. 286.
76. *Theosophy in Scotland* (Edinburgh), Nov. 1911, p. 89.
77. *Theosophy in Scotland* (Edinburgh), Apr. 1912. Jane Whyte was a member of a committee appointed by 'Abdu'l-Bahá which among other tasks had the mission of overseeing the publication of *'Abdu'l-Bahá in London* (see Weinberg, *Ethel Jenner Rosenberg*, pp. 142–4); since she was also closely connected with the Scottish Theosophical Society, it is thus probable that this initiative was suggested by her.
78. See for instance 'Theosophical Society in Scotland', *Scotsman* (Edinburgh), 4 Jan. 1913, p. 1.
79. 'Abdul Baha', *Theosophy in Scotland* (Edinburgh), Jan. 1913 (3:9), p. 1.
80. Sohrab, Letter to Harriet Magee, 6 Jan. 1913.
81. Sohrab, Letter to Harriet Magee, 9 Jan. 1913.
82. For Persian notes of this talk see 'Abdu'l-Bahá. *Majmu'ih-i-Khatábát-i-Hadrat-i-'Abdu'l-Bahá*, vol. 3, pp. 53–7.
83. 'Abdul Baha on Imitation Religions', *Scotsman* (Edinburgh), 10 Jan. 1913, p. 6.
84. 'Captive Religions', *Evening Dispatch* (Edinburgh), 10 Jan. 1913, p. 3.
85. 'Address to the Theosophical Society in Scotland by Abdul Baha', *Theosophy in Scotland* (Edinburgh), Feb. 1913 (3:10), pp. 167–70. Compare with ' Abdu'l-Bahá, *Promulgation*, pp. 306–8, talk delivered in Montreal on 1 Sept. 1912.
86. ibid. p. 175.
87. I would like to thank David Merrick for kindly sharing with me the text and images of this Tablet. According to Sohrab, 'Abdu'l-Bahá dictated several Tablets for individuals in Scotland on 27 February 1913. The letter bears a note indicating that the translation was done on the same day as its composition.
88. Sohrab, Letter to Harriet Magee, 28 Feb. 1913, p. 2.
89. 'Bahai Meetings', *Theosophy in Scotland* (Edinburgh), June 1913, p. 25.
90. 'Between the Covers', ibid. p. 31.
91. 'The Search for Truth', ibid. July 1913, p. 42; 'Unity of Mankind', Aug. 1913, p. 58; 'Love', Sept. 1913, p. 73; 'Religion and Science', Dec. 1913, p. 111.
92. 'Bahaia Beno', ibid. Sept. 1913, p. 79.
93. 'Letter from Abdul Baha', *Theosophy in Scotland* (Edinburgh), Oct. 1913, pp. 81–4. It was later published with some differences in *Reality* (New York), Feb. 1921, pp. 7–9, and Ahmad Sohrab, *Abdul Baha in Egypt*, pp. 2–5. The translation is dated 5 July 1913 and the Tablet was presumably written on 1 July.
94. ibid. pp. 83–4. Later published with some differences in *Reality* (New York), Feb. 1921, pp. 7–9, and Ahmad Sohrab, *Abdul Baha in Egypt*, pp. 2–5. The translation is dated 5 July 1913 and the Tablet was presumably written on 1 July.

95. 'Mrs. Besant as Seen by Abdul Baha', *Theosophy in Scotland* (Edinburgh), Feb. 1914, p. 143. For the full text of this letter see Ahmad Sohrab, *Abdul Baha in Egypt*, pp. 254–5.
96. For Persian notes of this talk see 'Abdu'l-Bahá. *Majmu'ih-i-Khatábát-i-Hadrat-i-'Abdu'l-Bahá*, vol. 3, pp. 57–61. For a summary see Sohrab, Letter to Harriet Magee, 13 Feb.1913, pp. 11–13.
97. 'Société Théosophique de France. Causerie par Abdou'l Baha', *Le Théosophe* (Paris), 1 Mar. 1913.
98. *Theosophy in Scotland* (Edinburgh), May 1913, p. 5.
99. 'Echos du Monde Théosophique', *Revue Théosophique Française* (Paris), 27 Mar. 1913, p. 23.
100. 'Revue de Revues', ibid. p. 27.
101. 'Revue de Revues', *Revue Théosophique Française* (Paris), 27 June 1913, p. 124.

35 Spiritualism and Esotericism

1. She sometimes used the pseudonym Felix Rudolph.
2. 'A Wise Man from the East', *International Psychic Gazette* (London), Jan. 1913 (6:1), p. 158.
3. 'Theosophical Magazines', *Review of Reviews* (London), Feb. 1913, p. 215, col. 2.
4. ibid.
5. 'The Bab and Babeeism', *Review of Reviews* (London), 15 July 1896, pp. 57–8. Review of J. D. Rees's 'The Bab and Babeeism', *Nineteenth Century* (London), July 1896, pp. 56–66.
6. 'The New Messiah? A Bahai Apostle', *Review of Reviews* (London), Mar. 1907, p. 251. Parts of this article were reproduced as 'Cosas', in the Spanish journal *La Publicidad* (Barcelona), 7 May 1907, p. 1, col. 5.
7. *Review of Reviews* (London), Mar. 1907, p. 291. Review of Sydney Sprague's 'Bahaism or a Universal Religion' in *Theosophical Review* (London), Jan. 1907, pp. 410–19 and Feb. 1907, pp. 495–502.
8. 'The Persian Messiah', *Review of Reviews* (London), Apr. 1907, p. 393. James Rendell Harris (1852–1941) was a biblical scholar, and discoverer and curator of several biblical manuscripts in Syriac. He was also a member of the Society of Friends and president of the Free Church Federation, an organization with which several nonconformist and independent churches in Britain were associated.
9. 'Abbas Effendi and the Bahaists', *Review of Reviews* (London), June 1911, p. 601.
10. 'The Reviews Reviewed', *Review of Reviews* (London), April 1912, p. 397.
11. Constance Maud, *Sparks Among the Stubble*, pp. 89–92.
12. 'A Universal Races Congress', *Light* (London), 29 Apr. 1911, p. 198, col. 2.
13. Ebenezer Wake Cook (1843–1926) was a well-known artist and art critic who exhibited regularly at the Royal Academy. He was also president of the Langham Sketch Club and honorary secretary of the Royal British-Colonial Society of Artists. He published various works on art and as a spiritualist also wrote several articles for periodicals such as *Occult Review*. He also published the essay 'Spiritualism' (1903).

14. *Light* (London), 23 Sept. 1911, p. 455, col. 1.
15. 'Le Bahaïsme, fera-t-il la conquête de Paris?', *Excelsior* (Paris), 7 Nov. 1911, p. 2, col. 6.
16. 'La journée', *Le Figaro* (Paris), 9 Nov. 1911, p. 4, col. 6.
17. For the text of this address see *Paris Talks*, pp. 83–8; 'Abdu'l-Bahá, *Majmu'ih-i-Khatábát-i-Hadrat-i-'Abdu'l-Bahá*, vol. 1, pp. 130–7, and *Star of the West*, 2 Feb. 1912 (2:18), pp. 11–12 (Persian section).
18. 'Le chef du Bahaïsme fait une conférence', *Excelsior* (Paris), 10 Nov. 1911.
19. 'Le Bahïsme en France', *Le Siècle* (Paris), 10 Nov. 1911, p. 1, col. 4 (translated by Elham Simmons).
20. Data for November 1912.
21. 'Mahomet complète sa doctrine à l'Athénée Saint-Germain par la voix d'Abdoul-Baha, fils de la Splendeur de Dieu', *La Petite République* (Paris), 10 Nov. 1911 (translated by Elham Simmons).
22. Émile Berr was a permanent redactor on *Le Figaro* and the author of ten novels.
23. Émile Berr, 'Un Prophéte', *Le Figaro* (Paris), 10 Nov. 1911, p. 4, col. 1 (translated by Elham Simmons). 'Abdu'l-Bahá made a reference to this article in a talk given on the same day. See 'Abdu'l-Bahá, *Majmu'ih-i-Khatábát-i-Hadrat-i-'Abdu'l-Bahá*, vol. 1, p. 138.
24. 'Prestige de l'Orient', *Le Gaulois* (Paris), 26 Nov. 1911, p. 1, col. 6 (translated by Elham Simmons).
25. *La Renaissance Contemporaine* (Paris), vol. 5, p. 1392.
26. *Alliance Spiritualiste* (Paris), Jan. 1912.
27. W. J. Colville, 'Abdul Baha Abbas – The Prophet and His Teachings,' *Occult Review* (London), Aug. 1912, pp. 93–7. Also published in the Foreign Edition of the *Occult Review* (New York), Sept. 1912.
28. 'Psychic and Occult Magazines', *Review of Reviews* (London), Aug. 1913, p. 232, col. 2.
29. On August 1913 it published a lengthy article on the Bahá'í Faith by Beatrice Irwin (see chapter 28) and on January 1916 it published a review of *Talks by Abdul Baha* ('Reviews', Jan. 1916, p. 60). These articles appeared in both the London and New York editions of the magazine.
30. Coinciding with 'Abdu'l-Bahá's sojourn in London, the January issue of the *International Psychic Gazette* published the above-mentioned article by Felicia Scatcherd as well as two more articles on the Bahá'í Faith. One was a one-page account of a talk by Arthur Cuthbert delivered to the International Club for Psychical Research on 28 November 1912 ['The Message of the Bahai Movement', Jan. 1913 (6:1), p. 160.]. The other was a brief note publicizing literature on the Bahá'í Faith available to the general public ['Bahai Notes', ibid. p. 179].
31. 'A Wise Man from the East', *International Psychic Gazette*, Jan, 1913 (6:1), p. 158.
32. See Sohrab, Letter to Harriet Magee, 2 Jan. 1913, p. 3.
33. 'Abdul Baha on Reincarnation', *International Psychic Gazette*, Feb. 1913 (7:1), p. 197.
34. See Sohrab, Letter to Harriet Magee, 2 Jan. 1913, p. 3.
35. ibid.
36. 'The Hands of Abdul Baha', *International Psychic Gazette*, Feb. 1913 (7:1), pp. 199–200.

37. Sohrab, Letter to Harriet Magee, 6 Mar. 1913, p. 5.
38. In May 1913 the magazine also carried the text of a talk delivered in Paris to the Alliance Spiritualiste (see below); a one-page article by Elizabeth Herrick on the feast of Riḍván ('The Feast of the Rizwan', May 1913 (10:1), p. 301); and a short report of a farewell meeting for two London Baháʼís, the Jenners, who were leaving for Tasmania ('A Bahai Farewell'. This was a report prepared by Elizabeth Herrick and included verbal statements by ʻAbduʼl-Bahá about the Jenners.). In December 1913 it included an article by Arthur Cuthbert on the Baháʼí Faith ('Bahai Love and Unity', Dec. 1913 (17:2), p. 138). In January 1914 it published a report of words of ʻAbduʼl-Bahá to Lua Getsinger and an account of a farewell meeting for a Persian Baháʼí visiting London (Mirza Hashma Tullah, 'Farewell Meeting to Mirza Ali Akbar', Jan. 1914 (18:2), p. 177). In February it published an article containing words attributed to ʻAbduʼl-Bahá on the meaning of sacrifice. In April of the same year a collection of five letters of ʻAbduʼl-Bahá to Louise R. Waite was published under the title 'The Bahai Nightingale' (Apr. 1914 (21:2), p. 263). Arthur Cuthbert published an article on the Baháʼí new year feast on May 1914 ('Nauroz, the Bahai New Year Feast', May 1914 (22:2), p. 291). In June 1914 a message of ʻAbduʼl-Bahá to the London Baháʼís was also published (see chapter 37). In July of the same year the journal carried a lengthy article by Louise R. Waite on the Baháʼí House of Worship in Chicago ('A Great Bahai Temple in America', July 1914 (24:2), pp. 339–40) and notes of comments made in Haifa by ʻAbduʼl-Bahá on the soul (see chapter 37).
39. 'Notes by the Way', *Light* (London), 22 Mar. 1913, p. 1, col. 1.
40. She gave a talk on the Baháʼí Faith for the Alliance Spiritualiste on 2 May 1912. See *Alliance Spiritualiste* (Paris), July 1912.
41. 'Réception DʻAbdoul Baha Abbas, Chef du Béhaisme, La Paix du Monde et la Fraternité de Lʼorient et de Lʼoccident', *Alliance Spiritualiste* (Paris), Apr. 1913, p. 99.
42. ibid. pp. 100–1.
43. ibid. pp. 102–4.
44. ibid. pp. 104–11. For an announcement of the publication of this talk see *Mysteria* (Paris), June 1913, p. 284.
45. 'Abdul Baha on Universal Peace', *International Psychic Gazette*, May 1913 (10:1), pp. 299–300.
46. For notes of this conversation see Sohrab, Letter to Harriet Magee, 26 Feb. 1913, pp. 2–11.
47. Bowers, *Spiritualismʼs Challenge*, p. 53.
48. ibid. p. 69.

36 Opposition

1. For a clear example see 'A Voice from the East', *Congregationalist and Christian World* (Boston), 4 July 1912, pp. 10–11.
2. *Christian* (London), 21 Sept. 1911, p. 10, col. 1.
3. *English Churchman and St. Jamesʼs Chronicle* (London), 14 Sept. 1911, p. 591, col. 3.
4. 'The Message of Bahaism', *English Churchman and St. Jamesʼs Chronicle*, 29 Sept. 1911, p. 626, col. 3.

5. 'Bahaism a Warning', *Evangelical Christendom* (London), Sept.–Oct. 1911, pp. 186–8. The same issue contained on page 166 an editorial about the article which quoted a lengthy portion of the account published in *The Christian Commonwealth* about the visit of 'Abdu'l-Bahá to the City Temple. The tone of this editorial was neutral.
6. 'Warns Americans Against Abdul Baha', *Sun* (New York), 21 Apr. 1912, p. 3b, col. 1.
7. 'Question Evaded by Abdul Baha', *Washington Herald*, 25 Apr. 1912, p. 6, col. 5.
8. 'Doctrine of Bahaism', *Washington Herald*, 28 Apr. 1912.
9. See, for instance, 'Babism. Its doctrines and relation to mission work', *Missionary Review of the World* (New York), July, 1894, pp. 894–904.
10. 'Bahaism and its Claims', *Missionary Review of the World* (New York), Oct. 1911, pp. 727–34.
11. 'Bahaism and its Claims', *Evangelical Christendom* (London), Nov.-Dec. 1911, pp. 210–14.
12. 'Bahaism', *British Weekly* (London), 7 Dec. 1911, p. 300, col. 4.
13. 'Bahaism', *Evangelical Christendom* (London), Nov.-Dec., 1911, pp. 199.
14. 'Encore le Behaïsme', *Le Christianisme au XX siècle* (Paris), 19 Jan. 1912, pp. 18–19.
15. *Missionary Review of the World* (New York), Sept. 1912 (35:9), pp. 699–700.
16. *Woman's Work* (New York), July 1912 (27:7).
17. Rice, 'Bahaism from the Christian Standpoint', *East and the West* (London), Jan. 1913, pp. 22–43.
18. 'Visit of Abdul Baha to Great Britain', *Moslem World* (London), Apr. 1913, p. 196. The same issue contains a highly critical review of Phelps's *Abbas Effendi* (pp. 206–10).
19. 'Episcopal Ban on Persian Leader', *Baltimore News* (Baltimore), 27 Apr. 1912. Information based on *The Churchman* (New York).
20. *Living Church* (Milwaukee), 6 July 1912.
21. 'Methodist', *Washington Herald* (Washington), 27 Apr. 1912, p. 4, col. 2.
22. 'Liken Abdul Baha to Forty Thieves', *Washington Herald*, 29 Apr. 1912, p. 7, col. 3.
23. 'Pray for Abdul Baha', *Washington Post*, 29 Apr. 1912, p. 7, col. 6.
24. 'Assails Bahai Leader and Persian Veracity', *Evening Star* (Washington), 6 May 1912.
25. 'Score Abdul Baha as False Prophet', *Star* (Baltimore), 27 May 1912.
26. 'Sermons Devoted to Peace', *Washington Post*, 16 Dec. 1912, p. 4, col. 5.
27. At the time of writing this article William Thomas McElroy (d. 1963) was minister at Louisville, Kentucky. He became the editor of *The Christian Observer* (Louisville, KY).
28. 'The Babi-Bahai Movement', *Christian Advocate* (Nashville, TN), 1 Nov. 1912.
29. Text reproduced in 'Beha Persian Messiah', *Illustrated Buffalo Express*, 7 Apr. 1912.
30. *Continent* (Chicago), 30 May 1912, p. 757.
31. 'The Real Bahaism and its Prophet', *Continent* (Chicago), 30 May 1912, p. 760. Ellis mentioned 'Abdu'l-Bahá twice more in his articles. In September 1916 he wrote about the concept of universal religion and stated that 'Abbas Effendi, one

memorable night in Egypt, expounded at length to me his theories about the universality of Behaism. This idea of world religion, which all men would one day accept, has an especial allurement for most thoughtful persons. To the intelligent Christian it is inwrought in his faith. He cannot believe in Christ at all unless he believes that Christ designed His message and His salvation for all mankind everywhere.' See 'The Final Faith of Man', *Augusta Chronicle*, 24 Sept. 1916, and 'Final Faith of Man', *Idaho Statesman* (Boise), 24 Sept. 1916, p. 5, col. 5. See chapter 38 for a brief reference by Ellis to the fact that 'Abdu'l-Bahá predicted the World War.

32. 'Church and its Work', *Evening Press* (Grand Rapids, MI), 20 June 1912, p. 6, col. 4.
33. This sermon was announced in at least one local paper: 'Holland–Michigan Street and North Ionia Avenue, Rev. B. A. Van Sluyters, pastor. 10:30 a.m., "Abdul Baha and His reminder".' See 'Sunday Services', *Evening Press* (Grand Rapids, MI), 22 June 1912, p. 6, col. 4.
34. 'Church and its Work', *Evening Press* (Grand Rapids, MI), 24 June 1912, p. 6, col. 4.
35. Dirk Dykstra, originally from Wjelsryp, Netherlands, was a member of the Reformed Church in America who held different missionary positions in Arab countries between 1907 and 1948.
36. 'Says Mormonism is as Bad as Painted', *Evening Press* (Grand Rapids, MI), 7 Oct. 1912, p. 3, col. 4.
37. *Unity* (Chicago), 6 June 1912, pp. 211–12.
38. 'Oriental Doctrines are not New', *Montreal Daily Witness*, 10 Sept. 1912, p. 2, col. 3.
39. See for instance 'The Coming of an Eastern Messiah', *Flaming Sword* (Estero, FL), Feb. 1912, pp. 50–1; *Flaming Sword* (Estero, FL), June 1912, p. 185. The issue of March 1912 reports an article in the New Thought magazine *Nautilus*, announcing, among other prophecies, that 'the religions of Rome, Russia, and Mohammed are to meet changes. The teachings of Abdul Baha will assume prominence.' (p. 89).
40. Rev. C. C. Martindale, 'Inter-Racial Problems', *Month* (London), Oct. 1911, pp. 353–63.
41. W. P. S., 'The Problem of Universal Peace', *Catholic World* (New York), July 1912 (95:568), pp. 516–26.
42. 'Baha', *San Francisco Monitor*, 5 Oct. 1912, p. 4, col. 3.
43. 'Bahai Leader a Stoic', *San Francisco Call*, 14 Oct. 1912, pp. 1–2.
44. 'Baha', *San Francisco Monitor*, 26 Oct. 1912, p. 2, col. 4.
45. *New Age* (London), 21 Sept. 1911 (9:21), p. 484, col. 2. Years earlier this magazine had published reviews of Sprague's *Bahaism* and of *Some Answered Questions*. See 'Mayle's Penny Series', *New Age* (London), 21 Mar. 1908 (2:21), p. 414, col. 2; and 'Some Answered Questions', 22 Aug. 1908 (3:17), p. 336, col. 1.
46. Charles Brookfarmer, 'Baa! or, Another False Prophet in Sheep's Clothing', *New Age* (London), 26 Feb. 1914 (14:17), pp. 524–5.
47. Abul Mutaqim, 'Prophet and Priest', *New Age* (London), 28 Jan. 1915 (16:13), p. 342.
48. Eric Hammond, 'Prophet and Peace, *New Age* (London), 25 Feb. 1915 (16:17), p. 471.

49. C. E. Bechhöfer, 'Letters from Russia', *New Age* (London), 7 Oct. 1915 (16:13), pp. 545–6. In an article on a different subject Bechhöfer mentions briefly 'Abdu'l-Bahá as the 'Bahai charlatan', see 'Letters from Russia', 18 Nov. 1915 (16:13), p. 64.
50. 'Blast', *The Blast* (London), 20 June 1914, p. 21.
51. 'Sweet Religion', *Daily Citizen* (Manchester ed.), 2 Jan. 1913, p. 4, col. 3. The magazine *Light* (London) mentions on 11 January 1913 another article about the Baháʼí Faith in the *Daily Citizen*, probably in the London edition. Since the collections of this journal are incomplete, the present author had been unable to locate it. According to *Light*, the article in the *Citizen* stated, among other things, that the Baháʼí Faith is not a religion. This prompted a letter to the editor published on 25 January and sent to Jessie Vesel in an attempt to correct the statements in the *Citizen*.
52. ibid. 6 Jan. 1913, p. 3, col. 4.
53. 'Bahaism and Christianity', *Evening Dispatch* (Edinburgh), 8 Jan. 1913, p. 4.
54. 'The Bahai Faith', *Evening Dispatch* (Edinburgh), 11 Jan. 1913, p. 4, cols. 2–3.
55. 'The Bahai Revelation', *Evening Dispatch* (Edinburgh), 13 Jan. 1913, p. 4, col. 2.
56. 'Bahaism and Christianity', *Scotsman* (Edinburgh), 13 Jan. 1913, p. 10.
57. 'Bahaism only New Theology', *Evening News* (Edinburgh), 11 Jan. 1913, p. 4, col. 9.
58. 'Abdul Baha's Farewell', *Christian Commonwealth*, 15 Jan. 1913, p. 292, col. 3.
59. 'A Dilemma About Demons', *Daily News and Leader* (London), 18 Jan. 1913, p. 4, col. 5.
60. 'The Apostle of Paradox', *Christian Commonwealth*, 22 Jan. 1913, p. 309, col. 2.
61. Henry Snell, 'Persian Idealism and Christian Orthodoxy', *Ethical World* (London), 15 Feb. 193, p. 20.
62. 'To Question Leader', *Evening News* (Kenosha, WI), 11 May 1912.
63. 'Abdul Baha Ready to Face Malcontents', *Chicago Examiner*, 7 May 1912, p. 4, col. 3.
64. 'Challenge for Bahai Chief', *Chicago Sunday Tribune*, 12 May 1912, p. 8, col. 2.
65. 'Challenge for Baha Chief', *Evening News* (Kenosha, WI), 28 May 1912.
66. 'Dove in Fight While Bearing Peace Message', *San Francisco Call*, 13 Oct. 1912, p. 17, col. 4; and 'Peace Advocates Row Over Power', p. 24, col. 7.
67. 'Abdul Baha in Los Angeles', *Los Angeles Examiner*, 20 Oct. 1912, p. 1, 11, col. 2. Portrait included.
68. 'Bahai Leader a Stoic', *San Francisco Call*, 14 Oct. 1912, p. 1, col. 5; and 'Abbas Turns Deaf Ear to Charges', p. 2, col. 6. The article included the portrait of 'Abdu'l-Bahá distributed by Underwood & Underwood.

37 Return to Haifa

1. 'Table Talk', *Christian Commonwealth* (London), 14 Jan. 1914, p. 290, col. 2.
2. Holbach, *Bible Ways in Bible Lands*, pp. 5–9. For a brief mention of 'Abdu'l-Bahá in connection with this work see 'New Publications', *Friend* (London), p. 95, col. 1.
3. See Sohrab, Letter to Harriet Magee, 20 May 1913, p. 3, and 21 May 1913, p. 5.
4. 'The Bahai Movement: With Some Recollections of Meetings with Abdul Baha', *Nineteenth Century and After* (London), Feb. 1915, pp. 452–66. This article was

advertised in *Army and Navy Gazette* (London), 30 Jan. 1915, p. 86.
5. 'The Bahai Movement: With Some Recollections of Meetings with Abdul Baha', *Nineteenth Century and After* (London), Feb. 1915, pp. 461–4.
6. ibid. p. 460.
7. ibid. p. 465.
8. 'Abdul Baha at Home', *Christian Commonwealth* (London), 21 Jan. 1914, p. 311, col. 3. The same journal published on 18 Feb. information about the activities of Mrs Stannard in India, see 'The Bahai Movement in India,' p. 377, col. 2. The article mentions the publication of an article on the Bahá'í Faith in the *Sind Gazette* (Karachi).
9. 'On Mount Carmel: A Modern Prophet and His Message', *Christian Commonwealth* (London), 28 Jan. 1914, p. 315, col. 1.
10. 'The Bahai Temple, Chicago', *Christian Commonwealth* (London), 6 Feb. 1914, p. 342, col. 3.
11. 'Death of Famous Bahai', *Christian Commonwealth* (London), 11 Feb. 1914, p. 364, col. 2.
12. 'Bahai Pilgrims at Haifa', *Christian Commonwealth* (London), 4 Mar. 1914, p. 399, col. 4.
13. 'Bahai Temple in Russia', *Christian Commonwealth* (London), 25 Mar. 1914, p. 459, col. 2.
14. ibid. p. 454.
15. 'Abdul Baha's Thanks for New Year's Greeting', *International Psychic Gazette* (London), June 1914, p. 315.
16. 'Mohammedans in Christian Churches', *Christian Commonwealth* (London), 1 April 1914, p. 473, col. 2.
17. 'Abdul Baha on the Divinity of Christ', *Christian Commonwealth* (London), 8 Apr. 1914, p. 491, col. 2. Letter dated 15 Mar. 1914.
18. 'Bahai News', *Christian Commonwealth* (London), 17 June 1914, p. 667, col. 4.
19. 'Abdul Baha at Home', *Christian Commonwealth* (London), 15 Apr. 1914, p. 508, col. 1.
20. 'News of the Bahai Movement', *Christian Commonwealth* (London), 22 Apr. 1914, p. 523, col. 1.
21. 'The Breaking Down of Caste', *Christian Commonwealth* (London), 29 Apr. 1914, p. 536, col. 2.
22. 'The Bahai Movement', *Christian Commonwealth* (London), 13 May 1914, p. 574, col. 3.
23. 'Bahai News', *Christian Commonwealth* (London), 27 May 1914, p. 608, col. 1.
24. 'Abdul Baha at Tiberias', *Christian Commonwealth* (London), 3 June 1914, p. 625, col. 2.
25. 'Bahai News', *Christian Commonwealth* (London), 24 June 1914, p. 681, col. 3.
26. 'Bahai News', *Christian Commonwealth* (London), 15 July 1914, p. 733, col. 3.
27. 'The Latest Photo of Abdul Baha', *Christian Commonwealth* (London), 22 July 1914, p. 749, col. 3.
28. 'Bahai News', *Christian Commonwealth* (London), 22 July 1914, p. 751, col. 2.
29. 'Bahai News', *Christian Commonwealth* (London), 30 Sept. 1914, p. 876, col. 4.
30. 'Bahai News', *Christian Commonwealth* (London), 7 Oct. 1914, p. 8 col. 4. A much lengthier account by Ahmad Sohrab was published in 'An Interview with

Abdul Baha', *Star of the West*, 28 April 1916 (7:3), pp. 20–2.
31. 'Abdul Baha's Correspondence', *Christian Commonwealth* (London), 11 Nov. 1914, p. 69, col. 3.
32. 'Bahai News', *Christian Commonwealth* (London), 6 Jan. 1915, p. 188, col. 2.
33. 'From Abdul Baha to T.K. Cheyne', *Christian Commonwealth* (London), 31 Dec. 1913, p. 261, col. 4.
34. 'Message from Abdul Baha', *Christian Commonwealth* (London), 25 Feb. 1914, p. 386, col. 2.
35. 'Bahai Pilgrims at Haifa', *Christian Commonwealth* (London), 4 Mar. 1914, p. 399, col. 4.
36. 'Sheffield Minister's Mission', *Sheffield Daily Telegraph*, 2 March 1914, p. 7, col. 6.
37. Archie Bell, 'Along Holy Bypaths – XXV', *Plain Dealer* (Cleveland, OH), 11 Aug. 1914, p. 8, col. 6.
38. Archie Bell, 'Along Holy Bypaths – XXIX', *Plain Dealer* (Cleveland, OH), 18 Aug. 1914, p. 6, col. 6.
39. Archie Bell, 'Along Holy Bypaths – XXX', *Plain Dealer* (Cleveland, OH), 19 Aug. 1914, p. 6, col. 6.
40. 'Survival and Salvation', *International Psychic Gazette* (London), July 1914, pp. 341–2.

38 The War Years

1. 'Religious Side of War in Europe Important Factor', *Idaho Statesman* (Boise), 9 Aug. 1914, p. 2, col. 5.
2. 'To Combat War', *Mercury* (Hobart, Australia), 8 Aug. 1914, p. 8.
3. 'Paroles Prophétiques Prononcées par Abdou'l-Baha, le Chef du Behaisme, lors de son Séjour a Paris en 1913', *Bulletin Théosophique* (Paris), Mar. 1916 (17:1), p. 41.
4. 'A Call to Peace from the Holy Land', *Christian Commonwealth* (London), 2 Sept.1914, p. 832, col. 3.
5. 'War and Peace', *Christian Commonwealth* (London), 16 Sept. 1914, p. 856, col. 2.
6. 'Bahai News', *Christian Commonwealth* (London), 18 Nov. 1914, p. 82, col. 2.
7. 'The Voice of Universal Peace', *Christian Commonwealth* (London), 9 Dec. 1914, p. 137, col. 1. This Tablet was later published as 'The Voice of Universal Peace', *Star of the West*, Feb. 1928 (18:11), pp. 342–6.
8. 'Bahai News', *Christian Commonwealth* (London), 16 Dec. 1914, p. 150, col. 1.
9. 'Bahai News', *Christian Commonwealth* (London), 30 Dec. 1914, p. 176, col. 3.
10. 'Bahai News', *Christian Commonwealth* (London), 17 Feb. 1915, p. 260, col. 1.
11. 'Bahai News', *Christian Commonwealth* (London), 24 Feb. 1915, p. 271, col. 3.
12. 'Bahai News', *Christian Commonwealth* (London), 3 Mar. 1915, p. 283, col. 3.
13. 'Bahai News', *Christian Commonwealth* (London), 10 Mar. 1915, p. 294, col. 2.
14. 'Bahai News ', *Christian Commonwealth* (London), 31 Mar. 1915, p. 335, col. 2.
15. Probably Sakinih Sultan, the widow of a Bahá'í martyr, and her grandson. See Balyuzi, *'Abdu'l-Bahá*, p. 534, note 233.
16. 'Bahai News', *Christian Commonwealth* (London), 12 May 1915, p. 407, col. 2.
17. 'Bahai News', *Christian Commonwealth* (London), 26 May 1915, p. 431, col. 4.

18. 'Bahai News', *Christian Commonwealth* (London), 9 June 1915, p. 448, col. 3.
19. 'News of Abdul Baha', *Christian Commonwealth* (London), 22 Sept. 1915, p. 636, col. 1. See 'Latest News of Abdul Baha', *Star of the West*, 24 June 1915 (6:6), p. 43.
20. 'Bahai News', *Christian Commonwealth* (London), 20 Oct. 1915, p. 39, col. 3.
21. 'Bahai News', *Christian Commonwealth* (London), 27 Oct. 1915, p. 52, col. 1.
22. 'Bahai News', *Christian Commonwealth* (London), 3 Nov. 1915, p. 64, col. 2.
23. 'Bahai News', *Christian Commonwealth* (London), 12 Jan. 1916.
24. 'Bahai News', *Christian Commonwealth* (London), 22 Mar. 1916, p. 332, col. 2.
25. 'Bahai News', *Christian Commonwealth* (London), 16 Aug. 1916, p. 584, col. 2; 'Bahai News', *Christian Commonwealth* (London), 1 Nov. 1916, p. 58, col. 2; 'Abdul Baha at Baha-jee', *Star of the West*, 1 Aug. 1916 (7:8), pp. 73–4.
26. 'Conditions in the Holy Land', *Christian Commonwealth* (London), 17 Jan. 1917, p. 213, col. 4.
27. See 'Bahai News', *Christian Commonwealth* (London), 28 Feb. 1917, p. 276, col. 4; 'News of Abdul Baha', *Christian Commonwealth* (London), 5 Sept. 1917, p. 608, col. 1.
28. 'News of Abdul Baha', *Christian Commonwealth* (London), 5 Dec. 1918, p. 123, col. 3.
29. 'Abdul Baha's Letter', *Christian Commonwealth* (London), 12 Dec. 1917, p. 137, col. 2.
30. See 'Prophet Praises Carnegie', *New York Times*, 11 Oct. 1913, p. 12, col. 5.
31. 'Persian Peace Cry Sent to Carnegie', *Sun* (New York), 29 Aug. 1915, p. 3, col. 4.
32. See 'Abdul Baha Abbas Honours Carnegie', *Standard Union* (Brooklyn), 29 Aug. 1915, p. 11, col. 4; 'Carnegie Exalted by Bahaist Leader', *New York Times*, 5 Sept. 1915, 9, col. 1; 'Abdul Baha to Mr. Carnegie on Theme of Universal Peace', *Washington Post*, 12 Sept. 1915, p. 8, col. 1; 'Calls Carnegie Peace King', *Atlantic News Telegraph* (IA), 13 Sept. 1915, p. 5, col. 3; 'Calls Carnegie Peace King', *Pocahontas County Sun* (Laurens, IA), 16 Sept. 1915, p. 3, col. 3; 'Carnegie Exalted by Bahaist Leader', *Buffalo Evening News*, 1 Oct. 1915, p. 6, col. 4.
33. 'Bahai News', *Christian Commonwealth* (London), 19 Jan. 1916, p. 222, col. 4.
34. 'Abdul Baha Abbas Farewell Described', *Christian Science Monitor* (Boston), 1 Nov. 1915, p. 1, col. 7. This sentence is not present in the portion of the letter published months later in *Star of the West*, 16 Oct. 1915 (6:12), p. 90. Lady Blomfield quotes an account by Mírzá Jalál about a visit to Nazareth 'in the beginning of the year 1916' in which 'Abdu'l-Bahá met some two hundred officers of the Turkish Army and personally spoke with Jamál Páshá (see Blomfield, *Chosen Highway*, pp. 204–5). Perhaps Lady Blomfield's dates are wrong and the visit to Nazareth she referred to is the same as the one mentioned by Getsinger as having taken place in late August 1915.
35. 'Abdul Baha of Syria Taken in Raid by Turks', *Christian Science Monitor* (Boston), 28 Oct. 1915, p. 1, col. 7.
36. 'Delenda est Carthago', *Christian Science Monitor* (Boston), 28 Oct. 1915, p. 18.
37. 'News of Abdul Baha', *Christian Commonwealth* (London), 5 Jan. 1916, p. 200, col. 1.

38. 'Turks Seize Bahaist Leader, Topakyan Says', *Evening Post* (New York), 20 Oct. 1915, p. 10, col. 3; 'Abdul Baha Reported Safe', *Evening Post* (New York), 6 Nov. 1915, p. 13, col. 5.
39. Quoted in 'Striking Speech on the Armenian Atrocities Given', *Christian Science Monitor* (Boston), 15 Dec. 1915, p. 2, col. 4. This speech was probably delivered on 12 October 1915.
40. 'Abdul Baha Safe and is Reported Near Tiberias', *Christian Science Monitor* (Boston), 29 Oct. 1915, p. 7, col. 1. Portrait of 'Abdu'l-Bahá included.
41. 'Abdul Baha Reported Safe', *Evening Post* (New York), 6 Nov. 1915, p. 13, col. 5.
42. 'Abdul Baha Now Reported Back in Haifa, Syria', *Christian Science Monitor* (Boston), 26 Nov. 1915, p. 7, col. 1.
43. 'British Troops Find Abdul Baha at Haifa', *New York Herald*, 18 Oct. 1918, p. 4, col. 7. Also published in 'Persian Prophet Discovered by British Troops', *Bridgeport Telegram* (CT), 18 Oct. 1918, p. 16, col. 5; 'Abdul Baha Found at Haifa', *Christian Science Monitor* (Boston), 18 Oct. 1918, p. 9, col. 4; 'Baha Prophet Rescued', *Daily Northwestern* (Oshkosh, WI), 18 Oct. 1918, p. 12, col. 6; *Herald Dispatch* (Utica, NY), 18 Oct. 1918, p. 10, col. 4; 'Find Prophet Abdul Baha', *Philadelphia Inquirer*, 18 Oct. 1918, p. 8, col. 2; 'British Troops Find Leader of Bahaists', *Sun* (New York), 18 Oct. 1918, p. 3, col. 3; 'Prophet Baha Found at Haifa', *Washington Post*, 18 Oct. 1918, p. 10, col. 6; 'British Troops Have Discovered Abdul Baha', *Waterloo Times-Tribune* (IA), 18 Oct. 1918, p. 2, col. 3. In Canada this news was published in at least the following newspapers: 'Persian Prophet Found by British', *Chronicle* (Shellbrook, Saskatchewan), 29 Oct. 1918, p. 2, col. 6; 'Persian Prophet Found by British', *Mail* (Drumheller, Alberta), 28 Nov. 1918, p. 5, col. 6; 'Persian Prophet Found by British', *Claresholm Review* (Alberta), 29 Nov. 1912, p. 2, col. 6; 'Persian Prophet Found by the British', *Empress Express* (Alberta), 5 Dec. 1918, p. 6; 'Persian Prophet Found by the British', *Rivers Gazette* (Manitoba), 5 Dec. 1918, p. 6, col. 6; 'Persian Prophet Found by the British', *Bow Island Review* (Alberta), 22 Dec. 1918, p. 2. Some articles added general information about 'Abdu'l-Bahá and the Bahá'í Faith. See 'Capture of the Babist Prophet', *Morning Oregonian* (Portland), 26 Oct. 1918, p. 8, col. 2; 'Abdul Baha the Head of the Bahaist Faith', *Kansas City Star*, 30 Oct. 1913, p. 12, col. 4.
44. See Blomfield, *Chosen Highway*, pp. 219–30 and *The Two Worlds of Wellesley Tudor Pole*, pp. 94–8.
45. 'Abdul Baha', *Palestine News*, 19 Dec. 1918, p. 11, col. 1.
46. 'Abdul Baha and Esperanto', *Palestine News*, 26 Dec. 1918, p. 3, col. 1.
47. 'Palestine of Tomorrow', *Christian Commonwealth* (London), 24 Sept. 1919, p. 614, col. 3.
48. 'News of Abdul Baha', *Christian Commonwealth* (London), 15 Jan. 1919, p. 174, col. 4.
49. 'News of Abdul Baha', *Christian Commonwealth* (London), 22 Jan. 1919, p. 196, col. 4.
50. 'Pilgrims in the Holy Land', *Times* (London), 17 Sept. 1919, p. 9, col. 1.
51. See 'A Modern Prophet', *Christian Commonwealth* (London), 24 Sept. 1919, p. 622, col. 3; 'The Prophets of Today Are Martyred as Those of Old', *Kansas City Star*, 10 Oct. 1919, p. 24, col. 4.

52. 'News in a Nutshell', *Evening Telegram* (New York), 16 Dec. 1918, p. 6, col. 1. Also published as 'Prophet is Alive and Well', in the *New York Times*, 16 Dec. 1918, p. 4, col. 4; 'Founder of Bahaist Cult Alive in East', *Plattsburgh Sentinel* (New York), 17 Dec. 1918, p. 5, col. 3.
53. Published under the title 'Religious Cult May Spread', *Cannelton Telephone* (IN), 9 Jan. 1919, p. 2, col. 3; *Auburn Citizen* (New York), 11 Jan. 1919; *Nunda News* (NY), 11 Jan. 1919; *Wanatah Mirror* (Indiana), 12 Jan. 1919; *Montour Fall Free Press* (NY), 16 Jan. 1919; *Newark Advocate* (OH), 16 Jan. 1919, p. 6, col. 4; *Hobart Daily Republican* (OK), 22 Jan. 1919; *Phelps Citizen* (NY), 23 Jan. 1919; *Tyrone Daily Herald* (PA), 25 Jan. 1919, p. 5, col. 6; *Ballston Spa Daily Journal* (NY), 28 Jan. 1919; *Herald* (New Orleans), 30 Jan. 1919, p. 3, col. 4; *Waterville Times* (NH), 7 Feb. 1919, p. 6, col. 3; *Alton Evening Telegraph* (IL), 11 Feb. 1919, p. 6, col. 4; *Kingston Daily Freeman* (NY), 11 Feb. 1919, p. 9, col. 7; *Hamilton Evening Journal* (OH), 27 Feb. 1919, p. 4, col. 5; *Alton Democrat* (IL), 8 Mar. 1919, p. 6, col. 5; *Manitowoc Herald-News* (WI), 8 Mar. 1919, p. 3, col. 3; *Twin Falls Daily Times* (ID), 10 Mar. 1919, p. 2, col. 4; *Kokoma Daily Tribune* (IN), 12 Mar. 1919, p. 6, col. 2; *Park Record* (UT), 14 Mar. 1919, p. 3, col. 4; *Creede Candle* (CO), 22 Mar. 1919, p. 5, col. 1; *Dispatch Democrat* (Ukiah, CA), 11 Apr. 1919, p. 6, col. 6; *Logansport Daily Tribune* (Logansport), 11 Apr. 1919, p. 2, col. 5; *Marshall News-Statesman* (MI), 18 Apr. 1919, p. 1, col. 5; *Mountain Democrat* (Placerville, CA), 10 May 1919, p. 19, col. 5; *Charleroi Mail* (PA), 11 July 1919, p. 2, col. 1; *Charleroi Mail* (PA), 11 July 1919, p. 2, col. 1; *Chehalis Bee-Nuget* (WA), 25 July 1919, p. 7, col. 4.
54. From 1895 to 1912 Sulzer was a member of the US House of Representatives. In 1913 he was elected governor of New York but he kept his position for only a few months after he was impeached. Sulzer was a close friend of the Bahá'í Wendell Dodge and had collaborated with the Persian–American Educational Society. He met 'Abdu'l-Bahá in 1912 and wrote a fine article on the Bahá'í Faith published as 'What is Bahaism?', *Broad Ax* (Chicago), 14 Feb. 1920, p. 2, col. 2.
55. *World* (New York), 6 Oct. 1919.
56. Fawcett, 'Two spring visits to Palestine', *Woman's Leader* and *Common Cause* (London), 19 Dec. 1924, p. 376, col. 1.
57. 'Palestina', *Nieuwe Rotterdamsche Courant* (Rotterdam), 2 Apr. 1921, p. 2c. Translated by Tina Vonhof.
58. 'Palestina', *Nieuwe Rotterdamsche Courant* (Rotterdam), 13 Aug. 1921, p. 1b. Translated by Tina Vonhof.
59. P. W. Wilson, 'At the Cross-Roads of Three Continents', *World's Work* (Garden City), July 1922, p. 328.
60. For details of the knighthood of 'Abdu'l-Bahá see Momen, *Bábí and Bahá'í Religions*, pp. 343–5.
61. *L'Asie Arabe* (Paris), 15 Jan. 1920, p. 4, col. 1.

39. The Passing of 'Abdu'l-Bahá

1. For an account of the passing of 'Abdu'l-Bahá see 'The Passing of Abdul Baha' (1922) prepared by Shoghi Effendi and Lady Blomfield.
2. 'Death of the Bahai', *Times* (London), 30 Nov. 1921, p. 9, col. 2. A brief note also appeared on p. 11, col. 1 of the same issue.

3. 'Death of Leader of Bahai Cult', *Aberdeen Journal*, 30 Nov. 1921, p. 6, col. 5; 'Death of Leader of Bahai Cult', *Glasgow Herald*, 30 Nov. 1921, p. 9, col. 4; 'Founder of Bahaism', *Irish Times* (Dublin), 30 Nov. 1921, p. 5; 'Sir Abdul Baha Dead', *Daily Mail* (London), 1 Dec. 1921, p. 5, col. 5; 'Personalities of the Week', *Illustrated News* (London), 10 Dec. 192; included a portrait.
4. 'Late Wire News', *Aberdeen Weekly News* (SD), 1 Dec. 1921, p. 1, col. 1; 'Abdul Baha Abbas, Bahai Leader, Death', *Anaconda Standard* (MT), 1 Dec. 1921, p. 1, col. 7; 'Bahai Movement Leader is Dead', *Los Angeles Times*, p. 1, col. 3; 'Peace by Unity in Religion Leader Dies', *Beatrice Daily Sun* (NE), 1 Dec. 1921, p. 1, col. 1; 'Abdul Baha, Leader of Bahaists, Dead', *Boston Daily Globe*, 1 Dec. 1921, p. 17, col. 5; 'Abdul Baha Abbas Dead', *Bradford Era* (PA), 1 Dec. 1921, p. 1, col. 3; 'Bahai Leader Dead', *Casper Daily Tribune* (Casper, WY), 1 Dec. 1921, p. 1, p. 4; 'Bahaists Mourn Leader's Death', *Chicago Daily Tribune*, 1 Dec. 1921, p. 11, col. 4; 'Abdul Baha Abbas Dies', *Dallas Morning News*, 1 Dec. 1921; 'Death Claims Abdul Baha, Who Led Move for World Religion', *Daily Kenneber Journal* (Augusta, ME), 1 Dec. 1921, p. 1, col. 3; 'Bahaist Leader Dead', *Evening Public Ledger* (Philadelphia), 1 Dec. 1921, p. 12, col. 2; included a portrait; 'Abdul Baha Abbas', *Evening Telegram* (New York), 1 Dec. 1921, p. 6, col. 8; 'Syrian leader dies', *Galveston Daily News* (TX), 1 Dec. 1921, p. 2, col. 6; 'Noted Persian Death', *Hamilton Daily News* (OH), 1 Dec. 1921, p. 5, col. 5; 'Leader of Bahaism Dead in Persia', *Hartford Courant* (CT), 1 Dec. 1921, p. 2, col. 7; 'Abdul Baha Dies', *Helena Independent* (Montana), 1 Dec. 1921, p. 1, col. 5; 'Bahai Leader Succumbs', *Idaho Daily Statesman* (Boise), 1 Dec. 1921, p. 2, col. 4; 'Abbas Effendi, Leader Among Bahaists, Dies', *Indianapolis Star*, 1 Dec. 1921, p. 5, col. 4; 'Man Who Advocated Religious Unity Dies', *Joplin Globe* (MO), 1 Dec. 1921, p. 5, col. 5; 'Bahai Move Leader Dead', *Lexington Herald* (KY), 1 Dec. 1921, p. 8, col. 5; 'Bahai Leader is Dead', *Morning Oregonian* (Portland), 1 Dec. 1921, p. 9, col. 3; 'Abdul Abbas Dies', *Logansport Morning Press* (IN), p. 1, col. 6; 'Death of the Bahai Leader', *Nebraska State Journal* (Lincoln), 1 Dec. 1921, p. 9, col. 1; 'Bahai Cult Leader Expires in Syria', *New York Times*, 1 Dec. 1921, p. 16, col. 5; 'Abdul Baha, Religious Leader, Dies in Persia', *New York Tribune*, 1 Dec. 1921, p. 1, col. 4; 'Leader of Turkish Brotherhood Cult Dies', *Oakland Tribune*, 1 Dec. 1921, p. 1, col. 7; 'Abdul Baha Dies', *Philadelphia Inquirer*, 1 Dec. 1921, p. 2, col. 8; 'Abdul Baha Dead', *Standard Union* (Brooklyn), 1 Dec. 1921, p. 7, col. 3; 'World Unity Leader Dies in Persia', *Syracuse Herald*, 1 Dec. 1921, p. 16, col. 2; 'Bahai Cult Leader Dead', *Troy Times* (Troy, NY), 1 Dec. 1921, p. 1, col. 4; 'Abdul Baha Abbad Dead', *Washington Post*, 1 Dec. 1921, p. 14, col. 1; 'Abdul Baha Dies After Long Life at Head of Cult', *World* (New York), 1 Dec. 1921, p. 1, col. 2; 'Abdul Baha Abbas Dies at Haifa, Persia', *Plattsburgh Sentinel* (New York), 2 Dec. 1921, p. 1, col. 7; 'No Successor to Baha, Council of 12 Directs World', *Evening Telegram* (New York), 2 Dec. 1921, p. 10, col. 6; 'Bahaist Mourn Leader's Death', *Broad Axe* (Chicago), 3 Dec. 1921, p. 1, col. 5; 'Twelve in Bahai Council to Direct Baha's Work', *Utica Morning Telegram* (Utica, NY), 3 Dec. 1921, p. 1, col. 2; 'Baha Left no Successor', *Washington Post*, 3 Dec. 1921, p. 4, col. 3; 'Foreign', *Starke County Democrat* (Knox, IN), 7 Dec. 1921, p. 2, col. 3; 'Foreign', *Altoona Herald* (IA), 8 Dec. 1921, p. 6, col. 2; 'Foreign', *Anita Tribune* (Iowa), 8 Dec.

1921, p. 6, col. 2; 'Foreign', *Darlington Herald* (IN), 8 Dec. 1921, p. 8, col. 2; 'Foreign', *Lytton Star* (IA), 8 Dec. 1921, p. 2, col. 4; 'Foreign', *Marble Rock Journal* (IA), 8 Dec. 1921, p. 4, col. 2; 'Foreign', *Roland Record* (IA), 8 Dec. 1921, p. 2, col. 2; 'Foreign', *Cannelton Telephone* (IA), 9 Dec. 1921, p. 7, col. 2.
5. 'Abdul Baha Abbas Dies', *Manitoba Free Press* (Winnipeg), 1 Dec. 1921, p. 3, col. 6.
6. 'Fallece en Siria el Jefe del Movimiento Religioso Bahai', *Diario de la Marina* (Havana, Cuba), 1 Dec. 1921, p. 4, col. 4.
7. 'Advocate of Uniting Religions Dies in Syria', *Japan Advertiser* (Tokyo), 1 Dec. 1921, p. 10, col. 4.
8. 'Bahai Cult Leader Expires in Syria', *New York Times*, 1 Dec. 1921, p. 16, col. 5.
9. 'Bahaists Mourn Leader's Death', *Chicago Daily Tribune*, 1 Dec. 1921, p. 11, col. 4.
10. 'Abdul Baha', *New-York Tribune*, 2 Dec. 1921, p. 12, col. 3.
11. 'Abdul Baha's Mission Ends', *Boston Herald*, 2 Dec. 1921, p. 22, col. 3.
12. 'Abdul Baha', *Standard Union* (Brooklyn), 2 Dec. 1921, p. 22.
13. 'Bahai', *Lima News* (OH), 6 Dec. 1921, p. 8, col. 2; 'Bahai', *Wichita Daily Times* (TX), 6 Dec. 1921, p. 6, col. 5.
14. 'The Bahaite of Manhattan, Disciples of the Late Abdul Baha, Prophet of World Peace Claimed by Death as Arms Parley Vindicates Cult', *Evening Telegram* (New York), 4 Dec. 1921, p. 4, col. 1. This article was advertised on the previous day, see 'Tomorrow's Evening Telegram', 3 Dec. 1921, p. 12, col. 1.
15. 'Father of Bahai Religion is Dead', *Wyoming State Journal* (Cheyenne), 5 Dec. 1921, p. 4, col. 1.
16. 'Death of Abdul', *Appeal* (St Paul, MN), 3 Dec. 1921, p. 2, col. 2. The same article was published several times in the same newspaper over a number of weeks: 'Death of Abdul Baha', ibid. 10 Dec. 1921, p. 2, col. 2 ; 17 Dec. 1921, p. 2, col. 2; 24 Dec. 1921, p. 2, col. 2; 31 Dec. 1921, p. 2, col. 2.
17. 'Abdul Baha Abbas', *Chicago Defender*, 10 Dec. 1921.
18. 'Gregory Sees Great Service of Abdul Baha', *Chicago Defender*, 31 Dec. 1921, p. 15, col. 4. The article included a portrait. The copy in the possession of the present author is defective and large portions of Gregory's letter are illegible.
19. Charles H. Joseph, 'Random Thoughts', *Jewish Criterion* (Pittsburgh), 9 Dec. 1921, p. 14, col. 2.
20. 'Death of Abdul Baha Stimulates Cause in U. S.', *Kalamazoo Gazette* (MI), 18 Dec. 1921, p. 23, col. 6.
21. See 'The Galley', *Miami Herald*, 14 Dec. 1921, p. 4, col. 6; 'Books and Authors', *New York Times*, 18 Dec. 1921, p. 23, col. 1.
22. 'Abdul Baha', *Christian Register* (Boston), 12 Jan. 1922, p. 43, col. 2.
23. Newspapers that published this article or portions of it include: 'Mourn Death of Abdul Baha', *Los Angeles Times*, 11 Jan. 1922, p. 14, col. 1; 'Abdul Baha the Founder of Bahaism', *Bismarck Tribune* (ND), 11 Jan. 1922, p. 8, col. 3; 'Abdas Hailed by Many as Prophet', *Bridgeport Telegram* (CT), 11 Jan. 1922; 'Abdul Baha has many followers', *Emporia Daily Gazette* (KA), 11 Jan. 1922, p. 3, col. 1; 'Abdul Bahah Abbas Was Great Figure', *Helena Independent* (MT), 11 Jan. 1922, p. 8, col. 1; 'Death of Bahai Chief Removes Famous Leader', *News-Sentinel* (Fort Wayne, IN), 11 Jan. 1922, p. 8, col. 4; 'Recent Death of Abdul

Baha Removes a Prophet', *Niagara Falls Gazette* (New York), 11 Jan. 1922, p. 15, col. 1; 'Leader of Bahai Movement is Dead', *Aberdeen Daily News* (SD), 12 Jan. 1922, p. 4, col. 2; 'Abdul Baha Abbas was Held as Prophet', *Connersville News-Examiner* (IN), 12 Jan. 1922, p. 10, col. 3; 'Bahaism Means Reformation of Men Everywhere', *Idaho Daily Statesman* (Boise), 12 Jan. 1922, p. 2, col. 1; 'Prophet Founder Bahai Movement', *Hutchinson News* (KS), 11 Jan. 1922, p. 5, col. 3; 'The End to Prophet', *Iola Daily Register* (KS), 11 Jan. 1922, p. 6, col. 1; 'Death of Founder of Bahai Creed Mourned by World', *Sheridan Post* (Sheridan, WY), 12 Jan. 1922, p. 4, col. 1; 'Abdul Baha Abbas is Famous in Death', *Eau Clear Leader* (WI), 13 Jan. 1922; 'World News in Brief', *Pattsburgh Sentinel* (New York), 13 Jan. 1922, p. 1, col. 5; 'Founder of the Bahai Movement Dies in Palestine', *Davenport Democrat and Leaders* (IO), 15 Jan. 1922, p. 9, col. 4; 'Founder of the Bahai Movement Dies at Haifa in Palestine', *San Jose Mercury Herald* (CA), 15 Jan. 1922; 'Abdul Baha, Founder Bahai Movement Dies', *Manitoba Free Press* (Winnipeg), 16 Jan. 1922, p. 18, col. 1; 'Looked Upon as a Prophet', *Nebraska State Journal*, 16 Jan. 1922, p. 5, col. 6; 'Bahaism Adherents Throughout the World Mourn for Prophet', *Brooklyn Daily Eagle*, 22 Jan. 1922, p. 22, col. 3; 'Abdul Baha Abbas Dies in Palestine', *Kingsport Times* (TN), 31 Jan. 1922.

24. See 'Murió Abdul Baha Abbas, Fundador del Bahaismo, Religión de Fraternidad', *El Universal* (Mexico City), 11 Jan. 1922, p. 4, col. 3; 'Las Religiones del Futuro', *La Revista del Yucatán* (Mérida), 22 Jan. 1922, p. 2, col. 4.
25. 'Abd-Ul Baha – Abbas Effendi', *Independent* (New York), 24 Dec. 1922, p. 322.
26. 'The Founder of Bahaism', *American Review of Reviews* (New York), Feb. 1922, p. 217.
27. 'Abdul Baha', *Outlook* (New York), 21 Dec. 1921, pp. 632–3.
28. 'Bahaism', *Youth's Companion* (Boston), 19 Jan. 1922, p. 30.
29. 'Bahais to Hold Memorial', *Morning Oregonian* (Portland), 7 Jan. 1922, p. 2, col. 7; 'Community Church', *New York Times*, 21 Jan. 1922, p. 22.
30. 'Necrology', *Albert City Appeal* (IA), 29 Dec. 1921, p. 2, col. 6; 'Necrology', *Anita Tribune* (IA), 29 Dec. 1921, p. 5, col. 6; 'Necrology', *Danville Republican* (IN), 29 Dec. 1921, p. 4, col. 6; 'Necrology', *Moville Mail* (IA), 29 Dec. 1921, p. 4, col. 6; 'Necrologies', *Neosho Times* (MO), 29 Dec. 1921, p. 3, col. 6; 'Necrology', *Bode Bugle* (IA), 30 Dec. 1921, p. 3, col. 6; 'Necrology', *Boonville Standard* (IN), 30 Dec. 1921, p. 2, col. 6; 'Necrology', *Cass City Chronicle* (Cass City, MI), 30 Dec. 1921, p. 7, col. 6; 'Necrology', *Record Gazette* (Bedford, PA), 30 Dec. 1921, p. 7, col. 5; 'Necrology', *Weston County Gazette* (Upton, WY), 30 Dec. 1921, p. 2, col. 6; 'Necrology', *Williamsport Pioneer* (IN), 30 Dec. 1921, p. 6, col. 6; 'Necrology', *Deaver Sentinel* (Big Horn, WY), 31 Dec. 1921, p. 6, col. 6; 'Necrology', *Racine Daily Journal* (Wisconsin), 31 Dec. 1921, p. 19, col. 6; 'Necrology', *Republican* (Gillete, WY), 31 Dec. 1921, p. 2, col. 6; 'Chronology of the year 1921', *Van Wert Daily Bulletin* (OH), 31 Dec. 1921, p. 5, col. 3; 'Necrology', *Miami Herald*, 1 Jan. 1922, p. 10, col. 5; 'Dead in 1921', *New York Times*, 1 Jan. 1922, p. 9e, col. 6; 'Necrology', *Attica Ledger and Tribune* (IN), 2 Jan. 1922, p. 3, col. 5; 'Necrology', *Attica Ledger and Tribune* (IN), 3 Jan. 1922, p. 5, col. 3; and a second reference in the same newspaper: 'Necrology', *Attica Ledger and Tribune* (IN), 3 Jan. 1922, p. 3, col. 5; 'Necrology', *Iola Register* (KS),

3 Jan. 1922, p. 3, col. 5; 'Necrology', *Montour Falls* (New York), 4 Jan. 1922; 'Necrology', *Ruthven Free Press* (IA), 4 Jan. 1922; 'Necrology', *Salem Democrat* (Indiana), 4 Jan. 1922, p. 3, col. 2; 'Necrology', *Elgin Echo* (IA), 5 Jan. 1922, p. 3, col. 5; 'Necrology', *Goshen County Journal* (Torrington, WY), 5 Jan. 1922, p. 2, col. 5; 'Necrology', *Wanatah Mirror* (Indiana), 5 Jan. 1922; 'Necrology', *Pinedale Roundup* (WY), 5 Jan. 1922, p. 8, col. 5; 'Necrology', *Adiromdack Record – Elizabethtown Post* (Au Sable Forks, NY), 6 Jan. 1922; 'Necrology', *Ignacio Chieftain* (Ignacio, CO), 6 Jan. 1922.

31. 'Sir Abbas Al Bahai', *Morning Post*, 1 Dec. 1921, p. 9, col. 4. The description of 'Abdu'l-Bahá was based on references to him in George Napier Whittingham's *The Home of Fadeless Splendour: Or, The Diary of a Pilgrimage to Palestine* (1921). The book was dedicated to Wellesley Tudor Pole and contained one of his writings as a preface.
32. 'Sir Abdul Baha Abbas El Bahai', *Daily Sketch* (London), 2 Dec. 1921.
33. 'Death', *Daily Mirror* (London), 2 Dec. 1921.
34. S. K. R., 'The Prophet of Acre', *Manchester Guardian*, 7 Dec. 1921, p. 14, col. 1.
35. 'Creed of the Bahaists', *Pall Mall Gazette* (London), 19 Dec. 1921, p. 15, col. 4.
36. 'Death of Abdul Baha Abbas', *Light* (London), 3 Dec. 1921, p. 786, col. 2.
37. 'Who was Abdul Baha?' *Children's Newspaper* (London), 14 Jan. 1922, p. 2, col. 4.
38. 'Nouvelles Diverses de L'Étranger', *Le Temps* (France), 9 Dec. 1921, p. 2, col. 3.
39. 'Un Conciliateur', *Le Temps* (France), 10 Dec. 1921, p. 1, col. 4.
40. 'Abdul Beha Abbas', *Journal des Débats* (Paris), 9 Dec. 1921, p. 2, col. 3.
41. 'Abdul Baha's Memory', *Egyptian Gazette* (Alexandria), 10 Dec. 1921, p. 3, col. 5.
42. 'Palestine', *Gazette de Lausanne*, 6 Dec. 1921, p. 2, col. 2.
43. 'Ein Prophet', *Neues Wiener Journal*, 20 Dec. 1921, p. 6, col. 1.
44. 'Death of Abdul Baha: A Great Personality of the Orient', *Egyptian Gazette* (Alexandria), 30 Nov. 1921, p. 3, col. 5.
45. 'The Passing of a Great Leader of Men', *Sphinx* (Cairo), 17 Dec. 1921, p. 195.
46. 'The Late Sir Abbas el Behai', *Bombay Chronicle*, 1 Jan. 1922, p. 18, col. 3.
47. 'Abdul-Baha', *Times of India* (Bombay), 2 Jan. 1922, p. 8.
48. 'Social and General', *Japan Advertiser* (Tokyo), 7 Jan. 1922, p. 8, col. 1.
49. 'Social and General', *Japan Advertiser* (Tokyo), 8 Jan. 1922, p. 8, col. 1.
50. 'Mortoj', *British Esperantist* (London) Jan. 1922, p. 32, col. 2.
51. 'Niaj Mortinoj', *British Esperantist* (London) Jan. 1922, p. 32, col. 2.
52. 'Haifa', *Palestine Weekly*, 2 Dec. 1921, pp. 782–3.
53. 'News from Haifa', *Egyptian Gazette* (Alexandria), 5 Dec. 1921, p. 7, col. 3.
54. *Al-Narif* (Haifa), 6 Dec. 1921, p. 2, col. 1. Translation by Zia Bagdadi in *Star of the West*, 19 Jan. 1922 (12:17), pp. 259–60.
55. *Al-Narif* (Haifa), 6 Dec. 1921, pp. 2–5, col. 1. Translation by Zia Bagdadi in *Star of the West*, 19 Jan. 1922 (12:17), pp. 260–3.
56. *Al-Narif* (Haifa), 17 Jan. 1922, pp. 1–3. Translation by Zia Bagdadi reproduced from *Star of the West*, 13 Apr. 1922 (13:2), pp. 40–4.
57. For a copy of the cablegram from the Greatest Holy Leaf, see *Star of the West*, 19 Jan. 1922 (12:17), p. 258.
58. See *Star of the West*, 2 Mar. 1922 (12:17), p. 293.
59. 'Succeeds Brother as Bahai Leader', *Coshocton Tribune* (OH), 6 Jan. 1922, p. 1,

col. 3; 'Succeeds Brother as Bahai Leader', *Newark Advocate* (OH), 7 Jan. 1922, p. 1, col. 2; 'Heads Bahai Movement', *Baltimore American*, 10 Jan. 1922, p. 5; 'Succeeds Brother as Bahai Leader', *Chronicle Telegram* (Elvira, OH), 10 Jan. 1922, p. 2, col. 7; 'Succeeds Brother as Bahai Leader', *Olean Evening Herald* (New York), 11 Jan. 1922, p. 6, col. 5; 'Succeeds Brother as Bahai Leader', *Racine Journal-News* (WI), 14 Jan. 1922, p. 2, col. 4; 'Succeeds Brother as Bahai Leader', *San Antonio Evening News* (TX), 14 Jan. 1922, p. 5, col. 2.
60. 'New Bahai Leader', *Chicago Daily Tribune*, 24 Jan. 1922, p. 26.
61. 'Name Leader of New World Faith', *Grand Rapids Press* (MI), 31 Jan. 1922, p. 18, col. 2.
62. 'The Bahai Movement', *Egyptian Gazette* (Alexandria), 22 Feb. 1922, p. 8, col. 4.

Appendix 1: Writings and Talks of 'Abdu'l Bahá Published in General Periodicals
1. The letters, Tablets and talks referred to in this Appendix are English translations unless otherwise indicated.

Appendix 3: Book Reviews
1. 'Les Leçons de Saint Jean d'Acre', *Revue du Monde Mussulman* (Paris), Mar. 1908, pp. 647–9.
2. 'Abd-ul-Béha: Les Leçons de Saint Jean d'Acre', *Revue Philosophique de la France* (Paris), July 1908, pp. 93–4.
3. 'Abd-ul-Béha: Les Leçons de Saint Jean d'Acre', *Revue de l'Histoire des Religions* (Paris), Jan. 1909, pp. 124–6.
4. 'Publications Récentes', *Journal des Débats* (Paris), 14 Mar. 1908.
5. *New York Herald* (Paris), 22 Mar. 1908, n.t.
6. *Mercure de France* (Paris), 1 Apr. 1908, n.t.
7. 'Les Leçons de Saint Jean d'Acre', *La Revue* (Paris), 15 Mar. 1908 and 10 Apr. 1908.
8. 'Histoire des Religions', *La Revue Critique* (Paris), 22 Oct. 1908 and 5 Nov. 1908.
9. *Polybiblion* (Paris), Nov. 1908.
10. 'Some Answered Questions', *Scotsman* (Edinburgh), 5 Mar. 1908, p. 2, col. 4.
11 'A Persian Mystic', *Morning Post* (London), 30 Mar. 1908, p. 2, col. 5.
12. 'The Review's Bookshop', *Review of Reviews* (London), Apr. 1908, p. 414.
13. 'Some Answered Questions', *New Age* (London), 22 Aug. 1908 (3:17), p. 336, col. 1.
14. 'In the Social World', *Washington Herald*, 28 Apr. 1909, p. 5, col. 3.
15. *Springfield Republican* (MA), 13 Sept. 1909, p. 11, col. 2, n.t.
16. 'Answered Questions', *Outlook* (New York), 5 Dec. 1908, p. 798.
17. *Vahan* (London), 1 Aug 1912.
18. 'A Modern Prophet', *Light* (London), 31 Aug. 1912, p. 412, col. 2; p. 419 of the same issue carried a summary of the episode included in *Abdul Baha in London* about the wedding of a Bahá'í couple in London.
19. 'Abdul Baha in London', *Theosophy in Scotland* (Edinburgh), Oct. 1911 (3:6), p. 98.
20. 'Talks with Abdul Baha Given in Paris', *Theosophy in Scotland* (Edinburgh), Aug. 1912 (3:4), p. 66.

NOTES AND REFERENCES

21. 'Abdul Baha in Europe', *Christian Commonwealth* (London), 19 June 1912, p. 612, col. 3.
22. 'Reviews', *Occult Review* (London), Jan. 1916, p. 60.

Appendix 4: Invitations to 'Abdu'l-Bahá
1. 'Prophet May Come', *Syracuse Herald* (NY), 11 May 1912, p. 7, col. 1.
2. 'Abdul Baha to Visit this City, Sunday, 23rd', *Telegraph* (New London, CT), 5 June 1912.
3. 'Distinguished Persian Philosopher is Heartily Welcomed to America', *Sunday Oregonian* (Portland, OR), 28 Apr. 1912, p. 5, col. 5.
4. 'The Bahais', ibid. p. 8, col. 3.
5. 'Some Bahai Teachings', *Morning Oregonian* (Portland, OR), 22 May 1912, p. 10, col. 1.
6. *Morning Oregonian* (Portland, OR), 15 Aug.1912, p. 8, col. 4, n.t.
7. 'New Cult is Exemplified', *Morning Oregonian*, (Portland, OR), 17 June 1912, p. 9, col. 1.
8. *Morning Oregonian* (Portland, OR), 29 July 1912, p. 7, col. 2.
9. 'Abdul Baha is Coming on Tour in the Interests of His Religion', *Sunday Oregonian* (Portland, OR), 1 Sept. 1912, p. 13, col. 1 (includes a portrait of 'Abdu'l-Bahá).
10. 'Abdul Baha, Wonderful Persian Mystic Expected to be Here Next Month', *Portland Telegram*, 16 Aug. 1912.
11. 'Persian Head of Bahais will Pay Portland a Visit', *Portland Journal*, 29 Aug. 1912.
12. 'Abdul Bahá to Arrive Soon', *Morning Oregonian* (Portland), 29 Sept. 1912.
13. *Morning Oregonian* (Portland), 4 Oct. 1912, p. 26, col. 3.
14. 'Abdul Baha Coming', *Portland Journal*, 13 Oct. 1912.
15. 'Persian Prophet Will Not Visit Portland', *Portland Telegram*, 14 Oct. 1912.
16. 'Abdul Baha to Be Visited', *Morning Oregonian* (Portland), 14 Oct.1912, p. 7, col. 2.
17. 'No Portland Church Invites Abdul Baha', *Portland Telegram*, 10 Oct. 1912.
18. 'A Pulpit for Abdul Baha', *Portland Telegram*, 12 Oct. 1912.
19. 'Makes plea for Christian Unity', *Seattle Daily Times*, 16 Sept. 1912, p. 10, col. 5.
20. *Seattle Daily Times*, 30 Apr. 1912, p. 6, col. 1, n.t.
21. 'Says Superstition Must be Eliminated', *Seattle Daily Times*, 30 Sept. 1912, p. 10, col. 1.
22. *Seattle Daily Times*, 6 Oct. 1912. By March 1912 four invitations had been extended to 'Abdu'l-Bahá to speak in Seattle (Ida G. Finch to Joseph Hannen, 14 Mar. and 19 Mar. 1912, Hannen-Knobloch family papers, B21, US National Bahá'í Archives).

Appendix 5: The Christian Commonwealth
1. Dawson wrote the biography *Joseph Parker: His Life and Ministry* (1901).
2. In his letter to Albert Windust of 19 August 1911, Tudor Pole states that 'I have at last induced the "Christian Commonwealth" to take a real interest in the Bahai message and as it has a circulation of over 50,000 all over the world it is carrying that message far and near.' Albert Windust papers B12, US National Bahá'í Archives.

3. Tudor Pole to Albert Windust, 3 Oct. 1911, Albert Windust Papers B12, US National Bahá'í Archives.
4. 'Table Talk', *Christian Commonwealth* (London), 13 Sept. 1911, p. 857, col. 4.
5. 'Table Talk', *Christian Commonwealth* (London), 28 Aug. 1912, p. 782, col. 2. See chapter 6 for the rest of the letter.
6. 'The Christian Commonwealth', SW, 16 Oct. 1912 (3:12), p. 8.
7. A copy of this letter in Sohrab, letter to Harriet Magee, 4 Jan. 1913.
8. For some of the reports written by Joseph Hannen about 'Abdu'l-Bahá in America see 'Abdul Baha's World Tour', 28 Feb. 1912, p. 362; 'Abdul Baha Abbas in America', 12 June 1912, p. 605; 'Abdul Baha Abbas in America', 26 June 1912, p. 631; 'Abdul Baha in America', 28 Aug. 1912, p. 788; 'Abdul Baha in America', 4 Sept. 1912, p. 802; 'With Abdul Baha in America', 16 Oct. 1912, p. 49; 'With Abdul Baha in America', 11 Dec. 1912, p. 199.
9. C.M. (probably Chris Massie who is listed among the contributors of the magazine), 'The Message of Abdul Baha', *New Commonwealth* (London), 8 Oct. 1919, p. 14.
10. Today only a few libraries hold complete sets of *The Christian Commonwealth* and of these only some volumes are accessible to researchers. At the same time no Bahá'í archive keeps a complete record of the hundreds of references to the Bahá'í Faith that appeared in this historically significant journal. The present author has consulted all issues from 1908 to 1919 and hopes to be able at some point to prepare a bibliography of its Bahá'í content during that period.

Appendix 6: Arts and Artists
1. For the work, see Atherton, *Julia France and Her Times*. For a review mentioning 'Abdu'l-Bahá see 'Gertrude Atherton and her book, as seen by Suzette', *Oakland Tribune*, 5 May 1912, p. 4, col. 2.
2. Réne T. Quélin, 'Little Bas Reliefs Issued by the Friends of the Medallions', *Arts and Decoration* (New York), Apr. 1913, pp. 197–8, 216 and 218. For other references to this medallion see Charles de Kat, 'Medals issued by the Circle of Friends of the Medallion', *Numismatist* (Federalsburg, MD), Mar. 1913, p. 136.
3. See the program of the exhibition, which was held from 7 Jan. to 6 Feb. 1919, *Portrait Reliefs and Medals by T. Spicer-Simon* (1919).
4. 'The Current Art', *Reality* (New York), Sept. 1921, p. 29.
5. Thompson, *Diary*, p. 313.
6. 'With the Artists', *American Art News* (New York), 17 May 1913, p. 3, cols. 1 and 3.
7. 'Portraits Creation of a Woman Artist', *Sun* (New York), 31 Aug. 1913, p. 8. The copyright of this work was given as 15 July 1912.
8. Windsor P. Daggett, 'The Spoken Word. The Voice Portrait', *Billboard* (New York), 1 Apr. 1922, p. 28.
9. *International Studio* (New York), Feb. 1915, p. 316.

INDEX

This index is alphabetized word for word; thus 'Free Religious Association' precedes 'Freeman'. Hyphenated names are considered as two separate words. The words 'a', 'an', 'and', 'de', 'for', 'in', 'is' 'of', 'on', 'the', 'to', 'with' and Mr, Mrs and Dr in entries are ignored.

Proper names are indexed according to the spelling most often found in this book, e.g. 'Mohammed', rather than the transliteration 'Muhammad'. The exceptions to this are the Báb, Bahá'u'lláh and 'Abdu'l-Bahá, the Bábí Faith and the Bahá'í Faith. Persian, Arabic and Turkish names with no clear surname are listed by the first element of the name.

Owing to the length and nature of the book, the index has been restricted to individuals, organizations and a few Bahá'í concepts and principles mentioned by 'Abdu'l-Bahá and reported in the press. As 'Abdu'l-Bahá discussed the same concepts in many places, it was not possible to list them all in the index. Thus foundational Bahá'í principles such as the oneness of humanity, the brotherhood of man, unity, peace, education, progressive revelation, the Manifestation of God and God Himself are not generally indexed, as they appear in most of 'Abdu'l-Bahá's talks and newspaper interviews. However, principles which 'Abdu'l-Bahá expanded upon and developed during His western travels and which were in some way new to the discourses about religion, for example, women's suffrage, gender quality, the harmony of science and religion, and the rights of workers and economics, have been indexed.

As the whole book is about 'Abdu'l-Bahá, only a few highlights about His life are indexed. Similarly, references to the Bahá'í Faith are limited.

Only those newspapers and journals that published a number of articles about 'Abdu'l-Bahá and the Bahá'í Faith, such as *The Christian Commonwealth*, have been indexed but a list of all the print media cited can be found in the Bibliography, in the section 'Newspapers, Journals and Periodicals', pages 496 to 501.

Abbott, Catherine, 178
'Abdu'l-Bahá ('Abbás Effendi, the Master), vii–viii
   cares for Haifa and 'Akká residents during war, 428
   comments of, on the press, xviii–xix
   family of, 374, 380, 410, 415
   funeral of, 450–2
   imprisonment in 'Akká, vii, viii, xi, 38, 86, 372, 394, 415, 420, 425, 449
   knighting of, 437–8
   liberation from prison, 80
   opposition to, 339–63
   palms read, 323–9, 469
   passing of, 439–56
   station of, viii–viii, xxi
   successor to, 452–3
   titles of, vii
   Will and Testament of, 452, 453
   writes in Bible of City Temple, 458
Abdul Ghani, 64
Abdul Hamid, Sultan, 162, 213, 389, 449
Abdul Hlatin Effendi, 148
Abdul Latif Effendi, 132, 146
Abdul Mazid, Dr, 64
Abraham, 9, 151, 272
Abú Sinán, 405
Abu'l-Faḍl-i-Gulpáygání, Mírzá (Mirza Abdu'l Fazl), 339–40, 375
Acre, *see* 'Akká
Adam, 21, 47, 94, 98, 144, 272, 306
Addams, Jane, 199, 214
Adelphi Hotel, 6, 15, 275
Adler, Felix, 83, 204
Agence France-Press, xv
Ahmed Riza, 310–11
Ahmadiyya movement, 68
'Akká (Acre, Acca), 319, 341, 367, 368, 373, 380, 379, 382, 389, 390, 391, 405, 410, 412, 427, 435, 437
   'Abdu'l-Bahá imprisonment in, *see* 'Abdu'l-Bahá, imprisonment in 'Akká
   taking of, in World War I, 426, 430–1
Alajos, Pairet, 145, 146, 514

Alexandria, 44, 80, 81, 155, 205, 212, 367, 403, 449
Ali, Rt Hon Ameer, P.C., 64
'Alíy-i-Bastámí, Mullá, xvi, xxi
Ali Kuli Khan, 219
Ali Syed, Ameer, M.A., 209
Allen, Aseyeh, 466
Allen, Bessie, 345
Allen, Mary S., 194
Allenby, General, 422, 426, 427, 437, 439, 443
America, 266–75
American Woman Suffrage Association, 170
Andre, Mrs Addie, 178
Andre, George G., 111, 112, 279, 289, 531
Angell, Norman, 78
Anthony, Susan B., 201–2
Armour, Mrs, 7, 275
Arréat, Jean Lucian, 471
Arundel, Lady, 62, 64
Arundel, Sir, 62, 64
Assadullah, Sheikh, 176
Assad'u'llah, Siyyid, 5, 468
d'Ange d'Astre, Madame, 330
Atherton, Gertrude, 489
Atta Ullah, Sheik, 64
Atwood, Thomas, 156–7
Austria, 131, 149, 156, 254, 402, 448, 515
Ayaz, Lieutenant Román, 235

the Báb ('Alí-Muḥammad), ix, xvi–xvii, xxi, 7, 42, 80, 85, 128, 154, 186, 189, 192, 255, 257, 260, 264, 393
   'Abdu'l-Bahá confused with, 52
   Shrine of, 99, 373, 374, 450, 451
Bábí religion/Bábís, vii–viii, xv–xvii, xxi
Bacon, Bishop, 80
Bagdadi, Zia, 429, 461, 468
Balogh, Vilma, 132–3
Bahá'í Faith/Bahá'ís
   and Christianity, 1
   first mention of, in western press, xxi
   history of, vii–viii, xv–xvii
Bahai Woman's Assembly (Chicago),

INDEX

177–8, 179
Bahá'u'lláh (Baha'o'llah), vii–viii
  exiles of, xvi, xxi
  imprisoned at 'Akká, 96, 436
Baldwin, Nellie H., 266
Balfour, Arthur James, 426
Balkan Peace Conference, 3, 5, 16, 17, 23, 24
Balkányi, Paulo, 251
Balkans, 11, 13, 14, 16, 17, 20, 25, 26, 31, 44, 125, 142, 154, 160, 162, 360, 369, 406, 407, 436, 464
Barbour, Dr Alexander H. Freeland, 91, 97, 105
Barbour, Benjamin McCall, 359
Barclay, Lord and Lady, 62, 64
Barclay, Sir Thomas, 16, 17, 18, 504
Barney, Alice Pike, *see* Hemmick, Mrs Christian
Barney, Laura Clifford/Laura Dreyfus-Barney, 81, 128, 202, 239, 471–2
Bashir Uddin, Syed, 64
Bassett, Mr W.M., 230
Beales, Helen, 178
Beauchamps, Jeanne, 316, 330, 336
Bechhöfer, Carl Erich (Charles Brook-farmer), 355–6
Beede, Alice R., 113, 510
Begum of Bhopal, 63
Béla, Vikár, 146, 515
Bell, Archie, 389–97, 470
Bennet, William Stiles, 180–2
Berman, Harold, 207
Bernhardt, Sarah, 491
Berr, Émile, 318–19, 534
Besant, Annie, 158, 255, 256, 259, 260, 261, 263, 275, 301–2, 528
Betts, Dr F.W., 478
Bible, 12, 58, 66, 105, 150, 352, 359, 382
  'Abdu'l-Bahá writes in, of City Temple, 458
Blackwelder, Gertrude, 178
Blaine, Mrs Emmons, 217
Blakeslee, Professor George Hubbard, 208
Blavatsky, Helena, 254, 529, 530

Blech, Charles, 262–3
Bliss, Howard Sweetser, 376–7
Blomfield, Lady, 26, 38, 48, 64, 71, 173, 189–90, 198, 222, 255, 256, 311, 324, 325, 368, 474, 541
Blomfield, Mary, 26
Boissons et Taponier studio, 467
Book of the Covenant, viii
Botay, Mrs M. L., 216
Bourlet, Carlo, 238–42, 535
Bowers, Edwin F., 337
Boyle, Nina, 172–3, 175, 516
Braun, Sándor (Alexander), 135, 513
Bridge, Rev. W.H., 111
Briggs, Rev. A., 377–8
Bristol, 54–62
Brookfarmer, Charles (Carl Erich Bechhöfer), 355–6
Brotherhood Movement, 458
Browne, Edward G., xvi, 341
Bryan, William Jennings, 390
Buckton, Alice, 16, 24, 26–7, 63, 64, 80, 91, 110–12, 209, 255, 298, 529, 531
Budapest, 113, 127, 128, 131–49, 154, 156, 161, 199–200, 201, 248, 250–1, 277, 469, 489, 512, 513
Buddha, 101, 123, 272, 289, 335, 349, 353, 395, 396, 446
Buddhism/Buddhists, 10, 29, 96, 100, 101, 123, 147, 156, 261, 285, 396, 442, 445, 446
Buisson Effendi, Abdon, 124–5

Caillet, Albert L., 115–20, 248, 510
Cambridge, 64
Campbell, Frances Souley, 490–2
Campbell, Reginald John, 54, 197, 288, 340, 344–5, 484, 488
Carmel, Mount, 80, 86, 96, 353–4, 368, 372–4, 378, 403, 416–17, 419, 420, 422, 424, 426, 427, 437, 440, 449, 451, 454
  see also Haifa
Carnegie, Andrew, 107–10, 417–19, 459, 460, 509
Carnegie Library, x

Cart, Professor Théophile, 246–7
Catholicism/Catholics, 5, 8, 46, 132, 145, 157, 218, 226, 235, 250, 320, 352–5, 379, 513, 520, 529
Catt, Carrie Chapman, 199–203
Cattanach, A.P., 131
Caxton Hall, 79–80, 209, 359, 360
Cedric, RMS, 188
Celtic, SS, 3, 4, 5, 15, 504
'century of light', 65, 72–3, 178, 179
Chaigneau, Camille, 241, 245, 465
Chapman, Mrs Cecil, 198
Chaussegros, Mr, 240
Chessel, A. Piquet, 207–8
Chesterton, Gilbert Keith, 78, 359–62
Cheyne, Elizabeth Gibson, 506
Cheyne, Rev. Professor Thomas K., 41–2, 44–6, 385–6, 506
Child, C.W., 323–9, 469
Christ, Jesus, xviii, xxi, 4, 9, 11–12, 13, 17, 19–20, 26–7, 32, 34–7, 40, 42, 45, 49, 50, 51, 55, 65, 70, 77, 82, 99, 101, 110, 115, 123, 140, 150, 151, 153, 192, 209, 225, 260, 272, 289, 306, 314, 332, 341, 342, 343, 344, 346, 347, 348, 350, 353–4, 383, 390, 395, 396, 401, 414, 446, 453, 475, 504, 511
Christaller, Professor Paul G., 237, 249
The Christian Commonwealth, xviii, 3–4, 27–32, 105, 128, 158–61, 457, 458, 459, 460, 461, 463, 464, 465, 470, 484–8, 550
Christian Science/Christian Scientists, 164, 355, 368, 395, 478, 491
Christianity/Christians, xviii, 4, 10, 12–13, 18, 28, 29, 39, 45, 46, 51, 52, 53, 63, 83, 91, 92, 93, 96, 98–9, 100, 101, 102, 103, 104, 107, 110, 123, 129, 147, 150, 153, 156–7, 163, 175, 192, 209, 216, 217, 225, 228, 241, 247, 261, 276, 285, 309, 312–14, 322, 335, 339, 340–54, 358, 359, 360–1, 371, 373, 377–8, 380, 386, 393, 414, 426, 428, 442, 444, 445, 446, 448, 450, 451, 482, 484–8, 505, 511, 537

see also missionaries, Christian
Church of the Ascension (New York), 346, 462
City Temple, 54, 173, 288, 340, 458, 461, 475, 484, 536
Clarke, Lieut. T.H.R., 213
Cleopatra, 181
Clifton, 54–62
Clifton Guest House, 54–7, 61, 62, 465
Colby, Mrs George, 178
Coles, Dr, 379–80
Colville, Wilbur Juvenal, 321–3
Confucius, 395
Constitution
 Persian, 176
 Turkish, 406, 436
Cook, Prof. and Mrs G.W., 213
Coon, Callie P., 178
Cosmos Club, 48–51, 464, 506
Courmes, Dominique Albert, 264–5, 530
Covenant-breakers, 340, 362–3
Csernoch, János, 149
Cuthbert, Arthur, 309, 310, 323, 520, 534, 535

Daggett, Windsor P., 491–2
Darwin, Elizabeth B., 337
Dawson, Albert, 27–30, 198, 277, 458, 460, 484–7, 488, 549
Dean, Frederic, 445–6
Decker, Frank, 336–8
Despard, Charlotte, 16, 17, 24–5, 169, 176, 188, 189, 195, 196
Dodge, Wendell Phillips, 179–80, 186–7, 543
Doré Gallery, 71–2
Dow, Mrs F.A., 178
Drakoulès, Platon, 310, 311
Dreyfus-Barney, Hippolyte, 4, 15, 25, 128, 129, 209, 239, 241, 242, 262, 264, 276, 316, 319, 331, 465, 471, 479, 504, 528
Drummond, Rev. R.B., 91, 97
Druse, 451
DuBois, William and Nina, 213, 216
Dudley, Rev. George F., 349

Dunlop, Daniel Nicolas, 280, 285, 459, 529, 531
Dúst Muḥammad Khán (Moayer el Mamelck Doust Mohamed Khan), 54, 61, 62
Dykstra, Rev. Dirk, 351, 537

Eager Heart (Buckton), 26–7, 209
Easton, Peter Z., 340–2, 346–7, 350
economics, 95–6, 274
Eddy, Mary Baker, 491
Edinburgh, 32, 89–112, 223–39, 245, 247, 252, 279, 287–302, 313, 358–9, 508, 509, 510, 531
Edinburgh Esperanto Society, *see* Esperanto Society, Edinburgh
Egypt, x, xi, 51, 81, 105, 128–9, 143, 155–65, 201, 205, 209, 211, 219, 237, 255, 285, 287, 299, 311, 315, 319, 323, 324, 349, 372, 402–3, 405, 409, 410, 413, 414, 417, 419, 422–4, 436, 449, 452, 457, 484, 489, 527, 537
Ekstein, Mr, 249
Elijah, 368
Ellis, William T., 349–51, 402–3, 536–7
Emanu-El Synagogue, 463
Esoteric Fraternity, 457
Esperanto/Esperantists, x, xi, 104, 106, 113, 131, 132, 141–2, 144, 149, 156, 218, 253, 307, 312, 384, 395, 425, 450, 455, 461, 464, 465, 487, 506, 515, 525, 527
  'Abdu'l-Bahá asks Bahá'ís to learn, 103–5
  American Esperantists, 219–21, 527
  Austrian Esperantists, 237
  Edinburgh Esperantists, 223–38
  First International Esperanto Conference, 218
  Hungarian Esperantists, 132, 250–1, 513
  London Esperantists, 221–3
  Paris Esperantists, 238–48
  Sixth International Congress, 219
  Stuttgart Esperantists, 248–250
  Universal Esperantist Conference, 252–3
  Universal Esperanto Association, 450
  Vienna Esperantists, 251–2
Esperanto Society
  Edinburgh, 89, 90, 91, 102, 103–4, 223, 237, 464, 528
  Germany, 154
  Hungary, 132, 139, 145, 254
Ethical Movement, 83–8
Eve, 144

Falkenstein, Esther, 178
Fareed, Dr Ameen (Amín'u'lláh Faríd), 178, 219–20, 267, 322, 457, 459, 468, 521
Fawcett, Millicent Garrett, 430
Federation of Women's Clubs, 176–80, 201, 462
feminism/feminists, 138–9, 144, 170, 175, 194, 201, 313, 513
Ferdinand, Archduke Franz, 402
Feridun, Omer, 146
Fischer, Dr Edwin, 131
Flament, Albert, 320
Ford, Mary Hanford, 170–1, 516
Fox, Margaret, Kate and Leah, 309
France, 262–6
Fraser, Rev. Donald B., 7, 15
Fraser, Isabel, xviii, 3, 4, 17–26, 32–7, 42–4, 89, 110, 111, 113–15, 120–3, 504, 507
Free Religious Association, 83, 388, 462, 511
Freeman, Elizabeth, 180, 182
Freemasonry, 288, 442

Gandhi, Mahatma, 208
Garrison, William Lloyd, 214
Geddes, Professor Patrick, 90, 91, 92, 99, 103, 104, 106–7, 111, 224, 226, 229, 529
Geißwein, Canon Dr Merzander, 138
gender equality, *see* women, equality with men
Germanus, Dr Gyula (Julius), 132, 133,

134, 138, 139, 140, 145, 148, 156, 513
Germany, xv, 80, 131, 132, 150–4, 156, 235, 237, 247, 250, 370, 402
Getsinger, Dr Edward C., 410–12, 372, 468
Getsinger, Lua, 164, 372, 413–15, 419, 468, 520, 535, 541
Ghuli, Aga Abbas, 416
Gibran, Khalil, 489
Giesswein, Canon Sándor (Alexander), 134, 139, 140, 143, 148, 199, 250
girls, education of, 22, 176, 186–7, 200, 257
Gobineau, Comte de, xvi
Goldziher, Professor Ignác, 144, 145, 146, 148, 514
Goudsmit, Jo, 431–7
Grainger, Minnie Starr, 178
Gray, Rev. James, 346–7
Greatest Holy Leaf (Bahiyyih Khánum), 547
Green, Perry J., 482–3
Green Acre, 527
Greener Professor Henry, 178
Gregory, Louis G., 211–13, 444, 520, 545
Gül Baba, 148

Habid Ullah Khan, 64
Hagara, Viktor, 146
Hague Tribunal of International Arbitration, 223
Haifa, 105
  'Abdu'l-Bahá in, 80, 155, 157, 219, 367–401
  effect of war on, 402–38
  liberation of, 422–30
  passing of 'Abdu'l-Bahá in, 439–56
  pilgrims to, 381, 385
  see also Carmel, Mount
Hakim, Dr Arastoo, 209
Hakim, Luṭfu'lláh (Lotfullah) S., 417, 460, 487
Hakim Mahmud, 70
Haldane, John Scott, 91
Hammer, Mrs D. Harry, 178

Hammond, Eric, 80, 209, 280, 356, 473, 476
Hannen, Joseph, 221, 461, 486, 521, 550
happiness, 37, 43, 76–7, 81 82, 95, 136–7, 140, 142–3, 274–5
Harris, Rendell, 313
Harris & Ewing agency, 467, 468
Harrison, Frederic, 28
Hart, Rev. E.I., 351
Hassan bey Checry, 438
Havas, Charles Louis, xv
health/healing, 10, 19, 28, 116, 122, 288, 368, 375
Hearst, Phoebe A., xvii
Hearst, William R., xvii
Hearst newspapers, xvii
Hemmick, Mrs Christian (Alice Pike Barney)/Mr Hemmick, 202, 203, 211
Herrick, Elizabeth, 4, 7, 15, 175, 464, 504, 535
Higher Thought Centre, 70–2
Hillis, Kathleen, 384
Hinduism/Hindu, 120, 127, 156, 200, 261, 285, 445, 455
Hirsch, Dr Emil G., 214
Hiscox, Elinor, 422–3
Hoar, H.P., 342
Hoffman, Eunice, 479
Holbach, Maude M., 368–75, 380, 382, 388, 470
Holley, Horace, 445
Hollins, Alfred, 224, 229
Holmes, Mrs, 189
Holt, Elizabeth L., 491–2
House of Worship, see Temple, Bahá'í
Howard, Ebenezer, 209
Howard University, 209–13
Huart, Clément, 471
Hull House, 214, 215, 217, 266, 461
humanity, oneness of, see oneness of humanity
Hungary, 131, 135, 143, 235, 237, 251, 277, 514, 515
  see also Budapest
Hussein Rouhy, 424

INDEX

Inayati Order (Sufi Order of the West), 510
International Congress of Moral Education (Second Universal Congress on Moral Education), 83, 458
International (World's) Congress of Religions, 124, 388
international language, 218–53
  see also Esperanto
international tribunals/courts, 23, 39, 60, 75, 138, 223, 339, 356, 404, 433, 435
International Woman Suffrage Alliance, 197, 199
Irwin, Beatrice, 126–7, 534
Islam, *see* Mohammedanism
Ives, Rev. Howard Colby, 107, 420

Jack, Marion E., 110, 111, 175
Jacobsen, Bernard M., 363
Jamál Pa<u>sh</u>á, 541
Japan, 405, 450, 455
Jesus, *see* Christ, Jesus
Johnson, Harrold, 83, 258, 461
Jordan, David Starr, 32
Joseph, Charles H., 444–5
Jounet, Albert, 330, 336
journalism/journalists, viii, xv, xvii, 133, 146, 312, 349, 356, 453, 484, 487, 509, 513, 514, 529
  see also newspapers/press
Jowett, Dr, 42
Judaism/Jews, 4, 10, 11–13, 17, 45, 46, 50, 62, 63, 64, 92, 96, 100, 101, 123, 131, 147, 163, 214, 217, 218, 243, 260, 261, 276, 285, 291, 335, 339, 371, 373, 377, 386, 393, 395, 396, 414, 436, 442, 445, 446, 451, 463, 505, 513
Judge, William Quan, 254

Kamal-ud-Din, Khwaja (Khaja Kamaluddbi), 62, 64, 68–70
Karavia, Thalia Flora, 489
Käsebier, Gertrude, 469, 470, 489
Keating, Dr, 217
Kelman (Kerman), Rev. Dr John, 97, 103, 104, 105, 224–5, 227, 229
Kenosha, 362–3
Kerew, Kate, 468
Khan, Inayat, 115–20, 123, 510
Khayyam, Omar, 337
Kheiralla, Dr Ibrahim, 362, 363
King's Weigh House Church, 38, 40–1
Kinnish, C.A., 275
Kitab-el-Akdas (Kitáb-i-Aqdas), 220
knighthood, of 'Abdu'l-Bahá, 437–8, 439, 451, 543
Knobloch, Alma, 131
Knobloch, Fannie, 520
Kochersperger, Mrs P., 178
Koran (Qur'án), 12–13, 66, 67, 74, 93, 119, 200, 202, 289, 343, 348, 381
Koreshan Unity, 352
Krishnamurti, J., 259, 261, 275, 528
Kúnos, Ignác, 132, 133, 135, 138, 513
Kurartul Ayn/Ṭáhirih (Kurratul Ayn, Kurret ul Aine, Kurrat Al Eyn, Qurratu'l'Ain), 171–2, 175, 176, 186, 188–90, 192–3, 194, 197, 198–9, 200, 201

Labaree, Benjamin, 344
Labaree, Robert McEwen, 344
Lafayette studios, 508
Lake Mohonk Conference on International Arbitration, 107, 351, 458, 462, 468
Lamington, Lord, 63, 64
Lange, Dr Christian Loius, 206–7, 519
language, universal, 6, 39–40, 56, 60–1, 75, 92, 95, 104, 140, 141–2, 143, 154, 156, 218–53, 339, 395, 430, 433, 450, 457
  see also Esperanto/Esperantists
Lathrop, Dr Claude F., 483
Latimer, George, 384–5
Latimer, Mrs J.W., 480, 482
League of Liberal Christian Thought and Social Service, 484
League of Nations, 429–30, 439
Leeder, Mr S.H., 209
Lefranc, Jean, 262, 448
Leitner, Sir Dr Gottlieb Wilhelm, 62–4

557

Leitner, Henry, 62–4, 67
Lerber, M., 239
Lesch, Fannie G., 198
Letchworth Garden City, 255, 298, 529, 531
Leu, Louis Le, 316, 330–1
Lewis, Rev. Edward, 40–1
Lewis, John, 323–5, 329
Lewis, Wyndham, 357
Lewis Institute (Chicago), 176
Liberal Christian League, 484
Linne, Ragna, 177
Liverpool, 3, 4–16, 32, 63, 275, 276, 278, 464, 531
Livingston, Rose, 182
lodges, Theosophical, 7, 131, 255, 260, 266, 275, 280, 287, 298, 464, 528, 529, 531
London, xvii, 3, 4, 7, 15–41, 48–53, 54, 62, 63, 64, 68, 69, 70–1, 72, 75, 79, 80, 81, 82–3, 89, 90, 102, 108, 111, 128, 131, 152, 170–1, 174, 176, 180, 188–203, 204–9, 214, 251, 255–6, 276, 287, 288, 289, 311, 315–16, 359, 376, 472, 475, 534
London News Agency, 467
Loränd, Mr, 145
love, 10, 19–21, 45, 58, 86, 387
Lovett, William O., 350–1

Mackey, Mr and Mrs Mabel, 239
MacNutt, Mary Stokes (Mrs Howard MacNutt), 183
Magee, Harriet, 108
Maḥmúd (Mahmoud), Mírzá (Mírzá Maḥmúd-i-Zarqání), 5, 107, 379, 513, 517
Maimutullah Shah, 64
Manchester College, 41–4, 646
Mann, William, 222–3, 234, 248
Margoliouth, Prof., 80
Martin, Eva M., 256–8
Martindale, Rev. C.C., 207, 352–3
Mary, mother of Christ, 12–13, 27, 35
Mary Magdalene, 192
Mathew, Louise (Louisa), 212–13
Matthew, Bishop, 209

Maud, Constance, 198–9, 313–15, 324
McCall, Mrs Robert, 177
McCormick, Mrs Cyrus, 217
McElroy, William Thomas, 349, 536
McEwen, Dr, 177
Mead, George R.S., 62–3, 64
Mee, Arthur, 447–8
Mehmet, His Highness, 64
Messiah, 4, 5, 27, 35, 306, 313
'Messiah' (Handel), 90, 105
Mészáros, Gyula, 146, 515
Middleton, Jessie A., 453
Militz, Annie Rix, 164–5, 460
Miller, Mildred, 215
Miller, Mrs Walter McNab, 203
Minerva Club, 183–4
missions/missionaries, Christian, xvi, 97, 98, 103, 105, 156, 211, 225, 313, 339–53, 358–9, 376–7, 379, 425, 447, 537
Mohamed Hasan, 64
Mohamed Nawas Khan, 64
Mohamed Yehya, Shah, 64
Mohammed (Mahomet, Muhammad), Prophet, 4, 9, 12, 45, 65, 70, 77, 93, 99, 101, 123, 289, 343, 348, 446, 537
Mohammed Hassan, Aga, 374
Mohammedanism/Muhammadism/ Islam/Mohammedans/Moslem/Mussulman/Muslims), 8, 10, 13, 29, 42, 45, 46, 52, 62, 63, 67, 68, 69, 70, 85, 92, 96, 98, 100, 101, 119, 123, 124, 125, 132, 147, 152, 156, 157, 162, 163, 176, 179, 192, 200, 214, 235, 236, 247, 260, 261, 263, 276, 285, 292–3, 311, 335, 339, 341, 342, 343, 344, 347, 348, 349, 371, 373, 377, 380, 381, 383, 396, 404, 414, 420, 428, 442, 443, 446, 448, 450, 471
Monckton, Miss, 17
Moneak, Elena, 177
Monnier, Pastor Henri, 123, 128, 511
Móntet, Edouard, 472
Montgomery, Rev. James S., 346–7
Moore, E.C., 512
Moral Instruction League, 83

Morehouse, Frederic Cook, 346
Morse, Samuel, xv
Moscheles, Felix Stone, 48, 221–2
Moscheles, Ignaz, 221
Moseley, Judge Henry (Mr B.S. Mosley), 209
Moses, xviii, 4, 9, 11–12, 17, 27, 35, 36, 45, 70, 93, 99, 101, 123, 192, 272, 289, 315, 353
Muhammad, Prophet, *see* Mohammed
Muḥammad-'Alí, Mírzá, 340, 362–3, 452
Munavvar Khánum (Monover, Monnavar), 410, 411, 415
Munro, Ion Smeaton, 99–102, 509
Murray, Bishop, 346
music/musicians, 26, 116–23, 328, 335, 491, 510
Mutaqim, Abdul, 355–6

Náṣiri'd-Dín Sháh, xvi, 54, 96
National American Woman Suffrage Association (NAWSA), 170, 199, 202–3
National Association for the Advancement of Colored People (NAACP), 213–17, 461–2
National Union of Women's Suffrage Societies (NUWSS), 169–71, 173, 430, 516
National Woman Suffrage Association, 170
nature, 43–4, 73–4, 280–2, 301
New Theology, 484
New Thought, 115, 164, 482, 510, 537
New York Peace Society, 107, 370
Newman, Emanuel M., 389, 470
newspapers/the press/media, ix–xix, xxi–xxii, 3, 78–9, 89, 91, 102, 131, 139, 145, 146, 149, 150, 151, 156, 197, 204, 210, 219, 276, 290, 340, 350, 354, 359, 362, 385, 386, 419, 467, 471, 472, 479, 489, 503, 513
'Abdu'l-Bahá's comments on, xviii–xix
attacks on 'Abdu'l-Bahá in, 339–63
passing of 'Abdu'l-Bahá reported in, 439–56

see also journalism/journalists
Nicholson, Ralph, 234
Norma-Smith, Marguerite, 171–2
North Canongate School, 111

occult/occultism, 185–6, 254, 315, 321, 510
Olcott, Henry Steel, 254
oneness of humanity, 9–11, 15, 21, 38, 55, 59, 66, 74, 75, 92–3, 101, 159, 160, 210, 228, 240, 244, 245, 270–1, 286, 298, 307, 333, 334, 336, 387, 388, 407, 429–30, 449
opposition, 339–63
Orage, Alfred Richard, 355
Orient–Occident Unity, *see* Persian–American Educational Society
Osborne, Thomas Mott, 421–2
Oslan, Prince, 370
Ottoman Empire, vii, viii, 124, 125, 138, 402, 419
Ouroussoff, Princess Cheref, 62, 64
Outlook Tower Committee, 89, 90, 91, 92, 98, 105, 106, 111, 225, 279, 465
Ovington, Mary White, 215
Oxford, xviii, 3, 32, 41–2, 44, 64, 80, 368, 385, 386, 439, 454, 464
Oxford movement, 348

Page, William M., 223, 229–30, 234, 528
palm-reading, 323–9, 469
Pankhurst, Christabel, 169, 194
Pankhurst, Emmeline, 169, 180, 194
Paris, xv, xvii, 4, 7, 32, 72, 79, 80, 81–2, 111, 113–30, 131, 154, 155, 216, 238–48, 251, 262–6, 285, 290, 302–8, 310, 311, 316–21, 330–6, 371, 403, 448, 460, 461, 465, 466, 467, 474, 475–6, 489, 505, 506, 512, 516, 531, 535
Paris Congress, 129–30
Parker, Rev. Joseph, 484
Parsons, Agnes (Mrs Arthur Jeffery Parsons), 221, 266
Passmore Edwards Settlement, 209
Patterson, Frances B., 351

peace, 5, 6
  universal/international, 4, 6, 7, 11, 15, 17, 21, 23, 26, 28, 30–1, 39, 44, 55, 56, 57, 59, 65–6, 74, 75, 82, 93–4, 100, 106, 108, 117, 139, 145, 152, 154, 158–60, 180–2, 188, 211, 217, 218, 228, 257, 264, 266–7, 277, 285–6, 307, 312, 322, 331, 334, 344, 370, 387, 403, 406–9, 417–19, 429–30, 441–3, 450, 453, 454, 481
Peeke, Benedict and Margaret B., 457
Pekár, Gyula, 146, 514
Pembroke Chapel, 3, 6, 7–15, 464
Penfield, E. Jean Nelson, 180, 182
Persian–American Educational Society (Orient–Occident Unity), xviii, 220, 349, 503, 527, 543
Pethick-Lawrence, Emmeline, 170–1
Phelps, Myron H., 53, 298, 330, 471, 528, 536
Philips, H.C., 458
Phillips, Charles, 354
Phillips, Jessie, 209
Pickard, Edward W., 447
photography/photographers, xvii, 3, 30, 42, 43, 64, 67, 68, 99, 111, 105, 108, 132, 134, 144, 189, 241, 277, 290, 299, 316, 318, 325, 382, 389, 397, 440, 447, 449, 450, 452, 453, 464, 467–70, 474, 475, 485, 489, 490, 491, 505, 507, 508, 512, 514, 521, 524, 530
Pickens, Prof. William, 214, 217
pilgrims/pilgrimage, 72, 89, 129, 156, 157, 310, 367, 372, 373–5, 378, 380–3, 390, 403, 404, 405, 415, 470
  western, viii, xi, 183, 212, 385, 471
Pinchot, Gifford, 202
poems/poetry/poets/poetic language, 105, 117–18, 172, 193, 264, 328, 369, 414, 489, 490, 506
Pole, David Graham, 112, 287–8, 290–1, 298–301, 460, 461, 531
Pole, Wellesley Tudor, *see* Tudor Pole, Wellesley
Pollard, Marguerite, 260–1

Pollen, Dr John, 63, 64, 67, 68
politics, 39
Ponsonaille, Victor and Fanny, 113–15
Poole, Rev. J.J., 53
Port Said, 81, 129, 155–61, 164, 299, 372, 405, 409, 410, 413, 419
Potter, Mrs Francis Squire, 178
Potter, Louis, 489
Powers, Rev. Jesse D. O., 483
prejudice, 4, 6, 12, 74, 85, 96, 193, 211, 212, 271–3, 388, 392
  caste, 126
  class, 444
  commercial/industrial/agriculture, 361
  national, 22, 39, 154, 271–2, 430
  patriotic, 22, 39, 59, 74, 75, 94, 206, 271–2, 273, 361
  political, 39, 59, 75, 94, 101, 206, 271–2, 389, 432
  race, 22, 39, 59, 74, 75, 92, 94, 101, 154, 204, 206, 210, 211, 212, 215, 216, 271–2, 361, 389, 430, 432, 444
  religious/creed, 20, 22, 39, 44, 59, 74, 75, 92, 94, 101, 126, 154, 206, 243, 271–2, 350, 361, 375, 377, 389, 430, 432
Privat, Edmon, 450
Protestants, 5, 8, 124, 131, 386, 511
Pulitzer, Joseph, xvii

Quakers (Society of Friends), ix, 51–3, 313, 370, 457, 533
Quddús, xvi
Quélin, Réne T., 489–90

racism, 432; *see also* prejudice, race
Radja, Sirday, 146
Rainy Hall, 90, 91–9, 103, 104, 106, 465, 508
Ramakrishna, Mr, 118
Ramazan, Hadji, 416–17
Ramleh, 157, 164–5, 409, 449, 457
Rana, Maharajah, 80
Raven-Hart, Major Roland, 425
Rean, W.F., 78–9

Reed, Clarence, 469
Reed, Edwin C., 220
Rees, J.D., 312
Reeves, William Pember, 205
reincarnation, 54, 259, 261, 264–5, 324–5, 330
religion,
  nature and purpose of, 10–11
  science and, *see* science, and reason/religion
Remey, Charles Mason, 384–5
Reuter, Paul J., xv
Revel, Gaston, 265, 530
Rice, Walter A., 53, 345
Robb, Rev. Alexander B., 91, 97, 98, 103, 105
Robertson MP, J.M., 206
Romeike, Henry, 503
Rónai, Károly, 146
Roosevelt, Theodore, 490
Root, Elihu, 202
Root, Martha, 202, 422, 423, 527, 528
Rosenberg, Ethel, 48, 173–4, 255, 413
Rosenwald, Julius, 217
Rouhah Khanoum (Ruha Khánum), 374
Royden, Agnes Maud, 173–5, 199, 201

Sadler, Professor Michael, 84
St John, Captain, 80
Salvation Army, 32–7, 646
Samuel, Sir Herbert, 445
Sanderson, Mrs Cobden, 80
Sarkisjan, V., 235–6
Scatcherd, Felicia R., 310–13, 323–5, 459, 534
Schäfer, Richard, 150
Schleyer, Martin, 218
science, 42–4, 92, 106, 112, 121, 130, 134, 191, 193, 197, 204, 223, 226, 231, 234, 242, 263, 281–2, 303–7, 309, 324, 336, 387, 441, 472
  and arts, 22, 39, 119, 194, 196, 231–3, 398
  and reason/religion, 21–2, 39, 59, 66, 75, 94, 165, 264, 271, 430, 432
scientists, 18, 76, 104, 129, 191, 224, 306

Scotland, 90, 98, 99, 102, 104, 107, 111, 129, 223, 254, 285, 287, 289, 298, 359, 371, 459, 460, 461, 465, 532
  see also Edinburgh
Scott, Coa, 309
Scott, Edwin, 128
Second Universal Congress on Moral Education (International Congress of Moral Education, 83, 458
Serbia, 402
Seven Candles of Unity, 313, 457
Shah, the, xvi, 54, 61, 63, 96–7, 179
Shedd, John Haskell, 343
Shedd, William Ambrose, 343–4
Sheierman, Nikolai, 248
Sherriff, Prince and Princess, 64
Shirazi, Mirza Jaffir, 374, 381
Shirley, Ralph, 321
Shlapp, Dr Otto, 111
Shoghi Effendi (Rabbani), viii, xxi, 439, 452–4, 543
Short, William H., 107–8, 370
shorthand, 267, 395
Shu'á'u'lláh, 362–3, 452
Sidley, Mr, 190
Sidley, Mrs, 80
Simkins, Henry Walter, 459
Simmons, T. Bayard, 222
Singh, Sirdar Urnam, 138–9
Sinnet, Alfred Percy, 256, 257, 529
Smith, Ernest, 347–8
Snell, Henry (Baron Snell), 361–2
socialism/socialists, 70, 83, 95, 107, 185, 194, 309, 310, 318, 340, 355–8, 361, 395, 472
Society of Friends, *see* Quakers
Sohrab, Ahmad, 5, 7, 8, 18, 26, 31, 32, 41, 42, 51, 54, 55, 57, 63, 64, 72, 80, 92, 100, 102, 108, 110, 117, 120, 126, 132, 133, 136, 139, 144, 149, 153, 157, 161, 164, 165, 188, 222, 230, 241, 248, 249, 277, 278, 287, 291, 302, 308, 323, 324, 331, 371, 384, 393, 405, 415, 416, 417, 420, 421, 426, 427, 458, 459, 466, 468, 504, 506, 509, 513, 532
Sós, Dr, 251–2

Sosnowsky, Mr, 239
Spencer, Charles, 71
Spencer, Colonel, 37
Spicer-Simon, Theodore, 489–90
Spiller, Gustav, 83, 520
Spiritualism/Spiritualists, xi, 113, 245, 309–38, 442, 447, 533
Sprague, Achsa, 309
Sprague, Sydney, 209, 222, 224, 248, 310, 312–13, 528, 533, 537
Springer, Hans, 384
Stanhope, Philip James, *see* Weardale, Baron/Lord
Stannard, Jean, 161, 209, 255, 372, 409, 449, 539
Stapley, Sir Richard, 48, 62, 64, 520, 529
Stark, Leopold (Lipót), 131–2, 133, 134, 144, 146, 147, 513
Stead, William Thomas, 221, 310, 312–14, 329, 457
Stevens, Ethel Stefana, 313
Stiles, Mr J., 7, 464
Stocker, Richard Dimsdale, 84–8
Storrs, Sir Ronald (Col. Storres) 423–4, 451
Straun, Bijou, 463
Street, Rev. Christopher J., 388–9
Strong, Rev. Sydney, 483
Stuttgart, 113, 127, 128, 131, 132, 150–4, 237, 248–9, 251, 513
suffrage, *see* women, suffrage of
suffragettes/suffragists, xi, 34, 140, 169, 170, 171, 172, 173, 180, 182, 187, 188, 194, 197, 199, 430, 489
sufism/sufis, 53, 116–19, 127, 510
Sufi Order of the West (Inayati Order), 510
Sulzer, William, 429–30, 461, 543
Súriy-i-Ghuṣn (Tablet of the Branch), vii–viii
Swanwick, Helena, 172, 516
Szikszay, Elemér, 250–1

Taft, President William, 312, 490
Ṭáhirih, *see* Kurartul Ayn
Taki, Mirza Mohamed, 423
Tammaddun'ul Mulk, 209
Tarbiat (Tarbiyat)School, 220
tea, 394
Teed, Cyrus R., 352
telegraph/telegrams, xv–xvi
Temple, Bahá'í (House of Worship), 375, 440, 441, 442, 454, 527, 535
Ten Commandments, 12
Theological Seminary, 123–5, 511
Theosophical Society/Theosophists, ix, xi, 6, 7, 15, 64, 89, 90, 105, 113, 115, 124, 127, 131, 132, 139, 178, 200, 219, 234, 245–6, 250, 251, 254–308, 325, 370, 442, 448, 459, 460, 461, 463, 464, 465, 473, 489, 506, 512, 528, 529, 530–2
Thompson, Juliet, 419, 421, 490
Thornburgh-Cropper, Mary Virginia, 48–51
Titanic, RMS, 312, 350
Tolstoy, Leo, 390, 450
Topakyan, Hayozoun H., 108, 110, 417, 419, 459, 469
Tudor Pole, Wellesley, 54, 55, 57, 61, 62, 176, 205, 207, 209, 255–6, 261, 287, 309, 315, 422, 423–6, 447, 453, 484, 529, 547, 549
Turanian Society, 145–9, 514
Turkish constitution, 406, 436

Underwood Agency/Underwood and Underwood, 440, 467, 538
Unitarianism/Unitarians, 157, 322, 350, 351, 388, 445, 450, 463, 468, 469, 483, 506, 511, 522
Universal Esperantist Congress, 252–3
Universal Races Congress, 83, 204–9, 214, 222, 315, 352–4, 458, 519, 520

Vakil, Mr, 381
Vámbéry, Arminius, 145, 161–3, 371, 513
Van Sluyter, Bernard Anthony, 350–1
Varqá, Valíyu'lláh (Mirza Waliallah Khan), 468
vegetarianism, 48
Vergara, Pastor Paul, 124

Victoria, Queen, 24, 39, 67, 397
Vienna, 113, 128, 149–50, 154, 156, 248, 251–2
del Villar, Antonio, 489
Villard, Oswald Garrison, 214
Volapük, 218
von Suttner, Baroness Bertha, 156
Vorney, Edouard de, 316

Wagner, Pastor, 475
Waite, Arthur Edward, 476–7
Waite, Louise R., 459, 535
Wake Cook, Ebenezer, 315, 533
Wallace, J. Bruce, 255
Wallis, E.W., 315
Warrington, Albert P., 267, 530–1
Washington, Elizabeth Fisher, 492
Washington DC, xv, 201, 209–13, 219, 220, 221, 266, 346–7, 348, 349, 393, 411, 421, 422, 441, 463, 489, 514, 521
Weardale, Baron/Lord (Philip James Stanhope), 16, 204, 208, 504
Wedgwood, James Ingall, 256, 277, 279, 308, 529
Wendte, Dr Charles William, 129, 459, 511
Westminster Palace Hotel, 16–26, 81, 464, 505
Whyte, Dr Alexander (Principal Whyte), 89, 90, 102, 103, 104, 105, 107
Whyte, Jane Elizabeth, 89, 91, 104, 223, 290, 313, 457, 523, 532
Wilberforce, Archdeacon Basil, 197, 288, 340, 341, 345, 475
Wildman, A., 64, 68, 469
William Rader & Son, 321
Williams, Aneurin, 420
Wilson, Andrew, 224, 229
Wilson, President Woodrow, 429, 490, 491
Windust, Albert, 484, 549
wisdom, 10, 17, 23, 86, 89, 277, 327, 384, 399, 409, 427, 480
    divine, 374

Wise, Rabbi Stephen Samuel, 199
Wishart, Rev. A.W., 350
Woking Mosque, 62–70, 72, 465, 469, 507
Wolff, Bernhard, xv
Wolffs Telegraphisches Bureau, xv
women, 64
    equality with men, 22, 39, 56, 60, 75, 94–5, 106, 134, 135, 137, 138, 139, 140, 142, 147, 169–203, 273, 315, 339, 397, 430, 433, 440
    oneness of the world of, 193
    suffrage of, 56, 78, 169–203, 395
Women's Freedom League, 16, 24, 169–70, 172, 175, 176, 188–90, 195–7, 464
Women's Social and Political Union (WSPU), 169–70, 175, 194
Wooly, Celeste Parker, 178
work/workers, 32, 60, 78, 87, 95, 182, 245, 265, 309
World's (International) Congress of Religions, 124, 388, 460

Yaḥyá, Mírzá, 341
Yazdi, Ahmed, 405, 413, 504
Young, Andrew, 111
Young Turk's revolution, viii, 80, 311, 436
Yuhanna Dawud, Mirza, 376

Zafar Ali Khan, 64
Zafrulla Khan, 64
Zakka, Elia and Soheil, 452
Zamenhof, Lidia, 253, 525
Zamenhof, Dr Ludwig L., 105, 218–21, 223, 230, 236–8, 240, 241, 244, 246, 252, 253
Zenobia, 171, 181, 191–2, 195
Zipernowsky, Károly, 132, 513
Zoroaster, 272, 395
Zoroastrianism/Zoroastrians, 10, 45, 46, 96, 163, 276, 285, 335, 382, 396, 442

www.ingramcontent.com/pod-product-compliance
Lightning Source LLC
Chambersburg PA
CBHW050131240426
43673CB00043B/1632